UNKNOWN

VALOR

UNKNOWN

VALOR

★

A Story of Family, Courage, and Sacrifice
from Pearl Harbor to Iwo Jima

MARTHA MACCALLUM

with Ronald J. Drez

HARPER
An Imprint of HarperCollinsPublishers

HarperCollins books may be purchased for educational, business, or sales promotional use. For information, please email the Special Markets Department at SPsales@harpercollins.com.

FIRST EDITION

Designed by Elina Cohen

Library of Congress Cataloging-in-Publication Data has been applied for.

ISBN 978-0-06-285385-1

20 21 22 23 24   LSC   10 9 8 7 6 5 4 3 2 1

For Dan, Elizabeth, Reed, and Harry

Among the Americans who served on Iwo Island, uncommon valor was a common virtue.

—Admiral Chester W. Nimitz

"Greater love than this no man hath," said Our Savior, "that a man lay down his life for his friends." And the soldier who dies to save his brothers, and to defend the hearths and altars of his country, reaches this highest of all degrees of charity.

—Cardinal Mercier's Pastoral Letter, as quoted by G. B. Erskine, Major General Commanding, 3rd Marine Division

Contents

Contents

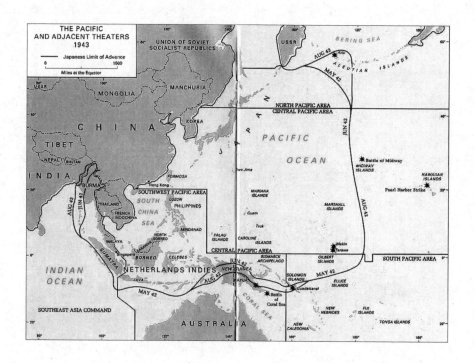

Introduction

War Plan Orange

So long as the sun shall warm the earth, let no Christian be so bold
as to come to Japan; and let all know that . . . if he violate this
command, [he] shall pay for it with his head.[1]

—Imperial inscription at mass grave site of Christians

It's almost impossible to understate how little Americans knew about
Japan before World War II.

In 1853, the empire of Japan was only known to the civilized
world as a shadowy, mist-covered island kingdom somewhere east
of China. There lived fierce warriors who brooked no intrusion from
outside. Their quarantine was absolute. No one had pried open their
door, although many had tried. Marco Polo had regaled his Venetian
audiences with enchanting tales of a "great island to the east" of Ca-
thay. It was 1295, and the explorer beguiled enraptured listeners with
tales of that enigmatic, alluring place. They imagined the equivalent
of the Lost Continent of Atlantis, the Fountain of Youth, or the Seven
Cities of Cibola. Explorers and merchants sought to lift the veil on
the Japanese kingdom, but all failed. Even the great armies of Kublai
Khan, who had overrun the rest of Asia and terrorized Europe, had
been hurled back in defeat when they had dared to storm the Japanese
wall.[2]

Only faith had opened the door, and only a little. Jesuit, Do-
minican, and Franciscan missionaries had been allowed entry in the
1500s. They had baptized more than 200,000 Japanese as Christians.

But in 1639, the door had slammed shut. The imperial establishment deemed Christianity a threat, and the backlash was brutal. Crucifixions, beheadings, and burnings at the stake laid waste to what was seen as heresy against the rulers. When the last Christians had been murdered, the black curtain of absolute exclusion and secrecy again shrouded Japan.[3] The Dutch were permitted a small trading post as a reward for having participated in the persecution, using their enormous cannons to batter down the walls of their fellow Christians' strongholds.

In 1831, a Japanese vessel sailing the eastern Pacific Ocean was engulfed by the wind and waves of a great storm. The battered vessel did not sink but was blown way off course. The crippled ship made landfall near the Columbia River on the coast of the Washington Territory of the United States. Local British and American settlers saved seven desperate Japanese seamen, but a return to their homeland, seven thousand miles away, was hopeless. They lived in exile in North America for six years. In 1837, an opportunity arose: a trading voyage was sailing to a small island off the coast of China. The homesick Japanese seamen would be taken to their motherland, ferried there by humanitarian Americans. The US government believed that the gesture would help soften the Japanese intransigence and pave the way to trade.

The final run to Japan from the island off the Chinese coast would be made by the USS *Morrison*, specially outfitted for the mission. To ensure that there would be no misunderstanding on the part of the Japanese that it was a peaceful approach, all of *Morrison*'s guns were removed. As the ship sailed for Japan and slowly entered the forbidden waters of Tokyo Bay, a fleet of Japanese junks appeared as out of nowhere, swarming the ship like moths around a flame. Waves slapped the sides of the ship as the American crew eyed the men bobbing below on the exotic fleet of painted boats with accordion sails of maroon and ocher. They felt a thousand eyes on them from the shore as well. Silence hovered around them. As it became clear that *Morrison* was unarmed, Japanese batteries opened fire from the shore. *Morrison* hastily unfurled more sail, moving to another anchorage off the island of Kyushu, but the batteries, firing unrelentingly, found them there as well. Defenseless, the Americans turned tail, leaving the hostile waters behind like so many before them. The long-lost Japanese sailors were still on board, tainted by foreign soil and now considered worthless to their homeland.[4]

Nine years later, President James K. Polk would try his luck. In 1846, Polk sent Commodore James Biddle with two ships on a mission to open trade with Japan. This time, there was to be no peace offering. Biddle would enter Tokyo Bay on the ninety-gun *Columbus*, the corvette *Vincennes* by its side, in an impressive show of US force and firepower.

The ships' entrance into the bay was greeted by swarming primitive Japanese boats loaded with hostile warriors. *Vincennes* was promptly boarded and proclaimed a Japanese possession. Biddle's request to go ashore and meet with the imperial ministers was flatly denied. For ten days, Biddle would stay anchored, leaving his ship only to make repeated demands to see the proper authorities. For ten days the Japanese declined.

Defeated, Biddle prepared to depart. As he stepped from a Japanese junk onto his own captain's barge, a Japanese sailor shoved him, sending him sprawling to the bottom of his own boat. Japanese officers feigned shock at the disrespect but simply looked on.[5]

Two years later, the United States and Japan would meet again. In June 1848, sixteen American sailors on the whaler *Lagoda* jumped ship off the coast of Japan to escape the treatment of a cruel captain. Staggering ashore on Japanese soil, they quickly realized that they had jumped from the frying pan into the fire. The Japanese arrested and imprisoned them. Close confinement was their fate, and they were forced to humiliate themselves by desecrating a Christian cross and crucifixes.

Eight months later, Captain James Glynn mounted a rescue expedition to liberate the captives. On board his sixteen-gun sloop, USS *Preble*, Glynn sailed into Japanese waters and was greeted with the now-familiar unwelcoming party of warriors signaling him to turn and leave. Undaunted, *Preble* bowled through the Japanese boats like a rampaging bull and beat them to a more favorable anchorage near the shoreline.

When the outraged Japanese finally caught up to him, they disembarked and mounted the high ground overlooking the bay, which bristled with sixty cannons. As they trained the guns on *Preble*, Captain Glynn was unimpressed. He stood tall on his deck and with his booming voice demanded the release of the imprisoned Americans.

The Japanese scoffed and reminded Glynn of the humiliation they had inflicted on the proud Commodore Biddle. Glynn was not to be pushed around, and from his lofty perch, he hurled insults and invectives back at them. The bravado seemed to stun those within the sound of his voice. Seizing on their momentary disorientation, Glynn forcefully demanded the prisoners' release and proclaimed that the United States had not only the power to protect its citizens but the will to use it.

All beheld the stunning scene. The moments passed slowly, and then the prisoners, one by one, surrounded by their guards, made their way down the winding hill toward Glynn. The triumphant American captain postured on the deck of his sloop and sailed away homeward with his crew.[6]

Glynn's success turned the tide. He recommended to Commodore Matthew C. Perry to strike with a new mission while the iron was hot. President Millard Fillmore commissioned Perry to lead an expedition. Fillmore penned a personal letter to the Japanese emperor and entrusted its delivery to Perry.

After an eight-month voyage from Norfolk, Virginia, Perry's squadron, called the "Black Ships," bore into Japanese waters. The steam frigate *Mississippi*, belching smoke, churned the waters white in the wake of its powerful screws. The Japanese marveled at the smoking beast with no sails pushing through a nine-knot headwind and creating open water as the Japanese junks scrambled to get out of the way.

Mississippi's decks had been cleared and rigged for combat, its guns loaded. Marines and other armed sentries stood at the rails.[7]

For the next ten days, Perry frustrated every Japanese demand to leave. He refused to meet with anyone but the governor; no subaltern would be entertained. As if to further aggravate the Japanese, he ordered his crew to man small boats and conduct a complete survey and sounding of Tokyo harbor. It was too much for the Japanese to bear, but despite their vigorous objections, Perry pressed on. When the swarming boats edged closer, he scattered them with the threat of cannon fire.[8]

In the end, Perry won the day. He departed on July 17 with a promise from the governor to give an imperial answer concerning trade upon Perry's return in the spring of 1854.

Perry's report revealed the success of his mission: "It not only taught the Japanese the folly of attempting to sway the Americans by bravado and sham exhibitions of force, but has proved to the world, for the first time, the practicality of sailing even to the capital of Japan."[9]

When Perry returned, the Japanese agreed to a trade understanding. But they also got something else that would be transformative: before Perry departed Tokyo Bay, to prove his friendly intent, he invited Japanese officials to dine on his flagship. He amazed them as he led them to explore the inner workings of his steam-powered vessel. They were enthralled and took it all in, awestruck at American inventiveness and ingenuity. They saw what it would take to rival the US Navy.

It took them only forty years. In just that time, the swarming junks morphed into one of the most powerful navies in all the world. The reclusive island empire became a global sea power. In 1894, they put that power to work, crushing the Chinese fleet in the Battle of the Yellow Sea. Eleven years later it shocked the world by vanquishing the Russian fleet in the Battle of Tsushima.[10]

In 1898, the Americans won their own pivotal battle, the Spanish-American War. The fruits of victory were Guam and the Philippine

Islands, and with that, the United States' naval presence was now in Japan's backyard.

X

The two powerful navies war-gamed all possibilities. If ever a future conflict could be predicted, this was it. The United States' War Plan Orange became the military strategy to react to an attack by Japan against the United States and its tempting targets of Guam and the Philippines.

War Plan Orange was an offensive plan to wage war once the "inevitable" attack on those far-flung outposts of US power took place. It anticipated an attack on those US possessions by any nation and was color-coded depending upon the adversary: Black was Germany, Red was Great Britain, Green was Mexico, and Orange was Japan. But after World War I, the only possible adversary was Japan, so the reaction plan became Orange, officially adopted in 1924. After its adoption, it became dogma at the US Naval War College.

As the historian Ronald H. Spector noted in *Eagle Against the Sun*, "A generation of officers debated, tested, and refined, War with Orange. One hundred twenty-seven times—in chart maneuvers and board games—the American fleet crossed the Pacific to do battle with its Japanese opponents."[11] It was axiomatic: the Blue (US) Navy would cross the vast expanse of seven thousand miles of Pacific Ocean for a showdown, or climactic battle, with the Orange (Japanese) Navy somewhere in the western Pacific in a winner-take-all confrontation. The fact that the US Navy had never fought such a battle was not a consideration. Nor was the fact that most planners reluctantly recognized that Guam and the Philippines would be lost in the opening hostilities of a war with Japan.

The only debate was how to bring about the "all-out attack and absolute victory."[12] Some thought it would be a mad dash across the Pacific to smite the Orange Navy with superior numbers. Others "proposed to march across the central Pacific step by step, securing small islands in succession, each step supported by the previous one."[13]

It embodied the concept of sea power defeating land power. It would be a systematic drive, an irresistible force pressing forward to isolate Japan and bring about her defeat through siege and final bombardment. From the beginning, there was no thought of an invasion of the Japanese homeland. All agreed that would be a strategy that would bring about a mutual bloodbath. "The siege would continue relentlessly until Japan was utterly exhausted and sued for peace."[14]

War Plan Orange evolved over many years, from 1906 until December 6, 1941. But during all of the additions and modifications made by several generations of war planners, it had occurred to almost no one that there was a possible scenario that had never been explored: that there would be no Blue Navy to cross the Pacific after the first day of war.

It had, however, occurred to General William "Billy" Mitchell, the Army aviator, who since fighting in World War I had rattled cages up and down the chain of command. He wrote extensive papers and carried out bombing exercises to prove that the future of war was airpower. He had been exiled to a post in Hawaii after his exhortations got him in trouble with the White House and most of his superiors. Mitchell traveled to Europe and Asia to study aviation advances and in 1924 wrote a prophetic document. Mitchell believed that Japan was preparing to do battle with the United States. He predicted that air attacks would be made by the Japanese on Pearl Harbor. The report was largely ignored.[15]

UNKNOWN

VALOR

Peekskill, 1971

Fifty-five Welcher Avenue in Peekskill, New York, is where my grandparents Frank and Helen Bowes lived. My mom was raised there, and my sisters and I went there all the time when we were growing up.

It was a compact house, with three floors, an attic that held hidden treasures, and a basement with Grandpa's workbench and an icebox. The day my parents were married in 1955, it was so hot, my grandmother said, she had to dress in front of the open icebox. The Bowes family's home was handsome and had a modest understated elegance, just as they did.

Frank and Helen Bowes had married a bit later than most, in their early thirties. They had one daughter, Elizabeth Jane Bowes, my mother, who as a little girl was known as "Betts." She was the light of their lives.

They were middle-class, educated, hardworking people whose lives were filled with friends and church and community. Grandpa was a handsome man with a shock of black hair. He wore a brimmed hat and an overcoat to work every day and attributed the full head of hair that he maintained well into his eighties to consistent hat wearing. In his lightly worn green velvet chair, each evening he would read the *New York Times* and *The Sun* or one of his books, such as *The Seven Storey Mountain* by Thomas Merton or the latest novel by Herman Wouk. The house smelled of his pipe, in a good way. He worked for Liberty Mutual Insurance Company in New York. Back during the war, he would take the train to Boston to see clients there and also visit his sister, Anne, and his niece and nephew, Nancy and Harry Gray.

Grandma was a gym teacher at a home for "wayward girls." As a kid, I wondered how exactly they'd lost their "way," but I knew there was no way they would put anything over on Grandma. She was kind but firm, and on Thanksgiving she could beat potatoes into perfect submission with a masher.

The Boweses delighted in taking my sisters and me on outings and buying us red wool coats with black buttons from Best & Co. They crossed the Atlantic on the *Queen Mary* and brought us little kilts from Scotland. In the winter, they would go to Florida with friends for a month and send us a crate of oranges and grapefruits. There was something about the arrival of that box in the middle of a New Jersey winter. You could smell the oranges right through the packaging, all citrusy and exotic with a smiling orange with long eyelashes on the outside.

But before those days, there was the war. It was that part of their story that I searched for in the attic. On Sunday afternoons at Welcher Avenue, I would slip away while the grown-ups talked in the living room about politics, color TV, and life.

My first stop was a spot near the top of the first staircase. Seated there, I could reach the box of Russell Stover chocolates that my aunt kept on top of the secretary desk below on the first floor. I would forage through it, gobble one or two, then replace the top and make my way to the second floor. There were four small square bedrooms: Grandma's, Grandpa's, Aunt Jane's, and Mom's old room in the corner at the back of the house, overlooking a magnolia tree and a small side lot. There was one shared bathroom in the hall with faded yellow and white tile. I was a nosy kid, and at one time or another, I'd looked through every nook and cranny, finding jewelry boxes with rings with big topazes and tourmalines brought home from a friend's stay in South America, Mom's pressed flowers from long-ago dances at West Point, matchbooks with friends' names written on them, and, on Grandpa's dresser, dishes with foreign coins and shirt stays mixed together.

To the right of Grandma's room, the staircase continued up. Behind the door were a rough unpainted staircase and banister, and as I ascended, a hint of cool mustiness and mothballs filled my nostrils, signaling an entry into the past. This place was separate and apart from the bustle downstairs.

Light streamed in through the one big window under the roof peak. Under the long rack of out-of-season clothing covered in plastic bags was a rectangular dry cleaning box with a sketched silhouette of a wedding dress on top. My sister, Lisa, would take me up there, and we would stare at it, knowing that one day, when one of us got engaged, we would get to open the box and try on the dress, but not until then.

On the other side of the room, past the Christmas decorations and boxes of slides and suitcases, was an old brown chest of drawers where the story was kept. On top of the chest was a handsome picture of Grandpa's nephew, Harry, in uniform, a jaunty smile across his face and sparkly eyes looking out from under his US Marine cover.

My grandfather's neatly stacked saved newspapers were preserved in plastic bags on top. I visited them over and over, carefully separating them, reading the screaming headlines: "Hitler Invades Poland." "Paris Falls." "Japan Wars on US, Britain; Makes Sudden Attack on Hawaii; Battles at Sea; Heavy Fighting at Sea Reported." "Great Britain at War; The King's Message to the Empire; Fighting to Save World from Bondage of Fear."

They told the story of the war that had consumed the family's lives from 1941 to 1945. Grandpa followed the movement of Adolf Hitler's march across Europe with pins on a map on his workshop wall. He, Helen, and their friends listened intently to the radio updates, sat rapt at newsreels at the movie theater, and argued with friends and neighbors about whether or not we should go to the aid of Great Britain; whether Hitler would storm down the Mall in front of Buckingham Palace or even Fifth Avenue in New York, as he had down the

Champs-Élysées, where Nazi flags flanked the thoroughfare in the nightmare that crept closer by the day.

In 1971, I discovered a long thin drawer at the top of the chest. In it was a dark green notebook with the gold-stamped Liberty Mutual Insurance Company logo. Inside were yellowed newspaper clippings, photos of Marines crawling up black beaches, and a photo with the headline "Wrecked and Abandoned Landing Craft Litter Beach." Toward the back there was a photo of Marines burying their dead in a cemetery. It was all a mystery to me; many of the words I could not read, but the images I could not forget. On the front was Grandpa's handwriting on a piece of paper slipped inside the plastic, the words in blue ballpoint pen: "The Story of Iwo Jima."

X

Iwo Jima, March 2019

Forty-eight years later, Frank Bowes's granddaughter is making her own way across the ocean to Iwo Jima.

I spent hours at the Japanese Embassy in New York getting my visa. It struck me as odd that the bloody battle to secure Iwo Jima ended in its return to Japan and now I need permission to go there.

I fly fourteen hours to Tokyo and another three to Guam. As we fly into Guam, the night sky is midnight blue and a full moon hangs over the sea, lighting the Mariana Islands. Below lies Tinian, to which the USS *Indianapolis* brought the parts of the first atomic bomb to be assembled. B-29s flew over these waters on their way to Iwo Jima, Okinawa, and Japan.

Tucked into my books are copies of the letters Harry Gray wrote my grandfather. My mother shared them with me as a child, and now I have shared them with my children. Like that of so many Americans, our story is woven into the wars waged and won for our freedom. These letters set me on this journey years ago. Deeper in my bag is a plastic bottle, to carry back sand for my aunt Nancy.

The Japanese open the island to veterans and their families, history buffs, and journalists only one day each year, on the anniversary of the battle in March.

I wake early, too restless to sleep, have coffee, and board the bus to the airport at 5:30 a.m. The security line is ridiculously long, and I'm annoyed by the lack of efficiency until I notice a man in his nineties in navy blazer and blue veteran's cap. He waits patiently, looking forward, and so will I.

We board the "Reunion of Honor" United flight. There is a jovial mood in our collection of travelers, most destined for a once-in-a-lifetime experience. Some have been here before, though. Bob Clemons is ninety-five and is traveling with his son and grandson. He is small in stature and stares out the window before drifting off to sleep. It will be his first time back since he was nineteen years old. I spoke with him yesterday and asked him what he remembered about Iwo. He said they had told them to kill any Japanese they encountered and to keep pushing until they reached the other side of the island. He also remembered running and tripping over scattered arms and legs. Bob said he loved Harry Truman because he ended the war and saved him from going to Okinawa. He said there was no way he was going there; he would've gone A.W.O.L. before he did.

Ronald "Rondo" Scharfe is standing in the aisle, chatting. He's ninety-one but moves like a seventy-two-year-old. He faked a baptismal certificate he stole from his church to join the Navy. At the age of sixteen, he drove a Higgins boat in the first wave and hit an underwater obstacle. The steering wheel ripped open his chest and crushed his nose and teeth. His company lost fourteen men.

Bob and Rondo say they never expected to get off the island alive. Rondo tells me that he always feels guilty that he got to have a life and get married and have kids when so many of the other guys did not. "I have a dream sometimes where I see two of my buddies as clear as day. I tell them to come on, I'll trade places with them. But just for the weekend," he says, his eyes brimming with tears. "But then I want to come back." Both men say they still have nightmares, seventy-four years later.

As we approach Iwo Jima, the United pilot tells us that we will soon see it on the left. He will fly two low circles over the island so everyone can take pictures and get a good look. There is a buzz of excitement as the gaping volcano Mount Suribachi comes into view, looming over the southern tip of the island. Those in the interior of the plane are passing their phones to the folks at the windows, craning their necks for a glimpse. Bob and Rondo stare down at the monster volcano in silence.

Once on the island, we walk the two-mile dirt road to Suribachi and climb it in the heat. The Japanese memorial stands large in the center. The American one is to the left. Next to it, the sawed-off end of the flagpole, on the spot where the famous flag-raising photo was taken, is in the ground, surrounded by a small patch of cement. People take turns taking photos; some have carried US flags to the spot, and they hold them up for the picture.

I look down at the stretches of black beaches below.

This is where Harry, Dom, Warren, Jay, George, Herman, and Charlie landed, among the sixty thousand boys of unimaginable courage from towns all across the United States, seven thousand miles away. Nearly seven thousand of them would die here on the eight-mile-square patch of nothing in the middle of nowhere in the costliest battle in the history of the US Marine Corps.

Admiral Chester W. Nimitz said after the war, "Among the Americans who served on Iwo Island, uncommon valor was a common virtue." For these young men and so many others whose tales of unknown valor lie only in their hearts, I tell their stories.

1

Arlington, Massachusetts, 1938

Frank Bowes heads up the hill, rifling in his overcoat pocket for the keys to his brother-in-law's house.

The always dapper Frank is a bit sweaty under the collar as he trudges north on Center Street. It is bitterly cold on this December night, and he pulls his coat tightly around. It has been a heck of a day. He barely made the train to Boston from Peekskill, then hustled through two meetings that morning: at a textile company north of Boston and the teachers' union, both his longtime clients at Liberty Mutual.

He walks and thinks, as the snow squeaks under the soles of his wing tips. Christmas wreaths are hung on the lampposts. Arlington is decked out. But it is going to be a rough Christmas. The red bows leave him unsettled, not merry.

Standing at the front door, he grips the key in his hand, separating it from his pocket change, his handkerchief, and his pipe. The worn black leather fob softened over time in another man's hand, in another man's pocket. On it are the worn words "Olmsted-Flint," where his brother-in-law, Harry Gray, Sr., worked. Olmsted made industrial belts for machinery, including the leather belts that powered the tallest wooden roller coaster at Revere Beach. Last summer, Harry Sr. went there to take the first test ride, to prove the belts would work.

"Better you than me," Frank joked. He wasn't much for rides, but

Harry Sr. loved anything fast and thrilling. As a boy in Long Island City, he spent his summers on the water on his fifteen-foot sailboat. He loved that boat, loved the water, remembers Frank.

Last winter, Harry Sr. made a model of it for young Harry. Frank could still smell the wood shavings, as the radio crackled and Harry Sr. hummed in the basement. It took him all of February to finish, but when it was done, Frank had to admit, it was a beauty.

She was two and a half feet long, with a tall mast and a little cabin with tiny benches inside. She had a wooden ship's wheel that turned and two perfectly scaled lifeboats with varnished seats. Harry Sr. made a polished stand, and Anne sewed three beautiful sails that hung on the mast, waiting for an imaginary wind. When Harry Sr. was done with it, he made a smaller one for little Nancy.

The two young families were as close as could be: four young parents with three little ones between them, starting their lives. The Great Depression was mostly over, and things were picking up. After years of angst and doubt, people were starting to feel pretty good about the future again.

Frank and his wife, Helen, and their four-year-old daughter, Betts, along with Harry Sr. and Anne and their two children, Harry Jr. and Nancy, often drove to Horseneck Beach to rent cabins for a week in the summer. Harry Sr. kept them laughing and singing, playing his mandolin in the kitchen after dinner. He was one of those guys, pretty good at most everything he tried. He played golf with his pals on Saturdays and Sundays, and with his family he was always the first one up, eagerly packing up the car. Then he'd scoop up Harry Jr. and Nancy from their beds, loudly announcing "Point of Pines or bust!"

There they'd run, laughing and shouting, on the paths until they all collapsed for lunch on a picnic blanket. Frank could still feel the mattress of thick pine needles under the wool plaid blanket. They were all in heaven under the umbrella of those heavily scented, towering trees.

They lay on their backs as the sun streamed down through the big bushy branches, and the world seemed just about perfect. When the day was over and they piled into the car, Harry would always have one more treat: "Who wants ice cream?" Sticky and drowsy, Harry Jr., Nancy, and Betts would fall asleep on one another's shoulders in the back seat on the way home. It was all as it should be, and they all just assumed it would be like that forever.

But it was not to be forever or anything close to it. Harry Sr. came home early from work on Saturday, December 3, not feeling right. He died in his bed that afternoon of heart failure.

Frank Bowes shakes the images from his head and turns the key at 17 Linwood, a house still in mourning. He opens the door, and they are all standing there to greet him: Anne takes his briefcase and hat as Harry Jr. and little eight-year-old Nancy look up at him.

"Well, ho, ho, ho!" he says, trying to lighten the mood. He hugs each one and musses Harry Jr.'s hair. Harry buries his face in his uncle's scratchy, manly coat. His senses fill with the sweet smell of pipe deep in the tweed, and he is relieved that Uncle Frank will sit at the head of the table tonight.

Anne Gray sits at the other end of the dinner table and smiles bravely to hold back her grief. She wants to try to forget her troubles for the moment, but she is still uneasy about the meeting she had that morning at Olmsted-Flint.

In her best dress and coat, the forty-year-old widow screwed up her courage and made her way to see her husband's former boss. He was very kind but explained that the new program known as Social Security would not cover her family because her husband's time at Olmsted fell just shy of the required three years to receive benefits. He was sorry but shrugged and said there was nothing they could do. Anne also went to the bank that morning. She and her husband had managed to put aside a little money, but there wasn't much; and after those savings ran out, she would be on her own.

Anne came from solid, hardworking stock, educated second-generation citizens of Massachusetts whose parents came from Ireland and England. Resourceful and proud, they lived within their means. No one complained. Like the rest of the family, she and Harry weathered the Great Depression, and they dreamed of owning their own home in the bustling town of Arlington. But that dream was from another life now. She gazes at her children, eating their dinner and laughing with Uncle Frank.

It will be first things first. She has to feed them and keep a roof over their heads. She has her mother to help, and she has her faith. She is smart and capable. She knows she will figure things out one way or the other. She's glad that Frank comes to Boston often for work. He will be the closest thing to a dad for young Harry—her pride-and-joy boy.

Young Harry is sharp as a tack, a bit of a prankster and a bit of an artist, too. He has a smile that melts everyone. Even the old man who runs the new roller rink in town has a soft spot for Harry when he and his chums roll through the door on Friday nights. Nancy is loving and chatty and admires everything about her big brother. But she has been quiet since losing her dad. Anne hopes that Nancy is young enough that she will forget all of this one day and just remember her adoring dad.

After dinner, Frank and Anne head upstairs and watch the kids brush their teeth and say their prayers. Frank lingers in young Harry's room, taking time to fold the boy's shirt and pants and lay them on the chair by the bed, just in case Harry feels like talking. He sits on the edge of the bed as Harry stares at the ceiling, and Uncle Frank rests his hand on the boy's forehead, gently brushing back his hair.

He unlocks a door with that touch, and tears well up in the twelve-year-old's eyes. On the nightstand is a picture of Harry, or "Junior," as they all call him, with his dad, fishing poles ready, smiles from ear to ear, both looking as though they are about to crack up. Frank kisses the boy on his forehead, and Harry closes his eyes and slowly, slowly drifts off to sleep. Frank sits motionless for a few minutes to be sure. Then he quietly stands, moves to the door, turns out the light. He goes downstairs to smoke his pipe and listen to the radio.

Anne is already downstairs, sitting in her chair.

The radio voices are deep and laced with static, bringing reports from across the ocean; from a world in flames. The war that President Franklin D. Roosevelt assures Americans is "not our fight." In London, Edward R. Murrow reports that Prime Minister Neville Chamberlain has spoken at a Jubilee Dinner for the Foreign Press Association. The prime minister said that British rearmament would continue unabated despite his commitment to the Munich Agreement and his belief that the British and German people are determined "never to go to war with one another again, and to settle any difference that might arise between us by the method of consultation."

Murrow says that at the press dinner there were empty seats. The German reporters had boycotted the evening. They had read an advance copy of Chamberlain's speech, and in it, the prime minister had chided them for the tone of their reporting and for rarely showing "any sign of a desire to understand our point of view."[1]

Anne and Frank listen as Murrow says that Jews have been ordered to stay off the streets of Germany during Nationalism Day. Hitler has declared that Jewish people have no role in German society. Their right to own real estate has been abolished, and business contracts with Jews are now considered void.

The news from the other side of the world continues. In Imperial Japan, Prime Minister Fumimaro Konoe has given a speech proclaiming a New Order of East Asia, encompassing Japan, Manchukuo, and China.[2] Where Manchukuo is, Frank and Anne don't know or particularly care. It all seems so far away from Arlington and all the quiet living rooms across the United States, where nearly all agree with their president that it is not their fight.

Anne is tired and has heard enough. She rises and walks toward the stairs. Her brother sees her sadness. "Hey, why the long face?" he chirps after her, just as he did when they were growing up in Worcester and his sister needed cheering up.

"How about we all go to the Capitol tomorrow night?" he says, looking at an ad in the paper. They made Dickens's *Christmas Carol* into a movie." Anne smiles a little and walks back to his chair.

"That would be wonderful, Frank. We'd like that. Good night."

She kisses him on the head and goes up to her room, to the bed that is now too big and empty. By Thursday, Frank will be back in Peekskill with Helen and Betts, and Anne will face the daunting prospect of Christmas without her husband, without the dad of those two precious children sleeping across the hall.

2

Infamy

On Saturday, December 6, 1941, Americans enjoy their last day of peace and isolation. Wars rage in Europe and Asia, but Americans have little interest. Of course, they watch the newsreels in the local theater. They shake their heads with pity when Edward R. Murrow recounts the unfathomable bombings in London. Great Britain is fighting for its very existence.

The Battle of Britain raged over the English Channel on July 10, 1940. Luftwaffe bombers roared overhead, rumbling the ground and striking terror into all below, battling to beat the British into submission. By September, it was an all-out assault against the civilian population of London to break the will of the people. Night after night, German raiders flew over the proud, historic city, pummeling its majestic buildings and streets with incendiary bombs. The Brits dug in during "the Blitz"; some huddled in wire cages made to fit under their beds, others fled to homemade bunkers in their small courtyards. As they weathered the onslaught by air, they watched the ocean for the expected invasion by sea.

On December 29, the 114th night of the Blitz, Murrow reported the unthinkable. In his deep staccato voice, he announced to the world that Saint Paul's Cathedral, with Christopher Wren's glorious dome, was engulfed in flames.

The queen mother continually encouraged her subjects to "keep calm and carry on" as parents huddled with their children in the Underground or loaded them onto trains to live with strangers outside the city. Their parents stayed behind, enduring the nightly raids by German bombers, not knowing if they would ever see their children again.

Americans shook their heads and talked about the war. In barbershops and corner stores, they shared their fears of what was to come, but when talk turned to US involvement, they drew the line. They were dead set against bailing out Europe as they had done in 1917.

They had seen it all in the catastrophic "war to end all wars," World War I: the anguish of the destroyed families of the 117,000 soldiers buried in the fields of France and of the 200,000 more who returned carrying the scars of that war and memories of which they could not speak.

Now European countries were fighting among themselves again. Did they not remember the gruesome war, the flesh and bone ripped apart by quick-fire machine guns in charges across no-man's-lands? The war that had driven so many of them to leave the continent behind for a new start. No, if the rest of the Western world was intent on destroying itself every few years, the United States would watch from the sidelines. Americans had other pursuits, such as the happiness promised by the framers of the Constitution. In reality, that happiness was still just out of their grasp. It was somewhere on the other side of war, the Depression, the Dust Bowl, bank foreclosures, and relentless unemployment.

According to Gallup, 81 percent of Americans were opposed to getting involved in Europe's war, and the president stood with them. Franklin Roosevelt was so adamant in his stance that anxious British officials, facing the full fury of the Germans, concluded that there wasn't the slightest chance of the United States entering the war unless the country itself was attacked.

Saturday nights, with the workweek behind them, Americans swayed to the sultry sounds of the big bands. It was a uniquely 1940s rhythm, a hip mover that made you want to dance or at least lean on the bar and tap your toe while sipping a martini. Glenn Miller, Sammy Kaye, and Jimmy Dorsey were an easy choice over war, setting the place hopping with "Chattanooga Choo Choo," "Daddy," and "Green Eyes." The Andrews Sisters softly crooned "I'll be with you in apple blossom time."

However, the bubble of peace in a world torn by war had not been easy to preserve. There had been enemy provocations. That fall, a German U-boat had torpedoed the US destroyer *Reuben James* off the coast of Iceland; 100 of the 144-man crew had perished at sea. Americans were outraged, and Woody Guthrie sang:

Now tonight there are lights in our country so bright
in the farms and in the cities, they're telling of the fight.
And now our mighty battleships will steam the bounding main
and remember the name of that good Reuben James.

President Roosevelt remembered the fallen with a black armband while assuring the nation that this attack would not alter German-American relations or escalate to war.

So young men went about their lives, finding jobs after the grim years of the Depression. They were enjoying life, and in 1941, that meant baseball! The New York Yankees' "Joltin' Joe" DiMaggio was on the path to a fifty-six-game hitting streak, and the Boston Red Sox slugger Ted Williams was sporting a rarified .400 batting average.

That spring, Harry Gray, now a freshman in high school, went roller-skating and to see *Gone with the Wind* at the Capitol Theatre in downtown Arlington.[1] It had been three years since his father died, and little by little, the Grays' life was finding a new normal. Anne had gone to typing school at night and landed herself a good job at Liberty Mutual, where her brother, Frank, worked. She was providing for her family and making ends meet. It was something she had never imagined having to do, but she was succeeding and was proud of it.

Fifteen hundred miles away in Gulfport, Mississippi, the Legion

Theatre had recently opened on 27th Avenue. It seated twelve hundred people, and, best of all, it had a balcony. Seventeen-year-old Jay Rebstock had been sent by his dad to the Gulf Coast Military Academy to get some "discipline" into his life. But on Saturday night, well, it was Saturday night and time to let off a little steam. Rebstock and his fellow cadets put on their best shirts and headed to town to catch Humphrey Bogart in *The Maltese Falcon*[2] and perhaps meet some girls on line to join them in the balcony seats.

The two young men, like so many others across the United States, had no idea what lay ahead, and they were, as they should be, blissfully lost in teenage life in their small towns in America. Adolf Hitler, Benito Mussolini, Emperor Hirohito, and Hideki Tojo were just names in the newspaper, monster characters in a faraway tragedy. Let Russia's and Germany's murderous empires devour each other. If they were bent on mutual destruction, so be it.

Still, the devil-may-care mood of the boys was not possible for their parents, who watched and worried as the Nazi black in the newsreel animations spilled farther and farther across Europe and Africa.

Young Harry Gray's uncle Frank feared that the United States could look away for only so long. When Helen and Betts were in bed, he would go down to his basement workshop. On the wall was his map with colored pins following the course of the war.

A year earlier, Germany, Italy, and Japan had signed the Tripartite Pact. In response, the United States and its European allies had banned steel and oil exports to Japan. Eventually, the Dutch colonial government in Jakarta hit Japan where it hurt most, freezing Japanese assets in Indonesia. Without Dutch petroleum, Japan's vast military machine would, in a short time, be gasping for air, unless they fought back.

Japan, an island nation, had few resources of its own and had absconded with China's bounty to scrape its way into the upper echelons of world power. Luckily, the Japanese were protected by huge expanses of sea and archipelagos barely worth colonization. Germany, nearly landlocked, had become an air power to subjugate its neighbors and rob their lands. Both seemed nearly impossible to stop, short of well-negotiated treaties.

𝕏

Frank takes another look at the map and wonders where it is all headed. He reaches up and pulls the cord that turns off the lightbulb over his workbench. As he walks upstairs, his thoughts go to Harry Jr. His memories of the boys fighting in the wretched trenches of World War I are still fresh; he hopes Harry can escape the madness, and stay safe at home in Arlington.

On that last peaceful evening, December 6, 1941, night falls on the continental forty-eight states. But far to the west, in the territory of Hawaii, it is still light. The last rays of the setting sun on the island of Oahu paint the sky orange and purple. It is Saturday night, liberty call has sounded, and grinning sailors in their pressed whites stroll out of the gates at Naval Station Pearl Harbor, a fresh pack of cigarettes and money in their pockets. They are off for a night on the town in Honolulu.

But not everyone is leaving. In fact, at the other entrance to the base, sailors and their girls buzz with excitement and squeeze through the crowded doorways of the Bloch Recreation Center for what is billed as the entertainment event of the year: the first annual "Battle of Music."[3]

Everybody has his or her favorite, and tonight is the semifinals of the big band–style competition that has been going since September. The crowd shuffles noisily for seats in the packed auditorium, laughing above the cacophony of the bands warming up. Tonight's semifinalists are the twenty-one-piece Navy bands from the battleships USS *Pennsylvania* and *Tennessee* and from the Navy fleet tender USS *Argonne*. A fourth band from the cruiser *Detroit* has made it to the semis but is missing because its ship has just left Pearl Harbor.

The band members from battleship *Arizona* line the wall behind the seats, watching the scene intently. They have already secured their spot in the next round and are there to size up the competition for the finals on December 20. They have a soft spot for the band from *Tennessee*, since they attended the Navy School of Music in Washington, DC, together.[4]

As the crowd settles down, the rules are simply spelled out: "Each band competes with a swing number, a ballad and a specialty tune, and performs for a jitterbug contest."[5]

It is the jitterbug contest that has the young sailors and Marines and their girlfriends sitting up in their seats. They are champing at the bit to get out there and start rocking, swinging, and flipping their dates. It is a perfect American night in that December of 1941. The kids are bursting with energy and ready to dance the night away.

Pennsylvania's band kicks off the program with a swing number, "There'll Be Some Changes Made," then moves into a sweet version of "Georgia on My Mind." But it is a roof-raising "Jingle Bells" for the jitterbug that gets everyone on their feet and starts the floor vibrating.[6]

Then the *Tennessee* and *Argonne* bands take their turns wowing the crowd, but in the end, it is *Pennsylvania*'s band that is whooping and hollering as the winner of the night. They advance to the finals, just two short weeks away. The band from USS *Nevada* packs up and leaves early. They need to be up to play morning colors at 8:00 a.m., out on "Battleship Row," where nine ships of the Pacific Fleet are lined up, two abreast, off Ford Island. The rest of the bands play long into the evening. It is a warm night and palm fronds rustle in the breeze over the harbor, but Christmas is in the air as the dancing goes on and on. Finally, after too many cocktails and too-swollen feet, the last dancers sway to one final song, singing "God bless America, land that I love . . ." Tuckered-out band members loosen their ties, pack up their instruments, and head back to the ships. Girls stroll down the walkways in bare feet, swinging their high heels in their hands. The men shuffle back on board and fall into their bunks, swaying to the gentle movement of the water below, sound asleep in no time.

Several hundred miles to the north of the sleeping sailors, the massive Japanese fleet churns the waters of this quiet night, ever closer with each passing minute. At exactly 6:00 a.m., the aircraft carriers halt and turn their bows into the wind. One after another, in practiced syncopation, 353 Japanese fighter pilots strap on their helmets and start their engines, then roar thunderously off the decks. By 7:30 a.m., in the distance they begin to make out the airfields they have studied, finally coming into view: Wheeler, Bellows, Ewa, and Hickam. Starting their descent through light cloud cover, they pierce the quiet air above the sleepy palm-lined harbor. US aircraft are lined up wingtip to wingtip on the airstrips, ready to be picked off. Anchored just off Ford Island, swaying on their chains at sunrise, are the ships of the US Pacific Fleet: *California*, *Maryland*, *Tennessee*, *Oklahoma*, *West Virginia*, *Nevada*, and *Arizona*, as well as *Utah*, which has been retired after thirty-three years. The battleship *Pennsylvania* is manned in dry dock. Eighty-six other Navy vessels jam the harbor.

The ships are full of slumbering young sailors, stacked three and four high in their racks. A few are already awake and up. They head into the galley for hot coffee, swap stories about shore leave and jitterbugging young ladies. Others are already at it, swabbing the decks and rubbing the brass to make it shine.

The Japanese squadron commander Mitsuo Fuchida, now over the target, determines that they have indeed caught the US Navy unawares. He shouts the signal to indicate it: "Tora! Tora! Tora!"

The morning calm is pierced by the guttural roar of propellers and screeching whistles of bombs rotating down in spirals to targets below. Dynamite rips through the ships' hulls, exploding their decks, slowly twisting the metal and then snapping the enormous masts. Oil and thick black smoke billow as the fighter planes sweep low across the water, dropping waves of bombs over and over. In all, 347 US warplanes and 18 warships, including all of the battleships, melt and twist into macabre hunks of metal, sinking in a stench of oil and fire. The Japanese lose just 29 planes. But 3,581 Americans are dead; more than half of them lie at the bottom of the shallow harbor, entombed in the *Arizona*. The killing blow to *Arizona* hit in between the first and second gun turrets. It is an armor-piercing round that goes through the decks and explodes in the powder magazine; this terrific explosion pancakes the front of the ship from the superstructure to the bow, instantly incinerating those inside. The ship goes down so quickly that in some parts, men are trapped under five feet of water. There is no way to get them out. For days after the attack, banging is heard from the men inside the ship, as they run out of oxygen. Among the dead are twenty-three sets of brothers, including the Beckers, the Dohertys, and the Murdocks, who had three brothers each on board; in each family, only one brother survived.[7]

X

History in ev'ry century
Records an act that lives forevermore.
We'll recall, as into line we fall,
The thing that happened on Hawaii's shore.

—Don Reid and Sammy Kaye, "Remember Pearl Harbor" (1941)

In Peekskill, New York, Frank Bowes decides it's a Howard Johnson's day, but he hasn't told anyone yet. He and his family walk down the steps of the Church of the Assumption after Sunday Mass. His daughter Betts and her best friend, Alice, skip down the stairs, hoping the grown-ups will head left at the bottom. That would mean they are going out for breakfast. Left it is! Betts and Alice run around the corner and pull open the big, heavy door. Coffee, toast, eggs, and chatter fill the air. They unbutton their church coats, and Frank hangs them on the hook built into the booth dividers. Betts and Alice swing their saddle-shoed feet and smile at each other. Helen's voice is loud and clear. "Hello, Joan," she says to the waitress. "Coffee, please, and two hot cocoas for the girls." Betts's and Alice's moms teach together, as does Helen's sister, Jane. They carefully pull off their church gloves and settle into chatter about school and husbands and Christmas lists, which the girls listen to intently to see what they can pick up, as seven-year-old girls will do. Frank and Larry settle in at a small table for two across from the booth and pull off their coats. Betts's eyes light up as Joan, who always piles on the whipped cream, slips the cups under their noses.

"It's hot, Betts, let it cool off." So Betts stares at the HoJo logo of the little boy and his dog, and the chef leaning down to show them the pancakes on his plate. Bing Crosby is on the radio singing "Silent Night" as she spins her spoon in the cup, blowing softly into it as the chocolate and cream swirl together.

Then she hears a grown-up gasp. She looks up.

Then, grown-up by grown-up, in a rising buzz, more gasps, then the words: Japanese. Bomb. Hawaii. What does it mean? She does not know, but suddenly everyone is shuffling, standing, chairs scraping across the linoleum floors. The parents start pulling on their coats. "What next?" they murmur. They forage in their pockets, leaving money on top of checks on the table, not waiting for change. "C'mon, girls, we have to go. We have to go." Mom grabs Betts by the hand, her hot cocoa still swirling in the cup. So terrible to leave it behind, she thinks.

At home, Helen and Aunt Jane sit down on the kitchen chairs, still in their coats. "What now?"

"We will enter the war, I imagine."

Betts has heard them all talk about "the war." They always told her not to worry, it is very far away. The maps down above the workbench in the basement are a different world.

Frank Bowes is down there already. Betts wanders over to the basement steps. She can smell his pipe. She holds the railing, goes down the wooden-slat steps, and sits on the last one. Frank rises from the step stool chair by the tool wall. He sweeps her up in his arms, leaving behind his maps and stacked newspapers, which show the movements of Hitler and Mussolini in Europe, and in the Pacific, the invasion of China by Emperor Hirohito and General Tojo. Frank had never imagined that the pushpins and arrows would sweep across the Pacific Ocean to the United States. He stares at the Hawaiian Islands in disbelief.

Later that night, Betts lies in bed, listening to the talk downstairs. A little girl in a house full of adults, she is used to staring up at the ceiling from her bed, hearing their chatter below, but tonight it is quieter, the words spaced farther apart. There are long gaps of silence that make her uneasy.

At noon the next day, Frank turns on the radio. Betts sits on the ottoman in front of his chair. Every American is doing the same thing, wherever they are. Everything has stopped. It is beginning to sink in: the United States is under attack. Where will they be hit next? What they dreaded and tried to push away has now landed on the back doorstep.[8]

The broadcast by the president from the House of Representatives in Washington, DC, is about to begin. They hear the raucousness inside the chamber as the rattled members of Congress settle into their chairs. President Roosevelt clears his throat and speaks.

Mr. Vice President, and Mr. Speaker, and Members of the Senate and House of Representatives:

Yesterday, December 7, 1941—a date which will live in infamy— the United States of America was suddenly and deliberately attacked by naval and air forces of the Empire of Japan.

The United States was at peace with that Nation and, at the solicitation of Japan, was still in conversation with its Government and its Emperor looking toward the maintenance of peace in the Pacific. Indeed, one hour after Japanese air squadrons had commenced bombing in the American Island of Oahu, the Japanese Ambassador to the United States and his colleague delivered to our Secretary of State a formal reply to a recent American message. And while this reply stated that it seemed useless to continue the existing diplomatic negotiations, it contained no threat or hint of war or of armed attack.

President Roosevelt's next sentences hammer at the perfidy of the enemy: the attack was "deliberately planned many days or even weeks ago," and the Japanese government "deliberately sought to deceive."

I regret to tell you that very many American lives have been lost. In addition, American ships have been reported torpedoed on the high seas between San Francisco and Honolulu.

Frank and Betts listen, spellbound, as the president goes on. There is much more.

Yesterday the Japanese Government also launched an attack against Malaya.
   Last night Japanese forces attacked Hong Kong.
   Last night Japanese forces attacked Guam.
   Last night Japanese forces attacked the Philippine Islands.
   Last night the Japanese attacked Wake Island.
   And this morning the Japanese attacked Midway Island.

The president's voice rises in fury at the unprovoked aggressions. His words, like hammer blows, land with incensed determination. He continues:

But always will our whole Nation remember the character of the onslaught against us. No matter how long it may take us to over-come this premeditated invasion, the American people in their righteous might will win through to absolute victory.
   I believe that I interpret the will of the Congress and of the people when I assert that we will not only defend ourselves to the uttermost but will make it very certain that this form of treachery shall never again endanger us.
   Hostilities exist. There is no blinking at the fact that our people, our territory, and our interests are in grave danger.
   With confidence in our armed forces—with the unbounding

determination of our people—we will gain the inevitable triumph so help us God.

His words hang in the air in the silence of the chamber, and in living rooms across America. In Roosevelt's strong, resolute voice, he concludes:

I ask that the Congress declare that since the unprovoked and dastardly attack by Japan on Sunday, December 7, 1941, a state of war has existed between the United States and the Japanese Empire.[9]

3

Outrage

Every valley shall be exalted, and every mountain and hill made low; and the crooked shall be made straight, and the rough places plain.

—Isaiah 40:4

In Gulfport, Mississippi, on the second Sunday of Advent, Reverend James N. Brown reads the words of Isaiah: fathers, mothers, and children bow their heads in unison. A baby is coming to save the world. King Herod fears the child will be a king, come to threaten his power. On his orders, his men ride through the villages, slaughtering all the young boys.

Meanwhile, across the Atlantic Ocean, far from First Presbyterian Church, modern-day Herod's henchmen storm neighborhoods of their own, forcing Jewish families out of their homes and loading them like cattle onto trucks. The crowded transports are packed with adults and children, some bewildered, others paralyzed with fear; they do not know where they are going. The sign over the gate at Auschwitz cruelly promises ARBEIT MACHT FREI, "Work sets you free," but most will never be free from Hitler's evil plan; they will be starved or gassed to death. These innocents stand between Hitler and his vision for the future, an Aryan nation cleansed of Jews.

Not far away from the sermon, Jay Rebstock is just happy to have the whole day off. On Sundays at the Gulf Coast Military Academy, in Gulfport, Mississippi, if you aren't in trouble and doing penalty drills, you're free to head into town.

From nearby Bay Saint Louis, Rebstock played football for Saint Stanislaus. His team last season was 12–0, thanks mostly to its full-back, Felix "Doc" Blanchard. He was unstoppable, pounding his hulking shoulders through every defense. Everybody wanted Doc: Army, Fordham, Notre Dame. But when Jay went to the military academy, Doc headed to the University of North Carolina and eventually to West Point.[1]

Jay's dad felt that his son would benefit from a bit of military structure, and perhaps he was right. Most Sundays, truth be told, Jay was doing discipline drills, but on this particular Sunday, Jay settles into his seat at the Paramount Theatre on 26th Avenue. There was a long line for tickets and Jay and his buddies rushed through the lobby and scrambled for a row of seats together to watch Gary Cooper as Sergeant York, the most decorated soldier in all of the Great War.

The newsreel projector sends flickering images across the screen. Marching music fills the theater, and the booming voice-over tells the hushed crowd of Germany's onslaught on Moscow in its winter offensive on the snow-covered battlefields of Russia. In Washington, DC, Japanese ministers shuffle through the halls of the State Department, meeting with Secretary of State Cordell Hull. They carry a letter from the emperor with a proposal to avoid confrontation with the United States.

About forty minutes into *Sergeant York*, as York is grappling with his newfound Christianity and the realities of war, the projector rattles, sputters, and then fails. This is not uncommon, and Jay and pals join in the usual chorus of boos and hisses. The house lights come on, and the harried-looking theater manager scampers up the stage steps and faces the audience.

They assume he's about to say they can get their money back at the box office, but instead he is agitated: "You should all head home; the theater is closing for the day. The Japanese have just bombed Pearl Harbor!" The manager pushes his glasses back up onto his nose and stands there a moment, not sure what else to say to the stunned crowd. There is nothing more to say. He hurriedly steps down and hustles back to the office.

His words hang in the air over the theater. Waves of panic and concern float across the voices. "Pearl Harbor?" "Pearl Harbor." "Where is Pearl Harbor?" Rebstock asks. Suddenly he feels a tap on his arm. An older cadet standing behind him leans over and says, "I know where that is; it's in Hawaii. My brother is there on a battleship named *Oklahoma*."[2]

X

"God, please get us out of here." The silent, desperate prayer comes from Seaman First Class Stephen Young. Gasping, he struggles and bounces to stay afloat in an upside-down watery world.

Some twenty trapped sailors cling to beams, braces, machinery, a half-submerged ladder—grabbing whatever is within reach.

Seven blasts heard from their bunks signaled danger. Moments later, Japanese torpedoes ripped open *Oklahoma*'s port side. Now, eleven minutes later, water is gushing through the open watertight doors. *Oklahoma* rolls with the weight of it, and now he can feel it in his bones. She is going down.

Three of the Pacific Fleet aircraft carriers are safely at sea. But *Arizona* and the capsized *Oklahoma* bear the brunt of the losses; two-thirds of the dead are in their hulls on the ocean floor.

A sailor hoists a lantern above his head, bobbing in the rising water. It is just now sinking in, as they orient themselves, that they are in an air pocket in the hull. The sailor with the lantern turns it off to save the batteries. In pitch blackness, as the water creeps slowly higher, each man grapples with what has happened and what it might mean.

Trapped upside down and submerged, Young remembers how only a moment ago, he was upright, combing his hair, patting his wallet in his pocket, about to hop up that same ladder, to catch the liberty boat ashore for a beach date with a lovely Hawaiian girl he'd met only the night before. "My girl and I were going to Nanakuli, where the surf was much better than Waikiki and the beach not nearly so crowded. For once I had plenty of money—a ten and a one-dollar bill."[3]

Then came the blare of the bugle, the *bong, bong, bong* of the ship's alarm. "What's this bullshit on a Sunday?" The question flew off the lips of hundreds of running men in dress uniforms, work uniforms, skivvy shirts, and shorts.

The voice on the PA system froze them in their tracks: "All hands, man your battle stations! On the double! This is no drill! Get going— they're real bombs!"[4]

Young had made it to his battle station—the powder hoist handling room of gun turret 4, the lowest deck on the ship—when an enormous explosion made the deck beneath his feet rock.

Now he is trapped in an air pocket, the *slam, slam, slam* of the torpedoes still ringing in his ears. His home away from home, the *Oklahoma*, is mortally wounded, listing badly.

The ship is almost on her side. Then suddenly it begins lurching. The deck slips out from under him; his hands snatch at empty air. As the ship rolls over, he is pitched into a dark mass of dead and dying, and with them he is buffeted and tossed about. Then the dark waters close over him as the ship stops, resting upside down on the bottom of the harbor.[5]

He swims frantically, not knowing in which direction. Then he has broken into a bubble of air. It is all coming back to him. How long has he been here? He does not know.

✕

The harbor is about forty-five feet deep. *Oklahoma*, resting on the bottom, is just visible above the water line.

"No talking," orders a voice out of the dark. "We've got to save the air."

"For what?" someone asks, and there is no answer.[6]

"How about a cold beer? I'm thirsty," Young blurts out, feeling around for his shipmate next to him. "I'll bet you a dollar we'll suffocate before we drown."

"Okay, you're on," agrees the shipmate. "I say we drown first." Each somehow manages to fish a soggy dollar bill from deep in his pocket.[7]

Time creeps by. Hours, maybe. No one knows how many. Is anyone searching for them? Does anyone know they are still alive? Have the Japanese captured Pearl Harbor? Someone is banging on the outside of the hull! But they hear the voices and realize that it is just other trapped sailors, also helplessly floating in a bubble on the other side.

Outside the *Oklahoma*, the Japanese have not captured Pearl Harbor, but they have dealt it a devastating blow. Still, the bombs that tore through hulls and snapped masts of the ships at Pearl Harbor are just the beginning. In the coming hours and days, the Japanese will strike General Douglas MacArthur's forces in the Philippines and British forces in Singapore and Hong Kong. They will conquer Guam, Wake Island, Borneo, Java, Malaya, the Solomons, the Marianas, Burma, and the Dutch West Indies in an appalling torrent of aggression.

But back on *Oklahoma*, hours pass, and Young and the others shiver and wait. It was morning when their world turned upside down. Is it now night? Some talk to keep one another going. Others drift into and out of sleep, dreaming for a few moments, then rocking back to their dire reality. Young's mind is like a kaleidoscope, with morphing school years, his mother and dad, faces of girls, laughing and full of life. Then he feels desperately sad and alone. He shouts to all and no one, "Damn it, I'm not even twenty and I'll never know or love a girl again!"[8]

Time ticks by. Anger begins to rumble within him. "Why couldn't we have died in the sun where we could have met death head on? That was the way to die, on your feet, like a man. But instead, it was to be a slow, useless death, imprisoned in our dark iron cell."[9]

In time, anger passes. Then comes submission, which is oddly calming as it settles over their watery tomb. There is only God left to come.

"Oh, God, relieve us of our torment," Young whispers in his head. "If it is Your will that we die here, please watch over our families and comfort them. We are delivered unto You and ask to be forgiven for our sins."[10]

But time does not bring death. The teeth of the soaking and shivering sailors chatter as they go into and out of shaking fits, into and out of sleep, descending deeper into the darkest parts, the lowest place a man can be.

Then comes a hammering, far away. It stops. The black bubble becomes deathly silent as the men strain to hear it again, but it is gone. They hear it again. Perhaps they are just imagining it. Then it is faint, but there is definitely someone there, hammering in the distance.

They take a dog wrench and hammer away at the steel bulkhead. Three dots—three dashes—three dots—SOS!

"They're trying to get us," someone says. They pound "SOS" again and again. They tap out their story: "We've been here a day—a whole twenty-four hours in this awful place. We were thirty, but now we're ten. The others are gone."

Suddenly there is a piercing, grinding noise; a drill bit flashes through the steel from the next compartment. The release of air forces a surge of water into their side.

The cutting tool begins its slow, sawing tear through the wall on the other side, now filled with light. They can see that the next compartment is empty; those men are saved. But the water is rushing in faster, shoulder high.

"Please hurry, for God's sake! We can't stop this flooding!" Young scans the morbid scenario in his head. We will be the ones to drown like rats at the last minute, just when rescue is within reach! They watch as the cutting saw makes a square; they begin pushing it open. Bending down three sides, one by one they squeeze their soaked bodies through the jagged metal edges. Each time a man forces himself through, the metal bends open a bit wider. There it is! Blue sky fills their eyes.

"I emerged from out of the cold darkness into the warm sunshine of a new day. It was 9 a.m., 8 December. Standing on the upturned hull, I gazed about me. It was the same world I had left twenty-five hours before, but as I looked at the smoke and wreckage of battle, the sunken ships Tennessee, West Virginia, and Arizona astern of us, I felt that life would never be the same, not for me—not for any of us."[11]

※

Young men across the United States knew their lives had been changed by that "day of infamy." There was no turning back. As Mark Antony knew, once the point of no return was met, the monarch's voice would "cry havoc and let slip the dogs of war!" The hounds had been released, and they would not return home until there was a victor.

And so they lined up and wrapped around blocks across the United States, young men straining to be unleashed against the enemy they called "the Japs." They wanted to fight; they wanted revenge. They poured into recruiting stations "in numbers unprecedented in the history of the nation."[12]

Their outrage was not fueled by a desire to save France and Great Britain. In fact, it had nothing to do with Europe at all. They wanted to come face-to-face with the bombers who had snuffed out the life of young men sleeping in their bunks or shuffling to breakfast. They wanted to end the Asian menace whose representatives talked diplomacy at the State Department while giving the order to annihilate our fleet at Pearl Harbor. Germany would declare war on the United States four days later, but to those men and boys on the long lines, the enemy that stirred their warrior blood was Japan.

At the University of Buffalo, the captain and star of the Bulls football team, Dominick Grossi, was one of them. Grossi's parents, Lena and Pasquale, called "Patsy," owned an Italian restaurant in their hometown of Lockport, New York. Dom was their adored son and big brother to Rose, Betty, Patrina, Marie, and his little brother, Junior. Dom left Buffalo early, packed his bag, and headed off to join the Marines and train at the University of Rochester. The Bulls' loss was U of R's gain as Grossi continued to take to the gridiron, but Grossi was turning his attention to the bigger battles across the ocean. He hoped to become an officer and head to the Pacific.

On December 10, the pride of the British Far Eastern Fleet, the battleship *Prince of Wales* and the battle cruiser *Repulse*, were hunted down and sunk by Japanese bomber and torpedo aircraft. Japanese forces took the Dutch oil fields in Borneo in mid-December and in the coming weeks managed to take over US- and British-built airstrips in Southeast Asia and the Philippines for their own use.[13]

In those early months of 1942, the existence of the United States was threatened in a way not felt since the dark days of the summer of 1814. Then it had been the rampaging British Army that swept Americans from their positions defending Washington, DC, and stormed the capital to destroy it. They breached the White House doors and helped themselves to the still warm food left behind in President James Madison and his family's hasty evacuation.[14]

The United States was now vulnerable again. The Japanese fleet had penetrated the ocean barrier and was moving undaunted across the Pacific. As with the British in their approach to the defenseless city of Washington, Americans were faced with the horror of the Japanese Navy sitting off our shores in a battle line between Hawaii and California.

With British and US naval forces destroyed or badly crippled, the Rising Sun flag was flying unchallenged in the Pacific.

)|(

Back in Tokyo, the forty-year-old Emperor Hirohito was a bit overwhelmed by his own success. His conquests had suddenly added 150 million new subjects in China and Southeast Asia to his kingdom. He told his lord keeper of the privy seal, "The fruits of war are tumbling into our mouth almost too quickly." The emperor had been told that he would likely lose a quarter of his ships in the early moves against the United States and Great Britain, but his only significant loss had been one destroyer. The Japanese war machine had surpassed all expectations. His imperial forces had vastly outmaneuvered the Allies with a larger and superior navy and air force and a masterful infantry that was better trained and more efficient. The days of just forty years prior, when the Japanese had been "awestruck at American ingenuity" and amazed by the technology of US ships, were long gone. Now they could see and taste dominance.[15]

This had been the plan for decades, and the work had gained momentum after the death of the Regent Hirohito's mentally ill father, Emperor Taisho, in December 1926. Despite the economic recession, the Imperial Diet had approved a yearlong enthronement extravaganza costing roughly the equivalent of $7 million, designed to deepen the bond of the people to their new leader in the tough economic times and dispel any tendencies toward communism that were simmering in the populace. The emperor's role as a god had to be reinforced, while any conspiratorial or radical movements against imperial rule had to be repressed. He was to be seen as father of the "divine land," a distant, all-powerful, benevolent leader. The distant part was a plus for Hirohito, who was awkward with people and plagued throughout his life by a "distinctly uncharismatic personality."[16]

The imperial court hierarchy sought to emulate the regal demeanor and pageantry they admired in the court of King George V, and with the dawn of mass media, albeit an obedient one, they sought to give Hirohito the royal treatment. It worked. A rapt nation witnessed his enthronement in Kyoto, which culminated with his oath "to maintain eternal world peace, and advance goodwill among nations through diplomacy." The final act of the ceremony involved donning ritual garments and traveling between three wooden structures in which he was purified; then he curled into the fetal position and was wrapped in a quilt to consummate his "marriage" to the sun goddess and his descent from the "plain of high heaven." This entire ritual was witnessed and assisted by members of the court.[17]

Twelve years later, the "maintenance of eternal world peace" was losing out to the ambitions of the Rising Sun. Now Emperor Hirohito and his minister of war, Hideki Tojo, were ready to seize opportunity.

On December 23, the US garrison at Wake Island surrenders to a Japanese invading force. On Christmas Day, the British at Hong

Kong also surrender, as US and Filipino forces hold out against overwhelming odds at Bataan, a province on the Philippine island of Luzon. In a horrific introduction to their ways of war, the Japanese force 70,000 prisoners, already weary from holding out, to march sixty-five miles north in the Bataan Death March. Thousands die along the way at the hands of the barbaric Japanese guards. Those who survive no doubt have many days when the alternative seems preferable, as they suffer at the hands of the inhumane prison guards, who take pleasure in beating and torturing them.[18]

The heaviest bombardment of the island known as "the Rock" comes on Hirohito's birthday, April 29. It is an all-day affair. Ten thousand shells blast the beach defenses. A powder magazine explodes, stripping the troops in the foxholes of their clothes and burning some men alive. The island is engulfed in flames and exploding ammunition that one ensign says made Dante's Inferno look like a backyard bonfire.[19]

One agonizing month after the fall of Bataan, the final US defensive stronghold in the western Pacific, Corregidor, falls. Thousands more Americans become prisoners of Japan.

They held the island for five long months after Pearl Harbor and, at the end of the battle on May 7, could hold it no longer. Defeated, the entire 4th Marines ceased to exist.

To all the Marines who watched events unfold in those early months of war, it is a gut punch. Though the Marines are seemingly always outnumbered, their fighting spirit captures the American imagination. The 147-man barracks at Guam fight tenaciously to the very end.

Major James Devereux's 449-man 1st Marine Defense Battalion on Wake Island seems to do the impossible. Devereux develops an Alamo-like defense that frustrates the Japanese, dashing their hope of a quick victory. Expertly deploying his guns and anticipating every Japanese maneuver, he blasts the Japanese out of the water, sinking two destroyers and an escort vessel. He damages two additional cruisers and two destroyers and destroys seventy-two Japanese aircraft.

Each morning, Americans at home grab their newspapers to follow the exploits of the daring Major Devereux. However, his men, who are the hope of bruised American morale, are up against the wall. They pin their hopes on a rescue naval force said to be racing to the scene. Americans read daily with bated breath, cheering on Devereux and his men. But the rescue never comes. Wake Island's brave defenders are finally overwhelmed two days before Christmas. The gallant Devereux and his surviving men become Japanese prisoners of war.

There is never any good news. The Japanese are never far away. There are muted reports that Japanese submarines are lurking along the California coast, shelling targets of opportunity. Then they are back at Pearl Harbor. Their mop-up operation frazzles Honolulu's already frayed nerves as the Japanese pummel the base with eight five-hundred-pound bombs, attempting to take out the dry docks and oil storage facilities they had missed on December 7.[20]

For all the young men standing in Marine recruiting lines, there are no illusions. The road back will be very long. They know next to nothing about what lies ahead. How many of them will it take? Will their little brothers be following them? These fresh-faced boys are eager to serve a cause bigger than themselves. If youthful enthusiasm could guarantee victory, then America was sure to win.

But the young warriors of the empire of Japan are also determined, and they are steeped in the "*bushido* spirit," based on the samurai code of honor. They embraced it for eight years in the bloody war in China, and they know in their bones that the code demands death before dishonor. Japan's minister of war, Tojo, made sure that each soldier has in his pocket his new booklet that explains the moral code of the fighting men: Running to your death, gun or sword raised high in a banzai charge, would be the only way to escape dishonor if your mission failed. Surrender would bring shame to everyone: the soldier, his family, his army, and the living-god emperor himself. The code demands, "Fear not to die for the cause of everlasting justice."[21]

They had little idea how fiercely that code would soon be tested.

4

The Changing Tide

The Rising Sun flew above the Dutch East Indies, it surmounted the French tricolor in Indo-China, it blotted out the Union Jack in Singapore. . . . Burma, Malaya, and Thailand were also Japanese. India's hundreds of millions were imperiled, great China was all but isolated from the world, Australia looked fearfully north to the Japanese bases on New Guinea.[1]

—Robert Leckie, historian and World War II veteran

On December 22, as the United States reels from the attack on Pearl Harbor, British prime minister Winston Churchill arrives in Washington, DC, to spend Christmas at the White House. He has invited himself. President Roosevelt tried to dissuade him, warning of the dangers of crossing the Atlantic Ocean, dodging U-boats and mines; still Churchill is undaunted. The prime minister knows the attack at Pearl Harbor has lit the fuse of the American people, but he is on a mission to bend Roosevelt's will to take the fight to Hitler in Europe first. He believes spending the Yuletide with the Roosevelts will help his cause.

It is nearly Christmas, but war precautions dictate that holiday lights are to be kept to a minimum. Cities are darkened at night, hoods are placed over fireboxes, and neon signs in cities are left unplugged. But that night, the Roosevelts and Churchill head out onto the South Portico in front of a large crowd to light the White House Christmas tree. In their respective homes in Arlington, Massachusetts, Gulfport,

Mississippi, and Lockport, New York, the Grays and Rebstocks and Grossis—and families all across the United States—sit in front of their radios to listen to their president and the prime minister. Churchill tells them that although he is far from his family and his homeland, he is glad to be among them in the country where his mother was born. He says that on this "strange Christmas eve," Americans should endeavor to "make the children happy in a world of storm," adding, "Now, by our sacrifice and daring, these same children shall not be robbed of their inheritance, or denied the right to live in a free and decent world."[2]

In the days that follow, Churchill and Roosevelt talk late into the night over cigars and scotch. The prime minister argues that the offensive against Hitler must push his forces back in North Africa first, while Roosevelt urges a France-first strategy. Churchill's stay stretches on for three weeks. He sleeps in the Blue Room and at times paces the room after his bath in just a towel and in at least one instance no towel at all, much to the surprise of President Roosevelt, who stops by to chat. The hours of talk forge a deep friendship and unshakable bond that Christmas of 1941 that will see them through the darkness to come. For each, the other is the one person who understands the enormous burden he bears.[3]

By January, Roosevelt is champing at the bit. He needs to punch back and soon. The American people must get the message that though they are down, they are not out. He wants to send Hirohito and Tojo a strong message close to home. He calls a secret meeting of his top brass at the White House. Huddled with the president are General Henry H. "Hap" Arnold, the chief of the Army Air Forces; General George C. Marshall, the chief of staff of the Army; Admiral Ernest J. King, the chief of staff of the Navy; Henry L. Stimson, the secretary of war; and William F. Knox, the secretary of the Navy.[4]

Roosevelt implores them to give him a plan that will bloody the nose of Japan and lift the sinking spirits of the American people. He pushes them again in a similar meeting on January 28. The obstacle is that the broadened ring of Japanese-controlled territory in the Pacific will require launching fighters from a great distance. But from where? The vast ocean offers no jumping-off point that is close enough to the Japanese mainland.[5]

The desperation of the president leads the military brain trust to propose a daring, if not impossible, plan. General Arnold lays it out to Roosevelt: The prime targets of the Japanese on December 7 were the United States' premier-class aircraft carriers. But by luck or the grace of God, they were not in the harbor that morning. Now those same vessels will be moved into position and act as floating airstrips, replacing the US strips on the nearby islands, which are now in Japanese hands.

The naval aircraft that typically launch off the carriers will not be used. They would never make it to the target. The plan calls for launching sixteen B-25 medium-range Army bombers (named for William "Billy" Mitchell) piloted by men from the US Army Air Corps from the deck of an aircraft carrier. There will be no chance of recovering the bombers since they were not built for a carrier landing; they are too big and have a nose wheel. They cannot be stored on the lower hangar deck, because they do not fit into the elevators. Instead, they will have to be lashed down on the flight deck, vastly shrinking the space left over for takeoff. The first plane will have just 467 feet to become airborne or plunge into the ocean.

To the crews who have trained on the carriers, the numbers do not add up. No aircraft with the standard 27,000-pound load has managed to become airborne in less than 600 feet. What they don't know is that the specially configured, stripped-down, combat-loaded planes, rigged with auxiliary fuel tanks, will tip the scales at a whopping 31,000 pounds. The aircraft, with their sixty-eight-foot wingspan, will somehow have to take off in less than 500 feet.

If they do make it into the air, they will need to fly 750 miles to drop their four five-hundred-pound bombs on targets in and around Tokyo, then hightail it for the Chinese coast, where, it is hoped, their pilots can locate the primitive landing areas marked out by the Chinese.[6] There are no guarantees; the pilots know that this is likely to be a one-way mission.

ж

The secret plan to bomb Japan has been in the works for more than three months. But after the designated carrier, *Hornet*, is spotted on its way toward Japan by the patrol boat *Nitto Maru*, the timetable has to be accelerated.

At 7:25 a.m. on April 18, 1942, the elite bomber crews, led by the esteemed aviator Lieutenant Colonel James Doolittle, get the call to man their aircraft. Just hours before, Doolittle bolstered his men with a wry smile as he attached ribbon-tied messages for the Japanese to their bombs. Now his fellow pilots snap into their seats, flash smiles and thumbs-up, their voices drowned out by the buzz of the massive spinning propellers and the roar of thirty-two engines. Sixteen B-25 bombers stand stacked like elephants, trunk to tail, practically touching, on the deck of the *Hornet*, as it lurches up and down on the sea.[7]

The bombers rumble for takeoff, with one wingtip nearly scraping the carrier superstructure, the other slightly sticking out over the water. Two painted white stripes run down the length of *Hornet*'s deck. The pilots are to keep their left wheel on the left-hand stripe and their nose wheel on the right-hand stripe. Any deviation would be deadly.

A sailor up ahead, his signal flag blowing in the fierce winds, is just forward and to the left of the first plane. He is the focal point of sixteen pilots as they stare down the axis of the deck. For those at the end of the line, this figure, his deck uniform plastered to his body by the howling thirty-knot wind, is "first silhouetted against the skyline, and then against the horizon, and finally against the boiling ocean as *Hornet* rose and fell from one wave to the next."[8]

He is known as "Fly One," and one by one he signals the moment for takeoff. Timing is everything. He eyes the bow of the ship and the ocean dashing against it. Like a child picking the exact moment to dive into dueling jump ropes, he watches as *Hornet*'s bow completes its lift toward the sky and then is well into its descent into the trough of the next wave; then he turns to Doolittle and whips his flag like a matador's cape. Colonel Doolittle releases his brakes. The big bomber strains at the leash; now the fully revved engines propel it forward. The B-25 begins its roll forward, downhill, on the flight deck that is now dipping toward the boiling ocean.

Breathing seems to stop, every eye now pinned to the moving aircraft. It gathers speed, lumbering toward the end of the piteously short runway. Then, at just fifty miles per hour into a thirty-knot headwind, with just a few feet of runway left, Doolittle pulls back on the yoke. The nose wheel lifts just as *Hornet* surges upward to crest the next wave. As her deck rises toward the sky, the B-25 is catapulted into the air to the cheer of the sailors. With one bomber aloft, yet only twenty-five feet above the water to avoid Japanese radar, confidence shoots through one pilot after another. In short order they take to the sky as well and set their course for Japan.

Within hours and now some seven hundred miles away, high above enemy territory, one after the other they hit the release and drop their bombs. Tokyo and five other cities in Japan are rocked by explosions as "Doolittle's Raiders" release five-hundred-pounders onto their targets.

In the end the physical damage is limited, but the psychological blow to Japan is significant. The Japanese wake up to a world where bombs have fallen in their own backyard. Fifty people are dead, including some civilians, and four hundred are injured. Japan is no longer a proudly isolated, invulnerable island. The long arm of Uncle Sam has jabbed and bloodied Hirohito's bespectacled nose.

Back in the United States, the president says nothing. He knows it is no time to take a victory lap. Though the mission succeeded, the pilots never found the makeshift airstrips in China, and the planes crash-landed in China and Russia. Three pilots are dead, and eight are now Japanese prisoners.

It will be from foreign sources that the US press picks up the news of the raid. Roosevelt lets the headlines speak for themselves. The *Santa Ana Register* blares:

YANKS BOMB TOKYO.

In smaller print in the middle of page 1, subheadlines follow: "Naval and Industrial Bases of Three Other Cities Also Attacked; Raid on Tokyo Brings Elation to Washington."[9]

The *Los Angeles Times* hits the streets with a "9 AM EXTRA":

TOKYO, KOBE, YOKOHAMA
BOMBED!

On April 21, three days after the raid and with the press frantic for answers, Roosevelt finally meets with reporters. They jockey for position to hear what he has to say. The president remains stoic and coy.

"Would you care to go so far as to confirm the truth of the Japanese reports that Tokyo was bombed?" fires off the first reporter.

"No, I couldn't even do that," Roosevelt replies. "I am depending on Japanese reports very largely."[10]

It's an odd choice of words, "very largely." Indeed, the Japanese media reported the raid just hours after the bombs fell. The *New York Times* picked up the story, setting off a scramble to fill it in.

Roosevelt remains mum and feigns ignorance, insisting that the reporters know as much about the incident as he does. But members of Congress are not as content to remain silent and eagerly entertain reporters with their own speculations. The most common of which is that the attack had to have been launched from China.

Colorado senator Edwin C. Johnson immediately jumps on the bandwagon: "That is about the only place from which an air attack could have been carried out successfully."

Pennsylvania representative John Buell Snyder chimes in, telling reporters, "This will prove TNT in boosting morale, not only at home, but especially in China and Russia."

And Senator D. Worth Clark of Idaho echoes the exhilaration felt by most Americans: at last, we have been able to strike back. "This is the only way we are going to win the war—start right in bombing them at home."[11]

But astute reporters continue to press on the most curious strategic detail: "From where did the attack originate?"

Finally, Roosevelt calls the press together to reveal the answer. Pencils poised above notepads, the reporters are ready to race off to the phones to call in the story, but the president takes his time as they close in for the scoop. Again, they ask, "Mr. President, where did the raid take off from?" "Shangri-La," he replies.

⋊

It is after midnight at 55 Welcher Avenue in Peekskill, New York, and Frank Bowes is at his workbench. He had taken a map out of the newspaper back when Hitler invaded Poland and put it on the wall there. He had marked it up and put pins into it to follow the expansion of Nazi territory. He had always wanted to go to Europe, and now he wondered if there would be a Europe when the war was over. He looked at the red pin he had pushed into Pearl Harbor.[12]

Now he holds a clipped newspaper headline and tacks it near Tokyo, where the Doolittle Raiders had hit. He steps back and takes a long draw on his pipe, the scent of which eventually wafts its way upstairs, letting Helen and Betts, already in their beds, know that he is still down there, deep in thought. The newly added pin seems defiantly alone, its gold color shining like a beacon on the western edge of his battle map. His young nephew, Harry Gray, now fifteen, is already itching to get in the fight. Uncle Frank has assured him that it will all be over by the time he is old enough to go. Frank wants Harry to stay right where he is on Linwood Street, in Arlington, not far from where he spent his own teenage years. He hopes maybe Harry will head off to Holy Cross for college and follow in his footsteps. Yes, he wants Harry to stay safely at home.

By May 6, 1942, any optimism Harry's uncle Frank had had about the Tokyo raid has vanished. In the Philippines, General Jonathan

Wainwright surrendered the US and Filipino forces that had bravely withstood the Japanese onslaught for five long, horrendous months. Though the details were scarce, stories of the Japanese forcing US soldiers to march hundreds of miles, many of them to their death, were starting to hit the home front. Americans could hardly bear the tales of their boys being mutilated, tortured, and starved to death, many left by the roadside unburied. It was simply unfathomable.

)(

After the Doolittle Raid, Japan lashes out against the Chinese, who they discover had laid out crude landing areas intended for the American pilots.

Japan's next priority is to shore up its southern defensive perimeter. That line is to run to the north of Australia and New Guinea. Japan has never lost a military confrontation at sea, and Hirohito, the 124th emperor, is determined to continue the unbroken chain of military success.

On the morning of May 4, 1942, the United States detects Japanese ship and troop movements toward Port Moresby, New Guinea. Admiral Chester Nimitz, the commander of the US Pacific Fleet, dispatches a naval task force. Severely depleted by the attack at Pearl Harbor, it is made up of some of the surviving cruisers and destroyers, which form around two of the last four carriers, *Lexington* and *Yorktown*. They make their way into the Coral Sea south of the Solomon Islands, searching for the enemy with orders "to destroy enemy ships, shipping, and aircraft at favorable opportunities in order to assist in checking advances by the enemy in the New Guinea–Solomon area."[13]

On May 7, 1942, a "favorable opportunity" arrives. The fleets spot each other on radar and signal for air attacks. Neither fleet sees the ships of the other side. But each land deadly blows, sinking ships in a storm of torpedo and dive-bomber attacks. In the end, the combatants back off to lick their wounds and count their casualties. The Japanese light carrier *Shoho* has sunk to the bottom of the ocean under the pounding of thirteen bombs and seven torpedoes. It was under attack only a short fifteen minutes.[14] The second carrier, *Shokaku*, lumbers along, wounded by the direct hits of six dive-bombers. The Japanese turn tail and abandon their mission to invade New Guinea and occupy Port Moresby.

But the US carriers are also hit hard. Gasoline fires roar across the deck of *Lexington*. Sailors scramble to put them out. Then the tank explodes in a fireball. The stinging smell of fuel burns in the sailors' nostrils and eyes, like Pearl Harbor all over again.[15] A gigantic column of dense black smoke rises skyward, and in the early hours of May 8, the order comes to abandon the "Lady Lex." US destroyers come in to finish her off, sinking her to the depths of the Pacific.

Yorktown, down but not out, sets course for Pearl Harbor for repairs. The Navy is now down to only two carriers, *Hornet* and *Enterprise*. Both sides have lost about seventy aircraft, and 1,500 sailors and aviators are dead.[16]

What neither side knows is that in this battle, in these days in May 1942 in the Coral Sea, the Japanese vision of southern territorial expansion by sea has been stopped cold in its tracks. But the battlegrounds to come lie dotted along stretches arching west and east on the path to the Japanese mainland.

〤

For the second time in three weeks, American newspapers hit the stands with screaming bold headlines. This time it is the battle news from the Coral Sea. *The Sun* of New York trumpets in big black letters:

15 JAP SHIPS SUNK,

LEXINGTON IS LOST,

IN CORAL SEA FIGHT[17]

That evening, Frank Bowes turns back the pages of the newspaper to the detailed maps, to read the reports of what unfolded on the Coral Sea. Helen sits in her maroon velvet chair and leafs through the papers as well. She is still in her dress and pumps after a long day at work. Betts scampers down the front staircase in her pajamas, her wet brown curls combed, ready for bed. She and her aunt Jane went to Woolworth's that afternoon after school, and Betts picked out a small box of American flags on pins. Helen looks over the top of her newspaper with a slight smile, watching as Betts holds them out in her small hands. She looks up at her father with her proud bright hazel eyes. "Daddy, these are for your map."

He smiles at her and pats her wet head. "Thank you, Betts. Tomorrow we will find Port Moresby, but now it is off to bed for you!" He holds her hand as they walk upstairs with Helen.

)(

One month later on June 7, days of press speculation continue as sketchy details emerge of yet another naval battle going on near the island of Midway. There are reports that the Americans are inflicting some real damage on the Japanese.

The *Sunday Telegram* of Elmira, New York, blares across page 1:

13 TO 15 JAP SHIPS SUNK OR DAMAGED
GREAT VICTORY IN MAKING, SAYS NIMITZ

There's more. The subhead reads:

2 OR 3 CARRIERS WITH PLANES AMONG ENEMY MIDWAY
LOSSES; BATTLE RAGES INTO THIRD DAY.[18]

A third day! Day three spells doom for a fourth Japanese carrier, which follows their carriers *Kaga*, *Akagi*, and *Soryu* to the ocean floor in a crushing blow for the Rising Sun.

It had begun, in the days prior, as the massive Japanese naval force moved toward Midway Island to push their eastern defensive line closer to Hawaii, and draw the United States' remaining aircraft carriers into battle.

Admiral of the Fleet Isoroku Yamamoto had sailed the Japanese Combined Fleet to the east in two battle formations. The first group of the huge armada had four carriers, two battleships, three cruisers, eleven destroyers, and five supply ships. On board the carriers, lined up head to toe, were 275 attack aircraft and the crews to man them. Several hundred miles to the rear were seven more battleships, one light carrier, three cruisers, and twenty destroyers. It was a daunting naval caravan as far as the eye could see.

On *Hornet*, *Enterprise*, and *Yorktown*, sweating work crews were still fixing and hammering and patching, as they sensed the enemy far out there in the distant rolling waves. But the Japanese commanders misjudged the location of the US carriers, believing them to be somewhere between the Coral Sea and Pearl Harbor.

They were wrong.

In fact, the Americans were less than an hour's flight from the Japanese carrier force.[19] The Japanese dive-bombers may have swept in on unsuspecting sailors on December 7, 1941, but six months later, at Midway, it was the Japanese who never saw the attack coming.

The American attack began midmorning on June 4, and within moments, three Japanese carriers and a heavy cruiser were ablaze. The fourth carrier, *Hiryu*, was the only one to initially escape major damage. It launched an attack against the *Yorktown* and severely damaged the American carrier. But by 5:00 p.m., dive-bombers delivered disabling attacks on *Hiryu*, and it, too, was scuttled by the next morning.

After Midway, the Japanese could no longer claim naval or air superiority in the Pacific. The four enemy carriers they lost were all attackers at Pearl Harbor. Unfortunately, the patched-up *Yorktown*, named for the pivotal battle of the American Revolution, also saw her last day at sea in the Battle of Midway. Torpedoed by the Japanese submarine I-168, the crew tried desperately to save her, but she was lost.

The morning after, Admiral Nimitz sent a message to his task force commanders: "You who have participated in the Battle of Midway today have written a glorious page in our history. I am proud to be associated with you."[20]

※

Weeks earlier, Frank Bowes had wondered how a sea of red and black ink could cover so much of the world map—and whether it was only a matter of time before it would cross the ocean to California and the US mainland—but tonight he and many in America have hope. The Battle of the Coral Sea has stopped the Japanese Empire's southern expansion, and the Battle of Midway has hemmed it in on the east. The bleeding has stopped, and it appears that the pushback is slowly getting under way.

※

Frank welcomes Harry for a visit just before his sixteenth birthday. It isn't often that the Bowes family have a boy in the house or that Anne can buy her son a train ticket, but everyone is glad to have Harry around. The house is too quiet much of the time with just one child, but Harry punches a hole through the silence with his laugh and hilarious stories about him and his friends sneaking into the movie theater in Arlington and taking their dates to the roller rink. Betts sits at the dinner table staring at him and hoping no one will shush him when he talks about teenage things with her parents. She loves the banter and how different her dad seems around him, since they are both "boys." Harry loves the change of scenery. Plus, he got to take the train and feels very grown up.

Talk turns to the war, as it does at every dinner table in 1942. When Harry talks about it, he gets that glimmer in his eye. He wants to be old enough to go fight the "Japs," as he calls them, and the Nazis. He doesn't want the war to pass him by. He wants the United States to win, yes, but not before he can get there. "I'm going to do it, Uncle Frank. I'm going to sign up as soon as I can," he says, gulping down his dinner. "I'm going to be a Marine."

Frank cuts his steak and nods. He knows just how Harry feels. But

Uncle Frank has told him not to enlist. "Wait to be drafted, Harry. You are the man of the house. Your mother needs you. Just be patient." But "patience" is a word wasted on sixteen-year-old boys. Frank knows that Harry looks up to him; he also knows when he looks in those bright green eyes and Harry smiles that warm, sweet smile back at him, as if nothing can touch him, that he isn't listening and there isn't much that Frank or anyone else can do about it.

So Frank does the only thing he can: every Sunday at the Church of the Assumption, when he is on his knees, he prays to God that it will all be over before next June 13, when Harry turns seventeen.[21]

5

What Hirohito Knew

I had presumed the news of the terrible losses sustained by the naval forces would have caused him untold anxiety, yet he was as calm as usual. He ordered [the Navy chief of staff] to ensure that future operations continue bold and aggressive.[1]

—From the diary of Koichi Kido, aide to Emperor Hirohito

The shock was all-encompassing. The Japanese navy once achieved great victories over its formidable foes China and Russia but now was suffering blows that cracked open the door to defeat by America and its allies. To the emperor, the first six months of 1942 seemed inexplicable. Until April 18, there had not been a shred of good news to bolster the flagging spirits of Americans and their allies. After April 18, good news was elusive for Japan.

Who deserved the blame for the catastrophe at Midway? The British and Americans had been on their knees. Had his leadership failed? Had his generals failed him? The Japanese had expected to push back the Americans in the central Pacific, but now the opposite was happening: they were losing dominance in the South and Southwest Pacific as well. The differences in culture and tactics appeared to be hurting the Japanese efforts rather than giving them an edge. They were now part of the wider world, and the forces against them were daunting.

After Commodore Perry pierced the veil of Japanese secrecy in 1853, Japan's rise as a military power was built on its own "rules of war." Those rules were formed in part by the fifth-century B.C. military strategist Sun Tzu, but largely, they were the creation of the Emperor Meiji, who came to the throne at age fifteen in 1867. Meiji brought Japan out of its dark age and into the light as a thriving industrial society with the military might to defeat China.

Meiji dictated "Japan will attack without warning."[2] And why not? Sucker-punching a nation with which you are at peace was anathema to the West, but Meiji's dictum was to conquer. Western rites of "proper" engagement were of no concern to him. An ancient samurai motto seemed to sanction it: "Win first, fight later." It was in sync as well with the great Sun Tzu's maxim: "In war the victorious strategist only seeks battle after the victory has been won."[3]

But the maxims of the samurai and Sun Tzu assume that hostilities have begun and two nations are at war; they propose that he who is victorious without fighting does so by presenting such a powerful posture that victory is certain. Meiji may have contorted his attack-without-warning strategy to resemble the win-first dictum of Sun Tzu. If so, he missed, or ignored, the second line of that dictum: "He who is destined to defeat first fights and afterwards looks for victory."[4]

✕

On December 25, 1926, at the age of twenty-five, Prince Regent Hirohito, a grandson of the late warrior Emperor Meiji, ascended the throne as the 124th emperor of Japan, after the death of his father. The Shinto religious ceremony celebrated him as the descendant of Amaterasu, the sun goddess, who had created the Japanese archipelago from the drops of water that fell from her spear.[5] In conformance with the custom of naming the upcoming era, Hirohito took the name "Showa," meaning "Enlightenment and Peace."[6]

Meiji possessed absolute divine rule. Hirohito was destined to struggle with a covey of powerful and often conniving advisers, but in all matters, he had the final word. He aspired to emulate the British model of constitutional monarchy, but two years into his reign, financial catastrophe thwarted his plans for the evolution of his government. First came the 1927 financial panic and the ensuing depression, then the calamity of a worldwide depression in 1929.

Japan's fragile economy could not risk any form of democracy in this fragile moment. Instead, Hirohito looked across the sea to China with a clenched fist. What China had, Japan must take; rich farmland, plentiful mines and coal. The Chinese were an easy target, and Manchuria was the obvious point of entry.

The United States had firmly signaled that Manchuria belonged to China, but Hirohito's prime minister, General Giichi Tanaka, had other ideas. He brazenly told his cabinet that a takeover of Manchuria was necessary.[7] So began the Japanese era of conquest, usually cloaked in multiple layers of deception, fraud, and feigned indignation. The drive for natural resources was the initial goal, but the taste for a growing empire was seductive. That hunger pulsed through the upper echelons of Japanese military and imperial advisers, but Hirohito, as sovereign, head of state, and supreme military commander, clearly wanted to make his mark on the world and prove the superiority of his dynasty and his people.

His father, Emperor Taisho, had been a weak leader, plagued by mental illness. As one story goes, on a rare occasion when he actually addressed the Imperial Diet of Japan, he stood before them all, rolled up his speech, and looked at them all through it, as if it were a spyglass.[8]

Hirohito took over as regent for his ailing father in 1921, becoming the effective ruler as Taisho retired to the country and died in December 1926.

Any suggestion that Hirohito was a bystander who watched as history unfolded is challenged by his every action. In 1928, many Japanese companies operated in Manchuria and defense was an integral part of the growing military-industrial complex. Rebellious soldiers plotted an "incident" to provoke China. Anticipating that it would work, the Imperial General Staff drew up secret operational orders to mobilize the army in Manchuria on May 22, 1928. But US intelligence uncovered the Japanese movements in Manchuria, and, suspecting that something was afoot, the US government demanded to know what Japan's intentions were, making clear that in the eyes of the West, Manchuria was Chinese territory.[9] The United States emphasized that any deviation from that understanding would constitute "a most serious matter."[10]

Tokyo got cold feet and backed down. But the rebels were furious and devised a plot to keep moving the ball forward. On June 4, 1928, at 5:20 a.m., a bomb they planted exploded under the railcar of a Manchurian warlord and killed him. Japanese soldiers approached the scene to investigate. They spotted three suspicious Chinese whom they approached to question. When one suddenly hurled a bomb, they were compelled to stab and kill two of them; the third escaped.

The three were in on the ruse and had been hired by the Japanese as backup assassins who were to rush in and finish off the warlord in case the bomb did not do its job. They did not know that the plan included killing them and, with them, their knowledge of the plot. But the third man escaped, made his way to the son of the slain Chinese warlord, and revealed the whole sordid plot.[11]

To stoke instability, the rebel soldiers went about bombing the homes and offices of Japanese residents as if it were the Chinese doing it, then offered the services of the Japanese Army to restore order. The plan fell flat on its face. In the end, the rebels' failures revealed their own duplicity.

Word quickly reached the Imperial Palace in Tokyo, and anxious advisers argued that the emperor be informed and the agitators punished. Others said no, fearing that escalating the situation would reflect badly on Japan and ignite rumors that the treachery had been sanctioned from the top.

Finally, the prime minister, Tanaka, went to Hirohito with the truth. The emperor demanded that the conspirators be punished. When it was not done quickly, he repeated his command. But there was no punishment; the Army secretly would not allow it, and the emperor let it lie. Some of the guilty officers resigned. Officially, the Army declared the incident closed, having found no evidence. In July 1929,

Tanaka stepped down in disgrace. In the end, Hirohito let those who had been responsible live, but their careers were over when the cabinet essentially collapsed.

It was not the last time Hirohito would butt heads with his military leaders. In 1930, despite enormous Japanese military and civilian opposition to the proposed London Naval Treaty, which sought limits on submarines and shipbuilding, Hirohito overcame the opposition and backed the treaty. Without him it was doomed to failure. The treaty was approved and ratified.[12]

A year later, the restless forces in the Japanese Army took another surreptitious run at amassing control over parts of Manchuria. Again Hirohito feigned disapproval, but his silence suggested otherwise. By the end of 1931, Manchuria was firmly under Japanese control. Like the parent of a rebellious child, Hirohito chose to look the other way while his officers moved in on Manchuria, stopping short of disciplining them as they achieved the desired goal. Japan signed an "agreement" with the last emperor of China, Puyi, in 1932, to demonstrate legitimacy in the eyes of the world, and established Manchuria as a puppet state.[13]

After a resolution by the League of Nations condemning the actions in Manchuria, Japan withdrew from the world body.

Japan was doubling down on its warrior culture, dynastic rule, and religious sovereignty of the emperor and moving farther away from any dream of constitutional monarchy. Hirohito embraced it. His father had been a weak ruler. His own personality was uncharismatic and awkward. He moved to bolster his stature as a deified leader. The Army instituted the Imperial Way with its patriotic pledge: "The Emperor, the people, the land and morality are one and indivisible."[14]

The youths of the nation were "reeducated" in the religion of emperor worship: "The entire nation regard[s] our emperor as a Living God." They were taught to die willingly for the emperor; they must always attack—never retreat.[15] Their training was brutal. Had he chosen to, Hirohito could have reined in that resurrection of the *bushido* code. But he did not. In the years to come, young men from the United

States would be astonished as Japanese soldiers ran into oncoming fire and exploded grenades into their own torsos, rather than humiliate their families and emperor by surrendering.

While the nation was being programmed in emperor worship, the Army officers continued their headstrong ways. On February 26, 1936, Army assassins mobilized to eliminate seven key figures in a coup of the Tokyo government leadership. They cloaked their actions as an effort to shore up the Divine Showa Restoration—done, of course, for the emperor's benefit.

Hirohito called in his minister of war and ordered that the rebellion be put down. Those who had surrounded the targets of assassination were now themselves surrounded by soldiers obeying the emperor's orders.[16] Despite the surreptitious moves and plots of his military to chart its own destiny, somehow Hirohito always had an inside track to their deviousness. He was leading from the shadows of the palace, always.

As Japan moved steadily toward its goal of Asian dominance, 1937 brought yet another opportunistic "incident" on the Chinese mainland. On July 7, a single Japanese infantry company decided to maneuver into a most unlikely area of the Twenty-ninth Chinese Army. In the confrontation, shots were exchanged on the disputed area of the Marco Polo Bridge. A cease-fire document was hastily drafted, but the Japanese left it unsigned for two days. At home the Japanese newspapers reported government-sanctioned accounts of the skirmish. It was a tale of anti-Japanese racism and exaggerated stories of Chinese atrocities.

The incident at the Marco Polo Bridge served the Japanese military's purpose of pushing the area of engagement beyond Manchuria into north China. The military leadership then went on to claim that the area of hostilities now went beyond north China and in fact that all of China was now in the Japanese sphere of influence. It was an argument made purely to justify the protection of Japanese interests wherever and whenever the Imperial Army saw fit. The military leaders pressed the emperor further and argued that, given the new circumstances, military reinforcements were necessary. They said it would take less than a month to subdue Chiang Kai-shek's armies and create peace in China.[17]

The emperor listened, fully aware that such a move would pull his country deeper into an aggressive path in Asia. He was told that five divisions from Japan, in addition to the existing army already in China, should do the trick; his advisers counseled that it wasn't really an act of war, more a show of force against the Chinese to *prevent* war. Hirohito gave the royal nod and his approval for the extended operation.

With that, he gave not only his blessing to the military leaders' lust for war but his confirmation of their distorted reasoning for the mission creep in China. He then unlocked the imperial war chest, without which his ambitious military advisers would be impotent.

Hirohito did not choose to weigh down progress with an over-attention to reason or thought when the possibility of a widening Japanese Empire was dangled before him.

Within a month, Hirohito was getting anxious. The promised quick victory was now nowhere in sight. The unsophisticated but fanatical Chinese Army was willing to sustain enormous losses against the modern Japanese Army. Hirohito called for an end to the fighting. A diplomatic solution would include land concessions, and that would be a win for now.

But it was too late. One "incident" or skirmish led to a response and then another, and now there was a full-scale mobilization of the Chinese armies and the emperor was left with no choice but to fight fire with fire.

Future apologists for Emperor Hirohito would proclaim that he had been personally opposed to war but had been powerless to stop it. The invasion that followed the incident at the Marco Polo Bridge refutes that notion, but a further examination of the events of the Second Sino-Japanese War proves that the emperor was very much in charge. Any doubt about his convictions was swept away that December in the Rape of Nanking.

By the end of 1937, the Japanese had the Chinese capital completely surrounded. Day and night, they pummeled the city with artillery and air strikes. Once the city was brought to its knees, the Japanese soldiers began a six-week massacre that would go down as one of the most brutal in the history of the world. It was a scene of unbounded degradation, torture, mutilation, and murder. Unborn children were sliced from their mothers' wombs. Sexual mutilation by the insertion of bayonets and sharpened bamboo poles into women's vaginas and breast amputations were giddily carried out and photographed by the rampaging Japanese soldiers.

The historian Edwin Hoyt attempted to explain the origins of the Japanese bloodlust:

> It was a result of the policy of brutalization of the troops from the day of enlistment. In the name of discipline, the most violent and inhumane actions had been taken against these soldiers . . . and had destroyed most of the admirable tender elements of the Japanese character. The new bushido had made them brutes, and they acted like brutes.[18]

That December, Reverend James M. McCallum, an American working at a hospital in a demilitarized enclave, made safe under German auspices and flying the Nazi flag, wrote in his diary:

> Never have I heard or read such brutality. Rape! Rape! Rape! We estimate at least 1,000 cases a night and many by day. In case of resistance or anything that seems like disapproval, there is a bayonet stab or a bullet. . . . People are hysterical. . . . Women are being carried off every morning, afternoon and evening. The whole Japanese army seems to be free to go and come as it pleases, and to do whatever it pleases.[19]

On December 23, 1937, George Fitch, an American Protestant missionary in Nanking, wrote that Nanking "is a city laid waste, ravaged, completely looted. . . . It is hell on earth. Hundreds of innocent civilians are shot before your eyes or used as bayonet practice. . . . A thousand women kneel before you crying hysterically, begging you to save them from the beasts who are preying on them. This is a hell I had never before envisaged."[20]

The butchery went on unmitigated for weeks. The officers saw a purpose in it. One of the regimental commanders confided to Hirohito's uncle General Yasuhiko Asaka that "the best bayonet training in the world was to let the troops work on people."[21]

Throughout the atrocities, Hirohito remained silent in his palace in Tokyo.

In Japan, newspapers glorified the butchery. One headline read:

Contest to Cut Down a Hundred!
Two Second Lieutenants Already Up to Eighty[22]

That was the headline on a story by Asami Kazuo and Suzuki Jiro on the murderous exploits of two Japanese officers, Mukai Toshiaki and Noda Tsuyoshi.[23] The two lieutenants bragged about their hand-to-hand combat with enemy soldiers, all of whom they claimed to have vanquished and dispatched with their swords alone. It was like a national sporting event to kill one hundred enemy soldiers first, and the Japanese public followed along. Every few days in December, the papers flashed updates and tallies of the kills until the final score was announced, 106–105. Both Japanese warriors outlasted more than two hundred Chinese rivals, somehow without sustaining even a scratch.[24]

But underneath the swashbuckling samurai spirit and *bushido* was a far less sportive, far more grim reality.

The truth leaked out rather ignominiously when one of the two lieutenants went home and detailed his exploits as if unaware of the lore. It turned out that the killings had been nothing more than extermination of prisoners. Neither of the Japanese warrior soldiers had suffered a scratch for the simple reason that none of the Chinese had been armed. They hadn't even been fighting back. After they surrendered, he admitted, "we'd line them up and cut them down, from one end of the line to the other."[25]

The soldiers in the Japanese Army were behaving just as they had been taught to. They had been conditioned to believe that they were part of a superior race. They pledged obedience to their officers and worshiped their emperor as a god. They were taught that anything or anyone non-Japanese was beneath them and therefore disposable.

It was all to the same ends to tell tales of valiant fighting that actually amounted to no more than systematic extinction. Lieutenant General Nakajima Kesago described his plan to murder the thousands of Chinese prisoners now under his control: "Divide them into groups of two hundred . . . and deal with them."[26]

In January 1938, Koki Hirota, the Japanese foreign minister, wrote, "I investigated reported atrocities committed by the Japanese army in Nanking and elsewhere. . . . Convincing proof. Japanese army continuing [to] behave in fashion reminiscent [of] Attila and his huns. . . . 300,000 Chinese civilians slaughtered [in] cold blood."[27]

That damning note found its way into the hands of a Nanking resident, Harold John Timperley, a reporter for England's *Manchester Guardian*. He immediately sent it on to the *Guardian* in enciphered English, which was intercepted and decoded by US intelligence and sent on to Washington.[28]

If Hirohito's foreign minister knew about the Nanking holocaust, how could the emperor not know? Hirota was not some low-level military officer on the faraway Chinese battlefield; he was part of the imperial cabinet and in the emperor's inner circle.

The rest of the world slowly became aware of the horror happening on the other side of the ocean, as diaries and photographs of Japanese soldiers murdering and raping helpless victims began to appear with all the ghastly details, including people being doused with gasoline and set afire. Their testimonies removed all doubt that anyone, anywhere could pretend not to know what was happening under the rule of Emperor Hirohito, who had taken for the name of his reign Showa, "Enlightenment and Peace."

In fact, it was a family affair. General Asaka, a prince of the royal family, had been personally appointed by the emperor, and the Nanking massacre had been carried out under his direct command. Hirohito himself had removed the constraints of international law for the protection of Chinese prisoners. For Hirohito, there was no such thing as a Chinese POW.[29] Neither Hirohito nor his uncle Asaka had stepped in to command an end to the slaughter that dragged on and on in Nanking. The historian Yoshida Yutaka wrote of the triumphant return of Asaka, who came bearing as gifts objects pilfered from the devastated city. He presented Hirohito with several Chinese art objects, saying, "We always bring back such things as booty."[30]

)(

After the Doolittle Raid, the Japanese captured eight elite US naval pilots. They were taken prisoner after they dropped their bombs on and near the Japanese capital and then crash-landed their planes. All of the pilots had known it was a mission from which they were unlikely to return.

General Tojo opposed putting them to death, fearing retaliation against Japanese citizens in the United States. The army generals urged the execution of all eight, to send a message. Hirohito commuted the sentences of five of the pilots and sanctioned the execution of three. Since all the prisoner-of-war records were later destroyed, no one knows why he let the five live.[31]

In 1942, after the Battle of Midway, US forces began to mobilize for what lay ahead. Midway had stopped the eastward expansion, but to the west lay the empire's hundreds of heavily fortified fortress-island outposts. The US Marine Corps's mission was to attack across the vast central Pacific, defeat the island-chain defenders, convert the captured islands into stepping-stones, and attack the heart of Japan. The young Marines who were unaware of the gruesome reports from Nanking enjoyed an innocence not shared by those who had paid attention. For them the images of how the Japanese had treated their vanquished were seared into their minds as they set sail.

The First Step: Say a Prayer for Your Pal on Guadalcanal

I've got spurs that jingle, jangle, jingle / As I go riding merrily along / And they sing, oh, ain't you glad you're single?

—Kay Kyser Orchestra, "Jingle Jangle Jingle" (1942)

Harry Gray hums along, "And that song ain't so very far from wrong." He likes what he sees in the mirror. He has grown at least another inch in the past year and is shaving pretty much every day now. Looking at his reflection, he can't help but smile a little, rubbing some Brylcreem into his hair and making a clean part to the right. The wide teeth of his comb carve his blondish-brown hair into a wave like ripples on the sea. He buttons up his shirt as he hears the *click-clack* out the window of Nancy, riding his creaky silver bike up the driveway. It is five o'clock, so she is just back from her route slinging *Saturday Evening Posts* on front stoops up and down the neighborhood streets.

"Oh, Naaaan-cy!" he hollers singsongy from upstairs as her saddle shoes slap up the front steps.

"Junior, I don't have any money!" she yells and runs like lightning into her room, slamming the door.

It's always the same: she adores her big brother, but she can't for the life of her figure out where his money goes. Every week she stuffs the $1.35 she makes for the magazine deliveries into the very back of her night table drawer. She is saving up for a bike of her own. But there he is again now, rapping lightly on her door. "Nance?" He cracks the door open just a bit, and she looks up at his sixteen-year-old eyes bearing down on her. "If you just lend me one dollar, I will pay you right back as soon as I get paid, and I will let you play touch football with me and Tom tomorrow after Mass." She looks up at him, trying to hold back a smile. She already has the dollar in her hand. It's a bargain he knows she will strike.

Tom is the handsome boy next door. He has a fox terrier named Riot. Nancy loves to play with them and race across the yard, squeezing the football tight in her arms. Sometimes her friends stroll by on the other side of the street, watching her running and laughing with the big boys. Other times, Harry puts Riot into the basket of his bike, and Nancy squeezes onto the front of the seat with him behind her, his arms on either side holding the handlebars, swerving from side to side and laughing as she screams, "Stop!" They come within a hairsbreadth of a tree or a fence or a parked car, but somehow at the last second Harry steers them onto the grass in front of the Linwood Street house, bumping up over the curb. Anne stands in the doorway watching it all, pretending to be just a little bit mad.

So of course Nancy gives him the dollar. He kisses her head and takes off like the wind. She swings around the doorway, watching him run down the stairs, hands hitting the walls instead of the banister as he goes and singing "Jingle, jangle, jingle . . ." The scent of his aftershave hangs in the air.

Tom and his sister, Kitty, pick up Harry, and they drive through town, the car windows down in the warm, still summer night. At a stoplight, Harry looks over at the old Winchester Savings Bank; a poster hangs in the window: "Even a little can help a lot—NOW." On the poster a little blond girl and her big sister crouch over a war stamps book, licking stamps and sticking them onto the page. Next to them on the floor lies a soldier's cap.

Harry feels a twinge of guilt about borrowing money to go bowling, but damn it, he wants to do more than lick stamps, he wants to lick "Japs." He is so ready! He kicks the floor of the car in frustration.

He does not want to wait another year. He can't imagine waiting another year. Three miles down the road, they pull up to Bowl Haven. Candlepin bowling on a Saturday night in New England; walk in the door, and you can forget all about the war. Taking a look around, Harry pushes his hands down into his pockets. The place is packed. The floor rumbles as balls roll down the alleys, pins crashing, steel bars slamming down to sweep them noisily into the pit. Underneath the sound of the balls shooting back up the ramp like earthquake tremors, teenagers jostle on the benches, one on each bench sitting at the lit score pad, pencil in his teeth, asking, "What'd you get? Are you sure?" They are whistling and slapping each other on the back. Harry takes it all in. There's that song again. It's on all the time: "Aren't you glad you're single?" He sips his Coke and settles onto a bench as Tom strolls up to roll his first ball. He takes another look over his shoulder; his eyes land on a slim blonde in the last lane. She is laughing and putting her hands over her face. Behind her, a ball meanders like a drunken sailor ever so slowly down the alley before plopping into the gutter. She slides onto the curved seat next to a boy about his own age. She has cherry-red lipstick and long legs crossed over each other under a straight skirt that skims the top of her smooth knees. Anybody going off to the war would want a picture of a girl like that in his pocket, thinks Harry. Staring over his shoulder, he watches her a bit longer. It suddenly seems as if there isn't anything else going on around them. If she were his girl, he would write to her every day from wherever he was, whoever she is.

"Harry, wake up, pal! What are ya looking at? Come on! It's your turn!"

)(

Charlie Gubish married his girlfriend, Ethel, on May 11, 1939, and their two boys, Charles and Richard, followed quickly thereafter. They live on a farm in Wassergass outside Hellertown, Pennsylvania. Their place isn't far from where Charlie grew up on his parents' 132-acre farm.

When Charlie gets home from a long day at work at the fire department at Bethlehem Steel, he plays with the boys, and sometimes when he looks at them, he sees the old days. In his family, as he was growing up, there were twelve brothers and sisters. Three of them died as babies, gone before they were five months old. Two were stepbrothers. Charlie left school at the age of twelve to help out on the farm, which was not unusual back then. His father needed the help. But it wasn't all work. Charlie and his sister, Helen, would run over the hills and into the woods when the work was done for the day. One spring day, they discovered what looked like a "tin man" propped up in the trees. Helen screamed, and then Charlie thought he saw the strange creature move, and they ran as fast as they could all the way home to tell their father about the strange man in the forest. Charlie's dad's face grew stern, and he looked them both square in the eyes. He scolded them for going that far and told them not to tell anyone what they had seen. In time, Charlie figured out that the "tin man" was busy making whiskey out there in the woods, during Prohibition. No doubt the men snuck a bit of it, when the whole family gathered at the Gubishes' farm on the weekends. The men would play cards and the women would cook for everyone.[1]

Charlie smiled thinking about it.

He bounces little Charles on his knee, and his thoughts turn to the present. Working at the mill makes him and the other men exempt from the draft since they are supporting the war effort. But when Charlie watches the young men shipping out in their smart uniforms, there are times when he longs to get onto a ship and sail away, see the world and maybe even a bit of action against the Japanese.

※

In the summer of 1942, the US victories in the Coral Sea and on Midway begin to dim a bit in their ability to keep Americans' spirits high. On the ground, the reality is that "our boys" are in a helluva fight against the soldiers of the Third Reich and those of the Rising Sun.

Field Marshal Erwin Rommel and his vaunted Afrika Korps appear to be unstoppable in North Africa as they capture Tobruk. On the eastern front, the Red Army reels under the devastating German onslaught; gruesome death is everywhere and casualties climb into the millions.[2] Americans do not know how bad it really is. By the end of the year, 35,000 of our brave young men will be dead: shot down in the air or blown up on the sea or the land.

Back home, American factories kick into high gear, working overtime to build the machines to fight the war. The auto factories that built 3 million cars in 1941 turn out only 139 new cars during the war years. Women flood into the workforce, as they did during World War I in England. Each morning, they pour through factory doors, lunch boxes and tools in hand, to build fuselages at Chrysler and engines at General Motors. At Ford, massively converted assembly lines build B-24 Liberator bombers, turning out one every sixty-three minutes.[3]

But the men to fly the new planes and fire from their gun turrets are nowhere near ready yet. As Americans sit in their cinema seats gazing up at newsreels of goose-stepping German soldiers and hearing reports of the treatment of our young men at the hands of their Japanese captors, they harbor secret doubts.

The United States' fighting strike force in the Pacific numbers only 15,000. What is that in the face of enemy armies in the millions? They are the men of the 1st Marine Division, a curious lot of holdovers from the 1930s who developed the new doctrine of amphibious warfare. They are the Marines who endured the privations of constant training, desolate posts and training grounds, and long separations from just about everyone and everything. The Corps is their home.

During World War I, Captain John Thomason wrote from France that the strange collection of fighting men were:

> a number of diverse people who ran curiously to type, with drilled shoulders and bone-deep sunburn, and a tolerant scorn for nearly everything on earth. They were the Leathernecks, the old breed

of American regular, regarding the service as home and war an occupation.[4]

Their home base was one only a "leatherneck" could love, New River Base, North Carolina: a recent Marine Corps acquisition described as "111,710 acres of water, coastal swamp and plain, theretofore inhabited largely by sandflies, ticks, chiggers, and snakes."[5]

To those being forged in that crucible, the grueling training and deprivations were to be not simply endured but relished and embraced as the path to a new level of esprit, camaraderie, teamwork, and disdain for all those who could never measure up. It was the chance for the new men to attempt to attain the never-to-be-attained title of "Old Breed."

Though that high-minded goal was not necessarily foremost in the minds of the Marines striving to achieve it, the idea of the ordeal itself was not lost on them. "This is the way they want things," growled one salty veteran. "You don't make a good fightin' man if you're in love with everybody. You got to be mad, so sore at everything you'd slug your best buddy at the drop of a pisscutter [slang for garrison cap]."

Recreation, when it came, was the occasional movie night, boxing match, or homegrown Marine talent show. Even the USO shows avoided the swamp in North Carolina. The men were largely shut off from the world, except for their rare, shared copies of the *Onslow County News*. Its editor seemed as salty and pissed off at the world as the Marines, hawking his weekly product as "the only paper in the world that gives a damn about Onslow County."[6]

That band of brothers, bound by their isolation and seemingly abandoned by all, wore their moniker, "the Raggedy Ass Marines," as a badge of honor. There was indeed a 2nd Marine Brigade stationed on the West Coast, but the Raggedy Asses delighted in distancing themselves from those "candy asses," and since the 2nd Brigade occasionally furnished Marines to the film industry, they labeled them "the Hollywood Marines," with all the disdain that the title conveyed.[7]

A Marine private's pay was $40 a month,[8] and the mess hall or field rations kept him fed. The Corps provided a roof over his head every night—even if it was a starry or stormy sky—and soon a refrain spread among them: "In the Corps, every day's a holiday and every meal's a banquet!" To many, they seemed a strange lot, but to one another, they were Marines.

In February 1941, the collection of "Old Breeders" that had been the nucleus of the 1st Marine Brigade since 1934 became the 1st Marine Division. During the seven previous years, the brigade had been the very essence of amphibious doctrine. It had conducted six fleet landing exercises training all services, and it had honed its unusual skill in warfare to the highest level. Now, on the day of its formation as a division, the men had no time for celebration; they embarked for Culebra for yet a seventh exercise.

A personnel officer noted of the new men, "The average age of the enlisted personnel is very low, probably not 20 years—about 90 percent of them enlisted since Pearl Harbor. They are full of patriotism and have the up-and-at-'em spirit."[9]

The naval brain trust, led by Admiral Ernest J. King, the chief of naval operations, was well aware that Japan's forces continued to fortify its outer-island defense system. Few people even knew where those far-flung places were, but during their whirlwind 1942 military expansion, Japanese forces had seized Rabaul in the previously British-held Northern Solomon chain. The rest of the chain, which ran from northwest to southeast, was also to be seized and fortified as an impregnable line blocking all communications and supply lines with Australia and New Zealand.

The historian John L. Zimmerman wrote of the Japanese, "In Rabaul they secured a prize of great strategic worth . . . as a point of departure for further offensives to the south . . . toward the all-important, slender U.S. line of supply and communications from the Hawaiian Islands to Australia and New Zealand."[10]

Despite the heady successes in the Coral Sea in the waters to the south of the Solomon chain and at Midway Island in the central Pacific, what was now at stake was complete control of the southern

Pacific Ocean and the installation of a phalanx of interlocked, fortified Japanese defensive lines. The foothold the Japanese had on those two spots enabled progress on two potential fronts. The northern route, from Pearl Harbor, could move from Tarawa to Saipan to Guam to Japan's own Iwo Jima. The southern route, up from New Zealand, would start with Guadalcanal, Leyte Gulf, Hong Kong, and on to Japan's own Okinawa. Both routes would involve amphibious assaults on heavily fortified Japanese bases. Most would require deadly close-quarters combat in order to drive out every last Japanese soldier. Battles at sea can sometimes provide easy victories, but there would be no easy land victories in the South Pacific. Every inch of wet jungle and barren rock would be paid for in blood.

Admiral King was determined to move the small band of leatherneck fighters along with his depleted navy to a position closer to possible combat. He ordered two-thirds of the 1st Marine Division, under the command of General Alexander Vandegrift, to Wellington, New Zealand. Vandegrift balked, complaining that the final combat training had not been completed. King assured him that combat was not expected to occur before January 1943, and there would be plenty of time, at least six months in Wellington, to complete training.

So on May 19, 1942, the 5th Marines sets sail from Norfolk. It passes through the Panama Canal, then continues toward the South Pacific. The 7th Marines was detached in April and assigned to the defense of Samoa, and it provides a ready force to be deployed to the Canal Zone if necessary. The 1st Marines, also bound for Wellington, will take a different route and has been entrained to the West Coast to sail from San Francisco.

The Marines who sail for the Pacific in May 1942 are the boys who first flocked to the recruiting stations in the aftermath of Pearl Harbor. Some enlisted fraudulently (they were too young); others, not yet eighteen, came armed with their parents' permissions; others came without their parents' permission but with forged parents' signatures; and the eighteen-year-olds stepped across the line on their own.

Thousands of other younger ones stand and watch their older

brothers and cousins board trains to bases for recruit training. Mothers, sisters, and girlfriends wave and weep. Each young boy who watches his hero brother wave good-bye is counting the days until he is old enough to join him.

X

Jay Rebstock is one of these boys. Back on December 7, when the theater manager announced the attack at Pearl Harbor in the middle of the afternoon at the movies and Jay heard the boy near him say, "I know where that is; it's in Hawaii. My brother is there on a battleship named *Oklahoma*," he scrambled out of his seat and ran to the nearest pay phone. The line at the phone booth wrapped around the block that afternoon as theatergoers frantically called family members to make sure they were okay and to talk about the shock and the "What next?" and try to understand what lay ahead. After Jay stood in line for three hours, change for the phone sweating inside the hand clenched in his pocket, Jay's father picked up the phone back home.

Suddenly, focused as never before, Jay said, "Daddy, I'm quitting school to join the Army to fight the Japs." His father at first was silent and then delivered his curt answer: if Jay walked away from school, the elder Rebstock would give him more fight than any Jap could ever give him. End of subject.[11]

X

Nineteen-year-old James Russell worked as a spot welder at a steel company in New Orleans, in a dark world of burning embers and blinding lights. As a barrel banged off the roller, Jim grabbed it, squared it, and hit a button on the robotic spot welder, which set into motion an impressive explosion of fiery bolts as the welder tacked the seams before the barrel moved along the belt to the next stop.

Russell was constantly snuffing out burning bits of metal that rained down on him. Goggles protected his eyes, but about every fifteen minutes he was handed a new pair of gloves, because that was how long it took for them to get riddled with small burn holes. For his work he earned sixteen cents an hour.

One day after work, one of the guys egged Jim on to join the service with him. It had to pay better than this, and it would get them out of the smoky inferno for a while. Jim thought it was a capital idea and told his grandmother that night that he was shaking off the dust of that factory and moving on. Like most families, she was stoic about his news, but her heart sank at the thought of him, just a kid really, facing the frightening menaces of the war. She tried to dissuade him, reminding him that in battle, some people get killed. But like most boys, he was fairly sure it wouldn't be him.

"Granny," he said. "Well somebody has to get killed, but it's better than that stupid spot welding!"[12]

✕

Pulling into King's Wharf in Wellington, New Zealand, the Raggedy Ass Marines, now known as the 1st Marine Division, hear a band playing. It is playing for them: "From the halls of Montezuma to the shores of Tripoli . . ."

It is June 1942, and these Marines are moving into the Pacific theater to train closer to the action. Wellington is the other side of the world in every way: a city in a mountainous and green foreign land. The Raggedy Ass Marines have kissed good-bye the sweaty boxing matches and bad talent shows under the hot, dingy tents in New River. The slithering snakes, chiggers, and sand fleas of that hellhole are now distant memories as they press together against the rail, craning their necks for a look at this first foreign port. Locals of all ages are waving and smiling up at them, and the band keeps playing welcome songs. The crowd's jubilance is an expression of their relief that the Americans are here to help defend them against the Japanese. They have watched the fall of Hong Kong and the surrender of Singapore; they have seen the British warships *Prince of Wales* and *Repulse* sunk; and they fear that their green island home will be next.

As the Marines come down the ramp, there begins a boisterous trade of coins for oranges and cigarettes; there are robust hand shaking and eye searching and crowd scanning as Marines lock eyes here and there with Kiwi girls and hearts on both sides race at the possibilities. Combat is still at least six months away. They will train for what lies ahead on the islands between here and Tokyo. But that day on the wharf, they drink ice-cold bottles of fresh farm milk offered to them from rattling carts, and for the moment, they forget all that lies ahead. The milk tastes so good, and this place looks more like home than anything they have seen in a long time.[13]

For the first time in a year and a half, these young men are "going ashore."[14]

But six days later, everything shifts. After his arrival in Auckland, General Vandegrift and his staff report to headquarters on June 26. They are there to meet with Vice Admiral Robert Ghormley, the commander of the South Pacific Area. Expecting that the first order of business will be the plans for training the division and coordinating activities with the New Zealand authorities, Vandegrift is handed a piece of paper. The Marine general quickly reads the thirty-seven words of an official military dispatch from the Joint Chiefs of Staff of the United States:

Occupy and defend Tulagi and adjacent positions (Guadalcanal and Florida Islands and the Santa Cruz Islands) in order to deny these areas to the enemy and to provide United States bases in preparation for further offensive action.[15]

Vandegrift asks who will be responsible for the occupying and defending. He is more than mildly shocked when the admiral blithely informs him that he and his 1st Marine Division are to execute the order—not in six months but in five weeks. The operation is provisionally set to begin on August 1, 1942.[16]

Unbeknownst to General Vandegrift, the change in plans has been set into motion by new movement of Japanese troops in the Solomon

Islands, especially at Tulagi. A Coastwatcher, British Colonial Service district officer Major Martin Clemens, from his hideout on a hill overlooking the Lunga River on Guadalcanal, has spotted a large Japanese force crossing the thirty miles from Tulagi to the northern shore of Guadalcanal. Two thousand Japanese troops and construction workers are now there building an airfield.[17]

Guadalcanal and Tulagi are small islands sitting at the southeastern end of the Solomon Islands chain. Guadalcanal is ninety miles long and twenty-five miles wide. It is separated from tiny Tulagi by Sealark Channel. The recent, frantic Japanese construction efforts are a red flag to Admiral King.

Admiral King seems to be almost alone in his urgent exhortation that the United States has to attack, seize the initiative, and do it now. This is no time for vacillation. It is time for the type of daring, offensive thinking that led to the stunning victory at Midway. The Japanese are on the march in the Solomons and in short order will complete the seizure of the entire formerly British island chain. There is no one to stop them. Their success in fortifying the Solomons would sever any and all lines between the United States and Australia.

Step by step the admiral manages to overcome all interservice rivalry, foot-dragging, and bickering, and Operation Watchtower comes to life.[18] The historian John Zimmerman describes Admiral Ghormley's understrength naval and Marine Corps force that is now to sail to confront the powerful Japanese forces surging ahead in the Solomon Islands:

Taken all in all, Ghormley could rely on a small, highly trained striking force . . . of less than one Marine division . . . surface forces of fluctuating and never overwhelming power (which nevertheless represented the maximum which Admiral Nimitz could spare), and an extremely scanty array of land-based aircraft. He had no assurances of reserve ground troops for the coming operation.[19]

It wasn't much, to be sure, but the commanders know that waiting is perilous and it is better to fight now with what they have than miss the moment to strike. Having lost *Lexington* and *Yorktown* at Coral Sea and Midway, they are down to three aircraft carriers. *Enterprise*, *Saratoga*, and the carrier *Wasp*, which had recently been transferred from the Atlantic, form the front line, along with the newly commissioned battleship *North Carolina* and a number of cruisers and destroyers.

In mid-July, from his lookout post, Clemens reports that the new Japanese airfield is nearly complete, and Admiral Nimitz orders the 1st Division to seize and hold it before they can get it done. The new invasion day will be August 7.[20]

The timeline advance is not enough, though. On August 5, one of Martin Clemens's native scouts reports to the Coastwatcher that the airfield on Guadalcanal has been completed (actually, only 2,600 feet of 3,800 feet has been finished) and will soon start receiving aircraft. Clemens is distraught. Japanese bombers will now be able to strike all surface ships bound for Australia, and Australia's isolation will be complete.[21]

But on August 7, the US naval force manages to arrive at Guadalcanal and Tulagi undetected, thanks to the cover of overcast skies and rain squalls. The weather has grounded all Japanese air activity at Rabaul.[22] The stealth and silence of this remarkable approach are broken at just after 6:00 a.m., when the bombardment fleet opens fire on the invasion beaches with its big guns.

The convoy carrying the 1st Marine Division anchors its transports, and under the lingering cloud cover the Marines begin disembarking. Almost 1,000 Marine officers and 18,000 Marine enlisted men begin the first US offensive against Japan. Tulagi and Guadalcanal are now under simultaneous attack.

Wellington is just a sweet, distant mirage as they shoulder eighty-four-plus pounds of gear (making them the most heavily weighted foot soldiers in the history of warfare) and pull all that weight over the side of the ship, clambering down the cargo nets, in their first death-defying feat of the attack.

There is no initial opposition upon landing. As Marines make it to the airfield, they discover full rice pots, still hot. The Japanese had run for the hills when they realized the Marines were there. Looking at the island, the first jungle most of these Marines have ever seen, they see the sweltering, hellish place that will be the arena of their first combat, the torrid jungle that will inspire their fellow troops to "say a prayer for your pal on Guadalcanal."

During the first two days of the landings, the Japanese soldiers work to disrupt further landings of troops and supplies. But a greater Japanese force is on the way. Late on August 8, a powerful cruiser force is dispatched from Kavieng and Rabaul with orders to "attack and destroy enemy transports in the Tulagi-Guadalcanal area."[23]

The vulnerable US troop transports are guarded by three cruisers and two destroyers of the Northern Group off Tulagi and two cruisers and two destroyers of the Southern Group off Guadalcanal. Separating the two groups positioned on opposite sides of Sealark Channel is the circular-shaped Savo Island.

At 1:30 a.m., August 8, the seven Japanese cruisers and one destroyer steam at twenty-six knots on a course to pass to the south of Savo Island. The Japanese attack force enters the channel waters undetected and closes on the unsuspecting ships of the Southern Group. As they come to bear on the US ships in their attack column, each ship in the column fires torpedoes. Explosions rock both heavy cruisers, inflicting damage—one later sinks.

Not missing a beat, the flying Japanese column now swings around Savo Island as if it were a revolving door, splits into two columns, and opens fire on the Northern Group.

Illuminating the US ships with searchlights, they open fire with their main deck guns at nearly point-blank range. The devastating fire rips through the US ships and sinks all three cruisers, and the Japanese sail away into the night. They have inflicted one of the worst losses ever on the US Navy.[24]

The rest of the transport ships and their escorts quickly leave the area. As dawn breaks, the Marines on shore look out on the now-vacant waters of Sealark Channel to discover that they are all alone with no sea or air support. In their isolation they nickname the Battle of Savo Island "the Battle of the Five Sitting Ducks."

X

On a steaming summer Wednesday, August 12, Frank Bowes settles into a sticky seat on the train on his way home to Peekskill and opens up his folded *Boston Post*.

"Gains on Solomons" blares the headline, and beneath, "U.S. Fighters Outpunching Japs in Invasion of Southwest Pacific Islands." Another item near the bottom catches his eye: "Clark Gable in Army as Private: Actor Joins to Be Airplane Gunner."[25]

The *Los Angeles Times* reports on the screen idol and Oscar nominee:

> Just as many another American male of proper physical, mental and moral qualifications is doing these days, Clark Gable, he-man of the motion-picture screen, yesterday held up his right hand and repeated the oath of enlistment in the Army of the United States.[26]

Gable, forty-one years old and devastated by the tragic death of his third wife, Carole Lombard, in a plane crash, decided to do his part. He enlisted in secret to avoid the crush of fans that swarmed his buddy Jimmy Stewart when he enlisted.

Gable says about being a man and a soldier, "He must be ready to choose death before dishonor without making too much song and dance about it. That's all there is to it."[27]

Although the Guadalcanal headlines are vastly encouraging to Americans at home, the death Gable speaks of is cutting down scores of boys no one ever saw on the silver screen in ways no one at home could even imagine.

✳

For the next six months, the Marines on Guadalcanal desperately cling to their island stronghold while the Japanese battle ceaselessly to evict them. The opposing forces on shore also have front-row seats at the nightly sea battles that rage in the waters offshore. While the US Navy mostly controls these waters during the daylight, at night the battle line of Japanese ships, nicknamed "the Tokyo Express," plows through "the Slot," the channel between the outer islands of the chain, to engage in the desperate struggle for control.

Each struggle brings more sunken ships, shelling of the Marine defenses, and bombardment of the crucial airfield. These attacks routinely crater the runway before it is frantically patched the next day. Some hits damage it to the point of full or partial shutdown.

There is never a day that Henderson Field is not under bombardment. "Almost daily, Japanese bombers from Rabaul attacked Henderson Field at noon during August, September, and October . . . warships and submarines sailed into Sealark Channel nearly every night to shell the airfield."[28]

The Henderson Field defenders call the noontime onslaught "Tojo Time." "There would be 18 to 24 of them, high in the sun and in their perfect V-of-V's formation. They would be accompanied by 20 or more Zeroes cavorting in batches of 3, nearby. Their bombing was accurate, and they would stay in formation and make their bombing run. . . .

"And the men would pull the chin straps of their helmets tighter and tense their muscles and press harder against the earth in their foxholes. And pray."[29]

Then: WHAM! (the first one hit) WHAM! (closer) WHAM! (walking right up to your foxhole) . . . WHAAA MM! (Oh Christ!) WHAM! (Thank God, they missed us!) WHAM! (the bombs were walking away) WHAM! (they still shook the earth, and dirt trickled in). WHAM![30]

As bad as the daily bombing is, the men prefer it to the naval shelling. That is much worse. "A bombing is bad," said one defender. ". . . But a bombing is over in a minute. A shelling, however, is unmitigated, indescribable hell. It can go on for a few minutes or four hours. When the shells scream overhead you cringe expecting a hit and when there is a let-up you tremble knowing that they are getting their range and the next one will be a hit."[31]

Then there is the other kind of trembling, the one that racks the body with dengue fever or malaria. On Guadalcanal, the men are as likely to die from the depletion of their bodies by these ravaging diseases as from bombing or shelling. And then there is the hunger that sets in after the supply ships leave. Men pick the maggots out of their white rice gruel or they just get used to eating them. The sun burns the men's skin daily, and when the rains come, it is never-ending deluge. Every day is like the next ring in Dante's Inferno.

The first two months in Guadalcanal hell is just a prelude to the next onslaught by the Japanese. The historian John Miller writes:

> Shortly before midnight of 13 October, a Japanese naval force including the battleships *Haruna* and *Kongo* sails unchallenged into Sealark Channel. While a cruiser plane illuminates the target area by dropping flares, the task force bombards the airfield for eighty minutes, the heaviest shelling of the campaign. The battleships fire 918 rounds . . . of which 625 are armor-piercing and 293 high explosive. They cover the field systematically. Explosions and burning gasoline light the night brightly.[32]

The bombardment has closed the field to US heavy bombers, and the perpetual shortage of aviation fuel is now dire.

In the weeks leading up to the October attack, the Japanese are unrelenting in their drive to fight hand to hand on the beaches and in the jungle to recapture the island. Though US air forces constantly interdict and destroy supply and troopships and bomb suspected Japanese assembly areas, some 27,000 Japanese soldiers try, on at least three separate occasions, to advance to the Marine lines and hurl themselves against the dug-in leathernecks. They are on a mission to break through the Marines' defenses and recapture the vital airfield, which now has a rudimentary secondary fighter plane strip that the Americans have simply demarcated on the bare ground. (This airstrip housed the famous Cactus Air Force, "cactus" being the code name for Guadalcanal.)

The desperate ground attacks surge against the line, and night after night the Marines hurl the banzai attackers back, ejecting them with frightful losses. Morning light reveals piles of broken bodies on and in front of the battle line.

In mid-September, on the orders of Lieutenant General Kiyotake Kawaguchi, 6,000 Japanese, laden with equipment in the hot swamp, cut a road through the thick mosquito-infested jungle. They attempt to fall on the Marine positions just south of the airfield, but are confronted and destroyed by Marines of the 1st Marine Raider Battalion and the 1st Marine Parachute Battalion. When it is over, 600 broken Japanese dead lie close to the Marine line on the ridge itself, smashed beyond recognition from point-blank artillery fire delivered into the charging mass.

To the extent that the military allows, reporters and their newspapers try to convey to readers back home the horrors of the first battle of the Pacific, but the message is often delayed, at times weeks or months later. But in time, Americans learn that the United States has lost yet another aircraft carrier, *Hornet*. The precious carrier force, after all the building and repairs the services have been working at breakneck pace to carry out, is now shockingly back to post–Pearl Harbor levels.

On October 30, the *Boston Daily Globe* tries to capture the vicious terror of the Japanese banzai attacks, but the paper reports that the Marines are equally ferocious in their response:

MARINES REPULSE JAPS 3 TIMES
GUADALCANAL TROOPS PLUG HOLE CUT IN LINE[33]

By mid-November, there are signs that the Japanese are being beaten. Their fleet pulls out of the battle area. Those still stuck on Guadalcanal continue to fight. Action will drag into February, but there are no more attempts to retake the island by ground attack. The Marines there have finally completed their mission; they have captured and completed Henderson Field, and they did it using the equipment left behind by the Japanese.

In the end, 24,000 Japanese soldiers are dead. The Americans have lost 1,600 and have 2,400 wounded. Several thousand more die from the diseases that infest the island. The six naval battles that raged in the waters around Guadalcanal have cost each side twenty-four ships and thousands of additional craft.[34] The waters off Guadalcanal, littered with sunken ships, become known as "Iron Bottom Sound."

Unbeknownst to the US Army command, now in control of the actions on Guadalcanal, Japanese plans are in motion to rescue more than 10,000 soldiers from the death that awaits them if they are left on the island.

On Christmas Day 1942, senior military officers of the Japanese Army and Navy meet at the Imperial Palace in Tokyo. The Army and Navy blame each other for the defeat at Guadalcanal. For days the two sides rage at each other. They must rescue their men from an island now held by US forces. The evacuation, which they plan for January, will require Hirohito's approval.

His Majesty is not at all happy to hear that his army and navy have been unable to drive the detested Americans from Guadalcanal in spite of more than four months of exhausting effort.[35] Hirohito is especially irked about the lost airfield. Why did it take Japanese construction crews more than a month to build an airfield when the Americans did it in days? Henderson Field was the key to the success or failure of the Japanese expansion and fortification in the Solomon Islands. It was the airfield that had triggered the US attack. He presses and grills his military leaders, putting them on the spot for another two hours before doing what he must: approving the troop withdrawal.[36]

With that, the emperor seals and sanctions the humiliating loss.

In a series of three-night evacuation operations the first week of February, Japanese destroyers rescue 10,828 soldiers. It is called Operation KE, and the US command assumes that the steady, increased naval activity is an attempt to reinforce the island for yet another attack, when exactly the opposite is the case: the Japanese are in retreat.

The rescued soldiers struggling off of the western shore of Guadalcanal are in terrible physical shape, hardly fit for a return to battle in the near future, or ever. The rescuing crews on the destroyers look aghast at the sight of the walking skeletons.

A Japanese officer on one of the destroyers writes that the pitiful men "wore only the remains of clothes . . . their physical deterioration was extreme. Probably they were happy but showed no expression. All had dengue or malaria . . . diarrhea sent them to the heads. Their digestive organs were so completely destroyed [we] couldn't give them good food, only porridge."[37]

The Marine Corps has struck the first successful blow in what will be a long trek across the vast expanse of the Pacific Ocean. The thinning, illusive ranks of the legendary "Old Breed" who were the minutemen of 1942 are now refilled.

)(

In February 1943, Frank Bowes places American flags on the tiny black specks of Savo, Tulagi, Santa Cruz, Guadalcanal, and Tassafaronga. How can these places, so small that some are barely on the map, matter so much in the effort to save the world? In the depths of his imagining, he cannot come close to understanding what is playing out on those godforsaken specks so many miles away. Americans in places such as Peekskill, and all across the land, have no idea what "their boys" are enduring overseas. Newspapers and newsreels do not report the horrors that will linger forever in the minds of the survivors, even into old age. These men will forever be haunted by tripping through darkness over charred limbs on beaches and in the jungles; the night sky lit with flares that shed light on the face of a buddy, his eyes wide open, a gaping wound deep, wet, and red across his midsection where his uniform was moments ago. Last night he was snickering with you about the absurdity of it all; now he is still. You can only move on; there is no time to stop and weep for him.

A Marine named Sid Philips remembers being sent with other troops to recover the bodies of US troops on Guadalcanal. When they found them, "they had been beheaded, their genitals stuck in their mouths." After that, says Philips, shaking his head, "we never took another prisoner."[38]

The *New York Times*, on February 10, 1943, spoke for Frank Bowes and so many others: "Every American heart must have thrilled yesterday at the news that the battle of Guadalcanal was over and the victory was ours."[39]

Although Frank knew there was so much sacrifice on the part of so many, he prays the silent prayer of parents and sweethearts across the country: "Just let it end before they need our boy."

)(

Harry Gray is determined to cross paths with the pretty blonde from the bowling alley. He sneaks the keys to the car while his mom is working late and drives by the house where she lives. He and his friends follow her and her friends as they head to the roller rink one night. Harry strolls in just a beat after she crosses the threshold, acting as if it is just the strangest coincidence to see her again. She is not with the boy this time, and Harry is not about to waste this golden opportunity. He sits next to her on the bench as she is putting on her roller skates and catches her eye. She locks onto his gaze and says yes, she does remember seeing him the other night. Her voice is harder than he imagined when he had watched her bowl and sway and sidle up to the older boy in the booth. Harry wants to know, so he asks. "Was that your boyfriend you were with at the bowling alley?" "No," she says, "well, not anymore." And then it is clear, she is not going to say any more about that. Harry doesn't care to hear any more on the subject, either, beyond that confirmation of what is relevant to him, and says, "Would you like to skate together?" Dorothy smiles and nods, and with that simple exchange, he and Dorothy skate off into the night. After that, they see each other pretty much all the time. He sometimes picks her up in his mom's car and takes her for ice cream on a weeknight. On Fridays, they go roller-skating. But on Saturdays, he takes her to the movies. He wants to sit close to her and put his arm around her shoulder. He slides his knee over to rest against hers and then moves to put his hand on her knee, which sends a quiet shiver through them both.

When the *tick-tick* of the newsreel begins, a different shiver courses through his veins. The movie rattles from the projector, and the audience tips up their heads in unison to get a good look at Hitler's army triumphantly goose-stepping past the Führer. Hitler, after suffering devastating blows the previous year, is imploring his people not to lose heart and to stand behind him.

Then the scene changes to the Pacific. The Marines are packing up and leaving Guadalcanal. Harry watches as they march thin Japanese prisoners in shirts and long white undershorts off the island. The grinning Marines have hollow cheeks, and their ribs jut out beneath their bare chests.

Harry knows the great landmarks of Europe. He has painstakingly drawn them in his sketchbooks. He wants to see the world and knows that if Hitler is not stopped, he never will. It is clear to him, though, that if the war lasts long enough, he will likely be sent to the Pacific. He wants to be a Marine. His friend Jim, who lives at the bottom of his street, has joined. He and Harry spent endless hours sitting on his front steps talking about how it isn't worth going if you aren't going in as a Marine. When Anne hears Harry coming up the front steps, she asks, "Where've you been?" If the answer is "At Jim's!"

she nods, her heart sinking a bit. She knows that Jim is filling his head with stories of the valiant Marines. If Harry has to go, she wants him to join the Navy. She tells him, "Harry, if you join the Navy, you'll sleep in a bed; if you join the Marines, you'll sleep in a ditch."[40]

Once the movie begins, Dorothy lets her head fall to the side against Harry's temple. He couldn't care less what is on the screen once the newsreels are over. He has it all planned out. He will enlist as soon as he turns seventeen. He will likely be part of the attack on Tokyo, and then he will come home a hero. He and Dorothy will get married and have a nice party at his mother's house, and then he will spend the rest of his days smelling Dorothy's skin and feeling her curls brush his cheek. She makes him happy, and he is 100 percent sure that he makes her happy, too. It's nice when life looks clear ahead; he can see it all perfectly.

On their way out of the theater, it starts to snow. Dorothy slips her arm into Harry's as they walk. Out of the corner of his eye as they pass the barber, Harry sees Tojo's toothy grin staring at him from a war bond poster saying mockingly, "Don't buy defense bonds, make me so happy—Thank you!"[41] Harry doesn't have any money to help the war effort, but before long, he will be doing his part against Tojo.

7

1943

A million men cannot take Tarawa in a hundred years.

—Admiral Keiji Shibazaki

Joseph Stalin could not make it to the Anfa Hotel in Casablanca, French Morocco, to discuss the next phase of the war with Churchill and Roosevelt in January 1943. His Red Army, which would ultimately lose 11 million men, was in the midst of the raging Battle of Stalingrad. Two-thirds of Hitler's forces were there fighting on the eastern front. On January 9, the Red Army would encircle Stalingrad, forcing Hitler's army to surrender there in a matter of weeks. To the north, it was on the verge of recovering Leningrad, and in the south, they were weakening the Germans' hold on the Caucasus.

Churchill and Roosevelt met in North Africa, and determined they could accept nothing short of unconditional surrender by the Axis powers. The first priority was to drive Hitler's Third Reich to its knees, followed by the complete capitulation of Imperial Japan.[1]

Churchill urged Roosevelt not to cross the English Channel to take on the Germans in France. The memories of trench warfare in France in World War I were still too fresh in the minds of the British people, and Churchill was determined to begin the pushback of Hitler's acquired territories in North Africa, then on to Italy.

By February, the Allies were on the offensive in Tunisia, where Hitler had given Field Marshal Erwin Rommel and General Hans-Jürgen von Arnim orders to "fight to the last." Rommel was a most dangerous opponent, and inexperienced US commanders and troops would learn the harshest of lessons in the hot sand before eventually starting to beat back "the Desert Fox."

While all eyes were on Europe, the Americans ran into a bit of luck combined with shrewd intelligence in the East. In April 1943, sixteen P-38 fighters took to the skies from Henderson Field and headed to Bougainville Island, based on intelligence that the revered Admiral Isoroku Yamamoto would be going there to inspect his troops. The poker-playing, Harvard-educated naval genius and architect of the Pearl Harbor attack called himself the sword of Emperor Hirohito and claimed that he would ride down Pennsylvania Avenue on a white horse and dictate the surrender of the United States in the White House.[2] As the plane carrying the commander in chief of the Japanese Combined Fleet was approaching the island, it was shot down by the US fighter jets and crashed into the jungle. His loss was devastating to Hirohito, who never discovered that US code breakers had deciphered intercepted messages detailing Yamamoto's location and itinerary for the day.

In May, Churchill and Roosevelt met at the Third Washington Conference in Washington, DC, code-named Trident, to plot the bombing in the Pacific theater, as well as the push to Sicily and then up the boot of Italy. Plans for an invasion of France across the Channel by combined US-British forces were also now well under way.[3]

On July 22, General Patton took Palermo, forcing the surrender of the Fascist dictator, Benito Mussolini, who had aligned himself with Hitler. Mussolini had been a miserable military failure, earning the ire of his own people. (Mussolini would hunker down in Milan until 1945. Under increasing pressure, he and his mistress, Claretta Petacci, tried to make a run for the Swiss border, but they were caught and their car was surrounded by Italian Communist partisans in a village near Lake Como. They were shot and hanged in the town square just two days before Hitler committed suicide.)

Hitler's soldiers would spend eighteen months in vicious combat to hold Italy, under strict orders from the Führer not to fail. The Allies lost 60,000 to 70,000 men before finally succeeding in the treacherous terrain of places such as Anzio and Monte Cassino. Meanwhile, in California, Washington, and Oregon, the fears of Hirohito's prime minister, Tojo, had come to pass. Tojo had argued that the US pilots who had been captured after the Doolittle Raid should all be allowed to live, fearing that if they were killed, there would be retribution against Japanese Americans. In 1943, President Roosevelt issued Executive Order 9066, forcing some 117,000 Americans of Japanese descent from their homes. They were put onto trains with only a suitcase and the clothes on their backs and forced to live in drafty one-room shedlike houses behind barbed-wire fences in internment camps in the West until the end of the war.

※

Across the Pacific, with Guadalcanal now secure, the southern Solomon Islands were firmly in US hands. The way forward would come only after an internal showdown between the powerful men leading the US Army and Navy.

Admiral Ernest J. King was the driving force behind the investment of men and resources in the Guadalcanal battles. But General George C. Marshall, the Army chief of staff and closest confidant of President Roosevelt, had done everything he could to sidetrack the venture. He wanted General Douglas MacArthur's army to lead the way. MacArthur was convinced that the way to the heart of Tokyo and victory was the western route through New Guinea and the Philippines. As far as King was concerned, Admiral Chester Nimitz's South Pacific route was the way to go. He felt the main thrust must be led by the Navy, under the command of Nimitz. After all, MacArthur and his troops were a thousand miles away from the battle area. King stood his ground, concluding his note to Marshall emphatically, "I think it is important that this [seizure of the initiative] be done even if no support of Army Forces in the South West Pacific is made available."[4]

Whatever the course, the Japanese military bulwark of Rabaul on the island of East New Britain in Papua New Guinea had to be taken. After the island's capture by the Japanese in 1942, it became a remote headquarters of the imperial forces in the South Pacific. General George Marshall wanted the Rabaul attack to be under the command of MacArthur, but the Navy balked. Admiral King was reluctant to turn command over to the Army, since the operations would not be possible without massive Navy ship participation.

King called for a unified strategic command under Admiral Nimitz. However, while the Third Washington Conference was under way to discuss the way forward, it was MacArthur's plan for the advance on Rabaul that was presented. The Navy would seize airfields in the Central Solomons, while MacArthur's forces would take airfields in the New Guinea area. Then, in subsequent stages, the Navy and Army would seize more airfields and other objectives in the tandem march to converge on Rabaul.

The plan they laid out would require five additional divisions and forty-five more air groups, a total of another 1,800 airplanes. The Washington brain trust balked. They saw the plan as impossible. Even if they were to commit a fraction of the aircraft and personnel to it, they wouldn't be able to transport them to the battle area.[5] MacArthur's people laid out their demands to the stunned gathering not as a suggestion but as a necessity. The conference adjourned in shock.[6]

Roosevelt had committed to Churchill's Hitler-first-and-then-Japan plan. He couldn't divert the Army's planes now; they were conducting a massive bombing campaign against the heart of Germany. The joint directive to the British and US air commanders had been unambiguous: "Your primary object will be the progressive destruction and dislocation of the German military, industrial, and economic system, and the undermining of the morale of the German people to a point where their capacity for armed resistance is fatally weakened."[7]

However, politically, Roosevelt could not let up on the Pacific push. The memories of the burning ships at Pearl Harbor and the loss of young sailors trapped in the *Arizona* at the bottom of the harbor had stoked the fire of revenge in the hearts of Americans. It was Japanese pilots who had dropped the bombs, and Japan must pay the price. "I'm going to kill Japs!" That was the cry of the boys on the recruiting lines and the fervent goal of the president who had declared that the day of the Pearl Harbor attack was a day of infamy and that victory over Japan was the only option.

Admiral King shared that desire. After the botched presentation of the MacArthur plan, King argued that if they didn't have the assets to take Rabaul, they would use what they had to neutralize the base. It would still require a large commitment of ships and naval assets in the advance to the northwest, up the long axis of the Solomon Islands. The advancing ships would be operating in confined waters and exposed to attack by land-based Japanese aircraft. To Admiral King, this was all unacceptable. The valuable carrier task forces should not be exposed to that danger.

At the Casablanca Conference, the British had given less-than-enthusiastic approval for a US drive against the Gilbert, Marshall, and Caroline Islands in the central Pacific once Rabaul was neutralized. To Admirals King and Nimitz and all of the other naval officers who had spent their entire careers embracing the dogma of War Plan Orange, that path must have looked very familiar.

In Washington, that new approach to a central Pacific offensive was met with favorable nods. It was a three-thousand-mile path across tiny islands clustered in groups like stepping-stones leading to the Philippines and to Japan itself. Even a novice tactician could see that there were no confining waters to hinder carrier operations or large landmasses that could provide bases for enemy air forces.

To the Navy, the central Pacific was the perfect operating area. Since the beginning of the war, it had been the opinion of the US Chiefs of Staff that Japan "could best be defeated by a series of amphibious attacks across the far reaches of the Pacific."[8] But there had been no chance to initiate such an offensive. The Marines' response to Japan's maneuvering in the Solomon Islands had been one of necessity, not of choice, to prevent the building of the airstrip at Guadalcanal.

A central Pacific drive was exactly what the old War Plan Orange had envisioned. If the enemy's navy chose to come out and challenge for control of the sea, so much the better, as it had been at Midway. If the enemy chose to defend an island, he could be isolated with little chance of reinforcement or resupply; and any attempts to reinforce or resupply would face interdicting attacks by US ships and aircraft.

On the other hand, there were disadvantages: Any attacking US force would be restricted in its tactics. It was not possible to land an overwhelmingly superior force against a smaller force of dug-in defenders. It would become a point-blank slugfest, ensuring many casualties on both sides, perhaps even to the point of mutual annihilation. How many men was an attacker willing to lose hurling itself against a rock-ribbed defensive position manned by defenders sworn to die at their posts? Would victory be so costly and the numbers of killed so ghastly that those on the home front would recoil in shock and demand a change of direction?

Plus, the defender would get to choose the battlefields. He controlled the islands the attackers would have to assault. The attacking Americans could never choose to bypass an island and let its defenders "die on the vine" if that island had an airfield. An advance to the next island could never proceed with an active enemy airfield left in the rear.

The Strategic Committee now decided that the central Pacific would be the primary approach with the Southwest Pacific thrust continuing as the secondary front.[9] The Japanese would have to deal with both drives. The committee's directive ordered the US forces to "maintain and extend unremitting pressure against Japan with the purpose of continually reducing her military power and attaining positions from which her ultimate surrender can be forced."[10]

On July 20, 1943, over vociferous objections from General MacArthur, the Joint Chiefs instructed Admiral Nimitz to capture bases in the Gilbert Islands and prepare detailed plans for the leap into the Marshalls.

※

Tarawa is an atoll of sixteen islands in the Gilberts, so small they can't be seen on most maps. The triangle they create lies across the equator, some 2,400 miles southwest of Pearl Harbor. Here Marines will battle first coral reefs and then malevolent tides that seem to be allied with the enemy; if and when they make it past that gauntlet, they will face a tightly constructed Japanese defense network designed to draw them to the island and its airfield and then make as many of them as possible sitting ducks.

These otherwise idyllic islands have on their western tip a tiny islet called Betio, the home of the Japanese airfield. Between two tips of the triangle is a submerged coral reef that opens in only one narrow place, the only unobstructed passageway to the beautiful, calm lagoon. Pilots say that Betio is shaped like a parrot, a long pier its feet. The whole thing is just two miles from head to tail, and at its widest point, it is not even seven hundred yards across.

Admiral Tomonari Saichiro does not want to see a repeat of Guadalcanal. When the Marines landed there, he began his work on Betio. He made the island that is home to the Tarawa airfield an impregnable fortress. Betio will be defended by massive firepower from sea and air, its beaches made into an obstacle course, creating a killing field for the unsuspecting Marines. The Japanese word for such a plan is *yogaki*, meaning "waylaying attack." "*Yogaki*'s purpose, to teach the Americans the prohibitive cost of invading fortified islands."[11]

Long-range bombers from Rabaul and short-range aircraft from Truk will provide decisive air support to Tarawa. The waters around the atoll will be teeming with Japanese vessels, ready to attack US shipping on the surface and with submarines from below.[12] It will be a repeat of the Tokyo Express, as it was in the waters around Guadalcanal.

In August 1943, Admiral Keiji Shibazaki arrives on Betio to oversee its final fortification and prepare to command the defense against the anticipated US attack. The admiral walks the entire perimeter, admiring the best-fortified position the world has ever seen.

The southern shore, with the airfield at its center, is heavily defended, aided by natural obstacles; the convex shape of the shore means that anyone trying to land there will be extremely vulnerable. It is also constantly lashed by winds and rough water. Thus the only way to approach Betio is through the coral reef and into the lagoon on the northern shore.

So it was there that Admiral Saichiro constructed his killing field. Twenty yards off the beach, he had his men build an ingenious coconut-log barrier wall. Pairs of logs were driven vertically into the earth less than two feet apart to form end supports for long logs stacked in rows on top of each other, creating four-foot-high walls. The whole wall construction was anchored and strapped at every point, and any gaps were filled with sand and coral.

The Allied attackers coming off the beaches will be forced to climb the wall in a hail of deadly grazing small-arms and automatic-weapons fire. If they choose to stay huddled behind the wall, they will be framed in a shooting gallery for preset mortar and high-angle-weapon fire. But even before they hit the unforgiving beach, they will need to make it across the eight-hundred-yard-long coral reef alive.

The approach will be possible for the "amtracs," tanklike vehicles, designed to claw their way up and onto the reef and grind across the coral, but most of the boats will never make it across, forcing the Marines up and out of them. As they wade into shore for hours, most will be shot and killed or wounded and drowned before they ever reach the sand.

Those who make it will then have to dodge fire coming from the pillboxes, blockhouses, and massive concrete-reinforced bunkers, some two stories high, that house every type and caliber of Japanese weapon. These fortresses are dug in, hardened against any aerial attack designed to soften the islet's defenses. In them are more than a hundred machine guns that can sweep every square foot of the battlefield. Twenty-three 37 mm antitank guns are dug in and concealed to back up thirty-four pieces of heavy artillery. Topping the list are four 5.5-inch and four huge 8-inch coastal guns, brought all the way from Singapore to do the job. They are capable of blasting holes in anything, including offshore ships. Almost 5,000 Japanese defenders man the bastion, each armed as well with an array of individual weapons for close confrontations.[13]

A 1942 Japanese order defined the mission:

> Wait until the enemy is within effective range (when assembling for landing) and direct your fire on the enemy transport group and destroy it. If the enemy starts a landing, knock out the landing boats with mountain gunfire, tank guns and infantry guns, then concentrate all fires on the enemy's landing point and destroy him at the water's edge.[14]

Admiral Shibazaki surveys it all from atop his two-story bombproof command post. He proudly announces to his assembled staff, "A million men cannot take Tarawa in a hundred years."[15]

Ever since Private James Russell had given up his sixteen-cents-an-hour spot-welding job and joined the Marine Corps in February 1943, boredom was no longer his problem. After surviving twelve grueling weeks at boot camp and three more weeks on the rifle range, he was off to several weeks of advanced infantry training at Camp Pendleton, California. He received orders that sent him to Tulagi while the Guadalcanal campaign was wrapping up, not to one of the regiments of the 1st Division but to the 2nd Division. After further training at Tulagi and New Hebrides, Russell sailed to Wellington, New Zealand, to become part of the cutting edge of the Marine force in the Pacific.[16]

Camp Wellington was a training ground the likes of which Marines had never seen. It wasn't just tactics and fire and maneuver that filled the training day, it was hours and hours of training for attacking a fortified beachhead. Previous training had stressed finding the least defended part of an enemy line and massing against it, overwhelming it with superior force. The training at Wellington stressed charging ashore from landing craft and immediately engaging the well-entrenched enemy. There was no room to maneuver; everything was a frontal assault.

If the men could bypass a position, they should bypass it, but they must keep moving, stopping for nothing, especially not to assist a fallen comrade. That would just slow down the impetus of the assault. "Move, move, move!" the sergeants screamed in their ears. They were to let follow-up forces finish off bypassed positions.[17]

Russell got his first glimpse of a landing vehicle, tracked (LVT) "Alligator" during that training. That latest addition to landing craft inventory was indeed revolutionary. It looked similar to a standard tank, but the Alligator could travel at seven miles per hour in the water and twelve on land. It didn't have to stop at the water's edge to discharge its troops; instead, it carried them up onto and over the beach. Men didn't exit the LVT, as they did a Higgins boat, by charging out the bow once the coxswain dropped the ramp. Instead, the outside ranks of the four columns of embarked troops did a low-profile roll-out over the sides, followed by the inside columns.

The Kiwis shared an easy camaraderie with the Marines from the United States. When the Japanese had been on their doorstep, looking south from already conquered lands with an eye on the green of New Zealand, the Marines had swept in to bolster the country's defenses. They had stood like pit bulls on the shore, looking north and forcing the Japanese to consider what they needed to defend, rather than prosecuting what had seemed to be a very appealing push into Oceania. Now the New Zealanders were returning the favor. They "adopted" the Marines of the 2nd Division, filling their bellies with home-cooked meals, listening to their stories, and giving them a bit of "home." For some it went beyond cooking; in the end, five hundred US Marines either stayed forever with Kiwi brides or took "down under" girls home to the United States as their wives.[18]

In mid-October, Russell watches as three battalions of his 2nd Marines quietly pack up, one battalion at a time. He is told, as he embarks on the USS *Biddle*, that they are heading for a final training exercise and then they'll all be back for a farewell party. The hotels in Wellington fill to the gills as dates and wives in party dresses anxiously await their return for one last shindig. The hours tick by as the women go from eager anticipation to frustration and then dismay as they realize their dates are not coming back. They slip off their white gloves and heels and put them away, wiping back tears with perfectly pressed handkerchiefs. They, like so many others back home, are sacrificing their happiness for the war; they will wait and pray for their young Americans to return safely.

The 2nd Marine Division sails as part of a naval task force for parts unknown. On the troop transports rumors spread like wildfire. "We were always going to Truk," says Russell. "Most Marines didn't know one place from another, but everybody seemed to know Truk. It was a nasty place with lots of Japs, and it would be a bitch to attack. It didn't matter where you were going, the speculation was always Truk."[19]

On November 14, the Marines on USS *Biddle* finish their morning exercise on deck and are called to a briefing. A lieutenant, brandishing a handful of maps and charts, points to the many islands of Tarawa Atoll and says the operation is code-named Galvanic; the target is the tiny island of Betio, the one shaped like a parrot.

Russell and the men of Company K, 2nd Marines, will land in LVTs on Red Beach 1 in the vicinity of the bird's neck and attack the large guns near the bird's beak. Rear Admiral Howard Kingman sends an unequivocal message to the landing force: "Gentlemen, we will not neutralize Betio. We will not destroy it. We will obliterate it."[20]

Three battleships, four cruisers, and more than twenty destroyers pummel Betio with three thousand tons of ordnance for two solid deafening hours. The bombardment ships are four miles off the western tip. On the decks of the transports, Marines wait for the order to roll over the sides and down the rope net into the landing craft, as they had practiced so many times. Suddenly, to the south, the bombardment fleet opens fire with salvo after salvo, like the finale at fireworks without the colors. The enormous cloud of smoke that hangs around afterward hovers and the whole two-mile island virtually disappears under the plumes. Cheers and hollers and whistles rise from the transports as for a moment it appears the job may already be done. Who could survive that?

But as the island shudders under the blows, Admiral Shibazaki, in his fortified two-story blockhouse, knows the attack is just beginning. He has built a fortress, but he is not without concern. The air and naval support he was promised has been siphoned off in recent weeks.

The US dual offensive has sent Japanese forces spreading out to cover their bases. To keep up their air strength in the Northern Solomons, they have borrowed from the airpower earmarked to support Tarawa. Naval vessels that had been held at Truk for the defense of the Pacific perimeter were sent to check the US forces' advance toward Rabaul. Adding insult to injury, the ships diverted to Rabaul were ambushed as they were about to refuel. US planes dived in, attacking with bombs and torpedoes. Of nine cruisers, seven were so crippled that they had to be sent back to Japan. As is often the case in a war of limited assets, the backup Shibazaki relied on is never coming to Tarawa.

The Americans, too, will see that on Tarawa, despite the briefings, nature and the enemy can combine to scoff at your plans. On the morning of November 20, 1943, the first three waves of LVTs cross the line of departure and head for Betio's Red beaches. Churning the water as they run, the Marines turn their eyes to the skies; they watch the final runs of fighters and bombers as they blast away, poking the bull of Tarawa like picadors stabbing to weaken it for the matador. But they soon notice that when the aircraft have banked off after dropping their last bombs, the tractors are still a good twenty minutes' distance from the beach. The crescendo of protective fire has ended, but the denouement is not yet ready to unwind. A heavy silence sets in.

Russell looks over both sides of his craft; the invasion line is well formed, and the tractors are advancing in unison. But in the momentary quiet, with no covering fire to pin them down, Japanese gunners begin to get the range on the advancing assault line. The lull is pierced by overhead whistles from the island and then the splash of geysers of water as exploding shells hit between and around the advancing Alligators.

Russell's tractor approaches the reef, its shallower green waters taking the place of the deep blue that had surrounded it, and then it hits the coral with a dull thud, throwing them forward a bit. The coxswain guns the engine, and the Alligator's tracks churn and jerk and lurch until it is on the reef. The beach is still well off in the distance, and what looks like a brown wall stretches across the sand.[21]

First on the beach are the assault forces of the 3rd Battalion, 2nd Marines, and two LVTs carrying part of Russell's Company K. The two Alligators have barely crawled ashore on the west end of Red Beach 1, when they are hit with raking fire coming from a position up to the left.

The blistering fire torches the Company K vehicles, stopping them in their tracks.[22] An LVT of Company I lands there as well; now it, too, is under the fire pounding at it from a hidden pillbox. Within moments, all the vehicles are knocked out; the steel hulks heave their last and sputter as they line up like dead whales on the beach.

Russell's LVT is taking a steady drumbeat of bullets on its port side when suddenly, to the left, a blistering hot orange flame shoots up as the next tank over explodes in a ball of fire. "Japanese fire whistles over our heads, and in the next instant, a large-caliber shell slams into the side of our LVT, killing both the coxswain and his assistant!"[23]

"Get out!" is the frantic order, and Russell rolls out, not over the side as he had practiced but anywhere—which turns out to be over the stern. He falls heavily on the sand, half in, half out of the water. "The rest of the men were out, running in a low crouch, crawling toward the wall. In their scramble out of the stricken vehicle, ammunition and other ordnance was dropped or left in the vessel."[24]

In the chaos of two hours, Companies I and K lose half their men and more than a third of their LVTs.[25] As the survivors run, they glance back across the beach at an eerie sea of bobbing bodies. Those who fought their way up the beach, only to be cut down, lie twisted as they fell, crumpled on the narrow strip of sand or pinned against Shibazaki's coconut-log trap.

Ironically, the destroyed LVTs have made it to precisely where they were supposed to land: at the neck of the bird. But in a gruesome plot twist, that has put them right into the path of Shibazaki's entrenched guns.

Now the surviving men from the two boats of Company K crouch on the sand and press against the wall as the world explodes all around them. The enemy fire is relentless and deafening. A sergeant named Gresham takes charge, yelling, "Move! Move!," exhorting the men to crawl west, toward the bird's beak. They scrape their way across the scrub and beach, dragging five of their wounded with them.

There is no other choice. Going left would take them away from their objective and into the teeth of the Japanese gun that blasted them from Red Beach 2. Going over the top of the wall would definitely be suicidal. Above their heads, certain death whistles over them; machine-gun bullets send a constant cascade of sand and log splinters down onto their heads and blurring their vision. The noise is so loud that they can only read their sergeant's lips and follow his hand signals.

Inch by inch they crawl along, dodging death, until Gresham's head turns toward the sound and he points at the sea. It is happening again: the tractors of the second wave are bearing down on the beach in a hail of gunfire and exploding shells. The Marines watch from their position as geysers erupt, shrouding the vehicles in walls of water and smoke. Some LVTs are knocked sideways like toys tossed in a stream; others erupt in flames as desperate Marines scramble to the water to escape the inferno.

Using the wall as continued cover, Jim Russell and his small band of Marines slowly muscle their way through the chaos, managing to skirt past one pillbox and then another until they hit a barbed-wire entanglement. One Marine deftly clips his way through with wire cutters. Their westward advance pushes them up against a third bunker, and now they are taking incoming. Japanese snipers are pinning them down. But now they have a position, and for the first time, they are firing back. Russell is unleashing a barrage of staccato fire from his Browning automatic rifle.

Popping up from behind the wall, firing, and ducking down again, for thirty minutes they chip away at the concrete surrounding the bunker's aperture. Some of their rounds are bull's-eyes inside the hole, and the shooters inside go silent. Gresham's group inches away under cover, crawling toward the bird's beak.

Russell's heart is pounding in his chest; he is a long way from the barrel line and right where his grandmother feared he would be. In a place where everyone seems to be dying, he finds his way to the beach and crouches down over the bodies of his fellow Marines as they float into and out of the water. He turns them, looking at their faces and wet uniforms caked in sand. He rifles through their pockets, looking for more ammo, just as he was taught to do. He finds some, but no grenades, the weapon he needs the most right now.[26]

Finally, as the unit moves along, there is water on both sides. The men have made it to the islet's tip—the bird's beak. They see that one large 8-inch gun has been knocked out by naval gunfire; but there is another, just inland, and it hammers away at the incoming Marines. As each round explodes, they watch helplessly as it cuts down their men.

The handful of still operational LVTs goes back for the rest of the invasion force, who are stuck waiting in Higgins boats at the edge of the reef they cannot cross. They were told that the tide would be with them, that the water would cover the reef and they would be able to float over. But the reading on the tides was wrong—dead wrong. One after the other, Higgins boats hit the reef. The Marines abandon their boats, climb out into the water, and wade across the jagged reef, through four hundred to five hundred yards of fire and water.[27] The men stretch across the lagoon, dotting the horizon, wading in, guns overhead, as they are picked off by Japanese fire, falling and sinking into the water over and over, going down in brutal, heartbreaking repetition, alone or in twos or threes as they stay in their lines. In a cruel twist of fate, the wounded Marines who cannot wade in lie on the reef waiting to be rescued, only to drown as the tide rises over them.

It is semi-ordered chaos. Communications have broken down, so small units resort to waving and shouting to one another. "There is no way to communicate with other units. The radios were inoperative, either from immersion in the salt water, or because they were riddled with machine-gun bullets."[28]

Russell and the rest of the Company K survivors dig in to defend their position on the bird's beak. They know nothing of the fate of the rest of their company, or what is going on beyond their sight lines. Their commander, Major John Schoettel, is hung up on the edge of the reef, trying to make it to the beach. He has some communication with parts of his three companies and seems to know the difficulties facing Companies I and K on the extreme right. He sends a message to Colonel David Shoup, commander of the 2nd Marines and the senior commander ashore, who has been blown out of his LVT and has taken shelter in the center of the landing area under the long pier. "Receiving heavy fire all along beach. Unable to land all. Issue in doubt."

Eight minutes later, with his remaining troops in the water and beginning the long wade-in with their rifles held over their heads, he signals, "Boats held up on reef of right flank RED 1. Troops receiving heavy fire in water."

Shoup signals back that he should try to land more to his left, toward Red Beach 2, and then try to work his way to the west. But during the short time between messages, the fate of Schoettel's wading Marines has become dire, and he transmits, "We have nothing left to land."[29]

There were 700 men in that battalion. How could there be none left?

He and his staff frantically wave to the Marines wading through the lagoon. Gaining their attention, they direct them to change direction and head for the pier. The pier will provide some shelter, at least, under which they can make their way to the beach.

For the Marines, who are chest high in water and laden with combat gear, currents swirling around them, shifting direction is nearly impossible. For some it is their last move. Japanese gunners in the trees follow them with their sights and pick them off; Marines tragically drop beneath the water one after the other. Those who make it to Shoup's position grab on to the wooden pilings of the pier like shipwreck survivors. (Shoup, who was born in a place called Battle Ground, Indiana, rose quickly through the ranks. He will win the Medal of Honor for his bravery at Tarawa and later become a general who is outspoken against the Vietnam War.)

Then, at the bird's beak, the small Marine force looks seaward and detects what looks like little "bobbing corks. In small groups and clusters, these bobbing objects move across the reef toward the shore. . . . Russell is held spellbound as the fourth assault wave wades in."[30]

As the Marines approach the shore, Japanese bullets pinging all around them, they make themselves into the smallest possible targets. They rest their rifles on their helmets and wade in with only their helmets above the water. On the extreme western flank of the reef, well removed from the main line of Marines struggling toward Red Beach 1, is a spread-out group of several hundred men. They are wading away from the line of approach to Red Beach 1 and directly toward the bird's beak.

They make better progress, and the Japanese fire is not as heavily concentrated against them, perhaps because the 8-inch gun has been destroyed and Russell's group has taken out some of the enemy on that shore.

This group is led by Major Michael Ryan with men from H&S Company and his own Company L. While waiting at the edge of the reef, his attention is diverted from the Red Beach 1 landing area to the extreme edge of Betio by the beak. His eye has caught sight of a solitary Marine from Company K jumping over the wall.

"It looked like a hopeless situation on Red Beach 1," Ryan will later say, "the boats hung up on the reef and the amtracs disabled.

Marines were forced to walk or crawl ashore directly into heavy fire, and it looked as if only a handful were surviving. I veered off to my right to avoid the guns on the left."[31]

It takes an hour for Ryan's group to wade in on this alternate line, and Japanese gunners are able to take down a third of the men. Finally, Ryan's men stagger into the Company K perimeter. The total force now on the northwestern tip of Betio is close to two hundred strong, and Major Ryan takes command of them all.

Out to sea, another strange procession seems headed for the bird's beak. A group of landing craft, mechanized (LCMs) carrying six medium Sherman tanks has discharged the Shermans at the edge of the reef, and the tanks have begun their crunching run in. Walking in front of the amphibious tanks and subjected to hostile fire are reconnaissance men carrying small flags to mark obstacles and potholes in the coral. When one flagman is shot, another heroically takes his place.

Only two of the tanks survive the harrowing trip to shore. Ryan takes command of them to spearhead an attack to the south, attempting to gain the upper hand on Tarawa for the first time. They will parallel the west coast along Green Beach and blast the enemy positions. Ryan's infantry will follow closely and clean out pockets of defensive positions.

At 2:00 p.m., the attack begins. The tanks blast the Japanese bunkers, but in the first minutes of the attack, the Sherman tank called *Cecilia*'s main gun is damaged when an enemy light tank gets off a round from its 37 mm gun and strikes the turret.[32] The other tank, *China Gal*, blasts the Japanese tank, and *Cecilia* continues on with her machine gun.

Russell and the other Marines follow in a furious charge, rolling up the Japanese positions, and in short order, they emerge on the other side of Betio, facing the blue water of the Pacific Ocean. The Marines have crossed the three hundred yards separating the contested Red landing beaches from the southern shore and have, unbelievably, outflanked the entire Japanese defensive force.[33]

The Marines dig in. They scrape out shallow holes to form a hasty defense facing the broken and shattered trees to the east. With their backs to the water, there are no Japanese defenders to confront them. Still, Major Ryan is uneasy in this advanced position. He has no way to signal anyone that he has outflanked the defenses of Betio and is on the southern shore. No one knows that Green Beach is secure for possible use. If the enemy counterattacks, he and his men will be alone.

He has two choices: to stay in his advanced position with the risk of being cut off or withdraw to his original position and try to establish communications.

Ryan is a veteran of the Guadalcanal campaign, and he understands Japanese cave and bunker fighting. The first grenade he threw into a bunker came flying right back out. He said, "I also learned that positions reduced only with grenades could come alive again a little later."

He has walked part of the battlefield at Tanambogo and observed that despite "a prolonged bombardment before the invasion . . . [there were] little mounded fortifications out of which scores of Japanese erupted in a kamikaze wave to push the Marines off the beach they had secured."[34]

All around him he sees many such innocent-looking mounds and bunkers that have undergone a massive shore bombardment but have never been cleaned out.

"When we managed to overrun most of the turrets and pill-boxes on the beak of Betio, I was convinced that without flamethrowers or explosives to clean them out we had to pull back the first night to a perimeter that could be defended against counter-attack by Japanese troops still hidden in the bunkers."[35]

He orders his force to withdraw. When Jim Russell hears the order to go back across the island to their original position, he cannot believe his ears. This is their only success of the day, and now they are going back? The tanks rumble alongside as they retrace their steps.

The sun is slowly setting on the wretched day. Exhausted, Russell stares out into the lagoon. Bodies float everywhere, swaying where the currents go. He is alive. Equipment and vehicles jam the beach, emasculated. Now their only service is as cover for the survivors who huddle behind them, shaken by their first combat day and first close-up views of death. They are so utterly exhausted that even these haunting images cannot keep them from sleep, fitful and short as it is when it comes.

To Russell's left and front, the Japanese still hold most of the island; at no time does their deadly fire seem to slacken. He and his fellow Marines dig in on the beak for a second time. They have no way of knowing that their landing and foray across the island have been the one enumerable success of the day.

✕

The Marines welcome first light on D + 1. The shattered state of Japanese communications has made a night attack impossible.

But during the night, Japanese soldiers reoccupied some of their old positions, including the hull of a sunken ship in the lagoon that provides a commanding view. Their bunkers along the beach are mostly intact. Few Marines have attempted to climb over the deadly coconut-log wall. The Japanese fields of fire are still as deadly as they were on D-Day.

The first new Marine attackers across the reef cross the line of departure in boats, expecting that the tide will lift them over. But the water is still shallow, and an agonizing repeat of D-Day is under way. Once again, boats catch on the reef and grind to a halt.

Japanese gunners in their blockhouses zero in on the stationary targets and blast away. *Time* correspondent Robert Sherrod lands on the first day and from his position on the beach watches the wholesale slaughter. "One boat blows up, then another. The survivors start swimming ashore, but machine gun bullets dot the water all around them. This is worse, far worse than yesterday."[36]

On the bird's beak, Major Ryan's force faces to the south for a renewed attack to clear the area behind Green Beach. During the night, a few stragglers joined him. Among them is Second Lieutenant

Thomas N. Greene, a naval gunfire spotter, who has a working radio.[37] Headquarters now knows their location and that they were able to make it across yesterday.

At 11:10 a.m., on this blistering hot Betio day, Ryan is ready to attack. The tanks are revving as the Marines watch the land in front of them explode in a thunderous display of naval gunfire. Lieutenant Greene, handset to his ear, rattles off adjustments to the ships offshore, the exploding salvos smashing into the Japanese defenses.

"Ryan's Orphans," as they will come to be known, wait for the bombardment to lift so they can step off into the attack. They have barely enough weapons, only what they managed to carry out of the initial attack. Jim Russell carries a single bazooka he found in the flotsam and jetsam on the beach, but there are only two rockets for it, and one of them has a damaged fin. The bazooka is a new weapon, and no one in the group has ever trained with it or fired it. As they have no hand grenades, explosives, or flamethrowers, this is the only weapon that can engage a bunker. No flamethrowers made it across the reef; the seventy-two-pound weapons had either been jettisoned or had dragged their gunners to the bottom.[38]

Overnight, Japanese soldiers found their way back to a large bunker that is so well hidden, it looks like a sand dune. Attacking it with naval gunfire is out of the question, and if *China Gal* were to try to maneuver into position for a shot, she could easily be blasted by the bunker's cannon. That would be the end of the armor on that end of the island.

Jim Russell is pinned down by enemy fire behind a large coconut log. Marines are returning fire at the bunker, to little effect. Russell knows they can't move on until the bunker and the men in it are cleared.

Russell and fellow Marine Private First Class Joseph Herberski discover that the large eighteen-inch log just in front of them rolls rather easily and they can move around behind it, changing their position without exposing themselves to the machine gun.

Major Ryan peeks out from his covered position to plan his next move and sees a large log suddenly roll forward with the two Marines pushing it from behind. Russell is dragging the bazooka and his single rocket along with him.

The Japanese gunners also see the rolling log and fire a burst in its direction.

At a turtle's pace, the log-rolling Marines get to the base of the bunker's slope. They are gasping for air and soaked in sweat, their muscles cramping and aching.

They move to lie on their backs with legs crouched against the log. They dig in the edges of their boots and push as hard as they can. The log rolls about a foot up the slope. Russell jams some rocks behind it so it can't roll back on them. Then they get behind it and crouch and push again, and again and again in this rhythm. Crouch, push, chock . . . crouch, push, chock!

They use their heads, arms, and shoulders as chocks to stop the log. The other Marines are firing at the bunker to keep the Japanese from firing at the log, but bullets are flying in both directions over the heads of Russell and Herberski and at the log. In one of their synchronized moves, Herberski gets too far above the log in his thrust and is hit, shot in the throat. Russell rushes to bandage him, but Herberski is undaunted, insisting it's just a nick. Sweating, straining, and under fire, they are now within fifteen feet of the bunker's shooting aperture. Herberski struggles with the bazooka and loads it, but he has lost too much blood and has no strength left to fire, so he passes it to Russell.

The other Marines are laying down tremendous fire that drives the Japanese gunners from the aperture; Russell braces himself for what he knows is his one and only shot. As the Marines pour fire into the bunker, he bolts upright to a kneeling position, takes a quick aim, and squeezes the trigger of the bazooka.[39]

The back blast of the weapon creates a dust cloud as the rocket sails straight into the bunker and detonates. The explosion knocks the log loose, and it rolls back down the hill, flattening Russell and Herberski.

The next bunker is eliminated with the help of the Marines' one Bangalore torpedo, and the Marines suddenly find themselves again looking at the blue waters of the Pacific off the southern shore.

Lieutenant Greene continues his calls for thunderous salvos of naval gunfire, and by 12:30 p.m., the western end of Betio has been swept clear of enemy resistance. Ryan's Orphans advance several hundred yards to the east and dig in.

Ryan signals back his success, and shortly afterward, the 1st Battalion, 6th Marines, lands without opposition, not in landing craft but in rubber boats, on Green Beach. The next day, they sweep the island in a flanking attack and roll up holdout Japanese positions. Knowing that the fight is over, most of the remaining Japanese soldiers run at the Marines in a suicidal banzai charge.

Russell and Herberski will receive the Navy Cross for their heroic actions at the bunker. But Joseph Herberski dies of his wound later that day. He is one of the 3,407 casualties in the 2nd Marines in just seventy-six hours of fighting. Among them more than a thousand lost their lives on Tarawa.

Some of the assault companies of the division lost more than 50 percent of their numbers. More than a hundred critically wounded Marines died of their wounds on board ships returning to Hawaii and are buried at sea.[40]

Of the 5,000 Japanese fighting on Tarawa, only 17 survived after the banzai charge. They were taken prisoner.

⅄

For the first time, back on the home front, Americans begin to really see the war. They see US Marines, not shiny faced and heading off to war, but lifeless and fallen in the unnatural crumpled posture of death by gunfire and shelling. They see young boys who will never come home floating facedown, tossed back and forth at the water's edge, thrown like shells crushed by waves, scattered on the shore. The Canadian illustrator Kerr Eby wrote, "Tarawa was a time of utmost savagery—I still don't know how they took the place."[41]

President Roosevelt was persuaded to sign off on the release of Norman Hatch's movie *With the Marines at Tarawa*, filmed during the battle. Hatch would later remember the stench of death and thick black smoke everywhere. His camera had captured the dead "just as they lay. This was the first time this type of death was shown; floating in the water . . . and this was just before Thanksgiving Day, which made it even worse."[42]

X

As Christmas 1943 approaches, Dominick Grossi writes home from boot camp at Parris Island. After a big send-off that made the newspapers in Buffalo, Grossi and his fellow University of Rochester football players turned enlisted men are now just head-shaven "numbers," like everyone else, getting taken down a few pegs and then built up stronger through the rigors of Marine training.

Grossi sends a postcard home to his younger siblings:

Hiya Kids,

Just returned from a movie. I called my rifle a gun and the sergeant had me write 100 times on toilet paper, "One hundred thousand Marines have a rifle, I'm lucky I've got a gun." You see we aren't supposed to call our rifles, guns.

Love to all, Dom.[43]

In Arlington, Massachusetts, Christmas and the end of 1943 turn Harry Gray's thoughts to his coming springtime graduation from high school. He will be eighteen then, and as he promised his mother, he will stay until graduation and then head to Parris Island to become a United States Marine. He will spend the next Thanksgiving and Christmas in the central Pacific.

8

Cracking the Inner Ring

Anne Gray, like her brother, Frank, now has a good job at Liberty Mutual Insurance Company. She is an executive secretary, a trusted employee, and her boss relies on her greatly. Anne is marching forward, and if she feels overwhelmed raising her children and holding down a full-time job, she keeps it to herself. Although life is very different for Nancy and Harry without their dad, they soldier on, without self-pity or complaint. They do not have much, but they have what they need and each other, as well as their grandmother, who still lives with them to keep an eye on things while Anne is at the office. The war, though, hangs over everything. "After the war, we will get a new car" or "After the war, when the boys come home" is a common refrain in every conversation. Life is suspended.

Harry is speeding through his senior-year spring homework and spending what seems like hours on the phone with Dorothy. The Grays share a party line with the neighbors, so Anne tells him all the time to keep it short. But as long as no one chimes in and barks at you to get off, you can get away with it, which they do. Anne is a bit concerned about all the time they spend together. She doesn't know all that much about Dorothy, just that she lives in a small house in a nearby town and has a job at the glove shop. They are still very young. She can't help but wonder what Harry Sr. would say. He'd probably tell her to leave them alone and let 'em have fun. If he were here, he would talk to Harry about it all.

On the home front, Americans are doing all they can for the war effort. They flatten their metal cans to be turned in to make weapons and save their bacon fat to be used to fuel explosives. It is a national way of life, and the Gray family does their part. They line up for butter only when it is Thanksgiving or someone's birthday. Nancy waits on line with her mother and smiles all the way home, thinking about spreading it on her bread when she gets home.

But Americans happily wait on line to go to the movies, which are the great wartime escape, even when they focus on the war. They are fascinated by the bombers and submarines being built across the country, and they thrill to watch them in action, with their boys—winning, of course—in films such as *Guadalcanal Diary* and *Cry Havoc*. Eighteen-year-old George Colburn and his buddies of Medford, Massachusetts, are among those at the Capitol Theater in Arlington, who settle in on a Saturday afternoon to watch *Guadalcanal Diary*. The picture lures them in with beautiful, sunny beaches and palm trees, and right then and there, George and his pal Bob decide they'll join the Marines and head to the Pacific. After all, their friends who had already enlisted were in Europe, where it was freezing cold and snowy.[1]

But the stories bring home the dark side of the war as well, revealing the barbarism of the enemy. In *Behind the Rising Sun*, a young Japanese man who has studied in the United States returns home, only to be sent to fight against the Chinese. He is horrified by the brutality of Japan's officers against the Chinese and he speaks out but is reprimanded by his commanding officer. He ends up hardening his heart for war but is then shot down in his plane. The movie's brutality gets it a rating of "not suitable for general exhibition."

The blockbuster musical *This Is the Army* shows the lighter side of military life and features Irving Berlin's showstopping "God Bless America." It seems as though everybody has a son in the war or one about to go or a husband or a future husband or an uncle or a brother.

All across the United States, people wait in long lines to be transported to their world or forget about it all. Each in its own way slightly eases the weight of the war at home.

In Japan, images of Midway, Guadalcanal, and Tarawa bring home a different reality. These losses have jolted the emperor and his top brass. As Japan's Navy and island defensive forces scramble to reposition themselves for the next US onslaught, Admiral Nimitz's Fast Carrier Task Force is retooled to iron out some of the deadly glitches of their equipment, such as the Alligator vehicles' difficulties on the reef at Tarawa. Now they are ready to strike again.

None of this feels good at the Imperial Palace, and Japanese leadership turns to the potent weapons of fantasy and denial to keep spirits up. Censorship is their weapon at home, to prevent the Japanese people from getting a "glimpse of the fate of their nation."[2]

The Battle of Midway was the first defeat in Japan's naval history. As its wounded fleet was limping home, Radio Tokyo was making up stories: two US carriers, a destroyer, and a cruiser had been sunk, it gleefully reported. If victory was an illusion, facts were pliable. In reality, only one US carrier and a destroyer had been lost. Radio Tokyo didn't stop at minimizing the United States' losses; it also pretended that the devastation of the Japanese fleet was a mirage, wiped away easily. It gleefully lied to the people of Japan, telling them they had lost only one carrier and another sustained a bit of damage. Clearly a victory for the Imperial Navy!

But the truth was this: all four of Japan's carriers were gone, as was a cruiser, and a second cruiser had been damaged, as had two destroyers, an oiler, and a battleship. Suddenly all the burning metal and dead sailors vanished into thin air as far as the Japanese media were concerned. Also unmentioned was the staggering loss of 322 planes and the better part of their highly skilled crews. Many of the planes had been incinerated on the exploding carriers or shot down by US fire. Some of the Japanese pilots had been killed when they came in for landings on carriers that were no longer there. Having no other choice, they had plunged into the ocean.

The Japanese leaders decided to hide the losses for the time being. Like gamblers, they bet that a later big win would make up for a dismal hand now. So when the rest of the fleet arrived back in Japan, the survivors disembarked under the cover of darkness and were essentially sent into hiding.[3] "All the enlisted men of the sunken carriers were sent to naval bases, confined to the bases, and shipped out . . . to the far reaches of the empire, such as Truk. So were many of the junior officers, and the others were sworn to secrecy."[4]

No one asked about the four missing carriers of Pearl Harbor fame or about the men who had served on them and had not returned home.

Fantastic reports of Japanese naval and air prowess, as well as incredible victories, were fed to the people in a steady stream. For the most part, they accepted it. They believed a report issued after Guadalcanal that thousands of US planes and 245 warships had been sunk during the previous four months—more than the United States could have ever produced—but no one dared to ask the obvious questions: If there had been such destruction of the enemy's forces, how was it possible for that enemy to be sitting on the doorstep of Japan's bastion at Rabaul; or, How did Guadalcanal and Tarawa fall?

On October 21, 1943, one month before the invasion of Betio, a senior literature student from Tokyo Imperial University, Shinshiro Ebashi, delivered an impassioned speech on the occasion of his call-up for military service. He was one of thousands of university students now called to fill Japan's burgeoning need for replacement manpower, especially in aviation. Those thousands were to march in a patriotic parade witnessed by 65,000 of their proud relatives and friends, wives and girlfriends.

Prime Minister Hideki Tojo was also there, proudly standing in the front in full military regalia. The parade was to be witnessed by thousands more and end at the Imperial Palace, where the students would shout a rousing triple cheer of "Banzai! Banzai! Banzai!" to honor the emperor. Such spectacles had been stoking the fervor of Japanese pride for years, but on this day, there was something decidedly different. A heretofore unspoken fatalism was expressed in Ebashi's speech: "We, of course, do not expect to return alive as we take up guns and bayonets as we embark on our glorious mission of crushing the stubborn enemy."[5]

Why would that be? Had not earlier Japanese warriors returned alive after their years of expansion, annexation, conquest, and "crushing the stubborn enemy"?

He then addressed those in the audience not yet called to service. He predicted that they "would follow in our footsteps, in the not distant future, and march over our dead bodies to win victory in the Greater East Asia War."[6] This was the *bushido* spirit that would characterize the coming months: the belief that the nation led by the emperor would win, even in losing. Ebashi's speech sent a prescient message: "Fight to the death, die proudly." In other words, the student told the people of Japan, we need your sacrifice, but wake up, things are not going well.

And what of the emperor? He would forever maintain that he, too, had been given rosy, deceptive reports. But did he really not know that his ships had never made it home? Could the descendent of the sun goddess be so much in the dark? As Prime Minister Tojo received the triple "Banzai!" cheer from the university students at the end of their march, did he feel a pang of guilt about sending off new recruits who could have no expectation to return alive?

In March and April 1946, shortly before the Tokyo war crimes trials were to begin, Hirohito would give eight hours of secret interviews about the war. In them he would reveal some of what he had thought during the war years, working to spin how he should be perceived in it all. He and his advisers had furiously worked to destroy any paper trail in the two weeks between surrender and occupation, and now he was filling in the blanks before the coming trial of his military leaders.

He stressed his "noninvolvement." He was a constitutional monarch, he said, not a supreme military commander.

The record and transcripts of the interviews disappeared shortly after their completion. They were never given to General MacArthur, and they remained missing for more than forty years, until they turned up in 1988 in a Wyoming home in the hands of the daughter of one of the interviewers.[7]

One interview segment was labeled "Table Talks on the Pacific War." In it, Hirohito revealed that he had been very much in command. He had been well aware of Japan's aggressive expansionism. He had been especially determined to hold on to his land acquisitions in the south and central Pacific. As the US offensive began late in 1942, he would say, "We can't give up our [newly-won] resources in the south half-way through exploiting them."[8]

Though the Japanese survived on the truism that to the victor go the spoils, the Americans upended it. The Japanese, living on an island nation with few resources of their own, considered a growing empire built on war to be the only path to long-term survival. The Americans, blessed with nearly unlimited resources, fought wars only to end them.

Hirohito further stated, "We thought we could achieve a draw with the US, or at best win by a six to four margin; but total victory was nearly impossible. . . . When the war actually began, however, we gained a miraculous victory at Pearl Harbor and our invasions of Malaya and Burma succeeded far quicker than expected."[9]

Hirohito declared that he would have sought for peace then, while he still had the upper hand, but he had been stymied from doing so. He blamed the Germans for having ruined his plans for seeking peace. He said he had been handicapped by the terms of a corollary agreement to the Tripartite Pact that he had signed with Germany. That corollary agreement forbade seeking a separate accord with the United States.

The emperor continued, "I knew we had lost any hope for victory when we failed to hold the Stanley Mountain Range on New Guinea."

This is nonsensical, since that battle in New Guinea went on late into 1942, while Japan was still actively expanding its empire to the south, into the Solomon Islands, and threatening Australia. The battle for Guadalcanal was still being fought, and it, too, was in doubt.

Hirohito himself indicated that he was hardly willing to fold before he had fully exploited his new landholdings.

He then again laid all blame for his continuing the war on the Germans: "I hoped to give the enemy one good bashing somewhere, and then seize a chance for peace. Yet I didn't want to ask for peace before Germany did because then we would lose trust in the international community for having violated that corollary agreement."[10]

So according to the emperor, Japan had continued the war while waiting for Germany's permission to surrender!

As Nimitz's Fast Carrier Task Force prepared to assault the inner ring of the Japanese defense line in the Marshall Islands, the emperor would have another opportunity to administer a good "bashing" to the Americans.

※

Legend has it that Admiral Isoroku Yamamoto, the commander of the Japanese Combined Fleet and architect of the Pearl Harbor attack, once said, "I fear all we have done is to awaken a sleeping giant and fill him with a terrible resolve."

At the end of January 1944, a massive US fleet plows its way through the Pacific. It moves westward toward the Marshall Islands, 620 miles northwest of Tarawa, along the War Plan Orange trail. Commanded by Vice Admiral Marc Mitscher, it is an armada the Japanese could only dream of building. Known as Task Force 58, it is actually a massive collection of four separate Navy task forces. Twelve aircraft carriers carry seven hundred planes, and these carriers are surrounded by eight new battleships and a ring of prowling cruisers and destroyers.[11]

For Japan, after the loss of Tarawa and the Gilbert Islands, the massive expanse of the Marshall Islands becomes the new forward rampart of her defense. But that rampart is not prepared for the aerial blitz that Mitscher unleashes with his 700 aircraft against 130 defending Zeros on January 29, 1944. The Americans swoop down like falcons from above and make short work of the Japanese planes; after two days, there are no more of them.

For the young Marines of the 4th Division, who attack into the Marshall Islands, this is their first action and the first fight of the division. There is no division history, as there was for the 1st and 2nd, which assaulted Guadalcanal and Tarawa. There is no Belleau Wood, Château-Thierry, Tripoli, or Chapultepec in their past. They are not part of the Old Corps or the Old Breed. They are the new Marines, a new breed that has expanded the Corps from 50,000 to a force now approaching half a million.

Their transports depart San Diego on January 13, 1944, and except for a twenty-four-hour layover in Hawaii, they are continuously at sea, zigzagging on a five-thousand-mile, eighteen-day trek to the battle. Several miles out of Hawaii, commanders show the eager Marines the operational maps and details of Kwajalein Atoll, in the heart of the Marshall Islands: a massive cluster of 32 atolls, more than 1,000 islands, and 867 reefs.

Yet in that vast expanse of ocean, reefs, and islands, the 4th Marine Division is focused on the tiny pinprick of a double island nestled within the huge Kwajalein Atoll called Roi-Namur. One look at the details of these twin islands evokes comparisons of the ordeal at Betio. On Roi there is an airfield, much like the one on tiny Tarawa Island; on Namur there are fifty-two pillboxes, coastal defense guns, heavy and medium antiaircraft guns, and numerous trenches, blockhouses, and tangles of barbed wire. Neither Roi nor Namur amounts to a square mile of land.

On the plus side, there are enough tractors for the attacking force and there will be no long wade-in across an exposed reef in the face of murderous enemy fire. And the massive force moving to attack Roi-Namur is far larger than that committed to Tarawa. It is comforting for the young Marines to stand at the rails of their transports and feel dwarfed within the body of the great naval task force that surrounds and escorts them.

One Marine, Private First Class Robert F. Graf, is eager to finally get his turn. Too young to join just after Pearl Harbor, Graf is among the legions of boys who envied the older ones who had gone off to fight the enemy and strained at the leash to join them. He will later say, "As I thought of the landing that I would be making on the morrow, I was both excited and anxious. Yes, I thought of death, but I wasn't afraid. Somehow I couldn't see myself as dead. . . . I was headed for great adventure, where I had wanted to be. This was just an adventure. It was 'grown up' Cowboys and Indians, it was 'grown up' Cops and Robbers. . . . Now it was my turn to 'carry the flag' into battle. It was my turn to be a part of history."[12]

Two days before the invasion, the US warships and aircraft carriers begin to bomb and shell every square yard of Roi-Namur. The battleships move into a bombardment position as close as 1,900 yards from the beach and fire into the island defenses. Waves of carrier planes sweep in for bombing and strafing, and the combined bombardment lays six thousand tons of steel on the twin islands.

The amphibious assault begins on February 1. The first wave of the 23rd Marines hits the beaches at noon, and as the Marines move inland, they are virtually unopposed. Immediately they see why: the devastating bombardments have left the airfield strewn with destroyed aircraft and caved-in defensive positions. The dead are everywhere; a few hundred dazed defenders are quickly mopped up. The rest of the force has fled to the more formidable positions on neighboring Namur.[13]

In fifteen minutes, Roi is neutralized, and at 12:15, a jubilant communications officer signals to the commanding general, "This is a pip. Give us the word and we'll take the island."[14]

After additional naval gunfire prep fires, the Marines continue the attack at 4:00 p.m. with tanks rolling ahead of the assault line. At 6:00 p.m. the island is secured in the quickest battle to ever be won in the Pacific. Hundreds of Japanese soldiers lay sprawled over the Roi battlefield. The bombardment caught them in various stages of fleeing for their lives and mutilated their bodies horribly.

Across the small causeway connecting the two islands, Namur is not a "pip." Not only are there multiple hardened defensive positions, but there is thick vegetation, concealing and camouflaging the enemy everywhere. The men of the 24th Marines hammer the Green beaches and are met with heavy gunfire as they are assaulted on the left. Scores are cut down within seconds of coming down out of their landing craft; all around them rifles and guns are firing at them at close range.

On the right, the Marines press ahead about two hundred yards and come upon a large enemy blockhouse. A lieutenant named Saul Stein leads his men to surround the building, and on his signal, a Marine carrying a shaped charge, used to penetrate concrete and steel, advances and places the explosive against the wall. After triggering the charge, he retreats to cover with the other Marines. The deafening blast rips a hole through the wall.[15]

The Japanese pour out from inside, firing wildly in all directions while making their escape. The surprised Marines fumble and scramble to engage them. Stein shouts for his men to throw in satchel charges in case any Japanese are still in there. The Marines hurl the charges with hissing fuses through the hole.

Within seconds, the world on the island of Namur explodes. An immense tower of black smoke and rubble jets into the sky, turning the heads of every man on shore and at sea toward the detonation. The cloud rises a thousand feet into the sky. From a ship offshore, an officer reports, "The whole of Namur Island disappeared from sight in a tremendous brown cloud of dust and sand."[16]

Major Charles Duchein, a Marine artillery spotter circling in an aircraft above the battlefield, suddenly feels his plane violently forced upward. "Great God Almighty!" he exclaims. "The whole damn island has blown up!"[17]

Men on Namur are knocked to their knees by the shock wave; they scramble for cover as tons of debris fall from the sky. One officer recalls, "Trunks of palm trees and chunks of concrete as large as packing crates were flying through the air like match sticks. . . . The hole left where the blockhouse stood was as large as a fair-sized swimming pool."[18]

The blockhouse was crammed with tons of torpedo warheads. Lieutenant Stein is among the twenty Marines who are killed by the massive detonation. Another hundred men are wounded. That evening, the attacking 24th Marines digs in for the night, fully expecting a Japanese night attack from the desperate surviving enemy, now pinned in a pocket against the northern shore.

It comes in the early-morning hours in the drizzling rain across the bombed-out landscape illuminated by star shells. Shrieking "Banzai!," several hundred Japanese begin the charge against the lines of the 3rd Battalion. The Marines pour fire into the onrushing enemy line. But the Japanese re-form their line and come on again. The firefight drags on for hours and at one point pushes the Marine lines back to a secondary defensive position. But the Marines charge back, regaining their ground, and in the end the attack fails.

In the early afternoon of the following day, Namur is declared secure. The operation is barely twenty-four hours old. As at Tarawa, the Japanese force is virtually annihilated, many of the soldiers committing suicide rather than surrender. Unlike the 3,400 casualties at Tarawa, the Marine casualties at Roi-Namur are 313 dead and 502 wounded, with 3,500 Japanese soldiers dead. Emperor Hirohito's wished-for "good bashing" has not materialized.

In a simultaneous attack, the Army secures the island of Kwajalein on the southern end of the atoll. In the Marshall Islands campaign, Japanese deaths reach a total of 8,122, twenty-seven times the number of Americans lost.

The swift wins in the Marshalls move up Admiral Nimitz's timetable by twenty weeks. US forces are now within 1,100 miles of the Mariana Islands, which will put them into a position to strike Japan with long-range bombers.

At home, in theaters across the United States, the dramatic voice of Hugh James of Movietone News narrates "Marshalls Invasion!" A preliminary image leads to the narration: "The victory is a major step in the Central Pacific offensive on the Road to Tokyo."

The short film, shot by Coast Guard, Navy, and Marine Corps combat cameramen, shows the great armada moving to battle and then the battle at Roi-Namur itself. The shore bombardment with its shattering sound vibrates the movie seats. The tractors running into the beaches as low-flying airplanes dropped their final bombs are high drama for Americans anxious to see victory.

James booms, "Enemy parties were wiped out in a war to the death." An orchestra plays "The Marines' Hymn" in the background, and there is a final tribute to those who did not make it out alive: "Americans who were defending their country's cause made the supreme sacrifice on a distant shore."[19]

9

Willing to Fight

As long as justice and injustice have not terminated their ever-renewing fight for ascendancy in the affairs of mankind, human beings must be willing . . . to do battle for the one against the other.[1]

In April 1862, the British philosopher John Stuart Mill penned those words about the American Civil War. As Mill saw it, the Union forces needed to prevail, and the citizenry of the Northern states needed to fight and defeat the new Southern Confederacy and end the perpetuation of the evil of slavery.

To Mill's way of thinking, the war was not to be won by military maneuver and a few defeats on the battlefield or even "by taking military possession of their country, or marching an army through it, but by wearing them out, exhausting their resources, depriving them of the comforts of life, encouraging their slaves to desert, and excluding them from communication with foreign countries."[2]

In a future time, Mill could have written those same words to describe the ongoing world war against Nazi Germany and Imperial Japan and the necessity to defeat their evil, totalitarian attempt to enslave the rest of the world.

The Casablanca Conference, in 1943, had called for the Allies to bring about the unconditional surrender of the Axis powers, not some negotiated peace that could leave their evil institutions intact.

Making peace would have meant "giving up the original cause of quarrel," Mill wrote.[3] Bringing about victory would require freedom-loving people to be willing to fight. Mill chastised those who were unwilling to fight and were willing to turn a blind eye to evil for the sake of peace in their time. In the 1930s, appeasement had enabled Hitler, Mussolini, and Hirohito to spread their subjugation and enslavement of innocent people under their vicious totalitarian rule. Now the wages of that unwillingness to fight would be paid by a new generation called upon to restore freedom to the world. Mill wrote:

> War, in a good cause, is not the greatest evil which a nation can suffer. War is an ugly thing, but not the ugliest of things: the decayed and degraded state of moral and patriotic feeling which thinks nothing worth a war, is worse. . . . A man who has nothing which he is willing to fight for, nothing which he cares more about than he does about his personal safety, is a miserable creature who has no chance of being free, unless made and kept so by the exertions of better men than himself.[4]

In Arlington, Massachusetts, "better men" had picked up the torch of freedom in 1775, when they had gathered to confront the British Army at Lexington and Concord. Dr. Joseph Warren, the president of the Massachusetts Provincial Congress, was willing to fight the tyranny of King George III. "To the persecution and tyranny of his cruel ministry we will not tamely submit; appealing to Heaven for the justice of our cause, we determine to die or be free."[5]

On a hot June graduation night in 1944, Harry Gray sits on the risers at Arlington High School, in cap and gown, sweat rising on his back. He is listening to the mayor talk about the history of Arlington and the battles at Lexington and Concord. As a little boy, he imagined himself in the spring of 1775, fighting for freedom and the future of a new kind of country. His mind drifts off to the place he dreamed up years ago. It puts him at the heart of the action.

He is a young minuteman, running, his worn boots covered in New England mud. Slung over his shoulder, a musket, and a hunting knife is deep in his pocket. He is racing back from the surprise attack at the North Bridge, his cheeks and jacket spattered with dirt and sweat. The cool Massachusetts air whips across his chest; his heart is pounding as he catches his first glimpse of the redcoats.

They are swarming the ridge in front of him in full retreat from the battle at Concord. Harry is crouching down behind the rock wall at Dr. Warren's farm. Watching them, breathing hard, he braces his musket against the rocks.

Before dawn this morning of April 19, 1775, the tensions between the local militias and the redcoats finally boiled over. At first light, the British marched out of Boston, and on Lexington Green the minutemen lined up to defy them, the tension between them rising in the air with every cool breath on that April morning. The redcoats, in their crisp uniforms, despise the scrappy bands of rebels and militiamen in mismatched farm garb. The rebels, though, have had more than enough of the stranglehold the king has on their money and their freedom. At some point, no one knows from whose rifle, a shot is fired, and within moments eight are dead on the ground, another ten are wounded,[6] and the stunned colonists fall back.

The poet Ralph Waldo Emerson wrote of the moment, "Here once the embattled farmers stood / And fired the shot heard round the world."

Down the road, the patriots at Concord have been tipped off. Paul Revere has warned the Massachusetts militias. Family by family, mile by mile on horseback, he bellowed the alert to the eleven towns between Lexington and Concord.

The militia scrambled to arm themselves, well aware that this day could be their last, as it was for their neighbors on Lexington Green. They are outmatched, outnumbered, undersupplied, and woefully trained. The only thing they have in spades is outrage.

At Concord there is a second skirmish, much like the one at Lexington, but this time the colonists have cobbled together more men than the redcoats, as they face off at the North Bridge. A first shot is fired that quickly deteriorates into a general melee, and the outgunned

British detachment falls back to rejoin the main column. Its officers, sensing that things have gotten out of hand, signal to the main column to begin retracing its steps back to Boston.

Now the colonists, amazed that the British are retreating, go in for more confrontation. They harass the red column on both flanks, ambushing them from all sides. The British, stunned by their mounting losses, hasten their retreat. This is where Harry sees them coming into Arlington over the ridge; he stays crouched down behind the stone wall.

The British column enters Arlington (known then as Menotomy), ripping through the town, looting along the way, reeling from the ferocity of the firepower from the mixed bag of farmers, armed with whatever they could find in the homes and barns.

But the spark has been lit, and the furious citizens simply won't stop shooting at them. Townsfolk gather, and the ambush is growing. Their weapons bristle and flame from every conceivable position: from just off the road, from behind the stone wall, from the taverns and the mills, even from the old cemetery.[7]

Lord Percy barks out orders for the British soldiers to clear every house and eliminate all snipers' nests. The soldiers bully their way in, ransacking and looting, then torching what is left. Flames soon engulf the buildings, and a black, choking cloud hangs over the streets.

Harry the minuteman hears the screams of his neighbors, bolts from the wall to Jason Russell's house, and takes cover with others in the cellar. Heart pounding and sweat streaking down the sides of his face, he braces his back against the cool stone cellar wall and holds his musket with his finger on the trigger.

Overhead, the redcoats stomp up the steps and into the house. Those in hiding hear Mr. Russell struggling with them and trying to push them back, then he cries out in agony and hits the ground above.

The redcoats are coming his way now. Harry's finger takes up the slack in the trigger as he hears the door creak open, and now black boots are on the step above his head. He holds his breath, as the boots take another step. Then he sees, through the open slats of the cellar stairs, the tips of the red coats. The others crouch back behind Harry, and he prays that they will stay still. As the redcoat comes down the steps, Harry waits a beat and then pulls the trigger. The flame leaps two feet from the barrel, and the recoil of the weapon drives Harry back. The slain redcoat's body drops heavily onto the stairs and then to the cellar floor. Harry hears the redcoats scatter from the house upstairs and rests his head on his musket as blood pools under the soldier on the floor. He has shot him squarely through his back; he is not breathing. Harry sneaks out the cellar door and sees the last of the redcoats making their way out of town.[8]

Harry's mind snaps back to the present, at his graduation, as the mayor goes on about the spirit of the patriots of the American Revolution and how that spirit is now at work in the world once again. He pays tribute to all the men in towns like theirs who are off fighting the war, now not in their backyards but in Europe, in the bombed-out villages and fields of France, and across the Pacific, facing the foe that killed so many at Pearl Harbor. Now Harry is getting antsy.

Finally they are calling names; his lifelong friends stand and walk across the stage, grinning as they receive their diplomas. "Harry . . . Eugene . . . Gray." Harry pops up with a big smile and strides across the stage. He shakes the principal's hand and shoots a side smile over at Dorothy, who is sitting with two of her friends. Then he finds his mom and Nancy, sitting in the bleachers. He can see how proud his mom is. She sits tall and holds the program against her chest, her hands folded over it. Her eyes are glistening a bit, and he smiles right back into them. The truth is that six years after his father's death, they are doing pretty well, and it is all because of his mom. She has held them together, kept a roof over their heads and shoes on their feet. For his part, Harry kept them all smiling. All in all, he thinks as he takes his seat, they are doing pretty okay.[9]

When Harry gets home, there is a small party under way. The table is full of pies and sandwiches. A couple of his buddies are there; they pat him on the back and mess up his hair. Everyone congratulates him. These are the pals he has played football and baseball with over on the sandlot ever since he was little. Two of Mom's friends from work are there and some of the neighbors. Looking around the room at them all, he sees them talking and laughing, but he feels somehow apart. So many boys have already left, and soon he will be on his way. Time has been standing still, but now he is about to leave Arlington and all of this behind. Uncle Frank sent him a graduation card and put some money into it for him. He said he knew Harry had worked hard and he was very proud of him. He signed it, "With lots of love, Uncle Frank and Aunt Helen and Betts." He is grateful for Uncle Frank's easy way and guidance over the years. Uncle Frank has never tried to tell him what to do; he always seemed to say just what Harry needed to hear when he needed to hear it. He knows that Uncle Frank did not want him to enlist. But he's glad he understands that Harry has to do what he has to do.

Suddenly his eyes are drawn to the doorway, and there is Dorothy. She looks perfect in her yellow fitted dress with a white collar and full skirt and her white gloves, her red lips and her short blond hair curling just below her ear. He excuses himself from Mrs. Newley, who has been talking his ear off, and slips through the crowd to her. Dorothy doesn't really know any of these people; Harry isn't sure *he* knows all of them. She is holding a cake on a plate. He smiles at her and takes it to free her hands. "Hi, Harry, congratulations," she says.

Harry smiles down at her. "C'mon, let's go put this in the kitchen." They work their way to the kitchen, and Harry puts the plate down on the table. "Did you make this?" he asks.

"Of course I did," she says. It has chocolate icing.

"What's inside?" he inquires with a sly smile.

"More chocolate," she answers, smiling back. Their words are just words; they are too busy staring into each other's eyes. Neither wants to talk about what the day means, which is that now there is nothing standing between Harry and leaving Arlington. Dorothy picks up the cake and goes through the swinging kitchen door, placing it prominently in the center of the desserts. He stands in the doorway and watches her. But then he catches his mother's eye. She is watching them as well. She looks at Dorothy. She worries that they've moved too fast, and the only thing she doesn't mind about Harry enlisting is that it will give him some time to figure it all out.[10]

)(

That June, Admiral Chester Nimitz's Fast Carrier Task Force is again on the move to the west. With the Gilbert Islands and the Marshall Islands secured, the next stop is the Mariana Islands, the inner ring of the Japanese defenses.

In Washington, the Joint Chiefs of Staff ponder the next Pacific objective and, after much discussion and argument, opt for a daring, far-reaching triple operation, to be called Operation Forager. The aim is to seize the islands of Saipan and Tinian and to recapture Guam, lost to the Japanese during the first days of the war. If the move is successful, the US forces will be just 1,250 miles from Japan[11] and within the range of a new long-range bomber coming off the assembly lines: the B-29.

The invasion force is already training in Hawaii. The 4th Marine Division, veterans of Roi-Namur, are on Maui; the 2nd Marine Division, veterans of Tarawa, are on the Big Island of Hawaii; and the Army's 27th Infantry Division is on Oahu.

Replacements have flooded into the 4th Division to fill the gaps left by the casualties suffered on Roi-Namur. They are green recruits and have completed only basic training, not nearly the training necessary to attack a fortified island. Lieutenant John C. Chapin will later report:

> Most of these replacements were boys fresh from boot camp, and they were ignorant of everything but the barest essentials. Week after week was filled with long marches, field combat problems, live firing, obstacle courses, street fighting, judo, calisthenics, night and day attacks and defenses, etc. There were also lectures on the errors we'd made at Namur. . . . We worked with demolition

charges of dynamite, TNT, and C-2 [plastic explosive], and with flame throwers till everyone knew them forward and backward.[12]

Late that spring, final maneuvers and practice landings are under way for the three divisions that will attack Saipan. The massive assault force that assembles at Pearl Harbor comprises eight hundred ships and more than 70,000 Marine and Army troops. This is a far cry from the dark days of 1942 and Guadalcanal, when a meager US naval force risked everything to face down the enemy in the Solomon Islands; or the even darker days during the Battles of the Coral Sea and Midway, when all that stood between survival and Japanese naval domination was three US aircraft carriers.

Now Task Force 58 is a juggernaut. Its main ships include sixteen fast carriers and seven new battleships, ringed by thirteen cruisers and fifty-eight destroyers.[13] The fleet weighs anchor from Pearl Harbor on May 25, 1944, to begin the 3,700-mile trek to the Mariana Islands.

Nine months earlier, in August 1943, the First Quebec Conference, code-named Quadrant, did not paint a rosy picture of the war in the Pacific. The conference had been convened to discuss strategy and a timetable for Europe, but at the end of it, the planners presented a timetable for the defeat of Japan. It was hardly encouraging for a quick end to the war.

The conference anticipated the defeat of Germany in 1944, but it envisioned a long-drawn-out conflict with Japan. "The plan called for capture of the Philippines, Formosa, Malaya, and the Ryukyus [Okinawa] in 1945 and 1946, with final operations against Japan itself to commence in 1947 and continue into 1948."[14]

※

Jay Rebstock graduated from Gulf Coast Military Academy in May 1943. He walked onstage on crutches to receive his diploma—he had torn cartilage in his knee playing football. He had intended to join the military service as school ended, but he had been declared 4F, unfit for military service. The surgery to remove torn cartilage had been successful, but the 4F classification had remained. His family was delighted.

From the day at the movies in 1941 when the manager had stopped the film to announce that Pearl Harbor had been bombed, he had been itching to get at it and join up. His father had shot down the idea in no uncertain terms.

Now that he was nineteen and free to do as he pleased, the doctors said no. None of his appeals to the recruiters were working. He dragged himself off to the Louisiana oil fields and became a roughneck doing backbreaking work on a drilling rig; he bitched every day that the strain on his knee as a roughneck was far worse than basic training.[15]

He tried to enlist in the Air Corps in Biloxi and was turned down; then he went to the merchant marine recruiter at Pass Christian, Mississippi, and was turned down. He could follow the war only as old men and shirkers followed it, through the newspapers and Movietone News. The billboard outside the recruiting office had said, "Uncle Sam wants you!," but he didn't seem to want Jay Rebstock. The headlines came and went: Midway, Guadalcanal, Bougainville. The war was passing him by. His friends were "over there," and he was over here. Like any young man who was still around at that point, he suffered taunts of "chicken" and "draft dodger," and he was tired of explaining his bum knee.

As the war progressed, the manpower shortage called for a mandatory draft; there would be few exceptions or deferrals. Rebstock decided to give it one more try. He hitchhiked from the oil fields to the town of Thibodaux and visited the draft board. He gave his name, and within two weeks, his summons came. He was ecstatic. At last he had found a way in.

His father was not pleased and told him it was a stupid move. Jay was adamant and told him that everybody was in this because of the sneak attack, and he felt left out and wanted to go. He argued that because his father was the head of the ration board, people were saying that he was pulling strings to keep his son out of the war.

Finally he reported to New Orleans for processing along with hundreds of other young men. He talked with some of his friends and said he wanted to go into the Marine Corps and especially mentioned the famous Raiders. He had read about their exploits in *Reader's Digest*. Echoing his bravado, his friends agreed and backslapped each other that they were going to be elite, too.

They were called to line up, and a series of recruiters spoke to them, outlining each service. The Army, Navy, and Coast Guard recruiters addressed them kindly: "Gentlemen" this and "Gentlemen" that and "Please fill this out" and "Please line up over there."[16]

The Marine Corps recruiter was altogether different. He was small and wiry, a sergeant who looked like a street fighter masked in his sharp, impeccable uniform: tailored shirt, military creases, and the distinctive red stripe down his trouser legs. He was a veteran of Guadalcanal, the newest of the Old Breed. His address to them was short, sneering, and caustic. The words that flew out of his mouth included "maggots," "scum," and "worthless."

Finally, standing with his arms folded in front of him, he called out to anyone "who thought they could make it in this man's Marine Corps" to take two steps forward and assume the position of attention. Young Jay did just that and even clicked his heels together after his two steps. The sergeant approached him and sent him right off for his physical exam.

It was then that Rebstock looked about and noticed that he had been the only one to step forward. His big-talking buddies were shaking their heads and avoiding his eyes. The sergeant told Rebstock to make sure that he revealed to the doctor any identifying scars; that "was so someone could identify your dead ass after your face was blown off."[17]

The exam was quick; he passed and sighed in relief. The young doctor asked him if he had any identifying scars, marks, or tattoos. Jay showed him every nick and cut, delighted that he was finally in. Then he showed him the large surgical scar on his knee, and he was suddenly out. The doctor shook his head and rejected him.

Rebstock's eyes welled up, he was so frustrated. He stammered out all the reasons he should not be rejected: he'd been working hard at manual labor; the knee never bothered him; he could bend his knee all the way—which he couldn't; and he could do anything anyone else could do. It wasn't fair.

The doctor was moved by the young man pleading with tears running down his face and gave his okay. Jay Rebstock finished boot camp at San Diego in December 1943 and joined the Raider Battalion for the toughest of training.

"You never went to bed without your weapon," said Rebstock. "You never took a shower without your weapon. There was no such thing as walking—everyplace you went you sort of jogged. When you got up in the morning, you brought a sock with you to the mess hall. They didn't care if you had been wearing it or if it was new, but you had to have a sock.

"When you got into that breakfast line, they gave you a handful of rice, a handful of raisins, two potatoes, and two slabs of Canadian bacon. You put that into your sock and tied it around your cartridge belt and that was your noon meal. It was long hours and lots of training. The Raiders were tough."[18]

Sometime in January, the paratroopers and the Raiders were broken up and he was assigned to the newly forming 5th Marine Division: Company E, 27th Marines. Rebstock promptly got himself a new "identifying mark," a tattoo of the Marine Corps emblem.[19]

⚔

That June night, after the small party at the house breaks up and the last guests have gone home, Harry takes Dorothy for a walk. They head down Center Street in the middle of town, past the movie theater and the soda shop. Harry takes her hand and walks her into the park near the *Menotomy Indian Hunter* statue, and they sit down on the bench.

"So, Dorothy, in a few days, I'll be off to Parris Island." She nods and looks at him. He is taking his time. He is nervous, she can tell.

"But I will always be thinking about you and telling everyone I meet about you, as much as they'll listen. They'll complain, because I will go on and on . . . about your sparkling blue eyes, your soft blond curls, your sweet red lips . . ." He touches her lips. She laughs and pulls away a bit, listening for what is coming next. "And when the guys pull out the pictures of their girls, I'll save mine until last. They will all go crazy when I show them your picture. But I'll say, 'Uh-uh-uh,' and I'll snag it back. 'She's mine, fellas, no more looking!'

"I'm keeping it right here in my pocket, always, wherever I go. I'm going to write you every day, every chance I get. And when I come back . . . I want us to get married, Dorothy.

"Will you marry me when I come home?"[20]

She puts her arms around his neck. "Yes, I will, of course I will, Harry!" She hugs him with all her strength. Then she pulls back. "But, Harry"—she takes a long pause—"why don't we get married now? You could take a job like your father at Olmsted-Flint, and we could get a little place right here in town. I don't care where we live. But we can start our lives together, we don't have to wait. Harry, maybe you don't have to go. Like your uncle Frank said, you're the man of the house, and the war will be over soon, anyway. Everyone says so."

"Listen to me, Dorothy. If I don't go now, I'll be drafted for sure. It won't be long, and I will be back, I promise."

He pulls her in to him, and she rests her head against his chest. He smells her hair against his downturned face and inhales it; he wants to be able to bring it all back when he is off at training. He closes his eyes and feels her heartbeat. He will lock all this away in his heart and take it everywhere he goes. One day they will look back at tonight and tell their kids about how they promised themselves to each other just a few days before Harry went off to the war. It is all going to turn out perfect. Harry is sure about that.

They talk some more and kiss good night, agreeing to see each other tomorrow and talk about it all some more.

Harry walks in the door after taking Dot home and sees the light on in the kitchen. His mom is sitting at the table, paying some bills. He tells her that he plans to marry Dorothy when he gets back.

Anne takes a deep breath. She is a bit taken aback. "Son, I know you feel grown up now that you've graduated, but trust me, Harry, you are still so young. You have your whole life ahead of you, and there will be other girls along the way." She puts her hands gently on his cheeks and looks into his eyes.

"You're just eighteen, and, my goodness, Dorothy's only sixteen. Give it a bit of time." Harry looks down at the floor and doesn't look as though he's going to say any more. So she changes the subject. She feels she's gotten through to him. He doesn't really want to get married now, she is fairly sure of that.

"Listen to me, Harry. Promise me you'll keep your head down and you won't volunteer for anything. If there's a safer job to be done, that's what you raise your hand for, do you hear me, son?"

He just looks at her. Her words falter, and she takes in a long breath. It is moments like these when she feels inadequate. It is too hard to be both mother and father, and sometimes she finds it easier not to say anything than to risk saying the wrong thing to her son.

She smiles. "I know you will be busy. But please write to me and your sister as often as you can. She is going to be so lonely here without you, Harry. She thinks you hang the moon, you know. Even though you battle sometimes, she's so proud of you, you know that's true, don't you? And write to Uncle Frank, he worries about you so. Send a note to Betts when you can. She is such a darling, and she adores you, Harry. We're all going to be praying for you. Remember to go to Mass every chance you get, and keep your rosary with you in your pocket. Introduce yourself to the chaplain. You're going to be just fine. Just do what you're told. Make sure you eat enough." There's nothing else she can think of, and he isn't leaving until Monday, so she takes both of his hands in hers and looks down at his long fingers. Her eyes are welling up, and she doesn't want him to see. "Okay, off to bed, you. Go get some sleep."[21] She reaches up and pats him on the head. "Good night, Mom," he says as he kisses her on the cheek. "Go on!" she says.

Harry lies in his bed, thoughts racing through his head. With his head on the pillow, he rolls left to look at the small framed picture of his girl. Dorothy's right, he thinks. He's going to do it; he'll marry her tomorrow. They'll go to the courthouse and get married. No one even needs to know. People do it all the time, especially fellows going off to the war. They still have a few days. He'll go to war a man, a husband. He likes how that sounds and how it makes him feel: bigger and older.

Harry wakes up early the next morning and runs to the corner market. Then, back home, he hops into his mother's car and takes off. He drives down Center Street, takes a left, and goes down the road to Dorothy's small house by the train station. His heart is pounding, he is so full of plans. He rings the bell, holding the flowers behind his back. Dorothy opens the door. Her hair is in a tiny ponytail, and her jeans are rolled up on top of her white sneakers. It is the first time he has seen her without her red lipstick on, and Harry thinks how young she looks without it. How wonderful it would be to wake up next to that soft, young face. "What are you up to?" she asks, turning her head to the side and leaning, arms crossed, in the open door.

He gives her the flowers and takes her hand. "Let's get married today, Dot. You're right about everything. Let's just do it, let's do it today. It will be our secret!"

Dorothy's eyes light up. "And you won't go? You'll stay here and not go?"

"No, Dorothy. I have to go. I'm going to get drafted if I stay. And I've already signed up. It's the right thing, and I want to go. My mother says we are too young. But she's wrong. I've never been more sure of anything in my life. But if we don't tell her and we go find a justice of the peace in Boston, no one will have to know. It will be the secret we can keep the whole time while I'm gone. If I know we are married, Dorothy, I will make sure I come home. I promise!"

Dorothy's smile droops. "Harry. No. We can't get married like that. I was carried away last night. I want a nice wedding and music and a dress. Harry, I won't go against your mother's wishes. You were right last night. I was wrong." She touches his cheek with her hand. "But don't you worry, Harry Gray. I will be right here waiting for you, when you come home."

X

Frank Bowes is in his green chair in the living room at 55 Welcher Avenue with the radio on. His pipe in his hand, he takes tobacco out of the fold-over bag from the drugstore and packs it in just right. He sets the pipe in his teeth, cups his hand around the bowl, and lights the match down low over it, taking a deep drag. The radio crackles.

A voice intones, "The Supreme Commander, Allied Expeditionary Force, General Dwight David Eisenhower."

This is the moment the country has been waiting for, and Frank settles in to listen closely. Helen and his sister-in-law, Jane, come in from the kitchen. Each sits in the chair she always sits in, just across from Frank and next to each other, facing the radio. Betts slides onto the edge of Helen's chair and pulls in close. After she settles in, it is perfectly quiet. General Eisenhower begins:

> People of Western Europe: A landing was made this morning on the coast of France by troops of the Allied Expeditionary Force. This landing is part of the concerted United Nations' plan for the liberation of Europe, made in conjunction with our great Russian allies.
>
> I have this message for all of you. Although the initial assault may not have been made in your own country, the hour of your liberation is approaching.

The world has been waiting for five anxious years for this announcement, often wondering if it will ever come. Can this be the beginning of the end of this war? The firm, calm voice of General Eisenhower continues:

> All patriots, men and women, young and old, have a part to play in the achievement of final victory. To members of resistance movements, I say, "Follow the instructions you have received." To patriots who are not members of organized resistance groups, I say, "Continue your passive resistance, but do not needlessly endanger your lives until I give you the signal to rise and strike the enemy. The day will come when I shall need your united strength." Until that day, I call on you for the hard task of discipline and restraint.[22]

Later that night they all gather again, like other families across the United States, to hear President Roosevelt's address to the nation, a national prayer. It is 10:00 p.m., but few have gone to bed.

> Almighty God: Our sons, pride of our Nation, this day have set upon a mighty endeavor, a struggle to preserve our Republic, our religion, and our civilization, and to set free a suffering humanity.

Frank, Helen, Jane, and Betts hang on every word. They say a silent prayer for Harry, who will be leaving soon. In Arlington, Anne, Harry, and Nancy listen at their radio. Anne sits up straight in her chair, as do Harry and Nancy—all silent, listening, feeling the weight of the president's words as he goes on:

> Lead them straight and true; give strength to their arms, stoutness to their hearts, steadfastness in their faith.
> They will need Thy blessings. Their road will be long and hard. For the enemy is strong. He may hurl back our forces. Success may not come with rushing speed, but we shall return again and again; and we know that by Thy grace, and by the righteousness of our cause, our sons will triumph.[23]

The next morning, Frank pores over the *New York Times*, featuring a prominent photo of General Eisenhower surrounded by paratroopers with blackened faces. The picture was snapped just prior to their being loaded on C-47s that will carry them across the English Channel to their airborne assault into France. The headlines blare:

HITLER'S SEA WALL BREACHED; INVADERS FIGHTING WAY INLAND; NEW ALLIED LANDINGS MADE[24]

The articles below report that in Philadelphia, the Liberty Bell was rung, and at Lexington and Boston's Old North Church, services are being held to pray for "our boys."

On June 15, 1944, Dominick Grossi, having been through Officer Candidates School in Quantico, Virginia, and graduating with a character assessment of "Excellent," is preparing to "shove off." He writes home to his girlfriend, Ruth, and his mother, Lena, on stationery that is embossed at the top: LIEUT. D. J. GROSSI. He tells his mom that he is headed to where his sister Marie is (San Diego). Her husband, Jim, who is also in the service, is Dom's closest buddy, and he hopes he will meet up with him when he gets there. He writes, "My outfit is all equipped and ready. I have 55 men. It certainly feels good to have an outfit of your own and look after them."

⅄

Warren Holloway Graham is the son of Jennie and Augustus Graham of Salisbury, North Carolina. He has a BS in chemistry from Virginia Polytechnic Institute in Blacksburg, and has just begun his training at Ashland Oil and Refining Company in Kentucky. That June, Graham, who according to his enlistment records is Methodist, five foot nine, and 164 pounds and has a slight speech defect, is about to shove off; he is headed to Parris Island.

⋊

At the same time, across the Pacific, the Marines of V Amphibious Corps have just smashed ashore on the island of Saipan in the Marianas. The landings of the 2nd and 4th Divisions are hotly contested by the dug-in Japanese defenders following the rigid principles of the "Tamura Doctrine," which calls for engaging the attackers at the water's edge and hurling them back into the sea.

10

D-Day: From Normandy to Saipan

They will be sore tried, by night and by day, without rest—until
the victory is won. The darkness will be rent by noise and flame.
Men's souls will be shaken with the violences of war.

—"Franklin Roosevelt's D-Day Prayer," June 6, 1944

As Task Force 58 readies for the long trek into the Marianas, General Vandegrift is back home speaking at a veterans' hall. The Medal of Honor recipient from Guadalcanal had become the eighteenth commandant of the United States Marine Corps. His audience includes men recovering from recent wounds and older vets from World War I.

The general begins, "Mr. Mayor, veterans, guests and friends—it is indeed a pleasure for me to be here tonight to do honor to those men from this community who have gone forth to fight for our country. They are here in spirit. They would appreciate your turning out to do them honor."[1]

It stirred the general's heart to hear the band play the same martial music he had heard on the docks in 1942 as his Marines boarded the ships that took them to the South Pacific. Now he looks into the eyes of men in the honor guard, and he recognizes some of them. They share the unspoken language of common experience. They know the jungle, the heat, the bodies, the deafening explosions, the darkness "rent by noise and flame," as FDR had so eloquently put it in his radio address. They know the awful cost but also the deep pride of victory together. The general continued:

> It is a special pleasure to talk to veterans, and to talk in the halls of the veterans of tomorrow. You veterans are graduates of the armed forces; we meet on common ground; we speak the same language.
>
> You, along with all Americans at home and overseas, are charged with the privilege of showing the Axis how far they underestimated us when they began this war—just as you did when Germany drew us into the last one.
>
> The Japanese in particular looked upon us Americans as constitutional weaklings. They were convinced our manpower had grown soft, spoiled by the luxury of the highest living standards in the world. I can assure you they are wrong![2]

✳

In late 1943, an interview with a Japanese fighter pilot somehow dodged the censors and found its way into *Fuji* magazine. Major Jiro Tsukushi revealed his prescient concerns about the enemy and the battles to come:

> If the mastery of the air is in enemy hands, it will be impossible to ship the necessary material to the island, and after about a week, the soldiers on the island will find it impossible to keep themselves alive from lack of foodstuffs. Then when the island falls, the enemy immediately builds an airbase there. The next island also meets the same fate . . . and the next . . . [3]

On the afternoon of June 11, 1944, at first they appear as thousands of specks, dots along the horizon; then, coming into view, they become clear: the ships of Task Force 58's massive armada are moving into the waters of the Marianas. There they will pummel the islands with unrelenting bombardment for three days. Overhead, the roar and rumble of the engines of hundreds of US planes fill the skies.

They swoop and dive on the Japanese targets, bombing and strafing, pounding at the island's defenses. It is like an orchestra of instruments with deadly aim. The battleships shell the islands with such force that the hulls and the men who stand on the decks of these ships rumble from within with each enormous explosion from the big guns.

The stunned Japanese watch from their bunkers. "All we could do was watch helplessly," wrote one who was on Saipan.

Another wrote from Tinian, "The planes which cover the sky are all the enemy's. They are far and away more skillful than Japanese planes. Now begins our cave life. Enemy planes overhead all day long—some 230 in number. They completely plaster our airfields. Where are our planes? Not one is sent up. Our AA [antiaircraft] guns spread black smoke where the enemy planes weren't. Not one hit out of a thousand shots."[4]

In two theaters of battle, ordinary American men—teachers, coaches, high schoolers, bookkeepers, and firemen, most between the ages of eighteen and twenty-four—who left their hometowns and traveled across the ocean, are now turning the tide against the evil that has paralyzed so much of the world. One week ago, the largest armada ever assembled in the history of man, nearly seven thousand vessels, landed on the beaches of Normandy, France, and now in June 1944 the "Normandy Invasion of the Pacific" is under way.

Since the devastation at Pearl Harbor, US forces have moved along the central Pacific Japanese perimeter. Under the direction of Admiral Nimitz, they have won at Midway, then secured the Gilbert and Marshall Islands, and moving up from the region just north of Australia, they ousted the Japanese from Port Moresby in New Guinea and Tulagi in the Solomon Islands. General MacArthur's forces are the secondary line, moving up the western sweep with the Philippines in their sights, but Guam and the Northern Marianas are the next priority. Guam, a US territory, had been captured by the Japanese in the days just after Pearl Harbor. The westernmost reach of US influence and central to the United States' access to the entire region, it must be liberated. Tinian and Saipan have essential airstrips on the path to the Japanese homeland, and then there are Iwo Jima and Okinawa, the doorstep of imperial territory. So it is the Marianas that the men of the US Navy must reclaim now.

On the ships, nervous, sweaty sailors and Marines try to stay loose. They huddle in the tight, dank spaces on the deck between the racks, dealing rounds of cards. The air smells of men and metal and sea salt. Faces light up as one Marine hangs his upper body down from his rack. In his hand is a pinup picture from his wallet. The others laugh and pass it around, whooping and hollering as they take turns looking. One corpsman lingers a bit too long, and another snatches it to get a look. Another young man, with the face of a boy, looks at a picture of his sweetheart and shares it so the guys can gaze at her for a moment, too.

Benny Goodman plays on the scratchy radio, which is bolted down like everything else on the ship. As the song ends, a young woman with perky English, whom they call Tokyo Rose—she calls herself Orphan Ann—taunts them with sweetly delivered jabs as she lures them in with music that takes them home, if only for a moment. How did she get her hands on all those records? they wonder.

"This is your favorite playmate and enemy, Ann. How are all you orphans in the Pacific? Are you enjoying yourselves while your wives and sweethearts are running around with 4Fs in the States? Here's another record to remind you of home."

She pokes at their homesick eighteen- or nineteen-year-old armor, she tugs at the strings in their hearts, she tries to scare them, warning them that their enemy is ready and waiting for them. But she barters music for her badgering, and they are willing to take the trade. Home is such a long way away.

Eventually fatigue conquers nerves, and they drift into a light sleep, the waves rolling beneath.

In the morning, their vessels churn through the salty sea under bright cerulean skies, heading to the Marianas, the islands that came under Japanese control under the terms of the Treaty of Versailles after World War I. Now Marines of the 2nd and 4th Divisions squint their eyes in the sun for a first look at the four-thousand-yard stretch of beach on Saipan.

The 2nd Division will land on the left, on the Red and Green beaches. The 4th Division will land on the right, on the Yellow and Blue beaches. Dividing the beaches is the old sugar dock that sticks prominently into the lagoon and the tall smokestack of the destroyed sugar mill just behind. North of the sugar dock and between the two divisions is Afetna Point. A shallow lagoon separates the deep blue water from the invasion beaches, just as on Tarawa. Here, thankfully, there is enough water to float the landing craft.

Private First Class James Russell received the Navy Cross at Tarawa for his deadly bazooka shot into the key Japanese bunker that opened the back door of the Japanese defensive line. Here he is in the first wave of attackers. As his LVT plows the water, he notices little colored flags that seem to be on floats scattered throughout the lagoon.[5]

Lieutenant General Yoshitsugu Saito, the commander of the Northern Marianas Army Group, knows the Americans will land on these two beaches. He has expertly placed his observation post on a spot the Americans have designated as Hill 500. His guns sit on the reverse slope, out of view from the air. His position puts him out of the line of fire during the US bombing runs.

He is the mastermind behind the little markers that sprinkle the blue waters and indicate target areas. His gunners know them by heart.

As a lieutenant colonel with the 4th Division later noted, "Wall diagrams in observation posts marked registration points on the reefs, the channels, the beach lines, roads and intersections adjacent to the beach."[6]

As the LVTs pass the bobbing tattletales, it is as if they trip a wire. Suddenly geysers of water shoot into the air as Japanese mortars hit. Russell and the others duck instinctively, staring at the floor of their rocking boats. They coil themselves into position, ready to vault over the sides, while all around them, landing craft are being blown to bits.

Sixty-eight armored amphibian tanks are in the 2nd Division's first wave, and thirty-one are knocked out in the lagoon or as they hit the beaches.[7] James Russell fears he has reentered Tarawa-hell.

In the first hour, the four battalion commanders of the 2nd Division's assault force are all wounded and out of action. Murderous flanking fire rakes the Marine lines; the 2nd Battalion, 6th Marines, goes through four battalion commanders.[8] Eight thousand Marines cram ashore during the first hour as enemy gunners continually rain fire down on them.

Afetna Point juts out into the lagoon between Green beaches 2 and 3. From this deadly post, antiboat guns fire down the shoreline as the landing craft approach the beaches. As the boats come in, the gunners wait until they pass in front of their muzzles, then blast away. The barrage of naval gunfire that had targeted the point in the days prior to the landing had been unable to take out this crucial firing line position.

Company G immediately turns south to attack Afetna Point, but the Japanese protecting the guns answer with a hail of rifle and machine-gun fire. The Marines are armed with Winchester Model 97 shotguns in addition to their regular arms. Since the point protrudes into the lagoon, regular rifle fire directed into the point could miss, continue down the beach, and hit the 4th Division Marines, just a few hundred yards away.

The shotgun-wielding Marines blast their way through the Japanese defensive lines, slowly clearing the bunkers and disabling nine antiboat guns. "Attached combat engineers, with their flamethrowers, bazookas and demolitions, were invaluable in destroying enemy pillboxes."[9]

Despite their progress, more enemy antiboat gunners refuse to abandon their guns and train them on the next wave of LVTs. They keep firing away, ready to die at their posts.

The Marine assault line slowly advances through the position with engineers brandishing twenty-pound satchel charges with high-velocity explosives. Any enemy who attempts to charge the Marine line is cut down by shotgun blasts with double-0 buckshot containing

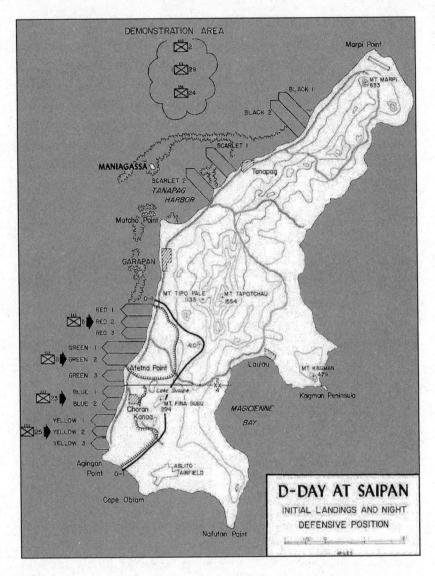

D-DAY AT SAIPAN

INITIAL LANDINGS AND NIGHT
DEFENSIVE POSITION

nine .33-caliber lead balls. The point is finally cleared during the late morning of the following day.[10]

On the other side of Afetna Point and the sugar dock, the 4th Division is pinned down. Some are dug in barely twelve yards off the water's edge. Only four of the fourteen medium tanks make it to the beach.

First Lieutenant John C. Chapin: "All around us was the chaotic debris of bitter combat: Jap and Marine bodies lying in mangled and grotesque positions; blasted and burnt-out pillboxes; the burning wrecks of LVTs . . . knocked out by Jap high velocity fire; the acrid smell of high explosives; the shattered trees; and the churned-up sand littered with discarded equipment."[11]

As the day winds down, the casualties are high: more than 2,000 killed, wounded, or missing.[12] The 2nd Division is hit the hardest—238 dead, 1,022 wounded, 355 missing—most of whom are later added to the dead.[13]

That night, 20,000 Marines cling to their toehold on the beach, while the Japanese light the dark night skies with tracers. They probe for targets. Their mortar rounds fall along the Marine line. Is a night attack coming?

These Japanese fighters are not like the abandoned defenders of earlier island battles, who had no hope of reinforcements. These defenders have been informed that their great fleet, including 9 carriers with 222 fighters and 200 dive- and torpedo bombers, has weighed anchor from their harbor at Tawi-Tawi Island, southwest of the Philippines. Help is on its way.

That morning, at 8:55 a.m., as the Americans conduct their amphibious operations, Admiral Soemu Toyoda, commander of the Japanese Combined Fleet, signals from his headquarters on the Inland Sea to all naval commanders: "The Combined Fleet will attack the enemy in the Marianas area and annihilate the invasion force."[14]

Back on May 3, 1944, Emperor Hirohito appointed Admiral Toyoda to command the Combined Fleet, and the next day, Toyoda messaged all commanders, "The war is drawing close to the lines vital to our national defense. The issue of our national existence is unprecedentedly serious; an unprecedented opportunity exists for deciding who shall be victorious and who defeated. . . . We will make this task our responsibility."[15]

His plan to strike this major blow is called Operation A-Go. When the time comes, detailed orders will be issued. "We must achieve our objectives by crushing with one stroke the nucleus of the great enemy concentration of forces, reversing the war situation . . . and shifting directly to the offensive."[16]

Toyoda's naval fantasy is rooted in Japan's great victories over the Chinese in 1895 and the Russians in 1905 and at Pearl Harbor. All were triumphant one-strike blows. He is determined to please the emperor by turning the tide with a stunning reversal sparked by a "divine wind," a climactic stroke.

While the Japanese fleet is on the move, darkness falls on the first night of battle on Saipan. Japanese attack forces form up in the town of Garapan, just to the north of the Marine invasion beaches, and begin moving south toward an assault line. The approach begins two miles north of the 6th Marines' positions, hastily dug in just off the Red beaches. This time, the Japanese make no attempt at stealth. They are coming in columns, some 2,000 strong; some ride trucks and tanks, some come on foot, "with the customary clamor of a traveling circus."[17]

Their swords flash in the moonlight; battle flags flutter in the night breeze; the clipped voices of the leaders can be heard as they make impassioned speeches, firing up their fighters. A bugle blares, and the massed force presses forward; first at a trot and then with increasing speed, it builds to a full charge.

US naval guns fire star shells that roll back the darkness, lighting the sky and revealing the pulsing, screaming Japanese attack columns streaming down from Garapan. Fire from the Marines pours into their ranks, shattering their momentum. It first slows the charge and then stops it cold. Mortar, bazooka, rifle, and machine-gun fire tear into the charging ranks, ripping them to pieces.

Staggering, the Japanese attackers fall back, perhaps to gather for another charge. But before they can regroup, land-based artillery and naval gunfire from offshore blanket them in pulverizing explosions.

Just before dawn, there is a second attack; this one comes from the east, accompanied by three tanks. Emerging from the gloom of the marshes around Lake Susupe, 200 Japanese slam into the lines of the 4th Division. Private First Class James Russell empties his Browning automatic rifle as fast as he can into the charging line, and then reloads. The weapon's barrel glows cherry red. He worries that it may melt down completely.[18]

Like the attack from Garapan, this one evaporates under withering Marine fire. When the sun rises in the morning, the bodies of 700 Japanese soldiers litter the road and the beaches down the coastline. Naval warships aim their guns onto Garapan and flatten the source of the attack.[19]

At 4:30 a.m. on the morning of June 16, a submarine lieutenant commander, Robert Risser, has his right eye glued to the lens of the periscope of his sub, the *Flying Fish*. He is looking for any sign of the Japanese offensive, and now he can barely believe his eyes: ship after ship, battleships, carriers, cruisers, silhouetted against the island's landmass, steam out of the San Bernardino Strait into the open waters of the Philippine Sea moving due east.

Risser's natural instinct is to launch all his torpedoes against the seemingly endless naval parade and then dive to the bottom, but his mission is not to attack; he is to watch and report. At this moment, he is the eyes of Task Force 58.

Finally the great parade passes him, and he surfaces the *Flying Fish*. He taps out a message to Admiral Raymond Spruance, the commander in chief of the Pacific Fleet: "The Japanese Fleet is heading for the Marianas."[20]

Emperor Hirohito has made clear that defeat is not an option. His empire is shrinking, and he has demanded the course that is now under way. He has told his admiral in no uncertain terms, "Rise to the challenge; make a tremendous effort; achieve a splendid victory." With Prime Minister Tojo, the man he elevated over the protestations of so many of his advisers, he has been even more direct: "If we ever lose Saipan, repeated air attacks on Tokyo will follow. No matter what it takes, we have to hold there." Tojo has filled the emperor's head with promises of "balloon bombs," a weapons program he is readying for the fall. Hirohito is buoyed by the knowledge that there is still a way to take the fight to the ever-encroaching Americans.[21]

Back on Saipan, on D + 1, artillery duels rage up and down the line. At nightfall, the order is to dig in. The Marine line has now advanced inland almost twice as far as on the first day.

Japanese general Saito has a bold plan for the night of D + 1. Confident that the naval Operation A-Go will soon be pummeling the US fleet and providing aerial support, he plans a large-scale attack against the 6th Marines—again against its left flank, facing Garapan. This will be an even greater, all-out effort than the attack of the previous night, which left 700 of his men dead. Saito will crush the enemy with tanks and infantry.[22]

On the southern outskirts of Garapan, Colonel Hideki Goto forms up the remaining thirty-seven tanks from his 9th Tank Regiment. He lost seven during the first night's abortive attack and certainly must have wondered why this all-out attack was not delivered then. He stands tall in the turret of his command tank and flourishes his saber overhead. Other commanders, steeling their courage, take their cue from him. Down the line, turrets pop open and warriors stand to face what is to come. Like Goto, they brandish their sabers aloft.[23]

The Japanese tanks are small, almost toylike, compared to the American Shermans. But they are fast, highly maneuverable, and well armed. Against other armor, they would be outmatched, but against infantry they are formidable. Three men squeeze into each tiny crew compartment.

The driver crouches down low on the right-hand side. Rubbing shoulders with him on the left, the machine gunner operates a .30-caliber gun with almost 1,200 rounds of ammunition. A second gun, operated by the tank commander in the turret and armed with another 1,800 rounds, faces almost to the rear. The 37 mm cannon with 130 rounds, also operated by the tank commander, is the main battle gun.[24]

At 3:30 a.m. on June 17, Saito's attack begins. Colonel Goto, like a cavalry leader of the Light Brigade at Balaclava, gives the side of his tank a slap with his saber, and at the sound of that metallic clank, the driver inches the vehicle forward. The other tank commanders clank the sides of their tanks to set them into motion, as if digging their spurs into their horses' sides. They are off, moving slowly forward in a cacophony of squeaks and rattles.

The Marines have nicknamed the Japanese tanks "kitchen sinks."[25]

As they approach some fifteen minutes later, the 6th Marines is waiting for them. With the Navy lighting the early-morning darkness, one Marine describes the furious firefight: "The battle evolved itself into a madhouse of noise, tracers, and flashing lights. As tanks were hit and set afire, they silhouetted other tanks coming out of the flickering shadows to the front or already on top of the squads."[26]

Amid the chaos and the blare of bugles, the Marine bazooka men take careful aim and send their rockets into the thin-skinned tanks with devastating results. Two privates first class, Herbert Hodges and Bob Reed, take out twelve tanks with eleven rockets and a grenade. As the Japanese attack disintegrates, Marine half-tracks move in. They scour the blazing battlefield like hyenas, finishing off Goto's wounded tanks. Twenty-four of the thirty-seven become smoldering, blackened hulks.[27]

The two night attacks have cost the Japanese dearly, but the Marines have also paid a Tarawa-like toll. By the morning of the third day, their casualty list tops 3,500, and the attacks that day that press the Japanese line farther back add 500 more.[28]

On D + 3, June 18, the Marine and Army infantrymen awaken to a sobering sight: the eight hundred ships that had their back are gone. The loneliness of the calm blue ocean and the gentle waves breaking in the lagoon tell them they are now on their own.[29] For some, it brings back memories of the dark days at Guadalcanal when the Japanese routinely drove the US Navy off, allowing them to blast away at the isolated Marines at will.

But this time, the Navy has not been driven away; it has gone out to prepare for a showdown with the advancing Japanese fleet. The support is still there; it is just out of sight, over the horizon.

The fifteen carriers, five hundred fighters, and four hundred bombers of Admiral Mitscher's Task Force 58 raced to an intercept point in the west. The battleships shield the island from their patrol positions twenty-five miles to the west. The smaller escort carriers are on call for aerial support for the invasion force—out of sight.[30]

But there is much more; in addition to the fifteen carriers and seven battleships, ten cruisers and fifty-eight destroyers complete the naval phalanx of ninety ships facing the approaching Japanese fleet.[31]

All this is unknown to the men ashore, who anxiously ask, "Where the hell are our ships? What about food and ammunition? Will we get back the supporting naval gunfire and the star shell illumination?"[32]

The supply transports have been moved out of harm's way to the vacant seas to the south and east. There they join the ships containing the men and materiel destined to assault Guam in the next phase of Operation Forager as soon as Saipan is secured.

At 5:42 a.m. on June 19, the sun rises over the Philippine Sea west of the Marianas. The first sign of enemy action isn't until 8:00 a.m. To the south over Guam, a large group of enemy planes approaches the island. Carrier planes from Task Force 58 vector out to intercept, and by 9:30 a.m., the F6F Hellcats have shot down thirty-five of them.[33]

At 10:04, the general alarm sounds throughout the carrier task force. Enemy planes are detected in great numbers all around the horizon. Admiral Mitscher rigs his carriers for combat, clearing his decks of all bombers and torpedo planes that are in the way, sending them to rendezvous to the east. This is to be a day for fighters, and fighters only. The decks are prepared for the task of launching, recovering, rearming, and servicing fighters in steady rotation. Mitscher anticipates a long battle.[34]

The first wave of Japanese attackers zeroes in on the battleships, but they are doomed from the start. Expert fighter-director officers on key US ships, especially on Admiral Mitscher's flagship, USS *Lexington*, analyze all aspects of the attack and guide the Hellcat fighters by radar to precise points in the sky to intercept the attackers.[35]

Part of the analysis includes some less-than-sophisticated eavesdropping. The coordination of the Japanese attacks is dependent on a senior squadron commander who takes a position flying high above the battlefield. The American fighter directors nickname him "Coordinator Joe."

On board *Lexington*, a team of officers, including a translator, listens intently for "Joe's" first transmission. When his voice comes up on the frequency, within moments, they know precisely every detail of the oncoming strike: location, numbers, direction, and tactics.[36]

Japanese pilots, poised to swoop down and fire, are blindsided by streaking, diving US fighters, which outnumber them and blast them from all sides. Japanese bombers are hit, catch fire, and free-fall from the skies. The Americans lose only one plane in that first wave, while thirty Japanese aircraft plunge to the sea.

The rest of the first wave tries to reverse course, but they run up against fierce antiaircraft fire thrown up by the US battle fleet. The wall of steel becomes so dense that more than a dozen more Japanese planes plunge into the ocean. The second wave sees nearly 125 Japanese planes rain down from the sky.

The third wave circles around to the north to try to avoid the US defensive battle line and make a run at one of Mitscher's carriers. Some forty enemy planes penetrate the defense. One scores a direct hit on the *South Dakota* with a 210-kilogram (462-pound) bomb; one crashes into the side of *Indiana*. There are near misses on a heavy cruiser and several carriers, doing slight damage and causing small personnel casualties.[37]

The fourth and final wave of Japanese planes is a chaotic last gasp. Many of the Japanese pilots never even sight the US carriers, much less attack them. Trying to escape, they fly toward Guam to attempt to land, but they are overtaken and shot down by avenging Hellcats. Of the 373 Japanese planes that attack that day, fewer than 100 are able to even attempt a return to their carriers. The Americans lose just 29 planes in the Battle of the Philippine Sea, which is quickly and forevermore nicknamed "the Great Marianas Turkey Shoot."[38]

The few Japanese planes that survive the "shoot" fly west. When they arrive at the spot where their carriers should be, the sea below them is empty. The pilots search in vain for the sunken carriers, *Taibo* and *Shokaku*, and then, with nowhere to land and no gas left in their tanks, they sputter, glide, and finally nose-dive into the ocean.

The 33,000-ton *Taibo* was the largest carrier in the Japanese fleet; it was torpedoed and sent to the bottom with its remaining planes and its entire crew compliments of the US submarine *Albacore*. The 22,000-ton *Shokaku* is also now at rest on the ocean floor, sunk by four torpedoes from the submarine *Cavalla*.[39]

The following day, June 20, Mitscher's task force detects what is left of the Japanese fleet fleeing south, already 250 miles away. Despite the waning light, the admiral makes the call to launch 216 planes to run down the enemy fleet and finish it off.

The pilots who fly the 216 planes know well that even if they catch up to the fleeing Japanese and attack, many will not have the fuel to make it back. Still, as has happened again and again, no one asks, "Why me?" No one seeks exemption. The squadron commander of USS *Yorktown*, Lieutenant Commander Bernard "Smoke" Strean, simply says, "Okay, gentlemen, we have our orders. I'll lead the entire strike. We'll be the first in to find the targets."[40]

They fly off and finally catch up to the enemy fleet in the waning light of the last rays of the sun. They sink another carrier, *Hiyo*, damage three others, and sink two oilers at the cost of twenty planes. The return flight is as predicted. Eighty planes are lost as they exhaust their fuel. Thirty-eight crew members perish; the rest are rescued. It might have been worse had Admiral Mitscher not ordered all the ships to turn on their lights to serve as beacons for the aircraft struggling home.[41]

For the Japanese, the defeat is devastating. They lost three aircraft carriers, one fewer than at Midway, and although the fleet escaped total annihilation, it is severely crippled. As the Navy reported, "The important result, Japanese carrier aviation was substantially finished as a naval force in the war."[42] Prime Minister Hideki Tojo no longer has the confidence of his government or the emperor and is forced to resign.

)X(

Back in Arlington, Massachusetts, Harry Gray is packing his small duffel bag. His mom, Anne, is next to him. She has lovingly washed and folded his underwear, T-shirts, and socks. She stacks it all neatly in his bag, even though he insists he can do it himself. She wants to touch his things, make sure they are just right. She presses it all down, leaving the scent of her hands on it all. Harry zips it up.

Nancy is on the bed, watching and swinging her feet. She doesn't want him to go. She worries that it will be lonely in the house with just her mom and grandma. She knows she will long for him to poke his head into her room and ask her if she has a couple of bucks he can borrow or if she wants to play some touch football.

Last night he said his good-byes to Dorothy. She slid her hand over the pocket of his shirt, where her picture was tucked inside. She kissed him and wrapped her arms around his back, burying her face in him, trying to imprint in her memory how his broad shoulders felt and the scent of his shirt, so she could summon him to her senses later. "Let's pretend we are already married," he whispered. She wished they had not listened to his mother, that they had just run off to the town hall and exchanged vows. But there is no going back now. She will have to wait, and when he comes back, their life will begin.

On that hot July morning at South Station, Harry kisses his mom and Nancy and hugs them tight. He tells them not to worry, he will be home soon. He shakes hands with Uncle Frank, who has come up to see him off. They stare hard into each other's eyes for a few seconds. "Take care of yourself, son," Frank says.

There isn't much for anyone to say now, so they stand for a moment, hearts in their throats. Anne breaks the tension by smiling up at her boy and giving him one more squeeze. "Off you go now, my boy. Don't forget to write. And we will see you when you get leave." Harry turns, beams back at them, and hops onto the train, flashing his million-dollar smile. He looks so young in his trousers and shirt, his sandy hair flopped over his forehead, as he looks back and then watches them through the windows as he takes his seat. They all keep watching and waving until they can't see each other anymore. Then, like other families all across the United States, Harry's family turns away from the departing train as it slips away, headed ultimately for boot camp at the Marine Corps Recruit Depot, Parris Island, South Carolina.

※

Miles away in Pennsylvania, Charlie Gubish is also packing his bag. His wife, Ethel, folds his things, and Charlie is lost in thought, hoping he made the right decision. Three-year-old Charlie Jr. is at his feet, playing with a wooden truck on the floor, and Richard, the baby, just four months old, naps on the hot summer night in the next room of their small farmhouse in Wassergass. Charlie thinks back to when he met Ethel. He and his dad took their produce to sell at a farm stand in South Bethlehem, where she lived. From town and the Bethlehem Steel Mill and back to the farm, that's all he ever knew. Here he knows or is related to just about everybody.

But there's a war on, and he feels he should go. Truth be told, he'd about had it working at the steel mill as a lieutenant fireman. The women who worked under him were always after him, asking if they could take breaks. The higher-ups kept giving him a hard time for taking pity on them once in a while. That was the kind of stuff he had to put up with and the kind of stuff that had made him "join the damn service."

One day, one of his buddies said he'd signed up and was heading to the Navy. He said it didn't matter that they were exempt because of their work at the steel mill, that you could go sign up anyway, and that was what Charlie decided to do. But when he got there, he saw the pictures of the uniforms and decided he would rather be a Marine. And that's why he's now packing his bag and leaving Bethlehem. He worked all his young life on the farm and then at the mill, like most everyone else.[43] But now life is changing. Bethlehem Steel built the rails on which he will soon be rattling off to Parris Island to become a Marine.

Between 1941 and 1945, 205,000 civilians were turned into Marines at Parris Island. In July 1944, each man went through eight weeks of basic training and eight weeks of basic field training, including 147.5 hours of rifle training.[44] When those young men stepped off their trains in South Carolina, they stepped into another world.

X

Harry's train pulls into the station near Parris Island the next morning. The whistle and the brakes shake the slumber off the young men in the cars. They are shuffled onto a bus that lumbers down the dusty road and past the sign at the gate. A drill instructor steps onto the bus and faces them. "Get off my bus!" he yells. "Say 'Yessir!' Louder!" Harry and the others stand and shout "Yessir" as loud as they can. The hot July sun pours through the windows, and the idle bus grows hotter by the second. A bead of sweat drips down Harry's back as he stares straight ahead. "Yessir!" he shouts again, as loud as his vocal cords can muster.

By the end of that day, his sandy blond hair is completely gone; he has a number—565110—a uniform, boots, and a rifle. He has been yelled at within an inch of his face to sit and stand and line up and pay attention. The process has begun; he is being transformed from a boy into a Marine. He has left behind all the trappings of his life at home. He has emptied his pockets and been told there is no "I"; he is to refer to himself only as "this recruit."

Warren Graham, the chemist from North Carolina, did not have as far to travel; he arrives at Parris Island on June 27, 1944. The military likes to do things alphabetically, so Gray, Graham, and another young man from Dayton, Ohio, named Herman Graeter are next to one another just about every time they line up or eat or run or scramble over a wall carrying a bucket of cement.

Herman Robert Graeter is the only son of Golda Marie and Herman Graeter, Sr., of Dayton. He was born in January 1926, so he is eighteen like Harry but six months older. Graeter played varsity football and basketball at Dayton High School. Under "Occupation" on his registration form, Graeter wrote in blue pen block letters "Part-time mail clerk and student" and said that he could type thirty-five words per minute. Under "Duty Desired" Herman requested "Radar Technician."

Charlie Gubish, the married father of two, has only just arrived at Parris Island when he starts thinking that his problems back at the mill look pretty darn manageable. His face, his uniform, his boots, and his rifle are caked in mud, and his drill instructor, a policeman from New York, is staring down into his face and calling him a "shit bird." When it is time for bed, he is exhausted and humiliated from being knocked around and cursed at, and pain racks his body from head to toe. He hears the guys near him say that one of the other guys tried to kill himself last night. He is so desperate for relief that he thinks to himself, I'd take my life, too, if it would save me from one more day of facing that New York drill instructor. But I can't, he realizes as he drifts off. They are watching all the time.[45]

By the end of week four, though, things are looking up. He and his fellow "shit birds" just beat the college boys on the obstacle course, carrying a bucket of cement the whole way. Something in Charlie is changing. It turns out that he can endure pain and punishment he never dreamed existed. They tell him they are going to turn him and the other "shit birds" into Marines, and Charlie nods to himself, thinking, I guess they are right.[46]

In Peekskill, New York, three weeks later, Frank Bowes sees a letter in the small pile of mail that has been pushed through the slot in the porch screen door. Under a couple of bills, the corner of a handwritten letter has this return address:

PVT H. E. Gray #565110 USMC
Platoon 409 6th BU
Marine Barracks
Parris Island, South Carolina

It is dated Sunday, Summer 1944.

Dear Uncle Frank,

Well here I am at Parris Island and everything is fine. I am in perfect health and have gained weight. I have had two shots and a blood test. Tomorrow we have 2 more.

We do calisthenics every morning until we almost collapse but try to keep on going. Yesterday we drilled in the sun at 120 degrees wearing full combat gear. We kept this up until 3 fellows collapsed, this place is so nerve wracking that one fellow from another platoon tried to commit suicide last night by cutting his throat. Just by chance they found him before he died.

Every morning we are up at 4:30 and between this time and 6:00 we sweep and wash the barracks, clean the windows, make our bunks, wash, shave, disassemble our rifle and clean it. At 6:00 we eat chow.

Next week our platoon has to appear for Colonel Inspection. We have to know many facts such as, "General Orders, all officers of rank, all parts of our rifle and many other items."

Well that's all my troubles. How is everyone in Peekskill? Fine I hope. Tell Betsy, Aunt Helen, Jane and Mr. Walsh I was asking for them.

I don't have much time to write, please thank Aunt Helen for her gift and Betsy's card. I appreciated them very much.

I have to go and study now so I will try and write later.

Lots of Love to All,
Harry

P.S. Tell Betsy I would love to receive a letter from her.

Frank reads it over several times, then tucks it carefully back into the envelope. He will show it to Helen and the family and will make sure Betts, now nine years old, sends off a letter of her own. He thinks Harry sounds pretty good, all things considered, and it's a load off his mind just to get the letter. He relaxes in his chair, opens the newspaper, and lights his pipe.

That night in Arlington, Nancy Gray lies in her brother's bed, about to fall asleep. Ever since her father died and her grandmother moved in, she's had to sleep in a twin bed in her mother's room, but since Harry left, she sleeps in his room. She feels so cozy, surrounded by his warm blanket, which still smells like him. She looks up at the stuffed gray owl on his dresser and wonders what he likes about that ugly thing. He thinks it's wonderful. She can't for the life of her imagine why, but he is a boy, so . . . She says her prayers and drifts off to sleep.[47]

11

Japan's Doorstep

I'll be seeing you in all the old familiar places / That this heart of mine embraces all day through. / In that small café, the park across the way.

—Bing Crosby singing "I'll Be Seeing You" in 1944

In hometowns across the United States, families were missing their boys abroad and factories were buzzing overtime, building weapons to win the war and bring them back home.

Ford, General Motors, and Rolls-Royce factories hummed around the clock, building parts, engines, aircraft, and tanks. The shipbuilder Bath Iron Works in Bath, Maine, was turning out destroyers for the Navy at a blistering pace of one every seventeen days.

The Boeing factory in Seattle rumbled day and night, turning out the B-17 bombers that were the workhorses of the European war. However, the Department of War had put out a call for a new bomber, one that could fly higher and faster and carry more bombs. The top secret project, at a cost of $3 billion, was by far the most expensive program of the war. It was known as the XB-29.

Ninety-eight feet long and metal from nose to tail, the aircraft that would become known as the Boeing B-29 Superfortress could fly at speeds of up to 350 miles per hour and at an altitude of 30,000 feet. It had a 4,000-mile range, making the stretch between the islands in the Pacific and mainland Japan attainable, even loaded down with 10,000 pounds of bombs and equipment. It was a flying silver dragon of cutting-edge technology that boasted the first-ever pressurized cabin. Dual-wheeled tricycle landing gear added stability on landing even for battle-damaged aircraft. The B-29's five General Electric–built remote-controlled machine guns, which were an early use of computer technology, ultimately made it the dominant, game-changing aircraft of the Pacific.[1]

But the endeavor to build the "plane that took down an empire" came at great cost. On February 18, 1943, during a secret test flight to measure climb and engine cooling, the XB-29's number one engine on the left wing caught fire. The highly regarded Chief Test Pilot Edmund P. Allen shut the engine down, and the fire extinguishers were activated. He began his descent and headed toward Boeing Field in Seattle. Then there was an explosion, and radio operator Harry Ralston said, "Allen, better get this thing down in a hurry, the wing spar is burning badly." In moments, the prototype burst into flames, metal was peeling and flying off, leaving a trail along the ground as Allen successfully avoided the buildings downtown. At 12:26 p.m., the plane crashed into the side of the Frye & Company meatpacking plant. Three crewmembers bailed out moments before impact, but they, along with Allen, seven crewmembers, and twenty employees at Frye, as well as a local fireman, all perished in one of the worst aviation disasters of the time.[2]

Around the same time in New Rochelle, New York, the Rex Manufacturing Company could barely keep up with the demand driven by the war. Under tremendous pressure and with a shortage of skilled workers and metal, Rex was a year late in delivery on its 1943 contract for the Navy. It took until 1944 to complete the order to the exact quality specifications, a measure of utmost importance. When the crate was ready for delivery, its precious cargo was intact: 135,000 Purple Hearts ready to be bestowed on those who had shed blood for our country and given to the families of those who were never coming home. The Navy was glad to receive them. Certain that a naval blockade of Japan was going to be the strategy, they were confident they would not be needing another shipment before the end of the war.[3]

X

After the Great Marianas Turkey Shoot, Fast Carrier Task Force 58, the indomitable strike force of the Pacific, sets its sights on its next mission: the Bonins, a chain of volcano islands stretching from five hundred to eight hundred miles directly south of Tokyo.

This is not just another stepping-stone. This is Japanese home-land. Sacred ground. Hirohito has pulled entire divisions out of China and Korea and rushed them to these islands to hold them. The United States and Great Britain have been quite successful in cracking the code of Japanese radio transmissions in order to gauge their next movements, but the Japanese have failed to do the same with the US transmissions. They can never be sure where their enemy is headed next.[4]

Navy pilots are the first to gaze down at the tiny pork chop–shaped island with the menacing volcano. Iwo Jima is an island of almost nothing, really, except a small fishing village, called Nishi, which would soon be evacuated. *Iwo* means "sulfur," and the foul element is the island's only "fruit." Nothing grows on the brown, moon-like, ash-covered stretch of rock. There is no water, barely any trees, and not a blade of grass. It is either scorchingly hot or bone-chillingly damp as the deep ocean surrounding it sends a cold wind across its shelterless rocks. Mount Suribachi's vents puff foul vapor into the air at the outer edge of Iwo's tiny eight-square-mile area. It is one of the most isolated places on Earth. The southern watchtower of Japan. The Americans have been inching closer, and Iwo's two precious airstrips are just the right distance to service B-29s coming from and going to bombing routes over mainland Japan, the ultimate target to end the war. The Japanese cannot lose this island, and the Allies can't move forward without it.[5]

But now, in mid-June 1944, the island is getting its first glimpses of battle. For two straight days, Task Force 58's seven carriers, and the fighter jets that line their decks, take to the skies over Iwo. Thirty-plus Japanese pilots get airborne to guard the hundred planes parked on the island. US fighters sweep most of the Zeros from the sky and take out almost all of those parked on the runways. When the strike force pulls out of the area after this initial pass, Iwo is wounded but far from dead.[6]

On June 24, Task Force 58 is back and takes another pass over the island. It is clear that the enemy has resupplied. Enemy planes meet the US fighters in the skies and launch attacks on the carriers themselves. But again they are outmatched. One hundred fourteen Japanese fighter planes are shot out of the sky or blown up on the island. Only nine US planes are lost.

On July 3, another fighter sweep of sixty-three aircraft sorties to Iwo. Again, Iwo staggers under the assault but stands.

X

On July 18, 1944, Imperial General Headquarters issues a report. The delusional propaganda describes wild imaginary successes.

Since the enemy task force came attacking the Marianas on June 11, the Japanese Air and Sea units gained the following war results:

1. Sank . . . Two aircraft carriers, three battleships, four cruisers, three destroyers, and one submarine, two warships of an unknown type, two transports.

2. Sank or damaged more than five aircraft carriers and over one battleship.

3. Damaged five or six aircraft carriers, one battleship, three cruisers, three destroyers, one warship of unknown type, seven transports.

4. Airplanes . . . shot down. More than 863.[7]

These are all fantastic lies, since during the Marianas campaign to date, Japan has managed to damage only one aircraft carrier, *Bunker Hill*; and a few other ships are in need of repair. The rest of the US fleet is intact.

The Japanese report ends with this oxymoronic conclusion: "It is indeed regrettable that despite such brilliant war results, we were unable to frustrate the enemy's malicious attempts."[8]

⋊

Guam is the second target of Operation Forager. Five hundred US servicemen have been imprisoned there for three years, since the day after the Pearl Harbor attack. Back when the smoke was still rising in Hawaii, Japanese bombers turned their sights to the other targets, including Guam. The Japanese swept the island almost effortlessly and began forcing the native Chamorro people into unpaid labor. Elvina Reyes Rios was thirteen years old. She worked in the rice fields. She was forced to walk four hours to be at work by 6:00 a.m. If she paused for a moment, she was slapped or hit with rocks. They were not paid or fed for their work. They complied because they feared they would be killed or put into prison camps if they did not. As the Americans got closer, the Japanese soldiers became nervous, and the abuse turned deadly. Barbara Dela Cruz saw three Chamorro men beheaded after they were accused of spying and assisting the one American holdout, George Tweed. The Japanese told Barbara and the others not to turn away during the killing, or they would be next. Days before the US invasion, forty-six men and women were massacred at Tinta and Faha, and that was the last straw for the Chamorros. They fought back, using whatever they could get their hands on, and killed every Japanese soldier they could find.[9]

On July 21, the island is awakened by earthshaking noise. Bombs are falling on the beaches, and this time it is a welcome violence coming from six battleships, nine cruisers, and destroyers and rocket ships of the US Navy.[10]

But the 19,000 Japanese defenders of Guam are ready. They have imposing defensive positions overlooking the invasion beaches to the north and south of the Orote Peninsula.

Lieutenant General Kiyoshi Shigematsu tells his men, "The enemy, overconfident because of his successful landing on Saipan, is planning a reckless and insufficiently prepared landing on Guam. We have an excellent opportunity to annihilate him on the beaches."[11]

The landings are hard; dug-in Japanese fire away as Americans hit the beaches and the hills. The labor of the enslaved Chamorros has created heavily fortified cave positions. Gunfire lights their apertures and shells rain down on the water and sand, some missing and throwing earth into the air, others exploding the amtracs and killing Marines fighting their way onto the beaches of Guam.

But during those first five days of battle, the Japanese play all their cards at once and launch two devastating banzai charges. The enormous casualties in these ill-fated attacks hasten the island's fate. The suicidal charges cost the lives of 3,500 men of the estimated 19,000-man force. But more critically, 95 percent of the Japanese officers are killed.[12]

Now the Marine and Army divisions are on the move, up the long axis of the island, chasing the remaining Japanese forces as they retreat deeper and deeper to the north.

Their commander, Lieutenant General Hideyoshi Obata, is living for the time being in a cave near Mount Mataguac. He is well hidden from planes above, but he hears the Americans getting closer. He knows his time is running out. He sends a message to Hirohito, one the emperor is growing weary of receiving: "We are continuing a desperate battle. We have only our hands to fight with. The holding of Guam has become hopeless. Our souls will defend the island to the very end. . . . I pray for the prosperity of the Empire."[13]

His final transmission before taking his own life: "I shall be the bulwark of the Pacific Ocean."[14]

Sixteen hundred Marines are killed on Guam, 5,000 wounded. More than 18,000 Japanese have made the final sacrifice for their emperor.

Operation Forager's focus now moves to the last of the Northern Marianas, Tinian. The veteran 2nd and 4th Marine Divisions, worn out from the grueling Saipan campaign, are "skinny" at only two-thirds strength.[15] Looking across the three miles of water to Tinian, they wonder, "Don't they have anyone else to fight this war?"[16]

Tinian is essentially a cane field. Mostly flat, it is 12 miles long and 6 miles at its widest. The boys from New York see a shape not unlike that of Manhattan, some 7,500 miles to the east.

On the island there are about 9,000 Japanese defenders, many of them hardened veterans of the war in Manchuria.

Tinian has only one real beach for landing, and it is on the southern end of the island on the harbor of Tinian Town. Every Japanese gun will have its sights squarely on that beach, ready and waiting for the Americans.

Admiral Harry W. Hill, the commander of the Northern Landing Force, will later note, "The more we looked at the Tinian Town beaches, the less we liked them."[17]

On the north side they find the only alternative: a small beach that is made up of more craggy sharp coral than sand.[18] It is divided by a protrusion of jagged coral, and each side has only about sixty-five yards clear enough for a vehicle to land. The rest is biting, skin-ripping rock and coral. Maybe four to eight men abreast can go ashore at a time. On Saipan they landed ninety-six across.[19]

Admiral Hill concludes, "My staff was of one mind: land on the northern end of the island."[20] Marine General Holland "Howlin' Mad" Smith recognizes the possible surprise factor of landing where it seems folly to try. Based on the reconnaissance reports showing that the area is almost undefended and only a few small defensive positions exist, he casts his vote with Hill.

However, Hill's superior, Admiral Richmond Turner, nixes the idea, saying it is impossible. He orders Hill to work on another plan. Hill does as he was told but lets some on his staff keep working on the northern landing.

A second attempt by Hill and Smith to convince Turner to land in the north turns the admiral testy. "You are not going to land on the White Beaches," he snaps at Holland Smith. "I won't land you there!"

Smith is not to be outdone. "Oh, yes, you will. You'll land me any goddamned place I tell you to," he booms back.

But Turner is unmoved. "I'm telling you now, it can't be done. It's absolutely impossible."

"How do you know it's impossible? You haven't studied the beaches thoroughly," Smith howls back. "You're just so goddamned scared that some of your boats will get hurt!"[21]

The matter is kicked upstairs to Admiral Raymond Spruance, the commander of the Fifth Fleet, who calls a meeting of all concerned, where all agree that they favor the northern beaches. Turner gives in.[22]

Indeed, Colonel Kiyoshi Ogata, commanding the Japanese 50th Infantry Regiment, confirmed Smith's hunch: "The enemy on Saipan . . . can be expected to be planning a landing on Tinian. The area of that landing is estimated to be either Tinian Harbor or Asiga (northeast coast) Harbor."[23]

As there has been no hint that the Marines will land in the north, the Japanese defenders have put just one 37 mm antitank gun into a covered position and two 7.7 mm machine guns into pillboxes.[24]

The newly acquired air base in Saipan has eased the way for preliminary aerial, artillery, and naval bombardment. Everything is moved from shore to shore across the less-than-three-mile stretch between the two islands. July is typhoon season in the Pacific, and they need a three-day window of good weather. Most of the reconnaissance and minesweeping go off without a hitch, except for the night before the attack, when Demolition Team 5 heads in on rubber boats to clear mines off the northern beaches and blast away some of the underwater rock formations. A squall moves in after the swimmers among them get into the water, and the visibility suddenly goes down to zero and the mission turns back.[25]

Jig Day, July 24: It's "go day," and the 2nd Marine Division is on the move. Plowing through the water in the direction of Tinian Town, they attempt to trick the Japanese gunners lodged in the hills just above the harbor into thinking they are coming in for the attack.

The coxswains gun their engines and head full bore toward the shore. The Japanese gunners immediately open up on the waves of incoming LVTs. Fountains of water shoot into the air as the LVTs hit the gas. But about two thousand yards from shore, the coxswains bank hard to the left and turn back. Another fifteen hundred yards, and they hit the brakes, hovering offshore. The Japanese try to figure out what's going on as they keep pummeling the Marines nonstop from the harbor. Water and shrapnel are flying everywhere, but no one has been hit.

Up in the hills, though, the 6-inch guns are blasting the battleship *Colorado* and the destroyer *Norman Scott*. *Colorado* is hit twenty-two times. Forty-five sailors lie dead on her decks, and 198 are injured. *Norman Scott* is hit six times. The captain is dead, along with 18 others; 47 others are wounded.[26]

It is now almost 8:00 a.m., and the first LVTs carrying Marines from the 4th Division are hitting the rocky White beaches, just a few abreast, firing back at the weak Japanese defense. The gunner and the pillbox fall silent.

They then begin their day's work, moving supporting arms and equipment onto this part of the island. By nightfall, 15,000 men have set up and dug into the sugarcane, creating foxholes wherever they can. They tip their helmets forward over their eyes to attempt to sleep in the cool breeze coming off the water. There has been steady progress so far, but no advance comes without a cost: 15 Marines are dead. Medics tend to the 225 wounded; those who won't mend here are being loaded onto the hospital ship.[27] Some wish they were headed there; a bit of relief it might be to get off these hot, thorny islands and rest in a hospital cot.

Night sets in, and a stinging, burning smell hangs over Tinian. It is rising off the charred Japanese bodies in the trenches and the singed palm trees. There is something about the preinvasion bombardment here that is eerily different.

In the past few months, Army Air Corps researchers at Eglin Air Force Base in Florida have been experimenting with a new weapon concoction. They have mixed diesel oil, gasoline, and a metallic salt

UNKNOWN VALOR

from naphtha that is used in the manufacture of soap. They have discovered that this sticky, thick, jellylike substance is highly flammable, sticks to surfaces, and burns with high intensity. They call it napalm.[28]

Admiral Hill has seen a film demonstrating its use and was impressed with its potential. Five days before the Marianas invasion, he signaled to Admiral Nimitz that they would need more. As the Marines tested its efficacy, they were awestruck. They watched as each firebomb released from their low-flying planes tumbled end over end to the ground and erupted in a rolling wave of fire, engulfing everything in a seventy-five-foot-wide-by-two-hundred-foot-long inferno.[29]

Those who fought in Saipan saw it in action first. Without the napalm gel, the emanating fire billowed and could be blown by the wind; with it, the tanks fired a virtual fire hose of flame speeding straight and steady toward the target.

The Marines establish a main line of resistance. They assign sectors of fire and ensure that all Marines know their jobs. Those who are to man the perimeter dig in. Experience has taught them that after nightfall, the desperate Japanese fighters will gather to die and will use whatever they have—guns, knives, and fists—to take out as many of them as they can. They will go down in the banzai charge attack, attempting to push the Marines back into the sea.

The Japanese forces are scrambling to catch up to the unexpected attack in the north. A thousand troops are shifted from the airfield to the new front. They head to the left of the Marine line. Fifteen hundred more converge on the center. To the right, 900 men, a battalion of the Japanese Mobile Counterattack Force, assemble. Marine intelligence reports lots of "Japanese chatter" along the front.[30]

At 2:00 a.m., a tightly formed group of Japanese appears a hundred yards in front of the 24th Marines' lines.

As the first Marine bullets and shells find their targets, the enemy bursts into a screaming, forward-thrusting mass. The shadows come alive as 600 leaping Japanese naval troops respond to the command "Banzai!"[31]

Tracers suddenly light the battlefield, and every Marine weapon is now ablaze as the massed enemy hurls toward them. The Japanese attackers move to within a hundred yards of the 1st Battalion's Company A. Six tanks join in the defense, and two 81 mm mortars fire more than fifteen hundred rounds. Company A is down to 30 men with usable weapons. Within a hundred yards of the Marines' lines, 476 Japanese bodies lay entangled on the battlefield.[32]

In the center, the first probes in the early-morning darkness are quickly repulsed but the banzai attackers reorganize and smash into the lines between the 24th and 25th Marines. Several hundred attackers find a "weak" point and pour through, threatening the Marine artillery on the beach and the rear area of the 25th Marines.

A reserve company of the 25th quickly moves in to clear them out, killing 91. The second group presses on to attack the artillery units near the beach as they start their direct fire missions to the front. All the rear-area Marines rush in to suppress the attack. The Japanese continue to push, but now they are the targets of two .50-caliber machine-gun teams laying down a devastating volume of fire, highlighted by streams of red tracers, tearing the Japanese to pieces.[33]

The remaining enemy troops regroup and advance again, this time with tanks. Personnel on the ships offshore see them and send up illumination rounds.

Lieutenant Jim G. Lucas recalls:

The three lead tanks broke through our wall of fire. One began to glow blood-red, turned crazily on its tracks, and careened into a ditch. A second, mortally wounded, turned its machine guns on its tormentors, firing into the ditches in a last desperate effort to fight its way free. One hundred yards more and it stopped dead in its tracks. The third tried frantically to turn and then retreat, but our men closed in, literally blasting it apart. . . . Bazookas knocked out the fourth tank with a direct hit which killed the driver. The rest of the crew piled out of the turret, screaming. The fifth tank, completely surrounded, attempted to flee. Bazookas made short work of it. Another hit set it afire, and its crew was cremated.[34]

Five tanks are destroyed and 267 men die in beating down the attack.

The operation grinds on for another eight days. The Japanese defending forces are basically broken. But the repetitive grisly sequence of securing the island is in motion. There is a final banzai charge, but then the Marines witness something they did not see before Saipan and now see on Tinian: the ritual suicide jump of desperate Japanese villagers.

They choose to die for the emperor and to avoid what they have been told will be brutal treatment if they fall into the hands of the enemy. *Time* reporter Robert Sherrod was embedded with the Marines on Saipan. He had heard of the mass ritual suicides and went to the cliffs to see for himself. A Marine had told him, "You wouldn't believe it, unless you saw it, hundreds of Jap civilians—men, women and children—up here on this cliff. In the most routine way, they would jump off, or climb down and wade into the sea. I saw a father throw his three children off, and then jump himself." Sherrod watched with them as a fifteen-year-old boy paced on the beach. "He swung his arms as if getting ready to dive; then he sat down at the edge and let the water play over his feet. Finally he eased himself slowly into the water."

"There he goes," the Marine shouted.[35]

Later they will be revered in Japan. A correspondent from the *Yomiuri Shimbun* praises the women who committed suicide with their children, writing that they were "the pride of Japanese women" and calling it "the finest act of the Showa period."[36]

The operation on tiny Tinian is dubbed the "perfect amphibious operation." General Clifton Cates, the commanding officer of the 4th Division, will later note:

The enemy, although long alerted to our intentions to attack Tinian, was tactically surprised when we avoided his prepared defenses and landed on two small beaches totaling in width only about 220 yards. Before he could recover from the shock, he was out-numbered and out-equipped on his own island. His subsequent effort to throw us into the water resulted in complete failure. We then pushed the length of the island in nine days, while suffering light casualties in comparison with those of most other island conquests.[37]

⚹

While the battle is still being fought, the Seabees are already at work, rolling out onto the old Japanese runways and converting them into what will be the largest airfield in the world.

Around the clock in scorching heat, they lay down six runways, each 8,500 feet long, ready for the B-29 bomber. Hundreds of the planes begin arriving in October. On November 24, 110 B-29s take off from Saipan on their first strikes against Tokyo. Shortly after, B-29s from Tinian join in, softening up the mainland of Japan for the invasion that is to come. The perch on the Marianas has brought them that much closer. Before the war is over, 19,000 combat missions against Japan will take off from Tinian.[38] One of them will be piloted by Colonel Paul Tibbets in a B-29 named for his mother, *Enola Gay*. It will carry the heaviest payload of all: the atomic bomb headed for Hiroshima.

⚹

As the B-29s begin their routes from Tinian that October 1944, the Marine Corps Recruit Depot on Parris Island is turning out fresh recruits. The newly minted Marines are lean and muscled from sixteen weeks of intense training. Private Harry Gray is in that proud number; like Charlie Gubish, Warren Graham, Herman Graeter, and George Colburn, he has his photograph taken in uniform. Anne Gray frames the photo and places it on the center table in her living room. The glimmer in her boy's eyes brings a tear to hers. She is glad that he looks happy and handsome, so she smiles back at him. She hopes that he is praying his rosary, the gift from his grandmother that Anne tucked into the leather pouch and put inside his bag. Prayer will give him support and strength. Work has been a good distraction for Anne. At night in bed, all she can think about is boot camp and the stories she hears about what it's like. Harry has spared her some of what he put into his letters to Uncle Frank, about the "nerve wracking" intensity and the suicide attempt by one of the guys.

The new Marines are given the customary weeklong leave after boot camp, and Harry heads for home on a hot September day. Riding the trolley from the train station down to the Linwood Street stop, he breathes in the crisp air and gazes at the people on the streets and the blue sky over Arlington. It is like a dream after the rigors of Parris Island, and he can't wait to walk through the front door, hug Mom and Nancy, and then sleep in his own bed.

As he walks the final steps to the house, his little sister, fourteen-year-old Nancy, is watching for him from the upstairs window. Since she got home from school that day, she has been there watching for Harry. Finally she sees a fellow walking up the street. She squints past the curtain. It looks like Harry, maybe, but his hair is practically gone and he is in uniform. She knows it is her big brother and her heart leaps as she runs down the stairs, but still, she can't get over it; he is like a different person.

That week, Harry spends most of his time with Dorothy. They are eighteen and sixteen, and they are in love and he is heading off to the war, so Anne and Nancy relish the moments they have with him and let them have their time together.[39]

Dominick Grossi, the broad-shouldered twenty-two-year-old from Lockport, New York, with the warm smile, was a football star back home. In fact, he turned down an offer to play for the New York Giants. In the military, he is enjoying his increasing responsibilities as a second lieutenant. Maybe the Giants will still be interested when he gets back. He doesn't plan to be gone too long. After all, the war is almost over.[40]

That fall of 1944, he writes home several times as he makes his way

Harry Eugene Gray and his little sister, Nancy, pictured in a friend's garden in Arlington, Massachusetts. Months later, Nancy recalls, "everything changed." (Nancy Gray Shade Family Archive)

"Uncle Frank" holds his "only boy," nephew Harry Gray, age two, at Horseneck Beach in Massachusetts. Frank Bowes would become "like a father" to Harry after his dad died. Frank urged Harry not to enlist. "The war is almost over," he told his seventeen-year-old nephew. (Nancy Gray Shade Family Archive)

Harry Gray waves the American flag as a Boy Scout. A few years later and 7,300 miles away, he would see it in the distance, raised on Mount Suribachi. (Nancy Gray Shade Family Archive)

The Grossi family of Lockport, New York. The parents, Pasquale ("Patsy") and Lena, are in the center, while Dominick (back row, second from the left) is surrounded by Rose, Marie, Elizabeth ("Betty"), Patrina, and Patsy Junior.

Lena and Patsy ran an Italian restaurant in town. Marie's husband, Jim, also served in the South Pacific and was Dom's "best buddy." While they were both overseas, on different islands, Dom wrote to him, "Keep plugging and the day will soon be when we are standing elbow to elbow over a bar, talking family troubles, instead of war." (Grossi Family Archive)

Anne Gray takes Nancy, Harry, and their cousin "Betts" Bowes (the author's mother) to the World's Fair in the spring of 1939. Called the "World of Tomorrow," the $135 million spectacular showcased the "Modern Electric Era." That year, on September 1, Hitler invaded Poland, beginning World War II. (Nancy Gray Shade Family Archive)

Private Charles Gubish, USMC, 968165. Charlie endured the grueling sixteen-week boot camp and the severe commands of his staff sergeant, a former New York City policeman. In the end, he says, "they made me a Marine." (Gubish Family Archive)

Marine on Iwo

MARINE PVT. GEORGE J. COLBURN, of 38 Grant ave., Medford, who has just written his parents from an Iwo Jima foxhole that "things were pretty hot." Pvt. Colburn, son of Mr. and Mrs. George W. Colburn is with the Third Division. He was graduated from Medford High in 1944.

Private George J. Colburn, of Medford, Massachusetts, played football against Harry Gray. Their mothers shared their boys' letters over the phone. (Colburn Family Archive)

Jefferson J. Rebstock, Jr. (Drez archives)

Private Harry Gray, USMC, 565110. (Nancy Gray Shade Family Archive)

James C. Russell, in the middle. (Drez archives)

Lieutenant Dominick Grossi, USMC, 395929. (Grossi Family Archive)

D-Day, Iwo Jima, February 19, 1945. As amtracs grind and falter in the volcanic ash, Marines in the first wave are forced out of their vehicles and have to climb the terraces on foot; with each step they take, the ash claws them in, like quicksand. At first they encounter little Japanese resistance on the beach, but then all hell breaks loose. (US Marine Corps)

Harry Gray writes: "I am in what they call 'Beach unloading party #3.' This means I am in the 3rd wave and unload supplies from Higgins boats. It is a very heavy job but not too much so for me. I think it will be ammunition, but don't know when. After the unloading is completed, we shall take our places in the lines or be held in reserve." (US Coast Guard)

Henry Hansen

Louis L. Charlo

Ernest I. Thomas, Jr.

Harold G. Schrier

Charles W. Lindberg

James R. Michels

February 23, 1945. The 2nd Battalion, 28th Marines, plant the first flag atop Mount Suribachi. The photograph was taken by Staff Sergeant Louis Lowery of Leatherneck magazine. When Secretary of the Navy James Forrestal saw the flag go up, he said to General Holland Smith, "The raising of that flag means a Marine Corps for the next five hundred years." (Louis R. Lowery)

The second flag raising, seen in AP photographer Joe Rosenthal's Pulitzer Prize–winning photo, is perhaps the most iconic image of World War II. The larger flag was greeted by cheers across the island and on ships offshore. As of October 2019, the correct names of the six flag raisers are, left to right, Ira Hayes, Harold Schultz, Michael Strank, Franklin Sousley, Harold Keller, and Harlon Block. Of those who raised the two flags on Mount Suribachi, six were killed in the coming weeks of the battle. (Associated Press)

Ira Hayes

Harold Schultz

Michael Strank

Franklin Sousley

Harold Keller

Harlon Block

Dominick Grossi's last letter home. "Remember I love you all so much. The Lord will see me through. Your son Dom, xxx (Grossi Family Archive)

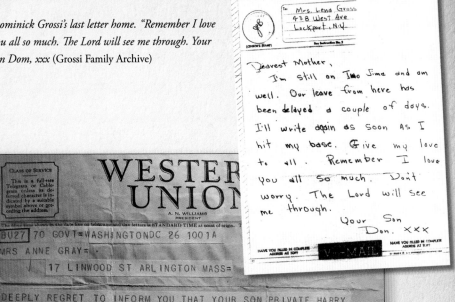

Telegram sent to Anne Gray, 17 Linwood St, Arlington, Massachusetts:
"DEEPLY REGRET TO INFORM YOU THAT YOUR SON PRIVATE HARRY E. GRAY USMCR WAS KILLED IN ACTION 13 MARCH 1945 AT IWO JIMA VOLCANO ISLANDS IN THE PERFORMANCE OF HIS DUTY AND THE SERVICE OF HIS COUNTRY. A.A. VANDEGRIFT, LT GENERAL USMC COMMANDANT OF THE UNITED STATES MARINE CORPS." (Dean Laubach)

Harry Gray wrote on the back page of his wallet prayer book before boarding the ship for Iwo Jima, "Treasurers, I beseech thee to bring this matter to a happy end, if it be for the glory of God and the good of my soul. Amen." The wallet, stained in his blood, was later returned to his mother. (Dean Laubach)

In Tokyo Bay, on September 2, 1945, US military personnel, photographers, and onlookers cram into every inch of the USS Missouri *to witness the official surrender of Japan.* (Department of Defense)

Below: Grave site, 3rd Marine Division Cemetery, Iwo Jima. (Nancy Gray Shade Family Archive)

Japanese dignitaries take their turns signing the Instrument of Surrender. After the ceremony, General MacArthur addresses the people of the United States: "Today the guns are silent. A great tragedy has ended. A great victory has been won. The skies no longer rain death—the seas bear only commerce, men everywhere walk upright in the sunlight. The entire world is quietly at peace." (Carl Mydans)

Martha MacCallum meets Charlie Gubish, age 100, for the first time. (Lori Frye)

The author at the US Memorial and site of the iconic flag raising on Mount Suribachi. (Briana Vota)

to San Diego and then sets out to sea. He writes to his mother, Lena, and she reads his letters to her husband, Patsy. Dom, now a second lieutenant, shares his thoughts about leadership and what lies ahead:

At times I'm tough but that is only when we have got work to do and do it fast. When I give orders they all cooperate and jump to. I'm sort of glad that I'm starting. I'm tired of standing by and waiting. I think I'm going to enjoy the coming adventure. The only thing that bothers me is you. I want you to promise that you will not cry and break down. I know you're going to worry, but please be strong. . . . Time does fly and in only a short while I'll be with you all again. Love to all, God Bless you xxxxx

Your devoted son, Dom

In another letter on November 28:

Dearest Mother,
    I am still at sea and still going strong. This beautiful morning I attended mass aboard the ship and received holy communion. The Chaplain who served the mass once taught at Niagara University.

Dom goes on to send a note to each of his siblings. This one is to the youngest, his brother, Junior.

HiYa Junior,
    How's your arm coming along? I haven't forgotten about the boxing gloves. You had better get in good shape because when I get back, you and I are going to box. One word of advice brother, I want you to stay away from the Canal Banks. I've heard that you have been there, but I don't want to hear of it again. Do you understand?

God Bless you, Goodnight xxxxx
Love, Dom[41]

[173]

12

"A Ghastly Relentlessness"

In late July, as Operation Forager ground on in the Marianas, the military brain trust of the United States was poring over maps and pondering its next steps. FDR and his admirals and generals were flush with victory. General Eisenhower and the Allied army in Normandy had broken out of the confined pocket that had hemmed them in since June 6. The German Army had fought furiously to keep them contained, but on July 25, the dam had finally broken.

Following a massive bombardment by 1,800 bombers from the Eighth Air Force, the German line at Saint-Lô was pulverized and the US Army poured through the gap. The American war correspondent Ernie Pyle wrote of the sheer force of the air attack, "Their march across the sky was slow and studied. I've never known anything that had about it the aura of such a ghastly relentlessness."[1]

A ghastly relentlessness! In the Pacific, the Marines stormed the beaches, clawed through the jungles, and clung to their gains, killing and moving, moving and killing, breaking the will of the Japanese with that same kind of "ghastly relentlessness."

By the end of the Marianas battles, the Marines had triumphed in seven major amphibious assaults across the stepping-stones of the central Pacific. The campaign had begun in August 1942 at Guadalcanal, and with the exception of a few surviving soldiers there, whom the emperor had deigned to rescue, the rest of the island defenders had chosen death over dishonor.

War Plan Orange, hatched thirty-seven years earlier, had for the most part been remarkably forward thinking and imaginative in an age when aviation was in its infancy and the range of airplanes was measured in a few hundred miles. The vision of future aerial capabilities had anticipated long-range bombers to bring about the defeat of Japan and detailed just how that plan should unfold. Despite interservice rivalries, arguments, and harangues, US forces were now poised on the inner ring of Japan's defenses to start the beginning of the end.

The capture and occupation of the Marianas had brought about significant events envisioned in War Plan Orange. The great climactic naval battle, anticipated by each side for forty years, had been fought in the Philippine Sea. The Japanese had joined battle with their Navy, risking everything in a winner-take-all showdown. And the Great Marianas Turkey Shoot had settled the question of naval supremacy once and for all.

Though early planners had envisioned China as the home base for the aerial assault against Japan, they had been wrong only as to the location. But as early as 1924, one of those visionaries had actually recognized that the Marianas were a great possibility.

General Billy Mitchell, the great Air Service hero of World War I, had said, "If we ever use a southern line of operations against Japan, Guam is a point of tremendous importance. It can hold any size air force."[2]

In 1944, Mitchell's prediction became reality and the Twentieth Air Force was in a position to conduct unrelenting war against what Mitchell had called the "vital centers" of the enemy. "The entire nation is, or should be considered, a combatant force," he said.[3]

Mitchell dismissed as folly the idea that war could be waged by detached armies on some romantic field of battle where the winner dictated a settlement and the loser lived to fight another day. He felt that waging war against an opposing army necessarily led to annihilation.

The Great War had been proof of that. The materiel of war would have to be stopped at the vital centers of production, before it got to the battlefield. Once it arrived, the battle area would become "a slaughterhouse from beginning to end . . . one side makes a few yards, or maybe a mile and thousands of men are killed."[4]

Although "humanitarians" shunned the thought of war against vital centers (always ensconced within the civilian population) and routinely opted for "more gentlemanly" battlefield slaughterhouses, US military planners had no such illusions. They knew that war is not a game played with a human chessboard laid out on some distant, remote battlefield.

The authors of War Plan Orange had, from the time of its original draft in 1906, defined the strategy for victory against Japan as "the destruction of Japanese capacity to resist."[5]

In January, at the Casablanca Conference, President Franklin Roosevelt had expressed his same understanding of the total capitulation of Japan when he called for the empire's "unconditional surrender." "Japan was to be occupied, disarmed, and stripped of all overseas possessions and its leaders unseated and prosecuted."[6]

Now, on July 26, the president had arrived in Pearl Harbor on the cruiser *Baltimore*, accompanied only by Admiral William Leahy, his personal chief of staff and closest confidant. Conspicuously missing were the rest of the Joint Chiefs. This meeting was to be with General MacArthur and Admiral Nimitz to settle upon the next military step against Japan. The gist of the argument was whether to advance against Luzon in the northern Philippines or to bypass it and attack Formosa to the north along the coast of China.

Admiral William "Bull" Halsey, commanding the part of Fast Carrier Task Force known as Task Force 38, had radioed Nimitz that he should cancel any cautious, deliberate approach to the Philippines. Halsey's recommendation was not just speculative. He was on the scene, and his carriers were hard at work blasting the enemy. His fleet stood within sight of land in the central Philippines, and there were no Japanese aircraft to challenge him. He had ordered 2,400 sorties and destroyed hundreds of Japanese planes, and still there was no reaction from the enemy.

The Fast Carrier Task Force was prowling the Philippine waters like an alpha dog spoiling for a fight, and there were no takers even as it continued to sink ships and bomb installations. As far as Halsey was concerned, attacking Yap, Palau, Morotai, and Mindanao would be a waste of effort. He argued for a leap forward to the north, a strike directly at Leyte.[7]

Nimitz concurred with Halsey's assessment, except that he nixed the bypassing of Palau. MacArthur was opposed to anything that would threaten his advance on Luzon, from which he had retreated in 1942, vowing, "I shall return." Luzon was not to be left out.

Now at Pearl Harbor, meeting with the president and Admiral Nimitz, MacArthur urged the president to side with him on the question of Luzon. He browbeat Roosevelt until he submitted, and the president left the three-hour ordeal feeling irritated and exhausted. "Give me an aspirin," he demanded. "In fact, give me another aspirin to take in the morning. In all my life, nobody has ever talked to me the way MacArthur did."[8]

Roosevelt put his irritation aside and agreed with MacArthur that the next military moves should be first against Leyte in October and then against Luzon in December. But a preliminary to the attacks on Leyte and Luzon was to secure Palau, 550 miles east of MacArthur's flank. Palau was a massive atoll 77 miles long by 20 miles wide. The military focus was not on the entire atoll but on the tiny island of Peleliu on the extreme southern tip, which contained its vital airfield.

There had been significant controversy as to the importance of Peleliu, and many thought it should be bypassed; but MacArthur and Nimitz wanted it to secure the right flank of the Philippine invasion, and D-Day was set for September 15, 1944. The attackers would be the veteran Marines of the 1st Division, together with the Army's 81st Infantry Division, with the Marines making the initial landings.

To many veterans of Guadalcanal and Cape Gloucester, the tiny islet of Peleliu eerily resembled Betio, which was located similarly on Tarawa Atoll. Everybody knew about the bloodbath at Tarawa. "Old salts" and "new guys" alike knew of the long wade-in across the fire-swept Betio lagoon; the Higgins boats that couldn't cross the reef; the rock-ribbed Japanese defenses; the deadly coconut wall; and the more than one thousand casualties a day. Before they had died, the Japanese defenders at Betio had decimated the 2nd Division.

The thin silver lining to Tarawa's terrible cloud had been that the battle had been short. The burning question now about Peleliu was: Would it be deadly but short, as Saipan and Guam had been? Or would it drag on, testing the limits of their endurance?

The 1st Division's commanding officer, General William Rupertus, was confident that the operation would be quick. Addressing his Marines four days before their ships weighed anchor at Pavuvu in the Russell Islands for the two-thousand-mile trek to Peleliu, he told them, "We're going to have some casualties. But let me assure you this is going to be a short one, a quickie. Rough but fast. We'll be through in three days. It might take only two."[9]

The general's optimistic assessment to his officers and senior NCOs was infectious. They returned to their ships' anchorage, sixty miles northwest of Guadalcanal, and happily repeated Rupertus's assessment to the Marines: "Three days, maybe two. It's gonna be in-again-out-again-Finnigan!"[10]

The word spread to the news correspondents, and many decided not to stick around for an operation that would be over so quickly.

But there was a lurking reality of which they were not aware. Captured enemy documents from Saipan revealed a significant difference from Tarawa: "Betio had been garrisoned by 4,836 Japanese, with no other substantial enemy forces within reach. . . . Early estimates placed 9,000 Japanese on Peleliu, and . . . upward of 25,000 additional troops posted on islands within practicable reinforcing distance."[11]

There had also been a change in the mind-set of the Japanese defenders. The traditional call of "Banzai!" would no longer be used.

Emotionalism and bombast were to be replaced with pragmatism. The *bushido* bravado of "Eat three of the American devils with each morning's bowl of rice"[12] was substituted with cold strategic reality. The Americans must be hammered with firepower, not flesh and bone.

"We must preserve personnel. . . . We must detect the opportunity for opening up accurate fire," declared Lieutenant General Sadae Inoue. "It is certain that if we repay the Americans with material power it will shock them beyond imagination."[13]

Aerial bombs were not to be feared. "The only fearful thing . . . is the psychological effect upon ignorant and inexperienced personnel. By observing very carefully the activity of enemy planes and the bombs while they are falling, avoiding thereby instantaneous explosions, and by taking advantage of gaps in bombardment in order to advance, it can cause no great damage."[14]

Concerning naval gunfire, Inoue was most optimistic: "The object of naval guns was to sink ships. . . . Their physical power is not very great against men who are advancing at a crawl, utilizing terrain, natural objects, and shell holes."[15]

General Rupertus had drummed into those attending the training exercises that commanders should be prepared for, and expect, a banzai charge during the first night after landing. Digging in for that attack should commence during daylight.

But there would be no banzai charge on Peleliu. Whereas the Marines had come to realize that those human-wave attacks actually shortened the battle by exposing the major part of a Japanese force to certain destruction in one climactic action, the new philosophy was designed to extract a fearsome toll on the attacking Marines. They would now have to dig each defender out of a hardened position.

Peleliu was six miles long and only two miles at its widest point. The airfield of hard-packed coral was located on the southern end. Rising above the airfield was a low, five-hundred-yard-wide, wooded ridge covered in greenery that ran from southwest to northeast for about two miles.

The Japanese had renamed the ridgeline Momiji Plateau after they had taken over the island as a result of the League of Nations mandate. The original Micronesians had called it Umurbrogol Mountain. Soon the Marines would rename it a third time: Bloody Nose Ridge.[16]

Intelligence revealed that the defenders were crack troops, mostly the 14th Division of the Imperial Japanese Army. They had been a part of the fierce Kwantung Army that had fought in China and had recently been rushed to the Pacific after the Japanese defeat in the Marshall Islands.[17]

Commanding all of Palau was Lieutenant General Sadae Inoue, who headquartered himself on the northern island of Babelthuap. His subordinate, Colonel Kunio Nakagawa, commanded at Peleliu.

In March 1944, General Inoue had met with then Japanese premier Hideki Tojo on a dire subject. Tojo saw that the continuing advance of the Americans meant that sooner or later they would attack Palau and that continued possession of the island was no longer possible. He urged a strong defense of the island to make its capture a lesson in blood for the Marines.

Inoue took command of the Japanese forces there and set about converting the island into a killing field. He would block, for as long as possible, its capture and use by the Americans. He concluded that Peleliu was the key to all of Palau.

The previous commander had built numerous blockhouses, reinforced-concrete structures, pillboxes, bunkers, and fighting positions, all above ground, and had also begun expanding the defensive positions by improving the existing caves and tunnels. Some of that excavation was the result of previous mining operations on Umurbrogol. Much of it was camouflaged under a canopy of overgrowing scrub and secondary growth.[18]

In March, the carriers of Task Force 58 had visited Peleliu, bombing and smashing the airfield and turning it into a junkyard. But the Japanese there, hunkered down in their underground tunnels and shelters, had escaped unscathed.[19]

Nakagawa knew how to convert Peleliu into a formidable fortress. In addition to registering artillery and mortar fire to cover every inch

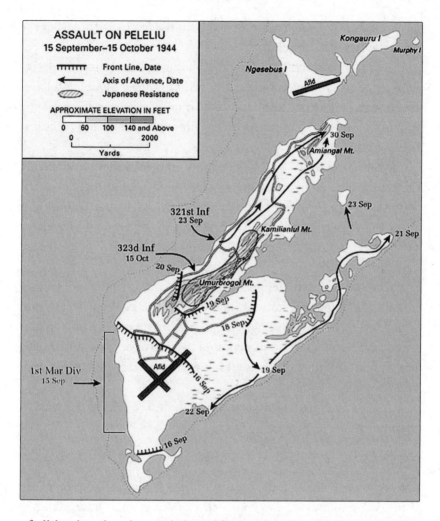

ASSAULT ON PELELIU
15 September–15 October 1944

 mmmmm Front Line, Date

← Axis of Advance, Date

◁▭▷ Japanese Resistance

APPROXIMATE ELEVATION IN FEET

0   60   100   140 and Above

0   2000

Yards

Kongauru I

Murphy I

Ngesebus I

Afld

30 Sep

Amiangal Mt.

321st Inf
23 Sep

23 Sep

323d Inf
15 Oct

Kamilianlul Mt.

21 Sep

20 Sep

Umurbrogol Mt.

19 Sep

19 Sep

18 Sep

1st Mar Div
15 Sep →

Afld

16 Sep

19 Sep

22 Sep

16 Sep

of all landing beaches and the reef immediately offshore, he had his
men plant five hundred wire-controlled mines in the shallow waters.
Seven hundred yards farther offshore, he registered massive concen-
trations at the edge of the reef, where he anticipated that the transfer
operations would occur to embark the assault forces into the attacking LVTs.[20]

But most important, he set all his forces to the task of digging,
tunneling, blasting, and boring into the most hostile collection of up-
thrusting, razor-sharp coral mutations that formed the myriad mazes

of Umurbrogol. Those badlands had been hidden by nature from the prying lenses of US aircraft.

The reconnaissance cameras had photographed a simple, continuous ridge covered with a lush, thin veil of innocent-looking foliage. But in fact, it was not lush at all but scrub growth surviving on the minuscule amount of moisture extracted from the coral and rocks just below its surface.

When Nakagawa had finished his unprecedented engineering project, he ordered his army into the interior of Umurbrogol's natural fortress. Except for a few battalions of infantry left to man positions along the western beaches and airfield, the massif swallowed soldiers, tanks, mortars, and artillery into its coral honeycomb of five hundred caves and tunnels.

"The tunnels were designed for . . . barracks, command centers, hospitals, storage and ammunition magazines, cooking areas complete with fresh water springs and seepage basins, and firing embrasures with elaborate concealment and protective devices, including a few sliding steel doors."[21] Everything was interconnected by horizontal and vertical tunnels.

Umurbrogol had been transformed into a "thousand-eyed"[22] mountain.

※

On September 15, the assault waves of the 1st Marine Division churn across the shallow reef and approach the White and Orange landing beaches on the southwestern tip of Peleliu. It is a blistering hot summer day: the temperature at Peleliu rarely dips below 100 degrees F.

There is an air of confidence among the Marines in the advancing first wave. Some hum the tunes they heard Tokyo Rose play on the radio last night; others smoke a cigarette and look out at the sea. One catches the eye of a pal and holds up four fingers: "In again, out again, buddy!" He hopes it will be true.

In no time, the tenor changes and tension creeps back into their bodies. The game is forever changing and moving, and expectations are thwarted by reality over and over again.

As soon as they hit the beach, it is on fire. Amtracs no sooner touch down than they are engulfed, turned into burning hulks by Japanese high-velocity antitank guns. Within an hour of the morning landing, sixty landing tractors are destroyed or disabled by the deadly guns firing relentlessly down the long axis of the beaches.[23]

The eighteen tanks landing to support the 1st Marines on the northern end of White Beach are also under fire. Seventeen of them are hit in the first hours. Nine are completely destroyed.[24]

All along the congested beaches is a sea of appalling human destruction. Fire from the dug-in Japanese beach defenders, as well as heavy mortar and artillery fire now unleashed from Umurbrogol, rake the pinned-down Marines: "Limbs, and heads, and pieces of flesh flying through the air; . . . men staggering about in the last throes of death, their lives spouting crimson from severed faces or stumps of arms."[25]

For eight hours, the savagery drags on, and then the Japanese make their only mistake of the day: they mount a massed tank assault across the northern portion of the airfield with infantry following closely behind. But once on the airstrip, the tankers rev their engines and leave the infantry in their dust, barreling forward to where the 1st and 5th Marines' lines join.

That thrust is short lived. All available Marine weapons, including three Sherman tanks and even a Navy dive-bomber, turn to meet the onslaught, raking the thirteen onrushing smaller tanks and blowing them apart. The Marines call them "tankettes." The fight is over almost before it starts.[26] It isn't a banzai charge, but except for a few probes of the Marine lines that first night, it is the only time that Colonel Nakagawa will expose his troops to the superior US firepower.

By nightfall, it is clear that "in again, out again" is not even a remote possibility. The 1st Marine Division carves out a beachhead three thousand yards long but only five hundred yards deep. It runs from the 1st Marines' positions on White Beach in the north to the 7th Marines on the southern Orange beaches, the 5th Marines sandwiched between.

They have run the gauntlet of devastating interlocking beach defensive fires, fought off an armored attack, and endured the first saturating salvos of dug-in Japanese artillery. There are 1,100 casualties, and 200 Marines are dead.[27]

The second day, the 1st Marines advance toward Umurbrogol. Whereas previously the features of that devastating defensive position had been shrouded, air strikes and naval gunfire have stripped away its disguise and reveal it to be a three-headed monster. The regimental narrative describes it:

> The ground of Peleliu's western peninsula was the worst . . . the rocky spine was heaved up in a contorted mass of decayed coral, strewn with rubble, crags, ridges and gulches thrown together in a confusing maze. There were no roads, scarcely any trails. The pock-marked surface offered no secure footing even in the few level places. It was impossible to dig in: the best the men could do was pile a little coral or wood debris around their positions. The jagged rock slashed their shoes and clothes, and tore their bodies. . . . It was impossible to get under the ground away from the Japanese mortar barrages. Each blast hurled chunks of coral in all directions, multiplying many times the fragmentation effect of every shell. Into this the enemy dug and tunneled like moles; and there they stayed to fight to the death.[28]

The 1st Marines' probe of the rugged coral ridges is an attack for which these veterans never prepared: a frontal assault against a dug-in, invisible enemy while scaling the steep slope of Umurbrogol. This first slope juts up two hundred feet.

The attacking Marines of the 2nd Battalion are constantly raked by small-arms and machine-gun fire as they claw their way up, but that is not the worst. Blasting them from close range are mountain guns and dual-purpose guns that appear and disappear as the Japanese gunners run them into and out of covered positions.[29]

The tanks and armed LVTs supporting the assault are blasted into flaming hulks. Nothing escapes the thousand-eyed mountain's observation. When at last the attacking Marines gain the top of Hill 200, there is still no respite or decrease in the enemy's fire. Just to the west of Hill 200 are the taller, steep-sided Hill 210 and yet another army of defenders and mountain guns.

The sole surviving company commander on Hill 200 reports, "We're up here, but we're knee-deep in Purple Hearts."[30] A *Time* magazine reporter describes the nightmare as "the incarnate evil of this war."[31]

The men of the 1st Marines continue cliff climbing, peak scaling, and cave clearing across boulders and rubble in the stifling heat through September 21, when they are finally forced by loss of men to grind to a halt.

Adding to the misery is a severe lack of water. When water finally arrives in fifty-five-gallon drums, the thirsty men drink it down quickly, ignoring its faint diesel taste from the poorly cleaned drums, leaving many of them very sick. The regiment's casualties climb to over 1,700.

They kill almost 4,000 enemy soldiers and overrun ten defended coral ridges, three large blockhouses, twenty-two pillboxes. They destroy thirteen antitank guns and clear or seal off 144 defended caves.[32] The enemy, worn out, is no longer a tactical fighting force.

After a solid week of the most tenacious fighting, the 1st Marine Division, with its 1st, 5th, and 7th Regiments, is in total control of the southern end of Peleliu. But the cost of that conquest has been severe: 4,000 Marine casualties, the equivalent of the loss of one entire regiment and the severe thinning of the other two.[33] The Army's 81st Infantry Division relieves the Marines.

MacArthur's flank for his attack in the Philippines is secure. The

Japanese have no means to threaten him. Critics say the Peleliu battle should not have happened at all; the forces should have been withdrawn and the Japanese defenders left "to die on the vine." But the battle grinds on.

"Finnegan" will hang around; he is not "out again" but rather dug in through the end of September and then October. The fighting continues on the godforsaken island for seventy-three days, until the days are indistinguishable, hellishly long, and seemingly endless.

On November 24, the same day that B-29s take off from Saipan for their first mission to Tokyo, Colonel Nakagawa acknowledges to his men, "Our sword is broken and we have run out of spears."[34] Nevertheless, he issues orders to his few remaining men to continue to attack and inflict casualties. His final message follows the pattern of those who have gone before him: accepting that his men are on the verge of annihilation, he has the 2nd Infantry Regiment flag destroyed, so as not to become a souvenir. The burning of all the documents follows, and then he sends his final message, telling its recipient that it will be the last he will hear from him.[35]

Colonel Nakagawa retires to a secluded section of his final command post and, like General Saito on Saipan, commits ritual seppuku. The act generally involved leaving behind a "death poem" and then stabbing oneself with a sword in the torso and grinding it upward to ensure death. Three days later, on November 27, the ghastly ordeal is over. Peleliu is secured.

The Japanese have inflicted 6,526 casualties on the 1st Marine Division and an additional 1,393 on the Army's 81st Infantry Division.[36] Of the reported 10,900 Japanese defenders, only 19 soldiers are captured. With no banzai attack option remaining, the Japanese soldiers are told to dig in, wait, and, when their moment comes, kill as many "invaders" as they can, before dying themselves for the emperor.

In Tokyo, Emperor Hirohito is having a tougher time selling the notion that his Imperial Army is prevailing, when the opposite is true. Day after day, US planes rain bombs down on the mainland, softening targets for the coming invasion into the "heart of the Empire."[37]

X

During those long days at Bloody Nose Ridge, Americans hope and pray that the war is almost over. But for Harry Gray, Charlie Gubish, Herman Graeter, George Colburn, and Warren Graham, it is just beginning. After a week at home, each boards a bus or train and makes his way to Marine Corps Base Camp Lejeune in North Carolina. At some point along their separate journeys, each presses his forehead against the cool window, watching America go by. Toughened by their long weeks at Parris Island, they are not the boys they were before, but now they venture a bit farther from home than any of them has been before.

In the morning heat, on the bus or the train, they move through the tall grasses and the farms of North Carolina. Dew beads on the outside of the window, and bugs stick smushed to the glass, their legs sometimes sticking some distance away from their flattened bodies. It is hotter down here than at home in September. Beyond these bits of information, they have little idea of what will come next. They do not know one another or that they are all ultimately headed to a tiny island in the middle of nowhere, a place they cannot imagine. The place they are in, rolling along through the tall grass, is different enough for now.

Harry is the youngest of them, having just turned eighteen that June. These are the answers he gave on his enlistment forms in Boston, days after his eighteenth birthday: "S" for his marital status and "2" for dependents, his mom and Nancy. He didn't support them, but they did depend on him, so that was how he answered the question. Under academics, he noted his diploma from Arlington High School and that he completed "Math thru Trig." Under "Sports in which qualified," he checked baseball, football, tennis. Under "School or Team," he put "Sandlot." Under "Talent for Furnishing Public Entertainment": "Piano." He could have written "Artist." He loved to draw Revolutionary War and biblical scenes in his large sketchbooks. His buddies found his sketches of pinup girls entertaining; his mother, on the other hand, did not. Under "Work experience":

"General Ice Cream Corp, Cambridge, Truck driver." "What did you do?" "Loaded up truck with ice cream, drove to various stores to deliver it. Some days drove from town to town. Drove days only, could make a few minor repairs." When the interviewer asked him "Duty desired?," Harry had written "AVN, Aerial Gun."

Herman Graeter, also eighteen and just a few months older than Harry, was from Cincinnati. He was the only son of Mr. and Mrs. Graeter of Melrose Avenue, Dayton, Ohio. Herman wrote on his enlistment form under "Employment" that he had been a "Duplication machine operator," a copy boy, at the local printer after school and in the summer.

Like Harry, he arrives at Camp Lejeune on September 13, 1944. In the next six months, they will go halfway around the world together, although neither knows it now.

13

"An Island of Sulphur: No Water, No Sparrow, and No Swallow"[1]

Five months before, as the assault waves of the 2nd and 4th Marine Divisions had hit the beaches of Saipan, Admiral Marc Mitscher's Fast Carrier Task Force had reached its long arm far to the north to destroy any Japanese air forces that might intrude into the battle. In doing so, they had swept over the Bonin island of Iwo Jima, 760 miles south of Tokyo.

The 7,000 Japanese defenders dug in frantically, scampering toward bomb shelters as sirens blared. Japanese aircraft hurried into the sky to meet the threat, engaging in a desperate dogfight. On the island below, the defenders watched the action above, as the Americans gained control. One discouraged defender wrote in his diary, "Somehow, my faith in our Navy air groups has been somewhat shaken."[2]

Four days later, on June 19, the Americans were back. This time, 101 Japanese fighters took off from Motoyama 1 airfield. "There was an air battle for about fifteen minutes, 5,000 meters south of Iwo Jima," said First Lieutenant Musashino. "Those who had been watching the battle felt very sad when none of our planes returned. After, some ten to twenty planes came to Iwo Jima from Japan . . . but all of them were destroyed. . . . There was now no Japanese planes and no vessels."[3]

Major Yoshitaka Horie, the officer in charge of the supply and communication base at Chichi Jima, lamented, "Now we have no fleet and no air forces. If American forces will assault this island it will fall into their hands in one month. Therefore, it is absolutely necessary not to let the enemy use this island. The best plan is to sink this island into the sea or cut the island in half. At least we must endeavour to sink the first airfield."[4]

X

On October 20, 1944, the US battle line faces the remnants of Japan's "Absolute National Defense Line."[5] That line's right flank is rock solid, with the Marines and Task Force 58 of the Fifth Fleet in total control of both the Marianas and the Palau islands. Nine hundred miles to the west, General Douglas MacArthur begins his long-anticipated return to the Philippines with his invasion of Leyte. The fall of the Philippines would mean the loss of all of Hirohito's expanded empire. His dreams of domination have shrunk to a desire simply to hold his own homeland. The loss of the Philippines would sever the few lines still open for industrial and oil supplies.

From October 23 to 26, Japan pours every last measure of its air and sea capability into an offensive that precipitates the biggest naval clash in history: the Battle of Leyte Gulf. Waves of kamikaze pilots dive out of the blue sky, spiraling down to attack enemy ships below. The human-guided suicide missiles bore full throttle into the US ships, crashing and detonating in their final heroic mission for the emperor.

Admiral Soemu Toyoda, the commander in chief of the Japanese Combined Fleet, fights with his back to the wall, knowing that for him, there is no tomorrow. He commanded the fleet during the disastrous Great Marianas Turkey Shoot and now faces his fleet's most desperate moment. His 69 ships face off against 166 of the US Navy. His 716 aircraft attempt to match the power of 1,280 US carrier-based aircraft.[6] Toyoda puts all of his chips in the center of the table. As he will later say:

Without the participation of the Combined Fleet, there was no possibility of the land-based forces in the Philippines having a chance. . . . It was decided to send the whole fleet, taking the gamble. If things went well, we might obtain unexpectedly good results; if the worst would happen, there was a chance we would lose the entire fleet; but I felt that chance had to be taken.[7]

The outcome is catastrophic: Japan loses 26 ships, the United States only 6. From October to December, Japan will lose 7,000 aircraft, including 722 kamikazes; during those months, the United States will lose 967.[8]

As 1944 grinds to an end, the strategic situation in the Pacific resembles a giant triangle. At the apex stands Japan. Forming the base angle on the left are MacArthur's forces in the Philippines; on the

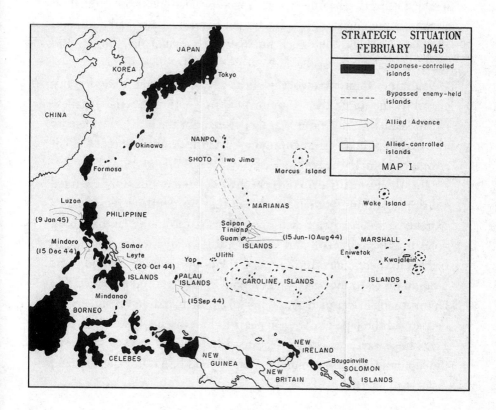

base angle on the right, Nimitz's forces are poised at Palau and the Marianas.

X

In May 1944, on Iwo Jima, Major General Kotau Osuga had directed his men to dig in at a frantic pace to the elevated, barren, rocky terrain to create an in-depth defense. But their work had been interrupted by the arrival of two of the highest-ranking Japanese general officers in the Pacific, Lieutenant General Yoshitomi Tamura and Lieutenant General Hideyoshi Obata, on an inspection tour. Tamura was the assistant chief of staff, and Obata commanded the newly created 21,000-man Thirty-first Army, responsible for the inner line of Japanese defenses protecting the homeland.

"What is the meaning of a beach line?" Tamura asked the assembled officers. The officers exchanged puzzled looks but offered no answer to the question. It is the border between water and land, and allowing for tides, "the beach line has to be defended," Tamura told them. It was there that the enemy could be annihilated.[9]

Tamura's vigorous advocacy of the beach-line defense was legendary; thus the name the "Tamura Doctrine." The Imperial Japanese Army Academy and Naval War College taught the beach-line defense as a matter of course and common sense; the annihilation of the enemy at the beach was key.

In answer to his demand, the Iwo defenders dutifully changed course; abandoning their work on the "in-depth defense," they switched to construct beach-line defensive positions, as had been done at Saipan, Tinian, and Guam. Guns located to the north, embedded and concealed in the rocky ridges on the high ground, were brought down to the beach and moored in bunkers and pillboxes. The Umurbrogol in-depth defense system constructed at Peleliu, which had served the Japanese well, appears to have been a lesson ignored.

A huge caveat existed in the teachings of the *Sakusen Yomurei*, the Japanese operations manual, that advised beach-line defense, and it somehow escaped the attention of General Tamura. In 1939, in a border clash with the Soviet Union—the Nomonhan Incident—the Japanese Army had been outgunned, outsupplied, and overwhelmed by the Soviets, who were armed with five hundred tanks, more than three hundred armored cars and five hundred aircraft.[10] Against those staggering numbers, the Japanese had fielded a pitiful fraction that had been humiliatingly defeated.

From then on, the *Sakusen Yomurei*, though continuing to teach the beach-line defense, added the proviso that "against an overwhelmingly armored enemy, a series of position groups must be made in depth."[11]

Generals Tamura and Obata then left the island, going their separate ways to Saipan and Guam to watch their beach-line defenses swept away in the first hours of battle by overwhelming US firepower. On Saipan, in the first two days, the Americans landed and cut to the opposite side of the island. In fourteen days, they pivoted to the north and succeeded in grinding the Japanese defenders underfoot. For two weeks the Japanese fought and fell back. Although they inflicted many casualties on the attacking Americans, they died by the thousands in the effort. On Guam, the story was similar. Ultimately, facing total defeat, Tamura and Obata chose to end their separate ordeals with the rite of seppuku—for their own honor and that of the emperor.

In Tokyo, Prime Minister Tojo had watched it all with dismay. The Americans had swept aside much of the inner defensive ring protecting the homeland and were poised for a final advance and potential invasion.

As they crept closer, all eyes turned to Iwo Jima. Just 760 miles from Tokyo, it was the obvious next target. A US conquest of the tiny volcanic island would be an invasion of Japan itself.

The "imperial decision" was to fight a bloody war of attrition, a war that would make the conquest of Japan so painful that the Americans would opt for negotiation, rather than Roosevelt's stated "unconditional surrender" and occupation. The final defensive efforts were to fortify Iwo Jima and Okinawa and turn them into massive killing fields.

Iwo Jima's barren, bleak, hostile terrain would be first. According to the historian and Marine Joseph Alexander:

> Mount Suribachi dominated the narrow southern end, overlooking the only potential landing beaches. To the north, the land rose unevenly onto the Motoyama Plateau, falling off sharply along the coasts into steep cliffs and canyons. The terrain in the north represented a defender's dream: broken, convoluted, cave-dotted, a "jungle of stone." Wreathed by volcanic steam, the twisted landscape appeared ungodly, almost moon-like . . . something out of Dante's Inferno.[12]

To command the defense of Iwo, before Tojo resigned, he had selected the fifty-three-year-old Lieutenant General Tadamichi Kuribayashi, a distinguished descendent of a samurai warrior family that had served in the Army under six emperors. Tojo told him, "Only you among all the generals are qualified and capable of holding this post. The entire army, and the nation, will depend on you."[13]

Kuribayashi's orders were perfectly clear, and he revealed his understanding of them in a letter to his brother: "I may not return alive from this assignment . . . but I shall fight to the best of my ability, so that no disgrace will be brought upon our family. I will fight as a son of Kuribayashi, the Samurai."

Kuribayashi had served as a military attaché in the United States from 1928 to 1930. He had written letters to his young son and drawn pictures of America for him. His son Taro later wrote:

> *While visiting Boston, he was lying sprawled on the gardens of Harvard University watching a clock tower, in another he is taking a walk in Buffalo, in another, playing with some American children and being invited to the house of Medical Doctor Furukohchi, etc.*

Throughout his letters, it is clear that my father used to drive in many directions in the United States, studied very hard late at night, and tried to be a gentleman. Also, he used to have many friends in foreign countries.[14]

On June 13, one month after Generals Tamura and Obata had inspected the defense preparations, General Kuribayashi arrived on Iwo Jima, although he was not to take command until the end of the month. A dilapidated car picked him up from his seaplane at the east boat basin and took him to a run-down headquarters. For two weeks he examined the progress made on the defenses, and on June 29, he met with Major Horie and told him, "The enemy will come to Iwo Jima without fail. When the enemy comes, we could contain him and our Combined Fleet would come from the homeland or Okinawa and slap his face. Our role could be a great containing operation."

Major Horie sat in stunned silence for a moment. Obviously the details of the great defeat of the fleet in the Philippine Sea had been kept from the general just as it had been concealed from most of the population. He finally spoke up in a low tone. "General, we have no more Combined Fleet in Japan. Some tiny naval forces still remain, but there are no more striking powers."

The general scoffed at Horie. "What a stupid man you are! This island belongs to Tokyo City."

Horie pressed on. "General, Japan died ten days ago on 19 June 1944."

"You must be drunk," said Kuribayashi.

The following day, the general and the major took the old car to the southern beaches to examine the land. Kuribayashi lay prone on the black sand as if he were an invading soldier. For the next two hours, they drove around the airfield, stopping often while the general examined the fields of fire. He ordered Major Horie to "stand here" and "lie down there" while he detailed places of concealment. As the inspection concluded, Kuribayashi lamented, "I had not known the facts."[15]

Now that he knew he must defend the island without any help from the homeland, he set about his task. He scrapped most of the work on the beach-line defenses but allowed some of it to continue for political reasons. The adversarial Navy headquarters, always at odds with the Army, had offered to deliver three hundred machine guns and the materials for building pillboxes for them, but only if they would be employed in a beach-line defense.

Major Horie objected in no uncertain terms: "I would like to know how long the seaside guns lasted at Saipan and Guam? Please teach me how the seaside pillboxes at Tarawa were effective? This is baby play. . . . The 40-centimeter naval guns of the enemy will blow up any pillbox."[16]

The Navy brass balked at Horie's rebuff, threatening to cancel the whole deal and provide nothing. Kuribayashi smoothed the ruffled feathers and offered to use half the Navy resources for the beach defense; he would provide, he said, 1,000 men a day for the pillbox construction if the rest of the guns and resources could be used in his defensive line. The Navy agreed and offered to send a total of 350 guns.

So 135 pillboxes were constructed for the beach defense, none of which would survive the initial US bombardment; the other 175 guns went into the cave and bunker defensive line.

Kuribayashi evacuated all the civilians from the island and received his final reinforcements, bringing his army's strength up to 21,000. Arriving with the last soldiers were the mining engineers who would convert Iwo Jima into a Pacific Gibraltar.

Digging and tunneling were grueling, backbreaking work, and many of the soldiers collapsed on the job. "Using an army pick, I continued digging the rock, and found that an average person could not continue work for ten minutes," said Major Horie. "Sulphur came up and it made our breathing hard. The key point of position construction was to make a cave from which we could snipe, and to link these caves with underground paths. Everybody, including the general, staff officers, and men made his position, and his tomb, by himself."[17]

They dug the underground tunnels sixty to ninety feet deep, creating side rooms, sleeping quarters, dining rooms, resting areas, and fighting positions, all connected to vertical and horizontal tunnels.[18]

General Kuribayashi even published his "Cave-Digging Discipline," whereby everyone was to accomplish his share—no exceptions. Some of the older men, knowing their final fate was ultimately death, grumbled about the digging: "Regardless of this cave-digging work," they said, "our deaths will be inevitable. Better to die without making this hard work."[19]

Colonel Takeichi Nishi, a tank commander and individual show jumping gold medalist in the 1932 Los Angeles Olympics, wrote, "We are going to dig the land 20 meters deep and make underground streets; then we won't worry about the enemy's one-ton bombs."[20]

Lieutenant Colonel Nakane cheerfully wrote home to his wife, "The enemy air raids come more than 10 times a day. Now we have saved enough water, and yesterday we made baths. Everybody was happy. We can get some fish because whenever the enemy makes air-raids, many fish come to the beach, being killed by their bombs. . . . So if they do not come, we miss them. . . . We're gladly waiting for the enemy."[21]

The 21,000 defenders on the surface of the island slowly disappeared one by one, gun by gun, into the island; 361 artillery pieces, 65 mortars, 33 large naval guns, and scores of large-caliber antiaircraft guns were swallowed into the earth. Kuribayashi's own command post, in the extreme badlands in the northern sector of the island, was seventy-five feet deep and connected with more than five hundred feet of tunnels.[22] "One installation inside Mount Suribachi ran seven stories deep."[23]

To a newcomer, the island would look completely deserted, just as the rock-ribbed Japanese defenses dug into Umurbrogol on Peleliu seemed to be nothing more than a peaceful, green forest landscape.

As the Japanese Army disappeared into the island, each fighting position prominently displayed Kuribayashi's "Courageous Battle Vows":

1. We shall defend with all-out effort.

2. We shall run over enemy tanks with explosives.

3. We shall infiltrate and annihilate.

4. We shall kill the enemy with one-shot, one-kill system.

5. We shall not die until [each] has killed ten men.

6. We shall harass the enemy even though only one man remains.[24]

X

To the Japanese, it was a foregone conclusion that Iwo Jima was an eventual target; the Americans were slower to come to that conclusion. It was not until the first launchings of the B-29 aerial offensive against Japan in early 1944 that Iwo Jima came clearly into focus.

There was a problem that stemmed from "a vexing little spit of volcanic rock lying halfway along the direct path from Saipan to Tokyo."[25] Iwo Jima's position directly in the path of the northbound bombers flying out of the Marianas gave mainland Japan a two-hour advance notice of the approaching strike.

It also gave the Japanese fighters on Iwo an opportunity to strike at the northbound B-29 Superfortresses, which had no fighter escort—and a second one on their way back, especially when some of the planes were shot up and crippled. Without escorts, the bombers were most vulnerable; and without possession of Iwo Jima, there was no possibility to stage escorting fighters.

Over the target areas on the Japanese mainland, enemy fighters forced the bombers to fly higher, and bombing from higher altitudes was most ineffective. Therefore the Joint Chiefs of Staff in Washington targeted Iwo Jima for attack; in October, they ordered Admiral Nimitz to plan to seize the island.[26] The Marine Corps was tasked to do the job.

For the first time in its long history, the Marine Corps would fight as a corps—three divisions—forming V Amphibious Corps. The newly created 5th Marine Division would join the veteran 3rd and 4th Divisions in the attack. The landings would storm ashore on the southern beaches of the rocky island—the 4th across the Yellow and

Blue beaches and the 5th across the Green and Red beaches. The 3rd Division would remain offshore as a ready reserve.

The Iwo Jima operation (code-named Detachment) consisted of almost five hundred ships, ten times the size of the 1942 Guadalcanal task force. US intelligence expected that the detachment would encounter 13,000 to 14,000 enemy and that the enemy would concentrate on "repelling or destroying our forces in the water and on the beach" and "counterattack our beachhead with all available reserve strength under the cover of darkness."[27]

General Kuribayashi's plans for his 21,000 defenders included none of those things.

꙰

On October 23, 1944, Harry Gray of Arlington, Massachusetts; George Colburn of neighboring Medford; Charles Gubish of Hellertown, Pennsylvania; Warren Graham of Salisbury, North Carolina; and Herman Graeter of Dayton, Ohio, are all assigned to the thirty-fourth replacement draft of the 3rd Marine Division and prepare to enter the war in the Pacific. Two days later, Harry writes:

Dear Uncle Frank,

I am sorry I haven't written you before but I have been terribly busy and haven't had much time to write. I am fine and in the best of health. The past two weeks, I have lived in a tent. I got very little food as I survived on K rations and one canteen of water per day. This was for drinking, washing and shaving purposes. We had actual combat fighting from 5:30 pm until 1:00 am with a half hour for [other] chores.

The first week was rugged being 10 and ¹/₂ miles from camp and carrying field transport packs weighing 60–80 lbs. The second week we spent on the combat range. I was there during the hurricane and many of the boys got soaked because their tents blew down but I was okay. I didn't change my clothes for two weeks.

I have been using all types of weapons, including BAR Browning

Automatic Rifle, M-1, Carbine, Flame thrower, Grenade launchers, TNT, Bangalore Torpedoes, rifle grenades, machine guns and bayonets. I have learned bayonet fighting, knife fighting, club fighting and hand to hand combat which is Judo.

I have had street fighting which is preparing me for the very near future. I have just received word that our 9th [unit] has become the 34th Replacement Draft. I also have been given word that we will be going overseas by Nov. 3. So this is it, all the furloughs have been cancelled along with 12 hour passes.

How is Betty, and Aunt Helen? I hope they are fine. Well I guess that's the highlights for now and hope this letter finds you all in good health.

Lots of love your Nephew,
Harry

He packs his bag in his barrack at Camp Lejeune. His name and number, 565110, are stenciled in black on the side. It is a methodical job for him now, arranging his clothes and gear tightly in his duffel. He feels years older than when he watched Nancy, Mom, and Uncle Frank disappear on the train platform, but it has actually been only a few short months since then.

As Harry gathers his belongings, he rolls his rosary beads in his palm, a gift from Grandma Bowes. Back home in Arlington, he dutifully went to Mass with his family. But most of the time, truth be known, he was staring at the stained-glass windows in Saint Agnes Church, thinking about Dorothy. But now he looks forward to the quiet of the Mass and the words that make him feel less alone. He is scared, and praying makes him feel as though God is watching over him and all the other men who kneel next to him at Mass each week at Camp Lejeune.

He holds the beads in his hand, silently prays an "Our Father," and safely tucks them deep inside. He glances at the signet ring Uncle Frank gave him for graduation and then opens the wallet from his mother and flips through its contents: photographs of Dorothy smiling at him in front, Nancy and Mom close behind. A tiny leather-bound prayer book fits perfectly inside, and a strap closes the folded wallet. With HEG embossed in gold letters across the front, it is a real man's wallet, and he likes the feel of it in his hand. He puts it deep into his front pants pocket. His most precious possessions accounted for, he yanks the strap through the metal-rimmed holes and hooks it to the handle. As he slings the bag over his shoulder, he glances down at the shiny object on his wrist, taking a longer second look and feeling the now-familiar pang of missing home.

The last night of leave, he and Dorothy went for a walk. They stopped in Robbins Park near the *Menotomy Indian Hunter* statue. He opened the small box wrapped in gold paper that she handed to him, and a smile broke out all over his face when he saw his name engraved on an ID bracelet, along with his number, 565110, and U.S.M.C. "Turn it over, Harry," Dorothy said. With his thumb and forefinger, he turned it over; on the back it was engraved LOVE, DOT. "Never take it off," she said, closing the clasp on his wrist and noticing the thick muscles that had grown in his forearms. Pressing the face of it onto his wrist, she said, "I will be right there with you, every time you look at this, no matter where you are."

To Harry, it was the closest thing to being married. It was the vow between them, the promise. He could not explain to her how much it meant to him, and tears were in his eyes that he did not want her to see. He kissed her. She looked up at him, staring straight into his now-glistening eyes, and it was a look that pained him: her wet, sparkling eyes.

The next day he proudly showed the bracelet to Anne and Nancy just before he got onto the trolley to head to South Station in Boston. Anne saw how deeply he cared for this girl she barely knew. He's so young, she thought. But his look of love was ageless, unmistakable. She had known it herself, she missed his dad so. She had dated in recent years. She had an offer of marriage, but passed on it. At age forty-five, she wondered if she would ever again feel what she saw in young

Harry's eyes. She was happy that he felt it now, that he knew that kind of love. Nancy, now fourteen, was tall and slender, with lovely brown curls. She turned the bracelet on her brother's wrist a bit to get a closer look. The giving of an ID bracelet was serious business. She wished she had someone to give one to, but most of the boys in town were off at war these days, like Harry. Certainly all the good ones. She reached up and put her arm around Harry's neck, teased him a bit about it, hugged him, and then waved good-bye.

After their final training in California, Harry and the rest of the draft board the troop carrier USS *Rochambeau* (AP-63), and on November 12, they sail from San Diego.

Their first stop is the Eniwetok Atoll in the Marshall Islands. A chain of forty coral islands, to Harry it is like pages in *National Geographic* come to life. Palms rustle against each other in the wind, making a dry, scratchy noise. The beach is like pink cake flour, and the water is crystal-clear blue, nothing like the thick deep sea green of the Atlantic with its seaweed scent, where he sailed with his dad a lifetime ago.

Back in February, Eniwetok was secured in a fierce battle. Abandoned machines lie along the beach, some half submerged and washed daily by the waves; the men who operated them have moved on to other islands or to God. He tries to picture the fighting, the noise of it all, in this now-blissful place. The atoll's spell is broken only by the bustling on the transport of the arriving Marines, moving and talking around him as they take it in.

They spend the morning in "work parties" on the ship and beach. On *Rochambeau*, Harry has reconnected with a football acquaintance from Medford, Massachusetts, George Colburn. Medford is right next to Arlington, and it warms Harry's heart to hear his familiar Boston accent in the rack below. George signed up for the Marines with his two buddies from Medford High: "Chubby" Cramer, who was no longer chubby after his weeks at Parris Island, and "Red" Francis, whom all the girls liked because of his russet head of hair.

(Back home, George's mother, Mary Ellen Colburn, and Anne Gray learned through the grapevine that their boys were both in the 34th Replacement Draft. They called each other every time one or the other heard from her son, to share their letters and any bits of information they could glean from them.)

It was so cramped for so many weeks on the ship, and so hot, they often slept out on the deck under the stars. In Eniwetok, one of the officers wisely decides it would be a good idea to get the men off the ship and let them run around and have a bit of fun. Everybody needed to let off some steam. There was too much young energy in too-tight quarters, and before it combusted, it was time to let the boys loose for a while. The officers let down a raft from the ship, and as soon as Harry gets wind of what's afoot, he smiles at George. "C'mon, buddy, no time like the present. This is paradise. C'mon, let's go!"

Suddenly, in a heartbeat, hundreds of them are out of their uniforms, tripping over their pants legs to be free, climbing onto the rafts, paddling into the beach. Harry jumps off the raft, disappearing into the cool blue-green silky water. He pops up smiling and laughing. "George! It feels so good. Have you ever felt anything this good?"

Then George jumps and disappears under the cool water, comes up smiling, shaking the water off his eyes, howling and laughing. "I think we must be dead, Harry."

"This is heaven, right?"

"We've died and gone to heaven. It was a hell of a battle, and you're a hero, my friend!"

All the men, most of them just teenagers, are having a ball! They splash water at each other, so happy just to be happy. There are even beers for them on the beach, like a party. "We were like boys that day. We were brothers, we would have done anything for each other," remembers George.[28]

In mid-December, *Rochambeau* docks at Naval Operations Base Guam. Harry writes to his uncle:

Dear Uncle Frank,

I have received your two v mail letters and was very pleased to hear from you. We have had mail twice since we left the States. Both were in Port, but I'm sorry to say I can't tell you where. I received 18 letters the first time and 12 the second.

I was sick at the beginning of the trip, but after a fashion I didn't mind it too much. It is very hot here and I sleep on the weather deck every night. Usually rains sometime during the night, but it never lasts.

We had a fair Thanksgiving, but of course couldn't compare with home. We had turkey, dressing, celery, squash, candy and a cigar. Now we are planning Christmas on board ship.

I think I will see George Smith, if I do he will be quite surprised.

I have been to confession three times since we left. To Mass every Sunday and some weekdays. The Chaplain comes from Jamaica Plain and knows the Priests at St. Agnes. I had quite a chat with him the other night. Bob, the boy from Newton is with me and there are many fellows from my section. I chum around with a fellow from Medford. Will write later. Hope everyone is fine.

Love, Harry[29]

Harry takes out his tiny wallet prayer book and reads the prayer he wrote there after his talk with the chaplain. In blue pen on the blank back page he has written in all caps, "HOLY ST. JOSEPH, SPOUSE OF MARY, BE MINDFUL OF ME, PRAY FOR ME, WATCH OVER ME. GUARDIAN OF THE PARADISE OF THE NEW ADAM, PROVIDE FOR MY SPIRITUAL AND TEMPORAL WANTS. FAITHFUL GUARDIAN OF THE MOST PRECIOUS OF ALL TREASURERS, I BESEECH THEE TO BRING THIS MATTER TO A HAPPY END IF IT BE FOR THE GLORY OF GOD AND THE GOOD OF MY SOUL. AMEN."

⚸

Charlie Gubish's wife back in Bethlehem waits faithfully in their home near the mill for his letters. Golda and Herman Graeter, Sr., in Dayton also keep an eye out for the mailman each day, hoping for word that their only child is safe. Like Harry's family, they have received the standard postcards with their names filled in by their sons at the top: "Dear _____, I have been transferred overseas and have arrived safely at my destination." The cards were prepared prior to their departure and are sent home after they arrive. They include a San Francisco address to send mail to but of course no indication of where they are now.

The same is true on the ship. Mail call is, for the men who get handfuls of letters at a time, the most uplifting moment of the day or week or weeks, since so much time can go by without any word at all. For those who do not receive any letters, mail drop is a morale killer. The men go their separate ways, to their bunk or any place else where they can take a moment to pore over the good wishes and news from home. It is what keeps them going. They read the letters over and over, sometimes sharing them with one another and talking about the people who sent them. They fill in some of the missing pieces about their families and life back home. Sometimes the letters make them miss home even more. They all try not to let on in their letters how homesick and uneasy they are. Harry, Warren, Charlie, Herman, and George lie in their bunks at night, talking, sometimes hiding tears from one another as they drift off to sleep.

One morning after they have settled in on Guam, Charlie wakes up and nudges "Gray," as he calls him, as they scramble out to line up for work party assignments. "What's up, Pop?" Harry always calls him that since he's twenty-four and Harry is only eighteen. "We never did get the 'beer-a-day' they promised us on the ship." "Yeah, so what are we going to do about it here?" "We are going to ask for it," says Charlie. A smile creeps across Harry's face; he just shakes his head at Pop.

Sure enough, on Saturday, someone takes pity on them and sneaks them a whole case. They down a few beers apiece and share some with their buddies. Harry never really had much beer back in Arlington, and it hits them both pretty fast. They are both leaner and stronger than when they left home and worn down from a week of heavy work rebuilding a church in the hills with the Seabees. With each beer the laughter comes easier, the stories spill out, and Harry is doubled over at Pop's tales of growing up on the farm in Pennsylvania. Harry passes around his picture of Dorothy, which all the guys look at longingly. Warren whistles and says, "Gray, you are a lucky man, my friend." But after a while, the laughter turns to melancholy. Charlie and Harry start talking about home. Charlie tells Harry about his wife and boys and wonders why he signed up for all this. Harry is homesick and hot and tired. Somehow they end up ambling over to the first officer's office. Both are now teary; they tell the officer their woes and say that they just want to go home. He gets their platoon sergeant, who's having none of it and yells, "Get these two goddamn guys out of here or throw 'em in the brig!" But the first officer is kind; he just takes away their guns and knives for the night, so they don't hurt themselves, and makes them get into their sacks. They are asleep in no time, exhausted from drinking and talking and crying and getting into trouble. In the morning, they decide it was all worth it. That spit-warm beer was the best thing they'd had in months.[30]

Warren Graham, the organic chemist from North Carolina, also tempts trouble. He watches the guard near the supplies and studies his pattern of movements. He waits for the perfect moment when the guard is on the opposite side, then gets down onto his belly, crawls over to where the crates of orange and grapefruit juice are kept, and steals a can. He dodges his way back to the guys, and they peel back the top of the can and pass it around, pleased that Graham has pulled it off. Pop chastises him, though. "If they catch you, they're going to kill you, you know," he says as he takes a big gulp.[31] He keeps at it, though he did get written up for something he did on October 17, back at Camp Lejeune. The guys don't know for what, though.[32]

Second Lieutenant Dominick Grossi, 18th Replacement Draft of the 3rd Marine Division, has been in Guam a few weeks already. His parents, at home in Lockport, New York, have received the yellow postcard in the mail that tells them he has safely reached his destination. That is all that Lena and Pasquale Grossi know, and their imaginations fill in the rest on many a night as they toss and turn in bed after their long nights working at their restaurant.

For the first time in years, this fall Dom is not spending the crisp afternoons at football practice. The all-state football star is now preparing for a very different kind of game. He lies in his rack and thinks back to the big send-off he and the other players received. The townspeople turned out in droves to wave their team, now in military uniforms, good-bye as they headed to Parris Island. Dom was always well thought of in Lockport. His earnest face had been splashed across the local sports page, showing him down on one knee, talking to the coach, preparing for Saturday's game. In the Sunday paper, a photo is titled "The Look Back," as Dom is shown running for a touchdown and glancing back over his shoulder to make sure no one is on his tail.

Like so many sailors and Marines, he has been at sea for Thanksgiving, and now Christmas is coming on Guam. In the heat and between rainstorms, he tries to imagine the kitchen at home: his mother stirring pots on the stove, his brother and sisters helping as always. He thinks of his girlfriend, Ruth, and tells his mother that they have been writing to each other; he confides that he has "told her how I feel." He asks his parents to "be good to her." In another letter, he writes:

Tuesday Dec 12, 1944
"12 more shopping days 'til Christmas"

Dearest Mother,
Have finally reached an island and am half settled, but not for long. Am standing by for new orders now. I may move to another part of this island, or move to another island. I'll give you more dope later.
On this particular island it rains eight to twelve times a day. The rainy season is just finishing so it won't be like this all the time.
I'm living in a large tent with six other officers and we have folding cots like those you use for camping. I am washing with rain water that we catch in barrels. We also have an improvised shower made up of a barrel with a pipe attachment that also catches water.

Today we took a ride to the other side of the island to get paid. I drew $100 and paid back $65 that I owed. (Gambling again.) We went about 20 miles and saw quite a bit of the island. We went through areas where a lot of fighting was done and saw many caves in which the Japs fortified themselves. I passed through a town and it was bombed flat. Some of the natives have returned to their shambles and rebuilt small shacks from the lumber they could salvage. The natives are half Korean and half Chamorro. They have American missionaries and all the children go to school every day.

We have movies every night and this evening we had a 15-piece orchestra that played some damn good music.

I received Patrina's letter dated Nov 28, but that was the only one from home. Evidently, some of my mail hasn't caught up with me. Glad to hear everyone is well, especially Junior.

Love Dom

On Christmas Day 1944, the 5th Marine Division begins loading its combat troops on the Big Island of Hawaii. The 4th Marine Division follows suit on December 27 on Maui. As Private Jay Rebstock of the 5th Division, Company E, 27th Marines, loads onto his troop transport, his destination is unknown. The scuttlebutt among the men of the 27th Marines, who are always second-guessing their destination, is that the target is either China or Formosa, which would be just a warm-up for the final target of Okinawa.

The final liberty call in Honolulu is jammed with Marines trying to enjoy the last bit of civilization. "There were ten men for every girl, hamburgers sold out, and the bars were loaded to capacity."[33]

On board the *Haskell*-class attack transports, Marines gear up for battle, cleaning and recleaning weapons; sharpening and resharpening knives. Rebstock loads machine-gun belts and magazines for his Browning automatic rifle. Belowdecks, they sleep five high in cramped quarters, and during the day there is nothing to see but the endless ocean.[34]

A week into the trip, company commanders assemble their men

wherever they can crowd together and crane to see, showing them their first look at where they are headed: Iwo Jima. The men of Company E look at one another and ask, "Where the hell is that?"[35]

When the convoy gets to Saipan, Rebstock reloads onto a landing ship tank (LST) and, after some practice assault runs, waits for D-Day. Briefings are held every day, and the men study the maps and terrain models. They figure that the 13,000 Japanese have to be sick and disoriented from the seventy days of bombardment. The fight should last four, maybe five, days, and once Suribachi is taken, that will be it. In the evenings, they listen to Tokyo Rose tell them that the Imperial Japanese forces are lying in wait for them on Iwo.[36]

The men of the 4th Marine Division sail from Maui on January 8, 1945, to begin their 3,700-mile trek to Iwo Jima. Eniwetok is their first stop, and then they will go on to Saipan and Tinian. In the eyes of the veterans of those previous invasions, the two islands have dramatically changed. Now endless white runways for B-29s replace the battlefield that was once littered with the rotting enemy dead.[37] On January 27, after final rehearsals, they are Iwo Jima bound and sail into the rendezvous area on February 11.

On February 8, 1945, the 3rd Division, now complete with its thirty-fourth replacement draft, begins combat loading in Guam.[38] "Marines write their last letters home. They are allowed to say they are at sea, going into combat—nothing more, except general statements about the weather."[39]

Harry Gray writes:

Jan 16, 1945
Central Pacific

Dear Uncle Frank and family,
    How is everyone? I have been going to write you many times but something always seemed to come up and I had to put it off. I want to thank you very much for your swell package. It was very delicious and sure came at the right time.

It was in swell shape. I looked for your friend George to give him some fruit cake but couldn't find him.

I had a letter written to you on the boat but was unable to mail it because many of our activities on the ship which I included were barred. I received your two magazines and Omni book, and thanks from the fellows too as everyone is enjoying them besides me. I also received your v mail of which the last one came yesterday.

I am fine and in good health. During the trip my medical records were lost and upon arrival had to have another physical. Everything is perfect except my teeth and had to have a tooth filled. The only thing I minded then was the two needles before they filled it. Novocain of course.

In our training we have been assigned to our duty when the beachhead is made, I am in what they call "Beach unloading party #3" this means I am in the 3rd wave and unload supplies from Higgins boats. It is a very heavy job but not too much so for me. I think it will be ammunition, but don't know when. After the unloading is completed we shall take our places in the lines or be held in reserve.

It is very warm here but the breeze is very pleasant and keeps the heat down. It usually rains once or twice in 24 hours mostly at night.

Yesterday we went on a twelve mile hike and it was pretty tough. We left camp at 7:20 and were back at 1:00. We made very good time considering the rough terrain.

We have quite a few recreational facilities but not much time. In the first place it is too hot and when the day is over I like to take it easy.

Well I guess that's the news for now. I'll sign off.

With love to everyone
Harry

The 34th Replacement Draft is now attached to the 3rd Pioneer Battalion as part of the division's shore party.[40] That means hitting the beach and handling the massive jobs of unloading and transporting supplies and ammunition, in addition to serving as replacements for the attacking regiments.

On February 17, Transport Squadron 11 weighs anchor in Guam to carry the 3rd Division to the battle area. Harry Gray, Charlie Gubish, George Colburn, Herman Graeter, and Warren Graham are on board USS *President Adams*. Two days later, the ship anchors eighty miles off the volcanic island of Iwo Jima.

14

"Hell with the Fire Out"

Put on the whole armour of God, that ye may be able to stand
against the wiles of the devil.

> —Ephesians 6:11, read by a Protestant chaplain on board
> the *Bunker Hill*[1]

For four months, air strikes pummel Iwo Jima. On December 8, the
horses of the Seventh Air Force join the hounds of the Navy to again
pound away at its defenses. In the greatest aerial attack of all the battles
of the Pacific theater, B-24 Liberators from the Marianas rain bombs
and explosives on the Bonin Islands for seventy-four straight days.[2]

General Kuribayashi writes letters to his wife; he warns her not
to expect him to return and to get her affairs in order. "Are you still
in Tokyo? Believe me, the bombings will get steadily worse, so I wish
that you'd go to a safe place."[3]

February 11 is the 2,605th anniversary of the founding of the nation of Japan. For the occasion, "Song for the Defense of Iwo," is
played on the radio. The battered men, huddled in their caves and
surviving on water and small vegetables, listen to the children sing.[4]

> *Down south from the imperial city*
> *a small lonely island floats.*
> *The fate of our imperial country*
> *lies in the hands of this island,*
> *Iwo Jima.*

Before D-Day, the Navy carries out three days of heavy bombardment at Iwo Jima. The Marines had requested ten days, but the Navy insists that its plan "would accomplish all the desired objectives."[5] At the end of day one, only seventeen targets were destroyed, with seven hundred more to go.[6]

Despite the Marines' frustration, they put on a good face. Major General Harry Schmidt, commanding V Amphibious Corps, says, "The landing force is ready for combat. . . . We expect to get on their tails and keep on their tails until we chop them off."[7]

For the old salts of the Corps, in combat in the Pacific for more than two years now, "life boil[s] down to a very simple formula: training for combat, combat, more training, followed by more combat . . . [and] the certainty that 'another rock' had to be taken."[8]

February 17 is a day of reconnaissance. Iwo Jima is unlike Tarawa, Saipan, and Roi-Namur with their reefs and lagoons. The landing vehicles will slam directly from deep water onto a steep black volcanic ash beach.

No one knows if the beaches or the land beyond will be mined. Will the tractors hit hard-packed sand, or will they sink in? Answering these questions is the work of the Underwater Demolitions Team (UDT).

Under gray skies, three battleships and the cruiser *Pensacola* ease in close to shore as protectors for the men of the UDT operation. The island is quiet, as it has been in all the reconnaissance photos and during all the flyovers. Minesweepers move into position just offshore; the battleships fire from three thousand yards at suspected enemy areas to deter any Japanese gunners who might be tempted to fire at the vulnerable minesweepers. *Pensacola* is just eight hundred yards off the sheer face of Suribachi, delivering its own cover fire.

At 9:00 a.m., an enemy shell explodes on *Tennessee*. It is just one and does little damage, but it stuns everyone on board and sets anxious eyes into motion, scanning with binoculars across every crevice on land, hoping to spot where the gun is that fired the shot. But the island gives nothing away. *Tennessee* continues its bombardment.

Inside Suribachi, the Japanese soldier behind the 6-inch gun tracks the cruiser *Pensacola*'s every move. The ship is so close to Suribachi that the gunner and his men are shocked that the US cruiser is such a clear target.

For a few moments, the battery's officer resists the temptation to open fire, which he knows will give away his position. But as *Pensacola* stares back at him, he knows that such a moment will not come again. "Fire!" he yells. The first 6-inch shell impacts just fifty yards off target, but in quick succession, the excited Japanese crew sends six more, and they smash into *Pensacola*, sending its men flying and igniting fires on the ship.⁹

The cruiser maneuvers farther offshore, trailed by columns of thick smoke and fire; the men of *Pensacola* frantically scramble onto the deck to extinguish the flames. But *Pensacola* is wounded: when the smoke clears, seventeen men are dead, including the executive officer, and ninety-eight others are wounded.¹⁰

Watching the smoke rise from *Pensacola*, the other bombardment ships back off their positions close to the island. But ten landing craft, infantry (guns), or LCI(G)s, move in to take their places. These 160-foot gunboats are like floating porcupines, sporting weapons rarely found together on one platform. Each has three 40 mm guns and four 20 mm guns to complement the firepower of its six .50-caliber machine guns. But their most impressive firepower comes from twelve rocket launchers positioned on each of their decks that can deliver rocket fire to support the beach landing.

They move in to within a thousand yards of Iwo Jima's eastern beaches to support the UDT frogmen and unleash a combined seven hundred rockets to flail the three-thousand-yard landing area; 40 mm cannons probe possible enemy concealed positions.

Watching all this through his binoculars, General Kuribayashi is sure that the landing is now under way, and he gives the order to unleash his barrage against the gunboats. It is a devastating bombardment, like a knockout punch.

All the LCI(G)s are hit, as if by volley fire, and in the twelve gunboats, 170 crewmen are killed. The first Japanese shell that slams into

Gunboat 449 wipes out the 40 mm gun mount and its 5-man crew. The second kills 12 more men stationed at the base of the conning tower, and the third hits the bridge, blowing out one side of it and slamming the commander to the deck, killing him.[11] All the other officers are killed or fatally wounded; the quieted gunboat is dead in the water, with no one at its helm.

Lieutenant (Junior Grade) Rufus Herring, hit three times and bleeding, barks over the intercom to the engine room to get the ship moving again as he drags himself to the helm. But he is too weak to stand, so he props himself up among some empty shell casings nearby and gives orders to his men, steering the ship out of the melee and thereby avoiding its destruction.[12] Lieutenant Herring will become the first recipient of the Medal of Honor at Iwo Jima. Before the bloody battle is over, for their extraordinary heroism, twenty-six others will qualify for the Medal of Honor; only half will survive to receive it. Ten valorous men will receive the Navy Cross.[13]

But the Japanese gunners pay a price for this initial victory. The guns that fired on the flotilla have exposed themselves to the searching eyes of the Navy spotters. The battleship *Nevada* trains its 14-inch guns on the discovered targets and pounds away at them. Then she, along with the battleships *Tennessee* and *Idaho*, lays down a thick smokescreen to cover the returning UDT frogmen.

"Swimmers reported beach and surf conditions suitable for a landing. No underwater or beach obstacles existed and the single mine found was destroyed."[14] The divers bring back a sample of sand and have left behind a small sign, WELCOME TO IWO JIMA. The path for invasion is clear.[15]

General Holland "Howlin' Mad" Smith will later say of the fight for the "stone fortress of the sea," "I was not afraid of the outcome of the battle. I knew we would win. We always had. But contemplation of the cost in lives caused me many sleepless nights."[16]

It became clear from reconnaissance before the battle that the sand would pose a problem and that Kuribayashi's defenses, guns, and blockhouses were disappearing underground.

Those who did the planning for the invasion seem to have a good sense of what lies ahead. Their ominous preparations reveal that for the first time in the Pacific theater, each division has its own hospital. Five thousand beds are readied in Saipan and Guam. A marked photo of the island shows where the cemeteries will be located.

The labeling and loading of supplies for Iwo Jima began four months ago, and the sheer volume of them presages a prolonged stay. The 8th Field Depot is the nucleus of combat logistics support for Operation Detachment. Their commanding officer is Lieutenant Colonel Leland Swindler. The Marines under his command include seven original companies plus four depot companies, which include the largest participation of African American supply personnel in the Pacific theater. They are known as the "Montford Point Marines," for their segregated boot camp in Montford Point, North Carolina. (These men, like all Marines, trained first as riflemen and then in logistics and will be among those pulled into active duty as the ranks on Iwo Jima thin.)[17]

The cargo includes enormous amounts of pencils, matches, toilet paper, gasoline, socks, bullets, prepainted wooden crosses, flares, dog food, holy water, fingerprint ink, cigars, and asphalt-laying machines, among a myriad of other things. "The Fifth Division alone carrie[s] 100 million cigarettes and enough food to feed Columbus, Ohio for thirty days."[18]

⋊

At 3:00 a.m. on D-Day, February 19, the landing force is called to chow. Amid the usual clanking of metal trays and utensils as the Marines eat their "warrior's breakfast" of steak and eggs, there is little chatter in the crowded galleys. The weight of what is upon them is sinking in. After the days at sea and the monotonous circling offshore, it is time to go. Some cannot eat; those whose stomachs are not knotted up by nerves happily wolf down what their buddies leave on their plates.

As the call to embark comes, Private First Class Jay Rebstock, in the 5th Division's 2nd Battalion, is in the well deck of an LST where the LVTs are revving their engines. Sergeants hand out extra supplies wherever they can be stashed in the wells: ammo, explosives, land mines, and in Rebstock's case, a five-gallon can of water.[19]

Private Rebstock is rough and ready, sporting a new tattoo. He hunkers in the well deck, glad that he will not have to climb over the side of a troop transport, dangling on a cargo net, where the slightest misstep into a bobbing and pitching Higgins boat can be fatal. Rebstock will ride into battle on the LST; then, when the well deck opens, he'll head down the ramp and splash into the blue Pacific.

Naval gunfire is in full force as the Marines hustle down to the tank deck of the LST, loaded for combat under their heavy packs. They swing over the sides of the tractors, and Rebstock pulls himself up, along with his heavy water can. Once they are in the well deck, the engine noise is deafening, and the men's nostrils burn with a quick intake of suffocating fumes.

A haze hovers above the tractors, and the men begin choking and grabbing for their gas masks, which do no good, because they are designed to filter, not provide fresh air. For thirty excruciating minutes the men sit in this metal tomb, coughing and gagging. The open air of the Higgins boat looks pretty good to Rebstock now as he fears he could die right here, suffocating before he even hits the beach.[20]

With a great bang, the bow doors of the LST open; air and sunlight hit Rebstock's face as the first tractor lurches forward. Like a great hippo, the ungainly tractor waddles down the ramp and into the water, nose first.[21]

It bobs to the surface, rights itself, and churns away just as the second tractor makes its plunge. Rebstock is next, and in seconds he and fifteen other Marines are part of a great swirling circle of tractors, like horses walking in circles before heading to a starting gate. They stay in motion to keep their momentum; they are champing at the bit, their breakfast lying heavily in their stomachs. The LVTs gather, form up, and move to the line of departure. The signal blares, and they are off; the run-in to the beaches has begun. Rebstock feels the sea air on his cheeks; he glances over the side of his tractor, and his chest swells at the sight of the small American flag on each LVT, flapping in the ocean wind.

Four hundred eighty-two amtracs sprawl across the sea, carrying eight assault battalions into combat.[22] All the while, the great bombardment ships are shelling the shoreline with their island-shaking blasts. He smiles as he and his buddies look knowingly at one another. There is no way anyone can survive this pounding. In amazement, they watch the island explode. They know that "when Suribachi falls, it's over."[23]

"We'd listened to Tokyo Rose a lot," Rebstock will later say, "and she told us we were going to Iwo. When we got briefed on the operation we were told it was a real small island with about 13,000 Japs: they were sickly and wounded, and wouldn't put up much of a fight. We'd been bombing them for [seventy-four] days and we were going in there to mop them up in three to five days."[24]

At 8:30 a.m., the assault wave crosses the line of departure, four thousand yards offshore. The run-in will take thirty minutes. Five minutes behind the first wave comes the second, and five minutes behind it, the third starts off.

Rebstock watches the steady, majestic march of the assault waves; he is proud to be part of them as they surge toward Iwo's black sands. He remembers his studies at Gulf Coast Military Academy and a poem by Alfred, Lord Tennyson, who wrote of the advancing cavalry in "The Charge of the Light Brigade":

Half a league, half a league,
Half a league onward,
All in the valley of Death
Rode the six hundred.

"They marched onward under the greatest cannonade of naval gunfire that they could ever imagine."[25] In those thirty minutes, US warships salvo more than eight thousand rounds.[26]

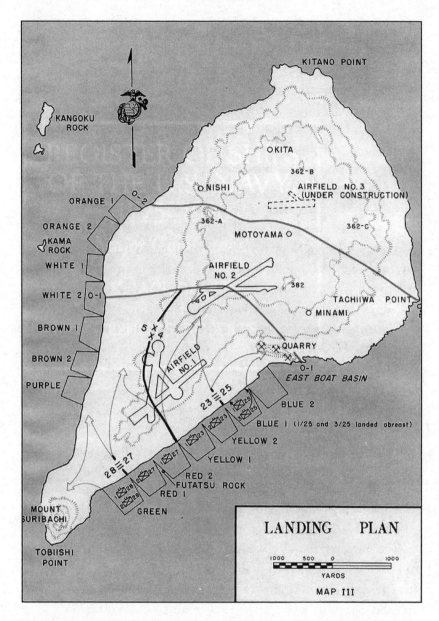

KITANO POINT

KANGOKU
ROCK

OKITA

362-B

ONISHI

AIRFIELD NO.3
(UNDER CONSTRUCTION)

ORANGE 1

O-2

ORANGE 2

KAMA
ROCK

362-A

MOTOYAMA O

362-C

WHITE 1

WHITE 2 O-1

AIRFIELD
NO. 2

382

TACHIIWA POINT

O MINAMI

BROWN 1

5

4

QUARRY

O-1

BROWN 2

AIRFIELD
NO. 1

EAST BOAT BASIN

PURPLE

23 25

BLUE 2

BLUE 1 (1/25 and 3/25 landed abreast)

YELLOW 2

YELLOW 1

28 27

RED 2

FUTATSU ROCK

RED 1

MOUNT
SURIBACHI

GREEN

LANDING   PLAN

TOBIISHI
POINT

1000   500   0   1000

YARDS

MAP III

Two minutes after 9:00 a.m., the first assault wave of troops (the
second wave behind the gunboats) slams onto the three-thousand-
yard-long beach. Marines from the 4th and 5th Divisions swarm over
the sides of their tracked vehicles "and hit the volcanic sand at a run

that slow[s] almost immediately to a laborious walk as their feet s[i]nk ankle deep into soft, loose volcanic ash."[27]

They feel as though they are being sucked into a strange glue; it feels like a nightmare in which you try to run, move forward, get away from something, but your legs are so heavy they can barely move. But this is real. It is only fifteen feet wide, the first terrace, but some of the men are crawling and reaching hand over hand as if swimming through a viscous pool. Others are upright but leaning so far forward that they are half bent; they gain a few steps, only to slide back down.

Private First Class Rebstock, on Red Beach 1, gasps as he fights halfway up the first terrace. His Browning automatic rifle and extra ammo weigh him down, and he can barely move. He curses the forty days at sea and feels out of shape until he looks down and sees that his right hand is still firmly clutching the five-gallon water can that he was supposed to have dropped on the beach.

Cursing under his breath, he shakes it out of his hand, and it rolls back down. He struggles to the top of the second terrace, finally out of the quicksand; his boots hit firmer ground, and he can now pick up the pace toward the western side.

It is less than a half mile across the narrow neck of Iwo Jima, but to the south of the neck looms Mount Suribachi.

Elements of the 28th Marines break off in that direction to surround the base, while Rebstock's 27th Marines presses on.

So far, gaining the beach itself has been the whole of the battle. Except for a brief fusillade from one blockhouse, their way is relatively easy. Again Rebstock wonders if maybe they are in for a cakewalk.[28]

The third and fourth waves now pile up on the beach behind them and begin their fight against the grip of the black sand. The 4th and 5th Divisions "[report] only scattered mortar, artillery, and small-arms fire, and excepting a few land mines, no man-made obstacles . . . on the beaches."[29] The first thirty minutes on Iwo Jima are passed in a strange, eerie calm, just a *pop-pop* from here and there, a last gasp, perhaps, from the survivors of the hellish bombardment.

From his post, Kuribayashi scans the beach through his binoculars. He is ready. He gives the signal, and the calm explodes into chaos.

The Japanese general's plan is in motion. His strategy: "Let the Marines land against light opposition. Make them lift naval gunfire and halt air support to avoid hitting their own troops. . . . Let the beaches pile up with men and equipment. Then cut off further landings with smothering artillery and mortar fire. . . . Let outfits ashore bleed to death with casualties."[30]

The second half hour is hell on Earth. In a single breath, the Marines' world dissolves into explosions, jettisoned body parts, and death. *Time* correspondent Robert Sherrod is there: "They died with the greatest possible violence. Nowhere in the Pacific have I seen such badly mangled bodies. Many were cut squarely in half. Legs and arms lay 50 feet away from any body."[31]

"The beaches were pulverized with every conceivable type of fire, and waves of raining shells swept back and forth like a giant scythe. Marine bodies were crushed, and landing crafts exploded. . . . Men from the first waves, already wounded and awaiting evacuation, were annihilated, along with the medical personnel attending them."[32]

One hour into the fight, Company B, including Private First Class Charles Tatum, is pinned down between the second and third terraces by the sudden enemy barrage.

"I could feel the hard concussions from nearby hits," Tatum will later say. "Fear was now a stark reality, as real as the hideous death and carnage occurring on all sides of us. . . . We moved out, crawling. It was the only option that seemed open to us."[33]

An explosion detonates in front of him, then another in the same place. He thinks the enemy gunners have him zeroed. Then two more come in the same place. As he burrows down into the sand, the concussions force grit into his eyes and mouth; he gags on it and spits it out.

A hand whacks him powerfully on the helmet. He looks up and sees the familiar snarling face of Marine Corps Gunnery Sergeant John Basilone staring down at him. The Medal of Honor recipient from Guadalcanal is shaking him and frantically pointing at the swirling sand, where the enemy mortars continue to land.

Tatum squints to see through the blinding sand and only then makes out the shape of a blockhouse. The explosions he thought were impacting mortar rounds were not mortars at all but concussions from the muzzle blasts of a Japanese gun.

Tatum brings his machine gun into action and pulls the trigger, but nothing happens. Sand and grit jam the breech. The Japanese gun continues to fire as Tatum rolls onto his side. "Why did this have to happen now?" he yells as he fumbles for a brush to clean the breech.[34]

He rolls back over, sets the gun in the tripod, and reloads. He instinctively pulls back on the bolt and lets it slam forward, chambering a .30-caliber round. Half expecting the gun not to fire again, he is relieved to hear it spring to life and watches as his tracer rounds bounce harmlessly off the wall of the blockhouse.

Basilone nudges him to move to the right, to face the blockhouse aperture at an angle. Tatum's second burst sends a stream of bullets into the enemy position. The Japanese slam the gun port closed.

Now the enemy is blind, and Tatum wants him to stay that way. He fires a few more short bursts. A demolitions man advances just wide of his streaming fire to hurl a satchel charge of composition C-2 at the base of the closed metal door. The explosion sends concrete and metal particles flying.

Before the Japanese can recover, Basilone signals for Tatum to keep firing and directs a flamethrower to advance on the same line, just wide of the covering machine-gun fire. Ignited napalm pours from the nozzle into the now-gaping hole in the bunker.

"There was a loud roar and it looked like a fire-spitting dragon's tongue had erupted," says Tatum. "The unsuspecting and stunned men inside . . . were cast instantly into the jaws of a roaring inferno: an incinerating hell."[35]

The attack is by the book, the way all the Marines have been trained and the way this island's defenses will have to be overcome. Basilone has just shown them how to do it.

Moments later, the hero of Guadalcanal and four members of his platoon, making their way across Motoyama 1, are hit by mortars that kill all of them. Basilone, who was sent home after Guadalcanal and then traveled the United States, telling his heroic story and promoting war bonds, had insisted on rejoining the fight in the Pacific, only to be killed on D-Day at Iwo Jima. When Basilone is hit and dies, the news travels up and down the landing beaches. Everyone realizes that if he didn't make it, they had better start fighting or they won't make it, either. The New Jersey native, who will posthumously receive the Navy Cross, was twenty-eight years old.[36]

In the initial calm on the beaches, eight assault battalions from the two divisions make it ashore. But they are surrounded by hulking, steaming wreckage.

Trucks carrying vital supplies are backed up on the beaches behind them or stuck in the sand. The men of the replacement drafts take on the backbreaking work of carrying them inland from the water while navigating wreckage, sand, and incoming fire. According to the historian Larry Smith, "Tanks and half-tracks lay crippled where they had bogged down in the coarse sand. Amphibian tractors . . . lay flopped on their backs. Cranes, brought ashore to unload cargo, tilted at insane angles, and bulldozers were smashed in their own roadways."[37]

Among the mangled bodies, many of them smashed beyond recognition, is the debris of war. According to a history of the 4th Division, "Packs, gas masks, rifles, and clothing, ripped and shattered by shell fragments, lay scattered across the beach. Toilet articles and even letters were strewn among the debris, as though war insisted on prying into the personal affairs of those it claimed."[38]

As the 5th Division pushes across the neck of the island, the Marines of the 4th Division, on the right, make it to the edge of the Motoyama 2 airfield, but they pay an enormous price for their advance: in taking the imposing ridges of the rock quarry on their right flank, overlooking the east boat basin, they lose 35 percent of their men.[39]

Twelve guns of the 14th Marines (artillery) attempt to land to provide fire for the 4th Division against the Japanese guns, but it proves disastrous. Only four guns make it to shore. Seven others are lost when the crafts transporting them are sunk, and the eighth and final gun lands with defective sights.

According to Lieutenant John Chapin, "There was no cover from enemy fire. Japs deep in reinforced concrete pillboxes laid down interlocking bands of fire that cut whole companies to ribbons."[40]

The Marines crowd onto the narrow beachhead in full view of the Japanese gunners looking down upon them. Protective counterbattery fire from artillery and offshore naval guns is mostly ineffective against the burrowed-in enemy, and any fire meant to impact on an observed enemy position explodes harmlessly on a now-empty position. As soon as the fire sweeps past, the enemy guns and gunners reemerge to hammer the pinned-down Marines.

According to combat correspondent David Dempsey, "The invasion beach of this island is a scene of indescribable wreckage—all of it ours. Japanese artillery, rockets and heavy mortars laid a curtain of fire along the shore. They couldn't miss and they didn't."[41]

The horrific losses experienced during the first two days lead the V Amphibious Corps commander, Major General Schmidt, to call for part of his floating reserves.

The 3rd Marine Division is anchored in an ocean corral for ships eighty miles southeast of Iwo Jima. With its three infantry regiments—the 3rd, 9th, and 21st Marines—the 3rd Division is the reserve of the V Amphibious Corps. The status of the two assault divisions, the 4th and 5th, already deep into the island and swamped with casualties, is unknown to the men on the ships offshore. Their job is to wait and, if called upon, to move in and do their part. When and if that call comes, the 21st Marines will be first into action.

The ships—*Cape Johnson, President Adams, Callaway, Frederick Funston*, and *Napa*—steam in like dark shadows. Just before midnight, the last of them arrives.[42] Among the small flotilla are two ships that carry a grim reminder of the reality of battle: *Fayette* and *James O'Hara* are transporting Marines designated as the 28th and 34th Replacement Drafts.

Every man in the invasion force has carefully studied the models and terrain maps of the pork chop–shaped barren rock, which translates from the Japanese name as "Sulfur Island," and sees it as another typical island invasion against strong beach defenses, backed up by a main line of resistance defended by a fanatical Japanese enemy who will, in final desperation, hurl himself at the Marines in a human wave, a banzai charge. There will be few enemy survivors when it is over, and then it will be time to look to the next island, and maybe, just maybe, that one will be the last.

The tactics are simple: There is always a frontal attack. There is no room on these tiny islands for grand maneuvers and flanking. The troops are to cut the island in half, sweep one half clear of all enemy resistance, and then attack the remaining half until the last remnants of the enemy are driven into the sea or left buried in caves. These are the bloody lessons of three years of fighting the Japanese from island to island: the need for close artillery support, the benefits of flame-throwers, demolitions, and tank infantry tactics when dealing with an enemy who will never surrender.[43]

The Japanese have no reinforcements; those days died at Guadalcanal. The banzai charges have been costly, flushing the enemy out into the Marines' field of fire. Despite the savagery and terror of the screaming charges, the Marines pray for them to come. The killing purges in the open fields mean they will not have to dig the enemy out of his caves.

The Japanese now have only the men on the island. There is no navy, and the few remaining aircraft they have cannot do much damage. This is 1945, not 1941, and the Rising Sun is setting, but it sits burning red on the horizon. Bitter fighting lies ahead, but two days into Iwo Jima, there is still the pervasive notion among the Americans that it might take only a few more days.

And then it will be on to the next island and then to Japan. They know that the road home runs through Tokyo. But first, this island, seven hundred miles south of the Japanese mainland, must fall.

The orders for the reserve division are to be ready, from D + 1 onward, to go wherever they are needed. Since the reserves are always called upon to save the day, to plug a gap in the lines, or to relieve a hard-pressed fighting force, they are trained to pass through the lines of a beleaguered force to keep the forward momentum of an attack.[44]

But there is another possible mission: "The division might be required to take up a defensive position to cover a withdrawal."[45]

A withdrawal! The word conjures up visions of defeat, heavy casualties, even capture. The 3rd Division's 21st Marines came into being because of a withdrawal. Formed to replace the lost regiment of the original 3rd Division, the 4th Marines ceased to exist in 1942, losing its colors in the crushing defeat at Corregidor. The Bataan Death March followed, and the specter of the fate of those lost Marines still looms large in the minds of Americans.

The call to action for the Marines of the 3rd Division comes quickly. The reserve flotilla weighs anchor and steams to within fifteen thousand yards of the Iwo invasion beaches. The klaxons and boatswains' pipes call the Marines to their debarkation stations, and all eyes strain to see the island. It is a blur, shrouded in explosions, smoke, and haze. Only the mouth of the volcano Suribachi thrusts above the haze into the blue-gray sky. An artillery observer says that it looks like "Hell with the fire out."[46]

As planned, the 21st Marines is committed first. Its Higgins boats lower into the water, and each of the coxswains maneuvers his forty-foot boat to just touch the sides of the ship. Cargo netting flaps down against the sides, toward the bobbing boats.

It's time to go. Four at a time, the men climb over, their feet finding the first horizontal strand, then searching for the next one as the nets slam against the ship. They must remember not to grip the rope where a buddy might crush their hand. A fall can be, and sometimes is, deadly, as they well know.

According to Private First Class Charles Tatum, "Climbing down rope nets with full gear and weapons require[s] the agility of a monkey, combined with the skill and daring of a trapeze artist, to avoid being slammed against the side of the APA and being crushed by the LCVP as it pitched and rolled."[47]

The regiment completes debarking at noon, and the landing craft move to the rendezvous area to circle, awaiting their time to cross the line of departure. Five minutes will separate the landings of the successive waves.

The circling is interminable: hour after hour of nauseating rocking, rolling, and pitching. The bottoms of the landing craft slosh with seawater and sometimes vomit, and still there is no call to land. Instead, late in the afternoon, the boats are sent back to their ships for the men to reembark. There is congestion on the beach, and waves of Marines are backed up, trying to land on the beach or stuck on it.

The climb back up the nets is even more treacherous. The men's packs and clothing are now sopped in seawater. In their frenzy to climb, dozens of men miss their leap to the cargo nets and fall into the heaving water below. Frantic recovery efforts ensue; some are pulled out, some slip beneath the surface—gone forever.

Several of the boats cannot maneuver back into position for the reembarkation, so they drift off and the men spend a miserable night tossing about, as a twenty-knot gale lashes the invasion area with seven-foot waves.[48]

But the next morning, February 21, the men of the 3rd Division's 21st Marines again load into their crafts, and this time they land on Yellow beaches 1 and 2. They are immediately attached to the 4th Marine Division for operations, and during the next two days, they attack up the terraced slopes while Japanese gunners pound away at them, devastating their ranks.

The men of the 21st Marines struggle to the edge of the Motoyama 2 airfield, where they pause to await the support of twelve tanks. Taking the runways is crucial to the capture of Iwo Jima.

The tanks come under direct large-caliber enemy fire and enemy mines as they hit the southern edge of the airfield. The infantry, without tank support, makes some progress on the western edge of the field, but there are hundreds of pillboxes and the Japanese have all the approaches covered in intersecting fields of fire. For four hours on February 23, the surviving Marines struggle against the hardened positions.

Among them is Corporal Hershel Woodrow "Woody" Williams of Quiet Dell, West Virginia. Woody is the youngest of eleven children, all delivered not by a doctor but by a neighbor of his mother. Williams says of his upbringing, "We were country, country. Dairy farmers." He never had any problem following orders, because his father always said, "I am only going to tell you one time, I'm not going to tell you twice." In 1942, he was too short to enlist, but in 1943, in need of more recruits, the Marines lowered the height requirement to five feet, two inches, and that was when Williams became a Marine.[49]

"We'd been there for two days, we had lost so many people. When we hit the beach, I had six Marines in my unit, flamethrower demolition people that could do either one. But we'd lost all those. So we gathered in a group, and the commanding officer asked me, the last flamethrower left, could I do something about some of these pillboxes that got us stalled? I was told I said, 'I'll try.' I picked four men to protect me while I'm using the flamethrower to try to eliminate the pillboxes. Two of those Marines sacrificed their lives protecting mine."[50]

Carrying the seventy-two-pound weapon on his back and with the cover of four riflemen who fire away and keep the Japanese pinned down or away from the pillbox apertures, Williams charges his first target. With his left hand, he squeezes the handle to light the sparking igniter. He braces himself for the recoil and, with his right hand, squeezes the trigger.

Williams shoots a fiery, seven-second stream of ignited jellied gasoline directly into the pillbox. Everyone inside is incinerated in an instant. "Killing with a rifle or a grenade is different than with a flamethrower. There is nothing like that smell, killing by consuming with fire." A Japanese soldier leaps from his hidden position near another pillbox, and Williams ignites him in his tracks. In quick succession, his four rifleman protectors are all dead or hit. "So then I began

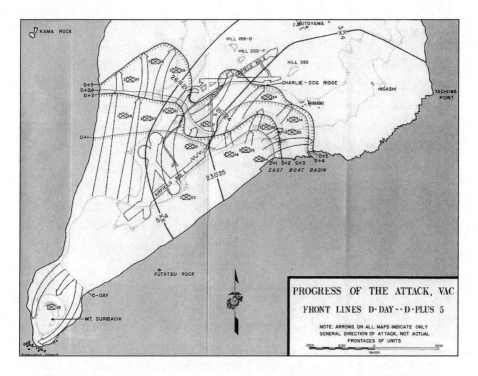

PROGRESS OF THE ATTACK, VAC
FRONT LINES D-DAY--D-PLUS 5

NOTE: ARROWS ON ALL MAPS INDICATE ONLY
GENERAL DIRECTION OF ATTACK, NOT ACTUAL
FRONTAGES OF UNITS

working by myself. I didn't have any more pole charge people. So in the process of four hours, I was able to use up six flamethrowers and eliminate the enemy within seven pillboxes. I have no explanation of how I did it. I don't remember how or when I got the other five flamethrowers. Why they didn't get me, why the mortars didn't get me, why the bullets didn't get me, I have no explanation for that."[51] For his "aggressive fighting spirit and valiant devotion to duty," Hershel Williams received the Medal of Honor for his heroism.[52]

But despite the heroics of the 21st Marines, it is unable to hold its hard-won positions and is forced to retreat to its initial position south of the runway.[53]

On February 22, D + 3, Lieutenant General Keller Rockey throws the entire 5th Division forward in an attempt to dislodge the enemy. Ten officers are killed, joining the ten killed the day before. Thirty-five men are lost in four days of combat.[54] Kuribayashi's killing fields carpet the island. There are no weak points.

The volcano, inert when the first waves hit the beach, roars to life like a beast disturbed in sleep. It is not lava that rumbles within but a hail of sniper and mortar fire that rains down on the men of the 28th Marines. They squint up its dusty, craggy ridges, trying to figure out where the shooters are. Inside, in interlocking rooms and caves, are several thousand Japanese fighters who live in the tunnels, having spent months digging them.

American GIs write letters home as the earth around them shakes with the unrelenting bombardment. Private Richard Wheeler will later say, "It was terrible, the worst [fire] I can remember us taking. The Jap mortarmen seemed to be playing checkers and using us as squares."[55] But on D + 4, February 23, the relentlessness of the 28th Marines pays off and it encircles the base of Suribachi.

Colonel Kanehire Atsuji, commanding the Suribachi sector's defenders, signals his dire situation to General Kuribayashi: "The enemy air, sea, and land attacks are serious. Now the enemy began to burn us with the flame throwers. If we keep ourselves intact, we shall just get nothing but self-extermination. We would like to go out for a banzai charge."[56]

Kuribayashi angrily replies to this challenge to his orders, "I had imagined the fact that the 1st airfield should fall into the enemy's hands. But what is the matter that Mt. Suribachi would fall within only 5 days?"[57]

At 8:00 a.m. on Friday, February 23, a tiny reconnaissance force of four men from Company F begins a slow crawl up the steep face of the mountain high above the invasion beaches. Four soldiers— Sergeant Sherman Watson and Privates Louis Charlo, Theodore White, and George Mercer—climb for forty minutes to the edge of the crater.

At the summit, they see an unattended battery of heavy machine guns with ammunition stacked neatly next to them. There are no Japanese in sight. Watson signals the men back down, and they slide to their starting point among the rocks below to report their findings.[58]

Quickly Lieutenant Colonel Chandler Johnson assigns the task to seize and hold the crest to First Lieutenant Harold G. Schrier of

Company E. He is to lead a forty-man patrol to the top, secure the crater, and raise a small fifty-four-by-forty-six-inch American flag so the whole island can see that the Marines now control the mountain.

The dramatic ascent of Lieutenant Schrier's patrol up the face of Suribachi is witnessed by all. The tiny figures are outlined against the steep, barren slope. One Marine quips, "Those guys ought to get flight pay."

Climbing Mount Suribachi with the Marines that day is Father Charles Suver, S.J., the chaplain of the 5th Marine Division, one of nineteen Catholic priests accompanying the invasion of Iwo Jima. Just days ago, a young lieutenant assured Father Suver that he intended to plant an American flag at the top of Suribachi. The priest told him that if he succeeded, he would say Mass right under that flag. Before they disembarked for the island, the men, many of whom were about to die, asked the priest about duty and courage. He told them, "A courageous man goes on fulfilling his duty despite the fear gnawing away inside. Many men are fearless, for many different reasons, but fewer are courageous." During the first hellish days of the battle, Father Suver, at great personal risk, ministered to the wounded and administered last rites to the dying. On February 23, he follows the men up the mountain and says Mass on the craggy ridges of Suribachi, under the misty skies, amid the chaos of war. He will later say he could hear the Japanese murmuring in their caves nearby.[59]

At 10:15 a.m., the patrol stands high atop the crest, almost six hundred feet above the sea. Sergeant Louis R. Lowery, a photographer from *Leatherneck* magazine, snaps photos all along the way.

Two Marines rummage in the rubble scattered in the crater and find a twenty-foot length of pipe that was part of the cistern to collect rainwater. Lieutenant Schrier and Sergeant Ernest Thomas, Jr., quickly attach the small flag to the pipe. Lowery positions himself slightly on the downslope of the crater wall to snap the picture as the flag goes up.

As the Marines push the pole into the rocky ground, the flag unfurls and snaps high in the wind. Private First Class Tatum is watching from his position with the 27th Marines but at the moment is looking away. His buddy slaps him on the back and points to the crest of Suribachi. "Tatum. Do you see that?"

He turns to see "our *Stars and Stripes* clearly on the peak, waving in the breeze. The 28th Marines . . . now, 'kings of Iwo Jima's hill!'"[60]

Jay Rebstock and his Company E men are preparing to continue their attack along the western coast. Suddenly there is cheering all across the front, and they hear the blasts and whistles from the ships at sea.

"The flag's up," someone says, and they all look to the top of the mountain and holler and yell with joy. Tears fill Rebstock's eyes as his chest swells with pride. Most important, this is the fifth day; all their briefings predicted that it would take five days to gain Suribachi, and when Suribachi falls, the end will be near.[61]

As Lou Lowery's camera shutter snaps the dramatic photo, two Japanese soldiers charge out from concealed positions, hurling grenades in a headlong attack. One heads straight for the flag raisers, brandishing his drawn sword. Private First Class James Robeson, who refused to be in the flag-raising picture, shoots him, and he falls head over heels into the crater below, his sword snapping under him as he careens downward.[62]

The other lobs his grenade toward Lowery, who vaults out of his position in the crater and over the rim to avoid it, but now he's sliding downward, his arms, legs, and hands clawing at the ground to slow down. He lands fifty feet down; his camera is smashed, but the precious film inside is intact.[63] When the photo is developed, he sees that he has captured the moment: the flag raisers planting Old Glory as one Marine looks outward, keeping watch, rifle at the ready.

From far below on the beach, the flag looks tiny, and Lieutenant Colonel Johnson fears that "some son of a bitch is going to want that flag, but he's not going to get it. That's our flag."[64]

So he dispatches a runner to the nearby beached LST 779, and Ensign Alan S. Wood gives him the ship's flag. It is fifty-six by ninety-six inches, twice the size of the one flying now. Johnson sends the large flag to the top and orders his men to "bring ours back." (Others report that Secretary of the Navy James Forrestal came ashore and said that the flag raised on Suribachi ensured that there would be a Marine Corps for another five hundred years, and he wanted it for posterity. That meant they would have to send up another one.)

Associated Press photographer Joe Rosenthal, who is covering the southern beaches that morning, missed the first flag raising and heads up to catch the second one. As he arrives at the top, the first flag is coming down, and six other Marines have already put the new flag on another pipe and are standing ready to place it into the existing hole. He has no chance to get a dual-action shot.

He scrambles to get a good angle, but time is running out. He piles a few lava stones on top of each other, and as he steps upon them, he sees, out of the corner of his eye, that the Marines with the new flag are moving the long pole forward. The first Marine crouches down to place his end of the flagpole into the rocky ground.

All Rosenthal can do is take a quick sight and hope for the best. "I swung my camera around and held it until I could guess that this was the peak of the action," he will later say, "and shot."[65] He continues to prowl the top of the mountain and shoots seventeen other photos. In the evening, he returns to his ship and sends the film off to Guam for development. He dropped the camera in the surf earlier in the day and just hopes that the film is still good.

The historian and former Marine Joseph Alexander will write that Lou Lowery's dramatic photograph "would become a valued collector's item. But Rosenthal's would enthrall the free world."[66] The six Marines whose pictures were hastily snapped as they raised the flag, not facing the camera, were:

Corporal Harlon Block
Corporal Harold Keller[67]
Private First Class Franklin Sousely
Sergeant Michael Strank
Private First Class Harold Schultz[68]
Private First Class Ira Hayes

On this fifth day of the savagery that is the Battle of Iwo Jima, the elation of the flag raising is short lived. In 1942, Winston Churchill spoke words that are so true on day five of this battle: "Now this is not the end. It is not even the beginning of the end, but it is, perhaps, the end of the beginning."[69] In less than a week, three of the flag raisers will be dead, and there is a long and brutal month of fighting yet to come.

As Father Suver will later observe, the most remarkable thing about Iwo Jima was the courage of the ordinary Marines and the care they showed for each other.[70]

15

The Badlands

After the flag raising, it was a horror.[1]

—George J. Colburn, 3rd Division, 9th Infantry Regiment

Bang! The supply crates on the beach rattle as explosions rock the ground up north. The ships offshore hurl 2,500 tons of exploding steel into enemy positions on airfield Motoyama 2. Air strikes quickly follow as the Marines attempt to attack the runway from the other direction.

Off the northern tip of Motoyama 1, two small taxiways connect the two airfields. The plan is to deploy a column of tanks to follow the taxiway from Motoyama 1 to the left flank of Motoyama 2 and attack from there.

It is 9:15 a.m. on Saturday, February 24. As the tanks lumber out onto the western end of the second airfield, Companies I and K of the 3rd Battalion, 21st Marines, will follow three other battalions of tanks across in a coordinated attack.[2]

But the plan implodes. The Japanese have seeded the connecting taxiway with antitank mines. The first tank in the column hits a mine and grinds to a halt. The column presses forward, but now the second tank is hit and explodes in a burst of scorching flame, triggered by a tremendous five-hundred-pound aerial torpedo rigged as a mine.[3]

Again the staggered column lurches forward, straight into the teeth of Japanese antitank fire coming from the fifty-foot ridge at the intersection of the northeast–southwest runway and the east–west runway eight hundred yards to the east. In minutes, three more tanks are hit and disabled. The remaining tanks, blocked by the five smoldering hulks to their front and outgunned by the Japanese high-velocity anti-titank weapons, abandon the attack and withdraw to the first airfield under cover of smoke grenades. Fifteen tank crewmen are killed or wounded.[4]

Major Holly Evans, commanding the 3rd Tank Battalion, will later say, "On the second day of fighting for Motoyama 2, only 19 of my original 46 tanks were operative. We were hit by anti-tank weapons, machine gun cannon, five-inch guns, and 150mm mortars, as well as mines of all descriptions. Most of our men and equipment were lost on the airfield—ten tanks were knocked out on the strip within a few hours."[5]

With no tank support for the Americans, the advantage shifts to the Japanese. The 21st Marines, poised to attack from the southern tip of the airfield as part of the tank and infantry assault, now have no choice but to go forward without support. Going forward is a bad idea, but it's the only idea available. Waiting is not an option on Iwo Jima.

As long as the Japanese can hold fast to their perch on Motoyama Plateau, they have eyes everywhere. The dirt-brown, barren island slopes downward and away from them. It is a near-perfect shooting gallery. Every bit of beach, every makeshift medical station, every foxhole and crater stretches out below. Bullets rain down on the advancing Marines and the already wounded men waiting for evacuation. They blow apart supplies, ignite crates of ammo, and keep every nerve on edge, every minute of every hour. They are ready and waiting for the next armored column that comes along to try again on Motoyama 1.

The two companies of the 3rd Battalion, 21st Marines, about to attack from just off the southern tip of the airfield, will be the first to test Kuribayashi's main line of resistance for the defense of Iwo Jima. After the fall of Suribachi, the general's plan left the south of the island passive and the beaches with a strong defense. The core of his resistance is a line across the middle, extending from northwest to southeast through Motoyama 2 airfield, with its flanks anchored on the opposite coasts. A final defensive line has been installed to the north in the vicinity of the unfinished airfield number 3.[6]

The V Amphibious Corps's commander, Major General Schmidt, knows there can be no pause while Kuribayashi relentlessly pounds the Marines from the plateau. He tells his aides, "We'll keep hitting them. They can't take it forever. We've got to keep pressing until they break."[7]

He has already committed one regiment of his reserve 3rd Division—the 21st—to the battle, and now he calls for a second regiment, the 9th. The battle is only five days old, and he is already reduced to a single reserve regiment, the 3rd.

The 21st Marines prepare to attack down the center of the Motoyama Plateau to seize the second airfield. It is wedged between the 5th Division, attacking on its left, and the 4th Division, to which it is attached, on its right.

Lieutenant Colonel Wendell H. Duplantis, commanding the 3rd Battalion, having observed the destruction of his supporting armored column, curses loudly and races to a foxhole near the southern tip of the airfield. Two of his company commanders are dug in, staring across the concrete flatland; they will have to negotiate under fire to seize the dominating high ground half a mile distant.

"We're in one sonuvabitchin' mess," he barks to twenty-two-year-old Captain Clayton Rockmore, the commander of Company I, and twenty-four-year-old Captain Rodney Heinze, commanding Company K. "But we've got to have the goddamned airstrip today."[8] At 9:10 a.m., Duplantis is ordered to "jump off on time, tanks or no tanks."[9]

At 9:30 a.m., fifteen minutes past the attack hour, Duplantis receives another order that there will not be three battalions of tanks, but there will be one company, six tanks from the 4th Marine Division, to support Company I against attacks from the pillboxes.[10]

The assault against the commanding heights to the north of the two airstrips is a daunting task with little to no tank support. Japanese artillery and high-velocity guns fire straight down the runways; their 47 mm antitank gun can penetrate up to four inches of tank armor.[11] To get to the high ground, the Marines will have to run the gauntlet of the long axis of the runway shooting alley.

It will be a frontal attack across an open field. If there is any silver lining at all, it is that with Suribachi quiet, they will not be shot at from behind. Ahead, it is a straight lunge into the line of fire. First Lieutenant Raoul Archambault, the Company K executive officer, looks out over the flat runways and thinks, "This is fighting on a pool table."[12]

The two companies of the 21st Marines move out thirty minutes late, with Company K advancing mostly on the mile-long northeast–southwest runway and Company I paralleling it on the right. The objective is eight hundred yards away.

As they set off, the eight hundred Japanese pillboxes that ring the field and the high ground to the north spring to life, and the Marines quicken their pace. The two captains are everywhere, shouting orders, pointing out targets, encouraging their men, and the green line surges forward. Captain Rockmore, at the head of Company I, leads his storming Marines toward the pillboxes on the right. He is shouting to his men, running crouched and moving forward, and then, in an instant, the twenty-two-year-old officer, who left Cornell University to enlist, is shot in the throat and falls dead on the airfield. Captain Heinze is also down. Two grenades thrown from a hidden spider trap blast his legs out from under him. Three lieutenants fall one after the other in the oncoming haze of bullets, and three sergeants step up to take the place of their fallen leaders without missing a beat.[13] Captain Daniel Marshall moves forward to take command of Company I.

Reeling, the two companies attempt to reorganize under the enemy fire as the lead tank of the six moving with Company I takes a direct hit from a Japanese antitank gun. The other five quickly withdraw until the big gun can be located lest they be picked off one by one.[14]

First Lieutenant Archambault races up to where Captain Heinze has fallen. Close behind him is Second Lieutenant Grossi. With Grossi are just twelve men; the rest of his forty-man platoon are either dead or wounded.[15]

The men take cover where they can, and focus on Archambault, waiting for his order. He is a man to be followed: a Silver Star at Bougainville, a Bronze Star at Guam. In a split second, he is off. He pulls up his Thompson submachine gun and a bag full of grenades and sprints across the runway, yelling back to Grossi, "Let's go, Dom!"[16]

The right-hand platoon of Company K charges across the runway directly toward the fifty-foot hill and into the first line of connected pillboxes and trenches. Nine minutes later, they are across.

With fixed bayonets and hurling grenades in all directions, the Marines begin the climb while howitzers pummel away at the ground above them. The Company I Marines have held their ground and move in with the 4th Marines on their right.[17]

But the friendly fire, smashing the Japanese crest, suddenly goes awry, and rounds begin falling on Archambault's men on the slope. It drives them off the hill, and for a half hour, they pull back and regroup to charge back up again. This time one platoon makes it to the crest, but it meets a hail of Japanese fire from every direction. Mortars rain down on the men on top of the ridge and those still climbing, but they keep going, moving forward despite the crushing onslaught. For fifteen excruciating minutes they battle hammer and tongs, but they cannot hold. The superior enemy firepower finally drives them back down.

Lieutenant Archambault's men scatter and slide to the jagged base of the hill, hunkering down against mortar fire in the enemy trenches, finding space among the dead from both sides. Dom Grossi's whittled-down platoon huddles nearby, and Archambault screams over the radio for more artillery fire. Colonel Duplantis yells that it is on the way and says that when he gets it, he's to "go after the *sonsabitches* again!"

"Will do, Colonel!" the frustrated lieutenant barks back. "But tell the bastard artillery to hit the fuckin' Nips and not us!"[18]

The artillery again smashes the hilltop, and when it lifts, Archambault and Grossi lead the attack back up the fire-streaked, unforgiving slope. But halfway up the hill, the Japanese defenders come down at them, swarming the exhausted Marines and driving them back down again. This time, Company K retreats to the south side of the runway. It is high noon.

Ships offshore and carrier aircraft hammer the hill while the men of Company K try to rearm, reload, evacuate casualties, and consolidate their thinned ranks. It takes them nearly two hours. But Archambault and Grossi are ready. Dominick Grossi's Navy Cross citation reads as follows:

> Second Lieutenant Grossi led his unit against the Japanese with dauntless courage, slashing right and left with his bayonet, thrusting grenades into massive emplacements sunk in the sands, dropping them behind rocks, sweeping aside the enemy, holding desperately and fighting furiously in hand-to-hand engagements as he smashed through a sector swarming with Japanese to gain the fifty-foot ridge on the opposite side of the airstrip.[19]

At 2:15, Company I finally crosses the runway and joins in the attack. In two minutes, the attacking Marine line sweeps over the crest against surprisingly light opposition. The surviving Japanese gather on the reverse slope for a final showdown, charging forward into the oncoming fire of the Marines.

The historian Bill Ross will later write, "Japanese officers swung ceremonial swords and were impaled on Marine bayonets. Japanese troops lunged at Marines with bayonetted rifles and were clubbed to death with weapon butts, entrenching picks, even rocks."[20] The official 3rd Marine Division report will call it "one of the most freakish nightmares of the Iwo battle."[21]

This time, it is over in ten minutes. Fifty more Japanese are killed in the final charge. Despite the heavy casualties, Marines are now on the north side of the airfield. The historian Frank Hough will later write of the 3rd Battalion's historic attack to take Motoyama 2, "They fought and died with the same valorous determination as General Pickett's men in the Confederate charge at Gettysburg."[22] But unlike General George Pickett and his men at Gettysburg, the Marines are not hurled back.

The attack gains eight hundred valuable yards from the jump-off point south of the runway to the high ground to the north of the airfield. The drive that began on D + 1, from the black-sand landing beaches to Archambault's hard-won position, cost V Amphibious Corps 5,338 additional casualties to be added to the more than 2,400 lost on D-Day.[23]

First Lieutenant Raoul Archambault's Navy Cross citation reads:

Assuming command after his company sustained heavy casualties and was badly disorganized, First Lieutenant Archambault quickly reorganized the company and, personally leading his men in furious hand-to-hand fighting while under hostile frontal, flanking and enfilade fire, succeeded in seizing a strongly fortified Japanese hill position. Counterattacked and driven from the hill three times, he repeatedly led his men against the enemy and finally regained the position. . . . Archambault was directly instrumental in making possible a break-through of the enemy's main line of defense.[24]

Wounded in the attack on the ridge, Dominick Grossi is taken to a hospital ship offshore from which he writes home. He does not mention his injury or anything about his heroic role in the battle.

February 27, 1945

Dearest Mother,
    I've been doing a little moving lately and that's the reason I haven't written. I know you're worried, but everything is alright. I'm on Iwo Jima and it's really a hot spot. It's just about secured

*now and we will move back to Guam in a day or two. There will
be another lapse of time before you get another letter, because I'll be
aboard ship. Don't worry Mom, I'm in good health and still going
strong. I just finished a hot bacon and egg cracker sandwich with a
hot cup of coffee. First hot stuff in about five days. I'm busy Mom, so
I have to sign off. Give my love to daddy and the children. Your son,*

Dom xxx

Don't worry everything is "O.K."

At the same time that Lieutenant Archambault and the 21st Marines crack the Japanese main line of resistance north of the airfield,
its sister regiment, the 9th, and the entire division headquarters are
landing at Black Beach, a redesignation of the area previously labeled
Red Beach 2 and Yellow Beach. By nightfall, the three infantry battalions have moved into an assembly area, ready to join the fight the
following day. Major General Graves Erskine sets up his division
headquarters just to the north of the first airfield.[25]

Landing with the 9th Marines is the 34th Replacement Draft.
Privates Harry Gray, Herman Graeter, Charles Gubish, Warren Graham, and George Colburn land at Black Beach and are immediately
attached to the 3rd Shore Party Battalion. It is their first glimpse of
the battlefield. Gray and the rest of the unit are immediately thrown
in among the scattered supplies and equipment strewn about everywhere at the supply depot on the beach.

The beehive of activity is an all-out effort to get desperately needed
supplies to the Marines clinging to the newly captured high ground
north of the second airfield. The call has gone out "for volunteers to
carry supplies to the front. Seabees cranked up bulldozers and pulled
loaded trailers up the terraces, across the first airstrip and to within
two hundred yards of the line."[26] Iwo Jima's terrain, with its sliding
terraces, boulders, and badlands, means they can shell any vehicle
that moves, and that reality has necessitated this resupply technique.

The "human conveyor belt, with hundreds of men packing crates and backpacks, pushing carts of ammo and water,"[27] will become the means of sustaining the attack for the rest of the battle.

But it is not the supplies and the chaos that deliver the rude awakening of war to Private Charles Gubish from Bethlehem, Pennsylvania. He will later say, "There is a pile, four or five feet high, covered with ponchos. And somebody says, 'Look at them Japs, they got boots like we do.' Then they pull the corner of the poncho up, and they aren't dead Japs, they are Marines." Before long Gubish, like so many Marines of his fellow replacements, is assigned the grimmest duty of all. "I was in the 34th Replacement Draft. I wasn't there to be a fighter; they use us where they need us. So my job is picking up the dead, taking off dog tags, carrying supplies to the front lines. That is my job."[28]

By day seven, the men of the 9th Marines have passed through the exhausted men of the 21st Marines and taken up their positions on and around the "pool table." Many more Japanese positions are dug in west and north of the runways, especially two rugged hills labeled "199 Oboe" and "Peter." Though Archambault's attack did indeed crack the defensive line, it is not yet broken.

⚔

On the northwest side of the island, the 26th and 27th Regiments of the 5th Division continue their attacks up the long axis of the island. They are bound by the water's edge on the left and the 3rd Division zone on the northern edges of the runways on the right. Each day is more of the same: prep fires to the front; attack as far as possible; dig in when pinned down; and continue to fire on the unseen enemy. At the end of each day, it is dig in for the night or fall back to the original position, depending on the progress of the 3rd Division on the right. The flanks of the attacking divisions are never to be left exposed.

Private Richard Wheeler of the 28th Marines, who had attacked around the base of Suribachi, will later say, "This was surely one of the strangest battlefields in history, with one side fighting wholly above the ground and the other side operating almost wholly within it."[29]

Aerial observers flying above the battlefield rarely if ever see Japanese troops moving above ground. To the southern end of the island, they observe thousands of Marines milling around, moving supplies off the beach, attacking along a line of resistance, or down in foxholes. The other side of the battle line seems deserted.

A captain in the 26th Marines will later say it best: "The Japs weren't *on* Iwo Jima, they were *in* Iwo Jima."[30]

On the western side of the island, Company E, 27th Marines, begins its advance again, keeping pace with the 3rd Division on the left. Jay Rebstock says of the advance that it was "strictly by the book: lay down a base of fire, bring up demolitions and the flamethrower, and destroy the positions; move to the next bunker and repeat all the steps."[31]

It becomes a continuous attack against one series of interlocking pillboxes after another. It is a bizarre existence. On Rebstock's right flank, the world is exploding; on his left, peaceful waves break on sandy beaches. His mind drifts over there for a fleeting moment: "What a marvelous spot it would be to spend a lazy afternoon."[32]

The fantasy shatters as Japanese artillery and mortar fire explode to his front. He aims and fires his BAR into the first strongpoint he sees on his right. The weapon bucks into his shoulder. He fires short bursts to drive the defenders away from the apertures. As he pours fire into the position, he sees his team rush to the flanks of the bunker to secure the area for the flame man to deliver the knockout blow.

Before he can close on the bunker, Japanese gunners knock him down. He increases his fire as a second Marine rushes forward to wrestle the seventy-two-pound weapon off another man's back and sling it onto his shoulders. But as soon as he stands to advance, he is gunned down.

Rebstock screams out at the bastards he can never see but who always see him. He changes magazines, pulls the bolt back, and fires a continuous stream into the entire area around the bunker. A third man now picks up the flamethrower, and as Rebstock fires, he suddenly hears the familiar *whoosh* and sees the blistering orange tongue licking at the rocks and boulders, trying to find the seams that will let it inside. Then the third flame man is hit.

The life expectancy of a flame man is brief. The very sight of him strikes fear and terror into the heart of the enemy, who envisions himself immolated in a fiery hell.

The squad moves forward in a rush, past the smoking position, and is immediately driven back by more small-arms and machine-gun fire. From his pinned-down position, Rebstock can fire only in the direction that other Marines gesture to. He can see nothing, and neither can they. They are firing at the roar of the lion, but the lion remains hidden. They fight this way all day and dig in for the night. They lick their wounds and count their casualties, with no enemy bodies in sight.

On February 25, the word comes down to try something else. The usual morning prep fire drives the Japs underground but also signals that an attack is coming. Today there will be no prep fires and no morning attack; instead, they will attack in the afternoon.

The terrain in front of them is as daunting as any in this fractured geological nightmare. From tip to tip, the island is contorted and scarred. It is death valley. A deep indentation crosses their line of advance and then descends a long slope to a level bottom, exiting on the other side by an equally exposed upward slope. There are no illusions that the advance will not be seen by the enemy. The Japanese defenders have stadium seats to watch the whole maneuver. The Americans' only hope is that a late start may turn the rhythm of battle in their favor.

As morning becomes afternoon, Rebstock and his fellow Marines of Company E nervously check, clean, and oil their weapons over and over—as if there is to be a general's inspection. As attack hour approaches, they exchange silent glances, and at exactly 3:00 p.m., they stand up in their lines.

But Rebstock's feet seem rooted to the ground, and he cannot take one step forward. "I guess that's what's called being scared shitless," he says. "I drank almost an entire canteen of water, and only then did my legs move forward."[33]

The hoped-for surprise, though, is no surprise at all. The line advances no more than fifty yards before its world explodes. Marines dive for cover. Rebstock jumps into a hole with three other men. Japanese bullets ping all around; one of the men in the hole is shot straight through his forehead. A second bullet smacks a man, bores a path between his helmet and liner, and miraculously worms its way around his head and out the other side, leaving him unscathed. Such is the randomness of life and death in battle.

Rebstock curls into the fetal position, sandwiched between the bodies of his squad leader and the dead and wounded. Japanese incoming fire then brackets them and thunders in, hurling shrapnel, stones, and dirt in every direction and partially burying them. No one can move in the eye of the artillery and mortar storm.[34]

Above the din, Rebstock hears the clanking of an approaching armored vehicle; almost on top of him, a US tank unleashes a shot with an earsplitting *boom*. That shot goads the squad leader and Rebstock into action as training wins out over fear. The BAR sends a chatter of rapid fire to the front, the stream highlighted with streaking red tracers.

Through the swirling dust, Rebstock glimpses a newly exposed enemy bunker and bangs away at the aperture. Other men creep forward as he changes magazines and targets the narrow slit. To his right he sees his friend Private First Class Leonard Nederveld moving up, clutching a white phosphorous grenade. He moves in low to the right side of the bunker, hoping for a chance to hurl it in and let its thick white smoke blind the gunners, providing cover for the pinned-down Marines.

Nederveld has seen a second opening in the bunker and under cover of Rebstock's constant fire charges the bunker and lobs the grenade in. He races back to his original position as the Marines around the bunker look on. Seconds later, they hear the soft explosion of the grenade. They wait for the choking smoke to pour out of the openings. All weapons are aimed to engage any Japanese who might bolt from the position to escape.

Instead, there is an enormous explosion, as if five hundred pounds of TNT have detonated. A shock wave emanates from the obliterated bunker, and thick smoke hovers over the battlefield. The concussion rips the Browning from Rebstock's hands and flattens him into his hole. Nederveld's grenade has found an ammunition dump; it explodes in rippling echoes.

Gathering his wits, Rebstock crawls out and stands to search for his weapon, but before he can find it, another giant explosion drives him back. The tank, which has taken a direct hit from the Japanese artillery, is engulfed in fire and smoke. The tank and the Japanese bunker detonate in dueling explosions as the ammunition cooks off.

It is over, and a strange silence settles over this tiny part of the battlefield. The ferocity and savagery have peaked and can no longer sustain themselves.

Dazed Marines rise as if from the dead, stagger around in a fog. Rebstock finds his broken weapon and swings it by its barrel, smashing it against a boulder. He replaces it with one from a fallen comrade nearby. Then someone calls out to return to the jump-off point, and the men of Company E stagger back, carrying their latest sixteen casualties.[35]

That night they shiver in the pouring rain, cursing the island and their bad luck of being on it. The next day, D + 7, comes and goes. A resupply of ammunition is brought forward, followed by the arrival of replacement troops.

They are told to stay in their holes, which they gladly do. In the late afternoon, they are alerted to the sight of a Japanese soldier crawling toward their lines. Rebstock trains his weapon on the man, who alternately crawls, stops, raises his hand, and crawls forward again.

As he approaches the line, someone realizes that the pathetic figure is not a Japanese soldier at all but a Marine. Rebstock yells for everyone to hold fire. He goes out and grabs the man under his arms, dragging him into their lines. Almost unrecognizable, his face caked in grime and mud, is Private Nederveld. Knocked senseless by the explosion created by his well-placed grenade, he has been trying for hours to get back to his men.[36]

"We were pulled out of the line because of our depleted numbers, and sent to the rest area in the rear," Rebstock says. "The rest area turned out to be anything but R&R." On the first night, Japanese artillery strikes the 5th Division ammo dump, igniting it in a spectacular series of explosions, not unlike the one Rebstock and the men came from.

The next day, they refurbish their arms and equipment, and each man is given a satchel charge and sent to the mountain. For the next six days, Company E is to clean the Japanese out of the caves of Suribachi or seal them in forever. "R&R," Rebstock says, "was killing more Japs!"[37]

✕

In the center of the island, the 9th Marines prepare to continue the attack initiated by the 21st. Resupply of the front lines continues by all possible means. Harry, Warren, Herman, Charlie, George, and the others trudge forward. After dark, when the Japanese observers cannot see, is the best time. Striking a match will guarantee incoming mortar fire.

Even so, along the Motoyama 2 runway, long after dark, two swinging flashlights appear like beacons in the night. Their beams play along the cratered runway, illuminating a path for a noisy bulldozer pulling a much needed, overloaded trailer of supplies.

A sergeant shakes his head and says with a laugh to those nearby, "In a lotta ways, you gotta be crazy to be in the Marine Corps."[38] The bulldozer and its men carry out their death-defying, heroic night duty.

Even on this desolate island, eventually, mercifully, there is mail call. For some, there might be a dozen letters at a time. At home, fathers, some of whom fought in World War I, encourage their daughters to write to the boys from their high school, knowing how much a letter will mean to them. Parents, aunts, uncles, and neighbors relate news from home, transporting the men, for a few moments, back to the place where things are predictable and sweet. There is no better sound than "Mail call! Colburn! Gray!"

George Colburn: "We all find a spot to open our letters and read them, and then we read them all over again and again. If your buddy didn't get a letter, you'd give him yours to read."[39]

At home in Massachusetts, George's mother, Mary Ellen Colburn, and Anne Gray let each other know every time a V-mail drops through the mail slot. They are searching for clues to where their boys might be. For a time, Harry put a middle initial into his mother's name to let her know: "Anne G. Gray," for Guam, for instance. But for whatever reason, from Iwo Jima he tells it to her straight:

Dear Mom and family,

How is everyone? I'm fine except a slight cold which I should be rid of soon. I suppose you are wondering where I am. Well the place is Iwo. I have been here a week and believe me it is no picnic. I am praying to get off this place and soon; but it looks like another week yet.

I have not been to the front lines yet but it sure has been hot where I am. The first few days I was dodging mortar shells and artillery every minute, but now it seems to be mostly over. Our Marine artillery is firing over our heads continually; right now it is bang and whistling of shells.

Two other fellows and myself are in a hole and you can bet it is very secure. We have worked hard on it by putting bags all around and on the roof. We had one air raid and Mom you can bet I was plenty scared. The living conditions are good and the chow is surprisingly good and plenty of it.

I can only write one letter a day so please tell Dot I'll write her tomorrow. Please don't worry as everything is under control. Well Mom I will go into it about this place later and will write every chance I get. Bob and George [Colburn] are here.

All my love,
Harry.[40]

The next morning is the dawn of another gray day on Iwo Jima. So far, there has been no other kind. The cold sweeps off the deep blue-black water and right inside Harry's uniform, sending a chill up his back as he looks across the crates of ammo and the tarps blowing in the wind on the beach. Another day is spent taking supplies to the front, dodging mortars, eating chow, and counting the days until they can get off this island and onto the next one. The worst duty is carrying the stretchers, taking the dead men to the beach, sorting their equipment, putting their helmets into piles, emptying their ammo, and putting it with the rest. There are hundreds of them, rolled in ponchos lined up on the beach. Then there are the hollers of "Corpsman! Corpsman!" coming from the front lines. Harry picks up one end of a stretcher; the wounded man on it clutches his gushing shiny red wound, trying to hold in what is torn and keep it intact; sometimes he is silent, sometimes he cries out, he wants his mother, he wants his wife, he wants to go home. Harry, too, desperately wants to go home. He's four months shy of nineteen, and he hopes to make it back by his birthday on June 13.

He can see it now: He will step off the train in Boston, and Dorothy will be there. He will be wearing a clean uniform, not this stinking set of herringbone twill utility stiff-caked with sweat and dust that he's had on his back for ten days. He will spin her around and say, "You didn't get married while I was gone, did you?," and she will laugh. "No, Harry, I did not get married. I was waiting for you, silly." They will have tears in their eyes, from smiling so hard. He will love every smell and sight in good ol' Arlington, where everything will look just as it always has, where they will get married and have two kids of their own, a boy and a girl.

He looks out at the beach, at the wreckage and the carnage. How will he ever explain to Mom and Uncle Frank and Nancy what he has done and seen?

He jolts back as a bang and then a whistle signal mortars toward the beach. He tucks in his chin and takes off in a low run to find cover in a crater. He lies flat, pressing his body in as deeply as he can, his rifle over his shoulder, as Herman Graeter, his foxhole buddy from

Ohio, dives in next to him. Harry shakes a bit and looks at the cold sky as shell fragments fly over his head.

That night, after a long afternoon of hauling supplies and men, they climb under the sandbag roof and back into their foxhole. Harry whispers, "Pop, you sleep, I'll watch!" Charlie Gubish closes his eyes, but the truth is that he can't relax. He worries that if he falls asleep, Harry will fall asleep, too, and then all of them in the foxhole will get killed. Charlie rests his eyes and listens to Warren and Harry quiz each other on chemistry questions. He has no idea why they do this, except that Harry is always calling Warren "College Boy" and testing his smarts. Charlie was done with school at age twelve, but he has the wisdom of his twenty-four years. They have lived a lifetime in the past months together. Charlie says they are all "good buddies." George says it's more than that, they are "closer than brothers." On the ship, they played endless rounds of pinochle, but here it's difficult to play cards. Herman Graeter is asleep now. Charlie drifts off. He wakes with a start to a sound. But it is nothing. He hears Harry and Warren quietly talking again; this time it is about home. Charlie squints through one eye under his helmet; Harry has his leather wallet out as he once again shows Warren the pictures of Dot and Nancy and his mom.

)(

On February 28, at his desk in Peekskill, New York, Frank Bowes takes out a pen to write a letter to Harry. He has been reading the accounts of Iwo Jima in the *New York Times* and looking at the photographs, captioned "Suribachi Reached in a Fiery Battle," "Wrecked and Abandoned Landing Craft Litter Iwo Beaches," and "Marines in the Final Mop-up Operations on Iwo Island." He scans the photos for a glimpse of his nephew. He puts another clipped-out article into the scrapbook he is keeping for Harry. "Blood Boats Went with Iwo Invaders," it reads. "For the first time in the Pacific war . . . blood has gone along on a special craft on an invasion with the men whose lives it is destined to save."[41]

He writes:

Dear Harry,

You can be sure we are all wondering what the story on you and the 3rd Division is as we are reading the news in the paper. It is hard to believe that you are tossed into one of the worst battles for the first experience. According to the paper it is certainly pretty bad and we are praying that you get through it OK and live to tell the story. We are anxious to hear from you whenever you can write. I had a letter from Grandma yesterday and she said they hadn't heard from you for three weeks. You were no doubt always pretty busy prior to the invasion. I am going over to Arlington Saturday, for a meeting in the office, Mon. Tues. Wed, so I will visit with the folks and have a good talk. You can imagine how your Mom must be worrying, but all Mothers are like that. I am having a hunch you will make it OK. It will be awful rough, but you have the courage kid and we have no doubt about that. Say a prayer when things look bad and we are praying also. Good luck and write when you can.

Uncle Frank

Now the men of the 1st Battalion, 9th Marines, of which Gray, Gubish, Graham, Graeter, and Colburn are a part, stare down the eastern end of Motoyama 2 and prepare to assault the menacing high ground just to the north: Hills 199 Oboe and Peter.

Dominick Grossi, like so many other injured Marines, has made it back from the hospital ship, after insisting to the doctors that he will return to the front lines. A surgeon, Lieutenant Evans, writes about these men:

We had 375 patients through here yesterday, to give you an idea. I've seen all the war surgery I want for a while. . . . They come in with wounds that make you sick to look at, and all they want to do is "Get back at those sons of bitches." You tell them they must be evacuated and they cry.[42]

The attack begins with two battalions abreast. The jump-off point is south of both runways and requires a double crossing of the pavement to advance toward the objectives.[43] Twenty-six tanks of the 3rd Tank Battalion support the assault.

At 9:30 a.m., the tanks crawl onto the southernmost runway and head north with three tanks of Company A in the lead: *Ateball*, *Agony*, and *Angel*. But they don't make it even to the second runway crossing before *Agony* and *Angel* explode in flames. *Ateball* is hit by a high-velocity shell and stopped in its tracks. Japanese gunners fire down the flat runways, unobstructed.

The 9th Marines press forward against murderous fire, but at the end of a five-hour fight, it has little to show for its mounting casualties. The 1st Battalion manages to advance only a hundred yards to the base of Hill Peter, and the 2nd Battalion just makes it across the double runway.[44] Nine tanks are lost.

The next day is more of the same, and after a little progress is

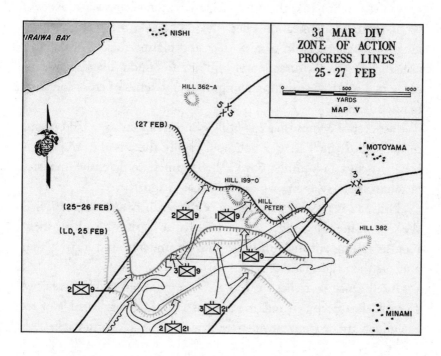

made in the morning, the Marines pause while the artillery fires a ten-minute saturating barrage onto the two hills. As soon as the fire lifts, the 1st Battalion rises and swarms over Hill Peter and then over Hill 199 Oboe to the north while the 2nd Battalion advances a dramatic fifteen hundred yards.[45]

On D + 8, Motoyama 2 is in the Marines' hands, and General Kuribayashi's main line has been completely breached. But the casualties are devastating. Jim Lucas, a veteran Marine correspondent, who witnessed the carnage at Tarawa, writes, "It was bad there, but it was all over in seventy-two hours. This bastardly battle goes on and on from one ridge to another. When will it end? And will anybody be alive when it does?"[46]

Harry Gray's buddy Private George Colburn will later say, "After the flag was raised on Suribachi, it was all a horror from there on out. The Japanese were everywhere in caves below us. We were just picking up bodies all the time. We paid an awful price for that island."[47]

On the right flank, the 4th Marine Division slugs away at its own set of Japanese fortifications, described as a "volcanic area [that] is a tangled conglomeration of torn trees and blasted rocks . . . crevices radiat[ing] from the direction of Hill 382 to fan out like spokes generally in a southeasterly direction providing a series of cross corridors to our advance."[48]

Just east of Motoyama 2 is Hill 382; to the south is a bald prominence called the Turkey Knob; and finally there is the Amphitheater, a rocky, stadiumlike bowl. This triumvirate defensive monster becomes collectively known as "the Meat Grinder."

Hill 382 is the most menacing of them all. After Suribachi, it is the second highest point, and General Kuribayashi's men have spent months toiling within, turning it into an underground fortress that anchors their right flank.[49]

Intelligence describes the hill as "a complicated mass of crevices, 15 to 50 feet deep . . . making it a bastion of defense capable of receiving an attack from any quarter. The crevices are worm-eaten with caves."[50] To guard all natural approaches, the Japanese have buried their tanks up to the turrets.

The three positions are mutually supporting, and defeating them will require simultaneously attacking all. They stand between the Marines and the ocean at the end of the island, and on Iwo Jima, the way to victory is through the Meat Grinder. For two vicious and bloody weeks, from February 25 to March 10, the three regiments of the 4th Division hurl themselves against the bulwarks. On Hill 382, the initial attempt appears to go well, and the 23rd Marines easily gains the summit, but it is a mirage; the men are jammed back to the base of the hill under a shroud of murderous fire and artillery.

The next day sees an act of gallantry almost beyond description. As elements of the 3rd Battalion attempt to seize the summit of Hill 382, a machine-gun burst strikes and kills a bazooka man. Reacting immediately, nineteen-year-old Private First Class Douglas T. Jacobson, a veteran of Saipan, picks up the bazooka and a satchel full of rockets and explosives and races forward. Weaving and zigzagging, he approaches the bunker containing the 20 mm gun and knocks it out with an explosive charge. His Congressional Medal of Honor citation reads:

> [H]e first destroyed two hostile machine-gun positions, then attacked a large blockhouse, completely neutralizing the fortification before dispatching the five-man crew of a second pillbox and exploding the installation with a terrific demolitions blast. Moving steadily forward, he wiped out an earth-covered rifle emplacement and . . . quickly reduced . . . six [more] positions to a shambles, killed 10 of the enemy, and enabled our forces to occupy the strongpoint. Determined to widen the breach thus forced, he volunteered his services to an adjacent assault company, neutralized a pillbox holding up its advance, opened fire on a Japanese tank pouring a steady stream of bullets on one of our supporting tanks, and smashed the enemy tank's gun turret in

a brief but furious action culminating in a singlehanded assault against still another blockhouse and the subsequent neutralization of its firepower. By his dauntless skill and valor, Pfc. Jacobson destroyed a total of 16 enemy positions and annihilated approximately 75 Japanese.[51]

Still, Hill 382 will not succumb, and at 4:30 p.m., the attack is called off, to be resumed the next day. The day has cost the Marines 512 casualties. As the days drag on, the story at the Meat Grinder remains the same: furious Marine attacks against a hail of fire delivered by unyielding, immovable Japanese defenders. Gains are measured in yards; sometimes there are no gains at all. A division officer will later report, "The enemy was determined to deny us Hill 382, and his unusually heavy mortar barrage on it twice forced our troops to retire after having occupied the hill area."[52]

Gradually, though, the Marines' battering ram begins to take a toll: the Japanese wall starts to splinter. On Hill 382, defensive positions are beaten down, incinerated, or exploded. On D + 12, March 3, it, too, is finally in Marine hands.

But six hundred yards to the south, the Turkey Knob and the Amphitheater are still in play. The massive blockhouse near the Turkey Knob is pounded daily, to little avail. The 4th Division is able to sweep forward around the two defensive positions, leaving a huge gap in the Japanese defensive line.[53]

On March 9, the Japanese defenders leave their positions and launch an ill-fated counterattack to break out. In the end, the Marines count 800 enemy dead.

On March 10, the two positions, surrounded and cut off from support, fall. The eastern end of the island is now in sight. The 4th Division's bloody two-week attack has cost 4,000 Marine casualties, including 450 dead.[54]

In the 3rd Division zone on the Motoyama Plateau, the Marines have overrun the incomplete airfield number 3 and at last are advancing toward the end of their long road, the eastern coast. No one knows

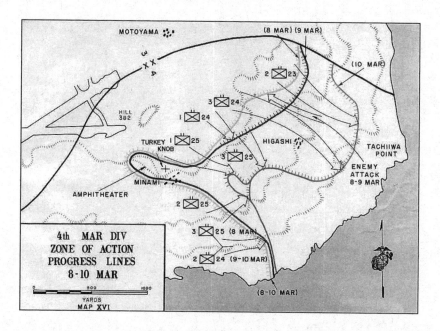

MAP XVI

what day it is, but it is Thursday, March 8, and the sun is peeking out for the first time in many days. The Marine line occupies the cliffs overlooking the sea, and a reconnaissance patrol, including Woody Williams, walks the hill down to the edge of the sand and scoops up ocean water in a canteen, proof that they have finally come to the end of the island. It is sent back to the corps commander, Major General Harry Schmidt, with a note: "For inspection, not consumption."[55]

But the heroic Dominick Grossi does not make it to the eastern shore. As he and his men attempt to move down the hill overlooking the beach, his unit comes under heavy flanking fire. The second lieutenant, Navy Cross recipient, and football star from Lockport, New York, is hit in the chest and torso, killed on the hill leading down to the sea.

Days before, he tucked this letter into the outgoing mailbag:

Dearest Mother,
I'm still on Iwo Jima and am well. Our leave from here has been delayed a couple of days. I'll write again as soon as I hit my base.

Give my love to all. Remember I love you all so much. Don't worry
The Lord will see me through.

Your son,
Dom xxx

"By evening of 10 March, except for the enemy pocket which held out for six more days . . . the 3d Division's zone of action up the center of the island was clear."[56] That holdout area, a thousand yards back from the island's east coast, is called "Cushman's Pocket" after the commander of the 2nd Battalion, 9th Marines, Lieutenant Colonel Robert E. Cushman, Jr., whose troops assailed it. It is a hornet's nest.

※

The 5th Marine Division smashes its way forward on the western side. The final fighting is in the badlands area known as the Bloody Gorge. The final Japanese defensive line is here, at the northeastern end of the island.

The division's report describes the situation: "The Japs were now cornered in a pocket of resistance approximately 200–500 yards wide and 700 yards long. This was a rocky gorge for the most part with precipitous sides. Scattered through this gorge there was a series of jagged rocky outcrops which were in effect minor gorges."[57]

The men of Company E, 27th Marines, including Private Jay Rebstock, move up onto the final ridgeline and stare down into the canyon below. Rebstock can see the rocky rim on the opposite canyon wall and the Marines there looking back at him. The last Japanese defenders are in between them, in the deep ravine below. Company E no longer resembles the company that landed on D-Day. Most of its men are new.

Rebstock will later count the faces of the men he has known for months. There are only thirty-one of them. There is a thirty-second man who is the only replacement left from the fifty that were sent up to the company.[58]

All the rifle companies are skeletons of what they once were. Company I, 24th Marines, has only 9 left of the 133 that landed. Company D, 26th Marines, has only 17 out of 250. Company B, 28th Marines, has gone through 9 company commanders. Seven hundred Marines have died for every square mile of Iwo Jima[59]—almost 7,000 men, with another 19,000 wounded.

Rebstock is an aberration. He is one of the very few who landed on D-Day and managed to stay on his feet for the entire thirty-six-day bloodbath. As he stands on that final ridgeline, the end is in sight. He makes sure he teams up with another veteran who knows the ropes. He can see the ocean to the northeast, and no one wants to be the last man killed. "The casualty rate among the new men was horrific," he will later say. "Without experience, they fell at an alarming rate. . . . They were cannon fodder."[60]

One of the Marines on the ridgeline slowly descends to the bottom of the gorge while everyone else watches, weapons at the ready. As he reaches the bottom, a sniper's shot rings out, and the man falls dead. A Japanese defender comes out, waving his hands over his head, but the Marines cut him down. A second one comes out, holding something under his arm, and despite a command to hold fire, the Marines pour down fire from above.

"I put my weapon down," Rebstock will later say. "I just couldn't kill anymore."[61]

※

In the center, the Japanese stronghold at Cushman's Pocket remains rock solid with tunneled caves and hundreds of spider traps. It bristles with an assortment of weapons, including the tanks dug into their turrets.

In an attempt to batter the stronghold into submission, four 7.2-inch rocket launchers, mounted on sleds, are towed into position by armored dozers. Each launcher has twenty rocket tubes capable of delivering a barrage of twenty rockets at a time into the pocket, equivalent to 640 pounds of TNT.[62]

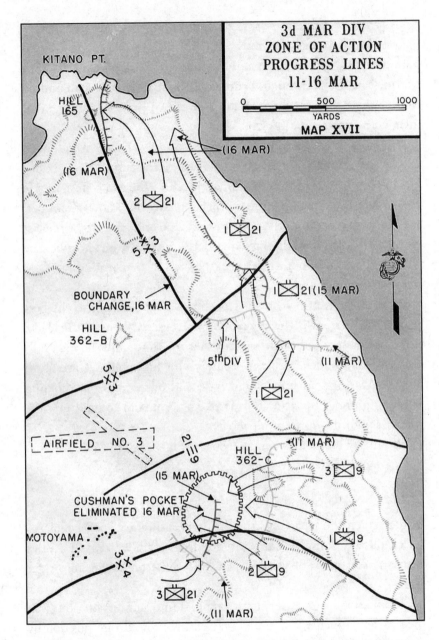

Early on the morning of March 11, these four launchers begin to hurl a combined, earsplitting ten barrages into Cushman's Pocket—more than three tons of explosives. When the smoke finally clears, the three Marine battalions attack from the west and south but make only incremental gains. The Japanese return fire keeps coming, the resistance as deadly as ever.[63]

On the rest of the island, there are pockets of calm in the rhythms of the battle and the routine of supplying the lines allow for small moments of normalcy, even fun. As Charlie, Herman, and Harry walk back from an ammo drop, there is a feeling that the end is near. Harry's steps are light as he runs up a rocky outcrop that has rebar and cement strewn about. "Hey, guys, come here!" With one hand on the top of the abandoned Japanese cave, he pops his head below for a look. "There's a bunch of Jap rifles in there. C'mon! We are going to take these home. We need to bring something back, or even we will never believe we were here."

Charlie warns him that they could be booby-trapped, and tells Harry to back away from the opening. Charlie fires a few rounds to be sure. They all stand looking in for a moment. Nothing in there, nothing alive anyway. Harry laughs and skips down inside. He gathers up the Japanese rifles and hands one to each of the guys. They turn them around, open them up, and inspect them to see what they feel like in their hands. It feels good to hold enemy weapons, inert and powerless, their owners no longer a threat. Harry later writes:

March 12, 1945

Dear Mom,

I suppose you are worried to death over me. Well I am in the best of health and feeling fine with the exception of a few scares. I told you I would write before but I really didn't have a chance. Also, I wrote another letter but couldn't mail it. Tell P.F. I got one for him. Also, tell Joe I have a couple of swell letters for him, but I couldn't mail them yet.

I have received quite a bit of mail from you, Nanc, Gram, Dorothy and Uncle Frank, but I also lost quite a bit of it. Haven't had any for 5 days.

I saw George C[olburn] yesterday and he is fine as far as I know. I haven't seen Bob since we left Guam and I am quite worried about him. The chow is pretty good mom as we eat C-Rations which fill me up pretty well. The weather is quite chilly here and haven't seen an all blue sky all day since I have been here.

Mom will you please buy Dot a nice corsage for Easter and have the tag say "To My Sweetheart with all my love, Harry." I will send five dollars to you.

Hope everyone, and everything is fine.

Love, your son,
Harry

The next morning, Harry, Herman, Warren, Charlie, and George shake off sleep and eat their breakfast, which has been warmed by an ingenious method of burying pots of coffee and eggs in the ground, where the sulfuric steam heats them, making them sort of, almost hot. They grab their rifles and head toward the resupply area up at Motoyama 2 airfield.

There is a bit of a lull, and they lie on their backs, shooting the breeze, waiting for the call. About an hour later they hear "Gubish, Graeter, Gray, Graham! Up to headquarters!" They look at one another and jump up, scrambling out of the crater they've been lounging in. "See ya, George!" Harry says, smiling back at his buddy from Medford, Massachusetts. George will later say, "I'll never forget that."[64]

They head up to the ammo dump at the front line. They will carry ammo and bring stretchers back. They know the drill. There is a line of nineteen men; Gray, Gubish, and Graeter are up front, and Graham is near the end of the line. George ends up joining the back of the line as well.

Charlie says, "We are supposed to go to the relieving outfit, to give them a break. And as we're marching, the mortars are coming from over there to the street. Nobody pays attention. We think they are ours. Then there is one on this side, the same distance, then I know it's coming from the other side. It's enemy fire, and I holler to Gray and Graeter, 'Hit the deck!' and I lay alongside of an engine, and that's when we got it. I see them laying there as sure as Christ, they got us right in the middle.

"Gray is hit direct. When I see him, he's bleeding from his head. He and Herman are both dead."

Nearly seventy-five years later, recalling this, Charlie stops. He's crying. "Graeter, the concussion killed him. I was knocked out, too, but I survived. But I still got shrapnel here. But Graeter, he only had a shrapnel in his leg. He would've lived but for the concussion, because it's that strong, it just kills you. Then I was out, I don't know how long. But then a corpsman passed by me. He was treating some of the others, and then he sees me standing up. He comes running back. He says, 'I thought you were dead!' I couldn't talk, I was in shock, but I saw Graeter and Gray laying there. And then I was crying. Then he saw that I was putting my hand over my left chest and he saw blood coming out of my fingers, so he pushed my hand down, he cut my jacket open, he put a compress on me. I'm still carrying that shrapnel in me today, I still have it in there. But Gray and Graeter, they lost their lives.

"It is a shame. We were great buddies. What are you going to do? War is war."[65]

Three days later, March 16, Cushman's Pocket is eliminated. At 6:00 p.m., after thirty-six days of hell, the volcano island of Iwo Jima is declared secure. By now, thanks to the Seabees, the runways are repaired and redone; B-29s have been landing, being repaired, and taking off again ever since the first one, the *Dinah Might*, came in on March 4. The landing stopped everyone in his tracks that day; the men marveled at the beautiful, lumbering aircraft as it touched down, and then they went back to clearing caves.

Their way of life on the island, to the extent that it exists, is shattered again on March 26. In a final spasm of death, 300 Japanese soldiers silently infiltrate from their defensive positions in the north and fall upon a tent city bivouac of the 5th Pioneer Battalion just off the edge of Motoyama 1. It is occupied by newly arrived Army pilots of the VII Fighter Command, who are to fly air cover for the B-29s flying north. While the men are sleeping, they are brutally attacked with grenades, swords, and automatic weapons in a violent and deadly last gasp. The Marines grab their weapons and engage in an hours-long defense. The only Marines besides the 5th Pioneer Battalion who stand between the attacking Japanese forces and the American airmen are members of the 36th Marine Depot Company and the 8th Marine Ammunition Company, both of 8th Field Depot. These are the African American units, known as the Montford Point Marines. The men served at the supply hub on the beach under Colonel Leland Swindler. The colonel integrated his beach-landing parties. Black and white Marines under Swindler worked side by side. In the last battle on Iwo Jima, as the banzai charge tore through the camp, they fought and died side by side. Two of these brave men received Bronze Stars for their heroism.[66] Corporal Archibald Mosley remembers, "The bullets didn't have color codes on them. I was more proud to have served under Colonel Swindler than if I had been tasked with raising the flag on Suribachi all by myself."[67] When the fighting ends, the 300 men of General Kuribayashi's last combat force are dead. It is said by Japanese survivors that he led the raid. His body is never found.

One hundred pilots and Seabees are killed in the last battle of Iwo Jima; two hundred more are wounded.[68]

The overall toll of Iwo Jima is ghastly: 6,800 Marines are dead, among them Harry Gray of Arlington, Massachusetts, and Herman Graeter of Dayton, Ohio, both eighteen years old; and Dominick Grossi of Lockport, New York, who was twenty-four. Nearly 20,000 are wounded, including Warren Graham and Charlie Gubish, who will spend weeks recovering in Guam. Only George Colburn is left. He remembers waiting in line for chow with the remaining men during the packing up. He hears someone yell, "What day is it?" The date is something none of them had thought of for days and days. But someone else hollers, "March 29!" George looks up and around, at the men on either side of him. "March 29? That's my birthday!" George Colburn has just turned nineteen.

When the ships come to take the last Marines away from Iwo Jima, the men gather at the 5th Marine Division cemetery for a last memorial service. A Jewish chaplain, Lieutenant Roland B. Gittelsohn, says this:

Here before us lie the bodies of comrades and friends. Men who until yesterday or last week laughed with us, joked with us, trained with us. Men who were on the same ships with us, and went over the sides with us as we prepared to hit the beaches of this island. Men who fought with us and feared with us. . . .

Some of us have buried our closest friends here. We saw these men killed before our very eyes. Any one of us might have died in their places. Indeed, some of us are alive and breathing at this very moment only because the men who lie here beneath us had the courage and strength to give their lives for ours. To speak in memory of such men as these is not easy. Of them too it can be said with utter truth: "The world will little note nor long remember what we say here. It can never forget what they did here."[69]

On March 26, 1945, the day that Iwo Jima is declared secured, the doorbell rings at 17 Linwood Street in Arlington. Anne is at work, and Harry's Grandma Bowes answers the door. She reluctantly takes the envelope. The delivery boy bows his head and turns down the steps. As she opens it, her eyes scan and fall on the only three words that matter: DEEPLY. REGRET. KILLED. She slides down into the hall chair and weeps.

DEEPLY REGRET TO INFORM YOU THAT YOUR SON PRIVATE HARRY E GRAY USMCR WAS KILLED IN ACTION 13 MARCH 1945 AT IWO

JIMA VOLCANO ISLANDS IN THE PERFORMANCE OF HIS DUTY AND
SERVICE OF HIS COUNTRY. WHEN INFORMATION IS RECEIVED RE-
GARDING BURIAL YOU WILL BE NOTIFIED.

TO PREVENT POSSIBLE AID TO OUR ENEMIES DO NOT DIVULGE
THE NAME OF HIS SHIP OR STATION. PLEASE ACCEPT MY HEART-
FELT SYMPATHY. LETTER FOLLOWS=

AA VANDEGRIFT LIEUT GENERAL USMC COMMANDANT OF THE
MARINE CORPS.

Nancy skips up the front steps and opens the door. Her grandmother looks up at her, eyes red and worn. There is a telegram on her
lap. Nancy doesn't know what to say or do. She is fourteen, and she
does not believe the news. It simply cannot be. There is some mistake.
Harry is so alive. He just wrote to them that he would be home soon
and to buy an Easter flower for Dot! But her grandmother is so very
sad. Nancy sits in shock and then falls onto the sofa. Her face pressed
into the cushion, she dissolves into tears. As she cries, she remembers
that the night before, she dreamed this moment. She dreamed that
Harry had been killed.

The neighbors have gone to get Anne at work. How to be the mes-
sengers who tell a mother that her son is gone? How many such mes-
sengers, by the thousands, across the country, are walking up front
steps, finding fathers and mothers at work, knocking on doors?

The priest comes. Anne wrestles the waves of grief; grief is an anvil
on her chest, shock leaves her struggling to breathe, disbelief tries to
poke holes in grief and shock. How can this be? Junior, her light, her
only boy, the one who was going to take care of her one day? He is
so alive. How can he be dead? The priest sits next to her. Bible on his
lap, he reads to her from the Song of Solomon: "Set me as a seal upon
your heart, as a seal upon your arm, for love is as strong as death." She
stares ahead in shock.

In Peekskill, Helen Bowes hangs up the phone and hangs her
head. She seats eleven-year-old Betts at the dinner table. Her little girl
knows that something is very wrong. Frank comes in the front door,

and Helen greets him with a kiss. She takes his black hat and gray coat; she is shaking. She wants him to sit and eat. She cannot bring herself to say the words. They sit at the table, and for a moment, it hangs all over the room. In the dreadful silence, Frank looks into his wife's eyes, which are now filled with tears. He puts his head in his hands. His shoulders begin to shake as he is overcome with sorrow. He pushes away from the table and goes to sit in his chair in the living room. Still no one has spoken a word. What is there to say? Harry is not ever coming home.

Two weeks later, Anne writes this letter:

Dear Frank and Helen,

I received your very lovely letter Helen, and I certainly appreciate all that you folks, your friends and the Nuns and girls have done spiritually for my little boy. I find it extremely difficult to be resigned to what God has permitted to happen to my son, but as life must go on, I will begin again.

I am going back to the office tomorrow and Nancy is starting her weeks vacation so she will be company for Mother another week.

Our friends have all been most kind and thoughtful and sometimes I wonder why I have deserved so much. Junior has received about 200 individual masses, 9 yearly enrollments and 4 perpetual enrollments.

Mother is getting along pretty well considering the terrible shock she has had. Nancy's friends and activities have kept her from thinking too much. We all have a long hard road ahead and I hope that God will help us to keep going.

Hope you all are well.

Love from,
Anne

These letters arrive for Anne Gray and Frank Bowes in the weeks that follow:

April 26, 1945, Central Pacific

Dear Mrs. Gray,

This is about the fifth letter I have started. I can't seem to put into writing just what I want to say. Harry and I were great buddies. It seemed we went every place together. We used to love to talk about home. He told me quite a bit about you, his little sister, and his girl, Dot.

I was with him up on Iwo Jima. I was also with him the day it happened. Harry was hit by a mortar shell, which killed three others. I'm sure he was killed instantly and there was no pain. He was wearing his rosary beads around his neck when it happened, and I'm sure he went to heaven. Harry was a very brave kid.

Well, Mrs. Gray I hope this letter makes you feel better. Oh, one more thing we (some more of Harry's buddies and myself) made a little gravestone and set it on his grave. It read, "Another Marine, from your buddies."

I'd like very much to hear from you, if you'd care to drop me a line. Until I hear from you then I'll say goodbye.

> *Sincerely,*
> *Harry's buddy George*

Friday, May 17, 1945

Dear Mrs. Gray,

My name is probably unfamiliar to you. I doubt Harry ever mentioned me in his letters to you, but I was almost constantly with him ever since Camp Lejeune. I liked Harry from the first day at Lejeune; he was always full of pranks and not afraid of the consequences. He was usually the leader in these undertakings, I tagged along.

I soon learned of his home, his mother and his sweetheart. He used to tell me how he sneaked the car without your knowledge. I remember Dot's name very clearly of the pictures of sweethearts in our group, hers always received the longest admiration. He told of his plans to marry her when he returned.

Harry and I were together in a beach party on Iwo Jima, sleeping in the same foxhole. We didn't have much time for horseplay but at night, we really carried on some intelligent conversations. He was always trying to catch me on questions about chemistry and physics because I was a "Rebel" who had been to college. It was there in the fox hole, just before going to sleep, that he talked of you and Dot. From listening to him, I could almost feel his love and desire to live up to the ideals that you had ingrained in him.

We stayed on the beach until March 7th and then moved up to the second airfield, we stayed there five days, helping to deliver ammo to the dump that was near the front lines, on the morning of March 13th, Harry and I were sent to the dump to carry ammunition and be stretcher-bearers. We arrived there about 8 o'clock and lounged around for about an hour waiting for a call. At 9 o'clock, 19 of us started out single file, each with a case of ammunition for the front lines. We were about a hundred yards from the dump when some Jap mortars landed. The first two shells were off but the third one landed near the lead of the column. I don't remember much after that and I didn't learn that Harry had been killed until I was back on Guam. A friend (Charlie) who was also wounded by the same mortar told me that Harry died almost instantly. I shall always remember Harry for his manliness and courage. I give credit to you, Mrs. Gray, for such a wonderful son, must have had a wonderful and courageous Mother.

Sincerely,
Warren Graham

May 27, 1945

Dear Uncle Frank,

Although, I've never met you, Harry told me much about you. I guess you were sort of like a father to him after his father died.

I met Harry coming overseas on the boat. Bob, Harry and I went swimming together on Eniwetok island in the Marshalls. We were great buddies, it seems we went every place together

Your right it was a job writing to his mother. But it had to be done. Harry was up the front only one day when he got hit. Like I said in my letter to Mrs. Gray, Harry was hit by a mortar shell and was killed instantly.

We left for Iwo together. I guess we were all pretty scared. He's buried in the third division cemetery on Iwo. There's a lot of things I'd like to tell you but I can't say in a letter. Maybe I'll get a chance to see you next time I'm home, and we'll talk it over. Drop me a line anytime you get a chance,

Harry's buddy,
George
PFC George J. Colburn 988282

On June 22, 1945, the Battle of Okinawa ends. It has been the largest amphibious assault ever mounted; Army and Marine forces stormed ashore at the end of March and fought for eighty-three days. With death and defeat at their door, the Japanese have mounted banzai-like attacks from the skies, pilots drilling down to crash their planes into US ships, a final sacrifice to the emperor, who demanded their death before their dishonor. The devastating kamikaze attacks have contributed to the losses of 763 US aircraft; the Navy has lost 36 ships, and another 368 have been damaged. Ten thousand sailors have been killed or wounded and 15,000 Marines. Army casualties have totaled another 25,000.[70]

On August 6, 1945, as the United States plans for the invasion of

Japan, Operation Downfall, the B-29 Superfortress *Enola Gay* drops a uranium atomic bomb, *Little Boy*, on the city of Hiroshima. Three days later, on August 9, the B-29 *Bock's Car* drops a plutonium atomic bomb, *Fat Man*, on the city of Nagasaki. The casualties are approximately 135,000 in Hiroshima and 64,000 in Nagasaki.[71]

Ignoring the Potsdam Declaration, which calls for unconditional surrender, Japan vows to fight on, even to the death of its 100 million people. Through back channels, the Truman administration transmits a glimmer of hope, an extraordinary face-saving measure: "The ultimate form of the government of Japan shall, in accordance with the Potsdam Declaration, be established by the freely expressed will of the Japanese people."[72] There will be no deposing of the emperor. Hirohito will live on, and there will be no war crimes trial for the imperial family. The man who orchestrated Japan's expansionist vision and urged his warriors to fight to the death in his honor fights to the bitter end to preserve himself and his family.

Then on August 15, for the very first time, the emperor deigns to speak to the people of Japan. They have never, until this moment, heard his high-pitched voice. They gather around radios all over Japan, as the death tolls from the two atomic bombs rise, and they hear this: "Our Empire accepts the provisions of their Joint Declaration."

The emperor does not concede defeat in his speech but declares that he is acting to save "human civilization" from "total extinction." He says that the original aim of the war he led was national "existence and self-defense."[73]

He finishes with this message, aimed at securing his place in the eyes of the future:

Having been able to safeguard and maintain the structure of the imperial state, we are always with ye, Our good and loyal subjects, relying upon your sincerity and integrity. Beware most strictly of any outbursts of emotion that can engender needless complications. . . . Let the entire nation continue as one family from generation to generation, ever firm in its faith of the

imperishability of its divine land, ever mindful of its heavy burden of responsibilities and of the long road before it.[74]

On September 2, 1945, Hirohito, the only surviving leader of an
Axis power, sends his emissaries to sign the Japanese Instrument of
Surrender. Some of his men are dressed in formal suits and top hats,
others are in their military uniforms. The representatives of the emperor stand in defeat on the deck of the USS *Missouri* in Tokyo Bay.
The decks of the ship are packed from top to bottom and bow to
stern, every inch and rail standing room only, with US military in
crisp uniform craning their necks to witness the historic event. You
can hear a pin drop. At a draped table, the men sign the surrender
documents as the world listens to the twenty-three-minute ceremony.
At 9:08 a.m., General of the Army Douglas MacArthur signs and
accepts the document on behalf of the Allied powers. Admiral of the
Fleet Chester Nimitz signs at 9:12, followed by the representatives of
the Allied powers.

The momentous ceremony over, Frank Bowes, Anne Gray, Patsy
and Lena Grossi, Golda and Herman Graeter, Sr., and other families
in their homes all across America turn off their radios and sit back
in their chairs. They weep for all they have lost. The scars of the war
will never leave them. They are grateful for the sacrifice of so many
Americans who fought to secure our freedom at such an enormous
cost. All the men who make it home carry their own Harrys, Her-
mans, and Doms in their hearts, always feeling that somehow it is
unfair that they themselves got to marry, have children, and have a
life when their buddies, who served with valor known only to those
with whom they were "closer than brothers," did not.

Epilogue

After the war ended, many of the men were shipped back to San Diego. The trains were packed full of people: soldiers and sailors heading home. Charlie Gubish couldn't get onto any of the first trains out, so he stayed an extra night in San Diego and went out for some chili with some of the guys. On the way back, they got involved in a scuffle with some sailors and some girls. It started with someone whistling at one of the girls and ended with a Marine being carted off by the MPs. But Charlie managed to slip out of the melee and spent the night at a YMCA.

A group of them finally got onto a train to Naval Station Great Lakes, near Chicago. There the men were discharged, and after that they had to find their own way home. Charlie made it to Philadelphia, where some of them put their money together and chipped in on a taxi. Charlie arrived at 4:00 a.m., his duffel bag slung over his shoulder. He rapped on the bedroom window to wake up his wife and tell her he had made it home.

Charlie Gubish went back to work at the fire department at Bethlehem Steel. He and Ethel raised their two boys, Charles and Richard, in their home on Mechanic Street. The family vacationed every summer in Atlantic City, New Jersey. Charlie and his brother-in-law, Stevie, liked to go to the racetrack on the weekends and bet on the horses. In 1981, Charlie retired as a captain. He and Ethel became proud grandparents to seven grandchildren, fourteen great-grandchildren, and twelve great-great-grandkids. They had Sheltie dogs, all named Rebel. After Ethel died, Rebel was Charlie's constant companion.

In 2015, Charles Gubish did an interview with a local reporter. He talked about the two buddies who were with him when he was hit. One was Herman Graeter, and the other was a young pal from Boston. At ninety-six, he couldn't remember his name.

Four years later, I connected with a young man through Shayne Jarosz and Raul "Art" Sifuentes at the Iwo Jima Association of America. Dean Laubach is an excellent researcher of all things World War II, and he became my door to a wealth of information. He knew a man named Charlie Gubish, one hundred years old and sharp as a tack, and he quickly figured out that Charlie was wounded the same day that Harry was killed. Although, in their initial conversation, Charlie didn't remember any other details, Dean asked me to send him a picture of Harry on my phone. Dean showed it to him and it stopped Charlie in his tracks. Tears sprung to his eyes and he stopped. "That's Gray. That's my buddy, Gray. He called me Pop."

Days later, I went to sit down with Charlie and he told me all he could remember about that day. Everything about Charlie's story of what happened on March 13, 1945, on Iwo Jima lined up with the accounts of George and Warren in their letters and the USMC records we used to put them all in that column of nineteen men, bringing ammo to the front lines. My aunt Nancy was shocked when I called her to say that I found someone, alive and living in Pennsylvania, who was with her brother when he was killed. Someone who could answer some of the questions she had carried with her, things unanswered by the telegrams and sketchy details from the War Department.

I brought her to meet Charlie; they hugged and she held his hand and they talked about Harry. Charlie shared the stories of their times together, having beers and grabbing Japanese rifles. Nancy showed Charlie the wallet and ID bracelet that had been sent home. Charlie was so glad to see them, amazed that in the chaos that he saw and worked in, anything had ever been recovered.

Charlie was able to share his firsthand account and a side of the "Marine" Harry that the family never really got to see. He described Harry as a "good buddy and very brave."

I am grateful that Charlie survived the mortar attack that day and came home to have a beautiful family. Several of them came to meet us and were part of that emotional reunion.

Like most of the men I've met from World War II, Charlie is humble and proud to have served, and lives daily with the memory of the sacrifice of so many of his buddies who did not make it home.

During the spring of 1945, the Grossi family went through a time when they didn't know if Dominick was alive or dead. Lena Grossi wrote to a friend whose son had also been on Iwo Jima, pleading for any information he might have. He wrote back that Dom had been wounded and evacuated and had returned to battle and been hit. But the young man said he had gone down to the 3rd Marine Division cemetery and could not find Dom's cross there. "Your hope of life for him may be well to hang on to—one really does sometimes make errors, I'm hoping so myself."

But the Grossis would soon receive the telegram that ended those hopes. An outpouring of letters from fellow Marines and friends followed, all praising Dom's kindness and heroism. Sam Ritz wrote, "This is the hardest letter I have had to write since I have been in the service these three years. I know nothing I say can console you, because your loss is so great. Dom was one of the nicest fellows I have ever known and I was always proud to be a friend of his."

James Quinn wrote, "As your boy's Chaplain, I can assure you that every Catholic was well cared for spiritually. Confessions and Communions before combat were 100 percent. In battle many of the men received four or five times. May our Blessed Mother, whose sorrow at witnessing the death of her Son was very great, aid and comfort you in your sorrow at the loss of your son."

Hundreds of people came to Dominick Grossi's funeral Mass in Saint Patrick's in Lockport, New York, to pay their respects.

That August, Lena and Patsy were notified that Dom would be

one of ten Marines to receive the Navy Cross for his selfless acts of heroism on Iwo Jima.

In May 1948, the path was cleared to return the dead from the cemeteries in the Pacific. They made their last voyage home in funeral fleets of white ships, marked from bow to stern with the purple band of mourning, as mandated by President Harry Truman. Their families were given the option of burying their dead at the National Memorial Cemetery of the Pacific in Hawaii, known as "the Punchbowl," or having them sent home for burial.

The ship that carried Dominick Grossi to New York for arrival on May 14, 1948, had a section that carried thirty-seven bodies, sent home in alphabetical order, according to the records kept by the Office of the Quartermaster General. Next to Grossi were the remains of another beloved young man who was headed to Boston, Massachusetts, Harry E. Gray.

Years later, in 2018, Dominick Grossi's niece Nicolena and Harry Gray's niece, the author of this book, had dinner together with their families in Florida. For all the years of my friendship with the Errico family, it wasn't until that night that I learned the story of their relative Second Lieutenant Dominick Grossi. Months later, while researching this book, my eyes fell upon the list of those transported back together that May, Grossi and Gray, side by side.

In Arlington in 1948, Harry's mother, Anne, had dutifully filled out the forms requesting his return. When the train pulled into South Station in Boston carrying Harry's body, Anne was there to receive it. It was the night of Nancy's high school prom, and Anne wanted her to enjoy it, so she had not mentioned where she was heading that afternoon. On the outside of his casket was a metal tag stamped HARRY E GRAY, 565110, USMC. An envelope also arrived with a list of belongings he had had with him and the items themselves: one brown leather wallet with pictures, one signet ring, one ID bracelet. As Anne took them out carefully and looked at the pictures of herself and then of Nancy and Dot, as well as the prayer her boy had so carefully written inside the small booklet, she saw that the things had been with him until the end. They were stained with his blood.

Dorothy did not come to Harry's memorial service or the funeral three years later. Anne and Nancy never knew why. They never saw her again. It always puzzled Nancy why Dorothy didn't come. Perhaps she was angry that Anne had not wanted them to marry, or maybe, at sixteen, the pain was just too much for her to bear. Many years later, Nancy heard that Dorothy had not had an easy life, that she had married shortly after the war and died young.

Harry was buried in a small military section of Arlington Cemetery. Although Anne and Nancy often could not find the words to talk to each other about their grief, they visited his grave together "all the time."

Years later, when the Gerald B. H. Solomon Saratoga National Cemetery was established in New York, Nancy decided she wanted her brother to have the honor of being buried there. Initially, Arlington Cemetery refused the disinterment, saying that, all these years later, they did not know what would be there. Nancy was adamant, replying that "even if it is a shovelful of dirt, I want him in the national cemetery." After fifty-two years and then five months of negotiations, Harry's casket was exhumed and found to be in perfect condition, the identification tag still attached. On May 18, 2000, a memorial Mass was held at Saint Edward the Confessor in Clifton Park, New York, after which there was a final burial with full military honors. My parents, Betty "Betts" Bowes MacCallum and her husband, Doug, were honored to attend.

The obituary of Herman Graeter, Jr., "Dayton Marine Is Killed on Iwo Jima," read, "The action in which he was killed was his first combat operation." He was the only child of Mr. and Mrs. Herman Graeter, Sr. Golda Graeter took on the sorrowful task of correspondence with the military, requesting information about her son and arranging for his burial. In December 1947, Golda wrote under the section titled "Remarks and Additional Instructions," "Would you please inform me if it is possible to visit the present grave of deceased on Iwo Jima, Mrs. Herman Graeter." She received a letter on December 30, advising her that it would not be possible as disinterment operations on the island had ended several months before. She later requested his burial at the National Memorial Cemetery of the Pacific. At home, Golda and Herman Sr. also received the contents of Herman's pockets: one knife, two keys, and an ID bracelet.

Charlie Gubish remembers that the morning they were all hit, Herman had asked him to carry his pocket watch and return it to his dad. Charlie had said, "What are you talking about, Graeter?" Herman had said, "Every day, somebody gets it." "I took it that he thought he was going to get killed. I didn't want to listen to him."[1] It always bothered Charlie that he hadn't taken Herman's watch that day. Later he tried to find Herman's family, to talk to them about it, but he was never successful. There was no pocket watch on the list of Herman's belongings.

George Colburn was sent to China after Iwo Jima, to round up Japanese prisoners from the Rape of Nanking. He was there a year and then got to go home because his mother was ill. He says that Harry Truman saved all their lives when he ordered the bombs to be dropped.

As George had promised, he went to see Harry's mom when he got back. Uncle Frank went up to talk with him as well. He answered as many of their questions as he could. He told them how close he and Harry had been, "closer than brothers," and how brave Harry was. He told Anne that if Harry had made it back, he would have been so badly wounded, it might have been difficult for them all. He remembers Anne looking at him and saying, "George, if I had to spoon-feed him every day for the rest of his life, I would still want him home."

Early on in the research, we could not find much on George Colburn. But when the book was nearly done, I took one more look at his file. In it, I found a form I had not seen before. It was one that George had filled out years after the war, requesting his military records. He wrote that when he moved from New England to Florida, the records had been lost. At the bottom was an address in Spring Hill, Florida.

I searched for the Florida address and then the name. As always in this research, I tried to find an obituary as a first step but found none. Within twenty-four hours, George, Dean Laubach, and I were on the phone. When I introduced myself to George and told him that I was Harry's "niece," and that Harry's sister, Nancy, was alive and living in New York, he went silent for a moment. He said he had thought of Harry so many times and that he had often thought that "he would've lived a better life than I did." I told him I was so happy to find him and he filled me in on their time together in Massachusetts, playing football against each other, and then connecting on *Rochambeau* on their way to the Pacific. He talked of he and Harry and the others "swimming on Eniwetok" and making an altar for one of the priests out of two barrels and a stretcher. He described the last time he saw Harry, when he ran off to join the column. How clearly he remembered him smiling back at him before he took off.

After Iwo Jima, George and the others went back to Guam, where they got to swim in the ocean again. Then they were off to China. When George came home he got a job with the railroad in Boston and worked on the trains for thirty years. He is father to six children and grandfather to many grandchildren and lives with his second wife in Melbourne Beach, Florida.

Writing this story was like being an archeologist, digging to see where the letters and files led me, to fill in the blanks and connect the dots between these heroes who were such great buddies. I never imagined that we would find so much. After all, there were more than 60,000 Marines on Iwo Jima.

In Japan, after the war, General Tadamichi Kuribayashi's son Taro spoke with Japanese survivors of Iwo Jima (of whom there were about 1,000) to try to put together his father's final hours there. They said he had been killed in the artillery barrage during the final devastating assault on March 26. Taro wrote:

> My father had believed it a shame to have his body discovered by
> his enemy, even after death. So he had previously asked his two

soldiers to come with him. One in front of him, one behind, with shovels in hand. In case of his death, he wanted them to bury his body then and there. It seems shells killed my father and the soldiers, and he was buried at the foot of a tall tree in Chidori Village along the beach near Oskaka mountain. Afterward, General Smith spent a whole day looking for his body to pay his respects accordingly and to perform a burial, but in vain.[2]

On September 27, 1945, Emperor Hirohito posed for a photograph next to the man who would oversee the United States' occupation of his country for the next six years. In the now-famous photo, Hirohito stands stiffly in his formal suit, looking straight ahead. General MacArthur is decidedly nondeferential; towering over the diminutive emperor, he looks casually at the camera, his hands in his back pockets. But together they would rebuild a nonmilitarized Japan. The plan was to avoid the devastation and leadership vacuum that had led to the rise of Hitler in Germany after World War I.

Tojo and five other generals received death sentences at the Tokyo Trial in 1946. They were charged with murder, which covered the attack at Pearl Harbor and the Rape of Nanking.[3] They were all executed by hanging. The bodies were cremated and their ashes dumped into the sea. "A Chamberlain alleges that on hearing the news of Tojo's death, Hirohito went into his office and wept."[4]

Adolf Hitler swallowed cyanide and shot himself in the head in a bunker in Berlin. Benito Mussolini's dead body was strung up on a crane in Milan after being kicked around in the piazza. Hirohito survived them all. He lived to see his country prosper, but like Dickens's Jacob Marley, he walked with the chains he forged in life, the blame he bore for the war that had killed approximately 3 million of his own people.[5] He died of cancer in January 1989 at the age of eighty-seven; by then Japan had the fourth-strongest economy in the world.

In the words of Eugene B. Sledge, who fought on Peleliu and Okinawa:

Epilogue

War is brutish, inglorious, and a terrible waste.

Combat leaves an indelible mark on those who are forced to endure it. The only redeeming factors were my comrades' incredible bravery and their devotion to each other. Marine Corps training taught us to kill efficiently and to try to survive. But it also taught us loyalty to each other—and love. That esprit de corps sustained us.[6]

May the memory of these men sustain us all and remind us of their sacrifice to secure our freedom. May we never forget their bravery and all they gave up so that we might live free. We are forever indebted to these heroes, whose unknown valor we are obligated to know.

Acknowledgments

Two years ago, I met with Eric Nelson at HarperCollins and told him the story of Harry Gray. Of my mother, Betty Bowes MacCallum, sharing his letters with us when we were growing up and of the tears that came to her eyes when she spoke of him. Harry was a smart, caring young man as we see so clearly in his letters. My aunt Anne (Gray) was one of my favorite people growing up. She and Grandpa had a wonderful brother-sister relationship. I had no idea, though, until I wrote this story and had extensive conversations with her daughter, my aunt Nancy (Gray/Shade), how hard her mother's life had been, how brave she was, and how much she had endured. My aunt Nancy is the last of that generation. I am grateful to her for the time we have spent talking about this family history and for her invaluable role in telling this story, and for her never-ending devotion to her brother and his memory. The Bowes-Gray families are an important part of our family legacy, and their strength and faith in God is at the core of what our generation and those to come should admire.

I thank my editor, Eric Nelson, for immediately sensing that this was the book I needed to write and for his steady hand on the tiller in seeing this project through.

It was always my desire to show the heroism of the men who died on the beaches and jagged rocks and ridges for whom no books are written or movies made. Their sacrifice was great, and families all across America have pictures of them in scrapbooks, and an empty space in their family where they should have been. By telling the story of Harry, I want to shine light on all of them as well.

My sincere thanks to my co-author, Ron Drez; his deep military knowledge is the backbone of this book. He tells the story of the origins of the war in the Pacific and the stepping-stones of the battle with clarity and an understanding of the Marines that only a Marine can know. He walked me through Japanese pillboxes in Guam and General Obata's cave. Then to Iwo Jima, where I walked the landing beaches and saw firsthand the airfields and buried tunnels. I climbed Mount Suribachi and looked down just as the flag raisers and Father Suver had on February 23, 1945. Ron took me to the now-grassy area of the Meat Grinder, where Harry was killed. Each year, Ron and the team at Ambrose Military History Tours take veterans of World War II, Korea, and Vietnam back to the battlefields where they fought. It was my honor to travel with some of them to Iwo Jima as well. I thank Ron for his service to our country as a Marine and as a historian.

Dean Laubach, founder and CEO of Corps Connections, has deep ties to the surviving veterans of World War II and is a trusted researcher who provided the links to the men who served alongside Harry Gray. He was always just a text message away as I was writing, often at midnight, and never failed to help me follow up on a lead or track down a detail. Best of all, he was as floored as I was when we found Charlie and then George, and as grateful to them as I was for openly sharing the joyful and painful memories they had locked away for so many years.

My thanks as well to Shayne Jarosz, a Marine, a teacher, and the vice president of Educational Programs for Military Historical Tours. Shayne and his team tirelessly bring our veterans back to the battlefield. On our flight to Iwo Jima were several men in their nineties, many returning for the first time. They came to attend the Reunion of Honor, which brings together Japanese and American veterans and dignitaries to pay tribute to those who lost their lives in that seminal battle. I am grateful for Shayne's guidance, which contributed to the telling of this story as well.

Briana Vota, Fox News producer, and Tommy Chiu, photographer, were with me every step of the way and beyond as they traveled to Saipan and Tinian and then to Hiroshima. Briana conducted some of the interviews, and she and Tommy shared my passion for this story from the beginning. Briana's sensitivity and respect are testaments to her humanity and professionalism. Tommy Chiu is the best, and whether I am in the jungle in Guam or in the crush of a political convention, for all these years, I've felt better at my job when he is by my side.

I am forever grateful to my friend Charlie Gubish for the hours he spent with me and my aunt Nancy. We are proud to know him and grateful for his service and sacrifice for our country, and above all for his friendship to Harry Gray in the final months of his life. I am grateful to the Gubish family, which sent me wonderful pictures of Charlie at Parris Island and in Guam, and recounted their rich family history for generations in Pennsylvania.

My thanks as well to George Colburn. I have had your letters in my files for years, and to hear your voice on the other end of the phone, speaking so warmly about Harry, was beyond words for me and my aunt Nancy. Your description of the friendship the Marines shared on Iwo Jima as being "closer than brothers" could well have been the title of this book. I thank George's daughter, Lisa Mitchell, for sending pictures of her father and of the USS *Rochambeau*, on which Harry, George, Charlie, Warren, and Herman sailed from California to Guam.

My friends Nicki and Bob Errico and Steve and Jennifer Errico led me to Donna Branch, whose mother, Betty, was Dom's sister. Nicki's mother was Dom's sister Rose. Donna opened up the family archives and shared with me wonderful pictures and heartbreaking letters that reveal the tenderness and love of Dom and his family.

I could not have completed this project without the endless hard work of Lori Frye. In addition to assisting in getting *The Story* on the air each day, she also took on the enormous task of coordinating research and edits. Her intelligence, attention to detail, and always-cheerful attitude made her such an asset to the entire process.

My husband, Dan, encouraged this project from the very start, and his understanding through endless nights of typing, as I was buried in documents and files, is just a small part of what makes him the love of my life. Through marriage, raising our three children, and juggling two busy careers, he has been "the wind beneath my wings," as he likes to joke. But the truth is, he is the far better half of our equation and I'm so lucky he's mine.

Our children, Elizabeth, Reed, and Harry, listened every time I gasped at an amazing connection or teared up at a moving letter. They gently nudged me forward and assured me it would turn out well. Someday, when you are parents, you'll know how much you are loved. Harry, I hope this story will stay with you always, as you understand the service to our country and the sacrifice made by your namesake. I have no doubt he would be proud that you are named Harry G. as well.

I'm thankful for the endless support of my dad, Douglas MacCallum. He came with us to meet Charlie Gubish and told me the story that my mom had shared with him about how the Boweses sat silently at dinner the night they learned of Harry's death, unable to speak the words.

Thanks as well to Karyn Shade, my cousin and the niece of Harry Gray, for her wonderful support and encouragement throughout.

To my agent, Olivia Metzger, I thank you for your constant friendship all these years. To David Larabell at CAA, who shared my enthusiasm for this story from the start. My thanks to Hannah Long, whose work with Eric Nelson at HarperCollins was tireless and committed. To my friend Dana Perino, who enthusiastically embraced my request to read my manuscript and offered sage advice. To Suzanne Scott and Jay Wallace and Rupert Murdoch and Lachlan Murdoch, whose support of my work all these years means so much to me.

I thank my executive producer, Brian Tully, and senior producer, Jenna Diaco, and our team at *The Story*. I truly appreciate their dedication to our mission to bring unique stories to our viewers each evening, and their commitment to telling the stories of our World War II heroes. Thanks as well go to Dion Baia, author and audio technician, for sharing the story of what fortunately turned out to be an overproduction of Purple Hearts, in preparation for the invasion of Japan, which mercifully did not happen.

Notes

Introduction: War Plan Orange

1. Matthew Calbraith Perry and Lambert Lilly, *Narrative of the Expedition of an American Squadron to the China Seas and Japan, Performed in the Years 1852, 1853, and 1854, Under the Command of Commodore M. C. Perry, United States Navy* (New York: D. Appleton, 1856), 5.

2. Ronald J. Drez, *Predicting Pearl Harbor: Billy Mitchell and the Path to War* (Gretna, LA: Pelican, 2017), 21.

3. Ibid., 22.

4. Perry and Lilly, *Narrative*, 5, 60.

5. William Elliot Griffis, "Our Navy in Asiatic Waters," *Harper's New Monthly Magazine*, October 1898, 741–42.

6. Perry and Lilly, *Narrative*, 61.

7. Ibid., 261–66.

8. Ibid., 273–76.

9. Ibid., 318.

10. Drez, *Predicting Pearl Harbor*, 35.

11. Ronald H. Spector, *Eagle Against the Sun: The American War with Japan* (New York: Vintage, 1985), 57.

12. Edward S. Miller, *War Plan Orange: The U.S. Strategy to Defeat Japan, 1897–1945* (Annapolis, MD: Naval Institute Press, 1991), 79.

13. Ibid., 79.

14. Ibid., 79.

15. C. V. Glines, "William 'Billy' Mitchell: Air Power Visionary," HistoryNet, quoted from *Aviation History* (September 1997), https://www.history net.com/william-billy-mitchell-an-air-power-visionary.htm.

1: Arlington, Massachusetts, 1938

1. David Darrah, "Chamberlain Rebukes Nazis; They Snub Him," *Chicago Daily Tribune*, December 14, 1938.

2. Edwin Palmer Hoyt, *Warlord: Tojo Against the World* (New York: Cooper Square Press, 2001), 114.

2: Infamy

1. Gray/Bowes family archives.

2. Ronald Drez, interview with Jay Rebstock, March 20, 1999.

3. Diane Diekman, "Battle of Music—USS ARIZONA Band," *Clear Lake Courier*, May 31, 1995, http://dianediekman.com/battle-of-music-uss -arizona-band/.

4. "U.S. Pacific Fleet Band: History," Commander, U.S. Pacific Fleet, https://www.cpf.navy.mil/band/history/.

5. Ibid.

6. Diekman, "Battle of Music."

7. "Brothers Assigned to the USS Arizona," National Park Service, July 2, 2019, https://www.nps.gov/valr/learn/historyculture/brothersassigned arizona.htm.

8. Gray/Bowes family archive.

9. Franklin D. Roosevelt, speech, December 8, 1941, Library of Congress, https://www.loc.gov/resource/afc1986022.afc1986022_ms2201/?st=text.

3: Outrage

1. Blanchard would enlist in the Army in 1943 and be stationed in New Mexico with a chemical warfare unit until he enrolled in the United States Military Academy at West Point in 1944. His three-year career led to three national championships, a 27–0–1 record, and a Heisman Trophy. See "Felix 'Doc' Blanchard, 1945," Heisman Trophy, http:// www.heisman.com/heisman-winners/felix-doc-blanchard/.

2. Ronald Drez, interview with Jay Rebstock, March 20, 1999.

3. Stephen Bower Young, "God, Please Get Us Out of This," *American Heritage*, April 1966, https://www.americanheritage.com/god-please-get-us-out.

4. Ibid.

5. Ibid.

6. Ibid.

7. Ibid.

8. Ibid.

9. Ibid.

10. Ibid.

11. Ibid. In all, 429 sailors from *Oklahoma* died in the attack. Stephen Young and 31 other men were rescued from entombment in the capsized hull of the ship. Many other men were trapped farther below. Tapping sounds were heard for many days, but the men could not be saved.

12. "Attack on Pearl Harbor—1941," Atomic Heritage Foundation, June 18, 2014, https://www.atomicheritage.org/history/attack-pearl-harbor-1941.

13. Herbert P. Bix, *Hirohito and the Making of Modern Japan* (New York: Harper, 2000), 445.

14. Ronald J. Drez, *The War of 1812: Conflict and Deception* (Baton Rouge: Louisiana State University Press, 2014), 183.

15. Bix, *Hirohito*, 188.

16. Ibid.

17. Ibid., 193.

18. Cesare Salmaggi and Alfredo Pallavisini, *2194 Days of War: An Illustrated Chronology of the Second World War* (New York: Milano Gallery Books, 1977), 179, 239.

19. Jack McClure, "Besieged on the Rock," *Military History Quarterly* 14, no. 4 (Summer 2002): 16.

20. Ronald J. Drez, *Predicting Pearl Harbor: Billy Mitchell and the Path to War* (Gretna, LA: Pelican, 2017), 229–30.

21. Edwin P. Hoyt, *Japan's War: The Great Pacific Conflict* (New York: Da Capo, 1986), 198.

4: The Changing Tide

1. Robert Leckie, *Strong Men Armed: The United States Marines Against Japan* (New York: Ballantine, 1962), 3.

2. Quoted in Meredith Hindley, "Christmas at the White House with Winston Churchill," *Humanities* 37, no. 4 (Fall 2016), https://www.neh.gov/humanities/2016/fall/feature/christmas-the-white-house-winston-churchill.

3. Ibid.

4. Henry H. Arnold, *Global Mission* (New York: Harper & Brothers, 1949), 274.

5. Ibid., 289.

6. Carroll V. Glines, *Doolittle's Tokyo Raiders* (New York: D. Van Nostrand, 1964), 12–19.

7. Thirteen of the crews successfully bombed their targets and then crash-landed in China. One crew had to land in Russia and was interned for the rest of the war, and two crews crashed, killing two members, with the remaining eight captured by the Japanese. The Japanese executed three, and a fourth died from harsh treatment.

8. Ronald J. Drez, *Twenty-five Yards of War: The Extraordinary Courage of Ordinary Men in World War II* (New York: Hyperion, 2001), 15.

9. "Yanks Bomb Tokyo," *Santa Ana Register*, April 18, 1942.

10. Ben Wolfgang, "News of Doolittle Raid Leaks Slowly as Roosevelt Keeps Silence," *Washington Times*, April 12, 2012, https://www.washingtontimes.com/news/2012/apr/12/news-doolittle-raid-leaks-slowly-roosevelt-silence/.

11. Ibid.

12. Gray/Bowes family archives.

13. Naval Analysis Division, *The Campaigns of the Pacific War: United States Strategic Bombing Survey (Pacific)* (Washington, DC: U.S. Government Printing Office, 1946), 52.

14. Ibid., 57.

15. Ibid., 52–53.

16. Ibid., 55.

17. "15 Jap Ships Sunk, Lexington Is Lost, in Coral Sea Fight," *The Sun*, June 12, 1942.

18. "13 to 15 Jap Ships Sunk or Damaged; Great Victory in Making, Says Nimitz," *Sunday Telegram*, June 7, 1942.

19. E. B. Potter and Chester W. Nimitz, *The Great Sea War: The Story of Naval Action in World War II* (New York: Bramhall House, 1960), 221–23.

20. "Battle of Midway: Timeline of Significant Events," Navy Live, June 2, 2013, https://navylive.dodlive.mil/2013/06/02/battle-of-midway-timeline-of-significant-events/.

21. Gray/Bowes archives.

5: What Hirohito Knew

1. Quoted in Herbert P. Bix, *Hirohito and the Making of Modern Japan* (New York: Harper, 2000), 450.

2. Edwin P. Hoyt, *Japan's War: The Great Pacific Conflict* (New York: Da Capo, 1986), 35.

3. Lionel Giles, trans., *The Art of War: Sun Tzu* (London: Luzac, 1910), 8.

4. Ibid.

5. Susan Chira, "Hirohito, 124th Emperor of Japan, Is Dead at 87," *New York Times*, January 7, 1989.

6. Hoyt, *Japan's War*, 59.

7. Ibid., 60.

8. Bix, *Hirohito*.

9. Hoyt, *Japan's War*, 66.

10. Ibid.

11. Ibid., 69.

12. Ibid., 74–75.

13. Ibid., 87.

14. Ibid., 111.

15. Ibid., 112–13.

16. Ibid., 112–30.

17. Ibid., 144.

18. Ibid., 173.

19. Quoted in Hua-ling Hu, *American Goddess at the Rape of Nanking: The Courage of Minnie Vautrin* (Carbondale: Southern Illinois University Press, 2000), 97.

20. Quoted in Iris Chang, *The Rape of Nanking: The Forgotten Holocaust of World War II* (New York: Perseus, 1997), 154.

21. Quoted in Hoyt, *Japan's War*, 172.

22. "Contest to Cut Down a Hundred! Two Second Lieutenants Already Up to Eighty," *Tokyo Nichinichi Shimbun*, November 30, 1937.

23. Masato Kajimoto, "Nanking War Crimes Tribunal," The Nanking Massacre; December 1937, https://thenankingmassacre.org/2015/07/04/nanking-war-crimes-tribunal/.

24. Honda Katsuichi, *The Nanjing Massacre: A Japanese Journalist Confronts Japan's National Shame* (Armonk, NY: M. E. Sharpe, 1999), 123–27.

25. Quoted in ibid., 125–27.

26. Ibid.

27. Quoted in Fei Fei Li, Robert Sabella, and David Liu, eds., *Nanking 1937: Memory and Healing* (Armonk, NY: M. E. Sharpe, 2002), 56.

28. John Gittings, "Japanese Rewrite Guardian History," *The Guardian*, October 4, 2002, https://www.theguardian.com/world/2002/oct/04/artsandhumanities.japan; Harold John Timperley, telegram, intercepted and deciphered by US intelligence on February 1, 1938, published by US National Archives and Records Administration (NARA) in September 1994, https://commons.wikimedia.org/wiki/File:Nanking_telegram_Harold_John_Timperley.gif.

29. Iris Chang, *The Rape of Nanking: The Forgotten Holocaust of World War II* (New York: Penguin, 1997), 40.

30. Bob Tadashi Wakabayashi, "Emperor Hirohito on Localized Aggression in China," *Sino-Japanese Studies* 4, no. 1 (October 1991): http://chinajapan.org/articles/04.1/04.1wakabayashi4-27.pdf, 7.

31. Bix, *Hirohito*, 448.

6: The First Step: Say a Prayer for Your Pal on Guadalcanal

1. Gubish family archives.

2. Cesare Salmaggi and Alfredo Pallavisini, *2194 Days of War: An Illustrated Chronology of the Second World War* (New York: Milano Gallery Books, 1977), 263–67.

3. Ken Burns and Lynn Novick, directors, *The War*, Public Broadcasting System, 2007, episode 2.

4. Quoted in George McMillan, *The Old Breed: A History of the First Marine Division in World War II* (Washington, DC: Infantry Journal Press, 1949), 3.

5. Quoted in ibid., 7.

6. Quoted in ibid., 10.

7. Ibid., 4.

8. "Enlisted Pay Chart 1941–1942," Navy CyberSpace, https://www.navy cs.com/charts/1941-military-pay-chart.html.

9. Quoted in McMillan, *The Old Breed*, 15.

10. John L. Zimmerman, *The Guadalcanal Campaign* (Washington, DC: Historical Section, Headquarters, United States Marine Corps, 1949), 1.

11. Ronald J. Drez, *Twenty-five Yards of War: The Extraordinary Courage of Ordinary Men in World War II* (New York: Hyperion, 2001), 217.

12. Ronald Drez, interview with James Russell, April 21, 1999, Drez archive; Drez, *Twenty-five Yards of War*, 89.

13. "US Forces in New Zealand," New Zealand History, https://nzhistory .govt.nz/war/us-forces-in-new-zealand.

14. McMillan, *The Old Breed*, 16.

15. Quoted in ibid., 18.

16. Ibid.

17. Clemens had left his government post at Aola on the northern coast of Guadalcanal on May 18 when the Japanese occupied the nearby island of Tulagi. Instead of evacuating, he chose to engage in the very dangerous duties of a Coastwatcher hiding in Japanese-occupied territory.

18. Zimmerman, *The Guadalcanal Campaign*, 10.

19. Ibid., 11.

20. James Bowen, "The Battle for Guadalcanal, 7 August 1942–7 February 1943," Pacific War Historical Society, http://www.pacificwar.org.au /Guadalcanal.html.

21. Ibid.

22. Zimmerman, *The Guadalcanal Campaign*, 24.

23. Naval Analysis Division, *The Campaigns of the Pacific War: United States Strategic Bombing Survey (Pacific)* (Washington, DC: U.S. Government Printing Office, 1946), 106.

24. Ibid., 107–9.

25. "Clark Gable in Army as Private," *Boston Post*, August 12, 1942.

26. Scott Harrison, "From the Archives: Clark Gable Joins the Army," *Los Angeles Times*, January 2, 2019, https://www.latimes.com/visuals /photography/la-me-fw-archives-clark-gable-joins-the-army-20190102 -htmlstory.html.

27. "Famous Veteran: Clark Gable," Military.com, 2019, https://www.mil itary.com/veteran-jobs/career-advice/military-transition/famous-veteran -clark-gable.html.

28. John Miller, Jr., *Guadalcanal: The First Offensive* (Washington, DC: Center of Military History, United States Army, 1995), 105.

29. Ibid., 109.

30. Ibid.

31. Ibid., 110.

32. Ibid., 149.

33. "Marines Repulse Japs 3 Times; Guadalcanal Troops Plug Hole Cut in Line," *Boston Globe*, October 30, 1942.

34. "Battle of Guadalcanal," Encyclopaedia Britannica, https://www .britannica.com/event/Battle-of-Guadalcanal.

35. David Alan Johnson, "Withdrawal from Guadalcanal: Abandoning the Island of Death," Warfare History Network, November 27, 2018, https://warfarehistorynetwork.com/daily/wwii/abandoning-the-island -of-death/.

36. Ibid.

37. Quoted in ibid.

38. Ken Burns and Lynn Novick, directors, *The War*, Public Broadcasting System, 2007, episode 1.

39. Quoted in Johnson, "Withdrawal from Guadalcanal."

40. Gray family archives; author's interview with Nancy Shade, October 18, 2018.

41. Gray/Bowes family archives.

7: 1943

1. Richard N. Armstrong, "1943: World War II's Forgotten Year of Victory," HistoryNet (originally published January 2013 in *Armchair General*), https://www.historynet.com/1943-world-war-iis-forgotten-year -victory.htm.

2. Robert F. Dorr, "Killing Yamamoto: How America Killed the Japanese Admiral Who Masterminded the Pearl Harbor Attack," *The National Interest*, August 4, 2018, https://nationalinterest.org/blog/buzz /killing-yamamoto-how-america-killed-japanese-admiral-who-master minded-pearl-harbor-attack.

3. Armstrong, "1943."

4. Quoted in John L. Zimmerman, *The Guadalcanal Campaign* (Washington, DC: Historical Section, Headquarters, United States Marine Corps, 1949), 6–7.

5. Ronald H. Spector, *Eagle Against the Sun: The American War with Japan* (New York: Vintage, 1985), 223–24.

6. Ibid.

7. United States Department of State, *Foreign Relations of the United States: The Conferences at Washington, 1941–1942, and Casablanca, 1943* (Washington, DC: U.S. Government Printing Office, 1968), 781.

8. James R. Stockman, *The Battle for Tarawa* (Washington, DC: Historical Section, Headquarters, United States Marine Corps, 1947), 1.

9. Spector, *Eagle Against the Sun*, 253.

10. Quoted in ibid., 255.

11. Quoted in Robert Leckie, *Strong Men Armed: The United States Marines Against Japan* (New York: Ballantine, 1962), 186.

12. Ibid.

13. Ibid., 185.

14. Quoted in Stockman, *The Battle for Tarawa*, 7.

15. Quoted in Leckie, *Strong Men Armed*, 191.

16. Ronald Drez, interview with James Russell, April 21, 1999.

17. Ronald J. Drez, *Twenty-five Yards of War: The Extraordinary Courage of Ordinary Men in World War II* (New York: Hyperion, 2001), 90–91.

18. Ibid.

19. Ronald Drez, interview with James Russell, April 21, 1999.

20. Quoted in Rafael Steinberg, *Island Fighting* (Alexandria, VA: Time-Life Books, 1978), 106.

21. Drez, *Twenty-five Yards of War*, 100.

22. Stockman, *The Battle for Tarawa*, 15–16.

23. Ronald Drez, interview with James Russell, April 21, 1999.

24. Drez, *Twenty-five Yards of War*, 100.

25. Ibid.

26. Ibid., 101.

27. Stockman, *The Battle for Tarawa*, 16.

28. Quoted in ibid., 16.

29. Quoted in ibid., 17.

30. Drez, *Twenty-five Yards of War*, 102.

31. Michael P. Ryan, "Tarawa," *Marine Corps Gazette* 68, no. 11 (November 1984): 122.

32. "Tarawa: The USMC's First Use of M4 Medium Tanks," The Sherman Tank Site, November 22, 2015, http://www.theshermantank.com/tag/tarawa/.

33. Drez, *Twenty-five Yards of War*, 104.

34. Quoted in Ryan, "Tarawa."

35. Quoted in ibid.

36. Quoted in Joseph H. Alexander, "Tarawa: The Ultimate Opposed Landing," *Marine Corps Gazette* 77, no. 11 (November 1993): 28.

37. Stockman, *The Battle for Tarawa*, 33.

38. Drez, *Twenty-five Yards of War*, 106.

39. Ibid., 107–8.

40. Joseph H. Alexander, "Issue in Doubt," *Marine Corps Gazette* 86, no. 11 (November 2003).

41. Robert Sherrod, "Kerr Eby: Combat Artist," *Leatherneck*, November 1992, 67.

42. Tom Bowman, "WWII Combat Cameraman: 'The Public Had to Know,'" NPR, March 21, 2010, https://www.npr.org/templates/story/story.php?storyId=124631492.

43. Grossi family archives.

8: Cracking the Inner Ring

1. Colburn archives.

2. Edwin P. Hoyt, *Japan's War: The Great Pacific Conflict* (New York: Da Capo, 1986), 335–38.

3. Ronald J. Drez, *Twenty-five Yards of War: The Extraordinary Courage of Ordinary Men in World War II* (New York: Hyperion, 2001), 54.

4. Hoyt, *Japan's War*, 301.

5. Quoted in ibid., 336.

6. Quoted in ibid., 336.

7. Bob Tadashi Wakabayashi, "Emperor Hirohito on Localized Aggression in China" *Sino-Japanese Studies* 4, no. 1 (October 1991), 5, http://chinajapan.org/articles/04.1/04.1wakabayashi4-27.pdf.

8. Ibid., 17.

9. Ibid., 17.

10. Ibid., 17–18.

11. Ronald H. Spector, *Eagle Against the Sun: The American War with Japan* (New York: Vintage, 1985), 269; Naval Analysis Division, *The Campaigns of the Pacific War: United States Strategic Bombing Survey (Pacific)* (Washington, DC: U.S. Government Printing Office, 1946), 193.

12. Quoted in John C. Chapin, *Breaking the Outer Ring: Marine Landings in the Marshall Islands* (Washington, DC: Marine Corps Historical Center, 1994), 4.

13. Ibid., 28.

14. Quoted in ibid., 29.

15. Robert Leckie, *Strong Men Armed: The United States Marines Against Japan* (New York: Ballantine, 1962), 286.

16. Quoted in Chapin, *Breaking the Outer Ring*, 9.

17. Quoted in ibid., 9.

18. Quoted in ibid., 9.

19. Movietone News, "Marshalls Invasion!," 1944; Movietone News, "U.S. Troops Capture Roi-Namur Island in Kwajalein Atoll," 1944, uploaded by CriticalPast, May 23, 2014, https://www.youtube.com/watch?v=mMoNh4wrEtY.

9: Willing to Fight

1. John Stuart Mill, "The Contest in America," *Harper's New Monthly Magazine*, April 1862, 683–84.

2. Ibid., 682.

3. Ibid.

4. Ibid., 683–84.

5. Joseph Warren, "Account of the Battle of Lexington," April 26, 1775, http://www.west-windsor-plainsboro.k12.nj.us/UserFiles/Servers/Server_10640642/File/bugge/Chapter%206/Account%20of%20the%20Battle%20of%20Lexington%201775.pdf.

6. Joseph B. Mitchell, *Decisive Battles of the American Revolution* (n.p., GA: Mockingbird Books, 1962), 27.

7. Gray/Bowes family archives.

8. Sally Rogers, "The Battle of Menotomy," Arlington Historical Society, https://arlingtonhistorical.org/learn/articles/the-battle-of-menotomy/.

9. Gray/Bowes family archives.

10. Ibid.

11. John C. Chapin, *Breaching the Marianas: The Battle for Saipan* (Washington, DC: Marine Corps Historical Center, 1994), 5.

12. Quoted in ibid., 6–7.

13. Robert Leckie, *Strong Men Armed: The United States Marines Against Japan* (New York: Ballantine, 1962), 315.

14. Ronald H. Spector, *Eagle Against the Sun: The American War with Japan* (New York: Vintage, 1985), 277.

15. Ronald J. Drez, *Twenty-five Yards of War: The Extraordinary Courage of Ordinary Men in World War II* (New York: Hyperion, 2001), 218.

16. Ibid., 219.

17. Ronald Drez, interview with Jay Rebstock, March 20, 1999.

18. Ibid.

19. Ibid.

20. Gray/Bowes family archives.

21. Gray/Bowes family archives.

22. Dwight D. Eisenhower, radio address, June 6, 1944, recording at Southwick House, Portsmouth, England, Imperial War Museum.

23. Franklin D. Roosevelt, "Franklin Roosevelt's D-Day Prayer," June 6, 1944, Franklin D. Roosevelt Presidential Library and Museum, http://docs.fdrlibrary.marist.edu/odddayp.html.

24. "Hitler's Sea Wall Breached; Invaders Fighting Way Inland; New Allied Landings Made," *New York Times*, June 7, 1944.

10: D-Day: From Normandy to Saipan

1. A. A. Vandegrift, speech, 1944, Marine Corps Combat Recordings, Library of Congress, Washington, DC.

2. Ibid.

3. Quoted in Edwin P. Hoyt, *Japan's War: The Great Pacific Conflict* (New York: Da Capo, 1986), 333.

4. Quoted in Carl W. Hoffman, *Saipan: The Beginning of the End* (Washington, DC: Historical Branch, Headquarters, United States Marine Corps, 1954), 36.

5. Ronald Drez, interview with James Russell, April 21, 1999.

6. Hoffman, *Saipan*, 60.

7. Ibid., 50.

8. Gordon L. Rottman, *Saipan & Tinian 1944: Piercing the Japanese Empire* (Oxford, UK: Osprey Publishing, 2004), 51.

9. Hoffman, *Saipan*, 54.

10. Rottman, *Saipan & Tinian*, 50.

11. John C. Chapin, *Breaching the Marianas: The Battle for Saipan* (Washington, DC: Marine Corps Historical Center, 1994), 3.

12. Hoffman, *Saipan*, 69.

13. Robert Leckie, *Strong Men Armed: The United States Marines Against Japan* (New York: Ballantine, 1962), 325.

14. Quoted in ibid., 326.

15. Quoted in Naval Analysis Division, *The Campaigns of the Pacific War: United States Strategic Bombing Survey (Pacific)* (Washington, DC: U.S. Government Printing Office, 1946), 233.

16. Quoted in ibid., 233.

17. Leckie, *Strong Men Armed*, 327.

18. Ronald Drez, interview with James Russell, April 21, 1999.

19. Leckie, *Strong Men Armed*, 327.

20. Quoted in ibid., 328; Ronald H. Spector, *Eagle Against the Sun: The American War with Japan* (New York: Vintage, 1985), 304–5.

21. Herbert P. Bix, *Hirohito and the Making of Modern Japan* (New York: Harper, 2000), 476.

22. Ibid., 330.

23. Ibid.

24. Rottman, *Saipan & Tinian*, 58.

25. Leckie, *Strong Men Armed*, 331.

26. Quoted in Chapin, *Breaching the Marianas*, 13.

27. Ibid.; Leckie, *Strong Men Armed*, 331–32.

28. Leckie, *Strong Men Armed*, 332.

29. Chapin, *Breaching the Marianas*, 16.

30. Leckie, *Strong Men Armed*, 328.

31. Naval Analysis Division, *The Campaigns of the Pacific War*, 234.

32. Chapin, *Breaching the Marianas*, 16.

33. Naval Analysis Division, *The Campaigns of the Pacific War*, 214.

34. Ibid.

35. Barrett Tillman, "Coaching the Fighters," *U.S. Naval Institute Proceedings*, January 1980, 41–43.

36. Spector, *Eagle Against the Sun*, 309.

37. Naval Analysis Division, *The Campaigns of the Pacific War*, 214.

38. Spector, *Eagle Against the Sun*, 309–10.

39. Leckie, *Strong Men Armed*, 336–37.

40. Ronald J. Drez, *Twenty-five Yards of War: The Extraordinary Courage of Ordinary Men in World War II* (New York: Hyperion, 2001), 153–54.

41. Naval Analysis Division, *The Campaigns of the Pacific War*, 215.

42. Ibid.

43. Author's interview with Charles Gubish, April 14, 2019.

44. "MCRD Parris Island: About," https://www.mcrdpi.marines.mil/About/; Elmore A. Champie, *A Brief History of the Marine Corps Recruit Depot, Parris Island, South Carolina* (Washington, DC: Department of the Navy, 1962), 10.

45. Author's interview with Charles Gubish, April 14, 2019.

46. Ibid.

47. Gray/Bowes archive.

11: Japan's Doorstep

1. "Historical Snapshot: B-29 Superfortress," Boeing, https://www.boeing.com/history/products/b-29-superfortress.page.

2. Bryan R. Swopes, "18 February 1943," This Day in Aviation, February 18, 2019, https://www.thisdayinaviation.com/18-february-1943/.

3. D. M. Giangreco, *Hell to Pay: Operation Downfall and the Invasion of Japan, 1945–1947* (Annapolis, MD: Naval Institute Press, 2009), 340.

Notes

4. Herbert P. Bix, *Hirohito and the Making of Modern Japan* (New York: Harper, 2000), 470.

5. Eric Hammel, *Iwo Jima: Portrait of a Battle: United States Marines at War in the Pacific* (St. Paul, MN: Zenith Press, 2006), 23.

6. Naval Analysis Division, *The Campaigns of the Pacific War: United States Strategic Bombing Survey (Pacific)* (Washington, DC: U.S. Government Printing Office, 1946), 212.

7. Quoted in Edwin P. Hoyt, *Japan's War: The Great Pacific Conflict* (New York: Da Capo, 1986), 428.

8. Quoted in ibid., 428.

9. Shannon J. Murphy, "WWII: Oral War Histories of the Chamoru People," Guampedia, October 13, 2019, https://www.guampedia.com/wwii-oral-war-histories-of-the-chamorro-people/.

10. Cyril J. O'Brien, *Liberation: Marines in the Recapture of Guam* (Washington, DC: History and Museums Division, Headquarters, United States Marine Corps, 1994), 1.

11. Quoted in ibid., 8.

12. Ronald H. Spector, *Eagle Against the Sun: The American War with Japan* (New York: Vintage, 1985), 320.

13. O'Brien, *Liberation*, 42–43.

14. Memorial standing in the South Pacific Memorial Park in Yigo, Guam.

15. Richard Harwood, *A Close Encounter: The Marine Landing at Tinian* (Washington, DC: History and Museums Division, Headquarters, United States Marine Corps, 1994), 5.

16. Ronald Drez, interview with James Russell, April 21, 1999.

17. Quoted in Carl W. Hoffman, *The Seizure of Tinian* (Washington, DC: Historical Division, Headquarters, United States Marine Corps, 1951), https://www.usmcu.edu/Portals/218/Hoffman_The%20Seizure%20of%20Tinian.pdf, 20.

18. Ibid., 3.

19. Spector, *Eagle Against the Sun*, 318.

20. Quoted in Hoffman, *The Seizure of Tinian*, 20.

21. Norman V. Cooper, "The Military Career of Lieutenant General Holland M. Smith," PhD dissertation, University of Alabama, 1974, 365–66.

22. Hoffman, *The Seizure of Tinian*, 23–24.

23. Quoted in ibid., 12.

24. Ibid., 15.

25. Commander in Chief, U.S. Pacific Fleet and Pacific Ocean Areas, "Operations in the Pacific Ocean Areas During the Month of July 1944," National Archives and Records Administration, EO 13526, declassified December 31, 2012.

26. Ibid., 43–44.

27. Ibid., 59.

28. Harwood, *A Close Encounter*, 6.

29. Ibid., 6–7.

30. Ibid., 13–14.

31. Hoffman, *The Seizure of Tinian*, 63.

32. Ibid.

33. Ibid., 64.

34. Quoted in ibid., 65.

35. Robert Sherrod, "The Nature of the Enemy," *Time*, August 7, 1944.

36. Quoted in "Turning Women into Weapons: Japan's Women, the Battle of Saipan, and the 'Nature of the Pacific War,'" in *Women and War in the 20th Century, Enlisted with or without Consent*, ed. Nicole A. Dombrowski (New York: Garland Press, 1999), 240–61.

37. Hoffman, *The Seizure of Tinian*, iii.

38. "Tinian," GlobalSecurity.org, https://www.globalsecurity.org/military/facility/tinian.htm.

39. Gray/Bowes family archives.

40. *Lockport Union-Sun & Journal*, May 4, 1999.

41. Grossi family archives.

12: "A Ghastly Relentlessness"

1. Ernie Pyle, *Ernie's War: The Best of Ernie Pyle's World War II Dispatches* (New York: Touchstone, 1986), 332.

2. Quoted in Ronald J. Drez, *Predicting Pearl Harbor: Billy Mitchell and the Path to War* (Gretna, LA: Pelican, 2017), 233.

3. Quoted in ibid., 56.

4. Quoted in ibid., 57.

5. Edward S. Miller, *War Plan Orange: The U.S. Strategy to Defeat Japan, 1897–1945* (Annapolis, MD: Naval Institute Press, 1991), 364.

6. Ibid.

7. Robert Leckie, *Strong Men Armed: The United States Marines Against Japan* (New York: Ballantine, 1962), 399–400.

8. Quoted in William Manchester, *American Caesar: Douglas MacArthur* (Boston: Little, Brown, 1978), 369.

9. Quoted in George McMillan, *The Old Breed: A History of the First Marine Division in World War II* (Washington, DC: Infantry Journal Press, 1949), 269.

10. Quoted in ibid., 270.

11. Frank Hough, *The Assault on Peleliu* (Nashville: Battery Press, 1990), 16–17.

12. Leckie, *Strong Men Armed*, 398.

13. Quoted in Hough, *Assault on Peleliu*, 192–93.

14. Quoted in ibid., 192–93.

15. Quoted in ibid., 192–93.

16. Leckie, *Strong Men Armed*, 396.

17. Hough, *Assault on Peleliu*, 17.

18. Gordon D. Gayle, *Bloody Beaches: The Marines at Peleliu* (Washington, DC: Marine Corps Historical Center, 1996), 8.

19. Ibid., 9.

20. Ibid.

21. Ibid., 10.

22. Leckie, *Strong Men Armed*, 401.

23. Hough, *Assault on Peleliu*, chapter 3, note 6.

24. Ibid., chapter 3, note 5.

25. Leckie, *Strong Men Armed*, 405.

26. Hough, *Assault on Peleliu*, 51.

27. Gayle, *Bloody Beaches*, 18; Hough, *Assault on Peleliu*, 57.

28. Quoted in Hough, *Assault on Peleliu*, 77.

29. Ibid., 78.

30. Quoted in Leckie, *Strong Men Armed*, 412.

31. Quoted in Hough, *Assault on Peleliu*, chapter 4, note 45.

32. Ibid., 88.

33. Ibid., 103.

34. Bill O'Reilly and Martin Dugard, *Killing the Rising Sun: How America Vanquished World War II Japan* (New York: Henry Holt, 2016), 33.

35. Hough, *Assault on Peleliu*, chapter 8, note 13.

36. Ibid., 183; "Battle of Peleliu," Howling Pixel, https://howlingpixel.com /i-en/Battle_of_Peleliu.

37. Leckie, *Strong Men Armed*, 427.

13: "An Island of Sulphur: No Water, No Sparrow, and No Swallow"

1. Yoshitaka Horie, "Explanation of Japanese Defense Plan and Battle of Iwo Jima," 1946, quoted in Whitman S. Bartley, *Iwo Jima: Amphibious Epic* (Washington, DC: Historical Branch, G-3 Division, Headquarters, United States Marine Corps, 1954), https://upload.wikimedia.org /wikipedia/commons/2/2e/Iwo_Jima-_Amphibious_Epic.pdf, 5.

2. Quoted in Bartley, *Iwo Jima*, 6.

3. Quoted in Yoshitaka Horie, "Fighting Spirit—Iwo Jima" (memoir, manuscript copy, 1965, Rebstock/Drez archives), 34.

4. Quoted in Bartley, *Iwo Jima*, 16.

5. Horie, "Fighting Spirit," 37.

6. Naval Analysis Division, *The Campaigns of the Pacific War: United States Strategic Bombing Survey (Pacific)* (Washington, DC: U.S. Government Printing Office, 1946), 315.

7. Quoted in ibid., 281.

8. Ibid., 317.

9. Horie, "Fighting Spirit," 39.

10. Viktor Suvorov, *The Chief Culprit: Stalin's Grand Design to Start World War II* (Annapolis, MD: Naval Institute Press, 2008); "Summary and Lessons," *Military History*, http://militera.lib.ru/h/kondratyev_v/09.html.

11. Horie, "Fighting Spirit," 40.

12. Joseph H. Alexander, *Closing In: Marines in the Seizure of Iwo Jima* (Washington, DC: History and Museums Division, Headquarters, United States Marine Corps, 1994), 3.

13. Quoted in Robert Leckie, *The Battle for Iwo Jima* (New York: Simon & Schuster, 2004), 11.

14. Tadamichi Kuribayashi, *"Gyokusai Sōshikikan" no etegami* (Picture Letters from Commander in Chief) (in Japanese), ed. Taro Kuribayashi (Tokyo: Shogakukan, 2002), quoted in Leckie, *The Battle for Iwo Jima*, 36.

15. Horie, "Fighting Spirit," 47.

16. Ibid., 63.

17. Ibid., 75.

18. Ibid., 77.

19. Ibid.

20. Quoted in ibid., 83.

21. Quoted in ibid., 83.

22. Ronald H. Spector, *Eagle Against the Sun: The American War with Japan* (New York: Vintage, 1985), 495.

23. Alexander, *Closing In*, 5.

24. Horie, "Fighting Spirit," 76.

25. Alexander, *Closing In*, 5.

26. Ibid., 3.

27. Bartley, *Iwo Jima*, 30.

28. Author's interview with George Colburn, October 10, 2019.

29. Gray/Bowes archives.

30. Author's interview with Charles Gubish, April 17, 2019.

31. Ibid.

32. Ibid.

33. Richard F. Newcomb, *Iwo Jima: The Dramatic Account of the Epic Battle That Turned the Tide of World War II* (New York: Signet Books, 1965), 40.

34. Ronald J. Drez, *Twenty-five Yards of War: The Extraordinary Courage of Ordinary Men in World War II* (New York: Hyperion, 2001), 228.

35. Ronald Drez, interview with Jay Rebstock, March 20, 1999.

36. Ibid.

37. John C. Chapin, *The 4th Marine Division in World War II* (Washington, DC: History and Museums Division, Headquarters, United States Marine Corps, 1974), 43–44.

38. G. B. Erskine, "3d Marine Division Reinforced, Iwo Jima Action Report, 31 October 1944–16 March 1945," April 30, 1945, https://www .scribd.com/document/110606038/Iwo-Jima-Campaign-1945, 1.

39. Newcomb, *Iwo Jima*, 41.

40. Erskine, "3d Marine Division Reinforced, Iwo Jima Action Report," 3.

14: "Hell with the Fire Out"

1. Richard F. Newcomb, *Iwo Jima: The Dramatic Account of the Epic Battle That Turned the Tide of World War II* (New York: Signet Books, 1965), 63.

2. Whitman S. Bartley, *Iwo Jima: Amphibious Epic* (Washington, DC: Historical Branch, G-3 Division, Headquarters, U.S. Marine Corps, 1954), https://upload.wikimedia.org/wikipedia/commons/2/2e/Iwo _Jima-_Amphibious_Epic.pdf, 39.

3. Quoted in Newcomb, *Iwo Jima*, 57.

4. Ibid., 58.

5. Bartley, *Iwo Jima*, 40.

6. Newcomb, *Iwo Jima*, 70.

7. Quoted in Robert Leckie, *Strong Men Armed: The United States Marines Against Japan* (New York: Ballantine, 1962), 441.

8. Bartley, *Iwo Jima*, 35.

9. Newcomb, *Iwo Jima*, 68.

10. Bartley, *Iwo Jima*, 44.

11. Newcomb, *Iwo Jima*, 68.

12. "World War II Medal of Honor Recipients (F–J): Herring, Rufus G.," https://ibiblio.org/hyperwar/MoH_F-J.html#herring.

Notes

13. Bartley, *Iwo Jima*, 45, n. 113.

14. Ibid., 47.

15. "Iwo Jima," SFR Productions, Freund Enterprises, 2012, https://www .youtube.com/watch?time_continue=2&v=fwmFBQZq9Z0.

16. Quoted in Newcomb, *Iwo Jima*, 29.

17. Author's interview with Dean Laubach, nephew of Coloner Swindler, Corps Connections, April 2019.

18. Newcomb, *Iwo Jima*, 37.

19. Ronald J. Drez, *Twenty-five Yards of War: The Extraordinary Courage of Ordinary Men in World War II* (New York: Hyperion, 2001), 230.

20. Ibid., 230–31.

21. Ibid., 231.

22. Bartley, *Iwo Jima*, 51.

23. Quoted in Drez, *Twenty-five Yards of War*, 232.

24. Ibid.

25. Ibid.

26. Ibid., 232–33.

27. Bartley, *Iwo Jima*, 53.

28. Ronald Drez, interview with Jay Rebstock, March 20, 1999.

29. Bartley, *Iwo Jima*, 53.

30. Quoted in Bill D. Ross, *Iwo Jima: Legacy of Valor* (New York: Vintage Books, 1986), 67.

31. Quoted in Newcomb, *Iwo Jima*, 103–4.

32. Drez, *Twenty-five Yards of War*, 236.

33. Charles W. Tatum, *Iwo Jima: Red Blood, Black Sand: Pacific Apocalypse* (Stockton, CA: Charles W. Tatum Publications, 2002), 156–57; Ronald Drez, interview with Charles Tatum, 2006.

34. Tatum, *Iwo Jima*, 157–58.

35. Ibid., 159.

36. J. D. Simkins, "Valor Friday: The Legend of John Basilone," *Marine Corps Times*, June 29, 2018, https://www.marinecorpstimes.com/news /your-army/2018/06/29/valor-friday-the-legend-of-john-basilone/.

37. Larry Smith, *Iwo Jima: World War II Veterans Remember the Greatest Battle of the Pacific* (New York: W. W. Norton, 2009), 4.

38. Carl W. Proehl, *The Fourth Marine Division in World War II* (Washington, DC: Infantry Journal Press, 1946), 152–53.

39. Ibid., 152.

40. Ibid., 152.

41. Quoted in Raymond Henri, *Iwo Jima: Springboard to Final Victory* (New York: U.S. Camera Publishing Corporation, 1945), 30.

42. G. B. Erskine, "3d Marine Division Reinforced, Iwo Jima Action Report, 31 October 1944–16 March 1945," April 30, 1945, https://www.scribd.com/document/110606038/Iwo-Jima-Campaign-1945, 1.

43. Ibid., 2.

44. Ibid.

45. Ibid., 3.

46. Joseph H. Alexander, "Iwo Jima: Hell with the Fire Out," *Leatherneck* 78, no. 2 (February 1995): 17–18.

47. Tatum, *Iwo Jima*, 79.

48. Ross, *Iwo Jima*, 140.

49. Author's interview with Hershel Williams, August 14, 2019.

50. Ibid.

51. Ibid.

52. "Williams, Hershel Woodrow," Congressional Medal of Honor Society, http://www.cmohs.org/recipient-detail/3066/williams-hershel-woodrow.php.

53. Erskine, "3d Marine Division Reinforced, Iwo Jima Action Report," 5–6.

54. Newcomb, *Iwo Jima*, 119.

55. Quoted in Joseph H. Alexander, *Closing In: Marines in the Seizure of Iwo Jima* (Washington, DC: History and Museums Division, Headquarters, United States Marine Corps, 1994), 24.

56. Quoted in Yoshitaka Horie, "Fighting Spirit—Iwo Jima" (memoir, manuscript copy, 1965, Rebstock/Drez archives), 93.

57. Quoted in ibid., 93.

58. Newcomb, *Iwo Jima*, 122.

59. Donald R. McClarey, "February 23, 1945: The Mass on Suribachi," *The American Catholic*, February 23, 2015, https://www.the-american -catholic.com/2015/02/23/the-mass-on-mount-suribachi-2/.

60. Tatum, *Iwo Jima*, 200.

61. Drez, *Twenty-five Yards of War*, 240.

62. Newcomb, *Iwo Jima*, 123.

63. Ibid.

64. Quoted in ibid., 124.

65. Quoted in Alexander, *Closing In*, 26.

66. Ibid., 27.

67. The Marine in the Rosenthal photo previously thought to be Private First Class Rene Gagnon was determined to be Corporal Harold "Pie" Keller. Confirmed by the U.S. Marine Corps on October 16, 2019.

68. For more than seventy years, Navy Corpsman John Bradley was misidentified as one of the famous flag raisers on Iwo Jima. In 2014, two amateur history buffs, Eric Krelle and Stephen Foley, forensically examined all the photos taken atop Mount Suribachi that day and proved that although Bradley was in the first flag raising, he was not in the second. Private Harold Schultz was the sixth Marine in Joe Rosenthal's famous photograph. See Matthew Hansen, "New Mystery Arises from Iconic Iwo Jima Image," *Omaha World Herald*, November 23, 2014, https://dataomaha.com/media/news/2014/iwo -jima/.

69. Winston Churchill, speech at the Lord Mayor's Luncheon, Mansion House, London, November 10, 1942, The Churchill Society, http:// www.churchill-society-london.org.uk/EndoBegn.html.

70. McClarey, "February 23, 1945: The Mass on Suribachi."

15: The Badlands

1. Author's interview with George Colburn, September 25, 2019.

2. G. B. Erskine, "3d Marine Division Reinforced, Iwo Jima Action Report, 31 October 1944–16 March 1945," April 30, 1945, https://www .scribd.com/document/110606038/Iwo-Jima-Campaign-1945, 3.

3. Whitman S. Bartley, *Iwo Jima: Amphibious Epic* (Washington, DC: Historical Branch, G-3 Division, Headquarters, U.S. Marine Corps, 1954), https://upload.wikimedia.org/wikipedia/commons/2/2e/Iwo _Jima-_Amphibious_Epic.pdf, 94.

4. Bill D. Ross, *Iwo Jima: Legacy of Valor* (New York: Vintage Books, 1986), 163.

5. Quoted in Raymond Henri, *Iwo Jima: Springboard to Final Victory* (New York: U.S. Camera Publishing Corporation, 1945), 78.

6. Erskine, "3d Marine Division Reinforced, Iwo Jima Action Report," 5.

7. Quoted in Ross, *Iwo Jima*, 161.

8. Ibid., 164.

9. Erskine, "3d Marine Division Reinforced, Iwo Jima Action Report," 3.

10. Ibid.

11. Ibid., 33.

12. Quoted in Richard F. Newcomb, *Iwo Jima: The Dramatic Account of the Epic Battle That Turned the Tide of World War II* (New York: Signet Books, 1965), 132.

13. Ibid., 132.

14. Erskine, "3d Marine Division Reinforced, Iwo Jima Action Report," 4.

15. Ross, *Iwo Jima*, 165.

16. Quoted in ibid., 165.

17. Erskine, "3d Marine Division Reinforced, Iwo Jima Action Report," 4.

18. Quoted in Ross, *Iwo Jima*, 166.

19. "Grossi, Dominick J.," Traces of War, https://www.tracesofwar.com /persons/31649/Grossi-Dominick-J.htm?c=aw.

20. Ross, *Iwo Jima*, 168.

21. U.S. Marine Corps, *Third Marine Division's Two Score and Ten History* (Paducah, KY: Turner Publishing Company, 1992), 133.

22. Quoted in Ross, *Iwo Jima*, 165.

23. Ibid., 98.

24. "Archambault, Raoul J.," Traces of War, https://www.tracesofwar.com /persons/30409/Archambault-Raoul-J.htm.

25. Erskine, "3d Marine Division Reinforced, Iwo Jima Action Report," 6–7.

26. Ross, *Iwo Jima*, 169.

27. Ibid.

28. Author's interview with Charles Gubish, April 17, 2019.

29. Quoted in Joseph H. Alexander, *Closing In: Marines in the Seizure of Iwo Jima* (Washington, DC: History and Museums Division, Headquarters, United States Marine Corps, 1994), 31.

30. Quoted in ibid., 31.

31. Quoted in Ronald J. Drez, *Twenty-five Yards of War: The Extraordinary Courage of Ordinary Men in World War II* (New York: Hyperion, 2001), 240.

32. Quoted in ibid., 240.

33. Ibid., 242.

34. Ibid.

35. Ibid.

36. Ibid., 244.

37. Ronald Drez, interview with Jay Rebstock, March 20, 1999.

38. Ross, *Iwo Jima*, 169.

39. Author's interview with George Colburn, September 25, 2019.

40. Author's archives.

41. Warren Moscow, "Blood Boats Went with Iwo Invaders," *New York Times*, February 24, 1945.

42. Quoted in Newcomb, *Iwo Jima*, 226.

43. Bartley, *Iwo Jima*, Map V.

44. See blue line of advance on ibid.

45. See green line of advance of February 27 on ibid.

46. Quoted in Ross, *Iwo Jima*, 219.

47. Author's interview with George Colburn, September 25, 2019.

48. Division intelligence report, quoted in Bartley, *Iwo Jima*, 150.

49. Bartley, *Iwo Jima*, Map V.

50. Quoted in Carl W. Proehl, *The Fourth Marine Division in World War II* (Washington, DC: Infantry Journal Press, 1946), 156.

51. "Jacobson, Douglas," Congressional Medal of Honor Recipients, https://themedalofhonor.com/medal-of-honor-recipients/recipients/jacobson-douglas-world-war-two.

52. Quoted in Bartley, *Iwo Jima*, 154.

53. Bartley, *Iwo Jima*, Map XVI.

54. Ibid., 177.

55. Quoted in ibid., 122.

56. Ibid.

57. John C. Chapin, *The Fifth Marine Division in World War II* (Washington, DC: Historical Division, Headquarters, United States Marine Corps, 1945), https://archive.org/details/fifthmarinedivis00chap/page/14, 15.

58. Drez, *Twenty-five Yards of War*, 248.

59. Alexander, *Closing In*, 47.

60. Ronald Drez, interview with Jay Rebstock, March 20, 1999.

61. Ibid.

62. Bartley, *Iwo Jima*, 178.

63. Ibid.; see also Map XVII.

64. Author's interview with George Colburn, September 25, 2019.

65. Author's interview with Charlie Gubish, April 17, 2019.

66. John J. Foster, *History of the Eighth Field Depot and Eighth Service Regiment, 1944–1946* (Lebanon, PA: 1989), 39.

67. Archibald Mosley, interview with Dean Laubach, Corps Connections, October 2015.

68. Alexander, *Closing In*, 46–47.

69. Quoted in Larry Smith, *Iwo Jima: World War II Veterans Remember the Greatest Battle of the Pacific* (New York: W. W. Norton, 2009), 316.

70. H. Avery Chenoweth, *Semper Fi: The Definitive Illustrated History of the U.S. Marines* (New York: Main Street, 2005), 368.

71. "The Atomic Bombings of Hiroshima and Nagasaki: Total Casualties," Atomic Archive, http://www.atomicarchive.com/Docs/MED/med_chp10.shtml.

72. Edwin P. Hoyt, *Japan's War: The Great Pacific Conflict* (New York: Da Capo, 1986), 407.

73. Quoted in Herbert P. Bix, *Hirohito and the Making of Modern Japan* (New York: Harper, 2000), 526.

74. Quoted in ibid., 527.

Epilogue

1. Quoted in David Venditta, "70 Years Later, Marine Veteran, 96, Recalls Battle for Iwo Jima," *The Morning Call*, February 21, 2015, https://www.mcall.com/news/local/mc-iwo-jima-anniversary-gubish -20150221-story.html.

2. Derrick Wright, *The Battle for Iwo Jima, 1945* (Stroud, Gloucestershire, UK: Sutton Publishing, 2007), 45.

3. Herbert P. Bix, *Hirohito and the Making of Modern Japan* (New York: Harper, 2000), 608.

4. Quoted in ibid., 610.

5. "2019 World Population by Country," World Population Review, http:// worldpopulationreview.com/.

6. Quoted in Donald R. McClarey, "February 23, 1945: The Mass on Suribachi," The American Catholic, February 23, 2015, https://www .the-american-catholic.com/2015/02/23/the-mass-on-mount-suri bachi-2/.

About the Author

Martha MacCallum serves as the anchor of *The Story with Martha MacCallum*. She joined the Fox News Channel in January 2004 and is based in New York.

Ronald J. Drez is an award-winning and bestselling author of ten books, among them his most recent works *The War of 1812* and *Predicting Pearl Harbor: Billy Mitchell and the Path to War*. As a captain of Marines, he is a decorated combat veteran of the Vietnam War.

Wrestling with Gravy

Wrestling with Gravy

A LIFE, WITH FOOD

JONATHAN REYNOLDS

RANDOM HOUSE

NEW YORK

TO THE LONG AND ENDURING LINE
OF REMICKS AND REYNOLDSES,
PARTICULARLY THOSE DESCENDING UPON
AND EMANATING FROM QUINCY, MASSACHUSETTS,
AND FORT WORTH, TEXAS

Copyright © 2006 by Jonathan Reynolds

Published in the United States by Random House, an imprint of
The Random House Publishing Group, a division of
Random House, Inc., New York.

RANDOM HOUSE and colophon are registered trademarks of
Random House, Inc.

LIBRARY OF CONGRESS CATALOGING-IN-PUBLICATION DATA

Reynolds, Jonathan.
Wrestling with gravy: a life, with food/Jonathan Reynolds—1st ed.
p. cm.
ISBN 1-4000-6274-8
1. Cookery.   2. Reynolds, Jonathan.   I. Title.

TX714.R496 2006
641.5—dc22   2006041765

Printed in the United States of America on acid-free paper

www.atrandom.com

2 4 6 8 9 7 5 3 1

First Edition

Book design by Simon M. Sullivan

I don't mind dying broke.
I just don't want to be broke the day before.
—Donald W. Reynolds

Be careful, Jonnie!
—Edith Remick Reynolds

Contents

Introduction: Exhuming the Lede

I've WRITTEN ABOUT food on the sly since the age of twenty-nine, never expecting any of it to see the light of day. In an attempt to make order of
what was then a chaotic life, I began making candid diary entries about
restaurants and dinners where I'd been either guest or host, noting not only
what was on each menu but evaluating it and the event's surroundings—and
occasionally throwing in the emotions and current events that went with it.
If I traveled to London or Atlanta or Alleghany County, North Carolina, or Los
Angeles or Manila, I'd take notes about the people and the food (though there
wasn't much to write about in Manila except for the mangoes). Between jobs,
I'd watch afternoon television cooking shows—The Julia, of course, and
Graham Kerr—for their technique and recipes. I'd kept a sports scrapbook as
a kid, cutting out pictures and (rarely) articles about stars in every conceivable
sport—I even had a few pages of swimmers—and now reverted to childhood
practice, only this time filling the scrapbook with recipes and (really rarely)
photographs. I was sure this was a sideline interest, possibly a psychotic one,
so I kept it secret. I should have realized that as I was spending more time describing the preparation for the small dinners I threw for eight to twelve people than on the script I was supposed to be working, and more time on the
preparation itself than on the descriptions, food was becoming more than a
way of not dying. It didn't occur to me that making scribbles in little notebooks
would one day inadvertently prepare me to turn future scribbles into magazine
columns.

A "lede" is newspaperese for the eye-catching topic of a story, the burying of which in someplace other than the first sentence or two is a sure sign of the amateur and a probable loss of the reader's attention. It is spelled as it is so as not to be confused with "lead" as in "leaden," perhaps for fear it might be mistaken as criticism of the writing. By squirreling away these notebooks, I was not only burying one of my life's ledes, I was burying the whole story.

Often, these dinners included some televised event—the Oscars, a World Series, the landing on the moon—to ensure that the guests wouldn't be bored if I was out of the room and they didn't like one another or, more frequently, to keep them happy when dinner was two or three hours late. In 1972, my longtime friend the abstract painter Gary Stephan and his girlfriend Linda Patton and I watched every night of the Summer Olympics—a joyful occasion until the terrorists arrived, then a riveting and somber one. I made all the food every night, liberally mixing cuisines—a bananas Foster preceded by *petits pois* braised with lettuce, preceded by Chinese woolly lamb (chunks of shoulder with cellophane noodles).

Food is controllable, while most of life isn't. And cooking is power: If you're the chef, you're determining what people eat. Cooking encourages freedom and invention, but if you're stuck, you can always fall back on a formula inside a cookbook or something cribbed from Batali on the Food Network. I cook most when feeling helpless: When I've been fired from a job or not hired for another, or a woman didn't phone back or did but said, "I don't think this is working," I'd zip to the stove, seek out Jeremiah Tower's blueberry *financier*, see if I could make a duck-liver mousse, find a new kind of heat to throw into a gumbo, and invite noisy people over. Not only would they be a distraction from my romantic or professional agony of the moment, but by being in charge of others for a few hours, I could be in charge of me for a few hours.

My first paid writing jobs were for David Frost's and Dick Cavett's television shows—the most exciting daily jobs I've ever had. In 1969, Frost was determined to change American television and so approached it like a journalist: get this story, that scoop, this embarrassment to surprise a guest, this confrontation between audience and pundit, all in the mold of an entertaining talk show like Johnny Carson's. Cavett was more cerebral and less rabble-rousing but appreciated guests who didn't usually appear on television. (He was much praised for an appearance by Noël Coward and the Lunts—which irritated him, since he knew they meant little in terms of national ratings.) At the Frost and Cavett shows, I booked and pre-interviewed a guest or two each day and, as a result, met just about everyone I ever wanted to: politicians, writers, movie stars, artists, singers, directors, Colonel Sanders his own self, and even occasionally the Right Woman. I strongly recommend this line of work for at least a year or two to everyone with a crush on adrenaline.

It was also immensely satisfying because whatever I wrote was usually seen on national television that very night. This instant gratification was ruinous for a writing career, and spoiled me for every other medium. When I was—*ahem*—excused from the Cavett show in 1972 and was seriously out of work for the first time in my life at the age of twenty-nine, I took up writing plays and movies—a Sisyphean task, considering my natural disinclination for self-motivation. After the razzle-dazzle of daily television, and now facing an electric typewriter in the stillness of my living room, either there was no feedback at all or it would dribble in months after the work was completed. I don't have now, and didn't have then, sufficient self-confidence to shore up a fathomless need for reinforcement, so I took up cooking. It was instantly creative, sensual, filled my tiny apartment with wonderful smells, and became a much-admired way to avoid writing. Other writers would say to me, "So that's how *you* don't write. Cool." And the reinforcement was as instantaneous as a daily talk show's, unless I was preparing thousand-year-old eggs.

Serendipitously, I learned that women find a man cooking seductive. I'm not sure why. Perhaps it's the surprise, or the role reversal, or some revelation of this warm fuzzy we men are secretly supposed to have if only we'd admit it, or the implied altruism—"He's taking the time to whip up that *riz à l'impératrice* just for *me*"—but every woman I've asked, married or un-, claims that a man cooking specifically for her is aphrodisiacal.

The converse is not true. Most men still find women who cook specifically for them scary, grasping, desperate, and clearly in search of a lifelong mate. Worst of all, it's expected—like men fixing the satellite dish. Women need to *not* cook for thirty or forty years so it becomes a novelty again.

My evidence is empirical. Two instances spring to mind. I wish I could brag about them over beers, but due to substantial defects in my personality, both failed to evolve into anything lasting longer than a few hours. The first woman, although sufficiently smitten by what I prepared, wouldn't go out with me for another five months, and that date was the last. Something terrible must have happened between the pear frangipane tart and breakfast, and I never knew what it was, though I am still willing to learn.

I'd been infatuated with the second woman for five years. After I made dinner, she, too, seemed smitten by my cooking just for her. I kissed her passionately after the dessert and could sense her breath shorten through her nose. I slipped my hand between her legs with ease—usually an encouraging sign. But just as the tension became deliciously unbearable and undergarments could no longer contain our heaving flesh, an alarm went off in her cortex, and she refastened snaps and clips, smoothed her skirt, and abruptly departed to meet another guy. She'd made an additional date at ten o'clock! The lucky beneficiary of all my toil and sweat was greeted with a well-fed, well-primed sleeping companion for whom he had to do no heavy lifting at all. True to form, I didn't see her again for ten years, when she wouldn't even hold hands.

Neither of these instances was calculated. I loved cooking and selflessly (well, sort of) wanted to thrill these young racehorses with vibrant new tastes. And since I wasn't making a dime at the time, it was actually quite a bit cheaper to stay home with a bottle of plonk and a *bavarois Clermont* than to go to a restaurant, even if it meant sweating over the soup for hours beforehand. Besides, taking a woman to a restaurant on a first date is about as original as carrying her books, and about as stressful as the night the *Times* critic comes to your play.

A man has to be truly obnoxious to impress a woman at a restaurant on a first date because he really has to perform. He's got a limited time frame and limited physical possibilities: About all he can do is talk and either show off about the wine or embarrass the waiter or in some way be completely thrilling. Women like to be thrilled.

But wielding a cleaver and sautéing diver scallops in his own kitchen, well, the work speaks for itself. He can bop around, show off scrapbooks and music, dance, do push-ups, and generally dazzle with displays of his possessions.

If you're lucky, there's a moment on a date when her eyes will forget the background and focus on you. She'll laugh at an idiosyncrasy, or you'll mesh on some point—a dislike of skiers, the weirdness of the name *Verizon*, a fear of heights, the realization that, despite Hollywood screenwriting rules, people usually *aren't* sympathetic—something. Even if all you make is farfalle with jarred tomato sauce (don't show her the jar), you will have her focus.

During my second single life, which only recently ended without remorse in a second marriage, I devised the following:

TEN RULES FOR SEDUCING A WOMAN BY COOKING HER DINNER

(which may also apply to men cooking for men and women cooking for women—
I don't know)

1. Find out if the seductee is allergic to anything. Find out what she loves but seldom gets, and get it.

2. Make something ambitious. Although I generally prefer simplicity at a restaurant, the perfectly cooked chicken breast isn't going to accomplish what you want unless your date is Rose Levy Beranbaum.

3. Balance the meal. You don't want it all heavily sauced, or neither one of you will feel thin enough to take your clothes off.

4. Serve something exotic—like cardoon. Though popular in France and Italy, and available here from late spring till early fall, it has never become popular in this country. It looks like celery, tastes like artichoke, and will make you seem a man of the world.

5. Have plenty of cayenne pepper on hand. Cayenne masks every conceivable cooking mistake except oversalting and burning. The former you can fix with sliced raw potato or a teaspoon of sugar and vinegar. If you burn something, you may be pleasantly surprised to find that she thinks you did it on purpose. Or you can always say, "I caramelized it."

6. Try to pull off at least one impressive cooking flourish. Throw things around in a wok or set something on fire. Don't froth anything—that's been over for years. Pour something from a great height,

like mint tea in a Moroccan restaurant. Think Baryshnikov, not one of those grunting tennis players.

7. Never consult a cookbook in public. Memorize the recipes or write them on little cards and hide them around your apartment, the way Marlon Brando did in *Last Tango*.

8. Clean your apartment to a better-than-postgraduate level.

9. Make sure the woman you're cooking for doesn't have another date at ten o'clock.

10. Make these:

CHICKEN LA TULIPE

La Tulipe was a wonderful restaurant on Thirteenth Street just off Sixth Avenue in New York that made a feast of a single chicken and had the pride to name it after itself. It is as close to an aphrodisiac as the date rape laws currently allow.

1 ½ ounces dried morels
2 tablespoons Cognac
2 tablespoons butter
1 ¼ cups light cream or crème fraîche
1 teaspoon salt, divided in half
Pinch of cayenne
One 3 ½-pound chicken, rinsed (neck, giblets, and liver removed)
¼ teaspoon pepper
¼ cup dry white wine

1. Preheat oven to 450 degrees. Wash morels carefully with cold water, making sure you get all the sand and grit out. Let morels soak in Cognac 15 minutes. Drain, reserving liquid.
2. Sauté morels in 1 tablespoon of the butter for 5 minutes; then add ½ cup of the light cream and reduce by half. Stir in ½ teaspoon of the salt and the cayenne.

3. Rub chicken with remaining butter and sprinkle with remaining salt and the pepper. Spoon morels into the body cavity. Roast chicken on one side for 15 minutes, baste, and then roast on the other side 15 minutes and baste again. Finally, roast it breast-side up for 20 minutes.

4. Remove chicken from the oven. Throw away most of the fat from the pan, add the wine and mushroomy Cognac, deglazing, and flambé immediately. *Make sure your guest sees this move.* Reduce over high heat.

5. Shake morels and juices from the chicken into the pot, add the rest of the light cream, and simmer for 5 minutes, until thickened. Taste for seasoning.

6. Cut the chicken into 8 serving pieces, arrange them on a platter, and pour the morel sauce over them. If it's that kind of evening, limit yourselves to two pieces each (see Rule Three on page xiii).

YIELD: 2 big servings.

BRAISED CARDOON
(or, Less Exotic but Still Formidable, Leeks)

4 cardoon stalks, peeled, split lengthwise, cut into 2-inch pieces, and
    washed well (or leeks, cleaned of all internal grit)
1 cup beef broth
1 tablespoon butter, in bits
Salt and freshly ground pepper

1. Preheat oven to 450 degrees. Grease a 1-quart baking dish. Cut cardoon crosswise into ½-inch pieces. Place in baking dish.

2. Bring beef broth to a boil and pour over the cardoon, top with butter, and sprinkle with salt and pepper.

3. Cover tightly with foil and bake 40 minutes, until tender.

YIELD: 2 servings.

BAKED FIGS

This is a freely adapted version of a recipe by Alain Senderens, the noted Parisian chef of Chez Lucas-Carton.

6 firm, ripe fresh figs, stems removed

1 ½ tablespoons butter, melted

1 ½ tablespoons sugar

Vanilla ice cream (or 1 cup raspberries, ½ cup heavy cream, and ¼ cup confectioners' sugar)

1. Preheat oven to 375 degrees and grease a medium-size baking dish.
2. Place figs in the baking dish and brush with butter and sprinkle with sugar. Bake 15 minutes, until bubbly and lightly caramelized.
3. With scissors or a knife, make an X in the top of each fig so that it opens like a flower.
4. Serve figs hot with ice cream, or with raspberries folded into heavy cream whipped with confectioners' sugar.

YIELD: 2 servings.

Wrestling with Gravy

Cut to the Chase

~~~~~~

MY PARENTS BATTLED through an acrimonious divorce right at the end of the war that supposedly made their generation the Greatest. They were almost central-castingly perfect opposites: Don Reynolds was short and fat, and at first meeting seemed like a hick from the dustbowls of Oklahoma and Texas; Edith Remick was a tall, dark-haired beauty, a refined and privately schooled graduate of Smith who had been brought up in Quincy, Massachusetts. She was given to upper-middle-class maladies like mild depression, frequently saw doctors for no apparent reason, and spent an inordinate amount of time resting at home. He was a whirlwind, she a lovely and fragile icicle.

In the late thirties, he briefly owned part of a Quincy newspaper. One of his biggest advertisers was an upscale department store specializing in men's clothing, named Remick's. They met at a company picnic, and he swept her off her feet. She'd never seen anyone like him: such energy, such surprising smarts, such wild visions of the future. And such a sexual drive. I don't know whether he loosed her panties the very first night or was forced to wait till marriage—but I would bet the ranch, if I had one, that it was on his mind, raging, from the moment they met and every moment thereafter. He told her—and her family—that he intended to live in Quincy for the rest of their lives together.

Within a month of their marriage, he sold his interest in the Quincy newspaper and announced that they were moving to Texas. He didn't ask her and hadn't forewarned her or anyone in the family; he just announced it, and off they went. Men could get away with things like that then. He then proceeded to hit the road in search of additional businesses. My sister, Nancy, was born in San Antonio in 1938, and the three of them moved to Fort Smith, Arkansas, where he established the Southwestern Publishing Company, a solely-owned enterprise that operated half a dozen small newspapers. I was born in February 1942, barely two months after the attack on Pearl Harbor, and Dad was drafted shortly after that. He grumbled about the army but finagled his way to Europe, where all the glamour was.

He returned home from adventures in London, France, and Australia, restless to continue his empire-building. Despite a wound received while being flown somewhere for *Stars and Stripes* (the military newspaper), he'd had a great time during the war, traveling everywhere and hobnobbing with bigs. As he was fond of saying, "It was a hell of a war, but better than no war at all!" After about five minutes of peacetime America, he looked at the open landscape and concluded he'd outgrown Mother, and definitely had outgrown children. He hit the road for good in pursuit of new ventures, thinking Mother was living with my sister and me back in Texas because that's where he'd last left us and that's where her letters were postmarked. Once Mother decided on a divorce—an iconoclastic choice in those days, unless you were a Hollywood star—all Dad had to do to protect his rapidly increasing wealth was stay out of Texas so he wouldn't be served with divorce papers.

Or so he thought. But Mother snuck us into Arkansas, where his headquarters was located. To establish residence, we hid out for six dusty months in Blytheville because she might have been recognized in Little Rock or Fort Smith. I remember surviving a tornado, watching Mother alone at an outdoor ironing board, and seeing a dog kill a rabbit. Nothing else.

With the help of a very determined lawyer named Fred Schlater, Mother found out Dad was driving into Arkansas late one night and hired a midnight paper-server to surprise Dad with divorce documents right there on the highway.

Angry? I was only three or four and didn't see the ambush, but he must have stomped around the countryside kicking up dust and biting dogs for weeks. He was so furious about the trap she'd laid—cop cars! Middle of the night! Those lying postmarks—that he wouldn't talk to her, except in a courtroom, for eleven years! Her treachery filled him with such righteous indignation that he felt he didn't have to see us more than fifteen minutes a year on moral grounds.

He stayed in the Southwest and frequently saw his son by his second marriage, Don Junior (Mother was his third of four wives), while Mother reared Nancy and me in New York. I do remember that once he began rolling in dough, he exaggerated his childhood poverty so as to make his substantial, self-made adult wealth all the more mythic.

The world operated by one set of values, and Dad lived by another, which changed whenever he wanted it to. And he bragged about that set! He believed in his right to complete self-expression regardless of whom it hurt; and he had the vision of an artist. He's one of the reasons I've thought artists are natural Republicans—they have vision and, like the best entrepreneurs, will do anything they must to realize it. Dad benefited thousands of people by employing them and gave everyone good benefits and low-cost loans for education. He was the only stockholder of his company, which meant he had to answer to no one.

I envied his fearlessness, his creativity, and his lack of concern for what others thought of him. I was tugged—yanked—between two radical extremes: on the one hand, a father who lived like a circus acrobat, balancing upside down on one finger atop a unicycle that he pedaled along a tightrope several thousand feet in the air; and on the other, a terrified, cautious, and passive mother who cared excessively what others thought. Envied him, simulated her. Saw no faults in him and in her nothing but. Perhaps it was because I was surrounded by her family and can remember seeing his only once.

Alice Waters Cooks Her Turkey Too Long

F OR CHILDREN, the end-of-year holidays—Thanksgiving, Christmas, New Year's—are cause for celebration bordering on delirium. For adults, they often signal obligation, and border on panic, and fear of disappointment.

By the time I was aware of Thanksgiving, at about six, the Remicks were as fractured as the Tyrones in *Long Day's Journey into Night*, though without the drugs or booze. Grammie was a determined widow, Mother was filled with repressed rage, and she and her brother, Bus, were both divorced at a time when it was considered a sign of mental disturbance, and Maymie, her sister, was what used to be called a spinster and possibly lesbian before it was fashionable. But we all temporarily regrouped for Thanksgiving in Quincy, as though posing for the cover of *The Saturday Evening Post*.

The highest compliment Grammie could pay a turkey was to say that its skin was just like wrapping paper. She'd always ask, "Would you like some wrapping paper, dear?" The turkey in those days seemed all right to me but hardly worth the long train ride. The sides were much more fun: candied sweet potatoes, sweetened cranberry jelly from the can, peas with sugar, corn with sugar, stuffing with sugar, endless pies of apple, mince, and canned peach. Unlike most nostalgics who revert to their childhoods for soothe, I've never had any of those exact recipes since: sweet potatoes and all the rest are much better without all the treacle. I wasn't paying much attention to food then—except for the single candy Grammie always offered each of us at meal's end from the Whitman's Sampler she kept in a cupboard. To me,

Thanksgiving was just the holiday without presents. It wasn't until much later that I discovered that eating was one of its pleasures, and that you could have your wrapping paper—and turn turkey into a destination.

A superbly roasted turkey (or any other poultry, for that matter) is welcome at any time of year. Even though they're bland, I love what these beautiful birds represent all the year round and rush to embrace new methods of preparation even in the summer because turkeys remind me of holidays as a child, and I want to re-create that feeling for others—an impossibility, of course.

Any day in May, when the suicide-and-euphoria holidays of the previous winter are a distant memory (as in childbirth, the pain forgotten or nobody would go through it again), is probably the perfect time to talk about cooking a turkey. Procrastinators can rejoice that they have 190+ days to plan but not execute, and the better-adjusted among us can analyze at leisure instead of rushing to the stove, ripped magazine recipe in hand, on Thanksgiving or Christmas morning, when it's too late. And tortured perfectionists like Barbra Streisand can practice, practice, practice.

The difficulty, as we have been told almost daily for the last quarter-century, is to cook the bird's drumsticks and thighs sufficiently without turning the white meat into washcloth.

All sorts of well-intentioned tricks are suggested for moisturizing the breast meat. Julia Child was said to massage butter between the breast and the skin, which lubricates the breast but makes the texture of the meat greasy and the taste overly buttery. Martha Stewart dips cheesecloth in melted butter, then drapes it over the white meat, but the melted butter fails to penetrate the more-or-less-waterproof skin. Alice Waters soaks the entire fowl in a home-concocted brine for seventy-two hours. This step is indeed helpful, though it takes so much time that you need to plan days ahead for even the simplest fowl. And she then defeats her noble aim by keeping the bird in the oven too long, drying it out.

There are two solutions. For those with successful hedge funds, buy two turkeys and cook one for the white meat and the other for the dark, then discard the overcooked white of one and the undercooked dark of the other. The rest of us can follow John Hess's method and have our twelve-pound dinner out of the oven in two hours, our sixteen-pounder in two and a half, and a twenty-pounder done perfectly in three.

Based on Hess's recipe, which appeared in *The New York Times* more than thirty years ago, a twelve-pound turkey is stuffed, slathered with a stick of butter, roasted at a very high temperature, first on one side, then the other, and basted every twenty minutes or so. True, all the basting is a nuisance, and the smoke caused by the high temperature may result in a visit from New York's Bravest, but this is a small price to pay for a standing ovation and the likelihood of hotel-room keys dropped in your direction by Casablanca models. Our bird will have juicy breasts, pinkless legs, and skin that crackles in your mouth like a UPS parcel.

Two important don'ts. First, don't truss the animal, whether you stuff it or not. Trussing is a matter of aesthetics: The perfectly bound, coquettishly trussed bird reminds me of a '50s debutante at a cotillion, not a hair out of place; untrussed, it looks like a ravished slut, disheveled and eager for more. But if you bind the turkey legs together, fifteen to thirty minutes must be added to the cooking time so the insides of the thighs and legs can reach the proper temperature—and at that point about the only thing you can do with the white meat is spackle the bathroom. If the purpose of trussing is to contain stuffing in the body cavity, a simple pin through the skin flap will do that; if the butcher has removed the flap, cover the opening with foil.

Second, don't, as some suggest, pour water into the roasting pan to prevent it from scorching, or you'll inadvertently steam the bird. Two tablespoons of oil will do the trick—as well as neutralize the burning properties of the stick of butter.

GRAMMIE NEVER PREPARED our Thanksgiving turkey, and I don't know how it was cooked. She had what used to be called a maid who did the culinary work. In those days, you could tell which hemisphere you were in by how the maid was addressed: if she was called "Miss" or "Mrs.," you were in the northern; if "Amice" or "Thelma," the southern.

Magically, Grammie's Mrs. O'Bannion would appear at exactly the right moment when the family—which included my sister, Nancy, and me now—was finished or ready for seconds.

"How does Mrs. O'Bannion know we're finished?" I asked Grammie time after time, which amused her no end. Over many Thanksgivings and summer holidays, I'd ask how Mrs. O'Bannion knew her entrance cue, and Grammie wouldn't tell me, just smiled slyly. I became increasingly frustrated and dazzled by this telepathy.

Finally, after an hour of pleading that threatened to last one entire Thanksgiving day, she decided that if she didn't tell me I might either 'splode or become an even greater danger to society than I turned out to be. "Look," she said, pointing to a bump in the rug near her chair. She pressed it with the ball of her foot, and Mrs. O'Bannion whooshed through the swinging door.

"What? What did you do?"

Grammie laughed. So did everyone else. "Go into the kitchen," she said.

I did, and after a moment heard a buzz. I didn't get it.

Then I did!

I ran back into the living room. "It's a buzzer! You operate it with your foot! It's hidden under the rug!"

"Yes, dear."

Nancy, three and a half years older, rolled her eyes. "Duh," she said, two or three decades before it became hip again.

I didn't care—I had discovered one of the wonders of electricity! If not electricity itself! "May I do it?"

"Yes."

I sat in her chair and toed the buzzer's button about thirty times, just stopping before everyone went insane. "That's enough, dear," Grammie finally said. "Now sit down and have some wrapping paper."

To serve ten people and have leftovers for sandwiches, here are two methods:

Two Ways to Roast a Turkey

1. Strangle and pluck a 12-pound turkey, preferably an anarchist that has been allowed to run around and eat grain whenever it wants. Remove whatever is inside (usually a neck and giblets) and cut off the wing tips, reserving them.

2. *Method One:* Twenty hours before cooking, swish 2 cups of kosher salt in 2–3 gallons of cold water until dissolved (no need to heat it) and submerge the turkey for 12 hours in this brine, using a weight to keep it underwater. (Waters suggests a more complicated mixture, but since the bird is rinsed thoroughly after brining, it just adds unnecessary work.) Either put this brining turkey in the fridge for those 12 hours or more, or if there's no room and the temperature is 33 degrees Fahrenheit or better and you live on a low floor, put it on the windowsill; or put lots of ice cubes in the brine, adding more when they melt. Skip to step 5.

3. *Method Two:* Instead of brining, after removing the neck, giblets, and wing tips, follow the recipe for Internal Turkey Brine (page 12), and inject the result into the turkey, as instructed. This will keep the bird as moist as the brining process does and gives it more flavor.

4. Pat the skin dry and refrigerate overnight (or at least 12 hours) so the skin will tighten and dry, increasing its eventual postalness.

5. Begin your stock by deeply scoring whatever was inside the turkey (except the liver, which may be chopped, sautéed, and added to a stuffing) and the wing tips and tossing them into a pot. Add a sliced carrot, a sliced celery stalk, a large quartered onion, and a handful of parsley and cover with water or with poultry, veal, or beef stock. Simmer for 3 hours, replenishing the liquid if it gets low or too salty. Because you are in charge, when the stock is done you get to eat the neck, which is delicious. You may also eat the vegetables, which are pretty tasty, too.

6. One hour before cooking the turkey, remove it from the fridge to bring it to room temperature and preheat the oven to 450 degrees. Pour a couple of tablespoons of oil into a roasting pan and either oil or use a nonstick V-shaped, nonadjustable rack. (Adjustable racks are too unreliable and may collapse under the turkey's weight.)

7. Stuff the turkey and rub its skin with a stick of softened butter. Place it on its side on the rack, place the rack in the roasting pan and the roasting pan into the blistering oven. Roast for 30 minutes. If smoke filters out of your oven, enjoy its spiritual qualities unless something actually catches fire. (If, however, your kitchen, the pan juices, or the turkey's skin ever approach blackness, turn the oven down to 400, or even 375 degrees.)

8. Baste the turkey with the pan juices. Then take the pan out of the oven, and with wads of wet paper towels (or large forks) placed at either end, turn the turkey over onto its other side, baste it, and put it back in the oven. (Turning the thing can get pretty ungraceful, so try not to be photographed right now, and don't try to turn the turkey at oven level unless you're wearing a truss. Instead, lift the pan from the oven rack, closing the oven door with your left heel; place the pan on a steady surface and wrestle the bird to its other side however you can.) Set the timer for 20 minutes and baste every 20 minutes, four times—your total cooking time will now be 110 minutes. Rotate the by-now-mahoganied beauty breast-side up, basting everything in sight.

9. Take the turkey's temperature in the fattest part of its thigh. It should read 135 to 145 degrees. (If it doesn't, leave it in a few more minutes.) If it does, take it out immediately and put it on a platter—it will continue to cook for the next 20 minutes or so while you make the sauce.

10. No flour or thickener is used in the sauce because it tastes better without. Pour off half the fat from the bottom of the roasting pan and place the pan over high heat (possibly two burners). Add 1 cup of the strained turkey stock and deglaze the pan, dislodging everything with a wooden spoon. Taste for saltiness and intensity—sometimes the sauce can go in those directions. If it does, add another cup of stock and reduce. If it is still too intense or salty, thin with a little water. Add ½ cup Cognac, white wine, or dry sherry and bring to a boil or set it afire to cook off the booze. This will not make more than 1 ½ cups of sauce—a tablespoon or two per serving, which is all that's needed. Some strain this concoction, but I prefer being surprised by tasty little scraps on top of my white meat.

When you roast the turkey on its sides, gravity drips what little fat exists in the dark meat into the white; like the basting, this helps moisten the meat. Some suggest cooking the bird breast-side down until the last 30 minutes, then browning the breast, but this makes basting about six times as difficult and the back of the turkey the brownest part of the body.

With the technique above, you'll be out of the kitchen an hour earlier than you have been at previous feasts. Your turkey will be sensual with juice, your wrapping paper will crackle, and you'll be ready to do battle with the next national holiday—the Academy Awards.

Internal Turkey Brine
¾ cup chopped onion
¾ cup chopped celery
3–6 tablespoons chopped garlic
4 tablespoons unsalted butter
2 tablespoons (or more) chopped hot peppers from pepper vinegar
2 tablespoons Worcestershire sauce
1 tablespoon plus 1 teaspoon salt
1 tablespoon cayenne
1 tablespoon black pepper
1 cup chicken stock

1. Sauté onion, celery, and garlic in butter until tender. Add hot peppers and Worcestershire sauce, then stir in the salt, cayenne, and black pepper. Add the chicken stock and bring to a boil.
2. Strain into a bowl, pressing the solids to extract as much juice as possible, to yield about 1½ cups.
3. With monster hypodermic, inject the turkey's breast in five places and each leg and wing in one place.
4. Pat the skin dry and refrigerate overnight, or 6–12 hours.

JOHN HESS'S SAUSAGE, BLACK OLIVE, AND WALNUT STUFFING

(Adapted from The Taste of America *by John L. Hess and Karen Hess, Viking, 1977)*
I've been making this basic stuffing for decades, and when I don't overcook it, it's marvelous. When I do, I add a little stock or fat to moisten it.

1 pound bulk pork sausage
1 turkey liver, minced

1 cup chopped onions

½ cup very thinly sliced celery

1 teaspoon chopped fresh thyme

1 loaf good bread, sliced

1 cup mild, pitted California-style black olives, sliced

1 cup walnut pieces

½ cup chopped Italian parsley

2 tablespoons Cognac or 4 tablespoons Madeira, port, or dry sherry

Kosher salt and freshly ground black pepper to taste

½–1 cup turkey stock, depending on desired moistness

1. Place the sausage and the turkey liver in a large heavy pan over medium heat, stirring until cooked and the sausage meat is well broken up, about 12 minutes.
2. Add the onions, celery, and thyme and cook, stirring frequently, until the onions are tender and pale yellow, about 10 minutes.
3. Toast the bread slices and dice; you should have about 3 cups. Place the sausage mixture in a bowl and add in the bread.
4. Mix in the olives, walnut pieces, Italian parsley, Cognac, salt, and pepper.
5. Add enough stock so the stuffing will hold together in the bird.

YIELD: About 4 cups.

If Alice Waters cooks her turkey too long, it's about the only thing in the culinary world she's ever done wrong. If most of the great professional chefs have been men for the last century, most of the great cookbook writers (and therefore influences on the home kitchen) have been women. Julia Child, Marcella Hazan, Madhur Jaffrey, Diana Kennedy, Eileen Yin-Fei Lo, and of course Elizabeth David, Jane Grigson, and the Fannie Farmer conglomerate spring to mind. There are many crossovers, of course—Mario Batali, Eric Ripert, and Thomas Keller helm kitchens and write excellent books. But none has done both to the degree Alice Waters has over the last thirty years. Her restaurant Chez Panisse in Berkeley is responsible for the California-cuisine explosion, and her cookbooks have spread the gospel to benighted urbanites the world over. She continues to be at the forefront of sustainable farming and cooking.

Now, good as the turkey above is, if you've got room for a vat of boiling oil and a propane tank to fire it, I strongly suggest deep-frying a turkey. Although bringing four to five gallons of oil to a bubble can take as much as forty-five minutes, the turkey takes only three and a half minutes per pound to deep-fry, little or no oil is absorbed because of the turkey's skin, and the resulting meat is the best turkey you'll ever taste. Though Louisianans have been boiling their birds for decades, I read about it in a piece for *The New Yorker* by Calvin Trillin and have since made about fifty of them without a single hitch in either flavor or conflagration. However, the potential for fire and oil-mess is great, which means you *must* do this procedure outdoors. Equipment made specifically for deep-frying turkeys (but useful for other preparations) is available at www .cabelas.com and many other outdoor outfitters.

Deep-Fried Turkey

(Adapted from The Prudhomme Family Cookbook *by Paul Prudhomme, William Morrow, 1987)*

One 14-pound turkey
4–5 gallons of peanut oil or lard
Internal Turkey Brine (page 12), minus the cayenne pepper
1 tablespoon cayenne or favorite Cajun spice

1. Follow instructions for Internal Turkey Brine, but omit the cayenne for now.
2. After injecting the turkey, with your bare hands, rub the cayenne into the turkey's breast *under the skin.*
3. You can either refrigerate, uncovered, 8–24 hours to dry out the skin or fry it immediately.
4. When you're ready to fry the turkey, remove it from the refrigerator, place it in the empty fryer, and cover completely with water. Then empty the pot, measuring the water.

5. Fill the fryer with the same amount of oil or lard, attach the extra-long thermometer to the pot, and heat the oil to 350–375 degrees.

6. Pierce the turkey with its holder and lower slowly into the oil.

7. Boil the turkey for 49 minutes or slightly longer (3–3 ½ minutes per pound).

8. Remove the turkey, let the excess oil drain off, and rest it on a platter for 10–20 minutes. Slice and dive in!

GRAMMIE WAS ALICE COOPER (yup) until she married Alfred Remick at the turn of the last century. Alfred was one of several brothers who owned Remick's, at the time a dry-goods store frequented by working men in Quincy. Although Alfred and Alice had three children—my mother, Edith, my uncle Bus, my aunt Mary, known as Maymie—their marriage was said to be relatively loveless. Alfred was a bayzo—fond of bay rum—and frequently could be heard by neighbors bellowing songs late at night as he wound his way up the hill from Remick's to the family house at 26 Fairmount Way. These noisy returns home infuriated Alice and got him banished from the bedroom. *Withholding* and *passive-aggressive* were not yet terms in fashion, simply because no professional jargonists knew Grammie. Ice. Silence. Cut-off.

But when Alfred died suddenly of a heart attack in his fifties, Grammie was heartbroken and went into deep mourning. She didn't exactly wear black the rest of her life like her mentor Queen Victoria, but she never married again. I don't think it occurred to her. By the time I knew her, she seemed loving and affable, with an easy, subdued laugh and the softest, wrinkliest skin. Her gift for inducing guilt was passed down to my mother, Edith, and it gave them both pleasure and the illusion of control.

Alfred left the store to his widow and three children, to be managed by the man in the family, Bus. He was a senior at Harvard and uninterested in the retail business but dutifully took on the assignment. Over the years, he turned Remick's into not only a success but the fashion center of downtown Quincy. He redesigned the interior, making its focal point a long, gracefully curved staircase, at the top of which he hung an enormous oil of Alfred. The portrait gave the store an aura of tradition, history, and permanence; the staircase and up-to-date fixtures transformed it from a boots-and-overalls store for the working stiff to an elegant emporium for the upper-middle-class aspirant. He improved the quality of the merchandise on sale, specializing in above-average men's haberdashery. He knew his customer base well enough not to attempt Armanitude, and was happy to be considered a competitor of Brooks Brothers. In the fifties, Bus mechanized the store windows at Christmas, as Saks and Lord & Taylor and B. Altman's had done in New York. None of these successes was accomplished without considerable personal sacrifice.

Most Elegant Fowl

FATHER OF ACTRESS Lee and would-be rancher Bruce, stepfather to three, and maternal uncle to my sister, Nancy, and me—Bus Remick was the most elegant man ever to grace the boulevards of New York, Boston, and Quincy, Massachusetts. Even given the hyperbole of memory, he remains the only person I never saw ruffle.

He loved good food, all the arts (on principle), laughing—slow, rolling baritone—his children, two wives at the appropriate times, and the retail business. He knew who he was; his view of the world was balanced, though occasionally Republican and decidedly anti-Kennedy, and his devotion was unconditional, as you'll see.

His real name was Frank, and his nickname was short for Buster, which he was called because he had once been a chubby kid—no remnant of which remained by the time I met him. Ever since I can remember, he looked like the love child of Cary Grant and William Holden and smoked cigarettes beautifully, using a long holder.

As a teenager, I didn't know what class I'd been born into or that there were classes. Certainly, the Remicks were middle class, and Bus's retail success and increasing prominence in the Quincy business community nudged the family toward upper-middle-classness. Dad was decidedly lower class by birth, but by virtue of all his money and the divorce settlement wrested from him by Mother, Nancy and I were New York City private-school kids and probably somewhere between middle and upper-middle. In any case, we both resented it—from the safe distance of being in it. Nancy wanted to dance professionally, and I emulated all the pop-idol bad boys, from Elvis to James Dean to Brando, dying to carry a switchblade, don a black leather jacket, and ride a motorcycle—though I was as far from being a tough guy as anyone at the Allen-Stevenson or Trinity schools who didn't learn to ride a bicycle (let alone a hog) till he was twenty-two could be. Still, as a teenager, I loved Brando's line (or rather the screenwriter John Paxton's line spoken by Brando) in *The Wild One*.

GIRL

What're you rebelling against, Johnny?

BAD BRANDO

Whaddaya got?

I'd made a study of cigarette-smoking styles and found myself torn between the soigné technique of Uncle Bus (from the Noël Coward School of Smoking) and how I imagined my father would have smoked—ciggie between thumb and first two fingers—if he had. And then there was the tortured cigarette manipulation of James Dean, which was mighty attractive. At a New Year's Eve party when I was fourteen, I toyed with Pall Malls and a holder and got a date, which I assumed was because the holder (or possibly the Bermuda shorts and knee-length socks) made me look grown up. I continued with the holder for a week or so before the whole process just became too unwieldy. But Uncle Bus always made it look smooth.

When, years later, he was forced to give it up because of a series of heart attacks, and his doctor advised gum as a stand-in, he became the suavest of chewers, slowly and subtly massaging the gum, never popping it or biting it frenetically, so that in his mouth even this activity looked magnolious.

The beaming black-and-white photograph of him on his mother's antimacassared Victorian tabletop in her dark Quincy parlor, brass buttons and gold braid spiking his double-breasted navy uniform, made him look more dashing—and a lot less show-bizzy—than Gary Cooper or Adolphe Menjou. His clothes were understated, though expensive. He frequented the theatre, loved the ballet even before my sister danced in the New York City Ballet under Balanchine. When in New York, he took me several times to Birdland, where, in sheer volume (let alone transcendence), the Count Basie Band with Joe Williams would have humbled the mongrel children of Limp Bizkit and Nine Inch Nails. We laughed every time we entered the place. Over the entrance was inscribed "Through These Portals Pass the Most." When I'd visit my uncle in his bachelor digs in Boston between his marriages, he'd put on a platter late at night, turn off the lights, and teach me how to listen to music: in the dark and L-O-U-D.

Bus had dreamed of high finance in London and Paris, but when his father died, he found his role in life: George Bailey, the character played by Jimmy Stewart in *It's a Wonderful Life*. If Bus hadn't agreed to run Remick's, his mother and two older sisters might have become penniless. Certainly, they were frightened. He embraced responsibility, took over the reins of the business for the sake of the women . . . and discovered he loved it. He held the company reins till shortly before he died of heart failure in 1983. Although needled by my father to open other branches of Remick's, or at least move out of downtown Quincy before it died, he remained civic-minded and kept only the one store, on Hancock Street. When it became successful, he took a box at Fenway.

This is how elegant he was: After Mother divorced, she sued Bus for paying her less than what she felt was her fair share of the family store, and Bus, not yet fifty, had his first heart attack. For years afterward, until a judge dismissed the case as frivolous and declared the price fair, Bus suffered considerable New England guilt. When I was twelve and found my eighty-third school in a row incompatible (actually, it found me), Mother had the nerve to phone him and ask for help as a paternal surrogate; Dad was empire-building out west and had little interest in counseling his children. He felt the million bucks Mother "stole" from him was sufficient contribution.

By rights, Bus didn't owe his litigious sister the time of day. She had brought him much misery and had nearly broken up the Remicks of Quincy—both commercially and personally. And he was trying to ease his own children through his divorce. But shortly after her phone call, Bus flew down to New York, never said a word against her, and introduced me to my first red wine, pheasant under glass, and steak without ketchup.

Though we moved to New York when I was six, my experience with "fine dining" had been limited to Mother's infrequent forays to Longchamps and

Schrafft's, which meant putting on a tie, Wildrooting down my hair, and sitting up straight (squirming actually) just in order to eat a "chopped sirloin" that wasn't nearly as good as the monster ground chuck at Hamburger Heaven next door. (It still isn't; chuck makes a better burger than sirloin.)

At home, I nourished myself with No-Cal cream soda, a forerunner of the diet-soda mania, and often requested Anne Pudding, named after a maid we had. The recipe is as follows:

ANNE PUDDING

1 slice pound cake
$\frac{1}{2}$ cup vanilla sauce, from powder
$\frac{1}{2}$ cup Nestle's milk-chocolate bits, more if I could get them

1. Put pound cake on plate.
2. Warm vanilla sauce and pour over pound cake.
3. Smother with chocolate bits.

YIELD: 1 serving.

So when Uncle Bus took me solo to the dining room of the old Westbury Hotel on Madison Avenue, I went eagerly—he was fun to be with, and he listened.

Until that night, he had seemed a pleasant, if distant relative, who was married to an energetic and breathtaking blonde and who was raising two golden children much more popular than I thought my sister and I were. I realized later we didn't see much of that side of the family because of Mother's lawsuit.

I didn't know what a pheasant was, but I'd heard it referred to in plays and books as the epitome of Upper East Side excess, and it appeared on the Westbury's menu. The restaurant's interior was considerably tonier than any I'd been to previously—filled with red velvet banquettes, golden lighting fixtures, perhaps a crystal chandelier. I wore a tie.

Mother certainly wouldn't have allowed me to have pheasant—too sybaritic and too expensive. But testing adults was the only behavior I felt comfortable with, and Uncle Bus was not only an adult, but also one who needed testing to see if he would leave like Dad. I had to ask. "What if I ordered the pheasant under glass?" Bus didn't raise an eyebrow at the expense or question my judgment.

"That's why I had them put it on the menu," he said. His eyes were playful. He had aced the test.

The bird didn't look nearly as glamorous as the "under glass" had promised. Instead of plumage and trumpets, here was a beige poultry breast under what I called gravy ("sauce," Uncle Bus said lightly), covered with a cloudy glass dome. When the waiter lifted the lid, I backed away to avoid the steam, but Uncle Bus waved the bird's perfume toward his nose. "That's the point, you see. The glass concentrates the aroma, so that you can smell it. Beautiful, isn't it?"

A bolt of lightning crashed through the Westbury's ceiling. Smelling was part of eating? Food could be . . . beautiful? It was the first time I realized food could be something more than fuel. I quickly waved my hands in imitation of Uncle Bus's, hoping to catch some of the pheasant vapor, but it had dissipated. "Just so you know for next time," he said.

If memory serves, the taste was bitter—not as bland or tender as the chicken and turkey my adolescent palate was accustomed to—and it was made worse by the unfamiliar taste of Cognac, softened though it was with cream and butter. In fact, Uncle Bus rescued me—the first of many times— by trading plates. When I asked for ketchup for the steak he'd given me, he said gently, "The meat is so good, maybe this once you should try it without." There were qualities of meat besides ground and not ground? I never ketchupped not-ground meat again and ever since have shunned sauces that overwhelm what they are supposed to complement.

I assumed his marching orders were to tell me to behave in school, which he did. But instead of questioning past performance, he said, "Do any of the subjects interest you?" After I'd dismissed them all, as befitted my professionally disgruntled student persona, he asked me about English.

"We're reading *A Tale of Two Cities*, which is pretty good, and I'm really good at diagramming sentences."

Math? "We just started percentages, and I'm actually pretty good at them."

American history (his major at Harvard)? "I can't wait to get to the Civil War!" He went through science and art—his minor—and music, and it turned out that I actually liked them all. "I'm glad to hear that," he said, "because you have so much to offer."

End of crit! He had tricked me into realizing I *did* like school and into wanting to do better at it! He didn't have to mention my underachievements in behavior. He must have known that taking pleasure in academics would straighten me out. I told him about Elvis, whom he thought fascinating, unlike any other person his age. And he loved the pheasant, a taste I've since acquired through diligence and education.

Uncle Bus didn't leave, and he was the best father substitute a boy, and then a man, could ask for. And the permission to order pheasant under glass was liberating: I wasn't ridiculous, my judgment was worth considering, and in his eyes I was on my way.

Pheasant Under Glass

Although this preparation is difficult to find on restaurant menus these days, it's a magnolious way of serving the bird. (Isn't magnolious a mellifluous word? I use it as often as I can.)

1 whole large pheasant breast, split and boned
2 tablespoons freshly squeezed lemon juice
½ teaspoon freshly ground black pepper
2 tablespoons unsalted butter
6 dried morels, brushed off
2 large shallots, peeled and chopped
2 large white mushrooms, wiped clean, trimmed, and sliced thin
2 tablespoons brandy
⅓ cup dry white wine
⅓ cup heavy cream

1 ½ teaspoons chicken demi-glace

Pinch cayenne pepper

---

1. Flatten pheasant breasts slightly with a mallet or rolling pin, then rub with 1 tablespoon of the lemon juice and season with black pepper.
2. Melt 1 tablespoon of the butter over medium-high heat in a 9-inch skillet. When it foams, sear the pheasant, skin-side down, about 5 minutes per side. Remove to a plate, cover, and keep warm.
3. Wash morels carefully with cold water, making sure you get all the sand and grit out. Steep the morels in ½ cup hot water for about 5 minutes. Drain and strain, reserving the soaking liquid. Discard stems and slice caps thinly.
4. Melt the remaining tablespoon of butter in the skillet and sauté the shallots for 2 minutes, until golden, then add the morels and mushrooms for 1 minute. Remove to a bowl and keep warm.
5. Boil the reserved morel-soaking liquid with the brandy and white wine until reduced by half, about 1 minute, then whisk in the cream and demi-glace and boil about 1 minute, until sauce is thickened and smooth. Whisk in the remaining lemon juice and the cayenne.
6. Place the pheasant breasts skin-side up on hot serving plates and top each with half the mushroom mixture, then the sauce.
7. Enclose each breast with (ideally) a glass cover. Alert your guests to the olfactory possibilities, so they don't blow the experience the way I did. Once they are seated and you have their attention, lift the cover and fan the essence toward them, if necessary.

YIELD: 2 servings.

IT TOOK MOTHER a while to get her money from Dad. She'd been awarded one third of his business in the 1947 judgment, but what good did that do if he reinvested every penny of profit back into the business? He paid himself a modest salary, but, as the only shareholder, he could allow himself an expense account that included homes, cars, fat watches, servants, fireplaces, travel, food, and the moon, with no one to say no. He loved showing off his belongings, and as soon as he could get a plane, he got one, then another, then jets, ultimately winding up toward the end of his life with his own 727, in which he installed a king-size bed.

I didn't understand any of this. Except for the dusty months in Blytheville, I didn't know what our circumstances meant. We moved to New York and a small apartment on Fifth Avenue in '48 or '49. Nancy went to Brearley, I to Allen-Stevenson—both private schools. I think it was hard on Mother, and I imagine she borrowed from her mother and sister.

Then in 1952, not long after she initiated the suit against Bus, Mother went back to court and convinced the judge that she was being rooked by her ex-husband. The judge awarded her a million bucks, and we immediately moved into a splendid three-bedroom duplex at 4 East 72nd Street. We had two TVs in a time when one was a luxury, an enormous living room, a separate dining room, and maid's quarters, which were occupied by a live maid. At ten, I was as savvy about money as I was about where babies came from—as far as I was concerned, the stork brought both. A friend visited and told me he didn't have a TV. I was incredulous and offered him some of my allowance. When I'd visit someone who lived in less elegant surroundings, I assumed his parents lived there by choice, and I'm sure I said some variation of "Jeez, you really should live in a better place" several times. I don't know why I was so thick in figuring out how the world worked. The curse is, I'm even thicker now.

I was curious about many things—TV, sports, movies, comic books, why some kids liked me and why others didn't, how grown-ups behaved, and more sports. But money? It was just lying around—for everybody, wasn't it? Blessed by New England guilt, Mother was ashamed of it, secretly felt she didn't deserve it (despite protestations of "I earned every penny, living with your father"), and so was tight-fisted. We never discussed it, and Dad—who was an encyclopedia on it—never bothered to clue me in about it or sex or much of anything else. I managed to learn something about sex and everything else, but never about money.

The Shot Heard 'Round the World

G ROWING UP IN NEW YORK, I was such a Yankee fan that in the fourth
grade I nicknamed myself Allie because of the great pitcher. When
the real Allie Reynolds threw two no-hitters in the same season, I was ecstatic, furtively hoping people would mistake me for him—a little early
schizoid behavior, since I was nine and he was thirty-six. Only slightly more
realistically, I hoped strangers would think I was his son.

In that fall of '51, while we still lived in the lightless uptown apartment, the
New York Giants and Brooklyn Dodgers were locked in the most dramatic
pennant race ever. The Giants fell into the cellar early in the season and
clawed their way to a tie with the Dodgers on the last day of the regular season. The commissioner decreed a best-of-three playoff for the pennant, and
the city could talk, breathe, or eat nothing else.

The Giants won the first game of the playoff, the Dodgers the second, and
they just about closed down the federal government for the final game. Despite their early integration of black ballplayers, the Giants were the white,
blue-collar team, and the Dodgers were the black street fighters from uncivi-
lized Brooklyn. The Yankees, of course, were the plantation owners who
didn't deign to integrate until Elston Howard joined the club in 1955—eight
years after Jackie Robinson had broken the barrier with the Dodgers.

The final game of the playoff was on October 3, 1951. I woke up that morning and told Mother I couldn't walk.

"What?" she said, amazed.

"I can't walk . . . see?" I slid around our faux-marble linoleum floor in my pajamas. She looked at me as if I were insane.

"Of course you can walk. Now get up and go to school."

"No, I can't walk." I made several theatrical attempts to stand but just couldn't. "I guess I'll have to stay home." She lifted me by the arms, but I became dead weight. "I want to walk, Mother, but I can't. I don't understand this," I said, suppressing my glee over this brilliant scheme to stay home and watch the game.

Nancy came in to breakfast. "What's the matter with Jonnie?"

"He can't walk," Mother said, laughing. Nancy had other things on her mind and thought this was about as important as an earache. "Well, I've got to go to school." She left. Mother had appointments out of the house, but our colored maid, Thelma, was coming.

"I know exactly what you're doing," Mother said. I think she was impressed by my ingenuity and amused by its foolishness. "You want to watch the ball game. Well, you can't. Our television is broken, and you can't go to the Crouses' next door. So you might as well go to school."

I couldn't very well admit I was faking, so I said, "But, Mother, I can't walk."

"Well, then, we better get you to a hospital," she bluffed.

"No, no, why don't we wait and see what I'm like this afternoon?"

"All right, that's enough—get up."

"But, Mother, I can't walk." I valiantly attempted to stand again and crumpled.

Whatever the equivalent of "Yeah, right" was then, she said it, and tried sixteen or seventeen times to get me up to my feet, but I was too proud to admit defeat. Finally, she left and wrote Thelma instructions not to let me leave the apartment.

I got tired of zipping around on my knees pretty quickly. Without TV, there wasn't much to do, and I had to be convincing as a cripple. Thelma was round and jolly, and when she arrived, I told her, "I can't walk." She laughed out loud. "That's the craziest thing I ever heard!" she said, and dusted the venetian blinds. The day dragged on. I kept acting the stricken victim, even in my room with the door closed.

Nancy, who was also a baseball fan, returned from school at three and immediately headed for the Crouses' working TV. By now, I was bored and anxious and wished I'd gone to school. At least I would have been able to see the last few innings like Nancy. In an hour, she returned.

"What happened?" I asked breathlessly.

"Oh, it was very exciting. The Giants were behind four to two in the bottom of the ninth, two men on, one out, and Bobby Thomson came up and hit a home run." My God, the Giants had won the pennant! The Giants had won the pennant! The most famous home run in baseball history, and I had been sliding around on the floor . . .

Almost immediately I recovered and stood up.

"What was this not-walking anyway?" Nancy said.

"I wanted to see the game," I admitted and asked her to explain the game in detail.

It's hard to remember that there was a time before instant replays, VCRs, and DVDs. Occasionally, I was lucky enough to see Bobby Thomson on film at the local Trans-Lux movie theatre around the corner as he rounded third and dove into a swarm of euphoric teammates at home plate. When a team wins a division or a pennant or the Series these days, it's mandatory that the dugout empties and the players enthuse; but in those days, the enthusiasm was spontaneous and for real.

I wondered several times afterward, What should I have done to be allowed to see the game? Told the truth? No, I would have been ordered to school. Gone to school, snuck back early to the Crouses' for the game? No, there'd be hell to pay later. Been picked up by the school bus, ducked out while everyone entered the building, gone to the Polo Grounds? No, I was nine, had no money, and didn't know how to get there. Chosen a more believable affliction? There was no perfect answer.

Two years later, I found the nerve to ask the headmaster at Trinity, where I'd transferred—a gruff, megalomaniacal hunchback—if I could be excused from classes to attend opening day at Yankee Stadium. To my astonishment (and the whole sixth grade's), he said yes. Although many of the players were before my time, I knew the Yankee numbers up to 30 by heart, and still do:

Billy Martin was number 1, then Crosetti, the Babe, Gehrig, DiMaggio, Bobby Brown, Mickey, Yogi, Hank Bauer, the Scooter, Johnny Sain, Gil McDougald, no number 13, Gene Woodling . . . then skip a few. Raschi was 17, Allie 22, and Lopat 30. Twenty-two years later, I wrote my first play, *Yanks 3 Detroit 0 Top of the 7th*, about a Yankee pitcher having a nervous breakdown on the mound in the seventh inning of a perfect game.

I was a spoiled kid in many ways, but none more than as a Yankee fan. They just won everything. So we Yankee sons believed this was our destiny, too. Sort of like America, 1945–1963. (Very good for self-image, very bad when it turned out they could also lose, because it meant so could we.) The few times when they did lose (say, not winning their fifth World Series in a row) became cause for tortured soul-searching: What had we done wrong? Why was God mad at us? And just as I didn't know that I was living a privileged childhood until it was too late to enjoy it, I didn't realize till too late that the Yankees weren't going to finish first forever. I was a fair-weather fan, it turns out; when they began failing—and I began growing up—the disillusionment was so crushing that I turned on them. Sort of like kids and parents.

I had brief success as a player—at age nine or ten, I pitched a no-hitter at camp. But I was a lousy batter, and whenever I played in the outfield, couldn't judge where a fly ball would descend. I'd invariably run toward the plate because that's where the ball seemed to be at that instant, then realize as it sailed overhead that I needed to run back, and it was too late; or I'd run back to protect myself from that error and have to race into the infield to even have a chance at it. Made me crazy.

As I grew and the players got better, balls came at me faster, and by the time I was in my early teens I was actually scared to death of a pitched base-ball—not so much because I might be hit by one but because I'd swing goofily at one three feet from the bat. So I usually determined to swing as the pitcher was winding up—not exactly a scientific choice unless you're a gambler betting they can't *all* be balls. But I remained a fan—and a talker.

I don't really remember the food in the Bronx. Like Jughead in the *Archie* comics, I preferred hamburgers to hot dogs, made alliances with boys who felt the same, and shunned those who liked dogs. I ate franks at the stadium only because the burgers were so bad. (Still are, at every ballpark—in order to murder bacteria, they're cooked beyond defeat.) But on recent visits to a few ballparks, I've been impressed how good the food is at the newer places and stunned to discover how sorry the food is at our local arenas.

After mother's milk, the three greatest cuisines in the world are French, Chinese, and Junque. (Italians, Japanese, and Myanmarians may argue the first two, but nobody disagrees with the third.) I'll go to the sainted Popeye's with anyone at any time. I'll follow those visits with a fistful of White Castle cheeseburgers or really good biscuits and sausage gravy at the Sparta Restaurant in North Carolina. So it's not with pleasure or from snobbism that I tell you that the food at Shea Stadium is possibly the worst food *in . . . the . . . world*. It's better at Yankee Stadium—but only if you consider that boring trumps putrid.

How did we—supposedly feeders in the culinary capital of America, snubbers of the mighty Ducasse, petulants if we don't get superlatives of everything—fall into such a wretched state? How is it we have allowed our prized ball clubs, with their fat payrolls and staggering TV revenues, to stiff us with near-toxic grub? Why hasn't there been a food riot in seventy-eight years?

It's not like this in San Francisco. At Pacific Bell Park, the relatively new home of the Giants that overlooks the sapphire bay, the menu explodes the notion of traditional ballpark food. More inclusive than the Republican party (well, at its convention), it features Mexican, Thai, Japanese, health, and vegetarian food as well as the more customary hot dogs and popcorn. Chief among them are the scrumptious American or French Gordon Biersch garlic fries, which are so inspired that even during a recent four-run Giant rally, the line to the stand was twenty persons strong. Antithetical to the chili fry, the garlic fry sizzles with a wonderfully concocted fresh garlic-parsley-oil sauce. Pac Bell also serves up surprisingly delicious edamame by the cupful. Admittedly, boiled soybeans would be a tough sell in New York, and we could teach them a thing or two about the pastrami-and-corned-beef sandwich, but whoever is in charge of food has hit several back-to-back grand slams.

The food at Yankee Stadium is exemplified by one teenager's critique of the gloppy and lumpy cheese fries, "But I like fake cheese." But it's Le

Bernardin compared with Shea, where, if you must eat, you better bring a mouth ambulance. The entire menu is truly borderline inedible. Most gruesome of all is a small, sticky-floored and tacky bar named after one of the great wits and cranks of the game—and the man not only responsible for most of the Mets' early popularity but also the one who gave them the sobriquet "Amazin' "—the justifiably legendary Casey Stengel, out from under whose hat once flew a bird. I guarantee you, if Mr. Doubleday (the owner, not the inventor) ever left his leathered and sequined bunker to buy anything here, he'd sell the club.

The game itself interests me less these days. The money is such an obvious factor—the Yankees just buy what they need—which it probably was when I was five and six and twenty-five, but which, like all other financial aspects of life, I chose to ignore till way too late.

GORDON BIERSCH GARLIC FRIES

9 ½ ounces olive oil
2 ½ ounces vegetable oil
3 pounds frozen shoestring fries, skin on
1 cup chopped garlic
1 tablespoon kosher salt
¾ cup chopped fresh parsley
1 tablespoon freshly ground pepper

1. Combine the oils and pour ¼ cup of it into a 12–14-inch skillet. Heat until hot and add a third of the potatoes. Cook, covered, stirring occasionally, until browned, about 5 minutes. Drain on paper towels. Repeat with the rest of the potatoes.
2. Crush the garlic and salt with the side of a knife until coarsely puréed. Mix in the parsley and pepper.
3. Add the potatoes to the garlic mixture and toss to coat. Serve hot.

YIELD: 6 servings.

Ship's Edamame (Boiled Soybeans)

6 cups (1 ½ pounds) fresh soybeans in the pod

1 gallon water

2 tablespoons salt

1. Wash the soybeans and drain.
2. Boil the water and add the salt and soybeans.
3. Boil 5–7 minutes, until tender but not soft.
4. Drain in a colander and cool with cold water.
5. Slip out the soybeans from the pod and eat.

YIELD: 6 servings.

Discovering Priapia

~~~~~~

Mother was depressed most of the time, and I think Nancy and I depressed her more. I'd visit friends in their apartments, and there was usually merriment to be found somewhere, even with the adults. Not in our home. Nancy and I weren't oppressed, or beaten, or deprived of much materially, though there were no Rollses outside. (Dad had those in Arkansas and Oklahoma.) Still, self-pity and defeat clung like humidity to the drapes, lowering the ceiling and replacing the nitrogen in the air. They seeped through our unsuspecting skins right into our marrows and lodged without a fight. Like most children and all dogs, we assumed that the home life we experienced was the norm, and that we were destined to ape its behavior, deepen it, and pass it on to our children. Over the years, I've fought depression like crazy, often beating it back, sometimes succumbing to it. I hate it— my own and whenever I find it in a companion. (I can spot it in anyone who sighs on the phone or drops an eyelid for an extra beat across a football field.) It's as familiar as socks and soon settles in comfortably around me. It's the way the world is supposed to be, and how issues usually work themselves out.

But we weren't as sodden with it as the Crouses next door. Sarah Crouse, who was Mother's age, had four daughters, three of them unmarried and living with her. She, too, was divorced and in her forties, but, unlike Mother, never managed to get out of bed. Whenever I visited Sandra, who was my age, or whenever Nancy visited Linda, who was hers, Sarah was in her nightgown and bathrobe under the covers. She read and slept and talked on the phone with the music of the thirties and forties playing on the *Make-Believe Ballroom* radio show quietly in the background—the family television miles away in the living room and too modern for her. Sarah generally had a glass filled with some brown liquid and ice cubes near her, and when I'd ask Mother why she was always in bed, Mother said, "She's not feeling well." The daughters were alive and full of high spirits, and their father, Otto, a successful lawyer, visited them often, which may have accounted for their resilience.

Years later, I understood why Dad had to get away from all this. He had lofty visions to realize, and with superhuman effort he could muster the energy to bring them to life. He couldn't possibly have done so if he had to bring Mother along with him. It would be like rappelling Mount McKinley with a knapsack full of rocks. And the knapsack was wet.

Leaving the Crouses' apartment and entering ours was like going to a ballgame by comparison. Mother, Nancy, and I had breakfast and dinner together almost every night. (The Crouse girls generally had dinner in their kitchen with their maid.) Mother wasn't interested in food, perhaps because the moment she drank a glass of water or ate five peanuts, they'd appear on her waistline. So in addition to everything else she was avoiding—like the world outside—she kept her distance from food. She tried to re-create a few interesting recipes she'd learned down south, but about all she could execute was a decent fried chicken with cream gravy and a baroque version of bread pudding made with chocolate. Once the divorce settlement became hers instead of a vending machine for Dad's expense account and we'd moved out of the dingy uptown apartment and into the sunny duplex, Anna, the Ukrainian maid, would emerge from her dark lair and serve generally uninspired basics, like well-done little lamb chops, gray chopped steak, and chicken so over-roasted you could dry your hair with it, all primly arranged on the plate with defrosted baby peas and a splot of mashed potatoes.

Unlike Sarah Crouse, Mother fought back against depression. In many ways, she was a pioneer. For six or seven years, she had tenaciously pursued that divorce and finally prevailed, at least financially—to the wonder of Dad and eventual congratulation of her female friends, many of whom had divorced and, in hopes of keeping the peace, settled for whatever their browbeating husbands offered. The women were invariably shortchanged, and there was never any peace. At least Mother had the pyrrhic victory of making a killing.

At the urging of her lawyer, Fred, and to a degree her ex-husband, she pursued the lawsuit against her brother Bus to the bitter end. That it broke her mother's and sister's hearts and alienated her brother for many years didn't dissuade her from this wrongheaded pursuit, but she saw it through.

She was also the first of anyone we knew to go to a psychiatrist. Laughable as this may seem today, when every other fetus is in some kind of therapy or at least reading a self-help book, only the certifiable or the extremely wealthy indulged in shrinks in the forties and fifties.

Ultimately, she paid fatal prices for her persistence: Dad's flight and fury were gasoline on the flames of her depression, just as her father's sudden death had been kerosene; and the damage done by the lawsuit with her brother was liquid oxygen. Psychiatry became my mother's addiction, at once enlightening her and imprisoning her in her own helplessness. It explained her to herself—and convinced her she was too fragile to make her own way in the world without the weekly, sometimes daily, ministrations of a shrink. When she confided to her two best girlfriends that she was seeing a psychiatrist, they viewed her as slightly odd and began treating her like a wounded china doll.

Self-esteem was called "confidence" in schoolyards then, and mine wasn't done much good when Mother decided I, too, should see a psychiatrist. I was ten or eleven and was instructed by her not to tell anyone—the shame! the shame!—which only reinforced my view of myself as even more of a misfit than I apparently was. I'd had a superb year in the fifth grade at Trinity, flourishing academically and socially under the guidance of a brilliant teacher named McLeod; in the sixth grade, I discovered jealousy and turned on all my friends for their accomplishments in sports, grades, popularity, bravery. The sixth-grade teacher, a man named Duncan, also suffered—from constant comparison to McLeod—and together we had a miserable year.

I'd like to blame my physical cowardice on Mother—she was afraid to do anything, and whenever I was in danger of rolling over in bed the wrong way (let alone playing football), she'd warn, "Be careful! Watch out! That's dangerous!" Certainly her cautious approach to the outdoors colored my view of it, but she wasn't the sole reason. In the fourth grade, I'd rounded an icy corner in the winter, slipped, and got poked just below the eye by the spike of an iron fence. Blood filled the lobby of our apartment building. And though the wound was easily bandaged, it was scary, and the scar lasted twenty years. In the fifth grade, I fell and broke my right wrist on an asphalt basketball court on Randalls Island and was treated at school like a war hero, everyone in the class trying to sign my cast. Nobody had seen someone with a broken bone before! In the sixth, I slipped in my own room and broke my *left* wrist—a far less glamorous venue and injury (though just as painful) and was greeted at school with some hostility and a big ho-hum, as though I had broken that bone to revive my flagging popularity. The sixth-grade cast itched, friends went out to play, and I got fat, despite all the No-Cal cream soda.

It was my own fear of falling that prevented me from learning to roller-skate till I was sixteen or ride a bicycle till I was twenty-two. I still find bicycles terrifying, whether I'm on one or some messenger is. They come at you in the middle of the night, lightless and silent as a sniper's bullet. Everything scared me then, except sex.

Sandra Crouse and I used to sleep at each other's apartments when we were seven or eight or nine, and one night curiosity seized us. We went into the bathroom and examined each other tentatively, both wildly aroused and breathing hard. We had no idea how to calm the tension, of course, and eventually went back to sleep. The next day, she told her mother, and we never had a sleepover together again.

In retrospect, sessions with the shrink were hilarious. They were full-frontal Freud: me at age ten stretched out on a couch, Dr. Becker behind my head, secretly opening his mail. I had no idea what free association meant or what I was supposed to do. The rigors of the philosophy prohibited him from asking direct questions, and it made me more nuts to speak to what I experienced as an empty room. Every now and then, he'd clear his throat and make some rustling noise, and I'd think, "Is he doing what I think he's doing? Is he coughing up phlegm, spitting it into a Kleenex, folding the Kleenex, and putting it back in his pocket? Yikkk!" He became increasingly impatient at my silences, which he considered a lack of cooperation, and I became increasingly anxious at his impatience.

"Why *can't* you remember the first thing that happened to you?" he said after repeated attempts to get at the gold mine of a first memory. I vaguely pictured myself walking into a bathroom, probably in Texas, being intrigued by Mother's dozen or so perfume bottles, and pouring them one by one into the toilet, so I told him that. It became locked in my head as "the first thing I can remember" and was the response I gave to a succession of shrinks, never knowing whether it really *was* the first thing I could remember or only something that came up to ease Dr. Becker's ill temper.

At one session, I fell asleep for the full fifty minutes, and he didn't disturb me—somehow I was supposed to learn a tremendous lesson from this. Trust or something. Mother was furious at this waste of money but sided with Dr. Becker, as she almost always did. To my regular questioning, "But Mother, what am I supposed to say?" the response, "Whatever comes into your head," was no help at all.

Things at Trinity deteriorated. I got angrier at and more resentful of my former friends, and basically turned into Iago, whispering plots behind their backs. They soon found friends who didn't get angry at them and weren't trying to sabotage them in some way. Showing off to new accomplices one lunchtime after some particularly wretched meat product aswim in gravy, I twisted three forks together and threw them into the opening for dirty dishes at the school cafeteria. The lower-school headmaster spotted me, and that together with my general overall pathological behavior became justification for my first NIBbing—Not-Invited-Back-ing. The only difference between being NIBbed and being expelled is that a NIB doesn't go on your record; the student simply decides to change schools. So at twelve, I "decided" to leave the wilds of the Upper West Side for the bucolic pleasures of Garrison, New York.

Boarding school wasn't much of an adjustment for me. When I was four, Mother sent Nancy and me to summer camp because of the nationwide polio scare. I continued to go to camp for the next twelve years, usually for eight weeks at a stretch, once or twice for as many as twelve weeks—longer than most school terms. So after a few minutes of homesickness the first year or two, I became so inured to it that I began counseling the other boys those first few nights. The food was the same at all camps and schools: a choice of hot cereals in the morning (oatmeal, cream of wheat, and the particularly odious farina), pancakes, French toast, reconstituted powdered eggs; lunch featured sandwiches and a bowl of canned pears; dinner was invariably some form of mystery meat—a thing floating in gravy or chipped beef on toast.

Malcolm Gordon was an unusual little school. It took in only twenty-eight boys, ranging in ages from eight to thirteen. The classes were so small—two or three students, max—that they were practically tutorials. It was the first of my three boarding schools, and resulted in the second of my three NIBs.

I was NIBbed at Malcolm Gordon for excessive letter-writing. We were all asked to write a letter of condolence to Arthur Debernarde, who had been attacked by his appendix and was hospitalized. I found the experience so much fun that I proceeded to write him a letter almost nightly—twenty-five or thirty of them over the next six weeks.

I had a great time writing them at the end of study hall every night. They were partially true, partially made up. I remember writing in one an elaborate description of Dad raping Mother, which to the best of my knowledge never happened, at least physically. Mr. and Mrs. David Gordon, who ran the school, encouraged imagination as long as it remained somewhat timid, and saw pederasty under every bed well before any of us students knew what it was. So after a few of my missives, the Gordons began opening them and, rather than reveling in discovering an incipient literary genius, were repelled at the prospect of a serial rapist in their midst, even one who never did any raping.

I had become very fond of the place and felt at home there. I felt betrayed and was stunned when I heard the news of my NIBbing from Mother over spring vacation and tearful when I said good-bye to the headmaster at commencement. (Under threats from Fred Schlater, the Gordons allowed me to finish the year.) I didn't know what it was I'd done wrong, but so great was my shame, it took me more than forty years to tell the story to anyone except a therapist.

I know now but didn't then that as an intensely priapic being, I would have ravished porcupines if that's all that was available in Garrison when I was twelve. When I was thirteen and a half (months are important at that age), my discovery of girls sent me reeling, spiraling, and ejaculating for the foreseeable rest of my life; but between twelve and thirteen and a half, I made the mistake of being surrounded exclusively by boys. This manifested itself not only actively and pragmatically, but literarily.

Lawrenceville used to be for boys only, and as an eighth grader the following year, I discovered written pornography unlike any I've seen since: One of the boys in the dorm got hold of photographs of the pages of a novel called *The She-Devil*, a wallowingly heterosexual romp through the bedrooms of southern France. For twenty-five cents he would rent out photographs *of the pages of the book*. No photos, no drawings—just words. Although we had access to *Playboy*, *Nugget*, *Gent*, and other deliriously breast-baring magazines, the suggestive written word was more thrilling than any realistic visual depiction because it hooked the imagination. But despite the swaggering prurience of all these publications, there weren't any actual women around, so I had to make do with what was at hand.

The '50s was not a good decade for homosexuality. It wasn't smart to be a homo then, even if it was through ignorance and lack of choice. (At thirteen, abstinence was not an option.) Every school and camp dedicated to boys was as terrified of homosexuality then as it is of drugs today because it was well-known to be a terrible disease. And the boys—even co-participants—were merciless. And there were many co-participants, as befits a boarding school. The showers were very busy in Thomas House, and I was a serial showerer. I thought all of it was just fun and either gender fair game—*Playboy* under my pillow, some kid with a hard-on in the next cubicle eager for experimentation. It was slightly naughty because sex is supposed to be slightly naughty, and I was relentless. My reputation grew.

One afternoon an attractive fellow named John Uhl from a nearby dorm suggestively lured me downstairs into the office of the lower-school newspaper, *The Recorder*, of which I was the editor, tricked me into confiding that I was perverted (which I did with some theatricality), and then revealed a tape recorder hidden under a desk nearby. I ran from the room, panicked and humiliated, while Uhl and the engineer of the prank, Webster Ford (at last, those scores settled!), proceeded to play the tape at all the lower-school dorms with considerable delight. Although filled with shame, I was able to stand back as if on Pluto and view the whole thing comically—this *was* pretty funny. I was the object of derision for months, and horrid as it felt, it also gave me a sort of swagger; I'd almost laugh at an innuendo said about me or a look exchanged between a couple of kids as though it were happening to someone else.

As if wanting to play the role of buffoon, I arranged my ultimate departure from Lawrenceville by writing a letter to a student I had unsuccessfully propositioned, suggesting we get together and work on some project together. In the back of my mind, I must have thought, "Well, writing letters got me thrown out of Malcolm Gordon, maybe it'll work here, too." And as if Euripides with several darker gods wandered into the lower school one afternoon, I stole a letter from this boy's mailbox, which I'd never done before and haven't done since. It was from his mother, saying that she had shown my letter to the lower-school headmaster, and that her son shouldn't worry—I'd be taken care of quickly. I read this calmly, with no sense of dread but with a tickle of pleasure, put the letter back in the envelope, the envelope back in the mailbox.

I knew for two weeks something drastic was about to happen, and it didn't faze me. A streak of asexual perversion, some naughty glee, was invigorating: "Oh, boy, I'm really going to get it now!" I thought. It wasn't masochism; it was the excitement that titillated. Then on a Sunday afternoon in October of my freshman year, the lower-school headmaster called me into his office.

"Is this serious?" I joked with him on the way downstairs from my dorm.

"Yes, it's serious," he said. It was exciting. But I knew it was about to be very painful.

Mother was in his office crying quietly. Other than that, the room was still. He gently read my letter aloud, then said, "You have a reputation which can't be tolerated. I've talked to Mr. Heely, the headmaster, and he's very upset about this. We can't have you stay here, but it won't appear on your transcript." More silence—except for Mother's sobs.

"When do I have to leave?" I asked.

"Right now. All the boys are out. You need to pack up everything." I did, and Mother had hired a car for the trip back to the city. We never talked about the sexual aspect of the NIBbing—not then, not ever—only what school I would go to next.

Although the actual expulsion was titillating, and I wished I could have stayed to see the look on all those boys' faces when they heard the news, I was miserable and felt tragic. It had also really devastated Mother, whom I never considered.

Years after I unhooked my date's bra for the first time, I continued to slink around with this shame: Was I secretly queer? Would I be NIBbed from another school, college, job, happy life, heaven? Clearly it was the worst offense a boy or a man could commit: Look what had happened to me because of it. And this propensity I had for the arts and aversion to towel-flicking locker-room prance—wasn't that indicative of effeminacy?

After Lawrenceville, I landed in a tutoring school in New York in hopes of getting the hell out of high school as fast as I could. It was a silly place: I took two years' worth of Regents exams in English and history in two months and suddenly was "ready" to be a junior at age fourteen.

I ENROLLED in an acting school run by John Cassavetes, a then relatively unknown actor and aspiring director. He was never there, but my teacher was Burt Lane, who wound up becoming Diane Lane's father. In one memorable assignment, he'd cast another actor and me in a scene from Robert Anderson's *Tea and Sympathy.* I played a college football player who teaches a sensitive college boy who fears he may be gay how to walk in a more manly way. I had James Dean on the brain then, and was so sensitive and tentative myself that Lane said at the end, "You two should have been playing opposite parts." Devastating. Stayed with me for about fifteen years.

That my cousin Lee was a movie star by the time I was fifteen had much to do with my wanting to be an actor. I was attracted to it for all the superficial reasons: its glam lifestyle; the moody sensitivity of Dean and Brando and Robert Mitchum; the suave clowning of Cary Grant; the money—was anybody paid more?; the outrageous behavior you were allowed if you reached stardom; and, of course, all the best-looking women were actresses. My mother was appalled.

Mother never tired of psychotherapy and trained Nancy and me to turn to it whenever problems arose. Immediately after the Lawrenceville exit, she sent me to the Ackerman brothers, two shrinks specializing in lost boys. They achieved a reputation by espousing a confrontational therapy. I don't remember if it was Nathan or Bernard, but whichever one was bald addressed me ferociously one day by saying, "Look at my head! What does it remind you of?"

"A bald head?"

"No! Something else." I groped for the answer he wanted.

"Uh, my father?"

"No! DOESN'T THIS REMIND YOU OF YOUR OWN PENIS?"

I was terrified. The prospect of a dick as large as his head charging straight for my precious heinie electrified every hair on my body—those on my underarms, legs, pubes. I ran out of the Ackerman office, and despite their many entreaties on the phone to capitalize on this "breakthrough," boy did I never go back.

Better Than Fontainebleau Lobster

MOTHER WAS ALFRED and Alice's middle child, beautiful (I'm told), and, even as a child, often withdrawn. Most of her life she felt betrayed by the four men most important to her—her stern, alcoholic father; her wild and entrepreneurial husband; her loving brother; and, I see in retrospect, me. Her father betrayed her by dying when she was barely in her twenties; her husband ran around on her for thirteen years, then abruptly divorced her and abandoned their children; her brother did not betray her at all, but she was convinced by her husband and her lawyer he had. And I took the fun out of having children. I was in combat as a teenager, and was a teenager for a very long time, until recently, really, which is probably why she kicked me out of the house so often.

As a single parent, she was overwhelmed, trying to raise a pair of temperamental and artistic children whose reaction to everything vaguely disciplinary could be measured in liters—sometimes imperial gallons—of defiance. By the early sixties—pre-Beatles, pre-Vietnam, late Freud—plays like *The Glass Menagerie* and *Gypsy* and movies like *Rebel Without a Cause* had created mothers so overbearing they were blamed for everything from juvenile delinquency to the crippling sickness of homosexuality. And since I flirted for about five minutes with both, barbells of guilt rounded her shoulders and made them sag.

When Nancy fled the more conventional life of private-school classes at Brearley and joined the City Ballet, to Mother it was worse than Nancy putting on a pair of stiletto heels and swinging a purse on Eighth Avenue. I wasn't aware of the enormous artistic achievement being blessed by George Balanchine till much later, but it ruled and anchored Nancy's life. She didn't want to finish school at all; only after many screaming arguments with Mother did she agree to finish her final year at the Professional Children's School, which would accommodate her rigorous performance and practice schedule. She became estranged from Mother, a split that was never repaired. Her life *was* the ballet, which Mother neither approved of nor understood.

If Nancy stayed pretty much within the law, I didn't always. I started having gin-and-tonics at fourteen, got away with a little shoplifting, stole money from Mother's friends, and, most dangerously, forged her driver's license.

I'd fallen in a big, big way for the photograph of a girl in shorts; her name was Pam and she lived in Miami Beach. She was a friend of a friend, and after boldly phoning her after school one day, I phoned her every day after that. I was determined to see her. With visions of Dad's grandiosity in my head, I wasn't just going to woo her but would knock her off her feet as well as offer up my virginity to her. I decided to fly to Miami, rent a convertible—already heady—and drive her to the beach, where we'd wind up rolling around as Burt Lancaster and Deborah Kerr had in *From Here to Eternity*.

The only problem was . . . I was fourteen. And didn't know how to drive.

Still, I gathered up the money a great aunt left me, ordered a goatee created by Eddie Senz, a leading Broadway makeup man, so I'd look old enough to rent the car (the minimum age was twenty-five), and stole Mother's driver's license. In those days, New York licenses were filled in in ink by the driver, and there were no pictures. I bought ink eradicator and slowly and carefully substituted my name, gender, and weight for hers.

After the Lawrenceville NIB, Mother had hired a companion for me to make sure I didn't get into trouble after school while she worked around the corner at a little pottery shop. She correctly feared I'd either veg out in front of the TV watching *American Bandstand* or come up with some kind of trouble. So she found a male nurse named Scott Olsen, who was not only gay but Extremely Gay. He was tremendous fun, but I don't think Mother quite figured out that an effeminate male role model wasn't exactly what I needed after the Malcolm Gordon and Lawrenceville episodes. Scott knew a lot of second-tier theatrical personalities, frequently said, "Oh, *jamais, jaMAIS*," and never minded when I'd order gin-and-tonics. He smoked and thought it was fine if I did. He roomed with an attractive black man who sometimes answered their apartment door in the nude. In imitation of Scott and his friends, I became more and more affected—while simultaneously pursuing every girl I thought exhibited the remotest chance of taking my virginity. Must have been quite confusing for the girls. And though I longed to be one of the red-blooded normals on *American Bandstand*, I knew if I ever got to Philly for the broadcast, I'd be treated as if I were wearing a clown suit.

I told Mother I was going to Miami Beach for the weekend, and to my astonishment, she said, "Okay, as long as you take Scott with you." It turned out that she'd been so advised by a psychiatrist named Hyman Spotnitz. She already knew I had stolen her license, and the progressive doctor told her, "Let him go. He'll get into a little trouble, but it'll teach him a lesson. How bad could it be?"

Bad enough.

The plane landed in Miami Beach, I spirit-gummed the beard to my chin in the men's room, and Scott and I headed for Hertz. I pulled off renting the car, though almost gave it away when I asked the salesman, "Uh, how do I get this in 'drive'?" He looked at me suspiciously and pointed out the PRND1D2 on the steering column. Scott quietly urged me to let him drive us to the Fontainebleau, which I did.

But not to Pam's house. That I had to do on my own—pantsless passion on the beach would not be aided by an older man driving us around. So I managed to get the convertible out of the Fontainebleau lot and pulled onto Collins Avenue. It was a lovely light-blue Chevy convertible with triangles of chrome telescoping from the exaggerated fins to the front doors. Couldn't have been cooler. And the night was breathtaking—sultry, warm, starlit.

I knew I had to turn left in the next few blocks, so I quickly switched on the radio, since that would be part of my entrance. I also had to have a cigarette to make the right impression, and I tried to light one. I realized I had missed the left, so while lighting the cigarette and turning to the right rock 'n' roll station, I impetuously jerked the wheel way to the left, zipped through the intersection out of control, bumped up onto the sidewalk, and scraped the entire right side of the immaculate Chevy to ribbons against a cement wall. It made a hell of a noise.

I wasn't hurt. I jumped out of the car to examine the damage, as I had seen people do in the movies. I had no idea what to do. The chrome had wrapped itself into tight little cylinders on both fins, there was an enormous dent for half the length of the car, and the wall was chalked with blue paint. In case someone was watching, I tried to blame the accident on the Chevy. I kicked the tires two or three times, not realizing that's what you do when buying a car, not wrecking one.

Within about three minutes, two Dade County police cars pulled up, sirens singing and lights flashing. Someone must have seen the accident and phoned it in. I wondered if I should retrieve the goatee and spirit gum, now in the glove compartment, and put it on, but the police were too quick.

"What happened?" an officer asked politely.

"I don't know," I said, acting as though we were old buddies and he surely knew as well as I did how crazy cars could get, sort of like wives. "Pulled over to the left . . . and it shot wide of the turn," I said, blaming the accident on General Motors. Two or three other cops were looking at the wall and the car—now part of the wall—and were whistling and scratching their heads in amazement. They were trying to figure out how such a wide turn was geometrically possible. The beautiful Chevy was totaled.

I'm not sure how I pulled the rest of it off. How could I possibly pass for twenty-five? I was fourteen, with some baby fat, not particularly tall or mature-looking. But I had seen twenty-five-year-olds in the movies and knew something about acting, so I just acted like one. In fact, I probably acted like a fifty-year-old. My demeanor was calm and serious but confident. I kept quiet, as though I had much on my mind. They examined my driver's license. It seemed to satisfy them, but they kept it. They radioed HQ while I sat in one of their squad cars. After half an hour, the pleasant officer said, "The car will be towed—all taken care of. We're going to have to go downtown, but it shouldn't take too long."

I knew I didn't want to go "downtown," whatever that meant. Would they examine the license? Find the goatee and spirit gum in the glove compartment?

"Mmmm, downtown," I said. By now I was wearing a mantle of gravitas that suggested I was missing a cabinet meeting with President Eisenhower.

That certainly would be an inconvenience. "I'd certainly prefer not to do that," I said, looking at my watch. "I'm late as it is. I'd really give anything not to go downtown."

"You would?" the officer said.

"Yes."

"What have you got?" He looked at me pleasantly. He'd been pleasant throughout the whole ordeal.

Thank God for all those movies I'd seen. I knew what he meant right away.

"I've got two hundred dollars in traveler's checks."

"No, sir, no traveler's checks."

"I've got, let's see, eighty to ninety dollars in cash." I was so happy—I was about to become fourteen again. Was this really how the world worked? I was doing it!

"That'll be fine." I gave him the ninety dollars. "Thank you, sir," he said. "Can we drop you somewhere?"

I told him Pam's address, never breaking my fifty- or seventy-five-year-old demeanor. "Lovely night," I said, as though I had grandchildren.

"Yes, sir."

He and his partner dropped me off at Pam's, courteously waiting for her to answer the door. They still had the license. But they didn't have me. Pam took one look at them and was immediately impressed. Was I so important I had a police escort?

"Thank you, men," I said.

"Yes, sir," the pleasant officer said, and drove off.

"Wow, what happened?" Pam asked. All my fingertips had pulses of their own, and they were haywire. I started to tell the story, and a few minutes in took a deeper look at her.

Pam was a dog.

The leggy photo hadn't misrepresented her exactly, but I had foolishly focused on the legs. I'd spent all this money, had a beard made, risked the federal pen for forgery, and endured a police inquisition seventeen hundred miles from home . . . for this? I immediately embraced her and kissed her. She was a good southern girl and wasn't used to this sort of assault. She was polite, and we rolled around on the floor for a while, but she was distinctly uninterested in my advances, and after a couple of hours, began to dislike me. I phoned for a taxi.

"See you tomorrow," I said.

"Yes . . . sure," she said.

Back at the Fontainebleau, I told Scott what had happened. He dropped about six pounds and four pints of blood in three seconds, as pictures of me on a Florida chain gang whizzed through his brain. "I've got to get that license back," he said.

I slept the sleep of the pure, and poor Scott was agitated all night. In the morning, he phoned Mother, who phoned Fred, still her lawyer. They devised some sort of plan. I went out on the beach to enjoy Miami.

But I don't actually like beaches. Windy, hot, too sunny to read, sand sticks to you, sweat collects in your navel. Pam appeared with another couple, who were engaged. In addition to the troubled adolescent stars, I also idolized Frank Sinatra and proceeded as I thought he would in this situation. So I offered Pam and her friends a few drinks and club sandwiches on the beach (turkey, bacon, lettuce, tomato, mayo, sand, toast), and when the guy wasn't looking I made a move on the other girl. She was flattered but not amused. Her fiancé was tough. Pam, who by this time *really* didn't like me, was crushed.

"You're a nice guy," the fiancé said to me, "but keep your hands to yourself." They left.

I had one more day in Miami and nothing to do but watch TV. I ordered lobster from room service for breakfast. It was dry and overcooked. I realized I'd had a rotten time in Miami Beach, and all of it was my doing.

But Scott had an even worse time. He was ready to mainline Miltown, the fifties' trank of choice. He'd spent all of Saturday and Sunday at the police station and was going to stay there until he got that license back. I left on my scheduled flight.

Mother met me at Idlewild Airport—as JFK used to be called—and the following morning I was driven to the Anderson School in Staatsburg, New York. I was told it was the last stop before reform school. I looked forward to

it. It was the first institution I'd been sent to that was coed. And by now I preferred the three cereals—even the farina—and the mystery meat to anything
the Ukrainian maid would serve.

BETTER THAN '56 FONTAINEBLEAU LOBSTER

*The best way to cook a lobster is to smother it in its own juices. But if you steam, roast,
or broil it, the juices will disappear. Try this, which may be prepared in an oven, in a
steamer, or on a grill.*

Two 1½-pound lobsters
¼ pound unsalted butter, cut into several pieces
4 cloves garlic, cut into slivers
½ cup chopped fresh cilantro
Handful of seaweed, optional
Salt and pepper, to taste
1 cup melted butter
Juice of 1 lemon

1. If using oven, preheat it to 375 degrees.
2. Stab the lobsters in the throat; this will kill them in the quickest and most
   efficient way.
3. With a nutcracker, crunch claws so they have openings large enough to
   stuff with butter, and make several incisions in the tails.
4. Insert butter slices and garlic slivers into these openings, sprinkle with
   salt, pepper, and cilantro, and drape with optional seaweed, which will
   give a taste of the sea. Wrap completely in aluminum foil.
5. Cook lobster for 12–15 minutes in oven, on outdoor grill, or in steamer.
6. Remove foil and serve with melted butter and lemon juice.

   YIELD: 2 servings.

Higher Learning

~~~~~~~~~~

ANDERSON DID THE TRICK. It was *filled* with misfits, mostly the misbehaving children of well-to-do parents. It also had its share of epileptics, the palate-clefted, and obsessive-compulsives. By comparison, I was school-president material. In fact, I became school president, an office for which no one who knew me would ever have considered me fit. It wasn't just that much of the student body seemed less able to function, though; the school's founder, V. V. Anderson, had been an industrial psychiatrist at Macy's and had some sense of how to keep order. The discipline was strict: Schedules were the same every day, we went everywhere in groups, no one was allowed to go to another building without a note (except to class). There was absolutely no unsupervised time. The rooms had no doors. The dances with the girls were strictly patrolled; there was no grinding or dirty dancing, absolutely positively no, you're-out-of-here-if-you-do, making out, no holding hands.

It gave me no latitude, exactly what was needed. I became a borderline goody-goody: got good grades, performed acceptably as an athlete, edited a yearbook, started a newspaper, acted in plays, held positions of responsibility. It cost three times as much as Lawrenceville, four times as much as Malcolm Gordon, and was year-round, with vacations between seasons. And it was worth every penny.

Unfortunately, it had no endowment, and when Dr. Anderson and then his son-in-law, the headmaster, died, no one picked up the torch. The school changed course considerably and currently takes only autistic students. Like

Malcolm Gordon, which has closed its doors, it was a singular place catering to a very narrow clientele in a very particular time in history.

A great pal of mine at Anderson was Ronnie Reuben, one of six grandchildren of Arnold, the feisty German immigrant who founded and maintained Reuben's restaurant. From the late teens till the sixties, when it closed, Reuben's was the show-biz-journalist-politico-occasional-mobster restaurant of choice. It was open twenty-four hours a day and was sort of a cross between Katz's Deli, Spice Market, and Nobu. When we were high school juniors, Ronnie introduced me to the most self-indulgent meal I had until I was thirty-three and ate at a German beer hall in Munich, after which I thought I was going to become an involuntary suicide bomber ahead of my time, spreading my own human shrapnel all over the Fatherland. And as you will see, on a Christmas day in the early sixties, Reuben's would be a personal lifesaver.

DURING MY LAST YEAR at Anderson, I thought I was in love with Pat Sutherland, the prettiest girl in school. I had lost—or, more accurately, flailingly flung away—my virginity two years before with a girl named Jo. Jo and I talked incessantly about *Other Voices, Other Rooms*; *Lolita*; and *On the Road* and decided that though fifteen, we were beats. We also discussed *Love Without Fear*, the paperback sex manual that encouraged use of the "ice-spurred special," the application of crushed ice to certain areas, and made out like mad on her parents' living-room floor in Basking Ridge, New Jersey.

My sexual initiation was not only inept, it was punitive. I had pictured a full afternoon's insatiable lust in my air-conditioned bedroom (Mother at work) followed by a titillating afterglow watching Brigitte Bardot in *And God Created Woman* at the Trans-Lux. I got the air-conditioning right but little else. Gropes, zero preparation, harsh strokes, completion, and depression—all in about ninety seconds. Complete failure! Not a hint of desire the rest of the day. And the spectacle of seeing the usually eroticizing Bardot turned out to be as tormented as De Niro squiring Cybill Shepherd to that porno movie in *Taxi Driver*. And—the punitive part—Jo told me a week later two pieces of news a young man never wants to hear: (a) "I think I'm pregnant," and (b) "I don't think you accomplished the task. I'm still a virgin." Neither, it turned out, was true.

The experience with Pat Sutherland was different. She had previously gone steady with a couple of the badder boys, and I had been with everyone I could talk into clandestinely holding hands. Pat was not only tough (in those days meaning gorgeous, as in the hit song "She's So Tough") but hot (in those days short for "hot to trot," not for gorgeous) and fast (same meaning it has today). She lived in Cuyahoga Falls, Ohio, and Mother allowed me out of her grasp for a few days during a vacation to visit her. Pat and I made incessant teenage love—in a haystack, in the front and back seats of her father's convertible, in her living room when no one was home. Anyplace, it seemed, that didn't have a bed. I finally learned to drive a convertible, and I was besotted with her.

When I visited colleges during my senior year at Anderson, I found that Denison University in Granville, Ohio, was the closest campus to Cuyahoga Falls. With my interesting record of NIBs and tutors and psychos, I wasn't exactly Ivy League material, and Pat wasn't going to college at all. I'd spent my young life in New York, where things can get pretty provincial, and Ohio seemed as far away as California and as exotic as Paris. Secondarily, I was sure I wanted to be an actor, and Denison had an excellent reputation as a theatre school. Hal Holbrook had graduated from there several years earlier. The campus was lovely and friendly. But the main reason I chose it was Pat.

But halfway through the summer, while I was working on a dairy farm in Vermont, she wrote that she was going to marry someone else. I wasn't the least crestfallen—I knew nothing would ever really come of our relationship besides the sex and some admiration that I had the best-looking girl in town on my arm. I went up to Pluto again, as I'd done at Lawrenceville and about thirty times since, and found it darkly hilarious: Here I'd chosen this school because of her, now didn't have her, and was going to the school anyway.

It turned out to be the best choice—or Godtrick—in the world. I wanted to be a fraternity boy, and I wanted to be in the theatre at the same time. Denison was segregated then: The artists (theatre folk, musicians, painters) were down the hill, and everyone else was up the hill. I was one of about one to straddle both worlds, and I loved it. I pledged ΣAE immediately; and because the theatre department had relatively few majors—no more than six the entire time I was there—but did so many plays every year, I was able to appear in about fifty by the time I graduated. This was roughly forty-seven more than my counterparts at Carnegie Tech, Northwestern, and Yale. I played nearly twenty leading roles—about nineteen more than my counterparts. Parts varied thrillingly from Leontes in *The Winter's Tale*, to the Father in Anouilh's *Eurydice*, to Ford in *The Merry Wives of Windsor*, to a Yiddish uncle in *49th Cousin*, Hialmar in *The Wild Duck*, Wilfred Shadbolt in *The Yeoman of the Guard*, a black chauffeur in whiteface in *You Can't Take It with You*. I was in bunches of musicals, and, in summer stock, popular Broadway shows. But whether *Antony and Cleopatra* or *Who Was That Lady I Saw You With?*, they were all approached with the same academic rigor—great introspection, suffering, scenery-chewing. When I understood a role and felt comfortable, I was transported; but far too often, I didn't get a grip on the character and was in torment.

My favorites were the Shaws. The second play I was ever in was George Bernard Shaw's *Too True to Be Good*—and miraculously, I was cast in the lead. This was a larger part than most Shakespearean roles, with language only slightly more modern and no less literate. *Back to Methuselah, You Never Can Tell, Pygmalion, Captain Brassbound's Conversion*: I loved swimming around in the language, wore it well, and attracted girls. What more could an actor ask from a playwright? The experience of being in a play is a much deeper one than simply reading it or seeing it performed. You live the literature, live the soul of the author.

Denison also had a summer theatre on its grounds—nine plays in ten weeks!—and I was in the company for two years, as well as two seasons of stock in Eagles Mere, Pennsylvania, run by Alvina Krause, the legendary acting teacher from Northwestern. If experience alone was the criterion, I was ready for the National Theatre of Great Britain.

I had some girlfriends at Denison, but way more rejections. I may have been scared of falling off a bicycle, but I was fairly fearless as a freshman calling juniors and seniors, who seemed amused by me. Over my college career, I put on forty pounds. I arranged for three illegal abortions in Cleveland, one of them mine, did mediocre work academically except for the theatre and English courses, wrote short stories for the literary magazine—the first about a man named Homer Glottis, who won an eating contest—and it felt so easy I didn't treat it seriously. It wasn't work. Acting was work—I was euphoric one day, depressed the next, like any college kid. There were just too many wild-and-woolly temptations at college to dive into.

Denison required a science, and as an alum of eight or nine years of serious psychoanalysis, I felt uniquely qualified to breeze through this requirement. But I had never met the behaviorists and their Skinner boxes, which proved to be a baffling—and to this day unilluminating—approach to the human mind. (The rat avoids electric shock! The chicken pecks for food when hungry!) It so unilluminated me that I failed the course twice, then finally got a D, necessitating an extra year in Granville. And a splendid year it was. Two semesters of six hours each, which included a course called Camping and Outdoor Life and creative writing. When I asked two of the psych profs if they'd ever had analysis or therapy of any kind, they looked at me as if I'd asked them if they'd ever been eaten by piranhas.

I paid no attention to food, though I ate plenty of it. My memories all fixate on midnight scrambies at the L&K Diner in nearby Newark. I was invited by my friend Rick Boyer to his house in Evanston, where he made something he called Eggs Sauternes—scrambled eggs, butter, and Sauternes wine. I thought to myself, "This is . . . unusual . . . this is . . . *good!*" The taste of it stayed with me.

Eggs Sauternes and, of course, the white apple.

About the only time I can remember not liking onions was a six-month period during and following my fraternity initiation at Denison, when the imaginative sadists at the Ohio Mu chapter of ΣAE put us pledges through what was grandiloquently called Hell Week. Denison was 90%+ Greek in that gentler era when you could still get into college without qualifying as an alcoholic (though you couldn't graduate without that honor). True, rumors abounded of a pledge somewhere in the South who had choked to death on a goldfish or a chunk of raw liver as part of his initiation, but, like the tales about that gearshift and Spanish fly, this was more urban legend than fact. Suffice it to say, the fraternities then were rather benevolent—every house on campus participated in a song contest, competed for grades, and played IMs (intramurals, not Instant Messages). I still find "The Sweetheart of ΣAE" a sweet and naïve and reverential song.

Which is not to say that Hell Week wasn't scary. It was. It actually lasted only a wimpy four days (and I understand that today's equivalent is Hell Day, and that tomorrow's will be Heck Afternoon) and was noted more for its cleverness than for corporal punishment. In addition to memorizing endlessly alliterative and scatological nicknames that were to be bellowed on command, sleeping on the unswept fraternity-house floor about three hours a night, the occasional paddling (we lived), and an inordinate number of practical jokes, we were instructed to wear a fat, raw onion—referred to as a "white apple"—on a string around our necks at all times, including to class, football practice, and ROTC (our neighbors, the Phi Delts, forced their pledges to wear burlap bags under their clothes). Whenever a brother decided we had done something wrong—like thinking for ourselves, or not doing two hundred push-ups in under ten seconds, or just staring into space bleary-eyed from lack of sleep—we were ordered to "take a chomp" of our white apple. Each of us munched through three or four of these monsters a day, which we discovered were not only extremely irritating to the gums but also lingered in our brains, perspirations, and general vapors for several weeks after we'd been activated.

I wasn't savvy enough to know then whether my white apples were Bermudas, Spanish, or big whites—but in retrospect I can tell you for sure that they weren't from Vidalia, Maui, or Walla Walla and weren't the Texas Supersweet variety known as 1015Y—all "sweet" onions with a higher sugar content and less sulfur than the "hot" ones. That's what gives them the sugary taste so enjoyable when chopped or sliced with a German Johnson tomato and a little ranch or Roquefort at Wolfgang's, the best steakhouse in New York (it has rib eye, Peter Luger's doesn't). It's a wonder any of us ΣAEs ever ate another white apple, and it must have been months before we had the nerve to grace our midnight burgers with an uncooked slice. But it's a good thing we persevered, because the absence of alliums—onions, leeks, scallions, shallots, garlic, chives, and their variations—would mean no more French, Italian, Indian, or Chinese food.

Vincent Scotto, formerly a partner at the estimable Scopa, now executive chef and, with his sister Donna, co-owner of Gonzo in New York, includes onions in almost every item on his menu except dessert and must be considered one of our town's leading *onioneurs*. "I love Vidalias raw, but it's a waste to cook them—if you cook a yellow very long and slow, you get the same result," he says. "Walla Wallas and other sweets are good, too, but the difference between all those sweet onions doesn't really blow my skirt up."

His onion salad is not only a modernist sculpture frequently worthy of MOMA's backyard; it constantly surprises the mouth as sweetness alternates with a slight burn. "I love all members of the lily family," he says, perspiring heavily as he works the Lilliputian kitchen at Gonzo, wearing shorts and clogs, frequently wiping down his fashionably hairless pate with a towel. "When I was at Scopa, I started making the salad with Vidalias, but since I couldn't get them all year round, I'd have to take them off the menu, and customers got mad. So I figured out that you can get the same sweetness with a yellow if you cook it long—forty minutes; don't be impatient—over low heat. And leave the skins on till they're done, so as not to lose extra layers."

Slow-cooked in this manner, the tops and bottoms caramelize, but when separated and nested with Parmesan, parsley, and croutons like a Russian doll, only the rims of each ring glisten with char.

Vincent Scotto's Onion Salad

4 large yellow onions, unpeeled
10 tablespoons olive oil
Kosher salt to taste
2 slices Tuscan bread, ¾-inch thick
1 clove garlic, unpeeled, halved
¼ cup fresh parsley leaves
¼ cup shaved Parmesan cheese
3 tablespoons fresh lemon juice

1. Preheat a griddle over medium-low heat until hot. Cut off the ends of each onion so that you can see the rings. Cut the onions crosswise into ¾-inch to 1-inch slices, keeping the rings intact and the skins on as much as possible. Use 4 tablespoons of the oil to brush cut sides of the onions and sprinkle them with salt. Grill slices until tender and caramelized, about

20 minutes per side. If they burn, scrape off the charred portion. (A little tastes okay.) Let cool.

2. Meanwhile, grill the bread until toasted, rub on both sides with the cut sides of the garlic, and sprinkle with 2 tablespoons of the oil and some salt. Cut into crouton-size pieces.

3. When onions are cool, remove remaining skins and separate into rings— they will resemble small, bottomless bowls. Divide half among 4 plates, sprinkle with half the parsley, half the Parmesan, and half the croutons. Repeat with the remaining ingredients on top. Drizzle with the lemon juice and the remaining oil.

YIELD: 4 servings.

The Plates Shift

I WAS A JUNIOR in 1963 when JFK was killed. One immediate concern—as it was when Pearl Harbor was attacked and on 9/11—was whether this was a single incident or the first military maneuver in a strategy to bomb, attack, and invade. Because other aspects of the murder became so prominent, it may be hard to remember that we didn't know what was going to happen next; our world had fallen in.

Nikita Khrushchev was every bit as scary as Osama bin Laden and when he banged his shoe on a rostrum at the U.N. and declared with certainty he would bury us, he gave us all just as many nightmares as bin Laden has. Though Khrushchev was talking economics, it was generally interpreted that he meant he would bury us militarily as well, so Kennedy's assassination—in addition to being a personal loss, and an emotional shock that eventually initiated a decade of political activism unseen since the Civil War—was, at least at first, terrifying.

I went into a theatre-history class at Denison that Friday, having heard the president was wounded, and emerged after a surprisingly low-key lecture from the most challenging professor in the school, William Brasmer, to find Kennedy had died. (Brasmer was normally given to bombastic and iconoclastic acting instructions such as throwing a set of keys on the floor and saying, "Make love to them," or firing off a starter pistol so he could observe our reactions.) The difference between "wounded" and "dead" was staggering. An unfortunate incident with optimistic hope of recovery and reversal became the

darkest finality. We all could sense this would change our sheltered, privileged lives. We didn't know how, and we didn't know what to do.

On Sunday, two days after the assassination, a bunch of us decided to act
rather than wallow in the helpless passivity of a numbed college campus four
hundred and fifty miles away from the nation's capital. Six of us scrunched
into my 1958 twelfth-hand starter Cadillac and headed for D.C. I had the
biggest car, probably because I inherited the Cadillac gene from Dad, who had
several new ones, and Uncle Bus, who had a yellow Cadillac convertible. We
would drive all night and arrive with little or no sleep in time for JFK's caisson and riderless horse with stirrups reversed to make its way up Pennsylvania Avenue.

We left at 9 P.M. in the dark and knew we had to be back for classes Tuesday.

Duane brought his book about theatrical lighting; Mary Kay, whom I was
dating, brought a small makeup kit. She and I were acting together in *Hecuba*,
the Greek tragedy by Euripides. She was Hecuba, I Polymestor, whom she
blinds for killing all her children. Paul toted underwear, Donna sheet music
(she was rehearsing a musical), and Bob brought nothing. I brought a tankful
of gas, a couple of maps, and just enough money for more gas, which was then
about thirty-two cents a gallon, threatening to go to thirty-three.

Despite the Cadillac's shabby grandeur, the fit was tight, three in back,
three in front. The mood was somber, though there was an undercurrent of
excitement and the knowledge that we were part of the national experience.
We discussed where we might crash for a couple of hours. Donna had friends
in D.C.

"How could this have happened?" Paul asked repeatedly. "I don't get it."

"Why did it happen? Who hated him so much?" I asked.

"The Russians," Mary Kay said. "The guy they caught was a Russian."

"They hate us that much?"

"Oh, yes."

" 'President Johnson,' " said Duane. "Sounds funny."

"That poor family," Donna said. "Those little children." She cried easily.

We remained respectful till we crossed into West Virginia, when we began
a game of Botticelli. After two or three rounds, we stopped at a gas station

where Donna could phone her D.C. friends. We tanked up, then ran next door, where a rival to McDonald's sold us bulging, divinely greasy cheeseburgers in paper bags, more bags of fries, and vanilla shakes. Someone had a fake I.D., so we bought two six-packs of Pabst.

Back on the road, emboldened by beer and comforted by food, we became less noble. Talk degenerated into remarks about other people in *Hecuba*, and their various drawbacks. *Schadenfreude* was a word in '63, and it got nasty. We were bitchy, just like real theatre folk, we thought. The name of the girl playing the second lead came up. "I've always thought she's, you know, depth-decrepit," said Mary Kay. I jumped on her for the use of the made-up word. "Well, you know," she said.

"How can I possibly play somebody blind?" I said. "I've never been blind. I've never really felt any serious pain," I said, forgetting my broken wrists and punctured cheek. Brasmer, the director, had shoved my hands under hot water, then cold, then hot again, to illustrate how pain screams at you, subsides, screams again. It was a brilliant acting lesson—no discussion, just action, and it made the experience visceral.

"Well, how am I supposed to act like all my children have been killed?"

"Mrs. Kennedy just had one of her children killed. Watch her," said Duane.

"I just don't want it to be phony, which I'll be unless I go off and blind myself." This got a laugh.

Brasmer was criticized. Euripides was criticized. How did you deal with the Chorus in Greek plays anyway? So unrealistic.

We crossed into Virginia, and Bob took the wheel. I held Mary Kay's thigh. Duane studied his lighting homework. Paul and Donna started singing, and everyone joined in. Duane fell asleep. We stopped again and got hot dogs. We got testy. We were cramped. We started laughing. We talked about the Kennedys. "What will this mean for Vaughn Meader?" Duane asked, referring to the successful comedian who impersonated JFK for a living. We all laughed and were then puzzled. Yes, what would this assassination do to the comedian?

We pulled into D.C. at about 5 A.M. and drove around for an hour, lost, in search of Donna's friends. We finally found them at daybreak. Donna's friend's parents welcomed us, urged a pile of buttery scrambies and bacon on us, and said we should sleep in the living room. We were all sure we wouldn't be able to fall asleep, then did in about thirty seconds.

We awoke at ten and headed for Pennsylvania Avenue. Thousands lined the streets. It was a cheerful crowd, though not boisterous. We stood for an hour waiting for the president's body. We talked to one another, and to many of the others standing there, and it was pleasant. We were all there for one purpose, and there was no anger. Suddenly I could see the caisson and the horse about a hundred yards away. The crowd turned silent. You couldn't hear a thing. Then, gradually, you could make out the scraping of the caisson wheels and the shoes of the riderless horse, and they became louder and louder, almost amplified. And then there was his casket in front of us, black and shiny and much larger than the man it contained, and it was unbearable. Silence except for the wheels and hooves. Suddenly a large Negro woman shouted out, "You did your job! Your time was short, but you did your job!" and now you could hear sniffles and sobs and clearing of throats all around. The reality was shocking, more shocking than the televised events, and the ride back to campus was relaxed and purifying.

It's important to go to the funerals of people who matter to you. Skipping them because they're unpleasant or watching them on TV if the person is famous doesn't let death scratch you, and it should. And when a funeral's over, the whole thing goes out to sea, and you can let go, if you've been there.

Of course, none of us let go of the repercussions that followed, or will ever forget the sense that even for a few days, the world had slipped out from under us, and we were without gravity and floating toward the moon.

Moonglow

~~~~~~

SHORTLY BEFORE THEY WERE married in the early sixties, Uncle Bus was rechristened by his second wife, Margaret, who said, "That's enough; that's a kid's name," and got us all to call him Frank.

Frank came to my rescue psychologically, socially, financially, and legally more than once. With Dad performing entrepreneurial calisthenics in Arkansas, Oklahoma, Nevada (by this time he'd bought the largest paper, the *Review-Journal*, and a TV station in Las Vegas), California, Alaska, and Hawaii, it was Frank, simultaneously masculine and effete, who introduced me not only to pheasant under glass and red wine, but to jazz and the proper perspective—all humor—toward *North by Northwest*.

In 1965, I motored across America with a college buddy named Weed. We drove a van with a motorcycle in the back, topping off our senior year at Denison with six weeks of adventures and mishaps from Cincinnati to Salt Lake, L.A., Tahoe, Las Vegas, and the Monterey County jail. One of us would ride the bike during the day (usually Weed, since I clung to my cowardice), and the other drive the van.

I've always liked big cars. They accommodate lots of people and in a pinch the backseat (or, more uncomfortably, the front) functions as a small motel room. Denison had strict rules for dormitory behavior then—no boys in girls' rooms and vice versa; girls in their rooms by eleven on weekdays and by one on weekends. This made physical intimacy quite a challenge, particularly in winter, which was the point.

In my first senior year, I stumbled across what I thought was the perfect solution: a hearse. Big enough in the back for a stretched-out body or two (by
definition), cheap, since there were few customers for a used hearse, and certainly attention-getting. I bought one for $750, and when it failed a year later,
bought another for $900. They were enormous successes, socially—twenty
people to a party! Twenty people *were* a party—and amorously, as girls actually *asked* to see the backseat. But they were unreliable, so I bought a van,
which had many of the same attributes. A big red van.

At night, Weed and I would sleep in the van (the second hearse had broken
down on the Pennsylvania Turnpike the year before), and thus made the entire round trip for less than $500.

I admired Weed, now a lawyer practicing in Atlanta, not only for his wit
and good company but also for his enviable height. He is six foot seven, which
made him ineligible for the draft, the luckiest inheritance of genes aside from
that of my friend John Schuck, whose allergy to eggs disqualified him.

After an eventful few weeks involving mostly junk food, a little gambling,
my initiation into prostitution (on the customer side), something resembling
a typhoon in Colorado, and a few days with Dad at Lake Tahoe, we headed to
San Francisco, then south. We burgered briefly in Carmel, and the cashier let
drop the news that Kim Novak's house was somewhere in the hills nearby.

There isn't much that jettisons me out of control—bullets headed in my direction might; a cardiologist's prescription for unlimited foie gras definitely
would—but ever since I developed an un-rein-in-able crush on her at age thirteen, the name or conjuring of Kim Novak has made me delirious. It does even
today, when she's in her seventies.

I saw *Picnic* thirteen times at age thirteen. It was a powerful, carnal story,
in which a sexy drifter played by William Holden runs off with the sexiest girl
in town, played by Kim, after the sexiest scene in all cinema, their dance to
"Moonglow and the Theme from *Picnic*."

Kim came to New York to promote the movie, and I phoned *The New York
Herald Tribune* to find out she was staying at the Sherry-Netherland (in those
days, newspapers were happy to impart information like that; you could even
phone the *Times* library at all hours of the day, and the staff librarians would
look things up for you, gratis, like an industrial-age Google.com). I tried to

woo Kim by sending flowers to her Sherry-Netherland suite three days in a row. This got me a telephone conversation with her that made my hands so sweaty I couldn't hold the phone. Her breathy vulnerability and husky thanks were more than my adolescent heart and knees could take. It also got me grounded for a week, since I'd charged the flowers to mother's account without telling her.

Now, even at twenty-three, being told she was less than twenty miles away in Big Sur, I knew I could never shave in a mirror again if I let this chance not only to meet her and impress her but also to . . . well, I don't exactly know what I wanted to do with or to her. This wasn't a case of lust, you see, and it wasn't simple infatuation. This was love, pure and selfless.

I should have known better. Actually, Weed *did* know better and argued strenuously that we should drop this pursuit—but it was my car. And so, around 9 or 10 P.M., we ventured past all the NO TRESPASSING signs into the Carmel Highlands, where, after an hour's drive, I found a mailbox that miraculously happened to have Kim Novak's *TV Guide* in it. I quickly flashed on what I imagined was a completely acceptable excuse for a stranger knocking on her door shortly before midnight: "Miss Novak, I've come to bring you your *TV Guide*."

She would be in lavender, her favorite color, look slightly wounded, as always, and part her lips, unbelievably grateful. She would invite me in. "Thank you so much—how kind, you young, strong man," she would say in that velvet voice, her platinumized hair shining. She would put on Sinatra or Mathis. (There was a rule left over from the fifties guaranteed to bring about successful seduction: Frank in the summer, Johnny in the winter, or the other way around, I forget which, but it was guaranteed. Even though I may not have wanted to seduce her, there was no harm in *her* seducing *me*.) She would offer pheasant under glass with the martinis, Weed would happily sleep in the van, and Kim and I would talk till dawn. I'd make her laugh huskily; she'd become even more vulnerable, until finally, just as the sun came up, she would invite me to stay for good. Weed could have the car and the motorcycle, free.

Encouraged by finding her mailbox, I insisted that Weed drive a few yards farther, where we came upon two stately houses. Did I really have the nerve to knock on Kim Novak's door? And which house did her door belong to? Until then, I had never acknowledged any obstacle to romance. The Miami Beach experience with Pam had taught me nothing. A year or two before this, I'd fallen for one of the summer-stock actresses who lived in Columbus and, mindless again of potential jail time, driven to her house with a friend, prized open a living-room window, and stolen two pictures of her from the piano. I still have them. I was, once again, thrust impulsively and ineluctably. Suddenly, just as I chose the house on the right, blaring headlights flooded the driveway and the air was filled with the barking of Dobermans. Weed wanted to either disappear or murder me, but I was unfazed. What higher justification could there be for trespassing than passion?

As it turned out, the driver of the car was an elderly woman, and the Dobermans toy poodles. "What are you doing here?" she demanded.

Assuming she would applaud the purity of my ardor, I said, "Looking for Kim Novak. I'm a friend of hers."

"If you're such a friend you'd know she's in Europe," the woman replied. "I'm calling the police." Weed and I were too well reared to yell anything back or run away, and besides, her car blocked ours from getting out. She disappeared into the house, and within minutes, the hands of some muscular representatives of the Monterey County sheriff's department were guiding our heads down into the backseat of their police car. It was the first time I'd seen car doors without inside handles.

Unamused by grand passion, the police took us to the Monterey County jail, where we were photographed and fingerprinted. Bail was set at $750 apiece—a hefty sum in those days. We were ordered impolitely into a cell with six or seven other overnight felons, all of us trying to sleep on one very hard floor. Concrete is unforgiving and retains heat only if there is any, which there wasn't. We spent a fitful and proto-pneumoniacal night. No blankets or pillows, no kind words, and no ways out.

Weed was livid at me, and it was hard to blame him. With a chilling lack of perspective, we were relatively unconcerned about our safety but were absolutely terrified about one thing: What were we going to tell our parents? He knew his would be furious, then hurt. I knew Dad would explode and say, "You got yourself into this—you get yourself out!" Mother would probably send the sheriff rent money to keep me there for another few weeks.

Morning came, and our shivering bodies were fed soupy, gruesome oatmeal and powdered eggs on a steel tray slid under the bars. I knew I was the ring-leader and felt bad for my trespassing friend, whom I had virtually kid-napped. It was up to me to come up with a solution, so I did, though quite by accident. I called Uncle Frank, three thousand miles away in Boston. One of his stepdaughters answered and said that he and Margaret were on vacation, golfing.

"Where?"

"Pebble Beach," she replied.

Pebble Beach? Pebble Beach just happened to be twenty-five miles from the Monterey County jail! I had called the right person, all right—he *knew* he was supposed to be at Pebble Beach just in case I got arrested!

Within an hour he and Margaret showed up with two certified checks for $750. He looked at me, amused. "Did you get to see Kim?" he asked.

"No, she's in Europe."

"Well, next time, better intelligence." He was so cool!

He took us to lunch at the Del Monte Golf Course Pro Shop. It may be all we know how to make, but no one knows how to make club sandwiches like WASPs (heavy mayo, crisp bacon, heirloom tomatoes, not too much lettuce, *toast*), and this was the finest meal an ex-con ever had.

That evening, Frank and Margaret and Weed and I returned to the scene of the crime to plead with the victim, her toy poodles, and her lawyer to drop the charges. Frank wanted his bail back, and we wanted to avoid having F.B.I. records for the rest of our lives, not to mention more Monterey County porridge.

Weed and I kept our mouths shut. Frank and Margaret did all the talking. They were quite intimidating, not because they raised their voices or were threatening but because they radiated a sort of aristocratic decency. The woman and her lawyer would somehow be *blessed* if they were allowed to drop the charges, which they did. They even wanted to stay in touch with Frank and Margaret! They were as grateful as I had imagined Kim would have been had I been able to present her with her midnight *TV Guide*.

In our current era, in which argumentative lawyers enrage even those with the noblest intentions, it's hard to imagine another, when refinement could change someone's mind. But that night it did.

I would like to say that Frank fed us pheasant under glass that night, but by then it was pretty much out of date, as would soon be his blue blazer, rep tie, gray flannels, and long cigarette holder. He and Margaret left to continue their vacation with nary a word of criticism. They knew how foolish I felt, which was lesson enough, as I haven't seen the wrong side of a jail since.

Weed and I headed south to visit and covet San Simeon, which I imagined Dad might someday buy, then farther to find Los Angeles aflame in the Watts riots and a world on the brink of catarrh. We didn't go into Watts, of course, but from the freeway could see fire and smoke fill the sky, and the radio told us it was lunatics in fury. The surreal juxtaposition of our prankish, college-kid night in jail with the bloody chaos in L.A. wasn't lost on us, but so shielded from the realities of the times had we been during our idyllic college daze in Granville, Ohio, that in our myopia we could only ask, "Why are they burning down their own neighborhoods?" It took an eerie repetition of those events in south-central L.A. twenty-seven years later, provoked by the decision in the Rodney King trial, for me to get a handle on the enormous rage and frustration and why they were released: The rioters had nothing to lose, and to the participants, riots are one hell of a good time.

One time, many Christmases after our incarceration, my wife and sons and I visited Frank in Boston. He put us up at the Ritz-Carlton—the first and most luxurious one—and over breakfast he laughed about that night in jail. We then ordered a delectable creamed finnan haddie, which had been on the Ritz's menu since the thirties and which turned out to be a perfect foil for the winter outside, shared as it was with this man who took me on as his son.

Monterey County Jail Oatmeal

Too much water
A lot of instant powdered oatmeal
As much sugar as the screws will let you have

1. Boil the water and stir in the oatmeal. Let steep.
2. Add sugar.
3. Eat with a steel spoon.

YIELD: 1 divided steel plateful.

THE BOSTON RITZ-CARLTON'S CREAMED FINNAN HADDIE

2 pounds finnan haddie (smoked haddock), skinned, boned, and cut into ½-inch dice
2 cups heavy cream
2 egg yolks
Cayenne pepper to taste
Your favorite hot buttered toast points (made from 6 slices of bread)

1. Cover the finnan haddie with water and simmer 6–8 minutes. Drain and keep warm.
2. Boil 1 ½ cups of the cream until reduced by half. In a bowl, beat the egg yolks with the remaining cream and whisk in the hot cream. Return the egg-yolk mixture to the saucepan and whisk constantly until hot but not boiling. Season with cayenne.
3. Divide the haddock over toast points, spoon sauce on top, and serve.

YIELD: 6 servings.

UNCLE BUS DIED in '83, after three or four more heart attacks. I asked him after his penultimate one if there was any pain. "No. My left arm hurt a little, then I woke up in the hospital." He was smiling. It was a great way to go—for him. And murder on the rest of us. I never got to tell him what he'd meant to me and what a shining example he was, and that in the competition between him and Dad for my soul, which neither of them knew anything about, he'd won.

Christians believe death is only the beginning of the good stuff—most religions do. Cheerful way to live. At his memorial service, they played the hymn

> *The strife is o'er,*
> *The ba-a-ttle done.*
> *The victory of life is won.*

The minister said something about his unconditional love. To me, this meant he'd have backed me if I'd spent one night in jail or five years, and I couldn't sing because of the burning in my throat and the tears that blinded me from seeing the words in the hymnal.

Be Like a Noble
Not a Knave
Caesar Uses
Burma-Shave

I LEARNED TO SHAVE from a magazine. *Esquire*, I think it was, or *GQ*, and I think I was in my twenties. Before I read that article, I had tried various techniques, found them all uncomfortable, and in my only attempt to shave upward from the Adam's apple to the earlobe drew droplets of blood at the root of every follicle.

The nonmetaphorical closest shave I ever had was at the hands of a hotel barber in London, who soaked my face in a hot, wet towel, then smoothed on various unguents and creams, stropped his straight razor, then minutely scalped every millimeter of my shaving area. My face felt smooth as a hockey rink after a Zamboni wash but subsequently so sensitive that I couldn't shave for several days. (My closest shave metaphorically was the midnight I fled Francis Ford Coppola's San Francisco mansion, inadvertently setting off the burglar alarm and dodging the police by seconds. But that's another story.)

I subsequently theorized that I had only one thing in common with Richard Nixon—translucent skin that made our beards look blacker than they would have if the skin were different. Nixon reportedly shaved twice a day when he had to make a public appearance, so I tried that a couple of times. My skin broke out in painful pink bumps, and I resolved never again to do anything that man did. So when the shaving recipe appeared, I was greatly relieved, and so was my face.

It wasn't that my father didn't have the knowledge to show me how to shave; he just wasn't around. By the time I was shaving, he was already into his thirtieth or fortieth million, and though you'd think he would be satisfied with that fortune and might have said to himself, "I think I'll feed the hungry in Sudan," or, "I think I'll go east and show my son how to shave," he wasn't and he didn't. Men like this (possibly women, don't know) aren't simply after wealth; they love playing the game. Not unlike Oprah or the Rolling Stones or Rafael Palmeiro, who, having made more money than any of them will ever possibly need, continue to play—and with increasingly record-breaking incomes. After the initial accomplishment—security—big money brings power, independence, a modicum of fame, and the ability to manipulate events. And it's fun! Dad could build an outdoor concert hall in Tulsa not only because it was deductible and good PR for his business in Tulsa but because of the prominence he achieved in town. So it's missing the point to say of a billionaire, "Why doesn't he quit working and do good? Doesn't he have enough money?" The answer is, "No, he doesn't."

He would also say that he *was* doing good. He was employing thousands of people, contributing to the tax base, delivering newspapers to families, wiring homes for cable TV, building concert halls in Tulsa, and benefiting charities.

To this day I don't know what fueled Dad's compulsion to leave such a footprint on the world. Perhaps he was driven by the need to surpass the lower-middle-class material accomplishments of his own father, about whom he felt contempt, embarrassment, and moderate affection. For the last fifty years of his life, Dad never needed to deprive himself of a single sensual experience or material object. But he went to his grave thinking he was deprived of them all.

THE PERFECT SHAVE

Hot water to taste
2 handfuls soap lather
2 squibs brushless shaving cream

1. Wash shaving area with hot water and 1 handful of the lather; leave lather on.
2. After 2 minutes, wash lather off with hot water, then rub in another handful of lather.
3. Massage in brushless shaving cream. Shave (downward if your face is sensitive).

"The Finest Restaurant in the World"

D ESPITE ALL THE experience I'd gained onstage at Denison and Eagles Mere, somewhere along the way I realized I didn't feel equipped to tackle Shakespeare or many of the British classics with the pros and that I wouldn't learn how to if I stayed in America. I remember cackling over Olivier's film of *Richard III* and being wowed by Albert Finney and Hugh Griffith and Edith Evans in *Tom Jones* and wondering, "How can I ever do *that*?" The times I enjoyed acting were getting fewer and farther between; I began to see actors as puppets, of secondary and tertiary importance to the play, after the author and the director. Miss Krause, the genius from Northwestern, continually stressed that as actors we were in service to the author, that he was the only creator in the process, and that everyone else was an interpreter.

Still, I'd trained all that time as an actor and lacked the imagination to pursue anything else. Much as I enjoyed the small, comfy community that was Granville, I knew there was a considerably bigger world out there. But at the moment, I had to do something to continue my education—there was a war going on in '65, and a draft, and I didn't want to take part in either. I had recently concluded that our involvement in Vietnam was unconscionable, thereby conveniently reinforcing self-interest with morality, not for the last time. I've always had wretched eyesight (glasses at ten, that first year at Trinity) and quickly found I was ineligible to become an officer—but not blind enough to avoid the service altogether. The most attractive option was to spend a year or two pursuing acting in London, and after I auditioned for

LAMDA—the London Academy of Music and Dramatic Art—in New York in the spring, they accepted me.

The idea of London sounded wildly romantic, far-off, and incredibly hip. It was the center of the universe then, thanks to the Beatles, Mary Quant, Richard Lester, and all those British movies made for a dime that were suddenly popular in America. And I thought I'd finally learn the secret of acting.

Mother wanted no part of this and refused to pay for it. Sometime during their marriage, she and Dad had set aside $75,000 to be split between Nancy and me when we became twenty-one. Nancy received her $37,500 at the appropriate age, but when I got there, Mother decided I was too irresponsible to manage it. The terms of the divorce dictated she pay for college—all of $900 per semester—and she liked the control over me it allowed her, as my summer-stock earnings amounted to about $400, total, over four years. However, the terms of the trust insisted that both parents had to agree to withhold the funds, and Dad delighted in not agreeing with her. I don't think he thought about my well-being for a second, only about thwarting her. She, in turn, enjoyed thwarting me—nice little triangle. So when Dad refused to agree, I received the trust, and Mother withheld—this time, in the fiduciary sense. I wound up paying for the last year of college, the shambles of serial Cadillac hearses, the midnight scrambled eggs, the beer. And LAMDA.

In another grandiloquent gesture, Dad gave me a first-class ticket on the S.S. *France* as a graduation present. This was the most spectacular ship on the water, and to be in first class was meant to be the experience of a lifetime—if you were eighty. At this point I didn't know whether he was continuing to open my eyes to the big world outside or competing with Mother—"What did *you* give him, Edith?"—or just showing off. But I was eager to see what would happen.

It was my first time on any kind of cruise, and the ship was indeed magnificent. Grand, stately public rooms, high ceilings, blue carpets, and ultra-*moderne* walls. Fire laws forbade using wood on the interior, so everything was decorated in aluminum, Formica, and plastic. I thought it magnificent. There seemed to be polished brass every three or four inches, officers and crew alike in snappy blue, gold, and white outfits. My cabin was small, but I soon learned all shipboard cabins are small by comparison to land.

Mother accompanied me to the departure and was quietly sarcastic. I didn't blame her when I figured it out some days later. She was confronted with a son she could no longer control, off on a mission of which she didn't approve, traveling on an extravagance she couldn't condone, presented by the man who had ruined her life and who was, at least symbolically, wooing her son away. She should have just put me in a cab.

I saw New York and its West Side piers disappear, and I immediately understood the term "all at sea." I was suddenly attached to nothing solid, literally and figuratively. I didn't know where I was going or, really, why. Didn't know a soul in London; didn't know a soul on board this behemoth.

The *France* was launched in 1960 and instantly became the rage of transatlanticers. DeGaulle desperately wanted to compete in the ocean-liner business as France once had with ships such as the *Liberté* and the *Normandie*, but had been outmatched by the *Queens Elizabeth* and *Mary* and the *United States*. He thought such a ship would build France's morale, in part compensating for the loss of its colony Algeria. And so this massive, white-atop-black structure, longer than three football fields, with two striking red smokestacks and a distinctive whale-back bow, was built in Saint-Nazaire and was the longest ship ever built until the *Queen Mary 2*. When it sailed into New York harbor on its maiden voyage, it was welcomed with a small armada of tug- and fireboats spewing waterfalls and helicopters and airplanes swooping and circling overhead in celebration. The *France* was enormously popular right from the start, attracting the famous and selling out on many of its cruises.

But it never made a dime. Despite its popularity, fuel costs necessitated constant subsidy from the French government, and demand for transatlantic crossings dampened with the advent of the jet. In 1974, when oil prices jumped almost sevenfold, the government decided it should subsidize the future, not the past, and sank its money into the Concorde.

On the *France*, by custom, the women in first class wore fancy dress and the men tuxedos to dinner except on the first and last nights out, when, presumably, butlers were unpacking or packing their shipboard wardrobes. We were assigned tables, and I was not only the youngest at mine, I was the youngest in first class. The main dining room was large, domed, and formal: beautiful flowers at every table, burnished hotel silver at every setting, linens so white you needed sunglasses and starched so crisp they might have inspired Kevlar.

What happened next redirected my life: I sat down to eat.

Out came baskets of breads and butters and rolls in many shapes and with different herbs, followed by caviar and vodka. I drank the vodka, and dipped the little spoon into the caviar. Not sure about that one. This was followed by a thick mushroom soup—I didn't know till then that I even liked mushrooms, since opening a can of Broiled in Butter was the limit of my experience. But I liked *these* mushrooms! A fillet of turbot or sole stuffed with what seemed like a white winey lobster mousse appeared, then disappeared down my gullet, followed by a beautiful fillet of beef encrusted with herbs, then a plate of fat, fresh asparagus on a napkin. (I knew just enough about food to say "yes" to the hollandaise.) I passed on the salad and the cheese—I'd have to learn about them later. Several desserts were presented, and through either thrift or curiosity (certainly not hunger), I asked for two. One was the richest chocolate éclair I'd ever seen, bulging with crème Chantilly front and back like a parade inflatable; the other was a Nesselrode pudding with chestnuts. I finished everything. The whole experience took two and a half hours, longer than any meal I'd ever eaten. I took a breath. I smoked then, and could barely smoke. I certainly couldn't move. This was the loveliest way of spending an evening since the night outside the Denison field house with Diane X in the back of the hearse.

The people at the table were impressed at the quantity I'd put away. I wasn't; I was impressed by the quality. I'd never tasted food like this, never even seen pictures of this, never knew it existed. The only hint I'd had were those Eggs Sauternes back at Rick Boyer's house in Evanston.

Craig Claiborne considered the *France* the finest restaurant in the world. It may have been then; it wouldn't be now because of the sheer weight of the food and plethora of sauces. The kitchen reportedly took on 15 tons of meat, 30 tons of vegetables, 70,000 eggs, and 330 pounds of caviar for every round trip. Some 18,000 bottles of nonvintage and 4,500 of vintage wine were consumed along with 25,000 rolls and breads. There was one waiter for every six passengers, and the kitchen never made the same dish twice on a voyage unless specifically requested. You could order anything from your room at any time of day, from a *langoustes à la parisienne* to the chef's version of corned-beef hash—included in the price of the ticket. And the visual displays! Operatically elaborate ducks coated in sauces and surrounded by tiny chestnuts and salsify in a pool of the same sauce, like something from a topiarist on opium, glistening *oeufs en gelée* crisscrossed with perfect *fleurs-de-lis* of truffles from Dumas, sculptures of fish encased in shiny pastries. Each scale and gill and eyeball carved into the shell. It was my first total sensory immersion since the photographs of the pornographic novel at Lawrenceville.

The next day at breakfast, which most of the guests skipped, another astonishing array was presented. I didn't know you were allowed to eat broiled fish or smoked salmon or *omelettes aux fines herbes* or grilled pork loins with Bordelaise sauce . . . for *breakfast!* Worried I might not taste them all, I ordered them all, requesting American cheese in the omelette and could I please have some hollandaise on it? (A table companion emboldened me to try *béarnaise* by the third day out; didn't need much encouragement.) The waiter was unabashed; if I'd asked, I think he would have brought Eukanuba *périgueux* (truffles) without blinking. When the omelette arrived, I realized my assignment on this trip: It wasn't shuffleboard or gambling or drinking and dancing or trying to pick up girls or reading books or swimming in the two indoor pools on deck; it wasn't even about getting to London. It was to eat every piece of food on that boat, and I had only five days to do it!

I followed breakfast with an overpowering lunch, then a return bout, tuxedoed this time, for dinner.

I remember clearly that I ate every meal. I probably put on five pounds, or possibly twelve, which, after all the sloth at Denison, I didn't need. But this was such a novel experience. I grew to like caviar, the soft and blander cheeses (smelly would come later), and the wine. I didn't yet have the nerve to embrace the raw oyster (that came a few years later, in New Orleans), but I don't remember turning anything else away. I *must* have turned away some fish; no kid of twenty-three likes every kind of fish, but I don't remember. I knew I wanted food to be a major part of my life, and never again would I suffer a meal not acutely aware of what was on the plate. It didn't have to be *haute*, but it had to be deliberate.

I also knew I didn't want to be an actor.

There wasn't much to do on the ship between meals; in fact, I was beginning to wonder if there was anything in life *worth* doing between meals. Everyone was older. I tried going downstairs into second class and introducing myself around, but as I was to find out later in the bar scene of the seventies, that wasn't much fun and I wasn't very good at it.

The ship showed two movies a day, so I watched them. In the course of those screenings, I realized I wanted to make them, not be in them. I'd gone to movies and plays since early childhood, and often cut classes at that tutoring school to see a daytime double feature. I saw everything, knew every name filling every job. I was particularly interested in movies about teenagers because they showed me how I was supposed to be behaving—not just James Dean, but goody-goody Pat Boone (well, at least you could understand the words), demented Sal Mineo, and troubled, intense John Cassavetes. Without probing much, I concluded movies and plays were about actors; so I wanted to be an actor. My cousin Lee was rapidly becoming a star, and I loved the glamour of her life. When I'd taken acting lessons at the Cassavetes school in dark rehearsal rooms on West Forty-sixth Street, that, too, had been glamorous: We boys and men were all fashionably depressed, like Brando and Dean; the girls and women were all beautiful and sulky, like Natalie Wood, Joan Collins, and of course Kim Novak. Being an actor gave me an identity at Denison, and occasionally, it was enjoyable. Now I realized it simply wasn't a good fit.

My aunt Maymie had told me many years before that I would be a writer, and anyone who knew me felt the same way—I should be writing plays or movies or books or letters, they said. Something. And certainly my experience with the post office at Malcolm Gordon and Lawrenceville pointed in that direction. Maybe on the basis of the S.S. *France*, recipes. But it's always taken me forever to turn conclusion into action—profession, marriage, divorce, where to live. I assume that on my morphine drip, I'll discover I was always meant to be a cabinetmaker and live in Delaware.

When the *France* docked in Southampton, all I knew was that I had to find a place to live in a city I knew nothing about and get out of a school that was my reason for coming to that city but to which I no longer wanted to go. Not unlike the situation where my undying love for Pat Sutherland inadvertently ushered me into Denison, I was in swinging London, but for the wrong reasons.

I found the London School of Film Technique, and the principal was eager to have my American dollars spent there; but the LAMDA principal said with some impatience that I had been chosen as one of only eleven Americans, and that I had guaranteed them £2,400 that year. I would have to pay it whether I attended the school or not. Though marginally better off than other students because I could afford to live by myself, I couldn't risk all that money on my newfound professional goal—what if it turned out to be a lark, too?

TOURNEDOS ROSSINI AS SERVED ON THE S.S. FRANCE
(Filet Mignon with Foie Gras, Truffles, and Madeira)
(Adapted from Classic French Cooking *by Craig Claiborne, Pierre Franey, and the editors of Time-Life Books, Little, Brown, 1970) You may cut corners, but don't blame me if the ghosts of Claiborne, Franey, and the master chef of the S.S. France, Henri Le Huédé, haunt your dreams.*

¾ cup dry Madeira
2 tablespoons juice from a can or jar of truffles
1 cup *Fond Lié* (see page 79)
6–10 tablespoons clarified butter
4 slices homemade white bread, ¼ inch thick, cut into 2 ½-inch-diameter rounds
Four 6-ounce *tournedos*, about 1 ½ inches thick
Salt and pepper, to taste
4 round slices *foie gras en bloc*, 2 inches in diameter, room temperature
4 round slices black truffle, 1 inch in diameter, ¼ inch thick
2 tablespoons butter, chilled and cut into ½-inch bits

1. Reduce ½ cup of the Madeira and the truffle juice to ¼ cup in a small saucepan. Add *Fond Lié* and set aside.
2. In a heavy saucepan, warm 3 tablespoons of the clarified butter, then brown bread rounds until crisp. Drain on paper towels and set aside on a warm platter.

3. Add 3 more tablespoons of the clarified butter, raise the heat, and after drying the *tournedos* with a paper towel, sauté them in the butter 3 minutes on each side, until rare. Season with salt and pepper.

4. Place a *tournedo* on each crouton, top with round of foie gras, then a truffle slice.

5. Working quickly, pour off the fat from the skillet and add remaining ¼ cup Madeira. Deglaze and stir in the *Fond Lié* mixture. Stir and heat the mixture through.

6. Strain the sauce through a fine sieve into a small saucepan, swirl in the butter bits, pour over the *tournedos*, and serve at once.

YIELD: 4 servings

That was simple enough. Now for the heavy lifting:

Fond Lié
1 quart *Fond Brun de Veau* (see page 80)
½ cup chopped mushrooms
3 sprigs fresh parsley
5 tablespoons arrowroot
⅓ cup cold water
¼ teaspoon Caramel Food Coloring (see page 81)

1. In a 2-quart saucepan, bring *Fond Brun de Veau*, mushrooms, and parsley to a simmer over moderate heat. Reduce heat and cook uncovered for about 15 minutes.

2. Dissolve arrowroot in water in a bowl, then whisk mixture into stock. Add Caramel Food Coloring, a few drops at a time, until the stock is a rich brown color.

3. Simmer the sauce until it thickens somewhat, about 15 minutes.

YIELD: 1 quart, which may be refrigerated for a week or frozen for three months.

Fond Brun de Veau

5 pounds meaty veal shanks sawed into 2-inch lengths

2 pounds meaty veal shinbones, sawed into 2-inch lengths

1 pound veal marrowbones

2 pounds chicken parts: necks, wings, backs

2 tablespoons clarified butter

2 medium onions, peeled and quartered

2 medium carrots, scraped and cut into 1-inch rounds

5–6 quarts cold water

2 medium celery stalks, including leaves, cut into 1-inch lengths

2 medium leeks, washed and quartered lengthwise (white parts and two inches of green only)

10 sprigs of parsley

2 fresh thyme sprigs, or ½ teaspoon dried thyme

1 large bay leaf

1 large unpeeled garlic clove, smashed

1 teaspoon salt

½ teaspoon whole black peppercorns

2 medium tomatoes, quartered

½ cup canned tomato purée (unflavored)

---

1. In a heavy 12-inch skillet, in batches, brown the shanks, shins, marrow, and chicken parts in clarified butter, turning frequently with tongs. Don't let them burn! Transfer to a 12-quart stockpot.
2. Brown onions and carrots in skillet, stirring, and add to stockpot. Pour 1 quart of water into skillet, boil, and deglaze. Add to stockpot with remaining 4–5 quarts of water (as much as you need to cover the bones).
3. Bring to a simmer slowly, skimming off foam and discarding it and scum. Don't let it boil, or stock will become cloudy. Add remaining vegetables and herbs, garlic, salt, and pepper.
4. Simmer stock for 7 hours.
5. Pick out meat and bones and vegetables and discard. Strain into a large bowl and let cool to room temperature. Refrigerate for up to 4 days, or

freeze for months. Before using, remove layer of fat that has accumulated at the top.

YIELD: about 2 quarts.

Thought you were done? Hey, this was the *France*!

Caramel Food Coloring
1 medium onion, peeled and cut into ¼-inch slices
1 cup water
1 ½ cups sugar

---

1. In a heavy saucepan over moderate heat, stir onions *without fat* until they're almost mahogany-black. Add ½ cup of the water and the sugar and cook until mixture foams up and rises in the pan. Stir in the remaining water and don't be alarmed if the caramel hardens at this point.
2. Still stirring, continue to cook until hardened caramel melts and syrup is smooth. Strain through a fine sieve into a heatproof jar. Cover with a lid.
3. Use to color food. It will keep almost indefinitely.

YIELD: 1 ½ cups.

Rules of the Game

S O A MONTH AFTER my night in jail, I began LAMDA classes. I wasn't the star I'd been at Denison—nobody was the star they'd been at college—and the atmosphere was competitive. We had classes in movement, breathing, dance, speech, and history, and we rehearsed scenes from Shakespeare, Molière, and Chekhov. I shivered through the fall in a studio flat near the (then) very down-market Notting Hill Gate and had to put pennies into a hallway meter several times in the course of a bath to keep the hot water four inches high in the tub. (Don't picture this.) I got on better with the English, for whom this was college, not grad school, and who were less combative than us Americans. I remember that a favorite riff with a British schoolmate named Roger Dunwell was our imitating Peter O'Toole's T. E. Lawrence after he'd trekked across the desert for days with an Arab lad and demanded of an astonished officers-only club, "We want . . . two . . . glahsses . . . of . . . le . . . mon . . . ade," and threatened to implode (as usual).

But most of all, there was the city itself, exploding with life and protest. Olivier, Gielgud, Finney, Richardson, Robert Stephens, Maggie Smith, Joyce Redmond, the Redgrave sisters—all were at the National Theatre in rep, night after night; Ian Holm, Glenda Jackson, and Janet Suzman were at the Royal Shakespeare Company. Noël Coward was live in the West End and Alec Guinness and Simone Signoret were in a dreadful but riveting *Macbeth* (performed in sweat suits) at the Royal Court. There were new plays by Pinter and Osborne, Peter Brook staged *The Persecution and Assassination of Jean-Paul Marat as Performed by the Inmates of the Asylum of Charenton Under the Direction of the*

Marquis de Sade, and nobody had ever seen anything like it. The RSC also mounted something called *US*, a shocking protest against America's involvement in Vietnam. It was all unbelievable! Everybody but Will Kemp and Aeschylus were in town and onstage. I think I spent about one night a month *not* in a theatre or cinema. You could *despise* the theatre and still see that it was making the earth shake in London. And there was always a race to the pubs afterward because they closed at eleven.

But, boy, was the food bad. On a student's budget, meals outside of beer consisted of sausages filled with highly questionable grains, soggy-crusted pub grub served at room temp, thin and runny custards poured over sweet "puddings," and something called a Wimpy, which was, if you can believe it, a really bad version of a McDonald's burger. After three months of this, for a reason I now forget, I ventured solo into Simpson's-in-the-Strand, a clubby British beef parlor with paneled walls, waiters in tails, and a serious air of condescension. I'm fairly sure I had the thinly sliced, red-juiced beef from the silver-domed carving trolley, brussels sprouts in cream, and something at the finish that was sticky with either golden syrup or treacle. At last, something one could eat in Britain—but not exactly the S.S. *France*.

What I remember most was watching a jolly fellow with a thickly veined nose and cheeks, ruddied from years of alcohol, dig two silver spoons into a ceramic tub of Stilton, which he then chased with a glass of port. He seemed sent for my delight from the casting department over at Ealing Studios, a Falstaffian Churchillian deliriously happy in his own, mostly unintelligible fog. After he left even jollier than when he arrived, I ordered the tub of cheese and a chaser of port—and found my own version of O'Toole's lemonade in this culinary desert: Stilton and port remains one of the great marriages in gastronomy.

None of us could afford that more than once or twice a year then—we were all 'umble hactors. LAMDA had eighty or so students, with our "advanced" class of twelve, who weren't English—eleven Americans and an Indian. I didn't think we were particularly advanced, just older, and had been to college. The English had grown up with Shakespeare in their bones and sausages, and we were doing our best to imitate them. They were amused by us Americans but had no respect for our playwrights; their reverence for

O'Neill, Miller, Williams, Mamet, and Neil Simon came much later. They did generally admire Brando and Robert Mitchum and Bette Davis, though.

The birds at LAMDA were elusive—Americans neurotic, English distant—and it was several months before I met Anna. She was on the rebound from Matthew Guinness, Sir Alec's son, and I was on the rebound from the world. The match only lasted a few months and was fairly fraught with minor disagreements—who got the extra pillow, and who paid for the bad sandwiches. I was nervous spending whole nights with girls. Not sure what to do. And all the beds were narrow. We visited Stonehenge and Salisbury and a dozen little inns (Six pounds a night! With breakfast!) and villages in a stick-shift, right-hand-drive Morris Minor I'd bought for twenty-five pounds. We ate frugally, talked about the theatre, and were clumsy lovers. The relationship ran out of fizz rather than exploding, though we remained friends. When I saw her twenty-five years later at a memorial for one of the students, she was just as lovely as she had been at age twenty.

But we did spend a week in Paris, and its reputation as the most romantic of cities asserted itself in contradictory ways on my first visit there, because Dad hit on her.

I didn't really blame him. Anna was blond and very bird-of-the-period, wonderfully well spoken, being British and an actress (sort of a Brit squared), and as brilliantly intimidating as women with English accents continue to be to American men. And Dad was bored.

She and I were on a spring break from LAMDA. We found floor space in someone's cluttered apartment near the Bois de Boulogne. We tussled with the metro, braved the open-air elevator on the Eiffel Tower, clinging to each other in terror (never again), and took pleasure in discovering the very thin slice of ham inside the thick, buttered baguette from the corner brasserie, which exemplified for me the difference between French and American sensibilities: at home, the sandwich would have been reversed—pounds of meat and mayo, overstuffed between sweet, spongy slices of Wonder bread.

After two days, Dad phoned. I don't remember how he found me—or why, since in the twenty-four years following my birth I hadn't seen him for more than a total of fifteen days. Perhaps he wanted to see if my experience on the S.S. *France* had improved me. He was impressed that I was going to school in London, though I don't think he focused much on the kind of school it was.

When I saw him in Paris, the movie *Goldfinger* was a recent rage, and between visiting a handful of newsprint suppliers to satisfy the IRS, he spent a few days in London picking up an Aston Martin. Never mind that, short, fat, middle-aged, and 94% bald, he looked more like Khrushchev than James Bond, Dad wanted that Aston Martin. He was driving it around Europe accumulating the 1,500 miles or so required to beat the import duty back into the States, even though tooling and hoteling around Europe was way more expensive than just paying the tariff. But since the tooling and hoteling was also deductible (in pursuit of business), the case could be made that the government was actually paying for him to buy the Aston Martin. Dad loved America, and nothing gave him more pleasure than working it for all its worth.

His lifelong M.O. was to interweave pleasure so thoroughly with business that the government couldn't distinguish between the two, and he deducted just about everything he did. He wasn't the first person to come up with this scheme, but possibly he was the boldest and certainly the most thorough, and conceivably could have been the reason for the alternative minimum tax. He bought houses concealed as offices, Mercedes that somehow became company cars, first-class plane tickets (and eventually first-class planes) and cruises to Hawaii that were "essential" for doing business. (Well, he *did* have newspapers and a shopping center in Hawaii, and he *did* talk business aboard those ocean liners.) For years he claimed the small house he bought on the G.I. Bill in Las Vegas was his legal residence so that the mansion he built across town would be considered an office.

He was a flamboyantly excessive devourer of failing newspapers, radio and TV stations, highway billboards, real estate, food, booze, women, the air we breathe—and the latest, trendiest possession.

"Where'd you like to have dinner?" he growled into the phone. Since I had seen not only *Goldfinger* but the movie *Gigi*, I suggested Maxim's, the wildly expensive museum of *haute cuisine* featured in the film. Because I didn't know he was always happy to be generous when it was his call, I expected him to counter with a neighborhood café featuring hard-boiled eggs and unlabeled wine on the table. He quickly turned me around: "Fine—see you at nine."

Anna and I got as gussied up as grad students could and swanned into Maxim's and *la belle époque*. It was like dining in an opera, surrounded as we were by dozens of Colettes and Chevaliers, and over there in the corner a couple of Leslie Carons. I remember ordering *duck l'orange* because it was the only thing I'd heard of except for *crêpes Suzette*, which I also ordered, not realizing both were laced with o.j. Dad had something with beef in it, Anna a lobster thermidor with a sauce so viscous that two George Foremans couldn't have finished it. It reminded me of the *France*. There was sauce on everything, all inspissated with butters, flours, crème fraîches. To me, it was all the *haute*st of *haute*, and delicious—though also somewhat oppressive. *Nouvelle cuisine* and its nasty little cousin *minceur* were a decade away. Dad was charming and funny, filled with war stories from his rambunctious life. He cheerfully announced that Scottish beef—not French—was the finest in the world, just to see the waiters blanch and make Anna laugh. She was pretty laughing.

The summer before, prior to my night in jail, I'd visited him for a week at his thirteen-acre lakefront property on the Nevada side of Lake Tahoe. He had two king-size beds right next to each other in his bedroom. It looked like a football field of mattresses. I couldn't figure out whether that was to fit more women in there with him or so he could sleep farther away from the one who was there. The guest quarters were considerably more spartan—he clearly didn't want to encourage anyone to stay for more than a few days. In keeping with his tax concerns, he'd built a dormitory filled with bunk beds and one bathroom, so that twice a year his executives would traipse up the mountain, climb into the bunk beds like little boys, and pee in a communal bathroom, and he could call it a business expense. It was also a none-too-subtle way of showing them the enormous gulf between employer and employee. I'd been thrilled and amazed to be with someone who seemed to have a complete handle on the way the world worked.

At one of the Tahoe dinners, he'd regaled his girlfriend *du jour*, a six-foot strawberry blonde named Jayne, my soon-to-be fellow convict Weed, and me with the story of his strike-breaking days in Las Vegas, and now he reembellished it for Anna at Maxim's. Anna was a socialist and both amused by the audacity of Dad's business manipulations and aghast at his selfishness.

"What are your labor contracts like?" she said.

"What labor contracts? Don't have any. Don't have any unions," Dad said proudly.

"However did you manage that?"

"A few years ago in Las Vegas my deliverers went out on strike. So I took one of the trucks out myself, delivered the newspapers all over town. When I got back, one of the strikers threw himself down in the driveway of the plant."

"Goodness, what did you do?"

"I drove right over him."

Anna inhaled sharply.

"Broke his back," he said cheerfully. He paused to let the shock register, then added, "But I broke the strike, too!" He grinned so hard his clenched teeth were almost crying.

Anna was speechless, and Dad loved it. He told the story with such joy, not cruelty, that if you hadn't heard the content, you'd swear he'd just related a story about curing a major disease or climbing a serious mountain.

I was completely enthralled. His action was bold and swashbuckling and in defense of everything he held most dear: his business, his art. He had made a pre-emptive strike—and a successful one—against thugs attempting to rape his family, destroy his religion, overthrow his country. It didn't occur to me then to empathize with the striker: He and his fellow thugs had tried to violate the religious sanctity of Dad's essence; they hadn't created this company, hadn't taken risks to preserve it, hadn't stayed up days on end to make it grow, hadn't *created* a single thing—*he* had. And now they felt entitled to a piece—an enormous piece—of his work of art. I felt nearly as triumphalist as he did: Those jobs wouldn't exist if it hadn't been for him, and now they were going to cripple him? Not without a fight! It felt like narration from a novel that I could comprehend but not grasp. I couldn't sympathize with the striker's broken back because I'd never experienced drama and violence like that.

And he was my father.

Over the years, Dad told the story repeatedly, and it was never clear how much of it—if any—was true. The threat of his rage made him too frightening to challenge with questions about its authenticity. But I'm sure the kernel was accurate. As far as I know, he broke every strike thrown at him till he ran into the unions of Hawaii, and if he didn't run over that picketer's back, surely the strikers thought he could and would.

"Only have to do something like that once, dear," he told Anna. "Word gets around."

"But . . . but . . . didn't the police arrest you or something?" she said.

"Why should they? It's my driveway. You don't expect somebody to be lying down in your own driveway, do you?" He glowed and glowed. He had defeated the Hun, the Japs, the slants, the towelheads. I envied him his joy—such was my moral compass at the time. Anna was taken aback as much by his shamelessness as by the deed itself.

When the dust settled, I tried to talk to him about my graduate program, but it bored him. "Graduate school's just another word for welfare!" he thundered. "Besides, didn't Jimmy Stewart just walk on the lot?"

I told him how much I'd like to have a house like his at Tahoe someday.

"Sure, son, everybody'd like to take a pill and be rich."

"Well, you've certainly been lucky."

That got him particularly peeved. "Lucky? Hell, my life didn't just *happen!*" he snapped.

All that o.j. kicked in, and I headed for the loo. When I returned a few minutes later, Anna had a startled look on her face. Dad must have told her about the nights he'd spent with Nat King Cole and General Eisenhower at the Dorchester during the blitz, or how he'd wound up as one of Nat King Cole's pallbearers, which may have been true.

He wanted to go, so we went outside and looked up at the Paris sky. It was a beautiful moonlit night. Suddenly a shooting star went by and, without missing a beat, he pointed to the star and wished on it. "Moneymoneymoneymoneymoneymoney!" he said exuberantly. Then he went off to the Elysée Palace, or wherever he was staying.

On the long, raggedy metro ride back to the Bois de Boulogne, I found out why Anna had looked so stunned.

"Your father asked me to go back to Las Vegas with him," she said.

"What?" I didn't know whether to be shocked or angered or flattered. After all, I finally had something he approved of so strongly that he wanted it for himself. My girlfriend! "What did you say?"

"I said, 'No, Mr. Reynolds, I don't think that would be proper. I'm in love with your son.' That stopped him, and he behaved like a perfect gentleman. 'Of course, dear, of course,' he said, and asked me about my parents and the war."

It stopped me, too, because Anna also hadn't told *me* she was in love with me. I wondered if she meant it or if she'd said it just to counter Dad's proposition. In any case, Paris had suddenly become surprisingly romantic for all three of us.

"Are all you Yanks like that?" she asked, amused.

"Yes! Come back to Las Vegas with me!" I said. She laughed, and we climbed the steps to our high-rise. Two or three months later we broke up—we couldn't seriously penetrate each other's self-protection—and I heard many years later that she had been married once or twice.

On my most recent visit to Paris a couple of years ago, I found no *duck l'orange* on any menus. Instead, I found a delectable—and, needless to say, lighter—*pissaladière*, a thin pastry lightly brushed with crème fraîche, caraway, and shredded duck at the heavily luxe Plaza Athénée, where Alain Ducasse recently set up shop. I went with Red, whose birth-certificate name is Heidi Ettinger and whom I'd been seeing for a few months, and there was much laughter, which I'm sure will become a memory for future visits. But not like the first.

I don't plan to take my sons to Maxim's anytime soon, with or without their girlfriends, just in case this sort of thing is genetic. On the other hand, maybe I will, because in some areas, at least, I behave a lot better than my father did.

But every time I've been in Paris, and at just about every meal, the image of my old man making a pass at my girlfriend refreshes itself in my memory. And despite his ruthlessness and lechery, I picture him adventurous, optimistic, unbridled, squoze behind the wheel of what was at the time the hottest (and possibly smallest) car in the world, grinning madly, mindless of his appearance and what rules he broke, zipping around Europe courtesy of the IRS.

Could he do this and still not get a crown?
Tuuuuuut, were it further off, he'd pluck it down!

PISSALADIÈRE AU CONFIT DE CANARD

You may make this dish, adapted from Le Relais Plaza at the Plaza Athénée, with pre-
pared duck confit and any thinly rolled pizza dough. Dad would have loved it—as long
as someone else put it together for him. You may make your own crème fraîche by mix-
ing 2 tablespoons of buttermilk with 2 cups of heavy cream and letting it stand until
thickened—a few hours or overnight, usually. Fromage blanc is very much like sour
cream, and yogurt makes an excellent substitute.

For the confit
4 whole duck legs
½ cup kosher salt
1 ½ teaspoons whole peppercorns
3 garlic cloves, peeled and crushed
3 sprigs fresh thyme
1 ½–2 cups duck fat

For the short-crust pastry
2 cups all-purpose flour
½ teaspoon salt
2 sticks unsalted butter, cut into ½-inch cubes
1 large egg
3–5 tablespoons cold water

For the toppings
8 ounces fromage blanc
½ cup crème fraîche
¼ teaspoon freshly grated nutmeg
¼ teaspoon kosher salt
¼ teaspoon freshly ground black pepper
2 Vidalia or other sweet onions, peeled and sliced into paper-thin rings

1 teaspoon caraway seeds

18 walnut halves

---

1. *To make the confit:* Seal the duck, salt, peppercorns, garlic, and thyme in a zip-top plastic bag. Refrigerate for 12 hours. Preheat the oven to 200 degrees. Remove and reserve the peppercorns, garlic, and thyme. Rinse the salt off the duck. Place the reserved seasonings and the duck in a deep casserole so that the legs fit together nicely. Cover with duck fat. Bake until a skewer inserted in the leg slides in and out easily, about 3 hours. Cool the casserole on a rack to room temperature. Refrigerate until needed, up to 1 week.

2. *To make the pastry:* In a large bowl, combine the flour and salt and mix well. Add the butter and cut in with a pastry blender or your fingers until crumbly. In a small bowl, beat the egg with 3 tablespoons of the water and sprinkle over the flour mixture. Toss with a fork until moistened. Drizzle in remaining water, 1 tablespoon at a time, if needed, until the mixture holds together. Divide the dough into 6 equal portions and shape each into a disk. Wrap in plastic and refrigerate for at least 2 hours.

3. *To make the* pissaladière: Preheat a pizza stone in a 500-degree oven. Drain the fromage blanc in a cheesecloth-lined sieve for at least 2 hours, squeezing out the liquid; place in a bowl with the crème fraîche, nutmeg, salt, and pepper and mix well. Remove the duck from the fat and pull the meat into thin shreds. On a floured surface, roll each disk of pastry into a thin round and trim the edges, using a plate as a guide. Spread with the cheese mixture, dividing it evenly. Top with the onions, caraway seeds, and duck, dividing them evenly. Crumble 3 walnut halves over each round and bake 3 at a time until crisp on the bottom, 3–5 minutes.

YIELD: 6 servings.

I remember trying to figure out then, and I often wonder now, What exactly is British food? Roast beef? The famously inedible Bovril and Marmite? Oh, I know: that comfort food with preschool names like bubble and squeak, toad-in-the-hole, and spotted dick. Well, every country has roast beef, and the

other caricatures sound like *Tonight Show* rim shots. But certainly British food
has the worst PR of any cuisine in the world, even today. Its sternest detractors (not just the French) claim it's causing the hole in the ozone layer. Although friends of mine say foreign food in Britain—French, Italian, Chinese,
and Indian, in particular—is often better than in its native land, the popular
belief is that the Brits still haven't figured out how to cook their own, despite
its renaissance of celeb chefs like Gordon Ramsay and Heston Blumenthal.
And it's not embraced by many outside the U.K.: There are probably more
Chinese, Thai, and Papawaiian restaurants on any one block of New York than
there are British restaurants in the entire city.

"Our country lost its way after World War Two with rationing and scarce
money," David Chambers told me. Chambers is chef at Rules, the 207-year-old
institution in Covent Garden that is the Englishest of all English restaurants.
For years, I thought roast beef, Stilton, and port were about all there was to
recommend English food. But I realized that, as with Hemingway and Beckett, it's merely easy to imitate badly. Just try the steak-and-kidney pie at Tea
& Sympathy in New York. Or read a little Mamet.

A favorite stomping ground of Dickens, Edward VII, and Graham Greene
(much of whose *End of the Affair* took place here), Rules boasts a private room
that was the setting for a celebrated dinner for Margaret Thatcher and her cabinet—at which she, upon being asked by a waiter, "And, Madame Prime Minister, what about the veg?" purportedly said, "They'll have what I'm having."

In a country that actually applauds eccentricity rather than simply paying
it lip service (John Ashcroft, call British Airways), Rules is probably the most
eccentric—and therefore most British—restaurant in London. Its interior
would give a case of shingles to any modern decorator outside of Las Vegas.
There on a wall of one of its three chandeliered rooms, cheek-by-jowl with a
huge gilt-framed oil of Hamlet holding Yorick's skull, hang black-and-white
cartoons and watercolored *Vanity Fair* portraits of the once-famous, and a couple of mounted ibex heads; over there, a quartet of women's busts in marble;
above is a stained-glass faux skylight in the Cubist style; and right *there*,
painted on a curved section of wall, is a full-color mural of Lady Thatcher—
Lady Thatcher's hair, mostly—revealing garters on one thigh and all armored
up as St. George, the Falklands in the background. In her hand she proudly

proffers a staff whose pennant is emblazoned, RULES. If, as Russell Baker once wrote, the white race is not really white but pink, surely the Brits are the pinkest of all, and the clientele at Rules the pinkest of the pink.

Aside from the more common (and milder) pheasant, venison, and grouse, at various times of year you can also get what might be called Extreme Game—animals I was sure only existed in *Alice's Adventures in Wonderland*: blackgame, pochard, snipe, teal, ptarmigan, and wigeon. Extreme Game is an acquired taste, often very liver-y. If you're not used to it, it can be a shock (and if you're squeamish, best not ask exactly what jugged hare is; for the stout-hearted, I've provided the definition on page 98). The smell of wigeon we had on one visit practically blew us out of the room.

But what I find most enjoyable about Rules is its singularly British fare—a slice of the most sensual goose liver cut with slivettes of wild duck, amazingly creamy and light at the same time; the lush and salty Stilton-broccoli-and-almond soup (or the Stilton-and-walnut quiche with a spiky pear chutney); the many fresh vegetables; or the steak-and-kidney pie (also called pudding) made with a suet crust and served with a baked oyster on top (if you don't like the bitter taste of kidney, don't eat it; it's delicious without, though better with). The desserts, particularly the Sticky Toffee Pudding with Butterscotch and Vanilla Custard and the Sauterne Crème Caramel and Armagnac Prunes will time-travel you back to a most urbane kindergarten.

A NIGHT AT RULES

STILTON-AND-BROCCOLI SOUP

2 tablespoons olive oil

2 ½ cups leeks (1 Holland leek or 2 medium leeks), tough outer green leaves removed and thinly sliced

1 cup chopped onions

½ cup finely chopped celery

2 ¾ pounds broccoli, the stalks peeled and diced, the tops separated into florets

7 cups chicken stock

1 cup heavy cream

¾ pound Stilton, coarsely grated

Freshly ground black pepper

Salt

1 cup thinly sliced almonds

1. Heat the oil over medium-low heat in a large stockpot. Sweat but don't brown the leeks, onions, and celery, about 20 minutes. Add the broccoli and sweat for 10 minutes more. Add stock.
2. Bring to a rolling boil over medium-high heat, then lower the heat and simmer till the vegetables are just tender, no more than 10 minutes.
3. Purée the vegetables and return them to the pan. (You're just about done.)
4. Ten minutes before serving, stir in cream, then grated Stilton. Once the cheese has melted, taste (Stilton is salty). Add pepper and, if necessary, salt.
5. Serve immediately, passing the almonds separately. Don't be afraid to scoop big spoonfuls of almonds into the soup—they give wonderful textural contrast.

YIELD: 12 cups.

ULTIMATE STEAK-AND-KIDNEY PUDDING

2 ½ pounds beef chuck, cut into 1-inch cubes

1 ½ teaspoons salt

¾ teaspoon freshly ground black pepper

3 tablespoons lard (way preferred) or (ho-hum) mildly flavored olive oil

⅓ cup finely chopped onions

⅓ cup finely chopped carrots

¾ pound veal kidney, cut into 1-inch pieces

⅔ cup all-purpose flour

8 cups hot beef stock

3 cups quartered mushrooms

5 tablespoons Worcestershire sauce
Savoury Suet Pastry (see page 96)
At least 6 oysters, but as many as you want, shucked

EQUIPMENT NOTE: You'll need enough pots and pans and racks to hold 6 pudding basins.

1. In a large pan, sprinkle the beef with salt and pepper, then brown in melted lard. Add onions and carrots and sauté 10 minutes more, then add the kidney and continue sautéing another 15 minutes.
2. Mix in the flour and cook another 10 minutes. Add stock, mushrooms, and Worcestershire sauce, scraping up whatever's stuck to the bottom. Simmer for 45 minutes, stirring occasionally. Taste for seasoning.
3. Cut off ⅕ of each pastry disk and roll the remaining pastry into circles about 10 ½ inches in diameter and ⅟₁₆-inch thick.
4. Line six 18- to 20-ounce pudding basins or 5-inch ramekins with the pastry, pressing dough evenly around the sides. Fill with steak-and-kidney mixture. Roll out the reserved pastry and cover each pudding, crimping the edges closed.
5. Here's the weird part: Wrap each basin *entirely* in plastic wrap (this makes it a steamed pudding rather than a browned pie—in fact, don't be alarmed when the pastry doesn't color much). Tie string around the basin, securing plastic wrap, and place the puddings on racks in pans of simmering water, covered, for 2 hours, making sure the water stays two thirds of the way up the sides of the basins.
6. Remove the puddings from the water bath and remove the plastic wrap. Just before serving, cut a small hole in top of each and insert as many oysters as you like (at Rules they put one oyster inside the pudding and another on the side in its shell).

YIELD: 6 puddings.

NOTE: These are best when the fillings are made a day ahead and refrigerated overnight—either in the pastry or not—and then steamed before serving. They can be kept for 3 days, cooked or uncooked, in the refrigerator. Reheat in a 375-degree oven until hot, about 30 minutes.

SAVOURY SUET PASTRY

3 cups all-purpose flour
1 cup, or 8 ounces, beef suet, coarsely chopped (preferred), or (ho-hum) unsalted butter placed in the freezer overnight, and cut into small chunks
About ⅔ cup hot water (½ cup cold water if using butter)
4 tablespoons finely chopped chives

1. In the bowl of a food processor pulse the flour and suet (or butter) until the fat is incorporated, about 9 times. Continue pulsing and add the water slowly, till the dough forms clumps and leaves the side of the bowl.
2. Knead the dough on a floured board till soft, incorporating chives. Make a thick disk about 6 inches in diameter.
3. Cut the dough into 6 equal portions, form smaller disks, wrap in plastic, and chill for at least two hours before using.

YIELD: pastry for 6 puddings, 18–20 ounces each.

STICKY TOFFEE PUDDING

4 tablespoons unsalted butter
⅔ cup firmly packed brown sugar
2 large eggs
1 cup self-rising flour
1⅓ cups pitted dates, coarsely chopped
1 cup water
6 tablespoons golden syrup
Butterscotch Sauce (see next page)

1. Preheat oven to 300 degrees.
2. In a mixing bowl, cream the butter with the brown sugar, then beat in the eggs and fold in the flour.
3. Purée dates with water and add to batter.
4. Film six 7-ounce custard cups with golden syrup, then fill with batter and bake in the oven 40–45 minutes or until a knife inserted at the edge comes out clean.
5. Immediately run a knife around the sides of the puddings and invert onto individual serving plates. Pour warm butterscotch sauce over each and serve.

YIELD: 6 puddings.

BUTTERSCOTCH SAUCE

1 cup heavy cream
½ cup brown sugar
½ cup white sugar

1. In a small heavy-bottomed saucepan mix all the ingredients and bring to a boil over medium heat. Cook, stirring almost constantly, until reduced and thickened, about 20 minutes. This is delicious not only on this pudding but on just about everything except steak.

YIELD: 1 cup.

If all this sounds heavy (and much of it is), be reminded that in addition to the delicate grilled Dover sole and the poached finnan haddock, game is practically fat free. To my mind, a perfect evening in London is spent eating the preceding menu at Rules, then walking a few blocks east, past Simpson's-in-the-Strand, crossing the night-black Thames on Waterloo Bridge—St. Paul's glowing on your left, Parliament alight on your right—and catching a play at the National; and then crossing Waterloo Bridge back—St. Paul's on your right now, Parliament on your left—and if you've got room, stopping back at Rules (or Simpson's) for a little Stilton, port, and highly civilized condescension.

Oh, and as promised, here is the definition of jugged hare (though in deference to the faint of heart, it can be read only in a mirror):

Jugged hare is a rabbit whose throat has been slit and is then cooked in its own blood.

How a Fat Apple Pancake Saved Christmas

~~ ~~ ~~ ~~ ~~

EATING CHRISTMAS DINNER alone for reasons tragic or trivial can be brutal. I've done it too many times—never voluntarily, but fortunately thus far for reasons fairly trivial.

When I was on Christmas vacation from grad school in London in '65, I missed the train for a tour of Moscow a bunch of us had signed up for—and when you miss the train for Moscow, you miss *the* train for Moscow; the next one was a week later. Not only does everything, absolutely everything, close for Christmas in London—restaurants, movie theatres, even the Turkish baths—but then the following day is Boxing Day, when even *more* establishments close. Every single friend was out of town, and I remember walking around for nearly two hours before finding an empty Indian restaurant serving a kebab so dry it crumbled in my mouth. The following year, a bunch of us spent Christmas day in East Berlin, the unmerriest city not named Wheeling in the history of the world. But it was like Fezziwig's office party compared with that holiday in London.

My most memorable holiday spent alone was the Christmas Mother threw me out of the house because I'd grown a beard.

My junior year in college, when I phoned her to say that I was coming home and had grown a beard for a role I'd be playing—Dogberry in *Much Ado About Nothing*—I was greeted with the pleasant amusement I'd come to know as a warning: "Oh, you have, have you?" Somewhere in the back of my head a little light about the size of the sun went on. I think by that time I'd already told her

I'd bought a hearse to drive around in—though I didn't tell her it was because the women's dorm hours were so limited.

Of course, context is everything. Our Seventy-second Street apartment was white-gloved and heavily doormanned, and I often felt it was unseemly to step into the elevator without a necktie. The first night home went smoothly enough, complete with my telling her how much smarter I'd become since the summer and her nodding pleasantly. She did mention that parking the hearse was my responsibility, not hers. "And you'll have to park it around the corner so the doormen don't get depressed."

The second night she mentioned sweetly over the well-done lamb chops with mint jelly *à la Ukraine*, "I don't know that I really like the beard, dear," which is basically New England–speak for "Get rid of that thing before I burn it off with a blowtorch." By the third or fourth day, she had become increasingly agitated. I had the sense she wasn't sleeping. Finally she told me over more well-done lamb chops: "You'll have to shave that beard. The doormen are laughing at you behind your back and calling you 'Fidel.' " Pause, pause, beat, beat. "And I hate that hearse!"

How could she? I thought the hearse regal and was insulted by the comparison to Castro, who had taken over Cuba four years earlier but was still fresh news.

"Mother, he can't even grow a beard—he's got bald spots all over his face."

"Shave it! I can't sleep!"

"No!"

"Shave it and move that hearse!"

"No, it's my right to grow a beard and drive a hearse"—or some such semi-Constitutional defense.

"Shave it or get out!"

"I'll get out!"

"You'll be out for Christmas unless you shave that beard!"

"I don't care!"

"Get out now!"

Was she kidding? Did she think I'd yield my masculinity, self-respect, and newly acquired devotion to the First and Second Amendments (if you consider either a beard or a hearse a firearm)? I wouldn't budge, and neither would she, and she had all the money. Not exactly William Inge, but it went something like that.

I was given a few bucks and checked into a flophouse over some railroad tracks way west on Forty-second Street, where Mayor Bloomberg once hoped to build a stadium for the Jets. I'd heard it was cheap, and it was. Either the room was clean and safe or I was in my immortal phase. I phoned a couple of friends, and they were mighty impressed by what they considered my strength of character. We bombed around the city, reveling in our freedom. Nancy phoned in tears. "How can you be away for Christmas? She can't do this!" But she could. And so could I.

Christmas day rolled around, and my friends became unavailable—all, I imagined, surrounded by loving families in plaid bathrobes, warm noggy drinks, fireplaces, gift certificates for Jaguars, and mountains of gift wrap. Christmases had always been happy high points for us. There was no arguing, Maymie and sometimes Grammie would visit, and we'd go to the theatre in the afternoon. But the sweetest and saddest aspect of Christmas was that Mother allowed herself to give us all presents without suffering the guilt she would have felt the rest of the year—and found she enjoyed it. She felt more constricted at birthdays, and presents were out of the question at any other time of year. Once or twice at Christmas, she hit home runs: After my first term at Malcolm Gordon—just before the letter-writing—she was so pleased by my change in personality that she gave me a reel-to-reel tape recorder, the only thing I really wanted. Usually, she'd ask us for a Christmas list, and then would automatically ignore whatever was at the top. I once told Nancy, "I know the trick of this. I'll put 'lump of coal' as my first choice and 'Triumph TR3' as my second, and I'll get a car." But her generous nature slipped out at Christmas. She'd deliver on the rest of our list and throw in some cute trinkets in addition.

But the climax generally came when Dad's presents were unwrapped. As far as I can remember, Nancy and I never asked him for anything because it wouldn't be big enough, and he had a better imagination. We also knew that if we asked him for something, he would conclude we were just after his money and wouldn't give it; but if the inspiration was up to him, he would astound us. The giving of gifts is so revelatory of character: Certainly it communicates how the giver feels about the givee financially; but it also reveals the taste and creativity of the giver as well as the time and thought devoted to the gift and the aptness for the recipient. Dad was the most visionary gift-giver ever, opening my eyes to the material world outside and extending the hope that someday I, too, could come up with inventions like these, or accomplishments that would allow me to attain these things, or the curiosity and nerve to leave my surroundings and explore the universe. They were challenges. He gave me a full Lionel train set when I was four, before I knew such a thing existed; at eight, the first Polaroid camera—a big clunky thing by today's standards, but magical (black-and-white pictures in sixty seconds!)—the first digital watch, also magical; and years later, a microwave oven before anyone except the Department of Defense knew what one was. He sent Nancy dolls and clothing wrapped in spectacular colors and gadgetry from Neiman Marcus. In his presents, he treated us like a doting, protective dad.

I don't remember feeling unhappy the Christmas I got thrown out. I remember feeling self-righteous—at least till about 11 A.M., when the self-pity kicked in. It was about that time that I remembered Reuben's.

The restaurant was cavernous—three immense floors at 6 East 58th Street, filled with the smartest of the smart. And most important, it was open Christmas day. My friend Ronnie had joined the army when his grandfather, the patriarch of the family, refused to pay for college because he himself had never been. He hoped Ronnie would one day take over the restaurant, so he worked him mercilessly, ten- to sixteen-hour days—because that's how he had worked. Ronnie's skin grew pasty, his heart despondent. Unable to afford tuition, he enlisted. So he wasn't in town.

Reuben's had no smart set on Christmas day. It did have forty-four combinations of sandwiches, most of them named after Sophie Tucker, and what might be considered early fusion—a haphazard marriage of deli and continental. It also had the sweetest, hottest, hugest German apple pancake in pancake history. When I'd gone to the restaurant with Ronnie and friends, we would order one of these monsters—about the size of a pizza—for three or four of us. But this Christmas, I decided I wanted a whole one for myself. No turkey, no sweet potatoes, no pies. Just that pancake.

The crust was thin, not puffed, with apples all through it, in, under, on top;

I never could figure out how those apples got interwoven in there. And on the very top, a blizzard of sugar. God, it was sweet. And hot—you had to let it cool for ten minutes or if you put the roof of your mouth near an Esso pump you'd start a fire. I ate it mouthful by piggy mouthful, way beyond the point of satiety. Take that, Mother! I'm having a great Christmas! I don't care if my face breaks out and I put on five pounds! And she did and I was and it did and I did. It was about the most delicious thing I'd eaten in my life. I loved it, and in the process learned how to cope not only with self-pity but with sorrow: hedonism!

Food supposedly stands for so many meaningful things other than food—love, sex, happy and unhappy childhoods, family, excitement, wealth. And sometimes, occasionally, discreetly, and admittedly for a short time, stuffing yourself delivers them all.

Reuben's Apple Pancake

There are many recipes for this pancake, all claiming to be authentic. After trying several and scrunching up my nose with dissatisfaction, I got in touch with Ronnie, now Ron, living in Los Angeles and in the export business, and he verified this one as the real thing.

The Granny Smith's tartness gives a little contrast to all the sugar in the recipe, and it's crisp enough to hold its shape despite all the heat.

1 large Granny Smith apple
Scant ½ cup sugar plus 1 ½ tablespoons sugar
½ teaspoon ground cinnamon
3 large eggs
½ cup milk
½ cup all-purpose flour
⅛ teaspoon vanilla extract
8 tablespoons unsalted butter

1. Peel and core apple and slice into moon-shaped pieces, ¼-inch thick. Place in a bowl and toss with 1 ½ tablespoons sugar and the cinnamon. Cover and refrigerate for at least 24 hours, stirring occasionally.

2. When ready, preheat oven to 400 degrees. Whisk eggs and milk in a bowl until blended. Whisk in flour and vanilla until smooth.

3. Heat 2 tablespoons of the butter over medium heat in a shallow 12-inch nonstick ovenproof skillet until it sizzles. Drain apples and add to the pan. Cook, stirring, until apples soften, about 5 minutes.

4. Melt 2 more tablespoons of the butter in pan. Pour in batter and quickly arrange apples evenly before batter sets. Increase heat to medium-high and pull edges away from pan to allow batter to flow underneath and cook, sliding a wooden spatula under pancake to keep it from sticking.

5. When batter is set but still wet, sprinkle with 2 tablespoons of the sugar. Place a cookie sheet over pan and invert the pancake onto it. Return pan to heat and add 2 more tablespoons of butter, swirling to coat. Slide pancake back into the pan to cook other side. Reduce heat to medium. Sprinkle top with 2 more tablespoons of the sugar. Cook until sugar on bottom side is caramelized, about 2 minutes.

6. Using a cookie sheet, flip pancake out again. Slide pancake back into pan 2 more times, adding 2 tablespoons of butter to pan and sprinkling with 2 tablespoons of sugar each time. Adjust heat so that the sugar caramelizes but pancake doesn't burn.

7. Bake in pan until brown and crisp, about 20 minutes. Slide onto a platter and serve hot.

YIELD: 2 servings.

Exit, Pursued by a Bear

I THOUGHT I'D BE an actor ever since those Cassavetes classes at fourteen, through those five years at Denison and summer stock, and fifteen months at LAMDA. As mentioned, I began to dislike the art shortly before LAMDA, and once I actually joined the profession, I was more convinced than ever it wasn't for me. For months in London I assumed I would spend most of my life in Europe; but when Mother died suddenly in January of '67, during my second year, I sped back to the States for her funeral and decided I was sick of schools and needed to enter the real world—even the not-very-real world of the theatre. It was all I knew. And swinging as London had been and would be for a few more months, America was where the world now focused.

A year looking for work convinced me what a horrid profession acting is, unless you love it. I was lucky and was mostly employed that year, but I hated being under the thumb of casting agents and directors with bright ideas, and, once ensconced in a long run of Tom Stoppard's *Rosencrantz & Guildenstern Are Dead*, couldn't stand the repetition. More than anything, I disliked being on call to be somebody else at 8 P.M. After all those years performing Shakespeare and Chekhov and Shaw in the comfort of academe, I was also pretty much appalled by the literature I was going to have to deal with as a pro (though the Stoppard play certainly sang beautifully).

Unless you're one of about twelve superstars, you're powerless as an actor—anyone in the business can tell you what to do. And I found people generally dislike talking to actors because everything eventually returns to their chief source of reference, themselves. I'd turned into that. Acting (and the shrinks) had made me so self-conscious that I'd observe myself doing everything from shaking hands to drinking coffee to kissing a girlfriend's inner thigh. There wasn't a spontaneous, un-microscoped bone in my body.

The audition process made me feel an inch tall, even when I landed the part. Auditioning is based on acceptance and rejection for the most intimate, personal reasons—and the ratio of acceptance to rejection is about 1:11, or in some cases 1:11,000. It's never enjoyable to be turned down for a job, but to be turned down three or four times a week solely on the basis of your personality is psychological demolition. Picture asking thirty-five or forty girls to dance on one night and not one of them saying yes. No matter what reasons are given—I'm in love, I'm busy, I have a headache, I don't know this dance—eventually you take it personally. As an actor you're told you're the wrong height, weight, color, shape, type; but in the end it's always interpreted as personal deficiency. Actors who steel themselves against this sort of assault (and every successful actor must) lose part of the very emotional life they need to mine: So much effort is spent building a fortress around the soul to ward off the rejection, they can't access this essential chunk of their animus. Those who manage to preserve the secret tunnel to their inner lives usually succeed when young and before the tunnel walls have been bashed down.

By 1967 I actively hated the profession, but having no Plan B, plodded on, stoking a fire somewhere in the back of my head. That summer, I had landed plum roles in the three Shakespeare plays being produced in Central Park, part of Joseph Papp's Shakespeare in the Park company that included Raul Julia, Charlie Durning, Olympia Dukakis, David Birney, and Harris Yulin, among others. For starters, I was to play Antipholus of Syracuse, one of a set of twins that were the leading roles in *The Comedy of Errors*. But before rehearsals began, the director had the bright idea to recast the twins with a single actor, resulting, I assume, from a "high concept" he'd dreamed up one night when feeling, as too many directors do, that he had to put his own stamp on Shakespeare. Peter Brook should be allowed this liberty . . . and *no one else*. Unfortunately, Gerry Freedman, an extremely enjoyable man and capable director, who now runs the North Carolina School of the Arts theatre program, was not Peter Brook. It became clear in early previews that the audience couldn't tell which twin the single actor was supposed to be. I had been reduced to a few lines as Solinus, the duke, which I played with a Cockney dialect, an equally pointless high concept of my own. Freedman saw the errors of his own comedy and recast the recast two nights before the first performance, but because I looked nothing like the single actor, I wasn't part of the recast.

But that was nothing compared to *King John*, in which I had only a few lines and from which I was fired by the legendary impresario Joseph Papp himself. Joe was one of the great producers and entrepreneurs in the history of the New York theatre, possibly *the* greatest, and a larger-than-life, professionally testy, street-savvy character; but he was a terrible director. Nothing he ever directed was well received, by either audiences or critics or, most important, by me. *True West*—possibly Sam Shepard's best and certainly funniest play—was initially considered one of his worst because it had been directed by Joe in 1980; only after the Steppenwolf company got hold of it five years later was the play viewed as the masterwork it is. So it was hard to know intellectually whether being fired by Joe Papp was a crushing setback or a badge of honor, but it was certainly a blow to my pride. I'd just returned from LAMDA and am sure I irritated him with my pompous English affectations; he preferred hiring cabdrivers and ex-cons and letting them run around the stage nude and improvising.

But he *was* a great theatrical force. He reassigned me to Third Spear Carrier status, and I think I earned a modicum of respect by telling him that no, I quit, forfeiting the salary. This stopped him. "Yeah?" he said with his street-tough accent. "You wanna do that? Okay. Okay. I'll get you unemployment." He liked people who stood up to him, even those with British pretensions. By the time the third play of the summer rolled around—what turned out to be a ludicrous production of *Titus Andronicus*, also directed by Gerry Freedman, in which everyone wore identical masks and costumes, which, coupled with the lunatic P.A. system in the park, made it impossible to tell who the hell was talking. I prayed nightly for rain.

Being cast as an understudy in *Rosencrantz*, the hot play of the year, was a coup. But despite all my training and experience, it turned out to be the runway off which I jettisoned out of the business. I was psychologically ill equipped for the job as understudy, since panic isn't what's needed in someone given thirty minutes' notice to confidently tackle an immense role. And to give you an idea of my importance to the play, I was also cast as a member of Claudius's court (as was Elizabeth Franz).

I was well rehearsed during the out-of-town in Washington, and in the previews in New York, but the night the real Rosencrantz—Brian Murray, youthful and hilarious—showed up flu-ish was terrifying. Brian was a naughty boy in those days and burned not only both ends of the candle but the middle of the wick. That winter night he appeared at half hour logy and flushed. Because of union rules, my Guildenstern understudy and I weren't ever allowed to rehearse on the set or in costume or with props or with lights.

The real Guildenstern—the superb and impossibly imperious John Wood—quickly ran the first few lines of the play with me. We'd barely met, let alone rehearsed, and I raced through the part. "You don't need to go so . . . *fast*, you know," he said, barely suppressing panic and rage and reminding me of O'Toole on the two glasses of lemonade. When we took another go at it, I suddenly couldn't remember many of the lines, and Wood's eyes saucered as if blinded by the headlights of an oncoming train. But I'd played all those classical roles, and old men and young pups, and gone on with only two and three days' rehearsal! I should be able to do this! And what about the two shows I'd just done in the park that I *didn't* get fired from?

But my heart beat as if someone had told me to wingwalk. I slipped into Brian's doublet only to find my love handles larger than his, and a costume assailing the source of my future sons' very existence like a jockstrap designed by the inventor of Brillo. Wood huddled with the stage manager and a representative from producer David Merrick's office; they all looked over at me across the stage in my too-tight Elizabethan garb and then plunged into heated discussion, stopped, looked at me, plunged in again. A phone call was made. Within minutes, a little man with a black doctor's bag appeared and marched into Brian's dressing room. A few minutes after that, Brian emerged whistling and ready for the decathlon.

The stage manager ambled over and said casually, "Brian's feeling better. You won't have to go on." Any other actor would have thrown his grandmother under a train to go on for Brian that night, but I nearly fainted with relief. When the blood returned to my loins, I determined to get the hell out of show business.

That wasn't the only reason to get out, but it was the reason to get out NOW.

It was also January 1968.

When I was in London, three of the more socially conscious Americans at LAMDA gave me a crash course in current events. Denison was a small, mostly Republican school delightfully—but provincially—removed from the outside world. Though my head was constantly aflame with schemes to avoid the draft, I paid little attention to politics then and so followed everyone in patriotically paying lip service to the war in Vietnam. But the Americans in London had been to Harvard and UC Berkeley and saw a fresh lamb chop in me. They opened my eyes to the horrors of the United States invasion, and though my eyes have re-opened since (the Vietnamese did invade Cambodia as predicted after we left), our involvement was butchery, catastrophic, and ill conceived (and probably led to the subsequent atrocities). That my generation was ordered to participate in this wretched destruction was not just galling, it was worth sacrifice, struggle, and activism. The world was on fire, and well before the understudy crisis, I would stew in the *Rosencrantz* dressing room night after night while waiting to go on in yet another pointless crowd scene: Life was happening everywhere around me, and all I was doing was this infuriating and insulting play. And it was one of the good ones!

I'd done my patriotic share earlier that year by dodging the draft, thanks to not one but two letters from psychiatrists, each claiming I was so troubled that neither would be held responsible if I were drafted—by implication putting the army on notice that I might pull a *Full Metal Jacket* on some barracks or go nuts in the motor pool or sue the United States government. The draft officers on Whitehall Street had seen every conceivable performance and excuse—burly heteros limply lisping with their hair dyed pink to pass for queer, guys with blood pressure of 800 over 90 from a week of sleeplessness and drugs, others whose urine was neon—but as far as I know, not a believable depressive with *two* letters claiming instability.

DRAFT OFFICER
(Reading psychiatrists' letters)
Do you often feel depressed?

ME
(Looking depressed, shoulders sagging)
Yes.

DRAFT OFFICER
Are you depressed now?

ME
(Hugging my clothes to my chest)
Yes.

DRAFT OFFICER
(Scribbling notes, stamping forms)
You're excused.

It was a much better performance that I was giving in *R&G Are D.* I was classified 4F, which meant I couldn't serve in the military unless all the build-ings in America were on fire and a nuclear explosive in transit fifty yards over-head.

I knew this was a rich kid's dodge and wanted to be patriotic by fighting against the war, not fighting in it. In retrospect, the tiny dollop of John Wayne in me wishes I'd gone and fought—but that's a tiny dollop indeed, and in any case, my 20/600 eyesight probably would have resulted in my being assigned to typing in D.C. or to Whitehall Street to judge draft-evasion performances.

There were millions of us anti-warriors in those heady days, as spirited in our objection to American participation in our war as the soldiers for World War II must have been in prosecution of theirs. There was nothing shameful about it; we were proud of it. And it has surprised me since that the very people—my friends—who were so against the war turned out thirty-six years later to champion John Kerry for his service but were mum on the subject of his subsequent repudiation of it, the exact reverse of the positions they'd held during the actual conflict. Actually, both were brave positions—probably op-portunistic, but brave nonetheless. And initially, I admired Bill Clinton for evading service and expected him to be proud of it. It was infuriating when he attempted to weasel his way out of it (though darkly amusing when he intricately re-revised his own revisionism during the Kerry campaign and said he should have joined up after all!). I don't see this as psychological growth but reprehensible politix a little too conveniently flexible.

In any event, the theatre had nothing to say to me or to the country or to the world then, and I fled the stage of the Alvin for a week to see an old girl-friend in Milwaukee and, when that became uncomfortable, joined Eugene McCarthy's presidential campaign. I stayed with the campaign for seven months, through the convention in Chicago. My back was so completely turned on the theatre that I felt like a reformed whore: Even seeing a play made me uncomfortable, and the nightmares I had of acting again constituted excellent aversion therapy. It wasn't until seven years later, in 1975, when I finished my first play, that I thought the theatre anything but worthless.

The Fastest Food

A FEW MONTHS BEFORE I left *Rosencrantz*, I signed a contract with the Tyrone Guthrie Theater in Minneapolis and regretted it almost immediately. The Guthrie and the ACT in San Francisco were the leading regional theatre companies in the country, and I had landed two strong roles in their season, and if I'd just graduated Denison, I'd have been thrilled. But I didn't really need any more experience (or if I did at this point, I was hopeless) and suffered instant signer's remorse: How would this differ from being back in school, really? Just more performances in classic plays; I certainly wouldn't find career advancement in the Midwest. Besides which, I continually forgot, I didn't like being onstage!

There wasn't much romance in my life, though I certainly pursued it frantically. If anything more than a one- or two-night involvement threatened, I panicked and found a reason to break it off—or better, for her to break it off. I was eager but clumsy sexually and was really only good at pleasing myself. I realized it, and it was infuriating. I simply didn't know what to do. Most distressing, I didn't enjoy sleeping with anyone—the actual going-to-sleep part—and would be up all night scared the person was moving in on me in some metaphysical way. If I wasn't already there, I was well on my way to becoming a choice New York neurotic male.

Then I met Etoile.

Marian Watson, who at the time was referred to as a Negro, was a translator at the U.N. and preferred the name "Etoile" because it was glam. She wore the shortest skirts, most beautiful silk turbans, and best underwear of anyone

I'd ever known. Though not as tall as Iman, Etoile had the same conversation-interrupting impact on a room when she entered it. People were generally speechless for a moment, then suddenly in a swarm around her, magnetized and helpless.

Uncle Bus and Margaret met her with me one night at Sardi's, and for just about the only time in his life, my uncle started stammering. I hadn't thought to "warn" him, though it was much rarer to see an interracial couple in 1968 than it is today, even in New York. My sister, Nancy, had recently married a man of Korean descent, and his ethnicity seemed completely irrelevant. Why should this be any different? But, of course, it was.

Etoile had some explaining to do with some of her black friends about me, but it didn't seem to faze her, and I never sensed even a raised eyebrow from anyone I knew—though I was well aware that Dad would have thrown me out of the universe if he'd found out. Fortunately, he wasn't in the habit of asking about my personal life.

Etoile and I agreed on everything, and I don't remember a single argument for the first eight months of our nine-month relationship—except about political candidates. She and all her friends were for Bobby Kennedy the moment he announced, and I was a Eugene McCarthy supporter the moment the New Hampshire primary heated up. I thought Kennedy a coward for not standing up to LBJ in New Hampshire despite being asked several million times. Only after McCarthy had risked everything and won a surprising 42% of the vote in New Hampshire did Bobby opportunistically throw his hat in the ring. But then, I had procrastinated, too, stewing with discontent in the *Rosencrantz* dressing room and wishing I were in New Hampshire to fight the quixotic battle but only taking action once McCarthy had done so well (or Johnson so poorly).

A week out of the play, I flew to Milwaukee and joined the campaign as a canvasser, and after a couple of days in the snow was brought inside to help run things. I didn't eat a home-cooked meal for the next seven months and came to value the paper bag's versatility as a portable dining table.

And what happened in the next two weeks reversed the direction of the Earth's spin. On March 31, after thousands of us had spent twenty-four well-shaved weeks doing whatever we could to be Clean for Gene, President Johnson announced that he wasn't running for re-election. The McCarthy headquarters in downtown Milwaukee, where I'd been sleeping vertically, went berserk: We were sure *we* had made him resign; I, in fact, was sure I *personally* had made him resign. We had unseated a president! We were going to elect another one! Us kids! The power we felt was heady, made headier still when our man won the Wisconsin primary with 56% of the vote.

I flew back to New York and Etoile drunk on power, envisioning a life of politics, revolutionary campaigns, priomary nights more exciting than theatrical opening nights.

Two days after this dizzying turn of events, Etoile and I were walking the streets at dusk, amiably arguing the virtues and demerits of Kennedy and McCarthy, when I glanced at an extra on the newsstand: the Reverend Martin Luther King, Jr., had been shot and killed in Memphis. Etoile crumpled and burst into tears. "Why are they doing this to us?" she cried. "Why Martin?"

We were near the apartment of a new friend whom I'd met in Milwaukee on the campaign. He was white and it turned out was married to a black woman, and it was the best place for Etoile and me to spend the evening while the rest of the country went mad, as it damn well should have.

She was inconsolable for days. Bobby Kennedy had made a heroic speech the night of King's assassination; McCarthy had barely noted it. Etoile and I re-rated our candidates: Mine had certainly dropped the ball. Or had he? He hated the notion of stirring a crowd for any reason. Meanwhile, the campaign and its fast-food bag lunches steamed uncontrollably along with no time to pause.

I was asked to set up a storefront for McCarthy in Indianapolis's inner city, and spent the next few weeks flying by the seat of my pants till the Indiana primary. Every minute was a new experience. Paul Newman and the senator held a rally opening the storefront but it attracted little attention: Kennedy was the favorite and the media darling. McCarthy seethed.

I talked to Etoile on the phone and rubbed my eyes red, longing for her endless, comforting body to sleep next to, which she'd taught me to enjoy and with which she calmed my sexual agitation. And then suddenly, she was there! Without warning, a few days before the primary, she showed up in Indianapolis, short skirt, heels, and silk turban, her chic a notch higher than anyone else's (as always), and canvassed the astonished neighborhoods . . . for McCarthy! No one had ever seen anyone like her.

In spite of her, Kennedy won the Indiana primary—the first in direct combat with McCarthy—in early May, and I was hustled off to Nebraska, where the next primary would take place. Etoile returned to New York. I didn't know how I felt about her now—she'd made such an extraordinary sacrifice by switching political allegiances, which I was sure she'd done just for me. But we had many disagreements, and I found she hadn't been completely candid about the work she was doing at the U.N. She would never let me visit her there, and it turned out she was a secretary, not a translator, which wouldn't have bothered me had she told me. But she was anxious just being Marian.

In Nebraska, I became an advance man for the senator, which meant preceding him to events and more or less producing them: arranging light and sound cues, deciding which hot dogs he'd eat and which babies he'd kiss. It also meant spending time with him, which was a treat: Courtly, witty, philosophical, understated, Gene McCarthy was an intellectual and a sincere Catholic who worried that his candidacy might seem vain and overreaching to his God. He was always interested in those of us who supported his campaign, and always respectful. It was no wonder Bobby Kennedy complained, "Why does McCarthy get all the A students and I get the B's?" (I was the exception.)

"An actor, huh?" McCarthy said to me as we drove to a speech he was making in Omaha. The poet Robert Lowell was in the backseat with him. "Which playwrights do you like?" the senator asked.

"Shaw and Chekhov and Beckett and Tennessee Williams and of course Shakespeare," I said, without much originality. "I'm going to the Guthrie in the summer." I'd turned my back on the theatre but thus far hadn't found a way to get out of my contract.

"I've been there," the senator from Minnesota said. He looked more interested. I told him and Lowell about *Rosencrantz*, which was a prestigious credit, and they nodded in recognition.

I then told the senator how my advance partner, Peter Ellyard, and I planned his entrance. It was a gymnasium, I think, and Allard Lowenstein would warm up the audience, then the lights would dim, the local band would blare. McCarthy would enter from a corner, the spotlight would pick him up. Cheers from the crowd would build, he'd climb a few stairs to the podium, shaking hands along the way, and as the laudation crescendoed, the band would die down and there would be a minute or so of pure, blissful, insane ovation. It would be a sensational entrance, a brilliant event.

Except for one problem.

Eugene McCarthy was a cerebral public speaker, not a rabble-rouser, and Allard Lowenstein, who regularly introduced him at rallies and later went on to become a one-term congressman from New York, was an incendiary one. Lowenstein could whip the cremated into an emotional frenzy, with the result that the audience was usually disappointed by the senator's professorial delivery, regardless of the brilliant content. If Lowenstein had intro'd the charismatic Kennedy at a rally, Bobby probably would have been crowned king well before the election. We learned to accommodate, which sadly meant asking Lowenstein to step aside.

Kennedy won in Nebraska, too, and in D.C. Just as our ship seemed ready to go under, we rallied in Oregon and handed the Kennedy family the first election defeat in its history.

Etoile flew out to Los Angeles for the California primary a week later, taking time off from the U.N., again supporting McCarthy. She arrived shortly before Kennedy won, which was shortly before he, too, was murdered. I was working at the Beverly Hilton that night and found her. We couldn't believe this had happened: first King, now RFK, all against the background of a raging war and even more raging war protest. We held each other for the rest of the night.

Despite the closeness we'd felt and the tragic events we'd shared, or perhaps because of them, or perhaps the divisions between us were as irreparable as were the country's, or perhaps because I was simply too immature to appreciate the possibilities of this relationship, we had grown apart in serious ways. We returned to New York—she to her job, I for the New York primary—and split up.

I ADVANCED MCCARTHY at his first event after the Robert Kennedy assassination. It was a speech at the Waldorf-Astoria in New York, and it was grim: He was pale, terrified by what had happened (not for himself, but of the maniacs the divisive campaign had unleashed).

We went up in the elevator together. He knew he knew me . . . just not exactly who I was. I introduced myself, then said, "Actor."

"Oh, yes," he said, brightening for a moment. "The Guthrie." He was immediately sober. "How many people?"

"Four hundred, maybe five. They're really looking forward to hearing what you have to say." I was trying to pump him up but succeeded only in adding a line or two to his face and fifty pounds to his shoulders. He didn't want the responsibility of leading anyone anywhere.

Instead of the inspirational, upbeat speech both his and RFK's supporters yearned to hear, he gave a plodding and unexciting one. It was then that those opposed to Lyndon Johnson and Hubert Humphrey decided they needed an additional candidate to pick up the fallen Kennedy banner, and recruited George McGovern.

DAD WAS A BIG DEAL in Las Vegas, and my experience with that city is so loaded that I don't know whether I love it or hate it, fear it or think it a jubilant expression of optimism and folly. The company of which he was sole shareholder, Donrey Media Group, owned the largest newspaper, the *Las Vegas Review-Journal*, many of the billboards (billboards . . . *in Las Vegas*), a radio station, a television station (for a while), real estate, and other businesses. At one point he owned more than sixty newspapers. He built an enormous office/home on its outskirts, and watched as the city expanded to his guard fence. When he wanted in to something, people jumped. While he was alive, I was welcome in any saloon, showroom, or main room in town, because I was his son. Someone made a phone call, and the elusive Siegfried and Roy tickets were suddenly available.

I had been almost whimsically put in charge of five western territories for Senator McCarthy. The regional directorship was something most campaign strategists would consider way over my head; but the McCarthy campaign was run almost entirely by college kids, and as I was almost one of them— and one of the more enthusiastic ones at that—a man named Curtis Gans decided, what the hell—let's put him in charge of Arizona, California, Nevada,

Hawaii, and Guam. Maybe he can swing a delegate or two away from Hubert Humphrey or George McGovern. Strategically, McCarthy should have picked up the fallen baton of the assassinated Robert Kennedy and been Humphrey's only opposition, but Kennedy and McCarthy had become such bitter rivals, and the supporters of each such enemies that they could not join forces.

And thus I was assigned to rally what few troops there were in the western states. Nevada and Arizona Democrats were seriously Establishment, and there was no chance of wresting a vote from them at the convention; California was slightly more in play. But I started with Nevada.

Because I'd seen Dad for only three weeks or so in my life, and this particular kingdom was so far away from New York, I was unaware at this time of his colossal importance in Las Vegas. He was certainly the subject of much discussion in the family, but whose father isn't? To me, Las Vegas big deals were Howard Hughes, Frank Sinatra, and Bugsy Siegel.

I made an appointment with Senator Alan Bible, an ultraconservative Democrat who today would be an ultraconservative Republican. My task was to ask his support for Senator McCarthy—tantamount today to asking Pat Buchanan to support Barney Frank for president. The appointment was granted immediately.

Dad, too, was a well-known conservative who, when asked to which candidate he gave a contribution, replied, "The winner." His first concern was business, and he regularly gave to both parties. He always seemed interested in my political opinions, without necessarily agreeing with them, but had recently come to realize the war in Vietnam was hopeless, costly, and stupid. But when I'd asked him what he'd think if I dodged the draft, he'd said, "I'd think you were a shirker."

After LBJ dangled an ambassadorship to Australia in exchange for money and Donrey newspaper support in 1964 and then reneged, Dad turned on him with rancor. He was already philosophically far to the president's right.

After we had exchanged pleasantries, Senator Bible said, "Let me get this straight. You're Don Reynolds's son . . . and you're working for Senator McCarthy?"

"Yes, sir," I said.

"And your father is backing him, too?"

"I'm not sure, but he has an open mind." He didn't, of course, but I didn't know that. For a few minutes, Senator Bible's world was upside down.

Later that day, I went to the *Review-Journal*—to ask its support for McCarthy, a quest that would have pleased Don Quixote. It was part of the routine we campaign workers were instructed to attempt. The editor, a pleasant man named Ralph something, said, "You're Mr. Reynolds's son and you're supporting Senator McCarthy?"

"Yes, sir."

"And your father knows you're here?"

I'd written Dad I was coming out. "Yes, sir." In retrospect, I think of myself as Candide, only less aware. Ralph, who as editor regularly pirouetted around many elements of the civilized underworld, as well as Kirk Kerkorian and Howard Hughes, without ever authorizing an investigative report in the newspaper, had met his match. So he rolled up his sleeves and joined in.

"Any chance of Senator McCarthy coming here?"

"I certainly think he should," I said firmly. Well, he should have—if the campaign had twenty or thirty months to go. He could have warmed up for Bobby Darin—that's how seriously he would have been taken in Nevada.

The next day, a photograph of me shaking hands with Ralph spread across the front page of the *Review-Journal* with the headline MCCARTHY MAY VISIT LAS VEGAS. I was impressed with my salesmanship and importance. Incredible as it may seem, it didn't occur to me that I'd been welcomed into Senator Bible's chambers and headlined by this paper not because of the newsworthiness of my candidate or the persuasive oratory of my silver tongue but solely and simply because of whose son I was.

That day, Dad phoned. "I see you got yourself on the front page of the paper," he said, quite amused by what he thought was my brazenness but which, alas, turned out to be naïveté. Why shouldn't he be amused? He had 364 other days that year to put what he wanted on the front page. Poor Ralph probably thought he was buttering up The Old Man. Whenever I reflect on those days, I turn beet red, and the image of the Tim Holt character in the film of *The Magnificent Ambersons* rears: Holt played the dim and narcissistic son of an influential midwestern family who's unable to grasp reality, and to the end believes the world revolves around him. Makes me laugh and wince to this day.

The Democratic convention in Chicago was a theatrical event unparalleled either in London or New York, complete with a circus at its center and the lion eating its lion tamer as a climax. Brilliantly and sometimes hilariously whipped to a frenzy by the comic activist Abbie Hoffman (and the considerably more insidious Jerry Rubin) and opposed by the equally hilarious *and* insidious Mayor Richard Daley (father of the city's current mayor), we McCarthy supporters tried to discredit the convention by staging nightly demonstrations and pulling pranks on the television journalists, the police, and the Establishment, as represented by the unfortunate Hubert Humphrey.

On the final night of the convention, the police and the mayor decided they'd had enough of their chains being pulled. I was in the streets and missed by a whisker their attack on the McCarthy and McGovern headquarters at the Hilton Hotel (with the complicity of the hotel management, whom I subsequently cursed by vowing never to stay at another Hilton for the rest of my life; because there are other hotels in the world more comfortable and inviting than those in the Hilton chain, it hasn't been much of a sacrifice). On the pretext that bottles were being dropped from hotel windows, the police invaded the offices and sleeping quarters of the campaign workers and beat many of their occupants brutally and bloodily.

Fully depressed by the nomination of Humphrey, whom we now despised more than Nixon even though about five minutes ago he'd been a champion of liberal causes, most notably in the area of civil rights, I joined a friend, Walter Dallenbach, in Santa Barbara to campaign for Stanley Sheinbaum, an academic and an economist who had married one of the daughters of one of the Warner brothers and was now running for Congress. Stan was the first of many interesting contradictions I would encounter on the Left: A rich Marxist, he married a millionairess and turned her considerable fortune into an even more considerable fortune by cleverly trading foreign currencies. He was staunchly against the war and intelligently reformist in social matters but was running against the popular, conservative lemon rancher Charles Teague, who had been elected to Congress seven times, soon to be eight.

One of the Left's whipping boys in California in '68 was the statewide superintendent of schools, Max Rafferty, usually referred to by us as "Fascist Max Rafferty," a sobriquet ascribed to just about anyone who didn't agree with us. When Teague came out in support of Rafferty, we plastered the voting district with ads that said TEAGUE ENDORSES RAFFERTY! This was tantamount to the Kerry campaign taking out an ad in Alabama that said BUSH 43 PRONOUNCES IT NOO-KYUH-LER! We might as well have given the good lemonist a campaign contribution: Not only did he defeat Sheinbaum two-to-one, but the district also voted heavily for Rafferty! But of course Stan never had a prayer in that part of the world then: He was a Jew, a beyond-Left liberal, and a public speaker who combined the many spoken ellipses of Bill Bradley with the drone of an uncomic Jackie Mason, and all the folksy lemon rancher had to do was put out a quaint singing commercial to trounce us. Stan went on to become a political force in Los Angeles, at one time serving as president of the police commission, but he never ran for office again.

In the bigger picture of 1968, the devil had been elected president. We were all sure it was the end of America. I wrote in McCarthy's name, though voting for the comedian Dick Gregory was the fad, and returned to New York to see what the rest of my life was going to be like.

Walt (a screenwriter) and his earth-mother wife, Em (now a therapist), and I hashed and rehashed the plight of the Left over joints of fine, but by today's standards mild, grass. In some sort of peculiar anti-Establishment protest, I gave up drinking and substituted pot for about a year, giving it up minutes before it made me terminally paranoid.

What worried the Dallenbachs and me about the campaigns we'd worked on—and the politics of the Left in general for the next fifteen years—was the comfort everyone seemed to take in failure. We were on God's side, fer sher . . . but we weren't actually supposed to win anything because that would mean we had copped out and betrayed all the victimization movements we championed—the persecuted Vietnamese, Americans of color, women, the incipient gay revolution. We were to continue to field noble kamikazes like McCarthy and McGovern and even Bobby Kennedy, and later on, Fritz Mondale, but they weren't actually supposed to *win*, were they? Martyrdom felt familiar and welcoming to me, at least partially because it echoed Mother's. So we'd do it through the back door: on campus.

A startling reinforcement had come from Hollywood the year before. The iconic movie of the era, *Bonnie and Clyde*, exemplified the notion of the noble loser. Hard to believe now, but post-WW2 Hollywood, despite toe-dipping into the rebellious worlds of Brando and Dean, overwhelmingly reinforced the status quo. *Bonnie and Clyde*, a love story with guns, changed all that, pitting a band of idealists, all emotionally wounded in one way or another, against an uncaring, and eventually overpowering, Authority. The writers Robert Benton and David Newman and the director Arthur Penn made the movie so representative of the era and so powerful, emotionally and aesthetically, by victimizing its glamorous characters. Its sexually magnetic lovers were criminals who robbed banks and killed people—a complete reversal of the usual Hollywood formula. It was also horrifyingly violent (for the period) and scary—I spent nights awake, brooding over the shoot-out at the motel, with Estelle Parsons and Gene Hackman at their absolute best. But I never found anyone my age who didn't side with the killers, though they couldn't have been more morally reprehensible. I was completely on their side, too. Played by Warren Beatty and Faye Dunaway, and valiant but defeated, they were our heroes. And they would have lost all validity if they hadn't been defeated.

I wrote Dad that I was looking around for a job, and he wrote back offering me one as a cub reporter on the *Review-Journal*. I accepted quickly, relishing the idea of contact with him and a chance to learn something about journalism. As the fateful day to board the plane to Las Vegas approached, however, I got cold feet. Stories Mother had told me about Dad's treatment of his associates—and most particularly, his son Don Junior—had me tossing with worry. Even given her bias, the stories had the ring of truth; it seemed the closer you were to Dad, the more he pushed you away, and not gently, but with a nightstick. And if it was a work situation, you became the class victim. A lawyer Dad retained in New York confirmed these concerns.

After days spent fretting whether to work for him, I decided not to. I regret it enormously and at the same time am relieved at the bullet I dodged. One of his longtime associates, Fred Smith, subsequently told me, "It was the smartest thing you ever did. Your father ruined Don Junior's life."

Not only did I dodge a bullet, I fell into a tub of butter. Closing the door on that career path immediately opened one on another. Dave Garth, who had been one of McCarthy's media advisers and was also New York mayor John Lindsay's, took a liking to me during the campaign. He phoned to ask if I'd like to be the mayor's assistant press secretary. I jumped. "I can be there in twelve minutes," I told him. He laughed, but he also knew what a great experience it would be. Lindsay was one of half-a-handful of great white hopes the American Left had, certain to run for the presidency—if only he could get reelected as mayor of New York. Though nominally a Republican in the most Democratically bureaucratic city west of Beijing, there was little doubt he sought the mantle of JFK, to whom he was constantly compared. And this was now 1969, an election year for the mayoralty in New York. I didn't ask about salary or responsibilities; I was now a career politician!

Except that the following day, Garth phoned to say, "Sorry—that job is filled. How'd you like to go work for David Frost?" I was heartbroken and unheartbroken in about thirty seconds, and in about sixty switched from career politician to career TV producer.

Frost was an Englishman who had made a reputation in the United States as an acerbic wit on the weekly satiric show *That Was the Week That Was*. He was a star in England, a great TV interviewer, and a popular host.

The format of American TV talk shows was fairly uniform in 1969: They were generally ninety minutes long, and the host sat behind a desk interviewing guests who were primarily involved in show biz. Occasionally, an author or politico would appear at the end for ten minutes, but the overall tenor was one of frivolity and amusement. The champ, of course, was Johnny Carson on NBC, and the streets of the unemployed were littered with pretenders. Two popular daytime shows were hosted by Merv Griffin, who appeared five times a week for Westinghouse Broadcasting, and Mike Douglas. CBS decided to go toe-to-toe against Carson and hired Merv away from Westinghouse. So Westinghouse brought Frost over to fill that slot, and Frost brought with him two energetic former newspapermen, Peter Baker and Neil Shand. The three of them wanted to revolutionize American television, and for a while, they did.

Frost and his men couldn't stand pontificators and other guests who just prattled; they weren't interested in actors talking about acting or novelists talking about interpreting life; they wanted *visceral* TV, in which the guest would be dramatic—by either embarrassing himself or being embarrassed by someone or getting into an argument or crying or in some other way revealing himself in a way he never had.

There were two bookers for the singers and comics, and four of us who were responsible for everything else: the writer John Berendt, the wild Woodstocker and writer Alice Turner, the socialite Jeanne Vanderbilt, and me. It was up to us to make the show different from all the others. So when I was put in charge of Jane Fonda, I got her to talk about her mother's suicide, her relationship with her father, and politics, none of which she'd ever done before (hard to imagine Jane as a political virgin, but she was then). We booked Jacqueline Susann, fresh from her triumph with *Valley of the Dolls,* and ambushed her with Rex Reed, Nora Ephron, and John Simon in the audience. Rex and Nora rolled over, but John accused her of writing "trash"; she countered by angrily calling him a Nazi; he countered by saying he was Yugoslavian, not German; she accused him of not reading the entire book; he shot back, "You don't have to go through the entire can to know the whole thing is garbage." Mayhem! Cheers from the Frosties!

I booked a debate on the antiballistic missile system between Dean Acheson and Senator Charles Percy, which network news departments had been trying to do for months, and Frost was an excellent referee; I booked one of my childhood heroes, Elia Kazan, with a film-clip retrospective. He revealed, among other things, that despite his sensitive and noble screen image, James Dean was rotten and selfish. We initiated the first of the shows with only one guest for the entire ninety minutes, and I was lucky enough to get the assignment: Orson Welles.

David Frost didn't study much of the research we so thoroughly prepared for him because he had a photographic memory and could command most subjects in a matter of minutes, and whenever seriously confronted, he was the single best interviewer I've ever seen. He was so good on his feet that I never saw anyone get the better of him. Adam Clayton Powell once innuendoed that he knew who had *really* killed President Kennedy.

"Who?" said Frost.

"We know, we know . . . don't we," said Powell, winking conspiratorially at the audience. These were days of black power and all the ABO (Anybody But Oswald) Kennedy-assassination theories, and most interviewers wouldn't have challenged Powell, a rascal and a media darling.

"You can't come on national television and say that. If you know who killed

President Kennedy, you have to substantiate it. Otherwise you're just being irresponsible," Frost said sternly. Powell was shocked and eventually backed down.

Dean Acheson had haughtily confronted David backstage before the ABM debate.

"Mr. Frost, I am sorry I agreed to do this program. You are not a serious person, and I believe you are ill equipped to participate in this discussion," Acheson said imperiously. The Frosties loved the *Guinness Book of World Records*, and the previous show, which Acheson had seen, featured a man who could put thirty or fifty or seventy lighted cigars in his mouth at the same time.

"That is very disrespectful, Mr. Acheson," Frost said sternly. "You clearly have not seen any programs I've done in England, and I assure you you will be treated intelligently and with respect. And I am extremely well informed on the subject." He wasn't, until he subsequently photo-memmed my notes, but Acheson, used to being addressed only by those on bended knee, capitulated and was, in turn, respectful to Frost.

What David wasn't good at was a talk show's lifeblood, the second-tier celebrities; he imitated what he considered to be American show-biz insincerity and wound up doubly insincere; hence unknown singers and mediocre comedians would become "one of the greatest in the history of the business" show after show. He was also a terrible monologuist, and though the comedy writing was often funny, he would read his opening monologue from a clipboard, which was distinctly unfunny. But he had brass; at one taping, the monologue received such little laughter that he said, "All right, stop tape. We're going to do this again, and this time, everybody please laugh." Which they did.

Frost won an Emmy or two, and the television world sat up and took notice, but eventually he wore out his welcome. He couldn't get folksy like Johnny or Merv. We were imitated, and it got harder to be fresh. Others took on the ninety-minute and Kazan film-clip ideas and, worst of all, David simply wasn't a comic. Rule Number One was that this sort of show had to be funny, and if it wasn't, it didn't matter whether you could book Garbo, Howard Hughes, and Charles Lindbergh, the Three Unbookables. David was amiable, he was immensely good-spirited, optimistic, energetic, and an extraordinary businessman; but actually getting the audience at home or in the studio to laugh on a regular basis was beyond him.

The Frosties were demanding and exciting to work for, and they paid each of us four horsemen the grand sum of $250 a week. They were aware of the talk-show perks: Besides all the movie screenings, free plays and concerts, glam dinners, and other events, there was a social life. Whenever possible, I tried to improve mine, booking and attempting to romance as many women as I could. It was as close to rock stardom as I would ever get.

The Frosties experimented with hiring a mini–repertory company to per-form comedy skits, and one of those chosen was an old friend from my acting days, Oliver Clark. We have remained the best of friends for nearly forty years.

Meat Loaf: The Musical

~~~~~~~~~~~~~~~~~~

U NLIKE ME, Oliver, not only actor but cook, magician, mechanical-
bank collector, folk-art enthusiast featured in *Architectural Digest*,
and one of the all-time ten-best dinner guests, has never stopped performing.
When I saw him recently, he was pouring olive oil into a pan and tossing in
half a head of garlic with the theatrical flourish that is one of his many trademarks. He was standing in Red's kitchen, whipping up meat loaf and rigatoni,
and it reminded me of the time we once wrote a musical together.

"I got this pasta from Malcolm and Kelley McDowell, and you must put the
garlic in the oil before the tomatoes, or the oil will never"—he relished the
word—"in-fu-u-se." Oliver is the only person I know who does imitations not
only of Gielgud, Ralph Richardson, and Albert Finney but also of Maya An-
gelou. The tomato-garlic homily was his Gielgud.

We met in 1965, shortly before I went west to get arrested with Weed. We
were appearing in a production of *She Stoops to Conquer* at the Cincinnati Play-
house in the Park. Oliver played Tony Lumpkin, one of the leads, and I played
both a butler and a footman, with a total of four lines.

Oliver achieved fame as one of the patients on *The Bob Newhart Show* and on
his own short-lived sitcom. We started composing our musical after I moved
from the Frost show to *The Dick Cavett Show* at ABC, selling my soul for network exposure and a raise to $400.

The show taped at 5:30 P.M., and when it was over at around 7, I'd frequently
meet Oliver for dinner. He weighed 320 then and has battled weight most of

his life, bungeeing all the way down to 170, only to fly up 100 pounds a few months later. Right now he's about 220 and, as always, on guard.

"When I die," he said once, "they'll come up with a pill that has your ideal weight on it. If you take a pill marked 178 in the morning, you can eat anything you want, and at day's end you'll weigh 178. But it won't happen in time for me to enjoy it."

Oliver's real name is Richard Mardirosian, which he changed for the stage before Barbra Streisand made using real names stylish. He chose Oliver because the musical *Oliver!* was running when he came to New York, and Clark because it went well with Oliver. He grew up working the grill in his dad's blue-collar restaurant in Buffalo, and so he likes direct food, like the meat loaf he was prepping at Red's. Back in our musical days, we'd usually have a prime rib and the tomato-onion-iceberg salad with blue cheese at Beefsteak Charlie's or some other midlevel red-meat palace, though occasionally we'd go on a bender (his acting career was flourishing, and in '71, $400 was handsome) at The Palm or Peter Luger, because, as Oliver intoned in his self-parodizing British baritone, "You can get many beeves, good Jonathan, all of them pri-i-ime." After dinner we'd often walk uptown, fooling ourselves into thinking that a postprandial of forty blocks would neutralize the billion or so calories we'd just horsed down. Usually the freewheeling conversation revolved around the theatre, politics, food, and people we knew. On one of those strolls ("Let us walk against the elements, wearing good tweeds, hands clasped behind backs," was a customary invitation; he was in his Victorian period), I must have mentioned my interest in writing a musical, because that's what we did for several weeks.

Outside of kindergarten pageants, the first play I saw was the musical *Where's Charley?* at about age six and remember singing "Once in Love with Amy" for what must have seemed to others several months afterward. My second was *Guys and Dolls* at age eight. Both were by Frank Loesser. I saw *Damn Yankees* twice as an early teen, and fantasized about the woman in pajama-tops-only from *The Pajama Game*. I continue to love *My Fair Lady* and *Carousel*. My favorites, though, are everything that Gilbert and Sullivan ever wrote and *The Music Man*—particularly but not exclusively with Robert Preston. It has the most sophisticated lyrics disguised as bumpkin writing—a goal that

Oscar Hammerstein II so frequently sought and achieved and at which Meredith Willson excelled—of any show I know. Its story line is simple, but perfect (perhaps not needing quite so many references to Balzac), every single melody is memorable, and above all, it is unpretentious and true to itself in theme and style. To me, there is nothing more infuriating than pretension in the theatre, whether it be a musical or a straight play, nothing worse than the layering on of importance for its own sake. This doesn't mean a musical can't be serious. I'm a great admirer of *Gypsy* and *Cabaret* and *Sweeney Todd*, but only of *West Side Story*'s music, lyrics, and choreography, and not at all of *Company*, which tries desperately to say something "important" about marriage and is on the level of a kid looking in the window. And *Movin' Out*, in my opinion the best musical in the last decade or so, couldn't be more serious. It gives its subject profound meaning honestly, not glibly or facilely.

I've tried to write two—one about *American Bandstand* (at exactly the moment *Hairspray* was in the works) and one about the 1968 campaign. Neither saw the light of day. I also doctored the brief Broadway revival of *Whoopee!*, which Brendan Gill called "this rouged cadaver of a musical" in 1979. Not much success there. When musicals are good, and intelligent, they are everything the theatre should be: thrills, spectacle, artifice, intellect, emotion.

"I remember that musical," Oliver said now, whacking away at the lids of a couple of portobellos for the meat loaf. "You were completely bamboozled. Now listen to me: You must chop everything the same size so nothing stands out texturally." He brought out a green pepper and made same-size pieces of it. "I love me m'green pepper, but some people hate it. I'll leave it out if you want." No, I assured him—anything he put together would be excellent.

"Excellent!" We used to say this to each other all the time, it being a line from the musical *Ben Franklin in Paris*, in which he played Louis XVI. "Excellent! A copy of this news to his Britannic majesty in London!" is how I remember it. He loved the line because it was so silly. Acting is often silly—that's part of its joy. We shortened it simply to "Excellent!" and said it so often that to this day, forty-plus years later, it is still part of my phraseology; and because it's difficult to spend an hour with Oliver without starting to sound like him, I say it with his intonation.

When we started our musical, I was amazed at how adept he was at it. He came up with snippets of music that sounded Broadway-commercial. He even came up with a credible story line: A repressed Englishwoman falls in love with a rambunctious American, their parents are against it, she discovers herself. Not *Phantom of the Opera* exactly, but something to hang a few songs and dances on.

And his lyrics not only rhymed, they made sense. "If you're smart," he'd start singing, boomba-ing the percussion between lines, "do something crazy just for once."

> *If you're sma-a-art*
> *(ba boomba boomba)*
> *Do something foolish just for once*
> *(ba boomba boomba)*
> *Lose your he-e-ad*
> *And you might find your*
> *he-a-art!*

I couldn't improve on this but offered something rather feeble for another song. He mused on it, then haltingly began what we called the heroine's "I Want" number:

> *The right finger of me left hand*
> *Is the loneliest place in town.*

The improvisation materialized into a song over several weeks. After a few minutes of working at it, we'd run out of steam and start in on how to stuff pork chops.

Back at Meat-Loaf Central, Oliver added cream cheese to the other ingredients, then pawed at the mixture with two forks. "If you mix too much, the meat gets tough." He pushed the loaf into the oven. "Now all we have to do is boil the rigatoni. And that, as they say in France . . . is . . . *that*."

After a month or so of our strolling songwriting sessions, we had a complete story line and four or five plausible songs. With titles! "The Right Finger

of Me Left Hand," "The Uncle Sam Rag," "I Feel Merely Marvelous." These
sound like possible Broadway tunes, don't they? Not as good as *The Music Man*,
maybe, but I found myself humming them at all hours.

I was having a clandestine relationship with a co-worker at the Cavett
show, Bridget Potter. She was a former political activist who ran with Abbie
Hoffman and had been part of the group that once dropped hundreds of dollar bills from the balcony of the New York Stock Exchange just to see if the
brokers would scurry after them. (They did.) She was a lively British expat
who wore skirts so short they were often referred to as wide belts, the tantalizing fashion of the day. Bridget had been married for a year to a widly radical radio personality who insisted they have sex once a day. After they
divorced she found she missed at least that part of the relationship and found
me searching for someone to calm my own raging energy level. We didn't want
anyone to know about the relationship and so would leave the Cavett taping
separately, then meet up at one or the other's apartment a few minutes later,
or at a screening or with Oliver for dinner. The next morning, we'd taxi to the
Cavett offices, and I'd get out a block away and we'd walk separately into the
office. To the best of my knowledge, no one found out until years later, and
this skulduggery inadvertently made the relationship juicier. Bridget went on
to become an executive at the upstart HBO, married, had two daughters, and
divorced. We're still friends, at least partially because she's inexhaustibly curious and she loves to cook.

Back in the musical days, I told her I thought Oliver and I had a real shot at
Broadway and fantasized entering some junior version of the Loesser-Lerner-
Hammerstein pantheon, and even entertained quitting the Cavett show.
"Most amazing is that Oliver has pretty much done the whole thing himself,"
I told her. "I come up with brainchildren, he has better ones. I had no idea he
could write music. And he's so clever with lyrics."

"This is amazing," she said. "But don't leave Cavett just yet."

I sang "our" songs constantly. After I'd announced our musical to several
friends and was about to go seriously public with our boffo smash, Oliver became less inspired in his tunesmithery. I was sure he was becoming inhibited
by the possibility of success, and encouraged him every time we did our

hands-clasped promenades. Then one night he stopped by my apartment, an LP tucked under his arm. "Listen to this, my lad," he said, plopping the record onto a turntable.

For those of you even less perceptive than I, what happened next may be a surprise. Out from the speakers came brassy, orchestrated maxi-versions of our songs. The lyrics differed slightly from ours, but only slightly. I was stunned. "What is this?" I said. Had he had our songs recorded?

"No, Jonathan. It was on Broadway. It was called *Redhead*."

I think my dropped jaw was the funniest thing he'd ever seen. *Redhead*, with a score by Albert Hague and Dorothy Fields, starred Gwen Verdon and Richard Kiley, was directed by Fosse, and was a memorable innocuity that opened in 1959 and ran for a year. Oliver was beside himself with laughter and dined out on the story many times. I wasn't angry, just bewildered—and felt foolish. When I told Bridget, she laughed for what seemed like a month. Actually, she laughed for months, just not all the time.

"What I loved most," said Oliver, laughing now as he swirled the rigatoni into Malcolm and Kelley's pink sauce, "is that you actually sang the songs for people!" We sat down to the meat loaf—direct, flavorful, and bursting with juices—and the subtle, delicious pasta, and chortled again over the many curious things we'd done together. Like the time in the seventies when he got me to invest in an antique Rolls just as the oil crisis hit . . . but that's another story.

At about that same time, Oliver moved to Los Angeles, landed his series and dozens of parts in movies-of-the-week and features. He also became one of the three or four leading cast-iron-mechanical-bank collectors in the country and a successful folk-art dealer, and bought three houses. I didn't see much of him during that decade, but when my screenwriting career took off in the eighties, and I had to be in L.A., we spent many evenings together. We'd dine either at Musso & Frank's, which reminded him of New York and at which he had a table, or at The Palm, where his caricature adorned the wall. He had arrived.

Seven years after the great *Redhead* fiasco, I decided to marry. There was no second choice for best man. At the rehearsal dinner at Lutèce, he could have charmed the jewelry off my aunt Maymie throat, persuaded my future father-in-law to put up seed money for his growing folk-art collection, and levitated the room. He did none of those things, except for the levitation of the room.

Oliver Clark's Meat Loaf

4 cloves garlic, chopped fine

4 tablespoons olive oil

2 medium onions, chopped fine

Salt and pepper

1 ½ large portobello mushroom caps, chopped fine

1 green pepper, chopped fine

2 pounds ground beef

1 pound ground pork or sausage

1 cup unflavored bread crumbs

½ teaspoon onion powder

1 teaspoon Dijon mustard

½ teaspoon Cajun seasoning

⅓ cup grated Parmesan cheese

4 tablespoons ketchup

1 tablespoon mayonnaise

2 tablespoons whipped cream cheese

3 eggs, beaten

½ pound bacon

1. Preheat oven to 350 degrees.
2. Sauté garlic and onions in 2 tablespoons of the oil until the garlic is lightly brown and the onions translucent. Remove to a bowl. Add a dash of salt and pepper.
3. Sauté mushrooms in the remaining oil until liquid is released, about 2 minutes, and remove them to the bowl. Add more salt and pepper.
4. Place the remaining ingredients, except the eggs and bacon, in another bowl. Paw at the mixture with two forks, combining thoroughly but not overmixing.

5. Add in the eggs and the mushroom-onion mixture and blend.
6. Bake in the oven for 30 minutes.
7. Meanwhile, sauté the bacon till half cooked, then adorn the meat loaf with it and bake for another 30 minutes.

Yield: 6–8 servings.

MALCOLM AND KELLEY McDOWELL'S PINK RIGATONI
(Adapted by Oliver Clark)

10 cloves garlic, roughly chopped
6 tablespoons olive oil
10–12 plum tomatoes, quartered (canned may be used off-season)
½ teaspoon salt
½ teaspoon pepper
½ cup red wine
1 pound rigatoni
¾ stick salted butter
½ cup grated Parmesan cheese
½ teaspoon sugar

1. Over medium heat, sauté garlic in oil till brown (but no darker).
2. Add the tomatoes, salt, and pepper and sauté for 30 minutes or until the liquid begins to evaporate.
3. Pour in the wine and cook an additional 20–30 minutes until thickened, then remove from heat and let stand for 10 minutes.
4. Boil the rigatoni until al dente.
5. Fold the butter, Parmesan, and sugar into the sauce until it turns the famous pink. Dump in the rigatoni, mix, and serve.

Yield: 4 servings.

Dinner for Kings

I was fired from the Cavett show in January 1972, after fourteen months, under circumstances about which I'm unclear to this day. One version is straightforward and political, the other tawdry and juicy. In the first, the producer of the show, John Gilroy, had been suddenly demoted by the arrival from *The Tonight Show* of Marshall Brickman. Brickman had been wooed away from Carson with the promise of taking over as producer, but his contract wasn't up for a few months, and during that time Gilroy had been appointed. Brickman, who went on to write *Sleeper*, *Annie Hall*, and *Manhattan* with Woody Allen as well as direct his own movies, was immensely entertaining, and one of the funniest monologue writers ever. Bridget and I immediately gravitated toward him when he arrived and unburdened ourselves of the many complaints we had regarding the stodginess of the Cavett show, which, we felt, kept us third in the ratings behind Johnny and Merv.

Cavett was a wit from both Nebraska and Yale; he had written for Jack Paar and Johnny Carson and starred on his own successful daytime talk show. ABC had been trying to figure out how to use him for some time. When elevated to the magic 11:30 P.M. slot, he quickly threw together a staff, a desk, some chairs, and the Bobby Rosengarten band. But, like Frost, he had no second banana (Frost had already broken the interior-design rules by not sitting behind a desk). Johnny had Ed McMahon and Merv had a butlery Englishman named Arthur Treacher. These number twos not only laughed at jokes and encouraged the audience to do so, but gave the host a pal to talk to and fence with. Frost's ebullient personality didn't need this shoring up, but Dick was and is a reactive comedian who plays best off strong personalities. Although he desperately wanted the show to be funny, it became the repository of serious topics and second-choice guests. Dick was comfortable with Gilroy's steadiness but was irritated that the shows weren't more exciting. The show became a critics' favorite—the kiss of death in television—and quickly earned considerable snob appeal, but the audience stayed away.

I wanted to bring some Frostian zest to the enterprise, pit warring factions against each other, and generally stir the pot; Bridget had similar notions. Gilroy resented Brickman's arrival; he'd been successfully producing the show for several months and protested to Dick that he should continue, and that Marshall should become head writer. Individually, Bridget and I told Dick that we thought Marshall becoming producer would enliven the show, and we backed him vehemently. Dick eventually lived up to the contract he'd made with Brickman, but erroneously didn't fire Gilroy, which meant he had a sniping second-guesser rolling his eyes in a "This didn't happen when I was producer" blamelessness whenever something went wrong.

We zipped up the show, all right—one installment featured a shouting match among onetime segregationist and ax-handle flailer Governor Lester Maddox of Georgia, black footballer and angry activist Jim Brown, and Truman Capote; in another, Gore Vidal and Norman Mailer verbally bitch-slapped each other for an hour; in another, Fred Astaire was the sole guest. Feeling my oats and beginning to appreciate the limitless possibilities of the medium, I somewhat legendarily suggested that in order to viscerally demonstrate the horrors of air pollution, we should put a rat in a plastic bag, tape the bag to a running automobile's exhaust, and watch with the rest of America how long it would take for the rat to die. After collapsing with laughter, Brickman said simply, "No."

The shows were more exciting—but more unpredictable as well. In our attempt to arrange theme shows and guests that fit or fought together, we frequently couldn't book them till the last minute, which unsettled Dick almost as much as being told to put on Rosencrantz's costume had me. We went to London for a week, hoping to book Laurence Olivier, Diana Rigg, and the Prince of Wales. Instead, we got Laurence Harvey, Fenella Fielding, and a random earl. Most of the guests were available in New York, so it appeared there was no reason to go to London. It was a disaster. Upon our return, Brickman decided producing wasn't for him and became the head writer. Gilroy was reinstated as producer and as first order of business fired his most vocal critic, who happened to be me. He couldn't fire Bridget, because she was Dick's favorite.

That's the first version. The second was told to me three years later, just as I was pulling out of my depression over the firing.

Gilroy had what was then called a secretary, whom I'll call "Jackie." Jackie was what is now called a babe, with extra-long legs emphasized by her skirt—not a wide belt, but a narrow belt. Dick taped two shows on Thursday so he could have a long weekend at his home in Montauk, but we had to come to work on Friday anyway, and every Friday afternoon, Jackie would disappear from her desk outside Gilroy's office *into* Gilroy's office, and the door would be locked. Twenty to two hundred minutes later, depending, I guess, on enthusiasm and acrobatics, Jackie would emerge red-faced and disheveled, smooth herself out, and assume her position behind her desk. A few minutes later, Gilroy would emerge, adjusting his necktie. The routine was so obvious it became comical, and whenever I'd ask Jackie why she was in Gilroy's office with the door locked, she'd say with quadruple entendre, "John had some . . . notes he wanted me to take."

Other days, Jackie would walk into my office, her naked right thigh pressing my left forearm as I tried to type, and would initiate an inane conversation.

JACKIE

Oh, hi. What are you doing?

ME

Typing up the notes on Erich Segal.

JACKIE

Oh, I loved *Love Story.*

ME

He's very pretentious. And now, he's very rich.

JACKIE

He has such a way of, you know . . . writing.

ME

We're putting him on with John Simon. That should cause some sparks.

JACKIE

Can I look?

ME

Sure.

JACKIE

(Leaning over me and the typewriter, her shirt appearing to be more unbuttoned
than usual, knee now on the arm of my chair, underwear exposed)

I love John Simon.

When we got to London, my first visit was with Bridget to Piccadilly Circus. I hadn't been there for five years, and I wanted to roam every street.

My second visit was to Jackie's hotel room. She was having trouble with her orgasm, she said. She'd never had one with a man. And then she told me how boring it was to have slept with Peter Lawford, a recent guest on the show.

When we got back from London, Gilroy fired me. Jackie told me three years later that he had found out we had spent several nights together in London, and though he was seriously seeing another woman had become enraged. It didn't seem plausible, but he's since died, so Jackie is the only one who knows for sure.

Being fired for whatever reason was devastating, made considerably worse by Bridget firing me, too. I wasn't a particularly faithful boyfriend—never claimed to be, too many heebie-jeebies—but when she heard of my liaisons with Jackie, her contempt knew no bounds. Besides, she was becoming involved with a heavyweight newsman at NBC who took her to NASA liftoffs and promised for the next several years to leave his wife. But then, this was the seventies, when all STDs could be cured with penicillin, and drugs were actually thought to be good for you. (Kerouac became liberated on pot; Freud and Sherlock Holmes got smart on coke; Gaudi did Barcelona on mushrooms—how could they have been wrong?)

Once fired, I suddenly had no life and no identity. I'd expected some of the perks to keep up—screenings, play openings—but they abruptly halted with my dismissal from the show. You mean all those PR people were interested only in the show all along, not in me? Yup. So there I was, alone on the Upper West Side, with a bedroom, a living room . . . and a kitchen. So I picked up a pot.

I began cooking to ward off uncertainty and depression, and it worked. But one of the drawbacks of cooking is also one of its joys—as creative works go, it's done quickly . . . and it's over quickly. Palliated as I was when planning and executing dinner for others (and even for myself), there was always a junkie's letdown the following day, when the euphoria evaporated and there was nothing tangible to show for it except garbage bags. I was faced not only with joblessness but aimlessness, and cooking's brief injection of purpose and a parade of brief and thrilling but ultimately hollow relationships didn't quite make up for the empty clamminess of free fall. I attempted several television and film projects, none of which got anywhere.

In 1974 I began writing a play, never planning to show it to anyone who might produce it. I simply enjoyed writing it. It was a lengthy one-act about a baseball pitcher at the top of his form who, for no discernible reason, talks himself into failure in the middle of a game at Yankee Stadium. It reminded me of me. It was bold, in that it took place right on the mound, and the character actually pitched a baseball to his offstage catcher twenty-seven times while articulating his woes in a stream of consciousness, many of them politically infuriating by today's standards. I had recently seen a Richard Foreman play, *Sophia = (Wisdom) Part 3: The Cliffs*, and so liked the title I gave mine the same syllabification: *Yanks 3 Detroit 0 Top of the 7th*.

When I finished the play, I gave copies to Oliver and Lee, solely for their amusement. Oliver gave it to Wynn Handman, who ran the American Place, at the time one of the top not-for-profit theatres in the city. Wynn phoned to say he wanted to produce it. I couldn't believe it—this had been written for my pleasure alone, a sort of psychic bloodletting. Lee, living in London, sent it to Stephen Sondheim, who phoned.

"Jonathan, I'd like to give this play to Hal Prince. I think he should direct it." This was impossible, part two! Hal was one of the leading directors on Broadway and *the* leading producer. He phoned the next day to say he wanted to direct it; we met with Wynn, and they agreed to do it at the American Place Theatre. Hal took me aside.

"Jonathan, Broadway's future is all about musicals. There's room for one straight play a year, no more. This is going to be it. This is the wave of the future—try out a play at a not-for-profit theatre, save all the out-of-town expense and gamble, and if the reviews warrant, move it to Broadway." This is conventional wisdom now, but no one had Hal's foresight thirty years ago.

Wynn told me, "We can put this on with someone else's one-act, but it's much better for you if it's on with another play of yours. Do you have one?" I didn't, but an item in the *Times* had caught my eye: A bill had been introduced in the New York State legislature in Albany forbidding the public display of contraceptives for fear of alarming children and easily offended grown-ups. It was hilarious, and all true! I wrote the first draft of *Rubbers* in a week. Both Wynn and Hal were enthusiastic, and I now had an entire evening to myself.

Jerry Orbach did a reading of *Yanks* and it was hot; he was perfect but unavailable, so Hal and I cast Tony LoBianco and the rest of the characters. Meanwhile, Hal's designer, Eugene Lee, planned a lavish set with an electronic scoreboard; Wynn balked—his budget for a set was $5,000, max, and this would cost $25,000, min. They argued. Wynn phoned.

"Jonathan, Hal doesn't understand your play. I don't like his way of working. And it will bankrupt us. I can't have him working in my theatre." He was adamant.

There were aspects of the production I didn't like, either. It seemed fraudulent, as I thought much of Hal's dramatic work was. He knew everything about the theatre but not about the world outside, and his productions often looked like tasteful reproductions of other productions, not life. "Wynn, this probably means no Broadway," I said.

"I don't care. I never did care whether this went to Broadway."

As usual, I was unmindful of the economic possibilities. I was itching to see what another director would do with it. "Well, you can't let Hal go until you've got someone else," I told Wynn.

Wynn phoned Alan Arkin, who said he would like to direct the plays, then phoned Hal and told him he was out. I phoned Hal. He was incredulous, but not angry. Amused.

"I can't believe it—for the first time in my life, I've been fired. And by Wynn Handman!" He started laughing. It was odd, all right—sort of like my boyhood friend Michael Eisner being fired by the ride operator at EuroDisney. "Well, good luck," he said.

Yanks and *Rubbers* did well by Clive Barnes, the chief critic at the *Times*, but were lionized by Jack Kroll at *Newsweek* and John Simon at *New York*. Initially scheduled to run six weeks, the show ran nine months. Among the people who saw it was Francis Ford Coppola, who said he wanted to put it on in Candlestick Park (then the San Francisco Giants' stadium), starring Jack Nicholson, and hang television monitors all over the stands so the crowd could see close-ups. Francis had recently finished *The Godfather: Part II* and was festooned with Oscars and generally considered creator of the universe, at least in southern California. After some badgering on my part, he suggested I join him in the Philippines, where he was about to start shooting *Apocalpyse Now*. "I don't get it," he said. "The Vietnam War is the most traumatic event in American history, and nobody except John Wayne has made a movie about it."

Tom Sternberg, an executive who worked for Francis, told me Francis wanted my opinion on a script. This was exciting.

"I'll read it right away and phone him."

"No, read it and fly out to San Francisco and meet with him." Couldn't it be done on the phone? Not how things work in the movie biz. And who'd want it any other way?

The script was written by Steve Martin, then primarily a stand-up comic, and Carl Gottlieb, who'd written the screenplay for *Jaws*. It was a comedy about the settling of California, and I didn't find it particularly funny, largely because I didn't know the California history the authors were satirizing and had never heard of Father Junípero Serra. I arrived in San Francisco just in time to accompany Francis, Tom, and some friends to a Steve Martin performance. Francis was energetic, filled with ideas outlandish and sensible, and seemed extremely interested in my opinion about things. I kept looking over my shoulder to see who he was talking to, but it was me.

Martin was truly fresh onstage and completely silly, with an arrow in his head and a cutting take on all things show biz, into which he saw the whole world descending. At the show's climax, he led the audience snaking through the San Francisco streets, and the show continued for another half hour.

"That's the funniest stand-up I've ever seen," I said to Francis. "But I have to say I wasn't crazy about the script."

"No, I don't like it at all," he said. So why exactly was I there if he'd already made up his mind?

The following day, Martin, Gottlieb, and I appeared in Francis's office on Kearny Street. Francis proceeded to talk about the screenplay as though he were eager to produce it. I kept my mouth shut. When Martin and Gottlieb left, I said, "I thought you didn't like it."

"I don't. We're not doing it." First lesson of Hollywood: You never do the dirty work. Your people do the dirty work.

Francis invited me to his mansion in Pacific Heights for dinner. He was attempting to start a Hollywood North with his film-school buddy George Lucas, with whom he'd had an enormous success on *American Graffiti*. His entrepreneurial vision, coupled with the two *Godfathers* and the cult hit *The Conversation*, plus the Oscar he'd already won for the screenplay of *Patton*, made him the hottest single figure in the industry. But film wasn't his only interest. He'd just announced the end of *City* magazine, a literary publication he'd founded, and though unhappy about closing it, his vision for the future was brilliant. What made his ideas unusual was not only their range but their practicality: He could actually pull them all off. We sat around an immense table with his petite wife, Ellie, three of their children, Roman, Gio, and Sofia, and a few other friends, and talked about movies, television, magazines, food, wine, Italy, and how he hoped to realize his childhood dream: "Just one more hit, and I can start my own studio," he said. "And what do you like to do?"

A bit out of my league, I said sheepishly, "Well, I like to cook . . ."

"You do? You do?" Food was his favorite subject, except for all the others. "Cook tomorrow night! Take the whole day, use my staff, use my kitchen, whatever you want!"

A staff? Occasionally a friend helped me out in the galley kitchen of my one-bedroom apartment in New York, but I had no idea what to do with a whole staff. But the next day, I found out.

I wanted to impress the hell out of Francis and Ellie and so remembered a few things from the S.S. *France*, like *tournedos Rossini*, and from my own repertoire, like the killer-diller *bavarois Clermont*, with all the glacéed chestnuts in the middle and the whole candied chestnuts dripping with chocolate spikes around the center.

His staff of four—one also took care of the children, another was his flirtatious projectionist, two others did whatever jobs needed doing around the house and office—and I spent the entire day making the stocks for the *tournedos* from scratch, then wrestling the chocolated *marrons glacés* to the earth. The kitchen was the first I'd ever worked in in which there was actually room and equipment to do everything. Sharp knives! A Chinese hat! Stockpots that didn't have to be stored under the bookcase!

I started off with Shrimp Toast à la Rothschild, creation of Raymond Oliver, chef at the Michelin-three-starred Grand Vefour in the only city where the guide's stars are remotely helpful, Paris. Loaves of bread are sliced fat, hollowed out, sautéed in clarified butter, then filled with a reduced, buttery fish stock made with crushed shrimp shells and fish frames, adorned with shrimp sautéed in more butter. I placed a truffle slice on top, then broiled these little toasted shrimp boxes till brown, and sped them out of the kitchen, feeling like a pro.

They're rich but small—three bites, perhaps—and they vanished immediately. The *tournedos* are incredibly rich, too—but also incredibly small, and Francis is a man of large appetites in every area of life. When he spotted the two little fillets on his plate, he began screaming in mock fury, "That's it? That's all there is? You spent the whole day cooking and this is all we get?" Ellie laughed and shushed him, but the *tournedos* were inhaled in seconds. Out came some sautéed green beans (boiled in water for thirty seconds, then sautéed till blackened in cast iron to remove all moisture, then slathered with butter, which they drank in like anxious sponges) and potatoes Anna, and they, too, were gone in an instant. I thought Francis was going to order up a couple of bowls of rigatoni and roll out some gnocchi to hold us all over until dessert, but the richness of the food began to take its toll, and by the time the *bavarois* made its *haute* appearance, the crowd was sufficiently butterfatted and mellow.

We sat and talked for another hour or two or three. Francis Coppola is certainly one of the ten greatest dinner guests in the world—or, in this case, hosts.

I lingered in the kitchen afterward, my eye caught by the flirtatious projectionist, and after the day's work we were on intimate terms. We eventually went upstairs to her room. It was a perfect day and a perfect night, except for one thing.

Around 3 A.M., I couldn't sleep (Etoile hadn't provided hypnagogics for every insomnious neurosis) and decided to go to the apartment Francis's company had arranged for me. I snuck quietly down the stairs . . . and the moment my right foot hit the floor at the bottom of the staircase, all hell broke loose. The entire mansion was suddenly alight, and a siren started shrieking. Then the lights began to flash. The whole place was one big security zone! I didn't want to ruin my relatively impressive introduction to the director of both *Godfathers*, panicked, and opened the first door I found. In true Feydeau fashion, it was a closet. The second led to another door, and that one led down some more stairs, which for all I knew could have opened onto a spewing Linda Blair. Finally I found a door that led out back, and I jumped a fence onto a back street just as two police cars pulled up to the front of the house. I walked away with as much nonchalance as I'd had all those years before, in Miami Beach, and made it to the apartment a free man.

The next day, the projectionist phoned and, assuming I had left her side before the alarm system was switched on, said, "The weirdest thing happened last night after you left. About three A.M. the alarm went off and the whole house went wild for about an hour. The police came and everything. Francis was pretty upset."

"Really? Hmmm, how bizarre."

"What time did you leave?"

"I forget. Around one. Two . . ."

"How are you?"

"Oh, fine, fine. How are you?" I didn't know Francis well enough then to realize he probably would have broken up over the story. But just to be on the safe side, I never told him.

I met with him that afternoon to discuss the movie he hoped would give him the clout to run his own studio, *Apocalypse Now*.

We sat in his San Francisco office while he tried to talk Al Pacino into playing Willard, the special-forces officer sent up the river into the heart of darkness to bring back Marlon Brando. "No, no," Pacino said good-humoredly into the speakerphone. "I know what's going to happen—I'll be down on the ground swimming around in the mud for three months, and you'll be up in a helicopter giving everybody orders and having a great time." Francis cast Harvey Keitel, a former marine.

Francis had already finished the screenplay with John Milius, so we worked out a generous arrangement in which I would write a book about the making of the movie. Francis wanted no financial participation in it, promised me total access to him except when sleeping or in the bathroom, and guaranteed no one from his camp or from United Artists, the financing studio, would look over my shoulder or insist upon reading my notes.

The following three months of '76 were almost as surreal as what eventually appeared on the screen. I practically lived in Francis's skin, accompanying him on every jaunt, boat trip, and plane ride, not to mention his own helicopter lessons, his bouts with the flu, and a loss of fifty-plus pounds. I witnessed directorial bravura and pettiness, brilliant cinematic insights and breathtaking sequences that he created with his good buddy Dean Tavoularis, the production designer. Movie sets are notoriously boring: Hours pass waiting for the right natural light or the construction of artificial light. Not this one. It was full-throttle pandemonium almost all the time, as extras misbehaved, choppers wouldn't take off (or went missing), explosives didn't detonate, props were stolen.

Francis is a professional Italian and had hired two Italians as his first assistant directors. "Firsts" (Lee's husband Kip was one) execute what the director wants—setting up the shots, arranging the background and foreground, marshaling the extras. But these Italians spoke neither English nor Tagalog (the

Filipino language) nor Vietnamese, and there were hundreds of Vietnamese and Filipino extras. After a month, Francis fired his two firsts, and, while waiting for a new one, appointed . . . me. Suddenly I was explaining to the extras (through a translator) how to dive into the dirt when the helicopters swooped in for attacks and staging scenes of village treachery—under Francis's instruction, of course, though he gave me wide latitude. It was heady stuff; nine months earlier I'd been grappling with sanity, scribbling a play onto yellow legal paper and making Roy Andries de Groot's *bifteck de Gruyère* and Simone Beck's *salade de broc;* now I was halfway around the world eating mangoes and being a general in the restaging of the Vietnam War! (About the only food I found edible in the Philippines were the golden, sun-bursting mangoes, sweetest fruit I've ever tasted. I had one every morning with a squeeze of lemon. The lunches on set were mostly local street food and much ground beef, reminiscent of boarding school.)

From the moment Harvey Keitel appeared on the screen in the dailies, it was clear he was the toughest soldier ever to appear in a war movie. He was actually frightening, both in person and onscreen, and seemed to me perfect casting. He wasn't an actor from New York playing at being a grunt; he was the real thing. After a few weeks' shooting and much of the movie in disarray, Francis told me he was firing Harvey "because he isn't sympathetic. We don't want to go up the river with him." I respectfully disagreed, and years later Harvey told me he was discharged because Francis wanted to put him under contract for his next venture—his own movie studio (megalomania doesn't get much more megalo)—and Harvey said no. Whatever the reason, Francis shaved his beard off over Easter weekend so he wouldn't be recognized at LAX (I was never sure exactly who would recognize him even with his beard) and snuck back into Los Angeles to recast.

"Who would you cast," he asked me, "Jack Nicholson or Marty Sheen?"

"Jack Nicholson, of course," I said.

Two days later he returned, having cast Sheen. I didn't think then and don't think now that Sheen was particularly believable as a military commander and murderer, and he had none of Keitel's mercurial ferocity; but since the movie became a theatricalized—if frequently astonishing—version of the war, he fit the style better. This was clearly an actor playing a soldier, and the movie was clearly an inspired director's vision of the war.

The production couldn't have been further behind schedule. Though it was initially slated for a three- or four-month shoot, at the end of three months, there were eight minutes of film in the can. During an early bout with the flu, Francis said weakly, "All the studios are betting against me. I don't even want to direct this anymore. I've asked about the availability of Steven Spielberg and Billy Friedkin—they're the only ones who could take this on. Well, George Lucas could, too, but he's in Africa shooting a sci-fi movie called *Star Wars*." I don't know if Francis had a change of heart or neither Friedkin nor Spielberg was available.

Spring is monsoon season in the South Pacific, and several days of pounding rain and unbelievable windstorms ransacked the Philippines. Many died in Manila, many more in the hinterlands, where we were shooting. Four of us were holed up in a completely safe house with Cyndi Wood, a former *Playboy* Playmate of the Year who had a tiny role in the movie along with two other Playmates. When the rains stopped, Francis surveyed the damage to the set. It was completely devastated. Boats, planes, huts, villages, all wiped out. After a few days of conferences, he announced a two-week hiatus for everyone. We would all be called back once the sets were rebuilt.

I was glad to get out of there and wondered whether I really wanted to finish this picture, as it looked as though it would take another year. Six weeks passed without word from the staff. Finally, a phone call from Tom Sternberg, an exec with Francis's company.

"Are you ready to go back?"

"Yes . . ." I said reluctantly.

"Good. The only thing is, U.A. is very concerned about what you're writing. They want to have a look at your notes."

"You know what that means—they want to change anything they see as unflattering. They want a puff piece."

"Maybe not. But those are the conditions. You ready?"

"Nope. I'm not doing it." He tried to talk me into going back, but returning would have been spineless.

I didn't go back and am glad I didn't. As Francis later said, "Little by little, we all went crazy." Stories that poured out of there indicated a crew gone berserk, lots of drugs, general looniness. Francis's wife, Ellie, who had been making a documentary about the movie, ended up writing the book about the making of the movie. When *Apocalypse Now* opened in 1979, it drew wildly conflicting reviews but was generally considered a major work by a major director and wound up an enormous success. After defying odds and gods, Francis felt, with some justification, that he could do anything. Although he was the first (aside from John Wayne) to start a movie about the war, he wasn't the first to release one. Michael Cimino, who began shooting after Francis, stole much of the *Apocalypse* thunder. His *Deer Hunter* was a financial and critical success, going on to win the Oscar for best picture (not that Oscars necessarily bestow critical merit; they usually indicate more heat than light).

I didn't talk to Francis for fifteen years. Though we'd been as close as two people not married to each other could be for three months, he never phoned or wrote after I'd said I wouldn't be returning. Though he's only two years older than I, his entrepreneurial soul reminded me of Dad's, and so he became something of an unwitting father figure. Oddly enough, when we got together in the early nineties, he followed through on his earlier plan, having convinced CBS that it should air a reworking of *Yanks 3 Detroit 0 Top of the 7th* at Dodger Stadium, live. Jack Nicholson was too old, but Kevin Kline and Alec Baldwin weren't. We spent several months rewriting the script on and off, only to have Francis abandon the project at the last minute in favor of an expensive production of *Pinocchio*, a pet project of his, in France, which never happened, either.

A few months after leaving the Philippines, I started a play centered around four men and a Playmate, working in the Philippines on a movie called *Parabola of Death*, who are stranded in a house during a typhoon with little to do but torment one another. At the end of the second act, the production designer, frustrated by the Playmate's refusal to sleep with him, attacks her and beats her savagely. In the third act, she turns the tables: Not only is she paid off handsomely by the all-powerful director, but she gets to beat up the designer.

The play was called *Geniuses*, and I hoped it was funny and dark and a little scary. The structure was based on Shaw's *The Devil's Disciple*, complete with a deus ex machina in the form of the director (my version of Shaw's Gentle-manly Johnny Burgoyne). It was turned down at every theatre in New York—except Playwrights Horizons, then run by André Bishop, who was in the process of becoming the most important producer off-Broadway after Joe Papp. *Geniuses* was preceded at his theatre by Chris Durang's *Sister Mary Ig-natius Explains It All for You* and A. R. Gurney's *The Dining Room*, and was fol-lowed almost immediately by the amazing musicals *Herringbone* and *Sunday in the Park with George*. André knew exactly what to do with my play and sug-gested Gerald Gutierrez as director, which was exactly right.

Geniuses received strong support from *The New York Times*, first from Mel Gussow, then Walter Kerr, and it ran for nearly a year. In the second act the men gather 'round to feast on dog—a Filipino specialty that I tried once and found highly agreeable and rather sweet (and actually environmental, since there were thousands of stray dogs running around the Filipino backwaters where *Apocalypse* was shooting).

Dad came to the opening night and walked away with several copies of the *Times* review under his arm and was, I think, pretty proud. Francis heard about the play and was reportedly apoplectic. I assume he felt betrayed by its satirical perspective—he thought he had the copyright on what happened offscreen in the Philippines as well as on. (Actually, he had neither—no direc-tor does. The studio owns the copyright to the property. God owns the copy-right to what happens offscreen.) Francis was also angered, so I heard, because he assumed the production designer Dean Tavoularis, his great friend in real life, was made the assailant in the play. We've never talked about it.

SIMPLIFIED SHRIMP TOAST À LA ROTHSCHILD

(Adapted from La Cuisine, *by Raymond Oliver, Tudor, 1969)*

4 slices firm white bread, crustless, 1 ½ inches thick

4 tablespoons peanut oil

½ cup butter

1 pound small shrimp (rock shrimp preferred)

2 tablespoons minced shallots

1 medium onion, minced

1 carrot, minced

1 tablespoon tomato paste

½ cup dry white wine

¾ cup fish stock or clam juice

1 bouquet garni

Salt and pepper

2 tablespoons crème fraîche

2 tablespoons Cognac

¼ cup grated Gruyère cheese

4 thin slices truffle

1. Scoop out center of each slice of bread so it looks like a lidless little box. Sauté each box on all sides until crisp and golden in 3 tablespoons of the oil and 3 tablespoons of the butter, then drain on paper towel or rack.

2. Shell the shrimp, then pound the shells to a paste in a mortar or whiz them in a blender.

3. Cook shallots, onion, and carrot until golden in 1 tablespoon each of oil and butter. Mix in the shrimp-shell paste, cook for 3 minutes, then add tomato paste, wine, fish stock or clam juice, and bouquet garni. Cover and simmer over low heat for 20 minutes, then strain into another saucepan and reduce to ¾ cup. Add salt and pepper.

4. Sauté the shrimp in 3 tablespoons of the butter until just barely pink, then transfer them to the sauce and heat for another minute. Remove the shrimp with a slotted spoon and divide them evenly into the bread boxes.

5. Stir crème fraîche into sauce, then the Cognac, and bring to a final boil. If sauce is runny, reduce further. Remove from heat, add remaining butter in bits, and ladle sauce over shrimp. Top with grated cheese and a truffle slice and brown quickly under a broiler.

YIELD: 4 servings.

Starter Marriage

~~~~~~~~~~

S HORTLY AFTER LEAVING the Philippines in 1976, I had said to my friend Jack Temchin, "I'm tired of dating all these show-business people. I want an heiress!" Remarkably, Jack produced one. He had been to college with her. I made countless phone calls to Chatzie Kirk and received a few back, but it took months for us to get together. I finally learned how to use the post office to my advantage: Two funny letters actually convinced her she should drop everything and meet me.

The decade was fast, the sexual revolution (Part 8,403) in full swing, AIDS only an undercurrent. Usually the idea (mine, anyway) was to open a bottle of wine and as quickly as possible start convincing the woman I was with to spend the night. This worked exactly 24% of the time, which meant it didn't 76% of the time. When Charlotte walked into my apartment on West End Avenue and said, "Water," when I asked her what she'd like to drink, I knew this was not your typical seventies girl. She was striking, with an angular jaw and splendid cheekbones and a carriage that exuded confidence, even arrogance, and professional success. She possessed a selectively photographic memory, was much smarter than I was, and was, in the best sense of the word, a dilettante. She knew about art and architecture (minor at Vassar, when it was the women's Yale), classical music, literature, history, politics local and international, sports (played several), had been president of her high school senior class, and made the impression on everyone she met that she was a woman destined for glory. She had formed a producing company with a partner, and wanted to become the next Sol Hurok, impresario of classical music and dance events. She loved to talk, and to listen, and to argue, as did I. I'd never met anyone like her.

As far as I was concerned, girls had long graduated from biological curiosities to potential lifelong companions and inspirations. I was thirty-four when I met Charlotte but had been part of only two long-term relationships. I think I was so tentative because I had grown up surrounded by divorced and single women. Unfortunately, like a good liberal, I could see both sides of my parents' divorce. I could see that Mother felt betrayed and wounded, and I could see that Dad felt tricked and gypped. My solution was simplified Chekhovian: work! If a woman worked as hard as a man and was treated equally, she would be less susceptible to the swooning depressions that had swallowed up Mother, and she would be able to stand on her own two feet financially, therefore having no need to bankrupt and infuriate her husband. I never thought to substitute the word *desire* for *need*.

I had been a feminist for as long as I could remember—but not one with an agenda Robin Morgan or Kitty McKinnon would appreciate. I believed not only should women be allowed to work, they should be forced to work just as men are (not by law, but by custom), thereby protecting themselves from dependency. Though Chekhov meant it ironically, I didn't: Work made people value themselves. I didn't want more women winding up like Mother. Later, when some critics (in Los Angeles, of course) criticized *Geniuses* as sexist for showing a vapid blond woman beaten up onstage, my response was that yes, she is, but by the end of the play she has fought back and emerged victorious— she hasn't stayed in bed like Sarah Crouse or collapsed onto psychiatric couches like Mother. Many feminists of that time would rather women be defeated by men and become martyrs to be pitied. Not my brand of feminism. And Charlotte was a living example of it. Her own vivacity, coupled with her family's comfort level, meant (in my simplistic interpretation) that I'd never need worry about her passivity or depression or financial dependency. She would always stand on her own two feet and perhaps exorcise my own temptations toward narcissism and depression.

Her family was as impressive as she was: handsome, as aristocratic as a southern family can be, immensely entertaining, athletic, filled with the confidence of the blessed (if not the chosen), Ivy Leaguers all; and most important, it was functional. They loved one another.

Cf.

Charlotte and I went to the theatre and the movies, and on trips to Europe, the Maryland shore, and California. Once things got going after a month or two, we ate dinner together almost every night. We each had wagonloads of friends and they all had to be introduced. We briefly tried cooking together, but the competition was fierce and we became testy. We examined this to see if it was symptomatic of deeper troubles. I worked out of my apartment—by then a three-bedroom in the Village—and had more time to cook, not to mention read up on how to cook. She saw what cooking meant to me and gave it up agreeably (I think) in exchange for making the apartment look beautiful when we had some of our wagonloads over to eat and watch the World Series or an election or the Oscars. And always, there was provocative conversation. Both of us were sensualists, but our lives were liveliest above the neck.

Shortly before proposing, I went to her apartment on a perfect spring day with two truffles poached in a combination of champagne and sherry, then smothered with a mousse of foie gras and placed inside puff pastry with a thin slice of ham. I baked them in her oven, and her response to this extraordinary dish, called *truffes en feuilletage Cendrillon* (Cinderella Truffles), from the kitchens of the Parisian restaurant Lasserre, was so appreciative and sexual that the afternoon was gone completely, and I knew this match would work.

A few weeks before or after we were married, Charlotte's producing company failed. I don't know how; I reasoned it was overambitious to expect windfall profits from producing John Curry, the Olympic Gold Medal–winning, classically trained ice dancer, and the Royal Danish Ballet. Her partner grumbled about something Charlotte had done, but I never found out what it was. I assumed the whole thing was a minor setback, and that she would entrepreneur another venture right away. She never did.

When I was talking to my cousin Lee about her failed first marriage and some disappointments in her second, she had told me, "Everything is there in front of you right at the beginning. You just don't choose to see some of it. You choose to keep the bad things in the background, out of focus, while all the good things about the person are in ECU (extreme close-up). But it's all there. Then, as the years go by, the background comes forward into focus"—she moved her hands, one sliding far in front of the other, indicating a near image receding—"and the ECU goes into the background."

Charlotte and I both thought we had our focuses sharp, and we were married on June 10, 1978, at Grace Church in New York City, the Reverend Paul Zahl presiding. The place was full, the day a cool and sunny seventy-four degrees. Oliver didn't drop the ring, and the bride and groom rode uptown in a hansom cab, she looking like a Victorian angel, he wearing her father's top hat.

HOW TO GET A WOMAN TO MARRY YOU

Truffes en Feuilletage Cendrillon (Cinderella Truffles)
(From Secrets of the Great French Restaurants by Louisette Bertholle, Macmillan, 1974)

Four 1 ½-ounce truffles, fresh (brushed and peeled) or canned
1 cup dry champagne
¼ cup sherry
3 ounces fresh or canned *mousse de foie gras*
4 ounces puff pastry
4 thin slices boiled, sliced ham
1 egg yolk, beaten and diluted with 2 drops of water

1. Preheat oven to 350 degrees.
2. Poach truffles gently in champagne and sherry 15 minutes. Cool. Mash foie gras with a fork and coat each truffle evenly with it.
3. Roll pastry into a 16-inch square and divide into four parts. Place a slice of ham on each sheet and a coated truffle in the center of the slice.

4. Moisten pastry corners and pinch them together to seal, twisting at the top to form a bundle. Brush each bundle with egg yolk and bake on a baking sheet for 15 minutes or until golden brown.

5. Serve immediately on a dish lined with a white napkin.

YIELD: 4 servings.

Birthday Nut

~~~~~~~~~~

DID YOU PHOTOGRAPH your first child more than the succeeding
one(s)? If he was a boy, did you believe him the only one ever born
destined to play the violin, quarterback the Giants, read at six months, speak
Czech at two? I did.

Frank was born in 1980 during performances of our well-intentioned but
ridiculously inept revue of the songs of the great Broadway and movie composer Jule Styne. Jule composed the scores for *Gentlemen Prefer Blondes, Peter
Pan, Gypsy, Funny Girl,* and a bunch of others. He also won an Oscar for the
treacly title song of *Three Coins in the Fountain,* one of his weaker movie efforts.

Our show, which Jule called with a somewhat wooden ear *Styne After Styne,*
was produced at the Manhattan Theatre Club, hot on the heels of its success
with *Ain't Misbehavin'.* It had been decided that our show needed a book—
even though we all should have realized that one of the reasons for *Ain't Misbehavin's* success was its lack of a single line of dialogue. Just all those
wonderful Fats Waller songs exuberantly sung by a sensational cast.

The highlight of the rehearsal period for me came with what seemed like
my eighty-seventh rewrite of the very inane concept dreamed up by the director, Fritz Holt, and agreed to by me because I couldn't think of anything better. I also couldn't think of anything worse: A group of show guys and gals are
about to put on a musical, but gosh darn it, lacking an eleven-o'-clock number,
the guys 'n' gals sing Jule's catalog, before—eureka, at the eleventh hour—
finding one. This simple-minded story line was augmented by unmemorable
staging and a competent but unexciting cast.

Jule didn't like Rewrite #87, and said he was thinking of withdrawing the show. "Oh, this version is shit," the artistic director, Lynne Meadow, said to Jule in front of me, endearing her to me forever, "but the show will work any-way." Jule was convinced because he wanted to be convinced, but the show *didn't* work anyway (musicals with bad books never do). The rehearsals had been unpleasant, the previews frustrating, the reviews dismissive.

Normally, I would have been wrecked, but our son's birth superseded everything, and against my will I became a jubilant and dutiful—if somewhat selfish—father. After a lengthy discussion of names, Charlotte said, "Let's name him Frank, after your uncle." When I called Uncle Frank to tell him, he broke down. Many tears followed on both ends of the phone.

I had heard about babies before Frank was born but hadn't had much business with them and considered them as dangerous to hold as porcu-pines (still do, sort of). At his birth, I concluded that he was unique—and not by the standards of *Rosemary's Baby*. Had there ever been such fascinat-ingly tiny feet, intricately wrinkled fingers, ebullient smiles, or riveting breathing even while asleep? I photographed and videoed incessantly and still have a forty-minute tape of my giving him a bath that would rival Warhol's *Empire* for torpor-inducement. I submitted adorable head shots to modeling agents and, when he wasn't chosen, turned my back on show biz forever and deliberately sabotaged most of the scripts I was then writing. (Unfortunately, the studios decided it wasn't so deliberate.) I put his name up for Harrow and Eton and insisted that he be clothed by Rowe's of Bond Street, a ridiculously expensive store specializing in Spoiled Children's Clothes so fancy that they were suitable only for coronations—and which were outgrown in a matchstrike.

I also determined that he would have an epicure's palate and so made sure all his food was fresh and puréed by hand, occasionally sprinkling it with sea-sonings that might have pleased Fredy Girardet but didn't particularly please Frank. Charlotte, the eldest of four children, was well aware that there were other babies besides Frank but humored me nonetheless, even allowing me to make his first three birthday cakes with chestnuts.

I'd always thought chestnuts were indigenous to France, because that's where I discovered them, on a break from LAMDA. The trees grow all over the

world, but a blight wiped out most of our American ones in the early twentieth century, forcing us to import fresh chestnuts from Europe.

Here, we generally associate them with Christmas and roasting, thanks in
no small part to Mel Tormé's song about Jack Frost nipping at your nose. But
in French hands they become a marvel of subtlety. The *mont blancs* (puréed
with cream), *coupe aux marrons* (in syrup, over ice cream), and the fat and crys-
tallized *marrons glacés* (candied) from Lyons all exploit the natural sugar of
chestnuts, and by luck or the lack of it, dessert served as my introduction to
them. I loved their smooth, starchy taste (they have less oil than other nuts)
and crumbly texture and the way sugars and syrups clung to them, softening
them in sweet embrace. Years later, I made many friends by bringing forth a
bavarois Clermont, a spectacular Bavarian cream studded with candied chestnuts and surrounded by candied chestnuts dipped in chocolate—which was
also served to Coppola.

Since then, I've discovered the virtue of unsweetened chestnuts, as in the
delicious soup devised by Patricia Yeo at the departed AZ restaurant and a
supremely complex chestnut-flour farfalle that Alain Ducasse surrounds with
slivers of pork breast, tiny chicken quenelles, cèpes, foie-gras grease, white-
truffle shavings, and more chestnuts. It wouldn't take you or me more than
three days to make, but it is one of the great dishes in New York. You should
sell the family liver and go to the restaurant and order it.

If there's a chestnut on a restaurant menu, I order it.

Chestnuts are so special and so difficult to deal with—it's practically impossible to shell them without crushing the meat—that they have their own
knife (with a curved, sharp edge) and their own roasting pan (with small per-
forations so the shells won't explode). Neither is of much use for anything
else. Slitting the shells and roasting the chestnuts is the traditional method of
separating one from the other, but the shells may also be slit and the nuts
dropped into 350-degree oil for twenty minutes and then cooled.

Back when Frank was about to be a year old, I determined that the best
was almost good enough for him and came up with an old recipe from the legendary French chef Paul Bocuse for a *gâteau aux marrons* that isn't difficult but
is unusual and sets off the nut's mild and chewy pleasures with a fail-safe film
of chocolate. And though it can be made with the more common chestnuts in

syrup, which you then purée, or a can of the purée itself, I opted for the billion-dollar candied version. I whipped it up for him and several of his closest one-year-old associates, and he wolfed it right down. So did his buddies. Their parents were amazed that this would be served as a birthday cake for onegenarians, but I thought, superciliously, What else would you expect for a Czech-speaking, violin-playing pro quarterback? Besides, Payard Patisserie hadn't opened yet. At his second birthday, the scene repeated itself, happy children gulping down this special dessert and parents who stayed just to taste it.

On his third birthday, however, a little snag developed. Flanked by apparently wiser friends, Frank dove into his birthday cake with glee once more, having advertised it at nursery school for days. He then asked rhetorically, "Isn't this great?" and his best friend, Jasper or Julian or Kenneth or something, took one bite, made a face as if he'd just swallowed a full glass of soy sauce, and emitted a noise something like "Eeeyoueccccchhh!" He dropped his fork and said, "This is *awful!*" Frank, who is today quite a freethinker and dazzles and infuriates the Upper West Side with his contrarian views on international politics, was not immune to peer pressure at age three. He suddenly realized that he was eating something weird, possibly poisonous, something that might lose him friends, and that certainly had no place in the junk-food duchy to which he'd become accustomed (his father having sometime before given up on the puréeing of fresh produce, unable to fight what was served at nursery school and in other people's homes). He looked at the *gâteau* in shock, as if double-crossed, and dropped his fork. All of his friends dropped their forks. We lived near Washington Square, but you could hear the crashing of cutlery in Washington Heights. Amid demands for ice cream and "real" cake, the wheels quickly came off the party.

I quietly put the recipe away in a drawer and never had the nerve to try it out on him again—or on his less-photographed but equally adored younger brother, Eddie.

Until '02.

Mindful that fall and winter—and particularly Christmas—are optimal seasons for the warmth and earthiness of chestnuts savory or sweet, and that nineteen years had passed since that "friend" brought my son's culinary world (and belief in his father's taste) crashing all around, I decided to spring the cake on Frank's considerably more experimental palate once more. The occasion wasn't Frank's birthday but his soon-to-be stepbrother Dodge's. Dodge Landesman has exceptionally precocious taste buds. And so, with some trepidation, I looked up the old concoction, scoured the city for *marrons glacés* (a seriously disappearing breed but available at Payard and Fauchon), whipped up batter for two cakes, and melted chocolate. My memory had rusted. The timing was off (longer baking was required), and I laid the chocolate on too thick, but the cakes were a success. "Great, Dad!" Frank exclaimed. Both he and twelve-year-old Dodge, whose mother, Red, I was main-squeezing—and the sixteen grown-up guests—polished off their cake and nibbled the dishes clean.

However, if I was expecting a Proustian remembrance, it didn't happen. Frank didn't recall that third birthday (or the preceding two), which once again made clear to me that individual moments shared by parent and child are so evanescent and subjective that what is indelible and traumatic to one might fail to crease the brain of the other. But that wouldn't be the worst thing.

GÂTEAU AUX MARRONS

1 cup candied chestnuts (*marrons glacés*), or drained chestnuts in syrup, or chestnut cream or spread

4 tablespoons unsalted butter, plus extra for greasing the pan

6 tablespoons heavy cream

4 eggs, separated

4 ounces bittersweet chocolate

1 teaspoon apricot jam

5 or 6 macaroons (preferably made with pine nuts), for garnish

5 or 6 *marrons glacés*, for garnish

1. Preheat the oven to 350 degrees. Butter an 8-inch round cake pan and line with a round of buttered parchment paper.

2. Purée the chestnuts in a food processor. Add the butter and cream and process until smooth. With the machine running, add the egg yolks, one at a time. Transfer the mixture to a large bowl. Beat the egg whites until stiff and fold into the mixture just until blended. Pour into the pan and smooth the top. Bake until the cake is firm to the touch, 30–40 minutes. Cool completely on a wire rack, then place on a serving dish.

3. Melt the chocolate in a double boiler and stir in the jam and enough water to thin mixture to a spreadable consistency. Ice cake with a thin layer and decorate with macaroons and *marrons glacés*.

YIELD: 6 to 8 servings.

SQUASH-AND-CHESTNUT SOUP WITH CHIPOTLE CREAM
(Adapted from AZ)

For the chipotle cream
1 cup ruby port
½ cup dry red wine
1 teaspoon chipotle peppers in adobo sauce or crushed dried chipotles
2 tablespoons tomato paste
1 cup crème fraîche or sour cream

For the soup
2 ½ pounds kabocha, acorn, or butternut squash
2 quarts chicken stock
10 ounces whole chestnuts (before peeled), roasted and peeled
2 tablespoons pure maple syrup
Kosher salt and freshly ground black pepper to taste

1. Combine the port, wine, chipotles, and tomato paste in a medium saucepan, bring to a boil, and then simmer until the mixture is a thick paste, about 15 minutes. Let cool, then whisk in the crème fraîche and refrigerate until serving.

2. Preheat the oven to 350 degrees. Cut the squash in half lengthwise and remove the seeds. Place cut-side down on a foil-lined baking sheet and bake
   until soft, about 1 hour. When the squash is cool, scoop out the flesh and
   place 6 cups in a large saucepan. Add the stock and the chestnuts and simmer until the chestnuts are soft, about 30 minutes. Stir in the syrup and
   purée with a hand blender or in batches in a blender. Return to the
   saucepan and season to taste.

3. Reheat the soup and ladle it into bowls. Drizzle with chipotle cream.

   YIELD: 8 servings.

   NOTE: The soup and cream can be made ahead and refrigerated for up to 3
   days.

Right Turn on Red

I MET FRANK RICH while he was a film critic at the *New York Post* in the late seventies, and we hit it off immediately. We shared a great interest in movies, food, and the theatre; in fact, I was surprised when he told me he had wanted for years to be the drama critic at the *Times*. He found plays more exciting than movies (I didn't then but do now), and, having grown up in D.C. in New York's cultural shadow, knew only too well that there were hundreds of film critics across the country—but only one important theatre critic. He is a great raconteur and conversationalist, and I considered him a good friend. I couldn't have predicted then that he would wind up the most popular general columnist at the paper twenty-five years later.

Still, I was surprised when he told me during dinner one night that the *Times* had made him an offer to be a second-string critic with no promise of taking over Walter Kerr's position when Kerr retired a few years down the road. As it turned out, Kerr had a heart attack, and after a little jockeying, Frank was appointed chief drama critic within months of moving to the *Times*.

Frank and I went to the theatre several times, though not nearly as frequently as he went with his friend Rafael Yglesias; the two ditched their wives every Thursday night, saw something Frank was to review, and then had dinner and got pleasantly drunk, sometimes with me tagging along at least for the food and booze. Elaine's was the favored watering hole for a year or two, then Orso was.

Frank disqualified himself from reviewing *Geniuses* because he'd read an early draft of it, but Gussow's review was so uncharacteristically effusive, it read as though Frank had given Mel some of his Kool-Aid.

André Bishop opened *Geniuses* at Playwrights Horizons less than a year after the little-noted but still embarrassing *Styne After Styne*, and since Hollywood likes plays that take notice of it, pro or con, the studios came calling.

Rafe Yglesias and his wife, Margaret, lived two blocks from Charlotte and son Frank and me, and we became instant friends. As Frank Rich and I fenced over his reviewing *Geniuses*, Rafe and I became closer. Rafe had dropped out of school at fifteen, written his first novel at sixteen, and had three novels published by the time he was twenty-one. He is smart and snappy and funny, and a good friend to this day, unless we get into a political discussion, at which point he becomes a serious combatant.

Although he had the markings of a New York liberal when I met him, he told me many times, "I'm not a liberal, I'm a Marxist." But he was the only cheerful one I'd ever met. I was becoming suspicious of the Left's hypocrisy: Everyone from every campaign seemed primarily interested in making lots of money and sending their children to the best private schools while vehemently criticizing greedy capitalists and privileged children. Most of my friends were great advocates for civil rights but no one actually knew anyone black. And for all the talk of peace-and-love, the malicious treatment of returning Vietnam veterans was appalling. The Left's self-righteousness seemed as anal and dictatorial as the Right's (hello, Elia Kazan), and every bit as obsessed with controlling other people's lives.

In 1974, William Shockley, who had won the Nobel Prize for physics some years earlier, was invited to speak at Yale about his theory that intelligence was determined by racial genetics. This flew in the face of everything I had been taught and believed, and I thought this excuse for segregation had been disproved years earlier. But since the question lurks at the unmentionable core of every racial debate (Are whites genetically smarter than blacks? Are Asians smarter than whites? Are Calcuttans born with a better business gene?), I was interested in hearing it disproved again, as it no doubt should be at least once per generation in order to set it to rest. But student Lefties at Yale not only protested Shockley's appearance, they heckled him so thoroughly that he was unable to speak. This paradoxically gave his theory new currency: What were the students so afraid of? Why wouldn't they allow him to voice these opinions and have them countered? I began to see more hypocrisy on the Left, which insists on free speech but, as Nat Hentoff so clearly limns in *Free Speech for Me but Not for Thee*, frequently won't tolerate the practice of it. It is precisely this unwitting hypocrisy—and the delusion that their actions were taken "for the greater good" (i.e., to prevent innocent victims from being exposed to Shockley's unbearable ideas)—that mushroomed into the culturally crippling political correctness of the last thirty years.

If my mother and sister didn't discuss politics growing up, Rafe's family had all the time, it seemed, so he was considerably more invested in it than I had ever been, even though I'd gone out and campaigned for mine. My religion was a sloppy Episcopalianism; his was an unflinching Marxism. As long as he and I stayed off the subject, we couldn't have been more congenial and frequently hilarious together. When I took an office two stories below his on East Eleventh Street, we had lunch several times a week. He was continuing to write novels and, together with his half-brother, Lewis Cole, made screenplay deals, though none were produced.

When Hollywood showed serious interest in me after *Geniuses* opened, I asked for help. I'd been an avid moviegoer, hookeying through many a tutoring-school afternoon, and had written a couple of passionate but formless screenplays. I didn't really know how they worked. At breakfast one morning, Rafe sat me down over a bagel and smoked salmon (oh, all right, lox), and said, "The first and most important thing you need to know is that all screenplays can be broken down into three acts." The scales fell from my eyes. Next? "There are many more characters in a movie than there are in a play." Of course, and not just because Actors Equity charges too much per actor. Unless you're a salmon, you see many more people in the course of a day than you see onstage in a play not by Sydney Kingsley. "Characters don't talk nearly as much as they do in plays." That much I knew. "Scenes are much shorter." Yup. "There must be conflict. There must be jeopardy. There must be somebody to root for, and there must be change." Though it sounds simple, it was exactly the structural underpinning I needed to know about.

"Also, screenplays are fraudulent. Producers and executives always want the leading characters to be sympathetic, and let's face it, people basically aren't sympathetic." He laughed in triumph.

I went to Hollywood and commuted for most of the eighties. After months of flailing around with a script, I somehow managed to get a Columbia project called *Micki & Maude* right. Dudley Moore was in my mind during the writing of it—and, by God, they cast him and made the movie. A writer is never as hot as when he's written a script that's being made—not *has been* made (unless it's hugely successful), but *is being made*. If the movie has been made, it's a real object with real success or lack of it, as measured by the box office. But in Hollywood, fantasy is the stuff of life, and everyone's reputation becomes better or worse than the wearer of that reputation could ever possibly be. Before *Micki & Maude* was released, I had two other assignments, and they were also green-lighted. During the next five years, I wrote five movies that were produced—three written by me alone, one a rewrite, and one that was rewritten by someone who turned it into pap. All but one were signed before *Micki & Maude* was even released.

I'd signed on with a business manager when my first screenplays hit, and he was worth every percentage point he took. Not only did his real estate advice prove wise and his investments pay handsomely, he looked after all the details of the money, which, now, since I can no longer afford him, consumes 10–20% of my day. He is just as lively today as he was twenty years ago, and flourishing.

THE FABULOUS BAKER BOY

CLOSE YOUR EYES and listen to him, and you're back under the Third Avenue El in a white T-shirt on a roasting summer's day with the guys, mostly Jewish or Italian, smoking Luckys and screaming about ball and Marciano and money, whistling at the skirts. WW2 just ended, your hair's all curly, you're about to marry your best girl, and the world is yer erster. And now, fifty-five years later, in his kitchen, after a thirteen-hour day in the office—"Four hundred fights I got into today! Four hundred!"—Bert Padell relaxes by baking, a stress reduction probably unimaginable back in the days under the El.

Midnight baker, poet, former Yankee batboy, friend of DiMaggio and Mantle, Joe Cocker and Montgomery Clift, business manager and lawyer to eminent enterprises as varied as Britney Spears, Jackie Mason, John Berendt, Mikhail Baryshnikov, P. Diddy, the rapper Rakim, and the restaurants of Robert De Niro (but not De Niro himself), Bert is as New York a New Yorker as New York has ever Yorked. Sometimes as soft-spoken as a courtier, he is usually a walking exclamation point, either surprised or outraged. And I love talking to him.

While stirring a pound of chunked chocolate into a pound of butter melting over the heat of his electric stove one night in 2003, Bert tells me about Madonna's lawsuit against him in 1999: "The BBC kept trying to get me to say something bad about her, but I wouldn't." He nudges the chocolate gently with a spoon. "Go slow now—don't burn it." He wheels around and pours sugar into a stainless-steel bowl filled with eggs. " 'But I got nothing against the woman,' I told them. 'Most people would say something bad about her,' this interviewer kept prodding me, and I said to him, 'Well, I'm not most people.' "

As they said in the thirties, I'll tell the world.

For years his pastries went—free—to several of the restaurants he handled (most notably, One if By Land, Two if By Sea), but now he bakes mostly for his family. He used to start at eleven at night and finish up at two but now limits that to Fridays. Tonight he is making chocolate-chip cookies and the densest, creamiest, most-likely-to-make-your-cardiologist-rich chocolate cake ever to be unavailable to the public (until now).

An easy-listenin' version of "You Were Meant for Me" plays softly on the radio, followed by "Everything's Up to Date in Kansas City" and a bunch of other show tunes. Would Jellybean Benitez, Kid Creole, and Alicia Keys drop themselves from Bert's client list if they were aware of his musical tastes? Doubtful. And what about rap? "I don't like it, but I accept it," he says, paddling the eggs in his Dito Dean mixer. Bert's is not the kitchen of a pro but of a successful couple whose kids have moved out—which he is one of and who have. "When I first started baking, all my people were guinea pigs. I'd bring an apple pie into the office, and when it fell on the floor and broke the floor, they'd say how much they liked it. So I didn't know who liked what.

"My tofu cheesecake was good, but then one night by accident—by accident!—I put it in the freezer, and that was it! I found the secret of making it jell. See? You understand what I'm saying? You have to learn and learn." Bitten by the pastry bug, Bert went to the Culinary Institute of America in Hyde Park, which normally turns out cookie-cutter chefs prepared to oversee two hundred covers at a big hotel, and took a weeklong accelerated course—what else would you expect from someone who gets into four hundred fights a day?

"A lotta people like the taste of coffee with chocolate," he says, anticipating my own recent addiction—and pouring boiling water into espresso powder—nothing better than the darkest 91% chocolate mixed with a black espresso. He pours the coffee, then the chocolate and butter, into the eggs, lets the mixer work until the batter is the texture of heavy cream, and looks at me impishly. "Are you ready?" he asks. I nod, and he pours the mixture into a buttered and floured springform pan and carefully walks it to his oven. It's soupy, and there's a danger of spilling.

After baking the cake, he refrigerates it for thirty minutes, then gives it to me and kicks me out with an admonition: "Don't eat it till it's cool. Hot cake is very bad for you." I never heard that one before, so on my way home, I swipe a finger through it and suck—it's a cream dream!—and sleep the sleep of the just with no digestive eruptions.

The next two days running, Bert phones to remind me to whip the tofu for his famous cheesecake until it's very creamy and to take the chocolate cake out of the fridge twelve to twenty-four hours before serving.

A few days later, having made the cheesecake—warmly and incredulously received by friends for its lightness and lack of tofuishness—I visit his offices, a full floor opposite the Carnegie Towers.

There's not an inch of space on the walls—they're covered with hundreds of gold and platinum records he's been involved with, autographed posters and pictures not only of his clients but of presidents FDR, JFK, RMN, GRF, and WJC. ("I don't take sides in politics," he says.) There is a private bathroom with a letter about personal freedom from Charlie Chaplin, a conference room filled with hundreds of signed photographs from Cy Young and

Christy Mathewson and just about every Yankee ever as well as sixty-five baseball bats, belonging to everyone from Stan Musial to Garth Brooks (who once went to spring training with the Mets). The most extraordinary artifact is a framed collection of 1937 Yankee photographs, *with each player's original signed contract!*

I had asked Bobby, Bert's wife of forty-four years, mother of their three children, grandmother of six, and an interior decorator, where she thought his collecting mania stemmed from. "He didn't have when he was a kid," she said, "so now he can, and he gets everything." My genes kick in: another self-made man.

He is seated about three feet from two secretaries. Liz has been with him for thirty-three years, Douglas only two. Everyone talks on various phones at the same time, and between Bert's instructions to me about the proper way to serve pinwheel cookies, he illustrates what a business manager does besides crunch numbers.

He sprinkles his sentences with a vocabulary enriched not only by a childhood in the Bronx but by his 1949–50 Yankee batboy stint, which job he acquired when his predecessor was killed in a hunting accident. (Bert secured his place in the record books in the sky by being the first batboy ever ejected from a game for stealing signs from the opposing team's catcher and coaches.) One word in particular—which I'll euphemize as "handkerchief" but whose referent wouldn't get past the elevator operator of a family publication—is used about as often as most people use *the*.

"Seymour," he shouts into the phone, "the guy can't appear in a concert, he's in the handkerchiefin' hospital! He's got no leg! . . . But, but, he's got no handkerchiefin' leg! It was a terrible accident! The bone is lying there in the street!"

An accountant who hasn't been putting in enough office hours is reprimanded in front of me. When he leaves, Bert says: "He's been doing that a long time. The nicer you are, they put a bullet up your keister."

Another call comes in on the speakerphone. "That house she moved into, the hot-water heater doesn't work. Do you get a warranty with a used house?" the caller asks.

"You don't call a house 'a used house,'" Bert says. "It's a resale. And no, there's no warranty on a house. But call up the guy who sold it and tell him there is."

Liz places a call for him, and he turns courtly. "Marty, I'm sorry for breaking your chops the other day. . . . No, but I'm saying I'm sorry. And I sent him the mortgage." An employee rushes in to say the underwriter of a client's insurance policy has been pocketing the premiums but not paying the benefits. Bert picks up the phone and gets the underwriter's broker on the horn. "You tell that underwriter guy I want him in this office Monday or I'm going to the handkerchiefin' district attorney and file a complaint." (Lots of protests from the phone.) "You tell him I'm going to ask the handkerchiefin' DISTRICT AT-TORNEY to examine his books. Do you understand? . . . YOU DON'T UN-DERSTAND! HE'S GOING TO JAIL!!" He hangs up and says to me, "You gotta get your demand in first—that keeps them on the defensive, which is what you want." Liz gets him another number, and his voice drops in decibels as he becomes concerned. "Hi. I need a good lawyer to represent someone's son against his mother. He's in a psychological ward, poor kid."

And it's then I remember why his clients pay him the 5 percent—it's not just for keeping their accounts straight and their taxes paid and the hot-water heaters repaired; it's because he connects with them. He has a heart as big as the Bronx—just read some of that poetry—and he's an unflagging optimist.

Eighty-six problems confronted and solved, more or less, in an hour. "Sometimes I think I should go to handkerchiefin' China and be a monk and help everybody—I never seen such a business where everybody just wants one handkerchiefin' thing."

He has a lunch date, and I walk him to the street. "Bert, I have two questions. First, what happened with Madonna?"

"She sued me for two-point-five million dollars because New York State said she'd been living here for a hundred and eighty-three days and I had her in California." He won't tell me the figures, but they settled. He smiles confidentially. "But it wasn't very smart of her people to do. What's the other question?"

"Did the Giants steal the signs from the Dodgers in the '51 playoffs? Did Thomson know Branca was going to throw a fastball?"

"Of course," Bert says—no question. "They did it from the outfield, with binoculars. Now don't forget to take that cheesecake outta the fridge an hour before. And bring me my handkerchiefin' pan back."

BERT PADELL'S CHOCOLATE CHOCOLATE CAKE

1 pound unsalted butter, plus extra for greasing the pan
Flour for dusting the pan
12 ounces bittersweet chocolate
4 ounces unsweetened chocolate
1 bar (3.5 ounces) milk chocolate with cappuccino filling
8 large eggs
1 cup plus 2 tablespoons sugar
2 tablespoons espresso powder dissolved in 1 cup boiling water
Whipped cream for garnish

1. Preheat the oven to 350 degrees. Butter and flour a 10-inch springform pan and line the bottom with parchment paper. Set the pan on a square of heavy-duty aluminum foil and bring the foil up around the sides of the pan to prevent leaks. Set aside.
2. Combine the butter and chocolates in a medium saucepan and melt over medium heat, whisking until smooth. Transfer to a heatproof measuring cup.
3. In the bowl of an electric mixer with the paddle attachment, beat the eggs and sugar for 5 minutes at medium-high speed. With the mixer running, pour in the espresso and beat until blended, then the butter-chocolate mixture, again beating until blended.
4. Pour the batter into the prepared pan and bake for 55 minutes. (The cake will crack around the rim.) Remove from the oven and cool on a wire rack for about 20 minutes. Cover with plastic wrap or aluminum foil and refrigerate for at least 30 minutes (or up to 1 month).
5. Twelve to 24 hours before serving, take the cake out of the refrigerator. Re-

move the sides of the pan, slide a metal spatula under the parchment paper, and slide the cake onto a serving plate. Serve with whipped cream.

Yield: 12–14 servings.

BERT PADELL'S TOFU CHEESECAKE

1 tablespoon butter, softened, plus 2 tablespoons, melted
11–12 graham crackers, crushed, or 1 ¾ cups graham-cracker crumbs
2 cups plus 2 tablespoons sugar
¼ teaspoon cinnamon
2 pounds soft (silken) tofu
1 ½ cups plain yogurt
1 teaspoon vanilla extract
3 tablespoons flour
Pinch salt
4 egg whites (½ cup)

1. Say to yourself, "No, just because it's that nasty tofu doesn't mean it can't possibly be good. Trust this guy—he tells Alice Cooper what to do with his money."
2. Roughly 36 hours before serving, preheat oven to 400 degrees. Smear the tablespoon of softened butter over bottom and sides of a 10-inch spring-form pan. Set prepared pan on a large square of heavy-duty aluminum foil and bring up foil around sides of pan to prevent leaks. Set aside.
3. In medium bowl, mix the 2 tablespoons melted butter with graham crackers, 2 tablespoons of the sugar, and cinnamon.
4. Cover the bottom of the springform pan with half the crumb mixture.
5. In a large bowl of an electric mixer, whisk the tofu until creamy, about 5 minutes at medium-high speed. Gradually beat in the 2 cups sugar, then the yogurt and vanilla. Sift in flour and salt.
6. In another mixer bowl, at medium-high speed, beat egg whites until soft peaks form when beaters are raised and fold into tofu mixture using a rub-

ber spatula. Pour batter into prepared springform and top with remaining crumbs.

7. Place in a large roasting pan and add enough boiling water to reach two thirds of the way up the sides of the pan. Bake 30 minutes. Reduce temperature to 300 degrees and bake an additional 90 minutes.

8. Remove from oven, bring to room temperature, then freeze overnight, or for at least 8 hours.

9. Defrost cake in refrigerator for 24 hours. To serve, remove cake from refrigerator 1 hour before serving. Remove sides of pan, slide a large metal spatula under parchment, and slide cake onto large, flat serving plate. Cut into slices and serve.

YIELD: 12–14 servings.

Will the Soufflé Rise?

～～～～～

WHILE I WAS proud of my plays, I was damn disappointed in my movies. Although *Micki & Maude* was respectable critically and financially, I'd really only enjoyed working on one film—*My Stepmother Is an Alien*—because its director, Richard Benjamin, was so much fun. He laughed at everything I said, and I laughed at everything he said. And the movie is loopy and out there. But Dan Aykroyd was an overweight leading man and his love scenes with Kim Basinger were creepy. The movie got moderate reviews, and opened the same weekend as the blockbuster *Twins*, starring Danny DeVito and the governor of California. It quickly fell off the radar screen. *Micki & Maude*, directed by Hollywood's most unappreciated director, Blake Edwards, wasn't any fun because Blake didn't much like me after I told him I thought one of his lines wasn't funny. It was a simple line, and a big mistake on my part: I believed him when he said he wanted to know how I felt about his rewrite, which is director-speak for "Tell me how good my rewrite is." In my version, rather than fictionalize names of minor characters, I threw in the names of people associated with Playwrights Horizons—Gurney, Durang, Wasserstein, Innaurato, Lapine, Bishop—and at the beginning of the script, while riding in the back of a limo, Dudley's character asks the chauffeur his name. "Finn, sir," the driver replies, using the composer Bill Finn's name. In response, Blake wrote that Dudley should say, "Well, Finnsir . . ." I thought it wasn't funny but looked as though it was trying to be.

"I don't think that line's funny, Blake," I said into the phone. Silence.

"Gee, I thought it was pretty funny," he said, muted. I could tell he wasn't used to being challenged. Directors aren't in Hollywood; hence the second remake of *King Kong* and the bloated length of *The New World*. But I plunged ahead. I mean, he *said* he wanted to know my opinion.

"I think it's forced. It's asking for a laugh."

"Oh," he said, and despite my being invited to all the casting sessions and many of the sets before that conversation, I wasn't invited to a single one afterward. But the movie was the best-realized of anything I wrote, both because Blake was brilliant at staging physical farce (though less so at verbal), and because Dudley Moore, the only actor since Cary Grant able to play farce with sexuality and intelligence, was its leading man.

For the record, the other pictures were *Switching Channels, Leonard Part 6,* and *The Distinguished Gentleman.*

Despite what appeared to be success, I was miserable. I'd wanted to be some kind of serious cultural force in New York, and instead was being dismissed (if mentioned at all) as a writer of trivial, throwaway comedies. I ranted about these highly enviable problems to Charlotte, but she had trouble understanding my gripes.

In 1983, our second son, Edward, was born. Frank had been a feisty baby given to waking in the middle of the night with terrors; he burned almost hyperactively. By comparison, Eddie was quiet and loving and doted on his parents. I felt both boys deserved better than New York, and probably better than me, both of which were in chaos in the eighties.

But for the first time in my life, serious money arrived on the doorstep. Oh, not Bill Gates money or, God forbid, Dadmoney, but bags of it larger than you get for writing off-Broadway plays. I bought a house on Jane Street in Manhattan. It was Charlotte's dream to raise our family in as warm and bustling a home as the fairy-tale farm on which she'd grown up, in Elkin, North Carolina. The Jane Street brownstone was built for a single family in the mid-nineteenth century but had since been converted into seven studio apartments. It now looked like a tenement. It needed a near-gut renovation, which didn't interest me. But Charlotte wanted to attack the job.

About five years, a million dollars, and 64,000 arguments later, we moved in. It was a nasty experience from beginning to end. I felt Charlotte wasn't moving fast enough, and she had complaints about me of her own. For one thing, every time I'd come home with another 10 G's, I'd see something that could be improved and would request a change—a better lighting fixture that took three weeks to order, a wider staircase when one had already been built, a ten-burner Garland industrial range with two ovens and a salamander instead of the G.E. we'd decided on. The Garland was so big and heavy it had to be disassembled outside, carried in in pieces, then reassembled inside, and there was some question whether the floor could support it. All these events caused architect and contractor alike to tear their hair out at the roots. Finally, as the thing approached completion, I looked at the back wall of the house, not unlike the artist Gully Jimpson in *The Horse's Mouth* looking at people's feet and seeing a potential canvas, and said there was nothing exciting about it. I brought in Joe D'Urso, a visionary designer, and asked for help. Joe produced three sweeping French windows that made the entire floor magical.

But I was an apartment kid who'd never lived in a house, and it was overwhelming: What do you do if the boiler goes wrong? How do you fix a roof? What's this about shoveling snow? Besides, it wasn't even finished when we moved in—not a stick of furniture in the wondrous D'Urso living room. The boys' schools and my office were on the other side of town and suddenly much farther away, and the new neighborhood was scary. Hard to believe now, since Woody Allen has christened Jane Street "the second most beautiful in New York" (I forget the first), and as of this writing it's become one of the central boulevards in the horrifically trendy, unhappily regentrified meatpacking district. It swarms with people and traffic day and night—now.

But in the late eighties, we were in the more menacing Koch-Dinkins era, and the meatpacking district was considered the transvestite-hooker capital of North America. Now I can understand the appeal of a female hooker, and of a male hooker; but I cannot for the life of me understand the appeal of a male hooker who looks like a female hooker but won't once you get to know her. But somebody can. Quite a few people can, in fact, because we found used condoms and syringes in front of our door just about every day. In addition, the police department had successfully chased the "Joints . . . loose joints!" sales force out of Washington Square Park, and it had moved west, near us. So, easily influenced by the *New York Post*, recently purchased by Rupert Murdoch, I'd return from my office every night with images of our young sons with axes in their heads. No doubt my overheated imagination presented this image as a defense against a more realistic catastrophe.

Then one winter night, I got held up at knifepoint by a pair of what seemed like eighteen-foot-tall African-Americans. They'd followed my solo self home from the subway, one as lookout, one as knife-wielding perp, and demanded money. The exchange was almost funny.

"Give it up," the wielder menaced, his foot-long jackknife glinting in the streetlight. This was shortly after Arsenio Hall popularized the expression, so I briefly thought, "You mean, applaud?" I didn't know what he meant. I really didn't. The wielder's eyes darted between me and his lookout.

"Give what up?" I said. I probably could have disarmed him with a feather, because his shoulders sagged and he came close to laughing. He was suddenly not as frightening as he was disgusted at this street-unsavvy honkie. But still scary.

"Your money," he said with contempt.

Which I gave him. Eleven Andrew Jacksons.

He was about to run off when he stopped and looked through the glass panels of our front door. I imagined that he considered for an instant forcing me to open the door and murdering my children. This was funny no longer. Then, almost whimsically, he ran.

I opened the door, not frightened but crestfallen. "What happened?" Charlotte said.

"I just got mugged. At knifepoint." I was defeated, but she wasn't.

"Call the police! Call the police right now!"

She was right. Even though there wasn't a prayer of catching them, the police came in five minutes, and together we prowled the neighborhood; no luck. By simply calling them, I felt my depression lift. I was suddenly less powerless. Active, not passive. Left to my own, I would have sulked into a stew.

A month or so later, my pocket was ripped open in Times Square and picked. The thief made off with fifteen Jacksons this time, and the change that flew about was quickly picked up by the onlookers—and pocketed.

A few months after that, I came home after a midday Sunday movie with Eddie, then age five, to find our electronics stacked in the living room—a

VCR (valuable in those days), a record player, tuner, amps—and the curtains of a living-room window blowing in the breeze. Apparently the thief heard us enter and jumped out the window. This time I called the police without any urging, and again they came in less than five minutes. The search was again futile.

I had begun to dislike the city for reasons other than its curiously personal hostility toward me and my family. Although New York is arguably the most cosmopolitan city in the world, it can also be the most provincial. It's imperious and condescending toward those who don't live there—particularly if they live somewhere between the coasts. It brags of its tolerance toward various lifestyles—unless someone disagrees with that tolerance and actually doesn't approve of abortion or gay marriage or church attendance. It touts its urbanity while disdaining those who don't share its enthusiasm. Politically, it's as close-minded as a small town in Alabama, only from a different point of view; and if you're in show business, you will asphyxiate from the lack of fresh political ideas and go deaf from the sound of lockstep.

By the end of the seventies, I was disheartened by the local and federal policies that seemed to idealize codification and restriction and the rusting of gears. The Democrats ruled all branches of federal and local New York City government in 1976 and hadn't had a fresh idea since FDR died—except for the Peace Corps and landing on the Moon. They seemed stale and claustrophobic, chanting the knee-jerk mantra that we must be more like Europe. And in New York, we were. Municipal unions controlled the city almost as much as the theatrical unions and *The New York Times* controlled Broadway. The desire to squash the appetites of those who would express themselves fully, whether in the arts or in business or in foreign policy, had led to what Jimmy Carter correctly called "a national malaise"—at least some of which he caused. It was suffocating.

In 1980, I did the unthinkable. I pulled the lever for Ronald Reagan, whose buoyancy and humor and challenge to the old way of doing things lifted my spirits. I, who had campaigned without end for Eugene McCarthy and Stanley Sheinbaum, who'd flown back to New York on Election Day, 1972, sure that my vote would help George McGovern upset Richard Nixon, who'd pulled the lever twice for Lindsay and once for—arrgghh!—Abe Beame, had come to this. I was the only one I knew who voted this way—and I knew lots of people. When I told friends, arguments inevitably followed—heated and angry arguments, as if I had insulted the Pope in a cathedralful of Catholics. This was no lighthearted matter to them. This was religion. They felt betrayed and furious.

I saw myself as entwined with the city, both clogging ourselves in cobwebs and grime, the city frozen into inaction by political correctness, the divisive racial demagoguery of Al Sharpton, and the inability to break free from union strangleholds that have led to its becoming, as of this writing, the worst state in the union in which to do business. The worst! Fiftieth! In that regard, at least, I was becoming my father's son.

I thought my friends had little curiosity regarding the rest of the country. Occasionally someone would fly to Miami for a weekend or, of course, to L.A.—but interest in finding out something about the national character, not merely the local, left them cold and contemptuous of anyone who felt otherwise. I wanted out.

MY PLAY *Fighting International Fat* began as a comic jab at the coming phenomenon of afternoon TV talk shows, then exemplified by Phil Donahue, Sally Jessy Raphaël, and hundreds of narcissistic guests. In the play, all the characters except the host belong to International Fat Fighters, a group run by a character named Roz and loosely based on Weight Watchers International. Each character has a horror story about being overweight, and each successfully has lost weight through Roz's strategy: Not unlike that of Alcoholics Anonymous, each character is assigned a Food Governess, whose responsibility it is to prevent her from eating—whether that meant smashing all the food in her house, running her up hill and down dale, or becoming sexually involved with her. As I delved deeper (or some might say, shallower), I began to see the play as a metaphor for individualism. When Roz's nemesis, a beautiful woman named D'Raleigh Bell, who has lost weight and became ravishing through hundreds of surgeries, teases the group members away from International Fat Fighters with promises of their favorite foods, Roz sees how weak people are and appreciates the person who can stand alone without the aid of others. No doubt this was somewhat inspired by my father's independence, somewhat by the thoughtless and clunky avarice of corporations, and somewhat by the unions that so throttled New York and show business. I gladly joined the Dramatists Guild, which represents playwrights, lyricists, and composers and is not a union. As owners of their own copyrights, playwrights are entrepreneurs; and because the Dramatists Guild is not a union, each can act individually for him- or herself—and for the good of others if he or she so chooses (I doubt many other DG members view themselves as small businessmen and businesswomen; most would rather the Dramatists Guild were a union). Artists, by and large, function as individuals, and I began to see small businesspeople as artists, too—those who, as Stephen Sondheim writes in "Finishing the Hat" from *Sunday in the Park with George*,

> *Look, I made a hat*
> *Where there never was a hat*

create an enterprise. I doubt Sondheim or his collaborator, James Lapine, would view their show or this song as a capitalist manifesto, but artists, visionary businesspeople, mathematicians, and scientists often create something where there was nothing, and to me, anything that wasn't corporate, governmental, unionized, or federated became worth championing.

The play wasn't well received by critics, mostly because it was sort of a goofy mess, with half-formed ideas bouncing off walls and exaggerated characters camping around. I hoped GBS would approve, but I don't think he would have. Certainly audiences didn't. There were walkouts every night, even though I thought, "If they'll only wait for the big food fight, they'll love it!" Unfortunately, the ones who waited for the big food fight didn't love it, either.

THE BEST HOLLYWOOD COMEDIES are anarchic, whether made in the thirties like most Marx Brothers movies or in the forties like *Sullivan's Travels* or in the fifties like *Sunset Blvd.* or in the sixties like *Dr. Strangelove* or in the seventies like *Animal House* and *The Heartbreak Kid* or in the eighties like *Ghostbusters* or in the nineties like *Dumb & Dumber* and *Flirting with Disaster*. First among comic equals is probably Charles Lederer and Howard Hawks's *His Girl Friday*, the rapid-fire, gender-switching, verbal gymnastic made in 1940 and based on *The Front Page* by Ben Hecht and Charles MacArthur. Remakes aren't usually an improvement on the original, but *His Girl Friday* proves the rule, and in my opinion is considerably better than any of the *Front Page* versions. Lederer and Hawks changed the original from a male-buddy picture featuring a battling editor and his star reporter to a romantic comedy featuring a battling editor played by Cary Grant who's been married to and separated from his star reporter, Rosalind Russell, who, in turn, is about to marry a stiff played by Ralph Bellamy. Wearing my hubristic screenwriting hat, I was wooed by Columbia into trying to rewrite it into an update for Michael Caine, Kathleen Turner, and Christopher Reeve.

Unfortunately, I succeeded, and it was made into something seriously unfunny called *Switching Channels*, though without Michael Caine, which was crucial.

Comedies need surprise, edge, wit whether physical or verbal, and helium. Instead of the wit and high wires of *His Girl Friday*, my script was heavy-handed and obvious, more or less like the actors, who were club-footed and showed no understanding of the nimble acting style Hawks elicited. Largely due to the influence of the Actors Studio, today's actors often feel they have to show the *process* of arriving at their emotions—the great effort they've exerted—rather than the emotion itself. This is why light-footed comedies are so rare nowadays.

Also rare in movie comedies of any era is the length of the *His Girl Friday* script—as much as 240 typed pages, almost all of it slam-bang dialogue. Most scripts in the eighties were about 120 pages in length and today come in at slightly over 90 pages. Hawks managed to have his actors spit dialogue at a machine-gun pace without drawing attention to it. They appeared to speak and act just as naturalistically as in any action-comedy of the time, giving this picture a sort of loony, heightened theatricalism and an amazing unity of style. In our version, the actors were only too happy to show how hard they were working.

The director, Ted Kotcheff, and I watched this disaster unfold during the shoot and tried to figure out how to combat it every day. We couldn't.

Part of its failure artistically (it was a complete failure at the box office) was due to the absence of Michael Caine. It's difficult to find a leading man in his forties or fifties who isn't an action hero and impossible to find Cary Grant, certainly my favorite movie star of all time—and not just because he looked like Uncle Bus. Dudley Moore and Michael Caine came close as comic actors, and I'd written it with Dudley in mind. He wasn't available. Michael was, and when he agreed to play the lead, jubilation broke out among Kotcheff, the producer, Marty Ransohoff, and me.

We had a reading of my script at the Ritz-Carlton in New York, and it was thrilling—hard to imagine when you see the finished result. Kotcheff had wanted another writer to take a pass at the script, and it turned out Kathleen liked the other writer's version. So we had a script-off. The three actors read both scripts back to back. When it was over, Michael said, "Well, there's no question which one is better—yours."

"That's the one we're doing!" said Marty. Ted agreed. My head swelled, and I was a Cainiac for life.

"I always alternate pictures—do one because I like it, then one for the money," Michael said.

"And this is for the money?" I kidded him.

"No, this one I like. *Jaws 4* is for the money." I was tickled. I really hadn't wanted to write this script since the original film was already perfect, and I knew the critics would be gunning for it because of its presumption. (I continue to believe that the only movies that should be remade are ones with promising premises that were botched; you can never hope to better the good ones. Look at *Sabrina*.) But my ego was flattered because of agents and producers calling and blowing in my ear and, of course, offering money. And now the future Sir Michael said how much he liked it.

I had written the first draft a year earlier and sent it in to Ransohoff. I was in midtown New York the next day when I picked up a message to phone him and darted into the Princeton Club, where I was permitted because my father-in-law was a graduate, to make the call.

"Hi, Marty."

"Where are you?"

"In New York—I'm calling from the Princeton Club."

"You went to Princeton?" It turned out Marty, who was not Jewish but was annoyed when anyone thought he was, highly prized the Ivy League.

"No, my father-in-law did. I went to Denison." He chose not to hear that, and from that moment on referred to me as a Princeton boy. I think he got the picture green-lighted so he could brag about his author's collegiate genealogy.

"I love the script," said Marty, who is almost as enormous in legend as he is in physical size. "I've sent it to Michael Caine."

"He'll be great!" I said.

"And he's British, so there won't be all that actor bullshit," Marty said.

"And he'll say all the words!"

Marty laughed. "Yes, I don't want them changing one line of your script." He sounded pugnacious. "It's too good."

"Thank you, Marty," I said, knowing he'd forget he'd said those words as quickly as he'd forgotten I hadn't gone to Princeton.

Michael would shoot our film as soon as he finished *Jaws 4* (*Jaws: The Revenge*), which would be in plenty of time.

Only it wasn't. The payoff in *Jaws: The Revenge* included the shark jumping out of the water to bite the wing off an airplane . . . and they couldn't get the shark to work.

We began shooting in Montreal, then moved to Toronto, made as usual to look like someplace else—sort of Atlanta, since the newsroom from *His Girl Friday* was now a cable-TV station not unlike CNN, a fresh idea in 1987.

The wizards at Universal couldn't get the shark to work. We shot every scene that Michael wasn't in for two weeks, praying the damn shark would jump up and bite off that fucking wing.

Somewhere during the first couple of weeks of shooting, Kathleen announced she was well into a pregnancy.

Marty, one of the toughest of the tough, became apoplectic. "That bitch! That cow!" he said to me over the phone from L.A. "She knew she was pregnant before we started—she just made sure there was footage of her so she couldn't be replaced!" I thought he was going to come through the telephone from Holmby Hills and choke me in place of her. For the rest of the shoot, Kathleen had to be costumed so she wouldn't look like a mother-to-be. When she was sideways, her jacket was always open so it would hide the extra inches.

I wasn't a Kathleen Turner or Christopher Reeve fan. I've known several actors who've spent a year or two on TV soap operas and become so used to manufacturing emotions quickly (literally, overnight) and repeating them so frequently (two to five times a week) that they have nothing fresh to bring up. Kathleen suffered from this. She always did a lot of heavy breathing in her serious roles, which I found unbelievable and which eventually were treated as camp. In the dark comedy *The War of the Roses*, she found a wonderful blend of humor and menace that was perfect, but this wasn't a dark comedy, and in her other comic roles such as *Romancing the Stone*, she was frantic and loud but not funny. Although not sexually attractive to me as, say, Kim Basinger was in *My Stepmother Is an Alien* or Amy Irving and Anne Reinking were in *Micki & Maude*, I thought she would do a workmanlike job, and she did.

Although it's heresy to say so now, Chris wasn't any better. He was a lousy actor in his non-Superman roles and very full of himself offscreen, which was perfect for the role in *Switching Channels*. However, sometimes the hardest thing for a bad actor to play is himself onscreen or onstage because he isn't aware that's who he is—particularly if the role is unflattering. So he plays an exaggerated version of himself, which is what Chris did.

I hoped the anticipation of working with Caine would keep Kathleen and Chris on their best performing behavior. He would be their mentor in the film, which we all believed would bring out better performances than they'd ever given. Michael could be superb when properly challenged, and they knew it. I hoped he'd get there soon. I stroked Buddha's belly that the actors would try to rise to his level—and I knew his observations would make the script better.

And I still think they would have. But I never got to find out. A few days before we had to shoot his scenes, Marty jetted in and said he had to replace Michael with Burt Reynolds. I pleaded with him not to—not because Burt couldn't be good in certain roles, but because he was in no way a nimble, verbal comedian and certainly not a Brit, for whom the lines and rhythm had been written. Marty said he had no choice—we had to shoot his scenes.

Two days later, *Jaws: The Revenge* wrapped. I again begged Marty to get Michael.

"But I've already hired Burt."

"Well, unhire him—he's not as good as Michael for this role."

"Jonathan," Marty said, for the first and last time in his life sincere, "I couldn't do that to Burt. Think of the man's feelings. I mean, he's a human being." Marty is a very funny man, and I thought he was joking, but he wasn't.

I gasped for air. Marty was a man famous for incinerating the carcasses of studio heads, CEOs, and the Spielbergs of the world and had just chewed out Kathleen for becoming pregnant without his permission, and who had fired me temporarily for a rewriter Kotcheff wanted without reference to the possibility that I was a human being or his pledge to change nothing in the script, then rehired me on Caine's say-so after the script-off. For Marty, steak tartare was too well done. And here he was, turning mawkish. The fact was, he'd already guaranteed Burt's price, and to have two leading men on the payroll would have sent the budget into the red.

"But if the movie's no good because of the casting, it'll be a lot further in the red," I said.

"No. Have a heart."

Kotcheff and I were despondent.

Burt showed up and went to work like a pro—just a different kind of pro from Michael. He'd been the top box-office star in the world for nearly five years but had recently been brought low by a couple of failures and a strange jaw disease the press had described as AIDS, which it wasn't. He had lost confidence. And after years of one-liners opposite Johnny Carson, with whom he was charming and funny, he was unable to speak a sentence longer than three or four words. Sweet as Burt was, what would have been warm-up stretches for Michael became Olympic lifting for him. Ted and I knew from that moment that the picture was doomed.

Oh, and Burt and Kathleen hated each other. He resented her top billing; at a cocktail party, he informed her he'd been nominated for an Oscar, expecting her to be well aware of it.

"Oh, for what?" she said tactlessly.

"A little thing called . . . *Deliverance*," he said between clenched teeth and stomped out. The war was on. See for yourself.

About halfway through shooting, Marty phoned.

"I want you on that set. I've seen the dailies. You can't let them change your lines."

"But, Marty, I can't make anyone stick to a script. I'm the writer. They won't listen to me. That's the director's job."

"I'll tell them to listen to you. I've phoned Ted. Protect your script!" He hung up.

I sweated through most of the night. I didn't mind if the actors changed my lines all they wanted if it made them funnier.

The next day I duly went to the set. Kotcheff wasn't particularly glad to see me but was courteous. Unlike the theatre, in films, writers do not overrule or even consult with directors unless summoned by the director. So Marty had put Ted's balls in a vise, which Ted was handling as gracefully as he could.

In a scene Chris has with Burt, Chris says superciliously of Kathleen's character, "She'll make a great wife. It'll be like having an extra appendage— another arm or a leg." And Burt responds sarcastically, "Make sure to tell her that," knowing she'll explode. It wasn't going well, and Ted called me over.

"What's the matter with this scene?"

"Chris shouldn't say it as though he thinks it's funny. He should say it as though he's thrilled with this observation. To him it makes perfect sense," I said. "And it's sort of Acting 101, but if Burt laughs after his line, the audience won't. He's hoping Chris will tell her that." By now I was thinking maybe the lines weren't funny after all. Was any of it funny? Had we all been on nitrous oxide at the Ritz-Carlton script-off?

Ted ambled over to Chris, who shot me a threatening Superman look. Writers aren't supposed to interfere. They did another take. It was still unbelievable and still unfunny. This time I walked over to Ted, unasked. "He's still saying it as though he thinks it's funny." Now Ted looked at me unhappily. He suddenly weighed twice as much and slowly went over to Chris again and whispered. Chris stiffened.

"I'll get it from him," Ted said to me. "Why don't you step into the next room during the next take?"

I left, and after the take, Chris found me in the hall. "My character would never say that, you know," he said curtly. I tried to accommodate.

"Well, he's very full of himself. He doesn't really realize what he's saying is so self-centered. He thinks it's a compliment, as if he's just said, 'She's a great lawyer. We'll make a great team.' But what do you think he'd say?"

"Never mind. It's done," he said, and walked off. In the final version, of course, Chris tips his hand to let the audience know he knows it's a comedy, and Burt keeps the laugh.

The following morning, I got a call from the line producer, Don Carmody. "You're banned from the set. Chris doesn't want you around. And that goes for the scenes he's not in, too."

I was stunned and zoomed out to Pluto again. It was pretty funny, considering the universe of the movie world. "But Marty said—"

"Marty knows and agrees with Chris," Carmody said.

I phoned Marty. "Chris kicked me off the set. What do I do now?"

"You fucked up, Jonathan. You can't talk to an actor that way."

"But you told me not to let them change any of my lines."

"Yeah, but you gotta give in every now and then."

I spent the rest of the shoot in a singularly unattractive hotel room with thin walls in Toronto. Toward the end, a couple fond of very audible lovemaking moved into the room next door. Occasionally Ted would ask for additional dialogue, which I dashed off quickly because by then I was way more fascinated by the couple on the other side of the wall.

Michael Caine's high standards (at least on every alternate movie) might have lifted all boats, mine included—I screened the movie recently, and it's a dud from page one. Without realizing it, I had copied the structure of *His Girl Friday*—almost scene for scene—but left out the fluff. Michael Caine might have turned it into a soufflé of a dud, but the minute it was out of the oven, it still would have collapsed.

1,095 Bread Puddings

PROFESSIONALLY, I FELT glummer than ever. *Fighting International Fat's* hilariously disastrous reviews were not so hilarious to me at the time. Despite the money, the dismissive reviews and minimal box office for *Stepmother* and *Switching Channels* had been painful and dispiriting. And unimportant as it may now seem, a sketch of mine scheduled to appear in a revue at the Manhattan Theatre Club (home of "this version is shit") was suddenly dropped from the show, which proved to be the last straw.

Charlotte and I argued all the time, mostly about the house. We almost never argued about the children: She wanted them on an Ivy League track, and I saw no reason they shouldn't be. I had missed the Ivy League, and I didn't regret it (surely it would have meant another expulsion for something or other), but I thought Frank and Eddie might profit from it—though I also knew it made little difference where you went to college in terms of education, but a big difference in terms of contacts afterward. I thought Ivy League contacts didn't matter, since both boys showed artistic gifts—Frank appearing in school plays, Eddie revealing a sensitivity and wit beyond his years.

Charlotte hadn't recovered professionally from the collapse of her company a decade earlier and never ventured out on her own again, at least not while we were married. She became a real estate broker, but missed appointments and found that nothing moved. I thought she was wasting her enormous potential and worried she might be sliding into the passivity with which I was so familiar.

One night I announced to her that we had to leave New York. I thought we all needed recharging. I didn't want my children growing up knowing only New York, as I had. The uniqueness of America did not spring from this city—this city was Europe. I love Europe, but it's not America.

I was furious at the world for not recognizing my genius and rattled on about the boys' safety. I now hated the city where I'd spent so many exciting years in and out of trouble, love, gastronomy, and success. Charlotte wasn't enthusiastic—she'd grown up outside New York and already knew more about the country than I did. But at one point, as she reminded me several times later, I shouted, "I'll kill myself if I have to live in New York!" and she gave in when she saw my desperation. And maybe a move would freshen the marriage.

The idea began to feel good. I'd lived in several places—London, Paris, college in a small Ohio town, months in Los Angeles, San Francisco, Atlanta, New Orleans—and still felt I didn't know America. I wanted to move someplace exciting—like Las Vegas!!—or to a town we'd never been, like Butte or Durango. I knew I didn't want to move to the company town of Los Angeles, fearing that familiarity might breed contempt—theirs. I was more exotic to the studios as a playwright from New York and therefore more attractive—at least until the movies mostly bombed. Darryl Zanuck, the legendary chief of production at Fox, said to me when I interviewed him for the Frost show, "Hollywood is a town of proven failures," which I was about to discover.

Charlotte was more down-to-earth. No Las Vegas, no Montana, no burg in Colorado. "Winston-Salem," she said. She knew her way around Winston-Salem because she had been born there and grew up thirty minutes away in the tiny town of Elkin. With what remained of the movie money, a few years before, I'd bought a house and twenty acres just off the Blue Ridge Parkway near Sparta. Sparta is not only featured as Charlotte Simmons's hometown in Tom Wolfe's novel; it's a few miles from the Roaring Gap Club, where my nonfiction Charlotte and her family spent summers. Her parents owned a house on club grounds, and we'd visit every summer. I loved the area but wanted us to be on our own.

Charlotte had moved to New York from North Carolina twenty-five years earlier to go to Vassar and had decided to stay. One of her dreams had been to host a literary salon through which all types of New York characters would wander. Though close to her parents, she didn't really want to live near them, so moving back was a considerable sacrifice on her part, for which she made me pay over the next few years.

I've loved the American South since age eight minutes. I was born in Fort Smith, Arkansas, though Dad dragged us out after six months for the rivers of San Antonio and hills of Virginia, where he attempted businesses. Once the divorce was definite, Mother moved us to New York, where southerners are often caricatured as either racist or redneck or ignorant. I've always thought it the most mysterious, romantic, and tragic section of the country. Dad and his family were from the Southwest, and though Yankees don't differentiate between the South and the Southwest, natives do. The South is older, it's greener, and it has a more literary history. There is no aristocracy in Oklahoma.

And then there were all those bread puddings! The simplest, comfiest, most versatile sweetgoo ever concocted into which you could throw just about anything as long as somewhere in there were bread, eggs, milk, and sugar. And in the South they did throw in everything—every restaurant had its own—bread puddings with bourbon, rum, or just about any booze except Fernet-Branca; with whipped cream, butterscotch, molasses, vanilla, and nutmeg sauces; with bananas, pineapple, bananas *and* pineapple, walnuts, raisins (of course), apricots, lemon peel, coconut, cayenne, even cocoa (reminding me of Mother's noble effort); bread from yesterday's dinner, leftover biscuits, buttered Wonder bread, for Pete's sake, Irish-soda or any other bread or muffin (except maybe rye), and you could cook it on the stovetop, in an oven, in a Crock-Pot, or probably in a solar cooker. Loved it since a child, probably through a very strong bread-pudding gene pool. And because it was available everywhere all over town, I never had to make it!

As much as I was drawn to the South, I've never understood it. I certainly didn't understand segregation or Jim Crow or how anyone could come up with laws that wouldn't allow people to drink from the same water fountain or kiss one another. I'm not saying I just didn't agree with it—I didn't *understand* it. What did those lawmakers think would happen if two races drank the same water? I'm not particularly *laissez-faire*, and I'm happy not to be—if I can make up my mind, I sit *in judgment*; but this cruel foolishness I just couldn't fathom: I couldn't understand why they did it or what they got from it. But the region fascinates me and always has.

I find the South's literature, the fondness for conversation and stories compelling, and its history completely absorbing, flaws and all. I continue to love Faulkner, think Willie Morris's memoir *North Toward Home* is masterful, and find Tennessee Williams endures as our most beautiful playwright. He lacks the tin ear of O'Neill and the earnest social conscience of Arthur Miller and shares the spirituality of Thornton Wilder. I like Charlie Rose and Bob Schieffer and used to like reading Tom Wicker and thought senators Sam Ervin, Howard Baker, and eventually Fred Thompson saved the country. David Brinkley was the best broadcaster ever. It's a broad generalization, of course, but I find a sweetness and fragility in the southern character that struggles against its outward masculinity and often redeems its meanness. It's not just the cordiality of the English, though there is that, but—they'll kill me for this—an effeminacy and appreciation for intellectual thoughtfulness that no other part of the country embodies in quite the same way.

In New York, I grew up feeling combat the moment I opened the front door—real and imagined. People in the street seemed fighting mad just getting out of bed. Every day was a struggle against other people, whether you knew them or not. Most of the South wasn't like this.

So it didn't take much for me to agree with Charlotte. If we had to move, the familiar South was preferable to the Wild Blue Yonder.

One of the Great Bread Poods

1 cup raisins

4 ounces Maker's Mark bourbon

1 loaf of day-old white bread in 1-inch cubes (6–7 cups)

2 cups milk

2 cups heavy cream

3 eggs, beaten

2 cups sugar

2 tablespoons Mexican vanilla (Madagascar will do)

¼ teaspoon allspice

½ teaspoon cinnamon

½ teaspoon cayenne

1 cup chopped pecans or walnuts

3 tablespoons unsalted butter

1. Soak raisins overnight in bourbon.
2. The following day, preheat oven to 350 degrees.
3. Soak the bread in milk and cream until absorbed. In a separate bowl, beat eggs, sugar, vanilla, and spices together. Add nuts, raisins, and soaked bread, stirring gently.
4. Grease a 9 × 13-inch baking pan with the butter and pour in the batter. Bake 35–45 minutes, until edges brown and pudding looks set (it's also fine if it's a little runny).
5. Serve hot with Bourbon Sauce (see below).

YIELD: 6–8 servings.

Bourbon Sauce

½ cup unsalted melted butter

1 cup sugar

1 egg

1 cup Maker's Mark bourbon

1. Whisk together butter, sugar, and egg in a saucepan over low heat until it thickens. Whisk in bourbon.
2. Let cool, then whisk again and serve immediately. It should be creamy, and don't let the eggs scramble!

YIELD: About 2 cups.

Daddy Dearest

~~~~~~

I eat my peas with honey
I've done it all my life
It makes the peas taste funny
But it keeps them on the knife.

—Anonymous

A BOUT THE ONLY PERSON I know who doesn't like peas is my son Eddie, and in Winston we once had a Joan Crawford showdown over them. When we were entrenched in Winston in the early nineties (anybody who's been there more than five minutes drops the "Salem"), we were frequently confused with the local royal families—either the R. J. Reynoldses, who introduced the first nationally successful pre-rolled cigarettes, Camels, or their cousins the R. S. Reynoldses, who made the foil destined to become Reynolds Wrap, which was initially used to wrap the pre-rolled ciggies. This was of no advantage to us whatever and regularly resulted either in keen disappointment when others found out we weren't royalty or in being overcharged twenty-five bucks for service calls by appliance repairmen who didn't believe us.

But the boys lived an idyllic childhood that Norman Rockwell would have envied—unlocked front door, bicycles in the yard, skinned knees for all the right reasons, friends and kids down the block, water and nature all around. When I wasn't in L.A., we had dinner together every night, a Rockwellian conceit I continue to recommend to even the most virulent Schnabelian.

At first, Frank and Eddie were distraught—yanked out of school, separated from beds and friends they knew in New York, forced into classes and onto sports teams where the only faces belonged to strangers. After only a month, our Jack Russell terrier, Louis, was hit by a car and killed. I thought I had ruined the lives of three people and murdered the family dog. But after the second month, when the boys realized how liberated they were from the confines of New York, how all the greenery and camaraderie was available to them without a parental escort, how they could trust strangers, and, most important, that TV was the same down there as it was up here, they grew into it. As far as I was concerned, I could open the front door and not feel confrontation in the air. People were polite, both by heritage and because they thought it was a better way to live. In Winston, at least the days *started* happy.

I would usually throw together breakfast for the boys, who'd watch with disbelief as I'd eat a faddish health-food concoction of broccoli and oat bran (eggs were against the law in the eighties). Charlotte would pack their lunches. At night, we discussed what they'd eat. No fish, of course, potatoes and creamy things, yes, burgers, chicken, an attempt at a green vegetable (could corn be considered green? They'd both eat that). I'd write during the day, then take a break around five to go to the Fresh Market in search of something that wouldn't result in protest.

Neither boy had particularly adventurous taste buds and had yet to appreciate anything foreign like, say, Chinese, Indian, or Italian outside of spaghetti marinara or carbonara. But with the mac-and-cheese served at Duke's and the brilliant butterscotch pie from Roy's in Elkin, thirty-five miles away, why should they? Southern cooking is mostly soothing: cheese grits, chicken-fried steak, fried pies, creamed corn, Mr. Pibb, and all those cakes and puddings.

I was certain that peas fresh from the pod—English peas, or garden peas, as they're sometimes called to distinguish them from dried peas like the black-eyed, the chick, and the cow—would seamlessly initiate my sons into solid green vegetables, which they ate willingly in infancy, when Gerber puréed them into custard. Besides, peas are naturally sweet, can be mushy and comforting, and, in the generally green-loathing preteen years, are harmless. (I know the country would be better-governed if people weren't allowed to vote until they passed a stiff green-vegetable-appreciation test.)

But Eddie despised them, as I found out one spring evening. Soothingly buttered and spooned next to some G-rated mashed potatoes and a forgotten brown meat, the first pick of the spring couldn't possibly offend.

But it did. Eddie refused to eat them, even with threats of limited television that night, extra piano practice, and banishment from playing in one of those five-hour Saturday baseball games in which the catcher misses every pitch, and the pitcher misses every throw from the catcher who has walked leisurely to the backstop, and the second baseman has retrieved the missed throw, only to throw it over the pitcher's head, so that each pitch takes about ten minutes, first to last.

It became a shootout worthy of the O.K. Corral between a supposedly mature adult and a seriously determined seven-year-old. I decided this might be the inevitable confrontation Philip Roth insists must take place between father and son if the son is to become a man (though in Roth's version, the son is considerably older). I dug in. Eddie dug in. His mother implored him to at least *try* the peas, and I attempted cowboy recklessness, swearing we'd both sit there all night till he finished the peas. Freeze frames of Faye Dunaway and the congealing beefsteak flashed through my head, followed for no logical reason by the "No wire hangers!" tantrum. As I became Faye Dunaway, he became The Rock.

Finally, after three or four minutes, he took a forkful, gagged, rolled his eyes, and made several gurgling noises that under different circumstances would have admitted him to an emergency room. Either this was a superb operatic performance or he really hated peas. He bravely started to take a second forkful. I caved pathetically. "I guess you really don't like them," I said. He looked at me with the equivalent of "Hel-LO" (right before it took over from "Duh") and put down his fork.

To the best of my knowledge, no pea has passed his lips since.

I've never known whether it was the grandstanding emotional gauntlet I foolishly threw down in North Carolina (and thankfully never repeated) that made it impossible for him to like peas, or a genuine dislike of the things. But at 23, he's got another 113 years—if he drinks his green tea and eats his dark chocolate—to shape up.

In *Jane Grigson's Vegetable Book*, the late British author introduces what is certainly the simplest and friendliest method of eating this supreme springtime vegetable: You boil the peas, in their pods, in salted water for ten minutes, drain them, and serve them in a big bowl, family-style, accompanied by a couple of bowls of melted butter. Each pea-eater takes a pod by the stem end, dips it into the butter, and sucks out the peas while pulling off the soft outer layer of pod with his teeth. Totally delicious, totally effortless, certainly Rockwellian.

Jane Grigson's Peas in the Pod
(Adapted from Jane Grigson's Vegetable Book, *Penguin Books, 1998)*

2 pounds fresh young peas in their pods
8 ounces (2 sticks) butter

1. Boil peas in their pods in salted water for 10 minutes. Drain and divide into individual bowls.
2. Melt butter over low heat and place in two or more serving bowls.
3. To eat, take a pod by the stem, dip it into the butter, and suck the peas out while scraping the thin, sweet layer of the pod.

YIELD: 6 servings.

Elevating the pea to gastronomic divinity doesn't need my help, but it might need Alfred Portale's. Portale, proprietor and chef of Gotham Bar and Grill in New York, makes a stunning creation that will make you look at the formerly trivial pea in amazement and say, "This . . . came from . . . *that?*" Complicated but celestial. Might even impress Eddie.

Alfred Portale's Spring Pea Soup with Morel Custard and White Truffle Oil

Morel Custard
1 ounce dried morels
1 teaspoon white truffle oil or extra-virgin olive oil

¾ cup heavy cream

2 egg yolks

¼ teaspoon kosher salt

⅛ teaspoon freshly ground white pepper

Sprig of chervil

1. Preheat oven to 300 degrees. Lightly butter four 2-ounce ramekins.
2. Wash morels carefully with cold water, making sure you get all the sand and grit out.
3. In a medium-size saucepan, bring morels, truffle oil, and heavy cream to a boil over medium heat. Reduce the heat to very low and simmer slowly until the mixture thickens, about 12 minutes.
4. Place the mixture into a blender and purée until smooth. Add the egg yolks and strain through a wire sieve or a strainer. Add salt and pepper to taste.
5. Place the ramekins in a large baking dish. Pour the mixture into the prepared ramekins and put the baking dish in the oven. Carefully pour enough hot water into the dish to come about ½ inch up the sides of the ramekins. Cover the pan with aluminum foil. Bake until the custards are set, 1¼–1½ hours. (The centers will still seem a little loose.) Remove from the water bath. If not serving immediately, cool completely, cover with plastic wrap, and refrigerate for a day, possibly two, but no longer.

While custard is cooking, prepare the soup:

Pea Soup

1 tablespoon olive oil

1 onion, chopped

½ rib celery, chopped

1 quart chicken stock

4 cups shelled fresh peas

Coarse salt and freshly ground pepper to taste

2 tablespoons sugar, or to taste (optional)

1. In a stockpot, heat the oil over a medium heat. Add the onion and celery and cook, stirring, for 3–4 minutes, or until softened. Add the stock, raise the heat to high, and bring to a boil.

2. Add the peas and return to a boil, reduce the heat, and simmer for about 12 minutes, or until the peas are tender. Remove from the heat and season with salt and pepper.

3. While the soup simmers, set a strainer over a bowl large enough to hold the stock. Set another bowl in a larger one holding ice cubes and ice water to chill the soup. Also, have a blender and ladle on hand. When the soup is ready, strain it into the bowl. Transfer the vegetables to the blender and purée, adding only enough of the strained stock to make a fine, thick purée.

4. Scrape the contents of the blender into the bowl set in the ice bath. Add the remaining stock, a little at a time, until the soup reaches the desired creamy consistency. Season with sugar, if desired, cover, and refrigerate.

To Assemble:

1. Turn custard upside down in the center of a round soup bowl. It should come out easily. If not, use a paring knife along the ramekin to loosen custard.

2. Carefully spoon the soup around the custard. The soup should come up to three quarters of the height of the custard.

3. Drizzle white truffle oil or virgin olive oil. Add chervil sprig for additional color if desired. The soup may be served at room temperature or warm.

YIELD: 4 servings.

I WAS PRETTY SURE I was a wretched parent, running off to L.A. all the time, but it turns out I suffered from the typical daddy fear: dependency. Men are generally terrified of anyone relying on them for emotional support. I was no exception. And if there's one word synonymous with *baby*, it's *dependency*. I assailed diaper-changing valiantly, attended all sporting events when in town, even became assistant basketball coach for Frank's team in Winston, went to school fairs, and drove the boys to sleepovers. I also paid for a lot and enjoyed being able to. I actually *loved* paying for things as long as I could.

Still, I never minded when the movie business pulled me away. We lived in Winston for three years, during which I spent about two thirds of the time in North Carolina and one third executing or pursuing screenplays in Los Angeles. My professional tide was turning after those five movies were made right in a row, and my ego, which was once too large to fit in the room, could now squeeze easily through a keyhole. During an earlier disastrous period, when I was writing a television pilot for Diana Rigg in London, a British lawyer said to me, "You're odd, Reynolds—you're arrogant but not confident." I hadn't learned my lesson. I continued to get assignments but not to have any of them made. And making movies—not just writing them—is the barometer of the industry. It seemed the more time I spent in L.A., the less successful I got.

I had lavish experiences in the hotels of Los Angeles and managed two weeks in a suite at the Dorchester in London while working with the director on *Leonard Part 6*. I ate at the hotel daily or else at The Connaught and the usual Indian joints in Soho and lamented that the working period was so short. It meant leaving those surroundings. In fact, I felt certain the movie bubble would burst sooner rather than later and spent just about as much time dreading the end of it as I did enjoying its luxuries. I spent a week in an enormous, marble-floored bungalow at the Beverly Hills Hotel convinced I was there under fraudulent circumstances and would be found out, until I realized everyone in Hollywood was there under fraudulent circumstances. I spent a deranged month at the Bel-Air watching Peter Bogdanovich systematically turn a green-lighted screenplay that I'd been hired to punch up back into a development deal. Criminal. He was in his Springsteen-worshipping period and arranged for us to fly clear from L.A. to Syracuse, New York, to see The Boss's final concerts of the year, stopping in Manhattan aboard the MGM plane to pick up Charlotte (we hadn't yet moved to Winston at this point). This had absolutely nothing to do with the movie we were working on, but was the movie business at its most delightfully zany, and only adds a penny or two to the price of a ticket. Jim Carrey adds the extra dollar every year, just as A-Rod does at Yankee Stadium.

By far the worst of these experiences was the ten-week shoot of *Switching Channels* in Montreal and Toronto, during which period I was alternately being told by Marty Ransohoff to keep the actors from changing a single line of my sainted script and being banned from the set. I was welcome at the director Ted Kotcheff's table but not at Miss Kathleen Turner's, bless her basso profundo, or at Chris Reeve's. Kotcheff, who is Canadian, introduced me to the most memorable of Toronto dishes, the great smoked-meat sandwich, which resembled a Reuben without the cheese and sauerkraut. Mostly, I spent solitary days in an undistinguished hotel changing all the Michael Caine lines to Burt Reynolds lines.

Charlotte and the boys came up for a weekend and ran around the set. Frank and Eddie were dazzled that their dad was working on a picture with Superman, though Superman wasn't dazzled in return.

Trips back to New York and Winston from these surrealistic sites were as different as waking and dreaming. The boys were in a bucolic school in Winston, they had playdates in the afternoons and on weekends, as well as practices and games, piano lessons. Weekends we'd try to spend at the house on the Blue Ridge Parkway (christened "Bullhead" by Charlotte, in reference not only to a nearby mountain of the same name, but to our willful personalities). I grew to love that house and the simplicity it represented much more than the Jane Street house, which we'd rented to a family and was a continual headache. It represented complication, New York, and the need for money to keep it up. We looked into selling it, but during the week we talked to brokers, a man was shot and killed making a telephone call at Jane and Greenwich streets, and *New York* magazine's cover story the following week not only sensationalized the murder but outed the lurking violence and rampant transvestite-hooker community of the area. Prices fell and stayed that way for ten years. The house took an inordinate amount of time to landlord, and it never made a dime.

Charlotte chose not to work in Winston, put on weight, and dove headfirst into a depression that lingered on and off for the next decade. I drank aquavit late at night and at least once mentioned—shouted, actually—I would trade the Jane Street house for a divorce. No takers.

It was easy to make friendly acquaintance with people in Winston, but, like London, it was a difficult place for deep friendships to develop. Charlotte's brother, Donny, and his wife, Ruthie, and their three children were regular companions, and a joy to be around. It's surprising on whom children model themselves. Charlotte and I were seldom publicly affectionate, but Ruthie would sit on Donny's lap after dinner, and he'd call her "Sweets." Years later, Frank replicated not his own parents' cordial aloofness with his most serious girlfriend but his uncle's playful-natured warmth. She sits on his lap, and he calls her "Sweets."

Despite the many attempts at hosting dinners, I still felt like a stranger in Winston, and Charlotte just plain didn't want to be there. We rented a search-light and threw an Oscar party attended by thirty or forty people and featuring Frank and Eddie with Instamatics pretending to be reporters and snapping photos outside as the guests arrived. It would have been a smashing success had I managed to get Fredy Girardet's *blanquette de saumon et crevettes* on the table before the Best Actor was announced around midnight, but such was my timing that I didn't.

At Bullhead, we hosted assorted Kirks, Remicks, and Reynoldses, who came from New York and Boston and Winston, on Thanksgiving and Christmas. Those were the best times: our house overstuffed with people, the people overstuffed with crisply roasted turkey or goose, pies or plum pudding, and spider cakes and mountains of pork products for breakfast. We were at our familiest then.

When summer heat chased us up to our house on the parkway, we left the rented house in Winston and welcomed friends who passed through for the camaraderie, the German Johnson heirloom tomatoes, and a flank steak smothered with chilies and cooked on the grill. We were away from real life (though I realized too late that this was also real life and could have been ours) and untroubled by financial and real estate arguments.

Shake It Up, Baby

〰〰〰〰

O F THE FOUR most perennially puzzling culinary mysteries—how do you cook perfect rice, who separates the juice of the pomegranate from its seeds, what the hell is in marshmallows, and where did my malted milk go—the only question I can answer with any authority is the last. Like Nesselrode pie and Danish pudding, Nicole Brown's real killer, Salinger's talent, and the friendship between Woody and Jean, malted milk has disappeared.

Well, almost. (But then, the same can still be said for Nicole Brown's real killer, still out there somewhere.)

Nothing conjures the small-town America of Andy Hardy, Thornton Wilder, and Norman Rockwell like a malted milkshake served in a carbuncular soda glass and blissfully slurped through a straw—unless perhaps it's the four-fingered baseball mitt or the blueberry pie cooling on a Kansas windowsill. I don't know if there's actually malt in all the Rockwell shakes or in the famous drugstore scenes from *Our Town* and *Shadow of a Doubt* or when Andy and Polly roll their eyes at each other, but I'd like to think there is, because those blessed drinks sure seemed to bring families close.

Though there is no single greatest American playwright or greatest play, there is none greater than Thornton Wilder or *Our Town*. The play transcends the brilliant realism of *Long Day's Journey into Night* and *Death of a Salesman* and will satisfy the test of time even more enduringly than the inspired language of *A Streetcar Named Desire* and *The Glass Menagerie*. Because of its sudden leap into spirituality, detailed atmosphere, and theatricalism and its deceptively bone-simple style, *Our Town* resonates universally. It also captures the unique-ness of the American character that isn't urban—as does *The Music Man*—by lovingly memorializing, with its own spare realism, the nation's vanishing small towns.

The country's ills are harder to salve these days. We've pretty much rejected Wilder's religion, Louis B. Mayer's comforting (if ultimately bogus) platitudes, and Rockwell's masterfully simple reassurances, mostly to our detriment. While I'm not suggesting we airlift refrigerated trucks of strawberry malteds to Baghdad or Tehran or Omaha (where bin Laden is actually hiding), the case can nevertheless be made that such an international policy would certainly make the principals feel better. A roomful of Zarqawis, Abdullahs, Faisals, Condoleezzas, and assorted mullahs all sipping date or figgy malteds with flexible straws could only speed up the peace process. You simply can't do war with a malted milkshake in your mouth. Cognac and bourbon, yes (Churchill and Truman), but a malted banana smoothie, never. The earthy, nutty contri-bution malt makes to a shake cuts the shrill sweetness of ice cream and syrup. (Some throats—mine, for one—get sugar burn from too much sweetness, whether from ice cream or candy bars. Mine burns after two or three slugs of a shake, and malt soothes it. And speaking of ice cream, if you eat too much too fast and your head aches or your throat swells terrifyingly, grab something really cold—ice or the glass the ice cream's in—and press it to an artery at ankle, wrist, or neck, and it will disappear.)

Malt adds not only complexity and maturity to an otherwise infantile con-coction but also surprise and a smile to pies and puddings and cakes and muffins—no one ever expects it because they think it's dead.

Malt is usually made from barley that has been soaked and allowed to sprout, converting much of the grain's starch into sugar. Further roasting the barley caramelizes its sugars and gives malt its unique taste. Malted milk was initially created in 1887 by the Horlick brothers of Racine, Wisconsin, as an easy digestible for invalids and infants. They combined malted barley with wheat and added dried milk and a few thousand other ingredients like sugar, whey, various oils, and that old standby thiamin mononitrate. But malted-milk powder is not for the faint of heart—literally. Though a tablespoon of pure malt has 21 calories and 4½ grams of carbohydrate, Horlicks has 60 and

12, and who wants to stop at one tablespoon? The pure malt is just as good—though stronger and less rich-tasting—and is eminently worth trying.

The closest I came to a corner soda fountain *was* a corner soda fountain, though it was on the corner of Madison and Eighty-fifth, not Grovers Corners. Sipping a vanilla malted and watching two short-order cooks whir up ten or twenty burgers, eggs, and hash browns seemed the height of excitement and glamour. But there wasn't much of a soda-shoppe culture in New York; I got most of mine through the Andy Hardy series of movies, which I watched eagerly, hoping they would instruct me how to be a teenager since Brando and Dean weren't helping much. But there weren't any jalopies in my neck of the woods or dazzling beauties like Lana Turner, and though there was a sister who could be annoying and a maiden aunt in Quincy, there was definitely no Judge Hardy to turn to for advice. The series took place about fifteen years before my time, and in a small town so remote it might as well have been in Greenland, but I yearned for the experience. Instead, I got life lessons from Steve McQueen, Burt Lancaster, Montgomery Clift, and Ernest Borgnine, and in place of Judge Hardy, I had the role model of Frank Sinatra.

I hadn't had a malted in twenty years, when, sometime during the summer of 1990, I was motoring around the mountains of North Carolina in search of a camp meeting. I was doing research for a screenplay in which Dolly Parton—with whom I had fallen in complete but unrequited love—would play an evangelist who sings with divine inspiration, performs healing miracles for real, and becomes a national phenomenon. Then, at the height of her success, she is brought low by some human failing.

Paramount wanted her character, Sister Sunshine, to be a fraud, but both Dolly and I thought it would be more original and challenging if she was a true believer, which made the execs nervous, since in Hollywood the only valid and commercial religion until *The Passion of the Christ* was a zealous atheism. The scandalous Jimmys Bakker and Swaggart were all over the front pages then, casting more doubt than ever on organized religion.

Bakker was an apple-cheeked preacher who appeared on a daily television show called *PTL* (which alternately stood for *Praise the Lord* and *People That Love*) with his wife, Tammy Faye, a heavenly choir, and several seriously religious guests. I don't remember him healing anyone, but I do remember him selling time-shares in a vacation community in South Carolina. He was enormously popular and great fun to watch, even when he went on one of his to-the-right-of-Beria rants about homosexuals, masturbation, and women with loose morals. Supposedly, the show pulled in $500,000 a day in contributions and earned the envy of other prominent televangelists like Jerry Falwell and John Ankerberg. Our friend the actor Ian McKellen came to visit us at Bullhead and wanted more than anything to drive to the *PTL* studios a few miles away but didn't have time. I think Sir Ian, who is famously gay, wanted to look the devil in the face and laugh at him. Bakker was eventually accused of molestation by Jessica Hahn, a local girl who claimed to be a devout Christian. Bakker's empire was investigated, and it turned out Jim had oversold the properties, spent wildly on personal luxuries (supposedly $60,000 for gold bathroom fixtures and an air-conditioned doghouse), and may have been a practicing homosexual himself. Too neat for fiction. Off he went weeping to prison. Jessica Hahn went to Hollywood, bought breast implants, and posed for *Playboy*. You can't make this stuff up.

Though Bakker wasn't much of a scholarly Christian, Jimmy Swaggart was a highly regarded biblical specialist. His regular television show pulled in eight million viewers and somewhere between $100 million and $150 million a year in his heyday—which was, coincidentally, parallel to Bakker's. Swaggart began as a gospel singer and was given to tear-jerking, emotional sermons. After publicly denouncing Bakker as "a cancer on the body of Christ" and defrocking a fellow minister for an extramarital affair, he was photographed by that minister picking up hookers, after which he took them to motels and masturbated in front of them. That's all he did, but it was enough. He went on the air, cried, prayed that his wife and family and God and the public would forgive him, which they all seemed to . . . and then he went and did it again. He went on television again, cried again, and asked for forgiveness a second time, and it was again granted. But he lost his enormous flock and as of this writing was back in the Assemblies of God church's good bosom, though more as a scholar and admitted sinner than as the rabble-rousing fund-raiser of old.

The story of the man rising from the dead always fascinated me, as it has billions. I knew it wasn't possible, but now and then I'd say to myself, "Of course it isn't possible . . . but what if it happened? I mean I know it couldn't . . . but what if it did? The disciples who claim to have seen Him may have been true believers and were at least superb at PR, but it couldn't happen. Only, what if it did? How come all those brilliant minds throughout the centuries thought it happened? It couldn't be true . . . but what if it was? It would certainly end all argument about religion. And if it wasn't, the story at the very least espoused a great philosophy."

Most (all?) movies about evangelists set out to prove them crooks—most famously, *Elmer Gantry*—and Dolly and I wanted to make one that didn't.

I've been wildly disposed toward southern women since childhood. My very first serious backseat session took place on a double date in New York at age fourteen with a girl from Tennessee. Her willing clotheslessness, the languor of her voice and gesture, the ease with which she succumbed to every frenetic maneuver I made (I was a Yankee, after all), made me feel older, stronger, more triumphant than my years would suggest. I wrote her several passionate and explicit letters after she went home, all unanswered. Deliriously in love, I finally phoned her. She said, "You got me in a whole lotta trouble. My daddy opens all my mail, and I can't ever talk to you again." My heart was broken. Undone by the post office again!

Dolly recorded a song called "He's Alive," told from the viewpoint of a visitor to the tomb where Christ was laid. The rhythm pulsates with mystery until she discovers the tomb is empty and realizes He's risen from the dead—which means He's alive. Here the song hits a smashing crescendo that Dolly rides beautifully, and with my own questions of faith whirling around, this thrilling song—what if it were *true?*—made me wonder if writing this film was more than coincidental.

When I first met with her in Los Angeles in 1989 (me already primed to fall, her mind so swift, perception so honest, self-invention so extraordinary, heart so pure, and inside a little girl so terrified occasionally peeked out . . . *and* she was a southerner), we talked over her character's Achilles' heel—alcohol, drugs, money, power, doubt, loss of faith—what would it be? She looked me gently but unapologetically in the eye and with a beguiling innocence said, "Jonathan, my weakness is . . . men," thereby setting in stone what would undo Sister Sunshine, as well as, I hoped, me.

Dolly wrote wonderful music and lyrics for the film but ultimately wound up disliking the script almost as much as Paramount did. I never found out why. As with most Hollywood rejections, you never do. I think she thought the role too complicated, and indeed she was at her best live onstage or on television, where she could be direct, extempore, and sincere. At any rate, without her participation, Paramount was only too delighted to shelve a project that had made them so anxious in the first place. Needless to say, my heart was completely broke, as it is by all southern women.

But months before that, there I was, somewhere near Dobson, North Carolina, searching for that camp meeting (a small revival with a minister going at it), and I found a little dinette selling chicken-fried steak—a slab o' beef battered and deep-fried—and also featuring malteds. I ordered one as a curiosity, recalling that soda fountain on Madison and Eighty-fifth. It was so cold and so thick and probably so bad for you that I ordered another, and almost every day for about two weeks returned for what was rapidly becoming a very fattening addiction.

And ever since then, two associations pop into my head every time I put straw to lip—my own childhood and Dolly Parton. It's not that the malteds in Dobson were so extraordinary—after all, you just shake a little powder into milkshake fixin's—but that they existed at all. Ovaltine contains malt, but unchocolated malt is difficult to find. The Vermont Country Store sells Horlicks, and I've occasionally seen jars of Carnation's version, and the pure stuff can be found in health-food stores. In Philadelphia, you might get lucky and come across a Dusty Miller—coffee ice cream sprinkled with malt. At places whose food curve changes glacially—like, say, country clubs—it can still be found, but malt isn't carried in most supermarkets.

Easier to find are malted-milk balls—a single detractor of which I have yet to find in North America or the British Isles after an extensive, though admittedly anecdotal, survey. Among the best purveyors—aside from the cinemas that mark up Whoppers so astronomically I once thought of scalping them outside—is Dylan's Candy Bar on the Upper East Side, named after and run by Ralph Lauren's daughter (and a person in her own right). There, among other delights, you can find balls covered with dense, dark chocolate. About 96% of the time I prefer dark or semisweet chocolate, but in the case of malted-milk balls, dark overwhelms and yields a slightly bitter taste. Milk chocolate isn't so competitive. At Oren's Daily Roast you can feast on ones shellacked with espresso. The Brits enter the competition with Maltesers, which even some patriotic Yanks prefer.

But don't eat them all from the bag if you can help it, because they can be taken home and chopped and crushed and strangled into delicious cakes, pies, ice creams, puddings, and muffins. If you can't find malted-milk balls easily, go to the movies and see anything with Gene Hackman or Keira Knightley or Diane Lane in it. Buy several boxes (or if sold in bulk, several pounds).

But whether you invest the time and effort to make a pie or cake or even a shake, use malt to flavor something, because it's a snap to use: Open the jar, insert the spoon, remove a heaper, and dust it on anything, ranging from oatmeal to the peanut butter of a sandwich. If you like sweet alcoholic drinks—a piña colada, say, or a good rum punch as the sun sinks over the yardarm late in July—malting them gives you the experience of being a child and an adult at the same time, possibly one in love with Dolly Parton. And bourbonless, it's a great remedy for a hangover.

A Great Malted

3 scoops (about 8 ounces) vanilla ice cream, slightly softened (aficionados claim the ice cream should be vanilla regardless of the flavor of the syrup)

½ cup 1-percent, 2-percent, or whole milk

¼ cup chocolate, strawberry, or any other flavored syrup

2 tablespoons malted-milk powder, or to taste

½ teaspoon vanilla extract

Pinch nutmeg or whipped cream (optional)

In a blender, pulse all the ingredients on low speed just until smooth, about 20 seconds. (Don't overblend—the shake will become too soupy.) Pour the shake into a soda glass and top with nutmeg or whipped cream, if desired.

YIELD: 1 serving.

NOTE: For a vanilla malted, increase the milk to ¾ cup and omit the syrup.

CHOCOLATE MALTED ICEBOX PUDDING

4 slices pumpernickel bread, torn into small pieces
4 ounces milk-chocolate squares
1 ounce semisweet chocolate squares
3 cups heavy or whipping cream
3 tablespoons malted-milk powder
1 tablespoon confectioners' sugar
½ teaspoon vanilla extract

1. In a food processor, pulse the bread into crumbs (you should have about 1 cup). Transfer to a bowl. Using the large holes of a grater, grate the two kinds of chocolate. Add to the bread crumbs and set aside.
2. In a large mixer bowl, beat 2½ cups of the cream, the malted-milk powder, confectioners' sugar, and vanilla until stiff. With a large rubber spatula, fold half the bread crumbs and chocolate into the whipped cream just until blended. Repeat with the remaining bread crumbs and chocolate.
3. Spoon the pudding into a 1½-quart soufflé dish or serving bowl; smooth the top. Cover and refrigerate overnight.
4. Just before serving, beat the remaining ½ cup cream until stiff and decoratively spread over the top of the pudding.

YIELD: 8 servings.

Lee and Me

⌒⌒⌒⌒⌒

B UT WHEN IT CAME to true love, there was only one.

I fell in love with her the way most people who met her did—at first sight, passionately, like a sheepdog. I was maybe three years old, and she was probably nine, and we were on a beach somewhere, and had anything come of it, we both would have been in a great deal of trouble in every state except Louisiana, because we were first cousins.

Those of us who adored her were transfixed not only by her perfect Episcopalian beauty, and the alluring carnality underneath, and that laugh—head thrown back, mouth open, teeth flashing the sky—but also because being with her made us feel so good. It's been said of Frank Sinatra that if you were ever around him, in whatever mood he was, you were by definition at the hippest spot on earth. With Lee, you were at the happiest.

She reminded me of a Fitzgerald heroine, and we were all wearing the gold hat and bouncing as high as we could to move her. She had many friends and loved nothing more than girdling her dining table with them and feeding them, though you'd never guess it from her waist, which, until the end, simply wouldn't expand. People fell for her, just fell for her; she was surrounded by the aura of the Charmed, chosen by God or one of His best friends for the graceful and glamorous glide through life afforded to a handful. No heartache, no setback, no sadness. Or so it seemed through my inverted binoculars from the other side of the family. Was it self-pity, resentment, or envy that made me idealize *those* Remicks so and excoriate *our* Remicks?

Those Remicks were golden—handsome Uncle Bus, his lively beauty of a first wife, Pat, their children of such promise and zest. Why did they seem untouched by the depression and uncertainty that cloaked us like a comfortable and familiar duvet? For one thing, Dad had rejected us, and though he never saw them, he hadn't rejected them.

Of course they were beautiful. The older child, Bruce, was all boy, full of mischief, and wanted to be a rancher and work with animals. Lee was training to be a ballerina, but when she converted to acting, she became successful in what seemed like minutes, but inevitable minutes—seasons of stock, out of town with Broadway shows, then appearing on Broadway at seventeen in a few-night wonder, *Be Your Age*. I wasn't jealous. I was in awe.

And then she was chosen in '57 by Elia Kazan, the greatest director of his generation and certainly the best manipulator of actors in the history of the medium, to be in *A Face in the Crowd*. He saw in her not only the spoiled, erotic teenage baton-twirler she played in that movie opposite Andy Griffith but also the repressed, erotic spinster in her best picture, the seldom-seen jewel *Wild River*, with Montgomery Clift.

Lots happened after *A Face in the Crowd* was released. She married a dashing television director with a bright future, Bill Colleran; she got pinched by Prince Philip and wooed by the president of the United States; she made one movie after another; she had two children. She and Bill invited me out to movies like *Sweet Smell of Success* and plays like *Long Day's Journey into Night*, the original—and if you think the recent run was something, you shoulda seen Fredric March and Jason Robards. You shoulda seen Lee. It wasn't just that every head turned; it was that every head turned and she still focused on you. On me, actually.

Even her failures were honorable: There hasn't been as respectable a financial disaster on Broadway since *Anyone Can Whistle* lasted only a week. She met Sondheim, and there were rumors of a romance with him. If true, it wouldn't have been her first or last involvement with a gay man. She made *Days of Wine and Roses* and was nominated for an Oscar.

No life is a glide, of course, and my cousin Lee's trajectory jerked. While driving home alone one night in Los Angeles, Bill smashed up his car—and his body. Lee, who was filming *Wild River* in Mississippi, flew to his hospital bed. "His head is the size of a watermelon," she told her father, "and he doesn't remember anything." She spent the better part of the next year nursing him. Bill had a short fuse and though he'd been very successful in television directing what used to be called "spectaculars" as well as the weekly *Your Hit Parade*, he was never popular with executives. The accident, coupled with his reputation, prevented him from regaining his position. He was no longer "promising"; he was Mr. Remick.

In those days, homosexuality was considered a neurotic disease that could be conquered, and Bill "had been" gay before he married Lee. He wanted a heterosexual family life and, for a while, succeeded. Lee knew about his past but also believed the contemporary psychiatric evaluation that someone gay could change if only he thought the right thoughts and disciplined himself. In the sixties, Bill re-exited the closet and shortly after I returned from London in '67, the two split up, after nine or ten years of marriage.

In memory, it seemed more difficult to tell who was gay and who was straight in those days; the assumption was that people were straight. Maybe .5% weren't; but they adopted straight mannerisms because being gay was so terribly, terribly horrible. Despite his occasional wild idea for a comeback— "How about this for a show? Lee and Harry Belafonte in a musical of *Rain!*"— I never thought Bill was anything but a good family man; I don't know if Lee's mother and father did or not.

Lee loved that I had spent fifteen months in London and wanted to hear every detail, night after night—about every stage performance, a description of every street corner, and not the number of times it rained but the size of the drops. So when she made the film *Hard Contract* in Spain in 1969, she was primed to fall for an Englishman—and did. His name was Kip Gowans, and he was the very straight assistant director on the film, a handsome and tough working-class bloke with sideburns and a flat stomach. I warned her about English food, but she said, "I don't care! I'll cook."

She moved to London with the kids, who proceeded to have what might be called extreme adolescence: constant nightmares, experimentation with sex and substances, confusion. Neither liked her second husband because he was a tough disciplinarian and wanted his wife all to himself. The household filled with repressed fury. Lee tried to side with everyone.

Her movie career waned as she hit the wall most actresses run into: the age of forty. She made small movies in England and played Churchill's mother in the miniseries *Jennie*. But she miraculously rebounded on American television, where she soon became the queen of the made-for-TV movie for more than a decade. It seemed that the American public responded to her essential decency, and whenever she went astray onscreen, it was not without conflict; her personal morality always came through.

Though Kip was in demand as an A.D. (assistant director) in England, when they all moved to Los Angeles to take advantage of her newfound television career, American unions wouldn't allow him to work. Always a man proud of his trade, he became a heavy drinker. Lee defended him all over town, made him her producer. But he, too, became Mr. Remick. Upper-middle-class Los Angeles can be a trap for teenagers: too much money, too many cars, guilty parents, competitive escapades, unlimited sex. The kids suffered from too much freedom.

I visited her and felt instantly close again, as I always did. This is how close: I took her to lunch one afternoon when I was thinking of marrying Charlotte, whom she knew and liked.

"Do you think I should get married?" I asked her. Her blue eyes danced—she thought I was kidding. People don't ask their cousins for permission to marry. But I thought she'd know—was there something I was missing? She reminded me that a few years earlier, she'd told me about her failed marriage to Bill: "Everything is there in front of you at the beginning; you just don't choose to see some of it."

Lee realized now I wasn't kidding, and that her response would make a difference.

"Yes," she said.

"Do you think I will?"

"I think you better!" she said, laughing. And I did.

She bought a splendid house in Osterville, on Cape Cod, and after Charlotte and I had Eddie and Frank, we spent Christmases there with her. She was an enthusiastic cook, and her house was filled with cookbooks. "I read them before I go to bed," she said, "the way other people read mysteries." When her daughter, Kate, turned eighteen, Lee handwrote a cookbook for her with special instructions, which included: "1. Always read entire recipe from start to finish. . . . Nothing makes you crazier than getting halfway through and finding out there's something missing. 2. When in any doubt, it's better to cook on a lower flame than a higher one—because burning things is boring. . . . 7. The most important single thing to remember is to clean up as you go along."

Then, in the spring of 1989, as I was trying to sell a pitch to Paramount, I visited her in her Brentwood home. She was filming a TV movie and said in passing, "I've had this temperature about one degree above normal for a few days."

I didn't know what this meant. "How many days?"

"About a month."

When the film wrapped, she was told the cancer had metastasized from her kidneys to her lungs and brain.

She was more astonished than upset. Her New England upbringing taught her to face this as she had all the other challenges in life: forthrightly and without bitterness. Isn't this curious, this happening to me, she thought. There was no question that she would recover—just a little chemo and some surgery, just another little hurdle to clear—and, by God, she did, and with good cheer. She was in remission, and she was signed to do Sondheim's *A Little Night Music* at the Ahmanson in L.A.

Then, during a follow-up scan, she was told that she had seventeen new tumors in her brain. Her longtime friend Karla Champion was at the hospital and remembers Lee being annoyed but asking her doctor, "Well, what do we do now?"

"Denial" is psychobabble jargon and currently in disrepute, but sometimes it's one of the more useful weapons in our arsenal, as Ibsen illustrated in *The Wild Duck* and O'Neill in *The Iceman Cometh*. And Lee's refusal to clearly see or believe her fate wasn't foolish—it was thrilling.

Also thrilling was the reaction of her friends. As her body and face became swollen from the steroids and she gradually lost the ability to walk, we gathered nightly to feed her—body and soul. And ours. She actually had rolling, raucous parties centered on her and food, at once comforting and uniting, and on laughs and enjoyment of her last days on earth. Roddy and Bobby gossiped, and Glover massaged her feet, and Nanny and David reminisced, and the Guests and Axelrods told funny stories, and Beverly helped make her favorite shepherd's pie, and everybody brought food.

After she died, I wondered if her constant attempt to accommodate, to absorb the problems with children and husbands and friends as her own, made her more susceptible to the disease, or if her weakened resistance allowed it in. She blamed herself for poor judgment with Bill, for Kip's unemployment and alcoholism, for being away on a set while her kids went haywire.

Did she do it to herself? What if she had said, "Fuck off! Rescue your own damn selves!" Would she have avoided the cancer? Unknowable, of course. But if she had, she would have been a different person.

I was tantalized by Chinese food then and made her one of her other favorites—a seriously Szechuan hacked chicken. Her children, Kate and Matt, and Kip and Karla nursed her. Of course, when anyone took a breath and stepped back, there was incredible sadness—but lugubriousness isn't allowed in New England, even if it is in Hollywood, and it wasn't in that Brentwood house. We watched her die, and in its curious way, it was uplifting. She wasn't "brave" or "valiant," but of course, she was. She watched her demise with the curiosity and wonder of a child. Occasionally there was a shriek of terror from the bedroom, and concern for her children's future, but little anger.

She would have thrilled to see her daughter, Kate, a landscaper and contented married mother of two girls, Remick and Georgia; and her son, Matt, a bicycle fiend and an important digital-sound recordist in the movie business.

I haven't wanted to see any of her movies since, preferring to keep her alive in my memory, which she is to this day as much as she was before she gently stopped breathing on July 2, 1991, at age fifty-five. But I keep being reminded how good she is in *Wine and Roses* and as Churchill's mother in *Jennie* and in her funniest role, in the miniseries *Nutcracker,* so one of these days I will, and you shouldn't wait for me.

Lee Remick's Barbecued Chinese Duck

Four 1-pound duck breasts

1 cup sherry

2 tablespoons brown sugar or honey

3 tablespoons soy sauce

1 teaspoon powdered ginger
1 teaspoon powdered mustard
Toasted sesame seeds for garnish

---

1. Trim excess fat and skin from the duck breasts. Combine the sherry, sugar, soy sauce, ginger, and mustard and pour over the duck. Marinate several hours or overnight, turning occasionally.
2. Drain the duck and reserve the marinade. Grill 20–25 minutes over medium heat, turning and moving duck to avoid flare-ups while basting frequently.
3. Allow the duck to rest for 5 minutes before slicing. Sprinkle with sesame seeds before serving.

YIELD: 6 servings.

SZECHUAN HACKED CHICKEN FOR LEE

1 tablespoon Szechuan peppercorns
1½ cups peanut oil
2¼ pounds chicken breasts
9 tablespoons peanut butter
3 tablespoons sesame oil
3 tablespoons soy sauce
3 tablespoons white vinegar
3 teaspoons MSG
4 teaspoons cayenne (or less, to taste)
4½ teaspoons minced ginger
5 teaspoons chopped scallions
5 teaspoons minced garlic
2–4 teaspoons crushed red-pepper flakes
2 tablespoons chopped fresh cilantro

---

1. Fry the Szechuan peppercorns in the oil for 15 minutes. Discard the peppercorns, and reserve 4½ tablespoons of oil for this recipe. (Save remainder for another purpose. It will keep for months in the fridge.)

2. Skin and bone the chicken, then plunge it into boiling water and simmer till just barely cooked through, about 5 minutes. Cut into ¼-inch-thick strips 3 inches long.

3. Blend the peanut butter and sesame oil until smooth. Stir in all the remaining ingredients except the red-pepper flakes and cilantro.

4. Add 2 teaspoons of the red-pepper flakes and then taste, adding up to 2 more, according to your tolerance. Then add as much of the reserved oil as necessary to make a sauce that isn't overly greasy.

5. Arrange the chicken on a platter, spoon the sauce over it, and sprinkle the cilantro on top. Serve at room temperature.

YIELD: 6 servings.

Fear of Frying

~~~~~~

I NEVER SANG for my father, to quote my friend the playwright Robert Anderson, but I did finally manage to cook for him. Twice. The first effort was so unsuccessful that I was banished from his kitchens forever. It happened during a family gathering at his house in Kona, Hawaii, at Christmastime, 1991, nearly six months after Lee died. By then, family meant not only his three children, our spouses, and six grandchildren, but his gorgeous new girlfriend, Virginia McCartney, who actually loved the old weasel, and three or four aides who knew him infinitely better than the rest of us did.

Dad's mental decline had been noticeable back at his eightieth birthday party in 1986. He stared blankly for a few extra seconds, or his eyes welled up with tears for no apparent reason, or he simply didn't recognize people he'd known all his life. He threw himself the party because, he said, with that merry glint in his eye, "I wanted to see all my old girlfriends." And they and lots of others came to his Las Vegas mansion that night and ate huge amounts of lobster and drank booze from a table adorned with a bust of him carved in lard and an ice sculpture made of the company logo. Outside, where dinner seating was formal, the swimming pool was covered over so a stage could be erected for the stand-up performance of George Burns and the songs of the two remaining Mills Brothers, one of his all-time favorite groups. Of course, they sang his favorite song, "Paper Doll," which years ago the original four had made a hit, and the lyrics of which were startlingly revealing:

I'm gonna buy a paper doll that I can call my own
A doll that other fellows cannot steal
And then the flirty, flirty guys with their flirty, flirty eyes
Will have to flirt with dollies that are real.

When I come home at night she will be waiting
She'll be the truest doll in all this world
I'd rather have a paper doll to call my own
Than have a fickle-minded real live girl.

I think he'd always wanted a two-dimensional relationship with a gorgeous, never-aging woman who'd provide snappy dialogue at dinner, do everything he asked, let him alone when he wanted but also be there when he wanted. That he would publicly announce this sentiment in a song—with the financial contract spelled out ("I'm gonna buy a paper doll that I can call my own")—was unusually candid for a businessman who kept such a low and cautious profile that he shredded all his company papers every few years. His chief associate, Fred Smith, who was in charge of the party, had also arranged for the more generic "My Way" to be played and sung incessantly—same as at any party or bar mitzvah where the honoree once had an unusual idea.

I met my half-brother, Don Junior, for the first time at that birthday. I was in my forties, Don in his fifties. He was the issue of Dad and his second wife and spent too many years of his life working for him. He had Dad's stocky build and exuberant speech intonations, and it was a fascinating meeting. We strolled around Dad's grounds feeling each other out, trying to see what, if anything, we had in common, both genetically and psychologically. We got on right away. Don was funny and ironic about our father's influence on him and we laughed and sighed a lot. Under his gruff and bouncy exterior, I sensed a serious, lifelong hurt with which I was familiar, a feeling that whatever he did, he could never measure up to Dad or his expectations. Perhaps I was projecting, but as I see it, it wasn't until Dad died that Don Junior picked up a pencil, some chalk, and a brush, and began to draw. In his sixties, after a lifetime flailing around trying to please our unpleasant father, he became an artist!

Dad's three chief business associates (they weren't partners—Dad was the only stockholder and answered to no one) convinced him that he should now enjoy the fruits of his labor, relax, and gradually withdraw from the day-to-day operations of Donrey Media Group. This was contingent, of course, on Fred Smith keeping him informed on a regular basis. To cap this retirement plan, Fred suggested Dad surround himself with his loving family, and urged us all to fly to Hawaii as often as we could and spend time with him.

A stupider man than Fred might have tried to keep the children away from their father in case he uncharacteristically fell in love with them and changed his will to include them and lock out any associates. But Fred knew Dad well—he'd had only one job in his life, and that was working for "Mr. Reynolds" since the mid-sixties. He knew Mr. Reynolds wasn't about to get softhearted, and that Mr. Reynolds had long since made a gas- and water-tight will that favored Fred and two other associates and didn't favor the Reynolds children. Fred also shrewdly calculated that should the children protest the will, at least they (that is, we) couldn't accuse Fred of trying to keep father from children. In fact, he was practically forcing us together after years of lack of interest. And, incidentally, Dad would have companionship and plenty of distraction to keep his mind off Donrey Media.

So twice a year for four years, Charlotte and I would first-class Eddie and Frank to Kona, for the sort of vacations game-show contestants scream about. For the first two visits, Hawaii was an entertaining novelty; and the boys loved every second of splashing around pools and taking scary sightseeing trips in helicopters, and swimming with their medicated, sweet old grand-dad. For me, the charms of humid and dull Hawaii quickly turned into biannual obligations. Dad was beyond having a meaningful conversation, and the trips there soon became an endless routine of unexpressive meals together. He didn't have Alzheimer's, Fred explained, but he did have dementia.

That first attempt to cook for him was an overambitious disaster, during which I loonily decided that the Swiss chef Fredy Girardet's recipe for a blanquette of salmon and shrimp (the same one that took so long on Oscar night in Winston) needed the improvement of masses of onions sweated in butter, on the theory that everything that goes in or on the human body can be improved by the addition of sautéed onions.

Not only did this upset the delicate symmetry of the Swiss master's creation; it also made such a mess of the presentation that my father, already wandering agonizingly around his own mental Sea of Tranquility, took a look at his plate and cried out: "What am I eating? What am I eating here?" He was panicky and mad. While the other relatives seemed sincere in their praise, though bullied by Dad's fury, I realized I had forever gummed up my chances of so much as boiling water for him in any state where he owned a newspaper.

Dad was at that dangerous state of mindlessness during which you never knew whether he understood what you were saying or not. Gregarious as hell and an aggressive-aggressive before his dementia struck, he'd now often be violently silent, increasingly reminding me of my mother, a noted passive-aggressive. At lunch for the two of us one day, just as I'd mustered the courage to delve into the lifetime of dreams and disappointments that I'd always been afraid to tell him about, I threw in an off-the-cuff reference to a failed business venture forty years earlier in Alaska. He called in a couple of Black Hawks. "I didn't fail in Alaska!" he roared back at me. "Sold that paper for twice what I bought it for!" Steam flew out of every orifice, and for a moment his anger almost levitated him, like a wildly spouting balloon.

So the effort to cook for him was more loaded than, say, the night the Michelin man comes to your restaurant. I visited him once or twice in Hot Springs, Arkansas, where he had a house I don't think he recognized and a Thoroughbred racehorse with whom he felt increasingly *simpático*. Four or five of us would lunch with him at the track whenever his horse ran, and Dad would order fried catfish every single time. It didn't take too many races for me to realize that if I was ever going to show him I could do something on a stove besides make a mess, it would have to be with fried catfish, hold the sautéed onions.

I invited him to Bullhead for a few days one summer, and much to my surprise, he accepted. He'd long ago replaced the Ten Commandments with about thirty of his own, and the first was, "Fish and houseguests smell after three days," so I knew his stay wouldn't be long, just Armageddonian. The frantic housecleaning that ensued was rivaled in scope only by his arrival on the Donrey 727 at the airport in Winston-Salem. With an entourage that would impress the current resident of 1600 Pennsylvania Avenue, I motored him up the mountain in a fifteen-year-old Lincoln, which he liked because the front passenger area was roughly the size of Kenya, providing him enough room to swing his arthritic legs out to the pavement without all the bending and scrambling required in the next-largest conveyance, the Bradley Fighting All-Terrain Vehicle.

By now I knew something about catfish. He liked the muddier taste of the wild catfish he had grown up with, not the blander farm-raised that's generally available now, and he liked a good crackle. At this point, annoyances like cholesterol didn't concern him. Once I heard he was coming, I broiled several, deep-fried some, and sent away for mail-order breaders, coatings, and batters. Finally, I decided on a simple cornmeal-and-spice breading and held my breath.

As soon as he arrived that afternoon, Dad took a nap and woke up in a blind rage. He was brought upstairs to our living room, and, eighty-three years old and deep into his senility, suddenly shouted in panic, "Where's my money? Where's my money!" I certainly didn't know. He sure hadn't given it to me. His aides, Lee and Dennis, and his companion, Virginia, couldn't calm him down.

"In a bank in Little Rock?" I tried to cool the boil. "Or Las Vegas. Or Kona?" I was bewildered by this man whom Forbes had recently dubbed a billionaire at a time when a billion dollars was a lot of money.

But he was unmollified. "How do you know? Have you seen it? Have you?"

"Well, no, but what about your associates, surely Fred, and Ross and Pat—"

"Those guys have been robbing me blind my whole life!" he shouted. He was hyperventilating. It took several minutes to talk him down from that window ledge. We assured him his money was safe and that Fred and company weren't robbing him. And then, just as suddenly as he'd flared up, he calmed right down and the panic left his face. I offered him Scotch. He politely accepted. But the specter of winding up poor like his father never left him.

I quickly threw together the fried catfish, first soaking the fillets in buttermilk, then dredging them in cornmeal and spices, and pan-fried them up. Couldn't have been simpler.

Charlotte presented an overflowing platter to my father, his aides, and Virginia. He took several bites and mashed them in what remained of his teeth, and something clicked. He looked up at me suspiciously—where had I had this flown in from? But then his milky, alcohol-drenched eyes softened, and for an instant there was connection—even appreciation.

"You . . . did . . . this . . . for me?" those eyes seemed to say.

Which was about the best that could be expected, and all I'd been after all along. And the man who could no longer shave himself or find his billion dollars at last took satisfaction in something that cost $2.49.

Dad died three years later, on a cruise near Spain. Both my parents spared me the anguish of caring for them in their declining years—Dad, by virtue of his wealth, with plenty of people around him, all taking care of him; Mother, by dying of a heart attack, suddenly and young, at sixty-two, with no apparent health problems except glaucoma.

Though Dad left us three Reynolds kids enough money to pay the rent—literally, the rent—we were removed from his posthumous enterprises by Fred Smith, not to be confused with the founder of Federal Express. After a few months feigning interest in our joining the board of the Donald W. Reynolds Foundation and allowing us to make a single generous gift from it (I gave mine to Denison), Fred became president of the foundation, installed his own family (and Dad's doctor . . . hmmm . . . call *CSI*? Just kidding) on the board, and baldly shut us out. The foundation's assets were $800 million at Dad's death and have grown substantially since then, despite the annual 5% distribution required by law. Dad's name is now plastered on several medical and journalism schools, and Fred engineered the building of several edifices in states where Dad's businesses flourished—chiefly Nevada, Arkansas, and Oklahoma—glorifying Dad's good name. Among them, the Donald W. Reynolds Razorback football stadium for the University of Arkansas in Fayetteville and a geriatric center in Little Rock stand out. And Fred saw to it that at least one building was named after himself, also at the University of Arkansas. Dad achieved a mean reputation as a boss, in keeping with his union-busting activities, and in hopes of repairing his reputation, the foundation gave the Smithsonian a $30 million grant to buy Gilbert Stuart's Lansdowne portrait of George Washington, and in 2005 gave the Smithsonian an additional $45 million to restore the Old Patent Office Building and rename it the Donald W. Reynolds Center for American Art and Portraiture. Though Don junior and I chuckled over Dad's sudden and posthumous interest in art—mostly what I remember are portraits of the houses he owned that he hung over fireplaces, and a few Remington sculptures of the Wild West—it's clear the advantage private funding has over government subsidy. Didn't quite repair the lesions in *my* house, but with the good works the foundation has done, I don't think I'd get much sympathy as a movie hero.

But with Dad's death, gone overnight and forever was that extra little privilege that inflated my chest whenever I set foot in McCarran airport. To be near him for the little time I was was to be associated not just with power and money, but with ambition, amazing energy, a great sense of humor, astonishing cruelty, and the unflagging religion of individualism. I thought some of those things might rub off, but the ones required for gargantuan success didn't. And I'd begun to re-evaluate that individualism. The world can tolerate a few thousand people who think only of themselves, and might even be stimulated by them—but not a few billion. The line between total self-expression and social detriment is fine and etched with responsibility. America risks becoming too individualistic in the world, and without a balance between the absolute Darwinian and total altruism, will do great damage.

Dad's body was brought back to Las Vegas in his 727, and he was cremated. Almost before the ashes were soft, the three associates sold his company and became very, very, very rich men.

I tried to sort out what he'd meant to me. By disappearing, fathers convey that their children aren't important—not to them, not to the world—whether they mean to or not. I surely missed love and affection from Dad, but I don't think I'd have had it if he were around all the time; he didn't have it to give. My half-brother, Don, had Dad in his life till he was almost sixty, and it was calamitous for him. I missed Dad's not being around so that I could see him realistically—well, as realistically as any child sees any parent—and could experience more of him rather than turning his life into a fairy tale of exaggerated evil and Hollywood megawattage. I didn't see him take his shirt off at night and know his muscles weren't perfect or hear him be boring at the dinner table or watch him fail occasionally at business or, God knows, observe him being tender with Mother, which he must have been, once or twice. I never saw him naked.

Given that just about every child feels his parents should have loved him more, what I missed most became, by default, practical. All hows: How did he get so much exuberance? How did he come by so much self-confidence? How come he was so smart? And how the hell do you get the world to work for you the way he did?

Buttermilk-and-Cornmeal Pan-Fried Catfish

1 cup buttermilk or water
2 cups yellow cornmeal
½ teaspoon salt
½ teaspoon pepper
3 tablespoons Cajun seasoning (or to taste)
½ cup peanut oil for frying
Four 8-ounce catfish fillets

1. Place buttermilk in a shallow bowl. In another shallow bowl combine cornmeal, salt, pepper, and Cajun seasoning.
2. Heat about ⅛ inch of the oil in large skillet over medium heat until a pinch of cornmeal mixture sizzles quickly.
3. Dip catfish fillets into buttermilk to coat on both sides. Drain excess and dredge fillets in cornmeal mixture, coating both sides. Shake off excess.
4. Fry fillets in oil, 3–4 minutes on each side, adding oil as necessary, until nicely browned and crisp.

YIELD: 4 servings.

Red-Cabbage-and-Roquefort Slaw

(Adapted from Nantucket Open-House Cookbook *by Sarah Leah Chase, Workman, 1987)*

2 medium heads red cabbage
2 cups finely chopped fresh parsley (about 4 bunches)

1½ cups crumbled Roquefort cheese (about 8 ounces)

3½ cups mayonnaise

½ cup grainy mustard

1. Remove a few outer leaves of the cabbages, rinse, dry, and use to line a large serving bowl. Quarter and core cabbages; cut wedges crosswise into thin shreds. Place in a large bowl with 1½ cups of the parsley and 1 cup of the cheese.

2. Combine mayonnaise and mustard in a medium bowl and whisk until blended. Pour into cabbage mixture and toss to coat. Sprinkle with remaining cheese and parsley. Cover and refrigerate at least 2 hours before serving.

YIELD: 16 servings.

Eating with the ★ ★ ★

AFTER THREE YEARS in Winston, Charlotte insisted that we move to L.A. if I was to continue going there so frequently. I'd always enjoyed visiting L.A. but shied away from setting up house there because it made the movie world inescapable. You were there, in it, like spiders climbing up the smooth side of a greasy trash can, unable to get traction and unable to get out. In New York and Winston-Salem, there was retreat—and perspective.

We were both right. Living there was better for the kids and, for a while, for us; and it was excruciatingly enlightening. In 1991, we rented a house in Santa Monica, where we were assured that the temperature was always ten degrees lower because it was west of the 405. (A true Angeleno refers to the notorious freeways by number rather than by name—so we first had to jettison the San Diego Freeway and the Ventura Freeway from our vocabularies in favor of the 405 and the 101. But then numbers have always carried more weight than poetry in Burbank. Up north, they drop the *the*.) Real estate is more expensive in Santa Monica than in Winston, but we all managed comfortably, and I continued to work at home.

Frank and Eddie were, again, horrified. Having just put down roots in the South, and loving those roots, they were once more yanked out of the ground and thrown into a much bigger cauldron of strangers, odd customs, different and disturbing social hierarchies. Personality didn't matter as much in L.A. as it did in North Carolina; money, fame, position, and which car you drove mattered most. In Winston, "My dad writes screenplays" ensured an otherworldly reputation. Out west, it carried the same prestige as "My dad drives a taxi" (actually less, since taxis in Los Angeles are pretty otherworldly). It was as though we'd moved to the Moon: On Earth I weighed 170; Out There, 55.

Fortunately, we still had Bullhead, to which I anticipated we would all return for holidays, summers, earthquakes, riots, and terrorist attacks—most of which we encountered in our first two years in Santa Monica. The headaches at Jane Street continued. A new boiler was needed. New windows. The roof leaked, ruining the tenant's grand piano! Meanwhile, we tried to sink roots into the Pacific.

Fat chance.

During my painful incarnation as a resident screenwriter, I once found myself seated in first class right behind Michael Jackson at the height of his inventive powers, well after "Billie Jean" and *Thriller*, and right next to his chef, who told me that she nearly always flew with him. Flying first class is one of the great joys—most say the only joy—of writing for the screen.

On this particular trip, however, the chef regaled me for three thousand miles across the country with descriptions of her recipes for the Gloved One—leaves and acorns, giraffe-shaped radishes and space sauces, granola fasts and all-grape regimens—none of which would I have then considered putting in my mouth either singly or in combination. At the time, I thought, I'm trapped with an L.A. vegan[3] and her Newly Galactic food.

The truth now, of course, is that Los Angeles is one of the great eating cities of the world, and it's been ages since anyone could make fun of it for its cuisine. Yes, there are health-food stores and more than the average number of pasty-faced vegans, but there are also too many excellent chefs and educated palates braising and feasting every night in the southern 90000 ZIP code to dismiss its cooking. Besides, the tofu and baby spelt legs we on the East Coast once thought lunatic are now sitting on Manhattan tables just possibly saving our lives. And because southern California is the tail that so often wags the American cultural dog, be warned: The fricassee of lobster face you roll your eyes at tonight may just wind up on your plate tomorrow.

In Hollywood, restaurants are a gauge of how well you're doing. Not just which restaurants you're taken to by agents, producers, stars, and studio heads, but the time of day they choose to take you there. If you're invited to dinner by a potential employer, you couldn't be hotter. At lunch, true, your heat is measured by which restaurant the boss has chosen—in the nineties, Spago, Chaya Brasserie, and Ivy at the Shore were indicators of heat; studio commissaries and Musso & Frank's meant you were in trouble. Breakfast, unless it was at the Hotel Bel-Air, meant not even the best golf swing in the county could resuscitate your career.

When you're hot, you don't notice the food—the meeting is too highly charged for anything sybaritic to take place; when you're not, your diary notes became voluminous, or at least mine did. I could chart my success by the length of the food entries in my notebook. In the eighties my notes were short and clipped, and in the nineties, several forests were chopped down to record my increasing gluttony.

The sad but happy fact is, I never learned how to tell a film story, particularly at a pitch meeting. Too many digressions, irrelevancies, inconclusions. Not enough mystery. Sad, because from the outside looking in, I thought I wanted to be in the movie business; happy, because, once in it for a while, I realized that aside from cashing some outsize checks, I didn't want to be in the movie business.

After *Micki & Maude* was released in 1984, it was clear to me that the only artistic power in the business lay in supermoviestardom or directing; I was advised by agents, producers, and friends that because of the success of that movie and my background in the theatre writing and working with actors, all I had to do was come up with my own brilliant screenplay—not one originated or owned by a studio—one the money people would be so desperate to make that they'd be happy for me to direct. And in the twenty years I worked at it (on and off), I never could. At the same time that David Mamet successfully moved from playwriting to screenwriting to directing, I was trying to figure out cause and effect, rising and falling action, and what the hell character arc meant. And all along, where to get a good piece of Patagonian toothfish (a.k.a. Chilean sea bass).

Despite having all those movies made, I took a couple of screenwriting courses, which reduced beloved films of the past like *Casablanca* to mathematics. None of the writers and directors I admired had taken screenwriting or film courses—not Welles or Mankiewicz or Kubrick or Terry Southern or Arthur Penn or Kazan or Benton & Newman or Lubitsch or Wilder or Izzy Diamond or Charles Lederer or Wyler or Elaine May or John Ford or Paddy Chayefsky (but only *The Americanization of Emily*), either Sturges or Woody Allen or Hawks or the Coen brothers or Blake Edwards. Coppola went to USC but it hadn't become the constricted academy it is today. I don't know if David O. Russell or the Farrelly brothers or Amy Heckerling went to film school, but if so, nothing damaging seems to have worn off.

The teaching gurus at the time were Syd Field, Robert McKee, and John Truby. Ironically, not only did aspiring writers and directors attend these script courses, but studio executives did, too. This explains why so many movies resemble one another. The fatuous analyses promulgated by these disappointed writers who were now teachers resulted in a dog-chasing-its-own-tail mentality: Though these courses were initially conceived for writers, studio executives decided they needed a more systematic method of judging scripts other than "I don't know; I liked it"—though that was good enough for Zanuck, Goldwyn, Cohen, and Thalberg—so they began taking the courses, too . . . which meant the execs were deciding to green-light or reject screenplays based on their interpretation of how well the screenwriters' interpretation of the Field/McKee/Truby interpretation of what makes a good movie measured up. If the movie was ever made, this aping the shell of successful movies of the past resulted in nicely shaped, hollow films without an original thought in their heads. The unprecedented and the clever were reserved for the special FX of *The Matrix* and *Crouching Tiger, Hidden Dragon*.

I tried to conform to these rules but couldn't. They exemplified what I disliked not only about the movies, but all the pop culture I couldn't stomach—and my own inability to manufacture some of it. Like so many who wind up in Hollywood, I was in constant struggle between an intense, if fantastical, desire for easy money and fame—which making movies always seems to be from the outside looking in—and the need for some sort of spiritual nourishment professionally. What I could stomach—and like a truant, spent most of my time pursuing—was finding the best source for Brandywine tomatoes or the way to complicate the sharp flavor of a Virginia ham by striating it with spinach and garlic or which downtown bar made the best lamb sandwich, complete with its own *jus* for dipping (Philippe's on Alameda Street). That was sensuality and passion! That was living in the moment! That was fun! It just never occurred to me to make a living at it.

Just like you and me, Hollywood's stars and power brokers have to eat. They just get to do it first. L.A. restaurants are the purest of meritocracies: It doesn't matter who your parents are or where you went to school; if you're famous, you get seated first.

And prominently, just the way your car is parked.

In November 2000, after I'd left Los Angeles, *The New York Times* sent me a list of the city's dining hot spots and asked for an article. Herewith, a sampling of the whos, whats, and wheres on November 12, 2000:

Warren Beatty (whose fingertips Woody Allen reportedly said were what he'd most like to be reincarnated as) regularly orders the sushi without rice at Hamasaku. (Only in Los Angeles would someone dream up riceless sushi and not call it sashimi—sort of like fatless duck confit.)

Annette Bening prefers the intriguing Japanese bouillabaisse. Gina Gershon's bee-stung lips lovingly caress the lamb chops with tomato-mint salsa from Chaya Brasserie, where George Clooney and Matt LeBlanc go for the Chaya steak. Leo No-Last-Name-Needed-for-Another-Ten-Minutes tosses off pretensions with ham and eggs at the Griddle Cafe. It should also be noted that in this weathercock city, Wolfgang Puck's remarkable Spago remained hot longer than just about any other bistro, perhaps, among other things, because of its "Jewish pizza"—a thin slab of smoked salmon dolloped with caviar. None of these restaurants is as hot as it was.

On the set, a rigid class system rules. While the stars sip their strawsful of sugarless broth fumes and vapor of fetal watercress leaf helicoptered to their trailers daily, everyone else gets fat. Grips and gaffers don't usually have personal nutritionists. Because working on a movie set is about as exciting as seeing the movie of *Flower Drum Song* thirty times or *The Hours* once, you blindly reach out for whatever the craft service wagon has on display to quell the boredom—usually an endless supply of doughnuts, meat loaves, fries, burgers and dogs, things in gravies, and quite cosmic pastries drowning in sugars and jams. On a ten-week shoot (or a regular weekly TV series), you don't have to look above the belt line to tell royalty from commoner.

I never got any recipes from Michael Jackson's chef. Michael himself was polite and talkative and quite normal—until the plane landed, the glove went on, and the surgical mask was slipped over one of his noses. He didn't eat a thing the entire journey—perhaps that's the best secret of all.

Special "Lobster"

(Adapted from Mr. Chow of Beverly Hills)

½ pound fresh jumbo shrimp, peeled and deveined

½ egg white

1 teaspoon cornstarch

2 teaspoons salt

1 teaspoon plus ¼ cup vegetable oil

3 tablespoons rice-wine vinegar

1 ½ teaspoons sugar

1 teaspoon potato starch or cornstarch

½ jalapeño chile, seeded and minced

1 teaspoon slivered fresh ginger

1 celery rib, julienned

½ green bell pepper, julienned

½ red bell pepper, julienned

1. In a medium bowl, combine the shrimp, egg white, cornstarch, 1 teaspoon of the salt, and 1 teaspoon of the oil. Mix well. Refrigerate anywhere from 1 to 12 hours.
2. In a small cup, mix the vinegar, remaining teaspoon salt, the sugar, and the potato starch until salt and sugar dissolve. Set aside.
3. Heat the ¼ cup oil in a wok over high heat until hot and add the shrimp mixture, stir-frying 1–1 ½ minutes, until shrimp are pink and curled but not cooked through.
4. Pour shrimp and oil into a sieve over a bowl. Return 1 tablespoon oil to the pan. Add the jalapeño, ginger, vinegar mixture, celery, bell peppers, and

shrimp and stir-fry 1 minute or until shrimp are shiny and evenly coated. (Do not overcook shrimp and vegetables.) Serve immediately.

YIELD: 2 servings.

CHAYA RIB-EYE STEAK
WITH PEPPERCORN BUTTER AND BASIL SAUCE
(Adapted from Chaya Brasserie)

For the peppercorn butter
½ pound unsalted butter, softened
¼ cup black peppercorns, coarsely crushed
¼ cup green peppercorns (not in brine)
¼ cup pink peppercorns
¼ cup finely chopped onions
¼ cup finely chopped shallots
2 tablespoons minced garlic
2 tablespoons chopped fresh chives
2 tablespoons bread crumbs
2 anchovies, rinsed and mashed
Juice from ½ lemon
1 ½ teaspoons chopped parsley
1 teaspoon rock salt or sea salt

For the garnish
2 tablespoons olive oil
15 baby white potatoes
1 head garlic, separated into cloves and peeled
Salt to taste

For the basil sauce
4 tablespoons unsalted butter
½ cup veal stock

1 large basil leaf, finely chopped
Salt to taste
Five 1-pound rib-eye steaks

---

1. To make the peppercorn butter, 3 hours or more before serving, place butter in a bowl and beat with a mixer at high speed until fluffy, about 5 minutes. Fold in the remaining ingredients. Line a loaf pan with plastic wrap, spread mixture in the prepared pan, cover with plastic wrap, and freeze until firm, at least 2 hours.
2. To make the garnish, preheat the oven to 350 degrees. Coat the bottom of a small roasting pan with the oil. Add the potatoes and garlic and sprinkle with salt. Cover tightly with foil and bake 1 hour, stirring every 15 minutes. Uncover the pan and cook 15 minutes, or until potatoes and garlic are tender when pierced.
3. About 30 minutes before making the steaks, take the peppercorn butter out of fridge, unwrap, and bring to room temperature.
4. To make the basil sauce, about 15 minutes before the potatoes are done, melt the butter in a small skillet over medium heat and cook until browned. Add the veal stock and basil and boil for 1 minute to reduce slightly. Season with salt.
5. Grill or broil the steaks to the desired doneness. Cut peppercorn butter into 5 pieces. Place one piece on top of each steak, spoon some basil sauce on top, and serve with the roasted potatoes and garlic.

YIELD: 5 servings.

GOLDEN GAZPACHO WITH AHI TUNA AND HEIRLOOM TOMATOES
(Adapted from Patina)

For the gazpacho
6 large yellow heirloom tomatoes, quartered and seeded
1 yellow bell pepper, roasted, peeled, seeded, and quartered

1 Kirby cucumber, cut into 1-inch chunks

3 tablespoons extra-virgin olive oil

1 tablespoon sherry vinegar

Juice of 1 orange

Juice of 1 lemon

Sea salt to taste

Freshly ground pepper to taste

For the garnish

½ pound sashimi-grade ahi tuna, cut into ¾-inch cubes

20 tiny heirloom tomatoes (5 different colors or varieties), halved

1 bulb baby fennel, finely slivered

12 fennel fronds

20 celery leaves

20 tiny basil leaves

20 sprigs chervil

1 teaspoon finely diced red onion

1 scallion green, sliced into 12 pieces

Sea salt to taste

Freshly ground pepper to taste

1 tablespoon extra-virgin olive oil

1. To make the gazpacho, process the tomatoes, bell pepper, and cucumber in a blender until smooth. Strain through a sieve into a medium bowl. Season with the olive oil, vinegar, orange and lemon juices, salt, and pepper.
2. To serve, arrange ¼ of the tuna, tomatoes, fennel, fennel fronds, celery leaves, basil, chervil, red onion, and scallion in each of 4 large bowls. Sprinkle with the salt, pepper, and olive oil. Ladle the gazpacho over the garnish.

YIELD: 4 servings.

Stargazy Pie

~~~~~~~

I N SANTA MONICA, Frank and Eddie found new friends and eventually settled in. I never did. Tom Baum, a novelist and screenwriter I'd known in New York, took over for Rafe. We had lunch all the time, endless philosophical discussions ("buttering the air," a friend called it), no political fireworks.

In a bizarre turn of events, Tom and his wife, Carol, a movie producer, bought Lee Remick's house in Brentwood shortly after she died. It was hard for me to visit them for about two years, and I regularly invited them to our house or suggested we meet at the movies or a restaurant. When I did go to their house, I felt jumpy and remorseful, though those feelings eventually disappeared. Carol would have been the producer of *Sister Sunshine*, had it advanced to the next stage. The world is the size of a pea in Hollywood.

It was difficult to work with Charlotte in the Santa Monica house. It was half the size of the one in Winston, where we could lose each other. I'd leave the office downstairs for a sandwich, and she'd be reading the paper. Passivity filled the place. She'd brought a set of bizarrely painted chairs and tables from North Carolina in hopes of selling them and starting a business for the artist who'd made them. She showed them to one person who didn't like them, and the set remained unexamined in the garage for another seven or eight years.

After a year, she landed a job as a secretary with another soccer mom who happened to be West Coast editor of *The New Yorker*. Tina Brown had recently taken over as editor, and, flush with her success at *Vanity Fair*, had fortuitously opened a small office in L.A., only three blocks from our house, just in time for the O.J. murders, an earthquake, and the Eisner-Ovitz marriage. It was a perfect jumping-off point for Charlotte, now beginning a new career. She was meant for the magazine world: literate, articulate, skilled in grammar and language, focused with ideas. Initially it was a godsend, and she'd return home at night bubbling with stories and the idiosyncrasies of her boss, a bouncy Brit named Caroline Graham who'd been a girlfriend of David Frost and a wife of Bill Graham of the *Washington Post* family. Unfortunately, Charlotte didn't advance beyond the assistant level or land a position with another magazine, and when Tina left and David Remnick took over, he de-L.A.'d the mag and closed the office, putting Charlotte out of work.

Except for screenwriting, it was a lively time to be in L.A. There were seasonal floods, annual fires, two substantial earthquakes, the Rodney King riot . . . and O. J. Simpson. Life surpassed the movies, and the place seemed to be the center of the universe, as London had been thirty years earlier. Initially, I had a run of luck: That's when Coppola called wanting to revive live television drama, with CBS's blessing and *Yanks 3* as his first project. Cable television was in its infancy then, and the vast majority of Americans still watched either the three networks or their local channels. Such exposure on network television would have made any writer's reputation. Francis talked repeatedly of the action-packed experience of directing a live TV drama on location inside a truck, and I realized it was that vision of himself pointing and snapping his fingers that made him excited about the project. As the weeks passed, I think he saw he might not get the spotlight he anticipated—unless he filmed himself directing.

I had known Laura Ziskin for several years. She produced *Pretty Woman*, *What About Bob?*, *To Die For*, and several other movies. She went on to produce the *Spider-Man* movies (taking a percentage instead of a fee!) and had been interested in developing a project with me. She currently had a deal at TriStar. I wrote a script for her about the coming phenom of afternoon television talk shows in which a young woman in the audience of a program resembling the Oprah Winfrey show lies about her misfortunes on the air, then lands a job on the show and gradually rises to the top of the show's production crew by stabbing everyone in the back and ultimately betraying the Oprah character. It had my own personal kitchen sink in it: evil and funny, New York smart and outrageous, juicy, sexy, with a lesbian twist before such things were mandatory. Laura wanted to make it right away. But the head of TriStar, Marc Platt, balked at the evil and the lesbianism and wouldn't green-light it. When she tried to set it up at another studio, he wouldn't let her, and when she was appointed head of production at Twentieth Century–Fox a year later, he wouldn't sell it to her for fear of it being a success and making him look like a fool for turning it down. In such a manner are weighty aesthetic decisions frequently made in Hollywood. Needless to say, if Marc Platt is ever found armless and legless, the local constabulary could do worse than to subpoena my DNA. At the same time, Coppola bailed out of the television project to do *Pinocchio*.

Everyone has bad luck, of course, but I also had bad ideas—or at least no salable ones. The sons of Zanuck looked at my grosses, and to paraphrase my favorite David Mamet line, they could see "the handwriting on the whatchamacallit." I consoled myself that at least I was being a good father to my children: with me as a failure, they wouldn't have the same big shoes to fill that I had had. This worked for about thirty minutes, and I quickly did what everybody in Hollywood does when discouraged: I went to a therapist.

In the nineties, southern-California therapy consisted of a mishmash of a spiritual life in which you were not supposed to attach yourself to any outcomes. If you succeeded, it didn't matter, and if you failed, it didn't matter, either. The purpose of this spirituality was unnamed, but its subtext was basically that you should avoid ever feeling bad about anything. If you got an Oscar or a wife or cancer, it didn't matter because you weren't "attached" to the outcome. This bastard Buddhism (the only four realities are life, death, pain, and suffering) embraced any belief system as long as it didn't belong to an established religion, and it allowed any sort of sexual behavior that wasn't unkind to women. In practice, it meant getting up in the morning to repeat affirmations in front of a mirror. Things like "I am perfect as I am. I draw power from the nosehead of the universe and accept my imperfections as blessings from a Greater Source" two or three hundred times until your resistance was lowered and your head shook like a tuning fork. When I complained to various therapists—I had about six over the seven years I was there—that all I really needed was a job, they would object adamantly and instruct me to attach myself to nothing. Let the outcome, if negative, slide away, and if positive, don't forget to thank the nosehead. When I asked if I was also supposed to attach myself to nothing human—like my wife and children—the response was shocked. Of course you must attach yourself to them! "But what if they die?" Then don't attach yourself. Accept all misfortunes as blessings.

The one observation I did think true came from a self-invented guru named John-Roger, most of whose other thoughts were no better than the affirmations. But he did say, and here I'm paraphrasing, "The only thing man needs to make himself happy is an idea to get excited about." And sitting in this morass of gloom and rejection, I tried to get excited.

Whether it was my cynical New York background or just common sense, this resulted in alternating periods of despair and laughter. I was so discouraged that I had trouble writing more than a page or two of anything. I'd write a line or two, then head for the nearest TV and watch first the Clarence Thomas hearings starring Anita Hill, and years later the O.J. trial starring Johnnie Cochran and Lance Ito. The latter was more addictive than heroin, completely absorbing, and professionally self-destructive. So I researched and found the foremost authority on ADD, a malady destined to be more popular than rap. Dr. Wallid Shekim first put me on Ritalin, which had no effect, then Dexedrine, which made me sad for an hour, then hyperactive for five. I tried to make him understand the difference between sad and depressed, but he seemed to think they were the same thing, so he added Prozac toward the end of the day. The Dex made me energetic, all right, but to no good end. Rather than writing, I'd run out and buy sand dabs or pompano at the Santa Monica Seafood Company or have lunch with Baum for too long or drive all the way into Hollywood to see another writing pal, David Freeman, effectively blowing the day. Dr. Shekim said, "This medicine is no good, you know, if it makes you energetic but all you do is paint the house."

So I did what I generally do when depressed: write something for the other coast. As I'd written successful movies on the East Coast, I assumed the trick to creating a successful play was to write it on the West Coast.

For relief, I became Captain New York. Having got out of town to L.A. when in New York and Winston, I now flew to New York three or four times a year to get out of L.A. Sometimes I'd keep on going, to London, where the National Theatre really revved up my soul. This was ostensibly on business, but it was clear to even the children of these therapists that I was much happier when not living where I was supposed to be living. I'd go to the theatre in New York, make notes about the plays, eat at restaurants, and make notes about them. I no longer hated the place. I didn't hate New York or Los Angeles unless I was there. Sort of like being allergic to your own skin.

The most fun I had in Los Angeles was at restaurants or on the way to restaurants listening to right-wing radio. Rush Limbaugh was only the tip of the iceberg. Later in the day, Dennis Prager would appear, and on an opposing station an old loony named George Putnam, two characters named John and Ken, Tom Lykes, and a former chapter head of NOW, a liberal lesbian turned conservative lesbian, Tammy Bruce. They were all fabulously and hilariously over the top. They tweaked the establishment Left, turning political correctness on its head. In fact, I began to think of them and the pols they bolstered as the true progressives, since all the Left seemed to want to do was advance socialism from the thirties, which seemed regressive, not progressive. These radio-talk jockeys set the bedrock for the coming Contract with America and the Gingrich revolution. When I couldn't sleep, I'd listen to Howard Stern in the morning. So did Baum, and we'd compare notes.

I cooked most of the time, if I was there. Although the kids hadn't developed much of a palate, Charlotte loved food—meat, in particular!—and I tried to make something from the Los Angeles Times food section every week. Despite the L.A. Times's pompous, ridiculously PC editorial stance in this one-newspaper town, its Wednesday food section was more fun than that in The New York Times. It was livelier, more experimental, and in color. Los Angeles was celebrating California cuisine, and New York was playing catch-up, still aping Europe, and now beginning to ape the West Coast—but not initiating anything on its own. Ruth Reichl wrote the restaurant reviews for the L.A. Times and was sparkling, so, like the Yankees, the New York version hired her away.

During my less energetic moments with Ritalin, Dexedrine, and Prozac, I pored over cookbooks and loved picturing bizarre recipes. I found a perfect show-biz dish called Stargazy Pie, perfect because it's uncomplicated and delicious, and just looking at it will make you laugh. When was the last time dinner made you laugh? Not the guests, the food . . . ?

Nasty with unpredictability and generally greeted with both horror and delight, the sardine-packed Stargazy Pie is a darkly witty surprise and guaranteed to kindle conversation. According to the tough British food writer Jane Grigson, the pie (sometimes spelled "Stargazey") is a Cornish creation traditionally made on Tom Bawcock's Eve, two days before Christmas, commemorating the night on which brave Bawcock went to sea to find sustenance for his foodless hometown of Mousehole. Against all odds, he returned with netsful of sardines, fed the town with this pie, and wound up with a dish and an extremely minor holiday named after him. (Asking where the townspeople found the bacon and hard-boiled eggs in the foodless burg is as irrelevant as questioning how the girl who married Cain got there.)

There are several variations on it, but all versions of Stargazy Pie involve sardines, and all feature their Clupeidae heads poking up from under the crust. Grigson isn't clear whether the pie is named after the sail at the top of a mast—a stargazer—or the horse of the same name, so called because it keeps its head back, which visually parallels the sight of the sardine faces poking out from the pie. But the appearance is arresting and festive, which is why I suggest serving it to guests who have at least the hint of a sense of humor.

STARGAZY PIE

(Adapted from Jane Grigson's Fish Book, *Penguin Books, 1994)*

Two 9-inch rounds short-crust or puff pastry, unbaked
8 fresh sardines, scaled, cleaned, filleted, heads on and tails removed
2 tablespoons Dijon mustard
2 tablespoons chopped fresh thyme or cilantro
2 tablespoons chopped fresh parsley
Finely grated rind and juice of 2 lemons
1 teaspoon kosher salt
¾ teaspoon freshly ground pepper
12 ounces bacon, chopped, lightly fried

4 hard-boiled eggs (do not overcook), shelled, coarsely chopped
Egg wash (1 egg mixed with 1 tablespoon water)
10 small sprigs fresh parsley, for garnish

1. Preheat oven to 425 degrees. Arrange one pastry round in a shallow pie plate or on a baking sheet. Butterfly the sardines. Brush insides of sardines with some mustard and sprinkle with chopped herbs, grated lemon rind, salt, and pepper. Arrange the sardines on pastry round equidistant from one another with filleted-side down and heads resting on edge of pastry. Scatter bacon and eggs and then sprinkle lemon juice over all.

2. Trim about ¼ inch from edge of second round of pastry and place round over sardines. Brush bottom pastry at edges with half the egg wash and press top pastry onto bottom pastry between sardines, arranging a pastry edge around each sardine neck so that just the heads peek out. Gently press pastry around the bodies of the sardines to make a wavy surface. Cut a small vent hole in the center of the top crust. Brush top with remaining egg wash.

3. Bake pie for 20 minutes. Reduce oven temperature to 350 degrees and bake 15–25 more minutes, until top of pie is a golden brown. Before serving, tuck a sprig of parsley in each sardine mouth. Or not.

YIELD: 8 servings.

GRILLED MOROCCAN SARDINES

(Adapted from The Moroccan Collection *by Hilaire Walden, Soma Books, 1998)*

2 pounds sardines, scaled and cleaned, heads and tails left on
3 garlic cloves, peeled and crushed into a paste
Finely grated zest and the juice of 1 lemon
3 tablespoons olive oil
1 ½ tablespoons chopped fresh cilantro
1 ½ tablespoons chopped fresh parsley

2 teaspoons paprika

1 teaspoon ground coriander

Pinch each saffron threads and hot-red-pepper flakes

1 teaspoon kosher salt

1. Place sardines in a single layer in a nonreactive dish. Mix the remaining ingredients in a bowl, pour over the sardines, and turn sardines to coat. Cover and let marinate 1 hour.

2. Grill or broil sardines until cooked through, about 2 minutes on each side.

YIELD: 4–6 servings.

L.A. *Confidential*

~~ ~~ ~~ ~~ ~~ ~~

W ANT TO MAKE a Hollywood screenwriter really mad? Just whisper
in her ear, "A Film by Rob Reiner" or "A Sydney Pollack Film" or any
other misattribution of the authorship of a movie to anyone who didn't write
it. Watch the top of her skull hit the ceiling, duck while her eyes shoot blood,
hear the smoke rifle from her ears! Transparent lies make people mad, and
screenwriters are people, mostly.

Want to make a Mexicana living in Los Angeles really mad? Just whisper in
her ear that you know where to buy really good tamales. She may not have the
same rampageous reaction as the screenwriter—the Mexicanas I whispered to
simply looked at me condescendingly, as if I had missed the second grade—
but she knows that is a lie, too.

I tried several places in search of a great tamale in L.A., beginning with a
much-touted take-out shop near the airport called Corn Maiden, but either
the proportions were wrong or the dough was too clunky, so I quit trying to
buy them. Although I look forward to your contradiction, I agree with the su-
percilious looks of those Mexican women: You can't *buy* a good tamale in L.A.*

Which is not to say you can't find one. You just need to motor to the west
side of town, knock on the door of a show-biz quadrillionaire or an out-in-time
NASDAQer, and ask if he or she has any female undocumented workers—

---

*A matrimonial lawyer told me he regularly buys tamales for breakfast at Tito's in Culver
City—though since matrimonial lawyers (euphemism for serial drug-dealing child molesters)
generally feast on either human flesh or wheelbarrows full of Ben Franklin federal reserve
notes and usually both, *caveat emptor*.

euphemism for "illegal aliens"—on staff, the harboring of which gave the forty-second and forty-third presidents of the United States supposedly just reason for withdrawing support from the cabinet nominations of Kimba Wood and Linda Chavez. If the quadrillionaire employs someone illegal, and I've yet to find one who doesn't, your chances of getting a decent-to-brilliant tamale are substantially increased.

In Mexico, tamales are for special occasions—fiestas, the New Year, and in honor of the dead the day after All Saints' Day. They were eaten by Mexican rulers long before Spaniards came to the New World and can be filled with just about anything except soup. Normally, they are two inches wide and two to four inches long, but Diana Kennedy, the doyenne of Mexican-cookbook authors, writes of a dusty pilgrimage she made to the tiny town of Pánuco to breakfast on a pork-filled two-footer (the three-footer was too many towns away). She also enjoyed one filled with iguana and eggs.

Making the masa, a gallimaufry of dried corn kernels, lime, salt, and the L-ingredient* all mushed together for several hours, is the most demanding aspect of preparation. But an excellent substitute is Maseca instant corn-masa mix (*not* masa harina), available in most Mexican food stores.

"It's not Christmas without tamales," Alejandrina, housekeeper for a TV producer, told me in the jumbo kitchen of one of the swanker homes north of Montana Avenue in the boonies of Santa Monica. She smoothed a tablespoon of the gluey masa over three quarters of a corn husk, then added on some *pollo en salsa verde*, nimbly folded it, and tied it at the center with a strip of corn husk. She repeated this several times, first with the *pollo*, then with *puerco*, which had been boiled in chicken stock with a full head of garlic, then sautéed with a puree of California chili peppers, the pork-boiling mixture, and more garlic. The smell is smoky and sexy. The key to the filling is in the chilies. Guajillo, jalapeño, pasilla, New Mexico—all give different smokes. "Mexican people here don't buy tamales in stores. They are not good from stores." I concur. "Now in Guatemala and some Mexican places, they wrap them in banana leaves, but this is how we do it from where I come from."

Alejandrina came from Sonora in 1981. "Like everybody who come from an-

*L͟A͟R͟D͟! (Better for you than butter.)

other country, I jump from a fence over the border. They throw me out. Two hours later, I jump from the same place in the same fence and stay for five years." She begins making dessert tamales, which differ little from the savories—she adds a couple of teaspoons of sugar to the masa, dabs a spoonful of it on the corn husk, then places three or four pineapple chunks and some dried cranberries into the center, might add some chopped walnuts, then folds and wraps it as she has done with the others.

"After five years, I get sick for my parents and go back to visit them, but I cannot get back in. So I hike over mountains like everybody all night. I get very tired, but I cannot get back in. The third time I try, an American Indian with a taxi says to me, 'For fifty dollars I will take you anywhere,' so I pay him fifty dollars and take a taxi into San Diego, where Gustavo was waiting." I never found out who Gustavo was because I have to grab the tamales and run as though I, too, am crossing the border, which I am—into the deadbeat borough of Bel-Air, where another undocumented worker of another quadrillionaire was also making tamales.

Lucrecia came to Los Angeles in 1990 after her husband, a truck driver, was killed in Mexico City. She lives in a two-bedroom apartment with her five children, a granddaughter, and the granddaughter's mother. Her life back in Mexico should bring whining in America to a standstill. "My grandmother, mother, and I make fifteen hundred tortillas every day for the rich people. We get up at three in the morning to make the masa. In very big balls." She gets down on her knees to illustrate how the three women rolled out the tortillas for five hours. "We make seven hundred in the morning, in stacks this high"— she gestures three feet off the floor—"and I put them on my back. We ring the bell at each house, and we have to move fast because people need tortillas warm, and we must sell all seven hundred between eight and nine in the morning for their breakfast."

She isn't bitter but seems rather surprised by her feats—though she clearly does not wish to revisit the experience anywhere but in memory. "Then we have lunch of tortillas filled with roasted pumpkinseeds and salt. We don't have for chicken, we don't have for meat. When we have money— chicken! Meat!" She lines a steamer with empty corn husks, places fifteen tamales on top, then covers them with a dishcloth and a lid. "When we finish the lunch, we buy wood. I carry big bunch on my head! We make eight hundred more tortillas in the afternoon, and we have one hour to sell them, three to four P.M. Then is time to go wash the maize for tomorrow." The tamales steam for about an hour. "I am very glad my grandmother teach me this because I love to work." She mentions the names of the people who employ her now in Bel-Air, friends of mine, who ask to be anonymous. "I love them very much. They try to get a green card for me but it takes seven years and it cost them twenty-two thousand dollars. When my grandmother die, they send me home and they phone me every day. They have a very big heart."

An hour or so later, the tamales are ready, and the four of us—Lucrecia, her generous employers, and I—unwrap the husks and dig in. The flavor bursts through the thin dough, some mild, some smoky, some hot as hell, and the dough tastes deliciously cornful. We bolt down three each, smile big, and rub our bellies, at least metaphorically. They are right, these women—you can't buy a tamale in L.A. anywhere near as good as the ones Alejandrina and Lucrecia make. Having cleared up that lie, perhaps they could now be of help to the Writers Guild.

Undocumented Tamale Dough (Masa)

3 ½ cups Maseca instant corn-masa mix for tamales
2 ¼ cups hot water
1 cup lard
1 ½ cups warm chicken broth
Salt to taste (depends on how salty the broth is)

1. Mix masa mix with hot water to make pliable dough and let cool.
2. In an electric mixer, beat the lard on medium speed until fluffy, 3–5 minutes; then beat in masa mixture in three handfuls. Add a cup of broth until dough is the texture of buttercream frosting. Add salt, cover, and refrigerate 1 hour. Remix, adding broth if too stiff.

YIELD: thirty 4-inch tamales.

NOTE: Maseca instant corn-masa mix is available in Mexican food stores and through the website www.kitchenmarket.com.

GREEN SALSA

3 pounds fresh tomatillos, husks removed and quartered
2 jalapeño chilies, halved and seeded
2 cups roughly chopped fresh cilantro leaves and tender stems
2 small onions, chopped
2 tablespoons corn oil
About 2 cups chicken broth
Salt to taste

1. Boil tomatillos and jalapeños in 1 cup of water until soft, 2–3 minutes. Drain in a sieve or over a bowl to collect juices for 5 minutes.
2. Purée tomatillos, jalapeños, and cilantro in blender with ½ cup drained-tomatillo liquid.
3. Sauté onion in oil until almost browned, about 3 minutes. Add tomatillo purée and cook, stirring frequently, for 10 minutes, until thick, adding as much broth as needed to keep from sticking to pan. Season with salt.

YIELD: 4 cups.

RED SALSA

6 ounces Guajillo or New Mexican chilies
4–5 cups chicken broth
1 large onion, peeled and cut in half lengthwise
1 head, plus 1 clove, garlic
2 cups sesame seeds, toasted
¼ teaspoon Mexican or other dried oregano
¼ teaspoon freshly ground black pepper

3 whole cloves
Pinch of cinnamon
2 tablespoons corn oil
5 sprigs fresh thyme
Salt to taste

---

1. Slit chilies on one side with scissors and remove seeds and ribs. With tongs, briefly char chilies over an open flame, then plunge into cold water. Tear each into small pieces and place in large skillet. Cover with broth (about 3 cups) and heat to boiling over medium heat. Simmer, covered, over medium-low heat, 20 minutes.
2. Wrap onion and 3 garlic cloves in foil and place on a burner on low heat. Cook 10 minutes; turn over foil package and cook 10 minutes longer. Unwrap.
3. Add onion to chile liquid and squeeze roasted garlic from skin into pan. Mix in sesame seeds, oregano, pepper, cloves, and cinnamon, and, in 3 or 4 batches, purée, adding broth as necessary.
4. Heat oil in large skillet, add chile purée and thyme, and cook, stirring constantly, 5 minutes, adding broth as necessary to keep consistency of mixture. Salt.

YIELD: 4 cups.

Assorted Tamales

1 pound beef brisket, cubed
5 sprigs fresh thyme
Salt to taste
3 cloves garlic, peeled
1 pound boneless, skinless chicken breasts
6 cups chicken broth
1 pound small shrimp, deveined
1 pound lean boneless pork

1 head of garlic, halved crosswise
Green and red salsas
30 corn husks
Undocumented Tamale Dough (Masa) (page 247)
12 ounces *queso fresco*, diced
4 ounces mozzarella, cut into thin, 3-finger-wide pieces

---

1. For the beef: Simmer beef, thyme, salt, and 1 clove peeled garlic in water to cover 45–60 minutes, covered, until tender. Drain and divide into two bowls. Salt.
2. Chicken: Simmer with 1 clove peeled garlic in broth to cover, 8–10 minutes, covered, until tender. Drain, shred into bite-size pieces, and divide into 2 bowls. Salt.
3. Shrimp: Simmer shrimp and 1 clove peeled garlic in chicken broth to cover, 2–3 minutes, covered, until just pink. Drain and divide into 2 bowls. Salt.
4. Pork: Simmer pork with head of garlic and 1 teaspoon of salt in chicken broth 8–10 minutes. Let cool in broth, then shred and divide into 2 bowls.
5. Toss half of each filling with green salsa to coat, and half with red.
6. To fill and steam tamales: Soak corn husks in warm water until pliable, rinse away all silk, and drain. With husk tops pointing away from you, spread each with a 4- to 5-inch square of masa to ⅛-inch thickness. Spoon about 2 tablespoons of meat, chicken, shrimp, or pork filling on top and fold husk over from the sides. Then either fold top and bottom of husk over the first fold or invert a second husk, fold it over the first and fold the pointed ends so that they overlap like a Christmas present. Tie with a strip of husk. Layer in a steamer, covering pot with damp towel and lid, and steam 45–60 minutes until the masa pulls easily away from the husk.
7. For cheese tamales, place 2 or 3 cubes of *queso fresco*, a piece of mozzarella, and 2 tablespoons of either salsa on top, fold, and wrap.

YIELD: 6 tamales per filling.

NOTE: Because husks add no flavor, 6-inch-wide strips of aluminum foil can be used instead, but the presentation will lack authenticity. But since authenticity is over as of 2006, according to *The New York Times*, it's okay.

Leaving Los Angeles (Without Nicolas Cage)

E VENTUALLY, I REALIZED Los Angeles had to be left. It's no fun being unemployed anyplace, but it's the least fun of all being unemployed in Los Angeles. So much significance is attached to what you do that if you don't do anything—or worse, do something but aren't successful at it—you might as well enter your next social function with a sign saying BEARER HAS BIRD FLU. Movie folk don't generally admire the writing process because it's too mysterious—guy or gal goes into a dark room and comes out with magic or with stink—and nobody knows how it happened or what the difference between the two is. The cinematography is understandable, and the music, and the direction—but the writing is just annoyingly incomprehensible.

Freelancers in every profession are usually out of work—that's the status quo. The condition is also entrepreneurial—you can, in theory, write, photograph, or paint yourself out of failure, make up your own style, create your own empire. Picasso and Tom Clancy did; at least one screenwriter, when hot for two to three years, took on UCLA students to write his many assignments and supervised them editorially, like Rubens. So as a playwright and screenwriter, I thought of myself as an artistic entrepreneur—which, of course, runs the risk of complete failure, like all entrepreneurial enterprises—and by 1998 I had become what Darryl Zanuck had predicted. Hollywood is a town of proven failures.

Most of my downturn in fortune was due to a combination of rebelliousness and not knowing what the canon was that I was rebelling against. I never differentiated between luck and talent in the movie business, but sooner or later you have to have one or the other.

I pitched stories to people half my age—comic ideas that were received with respect but dead faces. After seven years of this masochism, nothing budged. Aside from having a couple of close friends and enjoying generally sensational weather, I felt as out of place in Los Angeles as I had at those boarding schools I'd been thrown out of. People kept telling me, "You're such a New Yorker," and I was beginning to believe them.

So I decided I should switch professions to either I'm not sure what—Dad hovered entrepreneurially—or producing. I'd long since decided that the most important skill in writing a screenplay wasn't in its content but in the ability to pitch it. The overwhelming majority of screenplays are bad, just like most movies and all but about six directors. In the eighties, it was said that one movie was made for every ninety-nine that were in development—which meant one out of ninety-nine that someone had actually paid for was produced. (There is no record of the number of screenplays written and submitted every year. It's probably two per citizen.) But those in development were backed by the studios because of reputation, track record, good luck (Nicole Kidman likes it!), good story line, or, mostly, salesmanship. I'm sure David Mamet's background in sales has helped immeasurably both in achieving a reputation and in having so many movies produced that, on merit alone, wouldn't have been. But on merit alone, almost no movies would be made.

So I went to a few sales seminars at which most of the people were interested in real estate. The principles were the same, but they didn't really address how to create and sell a story, so they weren't that helpful, either.

Finally, I attended one of Tony Robbins's seminars. Robbins gained immense fame from a series of TV infomercials through which he sold hundreds of thousands of audio and videotape packages at a few hundred dollars each. Their theme was reassuring: There is no limit to what you can accomplish if only you get your head screwed on right. He was extremely upbeat and one of the first of the truly inspired motivational coaches. His reputation became so great that when Bill Clinton was undergoing his own personal first-term doldrums, he summoned Robbins to the White House, though I'm not sure what went on there. Maybe Robbins taught him how to make Bob Dole the Republican nominee.

On Robbins's tapes, and in his seminars, he insisted that greatness was in each of us, that we were complete as we were, and that our realities were limited only by our dreams. He was dynamic and convincing, like a great evangelist, though his books and tapes weren't much different in essence from previous self-help manuals like Norman Vincent Peale's *The Power of Positive Thinking*, Napoleon Hill's *Think and Grow Rich*, and the granddaddy of them all, Dale Carnegie's *Thirteen Proven Steps to Riches*. Robbins championed a theory called neurolinguistic programming (NLP), which, in the tiniest of nutshells, claims what you do physically determines your emotional state. If you're depressed but stand up and smile and wave your arms vigorously (in the privacy of your office), you'll no longer be depressed. This actually works. You *can* program yourself physically—for about twenty seconds. It's not clear what you do after that, but as a quick fix, it works.

Robbins gave great talks, filled with energy and insight that sounded good when you first heard them. "How am I going to live today in order to create the tomorrow I'm committed to?" is one of his better-known bromides. "Using the power of decision gives you the capacity to get past any excuse to change any and every part of your life in an instant" is a little more opaque. He constantly referred to his own business success, using it as a model for us to emulate—but since his business success was in telling us about his business success, it was hard to apply it to any other walk of life except motivational speaking. I spent many freeway hours with this man's tapes in the car. I still have them. They still sound good. They perk you up. For all I know, they may have helped many people. Maybe Bill Clinton wouldn't have been re-elected had he not followed Robbins's advice. But as far as I was concerned, they had no lasting effect.

Well, they had one lasting effect. I wrote a screenplay loosely based on Tony Robbins as Molière's Tartuffe, called *Flexing the Muscle Within* (one of Robbins's bestsellers was *Awaken the Giant Within*), in which a motivational coach moves in with a depressed billionaire and strips him of everything—his money, his corporation, his home, his wife and family. The screenplay winds up with everyone walking on red-hot coals—which Robbins used to "prove" mind over matter—and Tartuffe gets his comeuppance. The billionaire (in my mind) was to be played by Danny DeVito and Tartuffe by Bill Murray, but it turned out to be too nasty or not funny enough, I forget which. But that failure got me out of L.A., so in its own counterclockwise way, Tony Robbins's motivational coaching was, for me, a success.

During so much restless downtime in L.A., I'd finished a play about race, *Stonewall Jackson's House*, which had been well received and even created something of a controversy in Manhattan back at the American Place Theatre, where my first plays had been produced. It was anarchic, and the ultimate anarchist, Wynn Handman, disagreed with every political position in the play but was a true liberal and put it on because of that. The play had a circuitous and frustrating history. On one of my many trips to Bullhead, I stopped in at the house in Lexington, Virginia, where Stonewall Jackson lived prior to the Civil War. The tour was a little cheesy, with hardly any artifacts actually belonging to the Jacksons, and the guide, a sixteen- or seventeen-year-old African-American girl, was ill-informed about her subject. In fact, a distinctly countrified couple on the tour knew considerably more about the general than the docent did and grew increasingly irritated at her lack of knowledge. The docent, in turn, became defensive.

When I got to Bullhead and recounted the incident humorously over dinner, my brother-in-law Donny said, "Sounds like a play to me." I couldn't see how, and forgot about it.

But the scene stayed with me and got funnier as I thought about it. Had there ever been a play about a house tour—particularly a second-rate house? What if the blue-collar couple actually became furious at her, perhaps having traveled miles to see the tour of their hero's home, and threatened violence against the docent. What if the girl didn't want to be in that house—after all, Stonewall was a slaveowner—and in addition was completely flummoxed by her whole life? What if another couple on the tour—making a total of five characters—felt kindly toward her and came to her defense? I didn't know where this would go but started writing it. As I tightened the screws on both the docent and the redneck couple, I conjured the girl as miserable, not only for being a guide but for being alive. Then the incendiary part came from out of nowhere: What if she were so miserable and so confused that she craved for someone to take over her life and tell her what to do? What if she begged the benevolent couple (from Granville, Ohio) to take her away from all this and let her become their slave?

I wrote the play in three weeks, and decided to chance a reading of it at the Actors Studio, where Elia Kazan, Arthur Penn, and Joe Mankiewicz had revved up a Playwrights and Directors Unit—possibly the most star-studded ever assembled. Its members included Norman Mailer, Harold Brodkey, A. R. Gurney, Eric Bentley, William Goldman, Don DeLillo, George Roy Hill, Romulus Linney, Sydney Kingsley, several recognizable visitors, and about forty others, all with opinions. The Studio was famous for its contentiousness, which was what I needed.

After a few minutes of laughs at the situation, the illustrious audience grew quietly outraged. Forty-five minutes later, the docent named LaWanda, says to Barney, the male half of the kindly white couple from Granville

LAWANDA

Do you have any openings on your farm?

BARNEY

Well, we do have openings from time to time . . .

LAWANDA

Could I fill one . . . ? I want to be your slave. I'm not talking about employment, I'm talking about slavery—uncruel but abject. You can't beat me or be mean to me, but . . . I want to be your property . . . I'll work hard for you, hard as you want. And in return you handle my money, decide what I want to do in life, do my concentrating fuh me, get me to a doctor when I needs it. Figure out which sexuality I like, pick out my clothes and friends, and bury me when it's over. I don't want to figger out taxes or parking tickets, hafta choose a HMO, keep track of my frequent-flyer miles, go to school, hunt down no jobs, or decide if Jesse Jackson's right or not. And mainly what I don't want most is to make any more decisions after this one! You own me—the lock, the stock, and the barrel.

After a few more exchanges, the couple from Ohio agrees, and the play ends.

I might as well have gone directly to B'nai B'rith and sung "Springtime for Hitler." This was a house built on social realism, if not naturalism, and the posing of tough questions about civil rights with fanciful irreverence didn't sit comfortable. Complete silence. Then all hell broke loose.

The custom at the P.D. Unit was for the author to face the audience, somewhat protected by a moderator, and have verbal fruit and veg thrown at him. Unbelievably, my moderator was Kazan.

"If you put this play on, you'll be lynched," Norman Mailer said, somewhat admiringly.

A black woman named Bonnie Greer was furious and incredulous. "This is unbelievable! Insulting!"

"What I'd like to know is, why isn't it funny?" said Eric Bentley, caustically.

Nearly everyone in the audience had an angry opinion, and all but two were at least negative and sometimes outraged. Everyone read his and her own personal experience into the play whether it had to do with race, class, or their own parental and societal disappointments, and boy were they pissed. Kazan did an admirable job of defending my "bravery," and Romulus Linney and the director Mel Bernhardt said they thought the idea was important and should be encouraged. But everyone else lambasted it for more than an hour.

After about forty minutes, I realized that I had my second act: this boiling discussion. The play brought out so many divergent feelings about victimization and seemed to have struck nerves all over the room.

I've always enjoyed controversy in the theatre, the more incendiary the better, whether I agree with it or not. Maybe because of my involvement as a student and actor with Bernard Shaw and admiration for iconoclasts like Molière and John Osborne, the gunfights between articulate ideas—providing they're dramatically presented—rivet me to a stage more than "relationship" plays (Chekhov and Shakespeare notwithstanding). Larry Kramer's *Normal Heart*, Mamet's *Oleanna*, James Lapine's *Fran's Bed* are recent examples. I admired Kazan not only for his direction of so many wonderful plays and movies—most famously, *Streetcar*, *Death of a Salesman*, *Dark at the Top of the Stairs*, *On the Waterfront*—but for taking a stand against the Communists in show business at a time when it made him a pariah. He thought them intrusive bullies in the theatre and movie worlds who frequently insisted on changing scripts to fit the party line. It's one thing to give up your career for something you believe in, but ridiculous to give it up for something you're opposed to. As dangerous and buffoonish as the House on Un-American Activities was, and he hated it, he also hated the very notion of collectivism. Had he named the names of Nazis, he would have been treated like a hero, but because the Communist party in America was something of a joke (though not in the rest of the world) he would forever after be vilified for trying to save his own skin by "ratting" on fellow showbiz folk. Far from apologizing, he took out ads after his testimony saying, basically, he'd do it again.

The next twelve years weren't kind to *Stonewall Jackson's House.* I changed the first act into a play within a play—a play that was being given a workshop performance by an off-Broadway theatre company to see if it warranted a full production—and the second act into scenes inspired by what had transpired at the Actors Studio session. Because of the success of *Geniuses*, most theatres around the country were eager to read this new play—but not one was willing to risk doing it. The Manhattan Theatre Club—which always says it wants to do my next play after having turned down the one before—was horrified; the Goodman Theatre in Chicago was simply afraid of the audience reaction (and subsequently did a very lukewarm version of the subject matter, *Spinning Into Butter*); George Wolfe at the Public angrily said no, even though an associate told him it was exactly the kind of play he should be doing. A theatre in Detroit said yes, then changed its mind when it learned the author was white. It was turned down by every single theatre in the country for twelve years.

I assumed it would never be produced. Then one day in 1997 I happened to send it to Wynn Handman at the American Place. I hadn't sent it to Wynn earlier because he was a well-known Liberal (his wife, Bobbi, runs the New York office of People for the American Way) and I assumed he would find it anathema.

Wynn was due for cataract surgery. He was given a drug and told not to make any important decisions for twenty-four hours after the procedure. Fortunately, he read *Stonewall Jackson's House* immediately following the surgery— within those twenty-four hours!—and phoned to say he wanted to do it. I couldn't believe it.

We had trouble finding a director; we had trouble finding an actress to play the docent—several African-American women turned it down flat. But we found the right director, Jamie Richards, who had a nice sense of the ridiculous and the sledgehammer the play required, and a wonderful actress who tore into the play shamelessly, Lisa Louise Langord. The play ran six or seven months and has been done all over the country—except in the highly p.c. L.A. and D.C.—the two cities that need it most, and where it would probably cause the most trouble. There are rules in the theatre, of course, but they're more flexible. You have to entertain the audience in some manner—but the manners are considerably more varied than they are in the movies. And I'd finished another play, about a struggling television comedy writer at the end of his life, called *Vitreous Floaters*.

A playwright, to paraphrase Robert Anderson, can make a killing in the theatre but he can't make a living. But he is in charge of his own work. Thanks to the Dramatists Guild, he owns the copyright, not a studio or a producer, and no one can change a word or hire an actor or a lighting designer without his permission. I thought that as long as I was going to fail at making a living, I should at least fail at something that was 100% mine.

By this time, Frank was graduating from St. Andrew's and was on his way to Dartmouth. Eddie was about to follow at St. Andrew's. Charlotte and I had moved to Los Angeles when Frank was eleven and Eddie eight. Frank went to Curtis, a private school, and Eddie first to Franklin, a Santa Monica public school, then Curtis and Harvard-Westlake, private ones, when Franklin turned out to be unable to keep up with him. Frank developed into a good student and a terrific athlete, Eddie into a good athlete and a terrific student. Both had scads of friends, and the only difference was that Frank and his friends tortured Eddie and his.

When Frank was ready for high school in the ninth grade, I worried at his tendency to follow a crowd endemic to all big cities but particularly pronounced in L.A.—the one with too much dough, too many cars, and way too much license. Millions of children grow into prosperous and productive adults in L.A., and I don't want to libel the entire city, but I never took to living there and both Charlotte and I preferred the educations found on the East Coast.

You'd think I would have been prepared for any sort of wildass adolescence, considering my own, but I felt out of my shallow in curbing the suburban temptations of L.A., and Charlotte and I investigated boarding schools.

We settled on what turned out to be the single best school, boarding or day, that I'd ever experienced, and in case it's not clear, I was something of a jaded expert on the subject.

St. Andrew's, a small school of 250 students in Middletown, Delaware, was founded and thoroughly endowed by the DuPont family in the twenties and looked so much the way a prep school should that it was used as the location for the movie *Dead Poets Society.* Most of the teachers live on the campus and not only teach classes but also coach athletic teams and participate in the extracurricular activities that abound. So close do students and teachers become that it really is like one extra-large family, and in an era in which schools and colleges are scrambling away from the concept of *in loco parentis* for fear of lawsuits, St. Andrew's embraces the idea with a passion. Hardly anyone was a disciplinary problem during our eight-year involvement. There were few expulsions, fewer drug problems, and the faculty generally spoiled parents for any other academic experience by being in constant communication about their child's progress.

I took Frank to visit several schools and never urged any on him, nor even the idea of a boarding school. But when he set foot on the very first campus we visited—Woodberry Forest in Virginia—he said, "I want to go here." He then proceeded to say the same thing at every subsequent school we visited. Not only were most of the campuses beautiful, but the ease and freedom of being able to roll out of bed and onto the football field or into the comparative-religion class, without the endless driving L.A. required, made him feel less powerless. The kids looked happy and talked smart. I found Choate insufferably PC and the student body too unattended to at too early an age, but the others we visited were all contenders and all accepted Frank, who is a garrulous good interview. The choice boiled down to Middlesex in Massachusetts, Taft in Connecticut, and St. Andrew's. Charlotte and I favored St. Andrew's and at the moment of decision tried to nudge Frank in that direction, but it didn't take much nudging, and we wouldn't have minded had he chosen any of them.

But we loved St. Andrew's. At the school, he found focus, did well in classes, quickly and enduringly became part of the community, and wound up at graduation winning the prize as the best four-year athlete in the school, resulting in one very teary-eyed father. He played football in the fall and basketball in the winter and rowed crew in the spring.

The night before his SATs, during the final football game of the season and of his career, he was knocked unconscious, his only serious injury in four years. It threatened to be a concussion, so he was awakened every two or three hours during the night by the school nurse to make sure it wasn't. Despite this setback, or possibly because of it, he did well enough on the SATs the following morning to get into Dartmouth, from which he was graduated in '02, having rowed first boat for three years and majored in political science. His room was a major mess for eight solid years. He is currently fighting the investment-banking wars in New York, and I haven't checked his room recently, partly from fear and partly because I haven't been asked to.

Frank being three thousand miles away at boarding school freed Eddie from the tyranny of his older brother, and he started to find out who he was. He became an excellent and confident student, wrote beautifully, read all the time, did a few stints as a stand-up comic at school, and studiously played the piano. I'd always regretted not being forced to play an instrument because I never had the discipline to practice on my own, and Charlotte and I agreed both boys should take lessons and practice until the age of fourteen, at which time they could choose for themselves whether to continue. (Frank quit at fourteen; Eddie more or less stopped at eighteen. But at least it's in their background.) Frank was an outgoing, potentially hell-raising kid; Eddie was full of beans, too, but enormously affectionate, hugging and kissing his parents well after Frank had gone, "Yewww," at the idea.

Eddie also loved nature and exploring it. He climbed trees in our Santa Monica backyard and in the Sparta forests, loved overnights outdoors, and repeatedly requested to go to wilderness camp in the summer. I tried desperately not to think of him rappelling, but he always came back alive.

Four years after Frank entered St. Andrew's, Eddie thought he, too, might want to go to boarding school, but not necessarily St. Andrew's, which he had visited with us several times. He was an attractive candidate for just about any school, and he and I toured Deerfield, Andover, Groton, Taft, and a few others. As with Frank, the trips were joyful times, as we compared notes on the schools, discussed the future, and wrestled over the amount of time he could listen to the Beastie Boys on the car radio in exchange for an hour of *All Things Considered*. I'd recommend a school-visiting trip to every parent even if their son or daughter is going to stay home. Eddie boiled his choices down to St. Andrew's and Taft.

But something happened shortly before our second trip to Taft that may have figured in Eddie's decision to go away to school: I announced to the boys that I was leaving our marriage.

I had pretty much concluded this eighteen months earlier and told Charlotte. She didn't believe I was serious—hard to blame her, since I have a history of being emphatic one moment and doing an emphatic 180 the next. But I knew there was no changing this. Although she was always a lively and provocative conversationalist and good company, we had grown increasingly separate. I realized that, aside from our children, our goals were different. I remained insanely and unrealistically ambitious about my career, and she was indifferent about both hers and mine. There were money "issues," as they're now euphemistically referred to, and in truth, there had been compatibility "issues" ever since the tortured dramas involving the townhouse in New York, which I now oversaw and leased by myself. Charlotte assumed this was another impulsive announcement on my part and urged marriage counseling, which I undertook more out of curiosity than optimism. I held out little hope for success but thought it was the least I could do after nearly twenty years of marriage. We saw a few people, all enlightening but unsuccessful.

Divorce had hovered around our marriage for years, but as the product of one, my greatest concern was the effect it would have on the boys, and so I put it out of my mind until I thought them an age at which it would be less devastating. Because I grew up with only one parent, I thought that was the worst situation, and that with each increasing year of age, the damage to the children would diminish. But Rafe's parents divorced when they were in their sixties and he was in his thirties, and he said the experience was extremely traumatic even at that age. So years may make some difference but don't remove all pain by a long chalk. I also didn't want the boys to feel this a shattering moment that would forever change their lives. I'd heard many tales of fathers announcing separations, then leaving immediately for a hotel room or, in my case, New York. With Charlotte's agreement, I waited for a vacation period when Frank would be home from school so that we could tell them and I would then stay in the house for the rest of the vacation to talk about it. This, I thought, would show them that life could go on and they would see I was still very much part of their lives, that none of this was their fault, and that their day-to-day existence wouldn't change all that much.

But Frank's spring vacations were regularly filled with crew events, and Christmas was a poor choice. Finally, he came home in the spring of '98. Charlotte continued not to believe this was happening and left the house on the night I'd decided to tell them, as though not participating in the discussion would mean it *wasn't* really happening. But unlike marriage, divorce takes only one to tango.

After dinner, she left, and I told them.

Of course these moments can be planned meticulously and then turn out haywire, like a military campaign. Frank immediately began crying and desperately tried to fix things, as he was able to with many situations at school. Eddie went limp and shut down quietly. The three of us talked and talked for two hours. Finally, when most of the factual questions had been answered and initial angles explored, I suggested they might want to talk with each other, without me, and left. When I returned an hour later, they were watching television and had accepted the facts, if not the impact, of this revolutionary turn of events in their lives. We watched TV together for a while.

At one point, Eddie said, "Well, I'm definitely going away to school next year." The prospect of living at home shattered by divorce was unbearable.

When Charlotte finally returned, she asked the boys if they had any questions.

"No," said Frank.

"Not really," said Eddie. But of course they did, and they asked them and experienced the shifting of plates beneath their feet for many years, perhaps the rest of their lives. I stayed through the spring, attempting to show Eddie how unchanged his life would be. Charlotte and I took Eddie on one more visit to Taft and St. Andrew's, and to our surprise he chose St. Andrew's.

That summer, one week shy of our twentieth anniversary, I moved back to New York, and Charlotte stayed west. We agreed almost immediately on financial terms. But because this sort of thing is genetic (at least in my bloodline), the divorce became acrimonious, and, despite our agreeing on terms, took six years. The only winners, as usual, were the lawyers, vampire teeth exposed from the first phone call. I abhor class-action suits, but if anyone ever wants to file one against divorce lawyers (or "matrimonial attorneys," as they hilariously call themselves), I've got three names. And two of them were, at least technically, on my side.

After I left for New York, whenever I saw the boys, which was as frequently as possible, I would ask them how they felt or if they had any questions about the situation. "Fine" and "No" were the general responses. I wasn't sure how deeply the knife had cut or the situation had been examined. I suspect after the initial announcement they probably concluded it made sense and weren't all that surprised. As my friend Bridget Potter said, "Children hear the grass grow."

Then, three years later, when I was taking Eddie to see colleges in the Northeast, Frank urged us to visit Dartmouth. As their final exam, he and the other students in his drama class were presenting scenes they'd written, and Frank wanted us to see his. Eddie and I drove from Cambridge, Massachusetts, to Hanover, New Hampshire, in a blinding snowstorm, unable to go much faster than thirty miles an hour, but I sensed the importance of Frank's request and risked ramming into several trees to get there. We pulled up outside his classroom—the Dartmouth theatre—two minutes before the class was to begin, and we raced inside.

We sat down just in time to see the very scene of the divorce announcement I've just described. Frank played me, and two other students played him and his brother. Though on that night I was dry-eyed, Frank, to his own surprise, was unable to keep from choking with sobs while he played me. But he finished the scene, and the rest of the students put their scenes on, in which Frank was frequently a character. I was incredulous: saddened by it and guilty at the harm I'd done. But at the same time I felt relieved that he had indeed understood what the separation meant, acknowledged it, and wanted to show his brother and me the effect it had had on him. Eddie was upset by the scene, and by seeing his brother fight back tears, but other than a serious look on his face, revealed little more. When the class was over, the brothers assumed their traditional roles of bantering combatants. The scene had been as shattering to me as the deaths of Uncle Bus and Lee.

Eddie's career at St. Andrew's was stellar. After five minutes, he was no longer "Frank's brother" but his own boy, and a superior student. He was captain of his cross-country team and an eager swimmer and rower. Throughout his four years, he was the top student in his class, but breathing down his neck was his first cousin—Charlotte's sister Elizabeth's son, Ted Unger—and, in something of a cliff-hanger, at the graduation ceremony, paralleling Frank's achievement in the athletic world, Eddie was awarded best four-year academic student and more tears from Dad. He won early admission at Princeton, where, as of this writing, he is a senior. He remains very close to his mother and, from what I can tell, anxious about her.

Although it didn't concern me much whether the boys went to prestigious colleges, it meant everything to Charlotte, whose entire family is one long Ivy League pedigree. By those standards, the boys met their mother's greatest hopes; whatever expectations their father had for them at conception, they continue to exceed them wildly.

I'VE MISSED FAMILY celebrations and the house on the parkway, but I've just about never regretted the divorce and absolutely never regretted leaving L.A. One positive result is that I don't have to read the *Los Angeles Times* ever again, although I still occasionally look at the food section on the website.

New York seemed new and surprisingly clean. Despite the knee-jerk opposition to Rudolph Giuliani spearheaded by the former and future demagogue now reduced by failure to witty troublemaker Al Sharpton, there was little doubt in my mind that the mayor had changed the town and helped it thrive. Armed with a copy of my play *Vitreous Floaters*, and a few ideas for musicals, I started out like a kid.

After a few months, I heard from my old friend and critical overseer Frank Rich, at the time an op-ed columnist for the (real) *Times*.

"The Sunday magazine is looking for someone to go in a different direction with their food section. I suggested you," Frank said on the phone. He remembered all the restaurants we'd been to and the dinners I'd thrown.

"Thank you, Frank, but I don't really write prose."

"Why don't you write just one column? Then you can both decide."

"No, I don't know anything about this."

"Just write one."

I did, and it was published in March 2000 under the title "Alice Waters Cooks Her Turkey Too Long." The editors liked it and wanted one more. After the second, they asked me to write regularly.

I COULD EXPRESS myself comfortably in letters to friends and family, but when I first started writing for the *Times*, the prose style worried me—it exercises a different lobe from the one used to write dialogue for plays and screenplays. When I told Amy Spindler, the sparkling editor of the back of the *Times* magazine, and her assistant, Andy Port, that I hadn't written this way before, they were both encouraging and said they were sure I could. Okay, but how?

I felt about most food writing at the time the same way I did about most wine writing—it was self-important and pompous and deadly, deadly earnest, as though each new innovation—like a foam—or sauce for a snapper were an earth-shaking profundity. I almost never finished reading a food article: grab the initial point in the first graf or two, then cut to the recipe, which would explain it all. The Wednesday section of *The New York Times* was guilty of this, as were most food sections of most newspapers. The *Winston-Salem Journal* was folksier, and the *Los Angeles Times*, unlike its editorial page, was less inflated, but they were exceptions. Calvin Trillin was a decided exception (I hadn't yet discovered Liebling)—he didn't take the cult of food seriously—in fact, seemed to find it amusing—which I thought the right perspective. And when I read Nora Ephron's piece on foodies in her collection *Wallflower at the Orgy*, which actually made fun of deadly serious food professionals, I realized the subject wasn't and shouldn't be sacrosanct. This hasn't made me many friends in the foodistic world, but the approach was encouraged by Amy and Andy and, by implication, the magazine's editor, Adam Moss. After a few weeks, I took a chance and wrote about Uncle Bus and food and, when further encouraged by A. and A., decided to write about food very personally.

After I'd written about four pieces, something clicked. Maybe this was home. Sure felt like it. They asked me to write the column weekly, but I wanted to write another play, so we settled on biweekly. The money at the *Times* was pathetic compared to movie dough. But they said no to only one piece in four and a half years.

I bought back the remaining two months of the lease from my Jane Street tenant and moved back into the house, complete with that ten-burner Garland range, which now had a professional reason for being, and was ready for a second adolescence, this time, I hoped, more swinging than the first.

I dove back into New York with glee, expecting success on every front, as I always did when changing cities. I imagined, in no specific terms, a harem, extraordinary financial success, reverence as a playwright, regular quotations on Page Six as if I were George S. Kaufman, GBS, or Noël Coward. Young—well, not yet old—playwright spurns Hollywood, returns to a grateful Broadway, throws dinner parties attended by mayors and heiresses, sleeps in a tux! As with Lee's analysis of mates, the bad aspects of the city were all out of focus and in the b.g. Only the good ones were sharp and in ECU.

Summers in the East are hot and muggy, and there's catastrophic protoplasm in the air that clogs my sinuses and causes my eyes to itch for about a month. But the first summer back I didn't even notice. As hot-button as the Jane Street house had been during the marriage, the idea of living alone in a twenty-four-foot wide New York brownstone had thrilled me for the last year. I couldn't wait to cook for a dozen once a week, squire ladies to the rooftop overlooking the Village, and, if I could get them to lean over just right, point out the Hudson River.

Dad hadn't wanted to discourage any of his children from working, so he left each of us just enough money to avoid starvation—to keep us from initiating a suit against his will. (Remember that: If you want to cut important relatives out of your estate, leave them *something*.)

As well as re-establishing contact with Frank Rich, I also got back in touch with Rafe, the painter Gary Stephan, André Bishop, and Wendy Wasserstein, and before long Oliver Clark sold his L.A. houses and moved back. Everybody was in New York! I had even seen my old flame Bridget. She had jumped into HBO at its inception and become an important exec. Her marriage was over, and she was angry at her husband, who had walked out and then asked to come back. "I miss the family," she said he'd told her, and she'd replied, "That's not good enough." She wanted him to miss *her*, and to her credit said no. In a strange star-crossing of gods and time planes, she dated Rafe's half-brother, Lewis, for several months. *Fearless*—novel and movie—had become a *succès d'estime*, and Rafe's career in Hollywood had been launched in the early nineties.

By the time I moved back, Bridget and Lewis had split up. When I told her of my plans, she said, "You're my hero."

"Why?" I said. I was feeling positive but hardly heroic.

"Because you're changing your life the way you want to." So she did, too. Bridget had never been to college, but because she was English everyone assumed she had at least a Ph.D. She always felt her collegelessness a shortcoming, and in 2002 she enrolled as a freshman at Columbia University.

Pete Gurney (the playwright, A.R.) had warned me not to come back into town expecting a play of mine to be produced just because I'd written it, but of course I'd done just that and immediately gave *Vitreous Floaters* to André, who was now running Lincoln Center Theater. I planned to write plays, then musicals, then more plays and more musicals, and, taking a leaf from Michael Caine's book, wanted to alternate supremely successful boulevard comedies with infuriating experimentation like *Stonewall Jackson's House.*

The amount of theatre available in Los Angeles had been a constant surprise. *L.A. Weekly*, the spiritual cousin of *The Village Voice*, listed forty or fifty plays in production at any given time, and the *Los Angeles Times* tried to ape the real *Times* by hiring a West Coast Frank Rich or Walter Kerr for the prestigious productions at the Mark Taper Forum or the Ahmanson, but failed. A good critic is essential to a lively theatrical environment, but the paper never managed to find one who could write. More important, the theatre didn't really matter to the general audience in Los Angeles, only to those already in show business who invariably used it as a stepping-stone to television or the movies. The Baums and I saw three or four plays by a favorite author, Justin Tanner, and at one of them were the only people in the audience. Although Marlon Brando and Aaron Sorkin never returned to it after their successes, and Gene Hackman seldom did, the theatre in New York genuinely seemed to be an end in itself, and the playwright's participation vital. There are currently four

ways to make a name for yourself as a writer: write famous novels, write famous plays, marry Marilyn Monroe, or shoot someone. Recently, the myth
that directors of television shows are as responsible for their success as their
movie counterparts are because, after all, they have the final credit, has been
debunked, and writers have actually been given predominant credit for TV,
but quick—name a TV writer! Quick—name a screenwriter other than
William Goldman! (Ummm, there's that guy who wrote *Sideways*. Actually,
two guys.) So, naturally, I assumed my re-entry into the New York theatre
would finally pay off what had appeared to be good potential only fifteen
years before.

Red

I'VE ALWAYS BEEN drawn to women of purpose, particularly professional purpose. Women who dab at work or don't do it at all make me nervous—I sense a neediness in them that resembles my mother's. She didn't work, or didn't work much—a receptionist at *McCall's* magazine for a few years, a part-time salesgirl in a tiny shop around the corner for a few years; that was it as far as I knew—and I worry I have inherited her free-floating-aimlessness gene, against which I do battle on an almost daily basis. My tendrils sense passivity at a hundred yards, and my stomach tenses.

I've always been drawn to WASPs, too. They're my favorite minority, not just because I am one, or at least aspire to being one, but because I find the duplicity of the well-behaved, well-spoken woman camouflaging underground caverns of passion and juiciness tantalizing. After experiencing a fairly raucous sixties and seventies, during which I tried to draw women of every shape, age, class, ethnicity, hair color, eye color, and number of fingers into my tent, I came to the Hitchcockian conclusion that WASPs may be cool and serene on the outside, but if you're fortunate enough to unlock the medieval stone gates someone's built to protect them, you'll frequently find them molten with yearning and occasionally nymphomaniacal on the in-. Not just sexually: The desire for experience and the delicious revelations they discover about themselves and the world after years of being told, "Don't!" can be explosive. Of course this is anecdotal, but in my experience, women who parade sexuality and candor generally are less sexual and less candid than those who conceal them, not unlike the peace-and-lovers of the sixties and seventies who were

usually filled with more violence and hatred than the button-downs they re-
belled against.

The first time I saw Heidi Ettinger (then Landesman) was in 1988; she was
walking the set she'd designed for a terrible revue produced at the Manhattan
Theatre Club called *Urban Blight*, to which I had contributed a sketch that was
eventually yanked. She had recently won Tony awards for designing the set
and co-producing the musical *Big River* with her husband, Rocco. If, on the
most superficial level, women with yellow hair seem compliant and brunettes
seem assertive, women with red hair seem defiant. "I am so not like the others, they need an additional *gender* to define me," they might as well be saying.
From the moment I saw her on that stage, commanding stagehands with
pleasant but decisive authority, I thought her red hair, aristocratic face, and
slender body hinted at an undercurrent of unbridled and possibly untapped
sexuality. When I discovered who she was, I thought she must be the feminist's wet dream of Wonder Woman: at the top of her career, the only woman
in a field dominated by men, happily married to a successful producer, three
no doubt ravishing children, and gorgeous. Oh, and unattainable.

I didn't speak to her and didn't see her again for more than a decade, but occasionally I'd flash on that image of confidence and accomplishment under
which bubbled a juiciness someone, presumably her husband, was bathing in.
I'd think how lucky she must be, particularly compared to the floundering
chaos I found myself in.

It turned out that my grass-is-greenerism was just that. When I saw her
next, at a dinner hosted by Wendy Wasserstein, who had named her Pulitzer
Prize–winning play, *The Heidi Chronicles*, after her, she was divorced, and unhappy, and her children were out of control. I was separated and happy but
looking to be happier. We hit it off immediately. For a reason I don't remember,
I revealed at the dinner table the circumstances of my NIBbing from Malcolm
Gordon—the first time I'd ever had the boldness to say anything about that
letter-writing obsession outside of a therapist's office. I was in my mid-fifties
and still embarrassed by the experience, but in front of relative strangers, in
front of Heidi Ettinger, the story rolled out of me before I could stop it.

I wish I could tell you what we had for dinner, but all I can remember
about the evening was Heidi's sympathetic face turning toward me in what

seemed like slow motion. I saw possibility in her eyes. Interest. Apparently, the story hit a nerve.

I deliberately waited a week before phoning so as not to appear overanxious, and we agreed to meet to see a movie and then skipped it in favor of a very bright Chinese restaurant on Second Avenue and Thirteenth Street for dinner. I tried my best to be glib, and she looked at me with great understanding, appreciating the effort. We walked to her house, which happened to be only seven minutes from mine. I had no idea how I was doing—she seemed tolerant and interested, but I didn't sense encouragement. We talked for an hour. When I stood up to leave, I put my hand on her cheek, she came to me, almost gliding, and we kissed. When Heidi kisses, she kisses fully, not aggressively, but giving her lips and mouth over to you, then her body. We kissed for four hours, and I left.

It was like being a teenager again. We were ravenous for each other— Romeo and Juliet if only the monks had got the message right (or Friar Laurence hadn't interfered in the first place) every night.

I'd arrived back in New York determined to lead the rock-star single life (middle-aged version) that most married men envy, and before I could even *buy* a little black book, I was cut off at the knees by "Red" (the name felt more natural than "Heidi"). I'd always been afraid of telling any woman I loved her because I think the word *love* is so weighted. Though some people throw it around like rice in a paella, to me it's always been so loaded that I reserve it for immediate family and maybe one other person, period. So it took six weeks for me to tell Red I loved her. Her response was, more or less, "Duh." She knew I loved her well before I knew.

The sexuality of the relationship only seemed to heighten, which was impossible—ask any physicist. We went everywhere together, ate everything, lapped up New York, rented a summer home, and managed our children. I cooked for her two or three nights a week, which she liked—usually fairly simple things, like chicken stuffed with tarragon and butter, and spinach with garlic, and tried to hide a chopped-up vegetable in potatoes mashed with potato water and butter so her children would have at least one vitamin to combat the tsunamis of soda. But when I could get her alone, I'd ply her with her favorite desserts, zabaglione and Meyer-lemon ice cream.

She encouraged me to write a treatment for a musical based on the year 1968, which was right up my alley, and I did. In it, a college girl joins what amounts to the McCarthy campaign, and winds up in Los Angeles for the Robert Kennedy assassination—but in my version, Kennedy lives. When we passed around the first-act treatment, there was much interest, particularly in seeing how the second act would turn out. However, my politics ran away with the second act, and the result was an America turned fascist—not exactly what the producers (or indeed, much of the audience) was dying to see musicalized. Still, it was a heady exercise.

Obstacles cropped up. Charlotte, basically agreeing to the terms of the divorce, wouldn't sign anything that would advance it. A year dragged by, then another and another. My divorce lawyer said it was a first for him—usually the injured party was screaming for the money and the settlement and the more loaded spouse was fighting tooth and nail to protect his/her resources. But here, I was trying to force money on her, and she wouldn't take it. He brought the case up in front of his law class, which was just as dumbfounded as he was. A new law was passed in California regarding prenups, which we had, so I attempted to move the case there, where she still lived, just to get it moving. But the California lawyer I took on made misjudgment after misjudgment—except when sending his bills, which were quite meticulous. Another year went by.

In the meantime, I was writing my *New York Times* food column. Red and I ate and traveled to the South and the West and, memorably, to Paris and London whenever she could take time away from her three children, who were living with her and undergoing sometimes painful adolescences. Frank had graduated from Dartmouth and moved in with me for six months while chasing down an apartment and a job. Eddie had graduated from St. Andrew's and, after a summer of rappelling and braving the wilds of another wilderness camp, moved in at Princeton.

My relationships with women have been simultaneously impulsive and cautious. I'm much more fun in pursuit than as a steady diet. But with Red it was different. It was provocative all the time. This didn't prevent me from finding other women appealing, just as she found other men appealing, though I hope not ravishing. Ideally, you don't retire from life when you get married.

Return to Henley

～～～～～～

IN 1997, MY SON Frank, then seventeen, was invited with his high school crew team to row in the annual regatta at Henley-on-Thames in England. The Henley Regatta is more or less the World Series of rowing, and St. Andrew's, fresh from a season it dominated in the eastern United States, manned (or boyed) an extremely strong boat. On the very first day of the regatta, the eight-man crew powered its way through nearly 2,000 of the 2,112-meter course, well ahead of its only competition, the English school Canford (all the races at Henley are two-boat races). But about ten strokes short of the finish, one of the rowers made a mistake, crippling the boat and causing it to slide impotently onto the wooden barriers bordering the race lane. Canford crept ahead and won.

Rowing is a precision sport, requiring synchronization not unlike that of a symphony orchestra, acrobats on a trapeze, or the Rockettes—one slip and the cymbal falls, the 'bat hits the circus net, the chorus line collides in disarray, which is what happened in that race. One boy "caught a crab"—dug his oar so deeply into the water that he was unable to get it out in time for the next stroke—resulting in the rest of the rowers scrambling in chaos as their oars whacked into one another.

The scene back at the rowing sheds afterward, which only twenty minutes before had been one of ecstatic optimism and jubilant testosterone, was, while perhaps lacking the dimension of full tragedy, among the saddest I've ever seen: eight young men on the verge of adulthood suddenly returned to their cribs by the crushing disappointment, some crying, all bewildered. As a show of solidarity, each had shaved his head the night before; and now here they were, childlike baldies wondering what had happened. And what had? After fourteen weeks of intense practice—the last two, for six hours a day in England—arguably the strongest team in its category was instantly out of the running (one loss and you're through at Henley). To twist the sword, the boat St. Andrew's was ten strokes away from whipping so soundly went on to the finals.

So when Frank phoned four years later and said he and Dartmouth, his college team, had been invited to the regatta, I took the news with a sense of both hope and dread.

For fifty-one weeks a year, Henley is a picturesque countryside town along the River Thames, lying roughly equidistant between the glorious city of Oxford and the tawdry city of Reading. For fifty-one weeks a year, nothing particularly newsworthy happens in this town of 11,000. Then, in early summer, Henley welcomes some 250,000 visitors over a period of five days—which would be the same as if New York suddenly played host to 200 million. Almost like Brigadoon, Henley springs to life, transforming itself into an Edwardian sporting event–cum–costume show that rivals the World Cup as a tournament and Ascot and Wimbledon as a social event.

For those with the gnawing suspicion that they were born in the wrong century—say, the twentieth or twenty-first—the regatta at Henley-on-Thames is a paradise. It is not only the dress code established by the stewards of the Royal Regatta that makes the scene look like a mass audition for *The Importance of Being Earnest*—no trousers on ladies, dresses and skirts must be at least two inches below the knee (and are generally to the ankles); gents must be blazered and necktied or cravated. It is also the *choice* of those attending the posher section of the viewing areas. Frequently, the men outdo the women: Nearly mandatory Panamas and straw-boaters festoon the pink-cheeked faces of present-day Evelyn Waughs, often competing for color with their bright rowing-club jackets piped with opposing hues. Although most of the 1-mile-550-yard strip that parallels the course is open to the public, the regatta organization owns and administers the last 500 yards or so nearest the finish, and it is here, in the Stewards' Enclosure, that the regatta looks put together by Merchant and Ivory's production designer.

This time, Red was with me. She and Frank and Eddie were on good, if somewhat formal, terms. She and I discussed her coming to Henley because Charlotte would be there, then asked Frank if he'd like it, and he said he would. She and Charlotte were cordial, and Red stayed in the background, not wanting to upstage the boys' mother before and after the races. But she reveled in the Henley experience and loved dressing up in ankle-length blue silk and a broad-brimmed straw hat.

Dartmouth's rowing season had been a disappointment in 2001, and though its hopes were high for the regatta, no one expected the team to do particularly well. The two leading contenders were Yale—to whom Dartmouth had lost twice in the regular season—and the expected winner, Princeton, which placed first in the Eastern Sprints to Dartmouth's eighth. We outsiders prayed only that Dartmouth would win once, to prove that it belonged in the regatta, and I personally hoped the St. Andrew's curse would not revisit the river. That disaster had become somewhat famous in rowing circles—the expression "They're a St. Andrew's crab away from winning" was a reminder to those who knew about it that one little misstep could turn certain triumph into sudden catastrophe. Several onlookers remarked that they had either been present at or heard about the afternoon when the "strong, tough team" of high school boys in '97 had caught a crab after leading so decisively. And so touched with superstition and foreboding was the event that Eddie, also a rower and by this time attending St. Andrew's himself, refused to videotape it because that's what he'd been doing at the Great Humiliation four years earlier.

So I watched with unalloyed joy as the Dartmouth eight creamed its first draw, the Hollandia Rowing Club from the Netherlands, by more than two lengths—a substantial win in rowing measurements, as you'll see. I hurried back to the sheds to find the team relieved but hardly callithumping. The men (no longer boys) were already preparing for the match the following day with the dreaded Yale, who had won their race handily, and the oarsmen looked even grimmer than before the race. All were purposeful, too serious for college athletes. Or were they?

The days of the fun-loving, beer-drinking three-letter jock faded into the sunset sometime in the seventies: College athletics have demanded dedication bordering on fanaticism for decades now, and not just the more glamorous ball sports, which lead to all the lucrative contracts, exorbitant fame, and illegitimate children that eat up so much newsprint and clog so many airwaves. Rowing, in fact, differs from most sports because it promises no professional future, is hardly ever televised, and, even in England, gets very little space in the press. But as with any college sport, it demands three to four hours of exhausting practice every day for at least nine months of the year (and you better not get out of shape the other three), which, if you are juggling a rigorous academic schedule, can burn out the most driven of undergrads. A college athlete's schedule pretty much precludes a social life or sufficient sleep, not to mention the more hallowed extracurriculars like yearbook-editing and meetings with the Young Cartophiles. When Frank was in grade school and showed promise as an athlete, his headmaster advised me that crew would be perfect for him. "It's hard to get hurt, and if you can stick it out, it's indication of genuine inner strength and character that colleges admire." So perhaps the Dartmouth victors *weren't* taking the Yale race too seriously.

The following day, Charlotte and I rode out in the umpire's launch, which trails the two racing boats, accompanied by two imperious men, one of whom wore a blue blazer and was certain of Yale's victory. I am sometimes—many would say "always"—obtuse and prattled on with him about the various teams and even repeated the story of the St. Andrew's curse. His chatty confidence continued until halfway through the race—about three and a half minutes—when Yale had fallen behind by half a boat length. After seven minutes, a much less imperious man in a blue blazer stepped out of the umpire's boat, a forced smile straining his face. Dartmouth had pulled off the unthinkable—beaten Yale by more than a length!

I whooped and hollered like an Arkansas hog caller and told the stranger it was a great upset, and a great day for Dartmouth, and a terrible one for Yale. I'm sure he must have thought me the perfect fool—and in this case, "perfect" is appropriate. Charlotte said after we'd hit the shore, "Do you know who that was?"

"No."

"The Yale coach," she said. My mouth dropped open in mortification . . . and then we started laughing. It made the victory positively glucoid.

Again, the sheds were a tableau of intense, almost military concentration, not rapture. If you hadn't seen the race, you would have thought they'd lost. Again, the team returned to its lodgings (all in the private homes of rowing buffs in town) to eat pasta, meditate, and watch tapes of *The Simpsons*. As well they should have. There was no possibility of beating the invincible Princeton, and on the trophy for which they were competing, called the Ladies' Challenge Plate, there is no room for the name of the second-place finisher. And Princeton had just whupped Syracuse by two full lengths. But at least Dartmouth had shown it deserved to be at Henley.

On the twenty-seventh Sunday of the year (the day the finals at Henley are always held), what *The New York Times* called "the most exciting race of the day" broke into action at a cloudy, cool 2:40 P.M. One third of the way, Princeton led by a half-length, then by a three-quarters-length, and seemed to be breaking away. Then gradually, Dartmouth gained. They were never ahead or even even with the Princeton boat as the two teams hit the halfway mark, then the mile-and-an-eighth, or a hundred yards from the end. But at the very last moment, now neck-and-neck, the upstarts from Hanover, who were supposed to have been out of the contest on the second day and possibly the first, somehow pulled across the finish line first, winning by what is called a "canvas"—about two feet. They had defeated the best team on the Atlantic Coast! It was thrilling.

The enthusiastic but normally restrained onlookers burst into whoops and applause—not because they necessarily backed one team over the other but because the race had been so brilliant and exciting. Though I had been trying to videotape the race, with so many people jumping up and no clear angle, I mostly captured feet and hats, but cheered in the best British manner with everyone else when the results were known.

Back at the sheds, havoc erupted at last. We cheered the boat as it docked, and the victors peeled out—one rower with a chronically bad back had to be lifted from the scull, another rolled over onto the dock in agony, a third leaned over to throw up into the river. What appears to the casual spectator as an elegant and graceful activity—boats gliding silently by in beautiful surroundings under Constable skies—belies the effort and strain the sport requires. But most were simply exultant—they embraced, cheered, threw themselves and one another into the Thames. After they climbed back on the docks, a new realization set in—they had actually won! Frank cried in his mother's arms, Eddie in mine—they are emotional boys, thank God, and unafraid to show it, at least to us—and even the team's customarily reserved coach, Scott Armstrong, struggled to fight back tears. Nuclear tension was lanced and relieved—and the St. Andrew's crab exorcised.

The hoopla lasted nearly an hour, as first the coxswain, a young woman, then the coach, were tossed into the drink. A small boat motored by, and a group of Brits hollered, "Three cheers for Dartmouth!" Several other crews ran by to congratulate. The Princeton team came to the docks and everyone lined up and shook hands. Except for a canvas—those two feet!—this delirium could have been happening at another dock. I am told—and the size of Frank's headache the next day substantiated it—that the neighboring pubs were visited well past their normal closing hours that night.

If you can go to Henley, do; if you can make it during the regatta, the competition and the *mise-en-scène* are well worth it. If you can stay an extra week, Henley holds an annual festival, which recently featured Kiri Te Kanawa on a floating stage and the cellist Julian Lloyd Webber, among several other performers. And Red reminded me several times of the hunk multiplicand—the sight of hundreds of young men competing in perfect physical condition wearing what amounts to spandex underwear elicits in some the sensations similar to those of young girls at rock concerts.

The ubiquitous and unofficial official drink of the regatta, Pimm's (formerly Pimm's *Cup*) is sold everywhere in town, particularly during the regatta, but I found its best incarnation on the regatta grounds because the mixer isn't too sweet. The drink is basically Pimm's liquor topped off with lemonade, slices of cucumber, lemon, and orange, and a sprig of mint. Although Pimm's used to come in several varieties—Pimm's No. 1 was gin-based, No. 2 was vodka-based, No. 4 brandy, all the way up to No. 7—now all but No. 1 have disappeared. The drink used to be flavored with the herb borwich, but simplicity of preparation now leaves that out.

The secret of a successful Pimm's, it seems to me, is in the lemonade. At the Red Lion Inn, the drink was unhappily sweet because the lemonade was sweet; inside the Stewards' Enclosure, Schweppes bitter lemon was the mixer, and it turned out better. You might experiment with various lemonades the next time you're sporting rowing cap and club blazer if you want to imagine yourself back on the Thames, but basically, the less sweet the better.

STEWARDS' ENCLOSURE PIMM'S CUP

1 sprig of mint
1 slice cucumber
1 slice orange
1 slice lemon
50 milliliters Pimm's (or Pimm's No. 1)
One 8-ounce glass of ice
One 150-milliliter bottle of Schweppes bitter lemon

1. Bruise the mint and macerate it and the cucumber, orange, and lemon in the Pimm's for 15 minutes, or up to 2 days.
2. Pour the mixture over the ice in the glass.
3. Fill with Schweppes bitter lemon.

YIELD: 1 serving

If the tournament becomes overwhelming, nearby are the towns of beautiful Oxford, the very tatty Stratford-upon-Avon, and the truly modest Ayot St. Lawrence, home of the merriest prankster of the English language, George Bernard Shaw.

Pajama Food

~~~~~~

Isn't it redundant to call anything you put in your mouth voluntarily "comfort food"? All food is comforting, or we'd be eating nothing but hot dogs at Shea and warm tar (indistinguishable in a *Times* blind-testing), with possibly a few vitamins thrown in. Unless you're on some kind of nasty medical diet or undergoing a fraternity initiation or briefly lapse into Joan Crawford territory with one of your sons, there is no such thing as "punitive food." And at no time in my memory did the need for palate-pleasing palliatives seem so urgent as during the aftermath of the destruction of the World Trade Center.

Red and I were in Sydney, Australia, the last two weeks of August 2001. She was producing and designing *A Little Princess*, a musical based on the Frances Hodgson Burnett story, which has been made into about 360 movies, the most famous of which starred Shirley Temple. Australian investors wanted a look, so she and the director Susan H. Schulman put together a workshop of the first act, which was quite promising. The Australian stage star Anthony Warlow wanted to play the young girl's father, which thrilled the investors.

Red and I then spent a few days in the Hunter Valley, a winemaking area two hours outside Sydney. When she went back to town, I stayed on two more days to write about it for *Travel & Leisure*. We returned to New York the first week in September, and Red moved into my house with her youngest son, Dodge, then ten, because contractors were renovating hers. On September 4, her son Nash, fourteen, arrived from a trip abroad late at night and didn't have a key. He rang my bell around midnight, and Red flew down the stairs to let him in. At the bottom of the staircase, she twisted her ankle badly and sprained it. The following day, Dodge began school across town at Gateway, located at Fourteenth Street and Second Avenue. Red and I put him on the bus and then spent hours in doctors' offices having her ankle X-rayed and being told nothing much could be done about a sprain except staying off it for a month.

A week later, September 11, 2001, Red got up at seven to put Dodge on the school bus. I was half asleep, flipping through radio stations, which I often do between five and eight in the morning. The companionship of strangers keeps my mind off me, and, depending on the program, either makes me mad, makes me laugh, or puts me back to sleep, my goal. I regularly listened to Howard Stern, who, despite his adolescent obsession with human discharge, remains the most imaginative and funniest personality currently on terrestrial or satellite radio. I don't know if he's as creative or as hilarious on satellite radio, where he is allowed to say "fuck" and "cunt" as much as he wants, the terrestrial prohibition against which led to much of his humor (not unlike movie comedies of the thirties and forties, which had to use wit to circumnavigate the ludicrous censorship of the Hays Office instead of having the freedom to say or show anything commerce would allow, as they do now). When Stern hit a dull patch, I would switch to Imus, then at his commercials, NPR, then, when they get into fund-raising pitches (more aggravating than other commercials), to Curtis and Kuby (Curtis Sliwa and Ron Kuby, Right and Left politically) and possibly to WBAI for a few additional laughs and some nostalgia for my brief flirtation with sixties radicalism.

Unlike most grown-ups (or most who will admit it), I heard about the attacks on the World Trade Center from Howard Stern. While Red was preparing to go to the dentist, Stern announced that a plane had crashed into the World Trade Center. He and I both thought it a bizarre accident but nothing more. When he announced the second tower had been hit by a second plane, I, like the rest of America, figuratively flew out of bed.

Red phoned Trevor Day, Nash's school on the Upper West Side. The school wisely assured her it would keep everyone there. She then phoned Gateway and was told to pick up Dodge immediately—the school wouldn't keep the students there, a gross error in judgment, adding to the panic and congestion of the city, especially downtown.

I had always thought I'd be an embarrassment in a crisis but was surprisingly calm, though every sense was alert to the slightest ping. Frank was safely in New Hampshire at Dartmouth and Eddie in Delaware at St. Andrew's. Increasingly agitated, Red decided she had to rescue Dodge and finished dressing. I saw there was no way she could make it to the curb with her sprained ankle, let alone all the way to Second Avenue. It was ten extra-long blocks, which would have taken twenty minutes by bus on the best of days. I told her I would collect Dodge.

I grabbed my radio and walked fast to Greenwich Street, looked downtown, and could see plumes of beige and black smoke from the financial district. There wasn't a chance it would ignite anything this far north, at least not yet, and from this distance looked benign—another New York fire. Birds continued to sing on Jane Street, oblivious of the devastation less than two miles away. Didn't affect *them*. I looked for a taxi, and of course there were none. I headed for Fourteenth Street and jumped on a bus. It inched. I flipped between Howard Stern, CBS, and WINS, the all-news station, and Stern actually did the best job of reporting the events. Completely gone was the adolescent, and in his place an adult journalist who neither exaggerated nor panicked as many of the regular reporters did. Others wondered aloud whether the date and our national emergency phone number were a coincidence or intentional and whether the meaning of choosing United and American airlines was a clever, if literary, irony. Howard stuck to the story.

After twenty minutes and still between Seventh and Eighth avenues, I realized the entire city was gridlocked and quickly jumped off and headed east on foot.

I remembered the panic that had swept the nation in the seventies, when the Symbionese Liberation Army kidnapped Patricia Hearst and threatened to attack and blow up America. No one knew how large that army was but responded for a few days as though it were the entire Soviet Union. I wondered if this would turn out to be the same ridiculously small number of zealots or if another shoe would drop at any second. I marveled at the ingenuity of using our own planes against us. In this age of electronics and intricately complex plots shown nightly on television and at the movies, here was a perfect plan anachronistically low-tech and dirt cheap.

I finally made it to Second Avenue and picked up Dodge, who understood something bad had happened but was primarily cheerful because he didn't have to go to school that day. I tried to phone Red, but cell service was still overloaded. I found a pay phone—soon approaching the antique—and got her.

"I've got Dodge. He's fine. We're headed back."

"Where are you?"

"Third and Fourteenth. We'll be there in a few minutes." She didn't sound worried any longer. We had a pleasant stroll home to Jane Street. It was a beautiful day, but each step, for me, was becoming graver and graver. I knew none of us and our country would be the same again but didn't know how. Only the day before we thought ourselves envied, but on this day it was clear we were hated, which had never occurred to us—whether by a thousand or a billion would become clear later. Our belief in our invincibility and in our specialness in the eyes of God would be no more.

We returned home, and Red was calm and happy to see her son. We went to the corner café—the Tavern on Jane—which was jammed with people, everyone sober in every sense of the word, the television excitedly repeating facts, rumors, predictions. The number of dead rose and fell. Mayor Giuliani seemed like the one man—perhaps besides Howard Stern—who not only knew the truth but was telling it. The three of us ordered cheeseburgers and silently began to miss the days, now gone forever as of three hours ago, that could have been described as deliriously, if selfishly, carefree.

When we returned home, a message from Eddie at school sounded fearful. Another from his adviser said he was distraught, assuming I'd been in or near the World Trade Center during the attack and was dead. I was so caught up in events that I thoughtlessly forgot to call him and his brother to assure them I was all right. I phoned Eddie immediately, and we laughed with some relief. I phoned Frank and was reassured to find him still the optimist—he knew damn well I wasn't in any danger. In this case, Eddie got my gene and Frank his mother's.

IT'S NOT EXACTLY that we were eating abrasive food before September 11. Far from it. Diners scaled the zenith of decadence nightly, often at home and certainly in restaurants around town, where meals for $100 a person were almost considered thrifty. It was precisely that merry extravagance that felt not only unwelcome in the days immediately following the attacks, but also like something we didn't deserve.

It seemed no one would ever, ever go out again, and until our predicament could at last be joked about weeks later, pajamas were the perfect garments for those uncertain times—at once commodious and self-expressive, sloppy, and potentially elegant, perhaps the least self-conscious clothes in all fashion for eating in in. And they already had a cuisine to match.

Pajama food doesn't require caloric conservatism. Ideally meant to be eaten with one leg draped over the arm of a chair or sofa, pajama food can also be taken lying in bed on Sunday morning with *The McLaughlin Group* or at midnight with the door to the fridge wide open and a pair of chopsticks in your hand—or at any other time. The only real requirement is that it give you pleasure. This usually means it's soft. And since you might be half asleep, it shouldn't be complicated to prepare. (Make complicated things earlier, then nuke them in your jammies.) Although the all-stars of pajama food are probably peanut butter (practically illegal for adults to eat until the eighties), ice cream, and just about any form of mashed potatoes, pj food is, of course, entirely subjective. Customarily, it's a dish you had as a child, abandoned as childish when those things began to matter, and then re-embraced when you realized that, say, macaroni and cheese wasn't something to be ashamed of.

Most often, pajama food is eaten with one hand because the other is busy holding the container, whether it's the just-delivered Sautéed Spicy Whole Green Pepper (Mao's favorite) from Grand Sichuan International or the cauliflower risotto from Lotus or the mashed potatoes made with a pound of butter, the potato-cooking liquid, a full udder of cream, and slices of sautéed cabbage that's found at my place alone. They all reheat beautifully. The rumor that pj food must be white as well as soft was debunked not only by a friend from North Carolina who claimed that any kind of sausage will make her "admit to everything," but also by none other than Alain Ducasse, whose closet snack is a hot dog with everything on it. Eric Ripert, the chef at Le Bernardin, has no guilt about his midnight food: "I get excited about eggs. I think there's something sexy about them. Maybe I should see a doctor, I don't know, but I love to see egg yolks running." The simple bistro dish eggs *en cocotte*—in which two eggs are sandwiched between 2 tablespoons of cream, crème fraîche, or any sauce, then baked in a 375-degree oven for 7–10 minutes in a boiling-water bath—allows myriad enrichments. "I really like them on top of warmed ratatouille or tomato *concassé*," he said.

For the cholesterolically untroubled, it's hard to do better than a perfectly grilled rib-eye under a pair of gorgeous and silky sunny-side-up quail eggs. A chicken's will also do.

Except for steak and eggs, anything that needs cutting with a knife doesn't really qualify because the whole thing becomes hard work. (*Eating* with a knife is fine.) Unfortunately, this rules out my own personal favorite, osso bucco, as too messy. Pajama food, I decided, should be relatively neat. And it should be easy to make, like my longtime guiltiest pleasure: a midnight bowl of Cracklin' Oat Bran and heavy cream, for which I frequently need a jailer with soft handcuffs to prevent a second helping.

It goes without saying that puddings of all kinds are perfect. Wendy Wasserstein liked Jell-O because "it's colorful, it moves, and it goes down easy."

For many years, it seemed that a new Civil War might break out over the question of grits, the ground dried corn that visually resembles cream of wheat when cooked but outperforms it gustatorially. Northerners felt they were as inedible as poi, while southerners took pride in preparing them every which way: boiled, baked, fried, souffléed, boiled *then* baked, savory with butters and cheeses and garlics, sweet with honey or maple syrup. Though a Yankee, since my first grit as a child, I've found they cool my hot head and make me want to stay put.

I've concluded the only rule for pajama food is that there are no rules—except the one mentioned above, that it should please you. And, as if you needed to be told, you don't even have to wear the threads to eat the chow.

CHEESE GRITS WITH GARLIC

6 cloves garlic, peeled
1 teaspoon salt

¼ pound butter

1 cup grits, preferably white, preferably stone-ground

2 cups really sharp, shaved Cheddar cheese

1 teaspoon Worcestershire sauce

4 eggs, separated

1. Preheat the oven to 350 degrees. Grease a 2 ½-quart baking dish.
2. Using the side of a knife, mash garlic and salt until a paste forms.
3. Melt 1 tablespoon of the butter in a skillet and stir in garlic paste. Sauté over medium heat until golden, about 2 minutes.
4. Boil 4 cups of water in a saucepan. Stir in grits. Add garlic. Cook until thick, about 6 minutes, stirring constantly.
5. Add ½ cup of the cheese, remaining butter, and Worcestershire sauce.
6. Off the heat, beat in the egg yolks. Beat the egg whites in a bowl until they are stiff and then fold them into the grits. Spread mixture into casserole, top with the remaining cheese, and bake for 30 minutes.
7. Serve in pajamas or not, as your solo dish or accompanied by just about any protein or anything remotely breakfastlike.

YIELD: 8 servings.

MIDNIGHT CRACKLIN' OAT BRAN

2 cups Cracklin' Oat Bran, dry and crisp (refold the liner bag)

1 cup heavy cream, or to taste

1 TV

1. Wait until 11:55 P.M.
2. Pour cereal into a bowl and moisten, cover, or drown with heavy cream.
3. Turn on the TV; throw the rest of the cereal box away.

YIELD: 1 serving.

CORN PUDDING

½ stick butter

4 eggs

¼ cup masa harina or flour

2 cups heavy cream

One 18 ½-ounce can of creamed corn

1 teaspoon salt

1 ½ cups fresh or frozen corn

½ teaspoon cayenne

1. Preheat the oven to 375 degrees.
2. Melt the butter in a 1 ½-quart casserole.
3. Beat the eggs with a whisk till foamy.
4. Sift the flour into a large bowl and then stir in the cream until thickened. Add the beaten eggs, followed by the creamed corn, salt, fresh or frozen corn, and cayenne, stirring thoroughly after each addition.
5. Pour the mixture into the buttered casserole and stir to incorporate the butter. Bake for 10 minutes, then stir; bake another 10 minutes, stir; and another 10 minutes, stir. Finally, bake an additional 30 minutes without stirring. Serve almost immediately—when cooled just enough not to burn your tongue.

YIELD: 6 generous servings.

THERE WAS A POSITIVE result from the destruction of the World Trade Center: America was suddenly forced to recognize the rest of the world. Since the collapse of the Soviet Union and the crumbling of the Berlin Wall, we had retreated into a smug little cocoon, confident that we were the best, had the most, lived the justliest, and were far from all harm except small-town drugs, Howard Stern lesbianism, and board scores good enough for Brown but not Princeton. Other continents were for visiting on vacation and doing business with. The Hard Left continued to champion the European form of social democracy ("Christian" was excised for the folks back home), as it had the communism of an earlier era, and will probably continue to do so long after the model has failed—as it has begun to with the failure of the E.U. Constitution—just as it did with the former Soviet Union long after it was exposed as unworkable. Under the Clinton administration and the astonishing prosperity of the nineties, we inched toward the European ideal with guaranteed this and that until Newt Gingrich put a stop to it. We thought, to paraphrase the popular Las Vegas slogan, "What happens on the rest of the globe stays on the rest of the globe." We didn't need anything or anyone else. The Middle East was ignored the way finding an alternative to oil was—or used for bombing practice. While I hope I don't have to say I wish the attacks never happened and the people in the buildings never destroyed, in fact they shocked us into the state of mind much of the rest of the world had been living in for a generation: terror. When President Reagan pulled soldiers out of Lebanon, when President Clinton withdrew from Somalia and then refused to retaliate against the terrorist acts against our embassies and the S.S. *Cole*, it seemed that evil would be confined outside our borders. It was despicable, blah blah blah, but wouldn't really touch us personally or interfere with our jogging and single-minded pursuit of self-esteem unless a loved one happened to be involved in one of the events. September 11 changed all that, at least for a while. We suddenly, if briefly, discovered uncertainty and fragility—which the Europeans had been well aware of for years, if not centuries—and for about fifteen minutes finding the nearest parking spot at the mall wasn't a national priority. The day after the attacks, a Greyhound bus was hijacked, and it appeared the invaders might be everywhere and had a well-thought-out plan to cripple all our transportation systems. The peculiar and as-yet-unsolved anthrax mailings made us feel, as Don Imus is fond of saying, "that the wheels were coming off" the country.

The gloom was palpable, as though everyone were carrying an extra thirty pounds of free weights. We were all in this together, and there was the bond of a shared disaster, which led to a further bond of shared defiance. But almost immediately, we began patting ourselves on the back. While it took weeks for anyone to make a joke about the attack and the potential future attacks, the "we New Yorkers are so resilient" campaign began within two days. Yes, I thought, we're resilient—for a day. But real resilience could be found in

Palestine and Israel, both of which endured smaller versions of this assault al-most daily. Come back to me after six months or a year of perpetual bombings and destruction, *then* you can say we New Yorkers are resilient—if we have been.

As THE INVASION of Iraq was ramping up, a jingoistic sense of excitement over-flowed American satellite dishes and Internet sites, as did a sense of dread in Europe. For those of us who favored pre-emption over the tired (and unhelp-ful) yakking about the Middle East over the last several years, and were buoyed by what then appeared to be a quick and comprehensive victory in Afghanistan, there was hope an invasion would establish a second bastion of western principles. However, years of inner-child orientation palliated many into believing there was no such thing as a bad child and no such thing as evil—only misunderstood infants and equally valid differing points of view. Violence was never, ever a solution to anything, this lazy line of argument went—hadn't Phil Donahue and Oprah promised us that all disagreements could be talked through if only we poured compassion over them like syrup over morning pancakes? Weren't people the world over basically reasonable, and don't we all share pretty much the same values?

A few weeks before the invasion, a good-natured screaming match with dinner guests swung toward vituperation—I was the one in the room who thought the Middle East needed an intervention or the relentless terror there would continue for God knew how many years, and that our presence in Iraq would not only put the terrorists on the defensive instead of us, but put us right smack in the middle of everything geographically. Furthermore, politics being the art of the possible, Iraq looked easier to invade than Iran, regularly reported to be on the brink of youthful revolution, and more important than Syria.

"But, Jonathan," Pete Gurney said, "we have no business there. It's playing right into the hands of the terrorists."

"Not if we win right away. Look what happened in Afghanistan."

"The Bush people believe the Iraqis are going to welcome us with flowers!" Pete said. "That's ridiculous."

"No they don't," I said, giving the administration more credit than it turns out it deserved. "I was around for the Bay of Pigs, and so were they—they can't believe that. They have a plan."

"Which is what?" Rafe said.

"Who knows? They didn't tell me."

"That's always your problem—you never know." As mentioned, Rafe and I have a history of scratchy political discussions.

"Look, you were sympathetic to the Soviet Union, and still haven't admitted you were wrong. At least I admit it when I'm wrong."

"You're always wrong."

"I've never been wrong."

The wives and wives-to-be tsk-tsked. It's not easy being conservative in New York and it's against the law in show biz—even if you're conservative on only a few issues.

There was excitement in the American air, all right. The anticipation of instant vindication—as had been the case in Afghanistan—promised payback against the bastards who cheered on 9/11 (and for all the nightmares they had created since). It reminded me of the boys going to war at the beginning of *All Quiet on the Western Front*, filled with hope, romance, and bravery.

None of the evidence about "weapons of mass destruction" or a connection between Saddam and Osama bin Laden was convincing to me, and Colin Powell's testimony at the United Nations was pathetically transparent. I didn't think it mattered. I thought the Bush administration held a more farsighted view, but that announcing we were going to war to establish a threatening—and balancing—stance in the Middle East, which would warn against anyone doing us harm again, was too abstract to expect the American public to get behind. We needed an attack, or at least the threat of an attack. So the administration popularized one—that Iraq had weapons of mass destruction ready to be used—which it felt it could explain away after a quick and triumphant victory. And had the administration been successful *fast*, it could have. But I learned for about the thirty-eighth time that one can never overestimate the incompetence of the government, Democrat or Republican (the thirty-ninth time came when Hurricane Katrina devastated the Gulf areas of Louisiana, Alabama, and Mississippi). It never occurred to me that no one had a strategy for the post-invasion victory. Perhaps spoiled by movies and TV, in which our government was technologically superior, agile, and intelligent, I was suckered into believing the administration. But the nay-sayers had no convincing arguments.

One of the difficulties the anti-invasionists failed to surmount was its lack of countervailing ideas. I had no certainty an invasion would succeed and earnestly sought other possibilities. Everyone was articulate and vehement in their anti-war stances, but when asked before the invasion what an alternative might be, no one I knew or read or saw on television had anything to offer except "to talk" or to further involve the United Nations, which had recently nominated Libya to chair its Human Rights Commission. But talking and relying on the U.N. had helped us arrive at 9/11. Reagan's retreat in Lebanon and Clinton's generally passive strategy to deter terrorism were failures—though they continued to be the only ones offered. They're *still* the only ones offered. Three years after the invasion, I asked for an alternative to it during an argument, and all I got back was, "We should have continued to pressure them"—whatever that meant—but not to establish a forcible presence. With two symbolic acts, the retaliation against Qadafi and Libya for the Pan Am bombing and what seemed at the time to be the ridiculous invasion of Grenada, Ronald Reagan actually did more to prevent terrorism than any amount of rhetoric or diplomacy.

Michael Moore's film *Fahrenheit 9/11* also suffered from a lack of strategies. Though brilliant, if facile, at criticism and a moving antiwar film, it wasn't specifically an anti-Iraqi-war film: The bereaved American mother who had been such a loyal military supporter and then did an about-face when her son died could have been any mother in any war; the recruiting tactics lampooned could have been from any recruitment; the distraught Iraqis, moving as they were, could have been from any country; the connection between the Bush family and the Sauds wasn't convincingly proved to be evil, just conveniently political.

My support for invasion was pragmatic and hopeful, certainly naïve, based on a quick resolution, which didn't happen. With my perfect hindsight, I wouldn't have opposed the invasion, but would have embraced Colin Powell's strategy of overwhelming force. And I sure as hell oppose most of what's happened since.

In ten years, if the situation is resolved, it may appear to have been quick, after all, but right now it's beginning to look more and more like the end, not the beginning, of *All Quiet on the Western Front*, with soldiers returning home damaged and disillusioned, forever changed right along with their country.

IT TOOK WEEKS for humor about 9/11 to appear. The first instance I remember now was a sketch on *Saturday Night Live* in which actors playing the World Trade Center and Pentagon attackers had a change of heart and were in a cave begging Osama bin Laden for a slight postponement. What made it particularly funny was that it was performed in what sounded like the low-key, very reasonable English translation of the Arabic we'd grown accustomed to from the bin Laden videos.

The fear that we might be invaded by a large force vanished quickly when it became clear how cleverly and inexpensively the attacks had been accomplished, and a greater fear set in: If fewer than fifty people could pull this off, how much damage could sixty do? Or five, or ten? Despite a few crackdowns, we continued to have a liberal immigration policy and fenceless borders. Anyone with ill intent could certainly get together with a few friends and cause disasters on subways, in theatres, Grand Central Station, and ballparks. The enemy clearly had superior weaponry: It had suicide bombers, and all we had were puny old useless nukes.

As the second anniversary of 9/11 approached, The Fear subsided somewhat. The intellectual knowledge that all around us could be exploded and crushed RIGHT . . . NOW‼ continued, but the airplane engine overhead or the backfiring truck down the block no longer made us sit up in bed.

Cooking for friends and my magazine column at the *Times* brought a new sense of intimacy. People became less demanding and more cheerful, except for Rafe, whose wife, Margaret, had contracted gall-bladder cancer and was slowly dying. He was experiencing a personal tragedy within the national drama, and by and large most of us were experiencing just the national drama. Life went on or stopped, as before.

The Cafeteria Factor

~~~~~~

THE LITTLE-KNOWN PREDICTIVE that decides every political race, high or low, has nothing to do with policies, war strategies, pro or contra stands regarding pan-gender marriages, photogenics, or economic success. Every presidential victor since Truman, save one (the exception that proves the rule)* has been blessed with it. It's a complex theory substantiated by much sociology, Sunday-morning-TV tooth-gnashing, and several doctoral theses. Narrowed to its marrow, it's known among us professional pols as the "Cafeteria Factor."

You don't have to be Kevin Phillips to appreciate that the one quality Americans admire most is the same one they resent the most: other people's wealth. Take Michael Bloomberg, both Presidents Bush, Senators Kerry and Edwards, self-appointed poobah Trump: Your average citizen (me included) dreams about, obsesses about, or at least pines for the kind of wealth any one of them has and at the same time luxuriates in their public downfall, on the assumption that they deserve it because they are wealthy. Mayor Bloomberg is, by definition, "out of touch" because he's wealthy; President H. W. was out of touch because he was so wealthy he didn't know what a grocery scanner was (despite the fact that most of us yearn to be so wealthy that we never *have* to know what a grocery scanner is); W. may be in touch, but it's the wrong kind of touch because he's wealthy, too. And the hottest places in public-resentment hell are reserved for those who've inherited their wealth, like the Bushes, the Trump, and the Kerry.

*Richard Nixon

In the 2004 presidential race, all the final candidates and incumbents were at least millionaires except Dennis Kucinich (and Al Sharpton probably would have been if only he'd pocketed some of those lavish personal-appearance fees instead of spending them on hotels and jets; still, he lived like one). Senator Kerry got something of a pass because he served so endlessly honorably in Vietnam, and for a while voters didn't seem to mind that Edwards reached that exclusive club by silver-tongued ambulance-chasing, one of whose jury summations included an imitation of a baby in its birth canal. And of course Ralph Nader, who still gives all his money away, was the only one familiar with the verb *to iron*, and looks as though he *lives* in a cafeteria, was excused. Americans suspire for money—but vote for those who don't look as though they've got any: LBJ, Nixon, Carter, Reagan, and Clinton didn't look rich. Hence, the Cafeteria Factor: Regardless of fortune, how comfortable did each candidate look sliding a brown, rectangular tray down a stainless-steel track in front of a glassed-in steam table?

Although they're an artifact of the American past—perhaps exemplified by Horn & Hardart, long out of business—cafeterias may be making something of a comeback. For an example of the original, nothing beats Smith's Bar at Forty-fourth Street and Eighth Avenue, which has been around forever and is just what a cafeteria should be—friendly and loud, linoleum floor peeling slightly, not that recently painted, glassed-in steam tables, choice of hot meats and chickens that have been cooking for three or four years, big fat meat sandwiches, a full bar a few steps away. W. would probably fit in best here, eating lamb shanks as good as any in town with his fingers, slapping the barflies on the back, and nicknaming all the bartenders. And though it's hard to picture Ralph Nader ever relaxed, at least he'd feel guiltless about the prices. The Kerry rectitude might suffer in this jovial, sloppy hangout, and it would test Senator Edwards's noted pan-classism.

Providing the comestibles are delicious, there's little that's more liberating than a cafeteria: You get to pick your own food by pointing at it, and, master and commander of your own culinary fate, bring it to a table you select, eat it on the tray or not, and never, ever have to tip.

Certainly one of the wilder lunchtime scenes takes place at Veronica, right in the middle of the button-and-bead district on West Thirty-eighth Street. It is, believe it or not, an Italian cafeteria featuring all sorts of specialties, from stuffed shells to Monkfish Francese, and attracts roughly a billion customers between eleven and two.

"I'm a newcomer," says Veronica's head chef, Andy, beaming. "I've only been here thirty-six years. And this woman here, she's my boss." He gestures to his wife, Ceil. "Veronica was my mother's name." Did Veronica start the restaurant? "No, she started his appetite!" laughs Ceil, patting Andy's stomach, evidence that he at least tastes what he cooks. "But she was a good cook, and I grew up knowing what was good food and what wasn't."

This food shouldn't be confused with Felidia's or Babbo's—it's strictly steam-table fare, each dish cooked earlier, then warmed up specially for you in a microwave, which is historically tough on pasta. And someone with glove size XXXXL administers the bread crumbs, so that finding the veg in eggplant parmigiana is heavy going (but you can't put "Breadcrumbs Parmigiana" on the menu).

Still, it's a festive place, and by God the food is nourishing. The people on line all seem to be Italian, or at least inflect with Italian gestures, and they're half the reason to go there. To get filled up is the other half. I'd say all the candidates would have done well here except Mr. Nader. The noise might make him retreat farther into his shell.

But the junior senator from Massachusetts would have positively shone at the Condé Nast cafeteria. The striking, almost Brahmin, design by Frank Gehry—featuring smoky-blue transparent panels, curved and overlapping—defines three eating spaces, and the pickled floor and elliptical orange-topped tables comforted by puffy caramel banquettes encourage a brief rest, if not exactly an afternoon stay. I'm not suggesting W., Mr. Nader, and Senator Edwards aren't architecture buffs, but here Mr. Kerry could at last find a place where he didn't have to pretend to "get down."

Stations are arrayed at which you can order tailor-made stir-fries, burgers, and sandwiches, and two large steam tables serve domestic and "international" fare. Miracle of miracles, a burger ordered rare actually turns out that way—a feat most restaurants that *aren't* cafeterias seldom accomplish. And I would rush to the station from which came the yummy, jammy raspberry pudding and the scrumptious peach-crumb pie, both of which belong in any self-respecting crib right next to your copy of *Goodnight, Moon.*

The one drawback of the cafeteria is that you can't get into it unless you work for Condé Nast or know somebody who does. So this might be the time to wheedle friendships with Trillin, Wintour, or Steingarten, even if you're just opportunistically using them for a crack at the Black Forest cupcake.

In summary, the class-straddling Senator Edwards would probably fit most photogenically into all these places. On the other hand, one shouldn't underestimate the social dexterity of cowboy boots; W. might have won a second term simply by strolling in and rolling up a pant leg.

The Democrats wound up nominating one of the least interesting candidates, Senator Kerry, whose onscreen persona was moneyed but aloof, sometimes nasty, and though it radiated intellect, often came across as phony. Most things he said and did seemed calculated for effect, and though President Bush's were undoubtedly calculated for effect, too, they didn't seem so obvious, and consequently Kerry appeared stiff. He implied enormous intelligence but refused to release his Yale transcript, was declared a hero in Vietnam but refused to release his war records. Five months after the election was decided, he released his college records, and it turned out his grades were no better than those of the president, whom detractors regularly referred to as a moron. Senator Kerry was certainly a skilled debater, but his heroism, followed by his criticism of Vietnam in the sixties, followed by simultaneously trading on his heroism *and* that criticism for the sake of the election, made him seem either dishonest or at the very least confusing.

Meanwhile, President Bush had revealed himself to be the worst public speaker of anyone in the White House since the invention of recorded sound, and that included his father, who was also a marble-mouth public speaker, and his father's vice-president, Dan Quayle, who made "deer in the headlights" a popular descriptive, and appeared to be understudying Tommy Smothers at his dumbest (but Smothers's stupidity was an act). But because W. didn't appear to be pretending he was something he wasn't, supporters found his frequent tongue paralyses evidence of authenticity, which was as big a buzz word in political circles as it was in food circles. He was also upbeat and positive, and Senator Kerry, despite a pretense of optimism, seemed dour and eager to reimport the restrictive European social democracy that the Democrats had embraced since the sixties and had been rejected by the electorate so many times since the heady deceptions of Lyndon Johnson. It was a clash of personalities: the Brahmin Kerry versus the country-boy Bush—though both were from prestigious and wealthy families and Kerry had married way, way up. Kerry was the wealthiest man in Congress and certainly wealthier than the president. Both had gone to Yale, and it's probable that Bush won at least partially because he didn't let it rub off on him.

If it was a snap to dislike Kerry as a person, it wasn't easy to like Bush as a politician. Aside from his boldness in attempting to reshape the Middle East, he curried to the witless elements of his party. His staunchest campaign platform was to oppose all science, whether it be stem-cell research, any kind of abortion, an accurate depiction of the state of the environment, or Darwinism. He insinuated he might be a Creationist and opposed the legalization of any aspect of homosexual relationships. He allowed his FCC to censor radio and television personalities by fining the companies that employed them; he clearly had no idea what to do in Iraq after the initial military victory, and will probably continue making it up as he goes along until he's out of office.

Unfortunately, Senator Kerry had no alternative to President Bush's Iraq strategy. He backed the soldiers (Who didn't? It would be like saying, "I can't stand the environment!"); claimed, as Nixon did in 1968, to have a plan for ending the war but wouldn't let us in on it—either before or after the election. For me, the overriding issue was Iraq. I was certain the country as a whole wouldn't make abortion illegal, that some country would undertake stem-cell research, and that sooner or later, the revulsion against homosexual unions— whether called "marriage" or something else—would abate, and that Howard Stern would go on to satellite radio, where he could say whatever he wanted. So it wasn't an easy choice—until I happened to see a discussion between Christopher Hitchens and Andrew Sullivan on Tim Russert's show, which took place on MSNBC September 25, 2004, just five weeks before the election. This, for me, was decisive.

Hitchens and Sullivan framed the issue cogently: Regardless of other important domestic concerns, the war in Iraq was of primary consequence because it was bound to affect us directly sooner or later. The enemy was Islamo-fascism, or what might be called, for the sake of symmetry, the Islamic Right, and the conflict was who would control not just the Middle East, but larger and larger populations. "I think the United States needs to be defended against the forces of jihad," Hitchens said. "There is no possibility of having a moral-equivalence discussion here—I won't listen to a bar of that song." He re-gretted not realizing how serious and terrifying this war would be when his friend Salman Rushdie was threatened with a fatwa in 1989. "We are headed for a confrontation with Islamic totalitarianism. There's a civil war going on in the Muslim world. We must not let the tyrannical side win there."

Sullivan went further. "I don't want this to be a war between the Christian Right and the Islamic Right but between fundamentalism and liberal democ-racy."

They both agreed on the administration's incompetence, but the mixed messages sent by Kerry—for Vietnam, against it, for it, against it—and the blunders he made, exemplified by his saying that he voted for a bill before vot-ing against it (what one Republican strategist joked was "the gift that kept on giving") made him seem unfirm and weaselly.

"It's a campaign of the irresolute versus the incompetent," Hitchens said. Sullivan hated that Bush wouldn't tell the truth about what was happening on the ground and was furious that such a noble enterprise was being handled so clumsily. But Hitchens had just returned from Afghanistan and found that it worked and would really work if only the United States would give up its id-iotic war on drugs so the farmers might flourish. "We burn the only crop these people have and then tell them we're trying to win their hearts and minds. We should be *paying* them to grow this stuff. Painkillers have to come from opi-ate." He was so encouraged by Afghanistan that he hoped the same, eventu-ally, for Iraq.

They took Christianity, Judaism, and Islam to task for so many of history's wars, and Hitchens pointed out the irony of the Left in the Middle East gen-erally backing the Iraqi regime-change because it meant a tilt toward secular-ism in the region while the Left in the United States by and large opposed it. The roles were similarly reversed for the Right in both areas.

The discussion was more complex than my summary, but both agreed that in the end they supported Bush because he would take responsibility for the war he started and was the less likely of the two to give up on it, which both agreed would be disastrous for us and for the Middle East and a major, major victory for the dark forces of jihad.

Red went to her voting booth, and I went to mine.

RASPBERRY PUDDING
(Adapted from the Condé Nast cafeteria)

2 cups fresh or frozen raspberries

1 cup raspberry jam

2 ½ cups sifted cake flour

2 ½ teaspoons baking powder

½ teaspoon salt

12 tablespoons unsalted butter

1 ½ cups sugar

8 large egg yolks

1 teaspoon vanilla

1 teaspoon lemon juice

½ cup milk

1. Preheat the oven to 350 degrees.
2. In a small bowl, stir raspberries and jam together. Put the mixture into a 9-inch round cake pan.
3. Sift together cake flour, baking powder, and salt. Set aside.
4. In a mixing bowl, cream butter for 30 seconds. Gradually add sugar and beat this mixture on high speed 3–4 minutes, until light and fluffy. Set aside.
5. In another bowl, beat the eggs, vanilla, and lemon juice on high speed until they are thick and a pale yellow.
6. Beat the egg mixture into the butter mixture, making sure to scrape the sides as you go.

7. Add the flour mixture ⅓ at a time, alternating with the milk mixture, ½ at a time.

8. Pour the mixture on top of the berry mixture.

9. Place in the oven and bake 30–45 minutes.

10. Use a toothpick to test the cake. If the toothpick comes out clean, you have a beautiful raspberry pudding.

VARIATIONS: If you are in a super hurry, you can always use a yellow box cake, angel-food cake, or chocolate-cake mix. They are all superb with raspberries.

YIELD: 8–12 servings.

RED IS THE THIRD of six children (one was killed at twenty-four in an automobile crash when Red was twenty-two), and grew up privileged in northern California. She went to Miss Porter's, the exclusive girls' school in Farmington, Connecticut, at fourteen, then to Occidental College in L.A., where she majored in theatre and art, then to Yale for a master's degree in stage design, where she met Rocco, who was teaching there. She married him at twenty-six and divorced him at forty-three. "I married too young and divorced too old," she told me once, martini in hand.

Her grandfather was the co-founder of Prentice-Hall, at one time the leading textbook publisher in America. His son, Red's father, was the heir apparent, but in a fit of rebelliousness told his father he really wanted to be a farmer. He didn't want to be a farmer but no doubt enjoyed the effect it had on his old man. Needless to say, he didn't take over Prentice-Hall as he was supposed to. "My grandfather was cold and ruthless and ambitious—sort of like your father," Red said once, same martini.

"And he was disappointed in his son?" I asked.

"Oh, yes. He never thought his son was very bright." Red's father died of lymphoma in 1994, the same year she got her divorce. A terrible year for her.

Her children are all show-biz babies. "I had North in eighty-five, when I designed and co-produced *Big River*. I cut the show in the hospital," she laughed. "I had Nash during *Into the Woods*, and I had Dodge during *Secret Garden*— which proves there's no point in planning anything." Amazingly, she remains close to her ex, valuing his friendship and professional advice. I speak to Charlotte perhaps twice a year—her desire, not mine—but Red and Rocco talk almost daily. They have disagreements—mostly over whose weekend it is to take the kids—but otherwise are pretty much best friends. For a significant birthday recently, his current wife, Debby, asked him whom he'd like to have at dinner. "You and Heidi," he said.

Rocco recently became really rich. As president of the Jujamcyn Theaters in New York, he made a deal with the owner, James Binger, to buy the five theatres at then-market value upon Binger's death. Binger died in November 2004, and the theatres were then worth considerably more than Rocco had to pay. Although he and I are both in the theatre, our worlds couldn't be farther apart. His interests are largely, though not exclusively, financial and mine unfortunately aren't. And there is some closeted, if benign, competition. In 2004 he said to Heidi, comparing himself to me, "But I am smarter, right?" And if smarts are measured by business success, I'd say, "Way."

Red has two sisters and a mother on this coast, a brother and a sister on the other, and when I threw her a surprise fiftieth one year late, I asked her who her best friends were. "Actually, my best friends are my family," she said, and that's who showed up.

But first . . .

Six Redheads and a Fjord

~~~~~~~~~

I F YOU WANT to know how to capture the rapt attention of five redheads ranging in age from two to sixteen, take them forty-five minutes by boat from the high-end Solstrand Fjord Hotel just outside Bergen, Norway, across the Bjørnafjord to the island of Tysnesøy. This is where Eystein Michalsen and Nina Havn have set up a meticulously rustic retreat called Kubbervik. Eystein will take these redheads out on a boat, yank in the nets he has laid the night before, and, with luck, bring in a couple of cod (one weighing more than twelve pounds and worthy of gasps from several would-be Cousteaus) together with dozens of red and clear jellyfish, about which he will claim, "These are not good." He will then gut the cod to the wonder of all, describing each of the organs as he goes along, and toss the inedibles back into the fjord, where they'll be immediately dive-bombed by a trio of friendly seagulls and one graceful tern. Game Boys and Walkmen will be silenced and earphones pocketed as the kids (and, I might as well admit it, another ten or so adults) will be transfixed by his surgical skill in filleting the cod, which he does in under two minutes. Who would have thought marine biology so much fun?

In the summer of 2003, Red and I traveled to Norway with her family—three children, a mother, two sisters, their spouses and children, and so many cousins, aunts, and assorted friends that I began to feel like Sir Joseph Porter aboard H.M.S. *Pinafore*. The number, I think, got as high as twenty-six, and in ten days never fell below eleven. My sons couldn't make the trip—Frank was slaving at a law firm, Eddie going native in Italy.

Red is mother to two redheads and aunt to three—and is one herself. The occasion was the sixtieth birthday of her brother-in-law Sven, and it was a logistical undertaking worthy of Joel Silver on location. Sven is a native Norwegian, though he grew up on the Kenai Peninsula of Alaska and lived in Seattle from the age of six, and he and Barbara, Red's sister, had arranged an exhaustive—though mercifully voluntary—schedule of excursions to acquaint us with several high points of his homeland. Many of these included indigenous food, and there is little that five redheaded kids greet with more apprehension than victuals that stray from the domestic familiars of burgers and 'zza. So Eystein and Nina had their work cut out for them.

If you're lucky, you'll be able to visit Kubbervik, which is open from April through November, when it's overcast or rainy; if you're blessed by an even higher power, you'll get to see it when the sun is out. Approaching its wood boathouse in a drizzle, we could see a long pine table laid for lunch, the candles of the silver candelabra blazing like a scene from *Babette's Feast*. Eystein, who is handsome enough, and Nina, who is the paradigm of the Norwegian knockout, are married, and for four years, the former economist and the advertising executive have been reconstructing four cottages that sleep a total of twenty, none with electricity—and, oh, there is no road—for vacation hideaways that authentically replicate the primeval Norwegian countryside.

At the moment, the complex of six buildings—two of them dismantled at another location, transported here, then rebuilt—are rented out for corporate bonding and "team spirit" retreats. But we were the only ones retreating that day, and despite the light rain, the food, walks, and miniature fishing adventures, were comfy.

Even those who seriously don't like fish—four out of six redheads, one of whom had proclaimed, "I don't *do* fish," the day before we left New York— were swayed by the chowder that Eystein and Nina made for lunch: just fish stock, white wine, cream, butter, and the previous day's catch of flounder, pollock, and cod. We looked out over Bjørnafjord (*bjørn* means bear) as the rain softly plinked on the surface, and it couldn't have been more familial, safe as we all were under our sloping tile roof, with candles, strengthening soup, and a fortifying white Burgundy.

The kids, of course, eschewed soup superlatives and eventually grew restless, leaving the table to explore the grounds as the rest of us curled up like
slugs for naps in front of the fireplace in the main house or delved into some
of the hundreds of books (many in English) from a backless birch bookcase
hanging nearby. Eystein took me on a brief tour of the house. "I just made
those beds," he said, pointing proudly to two brightly painted blue wood
pedestals lying foot to head, with protective gingerbread cutouts that prevent
sleepers from rolling off and busting their pates. And he didn't mean he'd
tucked in the sheets; he meant he nailed and screwed the boards. Concerned
about dinner, he shipped out once more, scraped a few mussels from rocks
nearby, and began preparations for our seafood orgy. As the afternoon progressed, the ever-inventive redheads started a game of charades, cheating
wildly by adult standards. ("No, no, it's a *movie*," one actor-out corrected his
team of guessers, then, on a later title, announced, "No, no, it's MALCOLM *in
the Middle*.")

In the kitchen, Nina sautéed fresh, fat scallops in a little butter, removed
them, and made a simple but exquisite saffron sauce by adding a little stock,
cream, and a few pink peppercorns for color. Eystein dipped monkfish
chunks into an elemental flour batter for quick sautéing.

I've never subscribed to the marketeers' description of monkfish as the
"poor man's lobster"—it's like the Chicken Liver Council claiming its product
is foie gras for the homeless. I usually find monkfish combative in texture and
only mildly toothsome. If you see a whole monkfish at the market, you'll think
its massive mouth scarier than a shark's. And it's devious: It sits on the bottom
of the ocean passively, opens its Godzilla jaws, and waits for poor unsuspecting fishies to swim right into it, not unlike the latest recipients of W's capital-
gains cuts. So it has in common with lobster only reprehensibility of
character. But Eystein had the novel idea of freezing it first—even though it
had been netted the day before—to improve its texture, which indeed it did.
Perhaps this technique should be used on all passive-aggressives, human or
piscine: freeze them first to soften their fibers, then cut them into pieces.

As everyone assembled at another long dinner table, activity in the kitchen
increased, and the spirit grew jolly. Nina's team of attractive high school girls
bearded the mussels, and Eystein steamed them simultaneously with fistfuls

of toothpick asparagus. He poached two-inch cubes of the newly gutted cod in lightly lemoned and salted water, simmering them for a brief two to three minutes as Nina decorated each plate with superb wild salmon that had been juniper-smoked locally. It's more intense than Scottish but less blunt than Nova.

At the long dinner table, redheads young and old gathered 'round. Dodge, who was twelve years old at the time and a daring eater, zapped around the table begging other people's mussels and racking up twelve or fourteen shells on his plate; Nash, the sixteen-year-old fiske-a-phobe, moved his scallop around his plate with a fork and ultimately slipped it to an uncle. The younger ones looked suspiciously at their plates and were finally granted hamburgers. But the rest of us feasted and feasted—mussels, cod, salmon, monkfish, asparagus, the ubiquitous boiled potatoes—till the last sliver was done. It was nine at night by the time we finished, so naturally, the sun came out and stayed till midnight.

KUBBERVIK SCALLOPS

3 tablespoons butter
12 fat sea scallops, with coral attached, if possible
Salt and freshly ground pepper to taste
1 ¼ cups dry white wine
2 tablespoons Fish Stock (see page 307)
1 ¼ cups heavy cream
1 tablespoon lemon juice
½ teaspoon saffron threads
¼ cup minced chives
Cracked pink peppercorns, for garnish

1. Melt the butter in a large skillet over high heat. Season the scallops with salt and pepper and sauté until lightly browned, about 1 minute per side. Remove the scallops and set aside. Pour the remaining butter and liquid into a medium-size saucepan.

2. Add the wine, stock, cream, lemon juice, and saffron to the liquid in the saucepan and reduce over medium heat by about half, until you have a rich sauce. Season to taste with salt.

3. Gently reheat the scallops in the sauce and stir in the chives. Serve immediately, sprinkled with the pink peppercorns.

YIELD: 4 servings.

FISH SOUP FOR A RAINY DAY

4 tablespoons butter
4 tablespoons flour
5 cups Fish Stock (see page 307)
1 cup dry white wine
1 cup clam juice
1 ¼ cups crème fraîche
1 ¼ cups heavy cream
1 large carrot, peeled and julienned
1 small celery root, peeled and julienned
5 scallions, green part only, cut into half-inch slices
5 cups coarsely chopped spinach leaves
1 teaspoon sugar
Salt and freshly ground white pepper to taste
2 pounds skinless, boneless white fish such as cod, flounder, turbot, or
    catfish, cut into ¾-inch chunks
30 mussels (optional)
3 tablespoons chopped chives

1. Melt the butter in a large soup pot over medium heat. Stir in the flour and cook, stirring constantly, for 3 minutes. Stir in the stock, bring to a boil, and boil for 5 minutes, stirring occasionally. Stir in the wine, clam juice, crème fraîche, and cream. Reduce the heat to a simmer.

2. Add the carrot and celery root and cook 2 minutes. Add the scallions,

spinach, and sugar. Season to taste with salt and pepper. Add the fish (and mussels, if using). Cook for 3 minutes, or until the mussels open. Ladle the soup into bowls, sprinkle with chives, and serve immediately.

YIELD: 6 servings.

FISH STOCK

Bones and trimmings from 1 large white-fleshed fish
3 quarts water
¼ head celery root, rinsed and peeled
1 carrot
¼ leek, rinsed and chopped
Juice of half a lemon
Salt and freshly ground pepper to taste

1. Rinse the bones and place them and the vegetables into a stockpot. Add water and bring to a boil. Lower the heat and simmer for 20 minutes, skimming off and discarding any foam that forms on top of the liquid.
2. Strain the liquid, discard the solids, and return the liquid to the pot. Continue to simmer until reduced to 6 cups. Add the lemon juice and season to taste with salt and pepper.

YIELD: 6 cups.

Reform Reform'd

~~~~~~~~

ONE OF RED'S great attractions is her ambition. She's not Sammy Glick and she's not a wild-eyed dreamer, but hardheaded and realistic about her career and, fortunately for me, about mine. For herself, she wants to design one musical a year—that's all. Doable and manageable, what with me, three sons, and two stepsons to deal with.

I arrived in New York from California in '98 with *Vitreous Floaters*, in which an aging sitcom writer lures a much younger woman to front for him to sell a series to the age-conscious network, and while it made the rounds, Red led me through the writing of the musical *'68*. She then saw to it that producers I didn't know read it. When the assignment from the *Times* came up, she persuaded me to embrace it. ("But I'm a playwright," I said. "You're a writer," she said. "This is writing. And it pays.") Then she contributed ideas, accompanied me on trips, and as of this date has read every single column I've written for that and every other magazine I've written for. She suggested the battery of nominators that secured me a Guggenheim for playwriting (André Bishop, Robyn Goodman, Pete Gurney, Frank Rich). Since knowing her, I've felt part of a professional team, which I'd missed—with Charlotte I often felt I was the tumbler in a dangerous trapeze act and my catcher was missing.

In the fall of 2002, Red announced that Carole Rothman, the artistic director of the Second Stage Theatre, wanted to do a one-man show of my columns, starring . . . me. It was Red's suggestion, of course.

She had mentioned the idea before, but usually in an offhand way—"Might be interesting to see your columns onstage," she'd said casually—as though she'd said, "Wouldn't it be fun to visit Chicago?" I didn't respond positively, feeling as though I'd been transported to another Hollywood script conference in which a director airs a preposterous idea I was then forced to fly with for a few minutes until the preposterousness became so manifest even the director gives up on it. So I was astonished she'd even discussed it with Carole, let alone won Carole's green light. True, up to this point, what notoriety my food writing for the *Times* magazine had achieved was mostly due to the occasional autobiographical take on food experiences that the editors Amy Spindler and Andy Port encouraged. But I hadn't been on a stage since 1967, didn't want to be, and didn't really think the idea was so hot.

So when Red floored me with the announcement that Carole Rothman wanted to put me back onstage, all this baggage flooded up, covering me in alternating layers of wet terror . . . and curiosity. What would it possibly be like? I mean, if it didn't go well, I could always claim a heart attack on opening night, couldn't I? It's in my family.

Carole founded the Second Stage with Robyn Goodman in 1979, initially to give second productions to good plays that had received bad ones the first time around. Robyn left to become an independent producer (recently winning a Tony for *Avenue Q*), and over the years Carole maneuvered the theatre into one of the leading not-for-profit companies in the city. Carole has been so successful that she and her board built a handsome new theatre on Forty-third Street just off Eighth Avenue.

"This should only include autobiographical stories," she said in her office. "And Heidi could put an entire kitchen onstage," she added. She knows Red by her professional name, Heidi Ettinger, and they have been friends for more than twenty-five years. Once a month or so they used to call a meeting of the Red Meat Club, at which Red, Carole, and Wendy Wasserstein would devour obscene amounts of highly prime beef.

"Got to have a deep-fried turkey," I told Carole.

"Deep-fried turkey? On a stage? Can we do that?" she said, and loved it. A *coup de théâtre*, all that bubblin' oil crackling when the raw yellow bird went in, oohs and aahs when it came out forty-eight minutes later, glistening and golden brown. I volunteered that my character could cook a five-course meal while rattling off these vignettes.

"Really? Five courses?"

"And we can feed the audience! Onstage! Or, let's see, theatre capacity is three hundred . . . I guess we couldn't feed everybody and still make money." Every bit of it sounded like fun . . . except the part about my being in it. I wasn't exactly frightened, but was certainly hesitant. "What about getting another actor to play me?"

"I don't think so," she said firmly. "I mean you're not exactly famous—what would be the point?" She was sympathetic but intransigent.

Between columns for the *Times*, I wrote the show over the next eight months—more difficult than I thought it would be. Turning reflective prose into action and dialogue snaps you to attention. I understood why only one of America's great playwrights—Thornton Wilder—was able to master both forms. The director, Peter Askin, grew up in a well-to-do New York real estate family and also came from a private-school background, so could relate to my travails, as narrated in the play. Peter has made a specialty of one-performer shows—John Leguizamo's, *The Vagina Monologues*, *Hedwig and the Angry Inch*, among others.

We had many sessions working on the script, which though part of a director's job, is generally misunderstood by anyone who hasn't actually done much stage work. The best directors, like the best editors, have a serious understanding of the play and don't attempt rewrites. They try to help the author clarify and dramatize what he wants to say—rearranging and cutting the blubber, which often means persuading the author to get rid of his favorite passages.

Peter is a soft-spoken, sandy-haired man in his fifties, married twice, with one set of grown children and another of smalls. He's so reserved that if you were a bully you'd think you could walk right over him, which would be a mistake. "Get rid of as many of the *he saids* and *she saids* as you can," he said quietly at one of our first meetings. "Instead of ' "I'm hungry," she said,' *become the person* and say, 'I'm hungry.' Put it all in the present tense, so it's active." I did, and at the next meeting, he said, "Get rid of as many of the *he saids* and *she saids* as you can."

"I thought I had."

"Uh-huh," he said, which meant I hadn't. I again brought up the possibility of another actor. "Brian Cox's very good," he said. I couldn't tell if he was going to pursue the English Cox, a LAMDA alum, or was forcing me to say, "Hey, he can't play that part! It's mine!" but it made me quit talking about a different actor.

Toe in the water, but not full leg, I thought for my own protection that the show might play better with an additional actor and so invited Peter and Carole and Red and two fellows on the tech crew to lunch, during which I'd deep-fry a turkey with my friend Oliver Clark, the actor who'd tricked me into believing we were writing an original musical. Lunch would be a two-man show featuring our kitchen banter. Peter had a cold and ate lightly, but the "performance" was a success, though I didn't tell Oliver the lunch's ulterior motive in case it didn't work out. In fact, I've never told him. He's learning it for the first time reading this, but it's not payback for *Redhead*.

Afterward, Peter phoned and said, "I like the way you two interact. Would you like to do it with Oliver?"

"I think I would, yes."

"Well, let's think about it overnight," he said softly.

I thought having Oliver onstage would be easier for me and possibly the show would be more fun but that it was also sort of cowardly. The next day, I phoned Peter. "You know, I think having someone else onstage would dissipate the story. Like it or not, it's about me."

"Well, that's true," Peter said. Man, was he making me work.

Typically, I harrumphed and rationalized and came up with all sorts of reasons why it should be a two-man show and why it shouldn't. Finally, Peter put a stop to it.

"Uh-huh, okay," he said. "So you would like to do it by yourself."

"Ummm . . . yes." At last, he'd heard a commitment! I had wormed my way backward into a one-man show, and Peter understood the anxiety.

"Uh-huh. Okay. Now I really think you should cut out as many of those *he saids* and *she saids* as you can."

I don't know to this day whether Peter thought there should be one or two men on that stage, but he didn't gloat and he didn't object. Just straight ahead.

He urged me to cut indulgent passages that were significant to me but not to the audience. If I didn't by the next meeting or rehearsal, he'd bring up the cut again, quietly . . . and again and again and again until I had. Of all the cuts and suggestions he cajoled, I think only one three-line section remained by the time we opened. I mean, I had to protect my manhood somehow.

I began memorizing the script in September, a month before rehearsal. My old summer-stock teacher Alvina Krause believed an actor rehearsing with a book in his hand was just wasting time. So I calisthenically learned a page and a half of dialogue every day, and at first rehearsal had the whole script under my belt.

Red designed a wondrous and fanciful kitchen, cut it back when the budget was reduced (as it always is), framing me with transparent walls, a whimsical arch of gleaming copper pots, a fantastical cornucopia of produce gushing forth from the wings, and a magical dining table that suddenly slid in, fully laid, a second before the final curtain. And of course, everything on the stage was functional—running water, stove top, ovens, machinery. I wrote in music that was important to me—"Moonglow and the Theme from *Picnic*" because of Kim Novak, "All Right, Okay, You Win," sung by Joe Williams and played by the Count Basie Orchestra, because Uncle Bus used to take me to Birdland to see them.

Red and the techs set up a working kitchen for rehearsal. I showed up on the set feeling as if I'd never left the stage and just sort of bulldozed my way through the next thirty days and slept through the accompanying thirty nights with only marginal help from Sonata. There's a line in the play referring to Lee Remick's death: "Denial is murder in a relationship but sometimes can be one of the more useful weapons in our psychological arsenal." In my case denial was just the insulation I needed.

Although I acted the role of being an actor—outwardly nattering and worried, seeking consolation and approval from everyone 24/7, like every actor I've known—in fact, at the center, I was relatively unruffled. Perhaps because there was so much writing at night and so much arithmetic during the day— the potato soufflé has to come out of the oven *here*, so it has to go in *here*, so the potatoes have to be mashed *here*, the cardoon chopped *here*—this nifty negation set in, not unlike the time I underwent a massive general anesthetic for a sinus operation and just ignored the possibility that all the things I knew could go wrong in a hospital would. Only after the operation did I really focus on what had happened and what could have happened and decided never to get sick again. I did wonder which, if any, of the seven rules for seducing a woman through cooking her dinner would get laughs (three invariably did, sometimes four; never seven) and if I would be able to make it through the descriptions of Uncle Bus's death—I was making a Reuben's apple pancake—and of Lee's cancer—during which I drained the braising cardoon—without tearing up.

The dreaded first night of *Dinner with Demons* came and went with attendant but short-lived panic: There were too many tasks to perform in this play! I looked out at the audience—which I couldn't see individually, and began peeling tomatoes, as planned. The words flowed out, the tomatoes got peeled, the turkey glistened, Lee died of cancer, I welcomed my demons to dinner. BLACKOUT. Applause.

Aside from the second performance, when I got lost and called offstage, "Where are we now, Kyle?" to the production assistant, and one very brief fire—squelched with a tea towel—I never had a problem with the technical aspects of the lines or the performance. I could have been deeper or funnier or more this or that, but the lines came out one after another in the right order for eight straight weeks, and the cooking came off without a slip—a deep-fried turkey, tomato sorbet, braised cardoon, a potato soufflé, and a splendid Reuben's apple pancake theatrically flipped, like a circus trick, just before the final curtain—and the running time always ended within a minute or two of its desired length. So I could do it! I never quite got rid of the voice inside my head that said, right while I was talking, "You could forget this line! This one might not be funny! That guy in the front row isn't moving—is he listening, asleep, or dead? Someone there in the middle laughed where there's never been a laugh before . . . and now, where there's always been a laugh, nothing! Hey, why is Kyle reading a book—what if I go up? Watch it—you're going to fuck up!" Battling this internal CD was the most exhausting aspect of every performance. But I got through sixty-five of them without falling off the stage or giving in to the voices. The show became better, the script tighter, my performance more relaxed (or so I'm told—I couldn't tell because the CD never shut off).

Red came often but left early, too nervous to watch for long, she said. Nancy came five times and laughed at the mention of her ballet days and memories of our mother. Frank and Eddie each saw the show twice—once bringing friends, so I knew I hadn't embarrassed them too much. Don Junior flew in from Tulsa with his wife, Rose, and said tears came to his eyes when I played our father tersely appreciating a fried catfish I'd made for him—about the only appreciation he'd ever shown either of us. When my Uncle Bus's widow, Margaret, came with her children and husband, I got teary during the sequences about Bus and again during Lee's death, imagining their responses. When Rafe came with his wife, Margaret, who was dying of cancer, I thought I might not be able to make it through Lee's cancer, worrying how it would affect them.

Oliver saw it twice—I recognized his laugh when I imitated my mother smoking, and a bunch of chums from Denison enthused over the sequence where one of them and I got arrested for trespassing at Kim Novak's. I heard Wynn Handman, the cantankerous and wonderful force behind the American Place Theatre, which had produced my two one-acts, *Yanks 3 Detroit 0 Top of the 7th* and *Rubbers*, as well as the catastrophic *Tunnel Fever, or The Sheep Is Out*, and the controversial *Stonewall Jackson's House*, laugh at a matinee. Andy Port and Michael Boodro, two *Times* editors, came on a chilly afternoon and kept everyone awake.

There were other rewards. The reactions of the pros who saw it swelled my head. Mario Batali said it was the best thing he'd seen all year—and the year was almost over! Eric Ripert was flatteringly incredulous that I could say all those words while prepping a five-course meal. Rocco DiSpirito, in the middle of media hell because of his TV show, came backstage and effused. *This* was thrilling.

WOULD I DO IT again? I can't say I ever looked forward to the performance every day, nor was I sufficiently at ease on the stage to completely enjoy what

I was doing: It was work, first and last; discovering a half-full and unresponsive house on a freezing December-January matinee was uphill work; I never felt particularly refreshed by the applause and in fact told Peter that I'd be happy to forgo a curtain call if it would make the show better. He said, "I've never had an actor volunteer that," and then "no." The money was lousy. But after each performance, when the CD shut up and friends and strangers appeared backstage, all warm, all positive (fortunately, people who feel negative about a play seldom come backstage or, if they do, they lie), was the second most sublime moment of the day.

First most sublime was the eleven o'clock martini and many forms of mussels with Red at Café de Bruxelles on Greenwich Avenue, which also serves the best French fries in town. That made it worth doing. For a million dollars and those experiences, I'd do it all over again in a fingersnap.

POTATO SOUFFLÉ

(Adapted from Potatoes *by Annie Nichols, Ryland Peters & Small, 2003)*

For the almond parsley pesto
1 bunch flat leaf parsley, washed, stalks removed
⅓ cup almonds, skin on, roasted till golden
1 cup extra-virgin olive oil
¼ cup grated Parmesan
Salt and pepper

For the soufflé
3 tablespoons unsalted butter, melted
⅓ cup bread crumbs
3 pounds floury potatoes, skins on
¼ cup unsalted butter
⅔ cup milk, warmed
2 large eggs plus 1 large yolk
Salt and pepper

½ cup grated Parmesan

4 ounces mozzarella, drained and cubed

4 ounces Fontina or Emmental, cubed

---

1. In salted water to cover, boil potatoes till soft, about 30 minutes. Drain and peel. Preheat oven to 350 degrees.
2. Grease and coat soufflé dish with half the melted butter and half the bread crumbs.
3. Mash the potatoes and add unmelted butter and milk, then mix in eggs and egg yolk. Season with salt and pepper, then add Parmesan and mix again.
4. Spread half the mashed potatoes on bottom of the soufflé dish, creating a ½-inch lip headed up the sides. Lay the cheese cubes evenly over the potatoes, then cover with the remaining potatoes.
5. Brush with remaining melted butter and sprinkle with remaining bread crumbs. Bake at 350 degrees for 20 minutes, then at 425 degrees until golden, about 10 minutes.
6. While baking, prepare the pesto by grinding parsley, toasted almonds, and 2 tablespoons oil in a mortar or food processor until fairly coarse. Blend in Parmesan and remaining oil and season to taste.
7. To serve, spoon the soufflé onto plates with ribbons of pesto over it.

YIELD: 4 servings.

Stolen Moments

I WASN'T VERY NICE to my mother in *Dinner with Demons*. Although what the play says is true, it omits the concern and sense of helplessness that made her, like most people, paradoxical. She was a single parent with a hefty divorce settlement and so befuddled about her two children that she frequently overreacted with almost-comical extremes of punishment. But there were other moments.

Two days after a Christmas in the early fifties, she planned to take me to a classical piano concert and, as a special treat, dinner at Schrafft's, the upscale chain of restaurants that infiltrated New York in numbers rivaling the fire hydrant—at one point there were nearly fifty of them.

I didn't look forward to classical piano at all and didn't even look forward to Schrafft's—too stuffy for my taste. Furthermore, she had been particularly generous at Christmas and I had bought her almost nothing, so I felt considerable guilt.

The day before the outing, I walked by the neighborhood jeweler's window and fell in love with a gold-plated cigarette lighter completely covered in mother-of-pearl. Although it would look more like a souvenir of Las Vegas to my eyes today, when I was eight or nine it was the most dazzling object I'd ever seen. Mother loved to smoke Pall Malls, long unfiltered cigarettes that no doubt helped lead to her death.

On an allowance of sixty cents—thirty-five of which went toward the Saturday kids' matinee at the Trans-Lux around the corner—I hadn't saved a nickel, and the lighter cost twelve dollars.

So I stole the money for it.

From her.

She left her purse lying on the bureau every night, and late Friday, I popped it open while she was frying chicken for my sister and me and hurriedly grabbed a wad of bills. Early the next morning, I went to the jeweler and bought the lighter, its pink, turquoise, and lustrous white finish changing magically in front of my eyes. She was astonished and thrilled. "It's beautiful! How thoughtful of you," she said in true amazement. Within a minute or two, she had sussed out the situation and began the tenderest of third-degrees. "How ever could you afford it?"

"Oh, I have some money."

"It's the sweetest thing, and I'm filled with gratitude. But I know how much allowance you get. Where did the money come from?"

I decided to face the suspicion head on. "I didn't steal it!" The more I protested, of course, the deeper the hole I dug.

Just before the concert, I lacquered on a handful of Wildroot cream oil, despite instructions that urged only a dab. "Mmmm, there's so much of it," Mother said with a scowl, noting the shiny, greaseball helmet that had previously been my hair.

"I like it like this," I said and then, tightening my own handcuffs, "I didn't steal that money!" This time, she didn't respond.

We went to the concert, and I tried to sleep with my head on her shoulder, but she gently pushed it away because of the Wildroot bear grease. "This is new," she whispered of her houndstooth suit jacket. I dozed off, waking just in time to head for Schrafft's.

Schrafft's was by then an institution of middle-class comfort. Its first "store" (as they were always called) opened on Broad Street in 1906, thanks to Frank G. Shattuck, who had previously been the top candy salesman for W. F. Schrafft & Sons. It lost money until his sister Jane was recruited from Syracuse to create a brief menu with distinctly homemade dishes.

"It was Jane's idea of what a kitchen should really be," his great-grandson Frank M. Shattuck told me recently in his small tailoring shop. "It was a much more genteel time then—everyone wore hats and handmade suits. And if you were a lady, it was safe to go in there, sit at the soda fountain, and drink gin from a teacup." Frank M. has never been in the restaurant business; he is an actor and a tailor specializing in dashing $5,000 suits that he designs himself. One day in 1980 he went into the last remaining Schrafft's—"It wasn't really a Schrafft's, just a pizza place with a dirty sign"—and made off with 2,500 recipes from the safe. "I asked the guy there if it was okay to take them, and he said yes, and a week later I sent him a bottle of Jack Daniel's."

Frank M.'s uncle Gerald worked at several of the stores. "It all came out of the Victorian era," he said over the phone. "Menus changed every day—we didn't want people to get bored. My grandfather was very concerned with quality. He paid top price for every ingredient. And it was clean, which is not so unusual today but was then. The most popular dishes were Lobster Newburg, Creamed Chicken on Toast, Fillet of Sole, and of course the hot fudge sundae." It might be said that Schrafft's was bricked and mortared with chicken; of the 187-and-counting recipes for hot chicken dishes alone, more than a quarter were fricasséed, creamed, or dumplinged in some fashion, including such exotica as Creamed Chicken and Sweetbreads on Southern Spoon Bread, Spiced Peach and Peas. Seen that on a menu anywhere lately?

"We also had a wonderful cheese bread," Gerald said. "And a fresh fruit salad with our own dressing. And pies! Lamb pie, lobster pie, tuna fish, all cooked on Hall china so they wouldn't break in the oven. And our steaks would have put Peter Luger to shame. We were such big purchasers of beef that during the Second World War, we supplied the Carlyle, the Waldorf, and the Pierre. Toward the end, we had what's his name who did the soup cans—Andy Warhol—painting our ads."

These deluxe emporia had such devoted customers that some left their favorite waitresses money in their wills and often waited in line for their favorite waitress and table rather than be seated at any available spot. The employees may have been treated even better than the customers: They were also profit-sharing partners and were kept employed even during the dark days of the Depression. Primarily rosy-cheeked young Irish women straight off the boat, they voted down unionization three to one. They were lined up in military fashion for daily inspection and were proud of their work. "The same waitresses worked there year after year," George C. Shattuck, Frank M.'s father, told me on the phone. "Sometimes two or three generations of them. We really were a family." At one point, more than seven thousand large.

What made it so beloved? "Consistency of quality and friendly service," George said. Why did it go out of business? "Times change," Gerald said. "New York became quite a dangerous place in the sixties. Our main competitors were Longchamps and Childs, and we all stopped about the same time. Schrafft's lingered for quite a few years as an ice cream company. Then Pet Milk bought it, pretty much abandoned it, and eventually probably sold the land alone for more than the purchase price."

I didn't know about the store's history when I sat down with Mother after that piano concert; I knew only that it seemed hoity-toity, and the chopped steak with brown gravy I'd had on a previous visit wasn't as good as its down-market counterpart at Hamburger Heaven. *Plus* you had to wear a tie and sit up straight even though you thought you already were. Mother ordered the lobster pie.

"You'll have to return the lighter," she said quietly. I didn't fight. The jig was up.

"But I want you to have it."

"I know, dear, and it's the sweetest present I've ever received, but it wasn't your money."

"I could save up for it."

"Of course . . . but you need to return it now. When you have the money, then you can buy it." She knew me. I managed to save up a few cents for a couple of weeks, then Dubble Bubble got the better of me.

"Try some of this lobster." I screwed up my face. Nunh-unh. The Irish stew I'd ordered was exotic enough and, except for the turnips, warmed up the winter outside. Mother had a dark rhomboid on the shoulder of her new suit.

"What's that?" I said, slurping the gravied warm veggies and lamb chunks.

"You went to sleep. Your hair is very greasy." I didn't understand—wasn't she trying to keep my head *off* her shoulder? "Well, yes, but you looked so tired, and you're my son."

I took a bite of her lobster pie. It was thick and sweet, with the brilliant briny flavor of real lobster, and it was the first comfort food I can remember.

Schrafft's Lobster Thermidor

4 cooked lobsters, about 1¼ pounds each

6 tablespoons butter

1 shallot, minced

1 tablespoon lemon juice, plus more to taste

¾ teaspoon paprika

Pinch cayenne

Salt and pepper to taste

6 ounces small white button mushrooms, sliced

3 tablespoons flour

1¼ teaspoons powdered mustard

1½ cups chicken stock or mild seafood stock, or a combination

⅔ cup heavy cream

½ cup grated Parmesan cheese

1. Preheat oven to 450 degrees. Split lobsters down the middle and remove and reserve meat from tail and claws. Discard everything from the head and remove the front legs, without detaching the cartilage that holds the head and tail together. Rinse and dry shells and set aside.

2. Cut reserved meat into ½-inch dice. Sauté 2 tablespoons of the butter in a medium-size pan and add shallots, lemon juice, paprika, and cayenne until warmed through. Season with salt and pepper. In another pan, sauté mushrooms in 2 tablespoons of the butter until tender.

3. Set aside mushrooms and lobster meat. Melt the remaining butter in the pan the lobster was cooked in. Stir in the flour and mustard and cook for 2 minutes. Slowly whisk in the stock, then the cream, stirring constantly, until thickened, about 5 minutes. Add the lobster and mushrooms and cook 2 more minutes. Season with more salt, pepper, and lemon, if desired.

4. Spoon mixture into the shells, sprinkle with cheese, and bake until the cheese is lightly browned, 10–12 minutes. Serve immediately.

YIELD: 4 servings.

SIMMERING IRISH STEW WITH DUMPLINGS

For the stew
2 tablespoons vegetable oil
3 pounds lamb-stew meat, cut into 1 ½-inch cubes
12 cups water
1 teaspoon salt, plus more to taste
¼ teaspoon pepper, plus more to taste
6 carrots, peeled and cut into 2-inch pieces
2 turnips, peeled and cut into 1-inch chunks
1 small onion, sliced ⅛-inch thick
3 potatoes, peeled and sliced ¼-inch thick
4 tablespoons flour
Butter as needed

For the dumplings
1 ½ cups flour
2 ¼ teaspoons baking powder
¾ teaspoon salt
½ cup parsley
¾ cup milk
2 tablespoons butter

1. Heat oil in a large pot over high heat and brown the meat in two batches. Return meat to the pot and add water, 1 teaspoon salt, and ¼ teaspoon pepper. Simmer for 1 hour.
2. Add carrots, turnips, and onions and simmer for another hour. Place potatoes in a small pan and ladle enough broth over them to just cover. Simmer potatoes until just tender. Pour stock back into meat, leaving just enough to keep potatoes moist. Season with salt and set aside.
3. When vegetables and meat are very tender, strain the stew. Let the broth set until fat accumulates on top. Skim fat off and measure out 4 tablespoons (if you have less, use some butter).

4. Heat fat in the pot over medium heat. Add flour and stir for 2 minutes. Whisk in the broth. Cook, stirring, until mixture thickens. Add meat and vegetables and reduce heat to a simmer.

5. Whisk together flour, baking powder, and salt. Whisk in parsley. Heat milk and butter in a saucepan until butter melts, then stir it into the flour mixture until just combined. Drop rounded spoonfuls into the simmering stew. Cover and cook for 10 minutes. Serve with reheated potatoes.

YIELD: 6 servings.

Red All Over

~~~~~

I 'VE NEVER MET a human or a pet or a fish who wasn't dogmatic about his food. Let's face it—my taste buds are only mine, not yours or anybody else's, and as such deserve no special accolade just because they temporarily have access to a printing press. This is helpful to remember not only in matters culinary, but in matters artistic, financial, and romantic. For instance, if somebody said she thought the 2002 Pulitzer Prize–winning drama was the emperor's new clothes, featuring some nice dialogue but essentially a play without a point or any forward action and would be considered racist if written by someone white, or trivial and pretentious if written *about* someone white, well, that would only be HER taste buds about *Topdog/Underdog*, not yours or anyone else's. And if another person added that although the seriously credentialed Pulitzer committee occasionally gets it right, the guiding criteria are invariably ones of safety and correct politics, why that would also be just ONE set of taste buds, no more nor less valid than any other.

Similarly, your broker's recommendation to buy or sell MerkDizneySoft options is only one person's opinion; and one woman's droolful hunk will inevitably be another's appalling brute. And if I tell you that the food at the Venetian hotel in Las Vegas modeled after the city of Venice is considerably better than the food in Venice itself, that's only my opinion—even though in this case it's right. And if I add that the food in that Italian city is the Most Mediocre and Overpriced in the World (not the Worst—that belt is still comfortably worn by Shea Stadium), well, that again is entirely subjective and a potential field day for the deconstructionist.

It's harder to be dogmatic about people than it is about food unless you love them. Legally free to remarry at last in 2003—yes, the divorce took six years—I was shy about marriage because the barbaric divorce industry has made the prospect so treacherous and commercial. The practitioners practically demand prenuptial agreements, then make sure they are dismissed if challenged. Its lawyers have their most intense cosmic orgasms when people are at their most vulnerable, like buzzards—or is it vultures?

I can't think of a more despicable profession.

So infuriating and debilitating was this divorce that I was sure I'd never marry again. But when I saw the hope and delight for our future in Red's eyes, even the Hannibal Lecterian figure of the Los Angeles bar faded away. Who was going to determine our lives—us or the crummies?

2003–2004 had been an active season for us. Yale University Press finally published Nancy's book, *No Fixed Points: Dance in the Twentieth Century*, which she'd been writing with Malcolm McCormick for twenty years and which received genuine raves from the *Times*es on both coasts as well as all the major dance magazines. My column was proceeding smoothly, and *Dinner with Demons* had been a confidence-builder. Red's designs for the otherwise incomprehensible musicalization of *Dracula* were among her best. Art nouveau in style, they visually resembled what Gaudi might have done had he designed the show. They slithered on and offstage from the wings, flew down from the flies and popped up from the traps cinematically in a spooky evocation of time and place that would have made Bram Stoker shudder with approval if he ever got out from under his seat. And then there was Red offstage.

I was so intrigued by the mystery of her femininity, sexually beguiled by her deep and ambiguous WASP deviousness, and just happy, downright happy, to be around her, that over Christmas of 2003 I asked, and she said yes. She is flinty and straightforward when angry, cushy and pliable when in love, and laughs freely at just about everything I say, but brutal if she doesn't like what I put on paper.

A comparison of the improbable is "That's like Heidi saying no to her children." She spoils them mercilessly, either from guilt at being a single parent or at being a professional or from her own permissive upbringing or from living through the seventies or a combination of everything, but so far they thrive on it, though I wish they'd learn Spanish. Most important, she loves them, and her relationship with my sons is affectionate and relaxed.

Once we decided to get married, we agreed to tell all five boys together at a special dinner at "21." I was concerned about Eddie's reaction—he continued to be dutiful toward and protective about his mother, so I told him ahead of time. He sighed, then said, "I thought that was what this dinner was about. I'm happy for you, Dad."

My grand and theatrical plan turned out to be a miscalculation bordering on the farcical. Dodge, Red's twelve-year-old, burst into tears at the announcement, worrying aloud that this would mean he'd never see Rocco again. He left the table, crying. His brother North consoled him, then Red did. Nash looked stunned, no doubt wondering what this meant about his room— would he get to keep it or was everybody moving? Frank, to my surprise, was himself surprised. He hadn't seen this coming, despite all the arrangements for clearing calendars made for this one dinner. Eddie was good-humored but sober, worrying, I think, how Charlotte would feel. In short, the reactions ranged from misery to sobriety. All five boys wondered what this meant in terms of their own lives and real estate, and all were somewhat annoyed at being told something so shocking in public. The waitstaff didn't quite know what had happened: Why were three boys looking stunned and one crying hysterically? It had all begun so happily.

I had told Charlotte by phone beforehand and Red had told Rocco, neither of us wanting them to hear it from anyone else. Charlotte thanked me and was sweet about it, but the irreversibility of our split sank in.

Both Feet on the Ground?

~~~~~~~~

Love is lovelier, the second time around.
Just as wonderful, with both feet on the ground.
—"Second Time Around"

R ED AND I got married in May of '04 (sorry, boys), and if you haven't recently but are interested, there are a couple of ways to go about it. Of course you can always take the stressless, inexpensive, and most direct route by bringing a thirty-five-dollar money order to City Hall (1 Centre Street, actually, second-floor southwest, no blood test needed) to get your license and twenty-four hours later swarm the hallways with a much friendlier, if smaller and apolitical, United Nations, waiting for a JP.

But if you believe argument, anxiety, and financial deprivation make for a colorful introduction to your new life together, you can exercise your culinary and aesthetic vision by doing what we did: invite everybody you know and throw a party. To add *frisson*, make sure your Beloved is designing sets for the *Dracula* and *Little Princess* musicals, both due at roughly the same time—two weeks ago. Then try to get your publisher to phone and say, "You know that deadline of January '05? It's now July '04." And if you're tired of sleeping deeply without aquavit beforehand, you can intensify the time contingency to, say, two months.

We struck gold almost immediately. After visiting a handful of reception venues—mostly low-ceilinged, gold, "tasteful," and hideous, we stumbled upon the Angel Orensanz Foundation, a funky palace on Norfolk Street on the

Lower East Side with mile-high ceilings and a faint odor of religiosity, ruin, and Eastern Europe. It's the oldest extant synagogue in the city and is now used for events, parties, and, occasionally, as a synagogue. There was no runner-up to the Angel. But what were we going to eat there?

Wait a minute—first things first. Red and I, both lapsed Episcopalians (Red severely lapsed, as in atheistic, me still wondering, "Well, if he rose from the dead, isn't that pretty persuasive? And if he didn't . . . likewise, only the reverse?"), agreed to see a few churches on the theory—mostly mine—that you're not really married unless it's sanctioned by someone a little loftier than Governor Pataki. After rejecting Heavenly Rest's *Fountainhead* interior and the Gothic splendor of Grace because I'd already been married there, we wound up at what may be the loveliest treasure in the diocese: the Church of the Ascension on Tenth Street and Fifth Avenue. Designed in the Gothic Revival style, the church is adorned with an enormous canvas mural by John La Farge (once the largest painting in North America) and a Tiffany-style stained-glass window, and, most important, radiates an unpretentious sincerity of mission. All but the opportunistic are welcome. As the rector, Andrew Foster, implied, "This isn't a stage set for rent; we have to know you are serious of purpose." And thus, between food planning, wine tasting, heated discussions about music, photographers, transportation, invitations, dresses, suits, length of honeymoon, set designing, column writing, and book finishing, we met with Father Andrew weekly for a gentle exploration of the essentials. How did we feel about each other's children? Where were we going to live? What were we planning about money? What would our religious participation be? The process was surprisingly enlightening, and it forced us to focus on the marriage itself.

By this time, I'd contacted several caterers with serious reputations for hosting things like J.Lo's next three weddings and Madonna's Kabbalah ordination. All came up with menus that featured what I consider the teeny-tiny fussies: little phyllos with baby somethings, squirts of goat cheese, pancakes folded nine ways and drizzled with trendiness, taquitoettes stuffed with an *emincé* of cedar-planked shrimp loin embedded in a Meyer-lemon remoulade— the sort of preciosity that makes me want to run around the corner for a good pulled pork.

All bids were ambitious (on our behalf, of course) and expensive (on theirs). As one friend said, "When caterers hear the word 'wedding,' they start adding on the zeros." You might want to tell them you're planning a wake and see what happens.

Because I'm cheap, and like being cheap, and like even better being *thought of* as cheap, I phoned them all and asked them to cut their prices in half. One said he would and never phoned back, another never phoned at all, and another was suddenly busy on the day.

We wanted a menu that would surprise, mixing high—to show we could—and low—so that people might relax and smile. I conjured sea urchin juxtaposed with corn dogs, Osetra caviar next to mini-cheeseburgers, maybe little bags of those superb fries from Bruxelles with ortolans akimbo, or a fried meat pie from New Orleans, where North was enrolled at Loyola, with gratinéed cardoon wedges. And since cooking is so often performance (as I'd recently demonstrated), perhaps a station at which a chef would make bouillabaisse in front of your eyes, and the gent with the stainless cart from Fifty-third and Sixth Avenue would throw together his chicken curry in a pita (with the aluminum foil and all those mystery sauces, of course) accompanied by celeriac shoestrings.

From left field, enter Scarsdale.

Scarsdale? Lynn Sobel, an ebullient party planner, recommended a firm named Standing Room Only (SRO). A caterer from Scarsdale? How un-chic, how reverse-droll, how . . . *suburban.* But also how reasonable in both expense and control, how eager to please, how energetic! Sharon Snyder welcomed the challenge—even the requests to replicate the smoked duck from Grand Sichuan Eastern and Madhur Jaffrey's incomparable mango soup. We motored to Scarsdale to sample.

Snyder's chef, Herb Lindstrom, spun a superb sea-urchin cerviche by infusing it with lemongrass, chilies, and lime, excellent gingered green beans (to be served upright, in glasses), and brilliant little finger-food lamb chops (teeny-tiny, but not fussy), their bones wrapped in scallion blades. We discussed, made notes, drank wine, and threw some darts at the menu. We decided that with cocktails we'd pass the sea urchin, green beans, fries in bags, and lamb chops, plus pencil-thin sausages in square glass jars, warm fresh figs with honey, and little macs and cheese; that we'd serve wedges of iceberg with Roquefort and the mango soup at the table; that everyone would then visit stations, where bouillabaisse, lamb tagine, and smoked duck would be assembled in front of their eyes, and a street cart would sport pitas and chicken curry. If anyone was still standing, out would come a carrot wedding cake and bowls and bowls for banana splits.

We asked only that the duck be smokier and that physics be defied by standing the mac and cheese on its own, without redundantly starchy pastry or ramekins—impossible, of course—and fled to the city for the finale.

The clock ticks grew louder. The original florist with an estimate of $18,000 was replaced by someone who charged $6,000 and came up with original, almost confrontational arrangements consisting of boxes of grass; we found a mos' danceable band called the Manhattan Rhythm Machine (they'd sing gospel outside the church and doo-wop outside the Angel); Red arranged for double-decker buses and pedicabs to get us all from church to reception; the photog was engaged. We decided against the full Ascension choir and Handel's "Zadok the Priest" (usually reserved for English coronations and therefore, I'd thought, fitting), and in favor of Purcell strings. Sharon rushed into town with two carrot cakes under her arm for us to try—we chose pecans over walnuts—then zoomed back to Scarsdale. As we panicked, Lynn Sobel took over like the driver of one of those out-of-control stagecoaches in an old Western. Red's three boys and my two were suited and pink-tied alike so they could usher and act as givers-of-the-bride and best men respectively.

And suddenly we were at the altar. I don't remember any of it except that I knew I was doing the right thing and Red looked resplendent in a Gabrielle Carlson gilded oyster dress. I'm told Wendy Wasserstein and Oliver Clark read humorous marital quotes I'd assembled ("No man should marry until he has studied anatomy and dissected at least one woman"—Balzac) and that two of Red's sisters read Shakespeare's "Sonnet 30," and that my brother and sister read a few verses from "Song of Solomon" (not the usual ones). One hundred and fifty people filled the pews, Whoever Is in Charge arranged for a beautiful day (Red is reconsidering her atheism), and Father Andrew calmly wrapped our ringed hands in vestments. We kissed, and it was fact.

Out the church we headed, to startling applause, then everyone mounted the double-deckers and pedicabs and headed for the Angel, waving our hats. Pedestrians stopped to applaud as we went by.

Not everything came off exactly as planned. The band played "Moonglow" but not "Moonglow and the Theme from *Picnic*," and there wasn't enough rouille with the bouillabaise. But the variety and surprise of the food and the happiness in the ether made the guests laugh (or so they reported), and Sharon miraculously managed to get the mac and cheese to stand on its own! Lynn oversaw the works with her mighty sword, and the band played till eleven, and two years later, the bride and groom are very pleased with each other.

Of course, marriage, child-rearing, adolescence, death, birth, and life in general are excruciating and never quite work out. I'm amazed at how well they have for me so far, gripes, bitches, and a bad review in the *Times* for *Fighting International Fat* notwithstanding.

Two people together for a lifetime seems a sensational idea—providing one of them lives only to age thirty-six. In my experience 91% (or thereabouts) of the marriages I know about wind up either in divorce or as some version of *Who's Afraid of Virginia Woolf?* or with the participants eating dinner together in silence. It's almost never been *Love Finds Andy Hardy*. That doesn't mean all the people aren't eventually happy. Single lives, separate lives, remarried lives, are only failures in the eyes of those inside the box. But it doesn't mean Judge Hardy was a fool, either. And Red and I make a hell of a racket at dinner.

SEA-URCHIN CERVICHE

3 cups Tropicana orange juice

1 large shallot, finely chopped

1 tablespoon chopped ginger root

1 stalk lemongrass, split and cut into little pieces

2 chiles de arbole

3 garlic cloves, finely chopped

Juice of 1 ½ limes
½ bunch fresh cilantro, finely chopped
Salt and cayenne pepper to taste
6 sea urchins

1. In a medium saucepan, reduce orange juice, shallots, ginger, lemongrass, chilies, and garlic by two thirds over medium heat. Strain and cool.
2. When cool, add lime juice, cilantro, and seasonings.
3. With a pair of scissors, cut the top of each sea urchin and discard any shell that might have broken loose.
4. With a small spoon, detach the urchin from shell, taking only the pale roe.
5. Lightly toss sea urchin with the orange sauce and marinate 15 minutes.
6. Clean shells and fill with cerviche.

YIELD: 6 servings.

VERTICAL MAC 'N' CHEESE

1 pound elbow pasta
1 quart heavy cream
2 quarts shredded cheddar cheese
¼ pound shredded American cheese
Panko (Japanese) bread crumbs

1. Prepare a day in advance. Cook pasta until al dente in well-salted boiling water (do not add oil). Drain and allow to dry.
2. In a medium saucepan reduce heavy cream by half over medium heat. Stir in both cheeses and purée with immersion blender until smooth.
3. Add cooked pasta to cheese sauce and return to stove. Cook on high heat, constantly stirring, until very thick.
4. Pour mixture into a greased half sheet pan, filling it to the top.
5. Refrigerate overnight.
6. Preheat oven to 350 degrees.

7. Using a 1-inch ring mold, cut rounds of mac 'n' cheese and dredge in Panko (Japanese) bread crumbs.
8. Bake 5–7 minutes, or just until warm inside.

YIELD: forty-eight 1-inch rounds.

Marinated Grilled New Zealand Baby Lamb Chops with Sea Salt

1 rack New Zealand baby lamb, trimmed and Frenched
Sea salt and pepper, to taste
½ pint extra-virgin olive oil
3 cloves garlic, chopped
Leaves from 2 sprigs fresh rosemary, chopped
7 scallions, green-part only, cut long enough to cover bones

1. Preheat oven to 350 degrees and generously season lamb with salt and pepper.
2. Mix olive oil, garlic, and rosemary and spoon half over lamb.
3. Grill 1 minute on each side, then place on a sheet pan, pour remaining marinade over it, and roast 12–15 minutes, until lamb reaches internal temperature of 120 degrees.
4. Rest lamb for 5 minutes, then slice off individual chops, cover each bone with the scallion leaf, and serve with a ramekin of sea salt for dipping.

YIELD: 8 servings.

Acknowledgments

~~~~~~~~

FOR FIVE YEARS, I had about the best food-writing job of anyone since Petronius. In addition to biweekly exposure, *The New York Times Magazine* allowed me unusually free rein over subject matter, style, and opinion, all the while supplying me with ideas ranging from inspired to zany. For this I thank primarily the late, joyfully combustible Amy Spindler and my own special champion, Andy Port. Andy, a woman whose "invisible editing" and metaphorical handholding improved every single piece of mine she worked on and made me feel I was the best writer on the magazine, though there was plenty of evidence to the contrary.

Adam Moss, then editor in chief of the magazine, encouraged or allowed Amy and Andy to allow me that free range and is now eating everyone's lunch at *New York* magazine. His successor, Gerry Marzorati, made me feel welcome, too.

Frank Rich not only suggested me to the *Times* but more or less insisted I take the assignment when I was too dim to realize its possibilities. I'm most grateful for his prescience.

I had wonderfully sympathetic and incisive line editors at the *Times* in Michael Boodro and Maura Egan, and learned much from two accomplished and extremely patient recipe testers, Mary Johnson and Alice Thompson.

This book could not have been possible without the extraordinary skill, cooperation, and frequent touches of genius from the chefs whose recipes are included herein. Since that week on the S.S. *France*, I've admired the art and craft of serious cooks; but it surprised me when I began writing the *Times* column and other pieces for other magazines—but surprises me no longer—to discover how generous chefs are as a breed. I've never been turned down for any request by any chef, whether it involved printing a recipe or profiling them or didn't, and believe me, it wasn't because of my good looks. Well, there was one, a woman who runs a fashionable kitchen in the East Village, and that may have something to do with my looks. But every other serious cook was helpful, expansive, creative, and kept no secrets.

My agent, Kathy Robbins, tirelessly shepherded a ragged bunch of columns into just the right corral, and my team of editors—Daniel Menaker, Dana Isaacson, and Joan Benham—molded them into the manuscript that became this book. The cynical might add, "My God, what must this have been like without them?" and they'd be right.

Although I haven't yet met A. J. Liebling, Jane Grigson, and Calvin Trillin, I urge anyone interested in food or writing of any kind to read them, and to read R. W. Apple, whom I have met—as who has not? I assume the first word out of the pope's mouth on learning one works for the *Times* to be, "You work for the *Times*? Do you know Johnny Apple?" No one has been kinder or more encouraging.

I would like to praise the courage and patience of my sons, Eddie and Frank, for putting up with years and years of unreasonable food combinations, including fish liver, pig cheeks, and oatmeal topped with spinach and a fried egg that frequently drove them from the table but fortunately not from home. I'm pleased to see their palates are now more adventurous than mine. And I have deep appreciation for the culinary frustration I put my stepsons, North, Nash, and Dodge Landesman, through, exemplified by one of them saying, "Can't we ever eat anything normal?"

But I wouldn't have drawn a single happy breath nor written a single column without my wife, Red, professionally known as Heidi Ettinger, the cardinal editrix who pored over every single word of every single column before anyone else, focused pieces when they went haywire, and read three versions of this manuscript when some may have trouble with one. She is the center of my life for many reasons, thank God, not the least of which being that she inspired the first paragraph of *Lolita* without ever having met the author.

ABOUT THE AUTHOR

JONATHAN REYNOLDS is a playwright, actor, screenwriter, author, and television producer. His biweekly column on food appeared for five years in *The New York Times Magazine*. His plays include *Dinner with Demons, Stonewall Jackson's House,* which received a Pulitzer recommendation, and *Geniuses.* He lives in New York with his wife, the theatrical designer and producer Heidi Ettinger. He has two sons, Frank and Edward, and three stepsons, North, Nash, and Dodge Landesman.